PRAISE FOR

INVISIBLE
CHILD

"The result of this unflinching, tenacious reporting is a rare and powerful work whose stories will live inside you long after you've read them."

—MATTHEW DESMOND, *The New York Times Book Review*

"Destined to become one of the classics of the genre."

—*Newsweek*

"Stunning . . . a remarkable achievement that speaks to the heart and conscience of a nation."

—*Publishers Weekly* (starred review)

"What easily could have been, in lesser hands, voyeuristic or sensational is instead a rich narrative, empathetically told. Elliott is a masterful storyteller."

—NPR

"A classic to rank with Orwell . . . [Elliott's] characters are so vivid they leap off the pages. The prose fizzes. The dialogue crackles. The energy in the writing seems to match the energy of the characters, fighting, spitting, raging against the impossible odds. But they aren't characters and this isn't a story. These are real people and real lives."

—*The Sunday Times*

"Elliott's book is a triumph of in-depth reporting and storytelling. It is a visceral blow-by-blow depiction of what 'structural racism' has meant in the lives of generations of one family. But above all else it is a celebration of a girl—an unforgettable heroine whose frustration, elation, exhaustion, and intelligence will haunt your heart."

—ARIEL LEVY, author of *The Rules Do Not Apply*

"With her *Invisible Child*, Andrea Elliott has achieved a towering feat of reporting that paints, layer by layer, an extraordinary portrait of a child, a family, a city, and the nation that produced them. From start to finish, she sustains an insatiably curious and deeply empathetic focus on worlds that so many people work hard, if mostly unconsciously, to never really see."

—HOWARD W. FRENCH, author of *Born in Blackness: Africa, Africans, and the Making of the Modern World, 1471 to the Second World War*

"*Invisible Child* is hands down the best book I have read in years. This is a profoundly moving investigation into what it means to truly love other human beings. . . . A masterpiece."

—THOMAS HARDING, author of *Hanns and Rudolf* and *Blood on the Page*

"At once a tender portrait of a family, and a tour of America's broken welfare systems and racist policies." —*The Atlantic*

"A landmark account of American poverty and class immobility." —*Los Angeles Times*

INVISIBLE
CHILD

random house *new york*

INVISIBLE
CHILD

poverty, survival & hope
in an american city

ANDREA ELLIOTT

Published in the United States by Random House, an imprint and division
of Penguin Random House LLC, New York.

RANDOM HOUSE and the HOUSE colophon are registered trademarks
of Penguin Random House LLC.

RANDOM HOUSE BOOK CLUB and colophon are trademarks of Penguin Random House LLC.

Originally published in hardcover in the United States by Random House, an imprint and
division of Penguin Random House LLC, in 2021.

Portions of this work were originally published in *The New York Times*.

Grateful acknowledgment is made to the following for permission to
reprint previously published material:

Hal Leonard LLC: Excerpt from "Papa Was a Rolling Stone," words and music by Norman
Whitfield and Barrett Strong, copyright © 1972 by Stone Diamond Music Corp. Copyright
renewed. All rights administered by Sony Music Publishing LLC, 424 Church Street,
Suite 1200, Nashville, TN 37219. International copyright secured. All rights reserved.
Reprinted by permission of Hal Leonard LLC.

Alfred A. Knopf, an imprint of the Knopf Doubleday Publishing Group,
a division of Penguin Random House LLC and Harold Ober Associates: Excerpt from
"Harlem [2]" from *The Collected Poems of Langston Hughes* by Langston Hughes,
edited by Arnold Rampersad with David Roessel, Associate Editor, copyright © 1994
by the Estate of Langston Hughes. Digital and audio rights are controlled by
Harold Ober Associates. All rights reserved. Reprinted by permission of Alfred A. Knopf,
an imprint of the Knopf Doubleday Publishing Group, a division of
Penguin Random House LLC and Harold Ober Associates.

Library of Congress Cataloging-in-Publication Data
Names: Elliott, Andrea, author.
Title: Invisible child: poverty, survival, and hope in an American city / Andrea Elliott.
Description: | New York: Random House, an imprint and division of
Penguin Random House LLC, [2021] | Includes index.
Identifiers: LCCN 2021012357 (print) | LCCN 2021012358 (ebook) |
ISBN 9780812986952 (paperback) | ISBN 9780812986969 (ebook)
Subjects: LCSH: Coates, Dasani, 2001— | Homeless children—New York (State)—New York—
Biography. | African American homeless children—New York (State)—New York—Biography.
Classification: LCC HV4506.N6 E45 2021 (print) | LCC HV4506.N6 (ebook) |
DDC 362.7/75692097471—dc23
LC record available at lccn.loc.gov/2021012357
LC ebook record available at lccn.loc.gov/2021012358

Printed in the United States of America on acid-free paper

randomhousebooks.com
randomhousebookclub.com

9 8 7 6 5 4 3 2

Book design by Jo Anne Metsch

To Ava and Clara

For these are all our children.
We will all profit from, or pay for,
what they become.

—JAMES BALDWIN

contents

DASANI & HER FAMILY

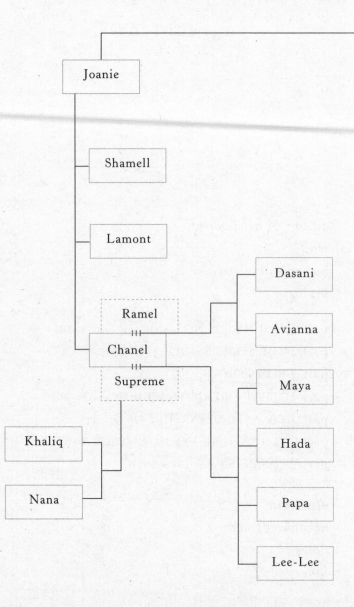

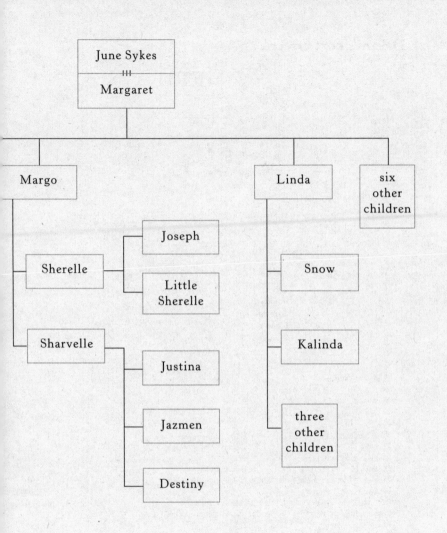

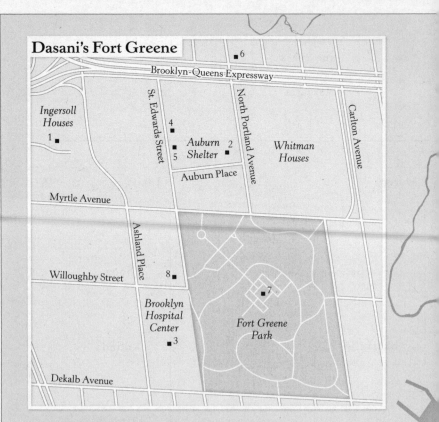

Dasani's Fort Greene

Brooklyn-Queens Expressway

Ingersoll Houses

Auburn Shelter

Auburn Place

Whitman Houses

St. Edwards Street

North Portland Avenue

Carlton Avenue

Myrtle Avenue

Ashland Place

Willoughby Street

Brooklyn Hospital Center

Fort Greene Park

Dekalb Avenue

1. Sykes family home, 1952–68
2. Joanie's birthplace, 1953
3. Dasani's birthplace, 2001
4. Charles A. Dorsey school
5. Walt Whitman Library
6. Dr. Susan S. McKinney school
7. Prison Ship Martyrs Monument
8. Brooklyn's first Black public school, 1845
9. Faith Hester's birthplace, 1964
10. Chanel's birthplace, 1978
11. Sherry's house
12. Supreme's childhood home
13. Chanel & Supreme's first rental, 2006–8
14. Joanie's final home
15. Dasani's group home, 2017–19
16. DHS family intake
17. Dasani's family shelter, 2014
18. Bartendaz base
19. Chanel & Supreme's first shelter, 2003–4
20. Fatima's hair salon
21. Dasani's family shelter, 2013–14
22. ACS Children's Center
23. HRA office
24. Staten Island family court
25. 120th Precinct
26. Chanel & Supreme's final rental, 2014–17
27. New York Foundling
28. Chanel & Supreme's final shelter, 2017–18

NORTH SHORE

Staten Island Expressway

STATEN ISLAND

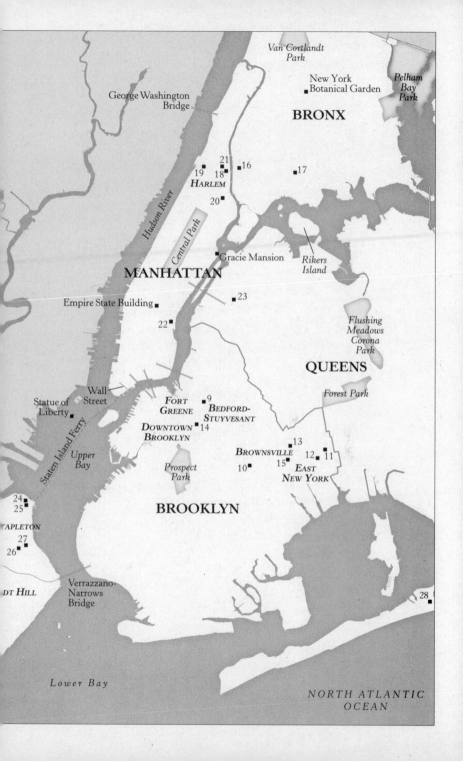

Van Cortlandt
Park

Pelham
Bay
Park

New York
Botanical Garden

BRONX

George Washington
Bridge

21
18   16
19
HARLEM

17

20

Hudson River

Central Park

Gracie Mansion

*Rikers
Island*

MANHATTAN

Empire State Building

23

*Flushing
Meadows
Corona
Park*

22

QUEENS

Wall
Street

Forest Park

Statue of
Liberty

9
*FORT
GREENE*   *BEDFORD-
STUYVESANT*

*DOWNTOWN
BROOKLYN*   14

*Upper
Bay*

13

Staten Island Ferry

BROWNSVILLE   12   11
15   *EAST
NEW YORK*

*Prospect
Park*

10

BROOKLYN

24
25

TAPLETON

27
26

DT HILL

Verrazzano-
Narrows
Bridge

28

Lower Bay

*NORTH ATLANTIC
OCEAN*

author's note

This is a work of nonfiction. No facts have been altered and no names have been changed. Ten of the children are identified by their nicknames, and several of the adults by their street names. I witnessed most of the scenes I describe in this book. My reporting also draws from thousands of records, hundreds of interviews, and many hours of video and audio recordings. For more detail, please see the afterword and notes.

prologue

First they came for Papa.

The eight-year-old boy asked no questions. He knew to be quiet in the presence of strangers. Two women led him into a silver van. Papa looked out the window as the ignition started. There was his school, a rectangle of brick that got smaller and smaller as the van pulled away.

Eleven miles south, another van collected Papa's brother from his school and four sisters from their schools, delivering all six siblings to the same place: the Staten Island office of New York City's child protection agency.

Only the youngest child remained.

The van turned east, heading up Laurel Avenue toward a white clapboard duplex with a boarded-up window. There, on the sidewalk, stood Baby Lee-Lee with her father. The toddler hid behind his legs.

As the van slowed to a halt, the father wiped his face. His daughter was too little to understand what was happening—that the people in the van were child protection workers. That the court had ordered them to take Lee-Lee and her siblings away. That the parents were being accused of "neglect." That they had neglected, among other things, the condition of their home.

A moment passed. The van door opened. A caseworker stepped

onto the sidewalk and paused. The father gathered Lee-Lee up and placed her in the van, promising to come for her tomorrow.

That evening, the siblings were transferred to a facility in Lower Manhattan, formerly the site of the Bellevue Hospital morgue. They stepped through a metal detector, trading their street clothes for matching maroon jumpsuits.

Their father's words kept ringing.

Whatever happens, stay together.

This much they had tried, for all of their short lives. Eight children, sixteen hands clasped into one chain. Like this they had dashed across the highway or played Ring Around the Rosie, lifting up and crashing down while never letting go. They had learned this from their parents, who had learned it from their parents.

Now the chain was breaking. The strongest link was already gone.

Her name was Dasani.

part 1

"A HOUSE IS NOT A HOME"

2012–2013

chapter 1

S HE WAKES TO the sound of breathing.

The smaller children lie tangled under coats and wool blankets, their chests rising and falling in the dark. They have yet to stir. Their sister is always first.

She looks around the room, seeing only silhouettes—the faint trace of a chin or brow, lit from the street below. Mice scurry across the floor. Roaches crawl to the ceiling. A little sink drips and drips, sprouting mold from a rusted pipe.

A few feet away is the yellow mop bucket they use as a toilet, and the mattress where the mother and father sleep clutched. Radiating out from them in all directions are the eight children they share: two boys and five girls whose beds zigzag around the baby, her crib warmed by a hair dryer perched on a milk crate.

They have learned to sleep through anything. They snore with the pull of asthma near a gash in the wall spewing sawdust. They cough or sometimes mutter in the throes of a dream. Only their sister Dasani is awake.

Dasani is tiny for an eleven-year-old and quick to startle. She has a delicate oval face and luminous eyes that watch everything, owl-like. Her expression veers from mischief to wonder. People often re-mark on her beauty—the high cheekbones and chestnut skin—but their comments never seem to register. What she knows is that she has been blessed with perfect teeth. When braces are the stuff of fantasy, straight teeth are a lottery win.

Slipping out from her covers, Dasani goes to the window. On mornings like this, she can see all the way past Brooklyn, over the rooftops and the projects and the shimmering East River. Her eyes can travel into Manhattan, to the top of the Empire State Building, the first New York skyscraper to reach a hundred floors. This is the type of fact that she recites in a singsong, look-what-I-know way. She fixes her gaze on that distant temple, its tip pointed celestially, its facade lit with promise.

"It makes me feel like there's something going on out there," she says. "I have a lot of possibility. I *do*, though. I have a lot of things to say."

One of the first things Dasani will say is that she was running before she walked. She loves being first—the first to be born, the first to go to school, the first to win a fight, the first to make the honor roll. She is a child of New York City.

Even Dasani's name speaks of a certain reach. The bottled water had come to Brooklyn's bodegas just before she was born, catching the fancy of her mother, who could not afford such indulgences. Who paid for water in a bottle? Just the sound of it—*Dasani*—conjured another life. It signaled the presence of a new people, at the turn of a new century, whose discovery of Brooklyn had just begun.

By the time Dasani came into the world, on May 26, 2001, the old Brooklyn was vanishing. Entire neighborhoods would be remade, their families displaced, their businesses shuttered, their histories erased by a gentrification so vast and meteoric that no brand of bottled water could have signaled it. And as prosperity rose for one group of people, poverty deepened for another, leaving Dasani to grow up—true to her name—in a novel kind of place.

Her skyline is filled with luxury towers, the beacons of a new Gilded Age. The city's wealth has flowed to its outer edges, bringing pour-over coffee and artisanal doughnuts to places once considered gritty. Among them is Dasani's birthplace, Fort Greene, Brooklyn, where renovated townhouses come with landscaped gardens and heated marble floors. Just steps away are two housing projects and, tucked among them, a city-run homeless shelter where the heat is off and the food is spoiled.

It is on the fourth floor of that shelter, at a window facing north, that Dasani now sits looking out. Nearly a quarter of her childhood has unfolded at the Auburn Family Residence, where Dasani's family—a total of ten people—live in one room. Beyond the shelter's walls, in the fall of 2012, Dasani belongs to an invisible tribe of more than twenty-two thousand homeless children—the highest number ever recorded, in the most unequal metropolis in America. Almost half of New York's 8.3 million residents are living near or below the poverty line.

Dasani can get lost looking out her window, until the sounds of Auburn interrupt. Different noises mean different things. She sorts them like laundry. The light noises bring no harm—the colicky cries of an infant down the hall, the hungry barks of the Puerto Rican lady's Chihuahuas, the addicts who wander the projects, hitting some crazy high. They can screech like alley cats, but no one is listening.

The sound that matters has a different pitch. It comes loud and fast, with a staccato rhythm. The popping of gunshots. The pounding of fists. The rap of a security guard's knuckles on the door. Whenever this happens, Dasani starts to count.

She counts her siblings in pairs, just like her mother said. The thumb-suckers first: six-year-old Hada and seven-year-old Maya, who share a small mattress. The ten-year-olds next: Avianna, who snores the loudest, and Nana, who is going blind. The brothers last: five-year-old Papa and eleven-year-old Khaliq, who have converted their metal bunk into a boys-only fort.

They are all here, six slumbering children breathing the same stale air. If danger comes, Dasani knows what to do. She will kick them awake. She will tell them to shut up. They will drop to the floor in silence.

Except for Baby Lee-Lee, who wails like a siren. Dasani keeps forgetting to count the newest child. She had been born in March, shattering the air with her cries. Until then, Dasani considered herself a baby expert. She could change diapers, pat for burps, check for fevers. She could even tell the difference between a cry for hunger and a cry for sleep.

Lee-Lee's cry was something else. Only a mother could answer it and their mother was gone.

Nearly a year ago, the city's child protection agency had separated thirty-four-year-old Chanel Sykes from her children after she got addicted to opioids. Her husband also had a drug history. But under court supervision, he had remained with the children, staying clean while his wife entered a drug treatment program.

Now Chanel is back, her custodial rights restored. Still, the baby howls. This is usually the sound that breaks Dasani's trance, causing her to leave the window and fetch Lee-Lee's bottle.

Dasani feels her way across the room that she calls "the house"— a 520-square-foot space containing her family and all their possessions. Toothbrushes, love letters, a dictionary, bicycles, an Xbox, birth certificates, Skippy peanut butter, underwear. Hidden in a box is Dasani's pet turtle, kept alive with bits of baloney and the occasional Dorito. Taped to the wall is the children's proudest art: a bright sun etched in marker, a field of flowers, a winding path. Every inch of the room is claimed.

"We each got our own spot," Dasani says.

Each spot is routinely swept and sprayed with bleach and laid with mousetraps. The mice used to terrorize Dasani, leaving pellets and bite marks. Nowadays, Room 449 is a battleground. On one side are the children, on the other the rodents—their carcasses numbering up to a dozen per week. To kill a mouse is to score a triumph.

"We burn them!" Dasani says with none of the tenderness reserved for her turtle. "We take the sticks and smash they eyes out! We break their necks. We suffocate them with the salt!"

In the dim chaos of Room 449, she struggles to find Lee-Lee's formula, which is donated by the shelter but often expired. Dasani squints to check the date. Now the bottle must be heated. The only way to do this is to leave the room, which brings its own dangers. Over the next year, 911 dispatchers will take some 350 calls from Auburn, logging twenty-four reports of assault, four reports of child abuse, and one report of rape.

Dasani opens a heavy metal door, stepping into the dark corridor. She is sure the place is haunted. Auburn used to be a hospital, back when nurses tended to the dying in open wards. Dasani's room was "where they put the crazies," she says, citing as proof the broken intercom on the wall. Right outside is a communal bathroom with a large industrial tub. A changing table for babies hangs off its hinge. Mothers shower quickly, posting their children as lookouts for the building's predators.

Dasani slips down three flights of stairs, passing a fire escape where drugs and weapons are smuggled in. She trots into the cafeteria, where more than a hundred families will soon stand in line to heat their prepackaged breakfast. With only two microwaves, this can take an hour. Tempers explode. Knife fights break out.

Luckily, in this predawn hour, the cafeteria is still empty. Dasani places the bottle in the microwave and presses a button. Baby Lee-Lee has yet to learn about hunger, or any of its attendant problems. If she cries, others answer. Her body is still small enough to warm with a hair dryer. She is the least of Dasani's worries.

"I have a lot on my plate," she likes to say, cataloging her troubles like the contents of a proper meal. "I got a fork and a spoon. I got rice, chicken, macaroni." The fork and spoon are her parents and the macaroni her siblings—except for Baby Lee-Lee, who is a plump chicken breast.

"So that's a lot on my plate—*with* some cornbread. That's a lot on my plate."

Dasani races back upstairs, handing her mother the bottle. Then she sets about her chores, dumping the mop bucket, tidying her dresser, and wiping down the small fridge. Her siblings will soon be scrambling to get dressed and make their beds before running to the cafeteria to beat the line.

Then they will head outside, into the bright light of morning.

Dasani ticks through their faces, the girls from the projects who know where she lives. Here in the neighborhood, the homeless are the lowest caste, the outliers, the "shelter boogies."

Some girls may be kind enough to keep Dasani's secret. Others will be distracted by the noise of this first day—the start of the sixth grade, the crisp uniforms, the fresh nails. She hopes to slip by them all unseen.

Sleek braids fall to one side of Dasani's face, clipped by yellow bows. Her polo shirt and khakis have been pressed with a hair straightener, because irons are forbidden at the Auburn shelter. This is the type of fact that nobody can know.

She irons her clothes with a hair straightener.

As Dasani walks to her new school on September 6, 2012, her heart is pounding. She will be sure to take a circuitous route home, traipsing two extra blocks to keep her address hidden. She will focus in class and mind her manners in the schoolyard. All she has to do is climb the school steps.

"Come on," says her mother, Chanel. "There's nothing to be scared about."

On a good day, Dasani walks like she is tall, her chin held high. More often she is running—to the monkey bars, to the library, to the A train that her grandmother cleaned for a living. No one on the block can outpace Dasani. She is forever in motion, doing backflips at the bus stop, dancing at the welfare office.

She makes do with what she has and covers what she lacks. To be poor in a rich city brings all kinds of ironies, perhaps none greater than this: The donated clothing is top shelf. Used purple Uggs and Patagonia fleeces cover thinning socks and fraying jeans. A Phil & Teds rain shell, fished from the garbage, protects the baby's creaky stroller.

Dasani tells herself that brand names don't matter. She knows such yearnings will go unanswered. But every once in a while, when by some miracle she scores a pair of Michael Jordans, she finds herself succumbing to the same exercise: She wears them sparingly, and only indoors, hoping to keep them spotless. It never works.

Best to try to blend in while not caring when you don't. She likes being small because "I can slip through things." She imagines herself with supergirl powers.

She would blink and turn invisible.

Sometimes she doesn't have to blink. In the blur of the city's streets, Dasani is just another face. Strangers do not see the opioid addiction that chases her mother, or the prisons that swallowed her uncles, or the cousins who have died from gang shootings and AIDS.

"That's not gonna be me," she says. "Nuh-uh. Nope."

Nor do strangers see where Dasani lives.

Children are not the face of New York's homeless. They rarely figure among the panhandlers, bag ladies, war vets, and untreated schizophrenics who have long been stock characters in this city of contrasts. They spend their days in school, their nights in the shelter. If they are seen at all, it is only in glimpses—pulling an overstuffed suitcase in the shadow of a tired parent, passing for a tourist rather than a local without a home.

Dasani landed at 39 Auburn Place more than two years ago. There was no sign announcing the shelter, which rises over the neighboring projects like an accidental fortress. Its stately neo-Georgian exterior dates back nearly a century, to when the building opened as a public hospital serving the poor.

Two sweeping sycamores shade the entrance, where smokers linger under brick arches. A concrete walkway leads to the lobby, which Dasani likens to a jail. She is among 432 homeless children and parents living at Auburn. Day after day, they step through a metal detector as security guards search their bags, taking anything that could be used as a weapon—a bottle of bleach, a can of Campbell's soup.

This harsh routine gives Auburn the feel of a rootless, transient place. But to Dasani, the shelter is far more than a random assignment. It is a private landmark—the very place where her beloved grandmother Joanie Sykes was born, back when this was Cumberland Hospital.

Every morning, Dasani leaves her grandmother's birthplace to wander the same streets where Joanie grew up, playing double Dutch in the same parks, seeking shade in the same library.

And now, on this bright September morning, Dasani will take her grandmother's path once again, into the promising middle school two blocks away.

To know Dasani Joanie-Lashawn Coates—to follow this child's life, from her first breaths in a Brooklyn hospital to the bloom of adulthood—is to reckon with the story of New York City and, beyond its borders, with America itself. It is a story that begins at the dawn of the twenty-first century, in a global financial capital riven by inequality.

It is also a story that reaches back in time, to one Black family making its way through history, from slavery to the Jim Crow South and then the Great Migration's passage north.

There is no separating Dasani's childhood from that of her matriarchs: her grandmother Joanie and her mother, Chanel. Their fleeting triumphs and deepest sorrows are, in Dasani's words, "my heart." The ground beneath her feet once belonged to them. Her city is paved over theirs. It was in Brooklyn that Chanel was also named for a fancy-sounding bottle, spotted in a magazine in 1978. Back then, from the ghetto's isolated corners, a perfume ad was the portal to a better place. Today, Dasani lives surrounded by wealth, whether she is peering into the boho chic shops near her shelter or surfing the Internet on Auburn's shared computer. She sees out to a world that rarely sees her.

To see Dasani is to see all the places of her life, from the corridors of school to the emergency rooms of hospitals to the crowded vestibules of family court and welfare. Some places are more felt than seen—the place of homelessness, of sisterhood, of a mother-child bond that nothing can break. They dwell within Dasani wherever she goes.

To follow Dasani, as she comes of age, is to follow her seven siblings. Whether they are riding the bus, switching trains, climbing steps, or jumping puddles, they always move as one. Only together have they learned to navigate poverty's systems—ones with names suggesting help. Child protection. Public assistance. Criminal justice. Homeless services.

To watch these systems play out in Dasani's life is to glimpse their power, their flaws, and the threat they pose to Dasani's own system of survival. Her siblings are her greatest solace; their separation, her greatest fear. This is freighted by other forces beyond her control—hunger, violence, racism, homelessness, parental drug addiction, pollution, segregated schools. Any one of these afflictions could derail a promising child.

As Dasani grows up, she must contend with them all.

chapter 2

"COME ON!" SAYS Chanel, losing patience with her daughter.

Dasani will not budge from the steps of her new school. Children stream past her as security guards patrol the sidewalk, taking stock of the new faces. More than five hundred students, from grades six to twelve, attend the Dr. Susan S. McKinney Secondary School of the Arts. Each class brings its bullies and its victims.

Dasani is her mother's daughter, a fearless fighter. But she is also an easy target. Nothing gnaws at her like the words "shelter boogie." A mucus-stained nose suggests a certain degradation—not just the absence of tissues, but of a parent willing to wipe; or a home so unclean that a runny nose makes no difference. Dasani and her siblings can get hungry enough to lose focus, but they are forever wiping their noses.

When Dasani hears "shelter boogie," all she can think to say is what her mother always says: that Auburn is a "pit stop." She is just passing through, whereas the projects are forever. Dasani says this out loud while walking by the Walt Whitman Houses: *"You* will live in the projects forever, as will your kids' kids, and your kids' kids' kids."

Dasani knows that the battle is asymmetrical. People stay in the projects for the same reason that a quarter million New Yorkers are currently on the public housing waitlist: the rent, for low-income families, is heavily subsidized. Dasani's parents have been on the waitlist six times. Even if they were lucky enough to land in the projects surrounding Auburn—Whitman or Ingersoll, where Dasani's grandmother grew up—they would still need to make the rent every month.

Public housing may represent all kinds of inertia. But to live at Auburn is to admit the ultimate failure—the inability to give your children a roof. There is no recovering from "shelter boogie." The most Dasani can do is duck the label.

Today, her cheeks have been "lotioned" to a high polish. This is the work of Chanel, who rose before dawn to get her children ready. There are three ways to be popular, in Chanel's estimation.

Dress fly. Do good in school. Or fight.

She knows Dasani can fight, but why not try for the first two things? A new school is a chance at reinvention. Dasani must look sharp. It does not matter that school uniforms are meant to temper such concerns, or that they only accentuate the things Dasani lacks— the manicure, the phone, the earrings.

Chanel puffs out her chest.

"Mommy, I'm not going in there," Dasani whispers.

Chanel sees no other choice. She shoves her daughter up the stairs, watching her disappear.

Students buzz along the hallway, trading gossip and hugs. Many are the sons and daughters of alumni who know the school by one name: McKinney.

Housed in a sprawling brick building by the underpass of the Brooklyn-Queens Expressway, McKinney is a refuge for the neighborhood's would-be starlets—a scrappy version of LaGuardia Arts, the elite Manhattan public school that inspired the 1980 film *Fame*.

Threadbare curtains adorn McKinney's theater. Stage props are salvaged from a nearby trash bin. The marching band plays with donated instruments, and the dance class is so crowded that students practice in shifts. Everyone at McKinney seems to be reaching. There is Officer Jamion Andrews, the security guard who moonlights as a rap lyricist, and Zakiya Harris, the dance teacher who runs a studio on the side. The drama teacher, Dale Smith, is a published playwright, and the English teacher, Faith Hester, wrote a self-help book titled *Create a Life You Love Living*.

McKinney's children also strive. Among them is a soprano who periodically lifts the school with an aria from *Madama Butterfly*. Whenever her voice rings out, everyone knows that a junior named Jasmine is singing a capella in the office of Principal Paula Holmes. The school matriarch closes her eyes. This may be her only tranquil moment.

Miss Holmes is a towering sixty-year-old woman, by turns steely and soft. She wears a Bluetooth like a permanent earring and tends toward power suits. She has been at McKinney's helm for fifteen years and runs the school like a naval ship, peering down its hallways as if searching the seas for enemy vessels.

Students stammer in her presence. She leaves her office door open, like a giant unblinking eye. The honor roll is posted right outside, near a poster of a man in jeans that sag. He is standing before the White House, opposite President Barack Obama. "To live in this crib," the poster reads, "you have to look the part." Miss Holmes has no tolerance for sagging—sartorial, attitudinal, or otherwise. She accepts "nothing less than one hundred percent."

McKinney's roots run deep. Like Dasani's grandmother Joanie, who attended McKinney in the 1960s, most of the middle school students are Black, live in the projects, and are poor enough to qualify for free or reduced price meals. They eat in shifts in the school's basement cafeteria, watched over by the avuncular Frank Heyward, who blasts oldies from a boom box, telling students, "I got shoes older than you."

For all of McKinney's pluck, its burdens are great. In the last six years, the city has cut the school's budget by a quarter as student enrollment continues to drop. After-school resources have shrunk, but not the needs of the students, for whom gun violence, domestic abuse, and murder are common enough that teachers have pushed for an on-site grief counselor.

And now a charter school is angling to move in. The proposed Success Academy Fort Greene plans to take over McKinney's treasured top floor, home to its theater class, dance studio, and art lab. This could be good or bad news, depending on one's perspective.

The guiding ethos of the charter movement has been "choice"— the power to choose a school rather than capitulating to a flawed education system and a muscular teachers' union. Champions of charter schools (which are publicly funded but privately operated) consider them the salvation of poor children, a way to close the achievement gap that many public schools cannot.

But in communities like McKinney, the "co-location" of charter and public schools can feel like the opposite of choice. Charters are known to exclude children with learning disabilities or behavioral issues. More than half of McKinney's children fall into these categories.

If the Success Academy comes to McKinney, its students will enter through different doors, eat their meals apart, and wear nicer uniforms. A website for the proposed school argues that parents "shouldn't have to trek to other Brooklyn neighborhoods or spend $30,000+ on a private school in order to find excellence and rigor."

McKinney is bracing for battle, with flyers warning of "apartheid" and a white "invasion." Half a century earlier, when Dasani's grandmother attended McKinney, the very notion of whites "invading" would have sounded extraterrestrial. The opposite was happening. Whites were fleeing.

New York City's school system—now the largest in the nation—is also among the most segregated. One percent of McKinney's students are white. It is also true that the vast majority of Success Academy's students (seven thousand are enrolled in fourteen schools) are Black or Latino and from low-income families. But they possess an advantage over Dasani: They win their spot by lottery, which requires the help of an adult—one with a reliable email account or at least a cellphone that doesn't shut off. None of these conditions exist for Dasani.

What she knows is the other side.

The bell is about to ring as Dasani makes her way down McKinney's halls. She wants to find the dance studio. She has never worn a leotard, or leaped across a dance floor. She won't believe it until she sees it.

But first Dasani must report to her homeroom teacher. As luck would have it, she has landed in the class of Faith Hester.

Miss Hester can best be described as electric. She paces the room, throwing her arms into the air as her voice echoes along McKinney's hallways. Long after she gave up dreams of acting, the classroom has become her stage, the students her rapt audience.

Sometimes she arrives in an Aretha Franklin beehive, batting extended eyelashes. Other days, she wears the brightly patterned prints of Senegal, purchased during a trip to "learn the truth about my motherland." She says things that her students remember long after they have graduated—expressions like "Oh my gooney goo hoo!" and "Okey dokey pokey shmokey!"

If a child is stumped, she will break into improvised song, with the class soon chanting: "I know you know it!"—clap, clap—"I know you know it!"—clap, clap.

Miss Hester, forty-eight, knows that her students learn when they get excited. She was the same way. She grew up in Brooklyn's Marcy projects, a monotonous spread of twenty-seven brick buildings where Jay-Z spent his boyhood. Miss Hester could never get used to the violence she saw. In the song "Where I'm From," Jay-Z describes a place

> *Where we call the cops the A-Team*
> *Cause they hop outta vans and spray things*
> *And life expectancy so low we makin out wills at eighteens*

Even today, many of Miss Hester's students don't expect to live much past age twenty. Two of her former students have been killed. One of them was a boy named Angel, who used to visit McKinney every summer to help Miss Hester set up the classroom for her incoming class.

Lately, Miss Hester has been trying a risky exercise: She asks her students to write their own obituary. When given the option of choosing their lifespan, most of them aim for seventy. Then they must imagine all the things they would have accomplished.

"I want them to see that they are the authors of their lives," she says.

Miss Hester's own salvation came at church and in school. She was one of the first Black students to be bused, in 1977, from the projects to a predominantly white school in Brooklyn. A group of local boys ran after her yelling, "Get out of our neighborhood!" She graduated from high school early, bound for SUNY Cortland. And now, thirty-one years (and two master's degrees) later, Miss Hester has returned to her birthplace, just a short drive from McKinney. Nothing else feels like home.

When Miss Hester looks around her classroom, she sees young versions of herself. She wants her students to do the same in reverse, to see a future for themselves in her example.

Dasani is watching Miss Hester carefully. She has the longest eyelashes Dasani has ever seen. They protrude like delicate fans, charting the teacher's moods. They flutter when she is being funny. They drop to half-mast when she is annoyed.

The teacher strikes Dasani as both "weird" and familiar. Miss Hester's birthplace—Bedford-Stuyvesant—is a neighborhood that Dasani knows block by block. It's the place where Dasani's own mother, Chanel, grew into an adult. Yet Chanel seems nothing like Miss Hester, who speaks with a polish that Dasani finds impressive. The teacher enunciates every consonant, while dropping the occasional "ain't"—almost like a tip of the hat. This is Miss Hester's way of saying, *If I can talk like you, the reverse is also true.*

For Miss Hester's lesson on "context clues," she begins in a simple manner.

"You come across an unfamiliar word," Miss Hester tells the class. "You look at the surrounding words and ideas and you unpack that word."

The theatrics begin.

"Flabbergasted," Miss Hester says. "I was *flabbergasted* when I found a million dollars in my purse."

Dasani bursts into laughter.

"A million dollars!" Miss Hester hoots. "I know that that's a lot of money. And it's in my purse. And I'm supposed to be *broke*," she says, batting her long lashes. "'Flabbergasted' means 'delightfully surprised.'"

Teachers are the happiest adults that Dasani knows. When asked "What will you be when you grow up?" she and her siblings all say the same thing: "A teacher."

In class, Dasani raises her hand high and speaks in forceful sentences. She seems unaware of how tiny she is—exuding a muscular confidence that carries over into the schoolyard.

The popular girls dote on Dasani, calling her "Shorty." But say the wrong thing, and she turns fierce. In a matter of days, Dasani is running around the school declaring herself "the Terminator."

It is still September when Dasani lands in the principal's office.

"There are no terminators here," says Miss Holmes.

"Please don't call my mother," Dasani whispers.

Miss Holmes is seated in a rolling pleather chair held together by duct tape. She takes a hard look at Dasani. Whenever a child says, "Please don't call my mother," Miss Holmes goes into "radar mode." She has been at McKinney long enough to know that a student's transgressions at school might bring a beating at home.

The principal slowly scoots her chair up to Dasani and leans within inches of her face.

"Okay," she says softly. "Let's make a deal." From this day forward, Dasani agrees to be on her best behavior. No more cursing, or mischief in the bathroom. No more calling herself Terminator.

In return, the principal will keep what happens at school in school.

Dasani's face relaxes.

With that, Miss Holmes waves Dasani off, fighting the urge to smile. She cannot help liking this little girl.

It is something of an art to sleep among ten people. You learn not to hear certain sounds, or inhale certain smells.

But other things intrude on Dasani's sleep. There is the ceaseless drip of the decaying sink, and the scratching of mice. It makes no difference that the family lays out traps or hangs food from the ceiling in a plastic bag. Auburn's mice always return, as stubborn as the "ghetto squirrels," in Chanel's words, that forage the projects for Chinese fried chicken.

Dasani shares a twin mattress with her closest sister, Avianna, whose name was inspired by the pricier Evian brand of water. Their room is the scene of debilitating chaos: stacks of unwashed laundry, shoes stuffed under a mattress, bicycles and coats piled high. Metal grates cover the windows, obscuring the view like in prison. A sticky fly trap dangles overhead, dotted with dead insects.

When the lights are on, the room is flatly fluorescent—a problem Dasani and her siblings try to fix with their usual inventiveness. They climb a dresser to reach the ceiling lamp, removing the plastic cover and coloring it with crayons in the shades of a rainbow. Finding a way to do homework is the hardest assignment of all. With no desk or chair—just a maze of mattresses—the children study crouched on sheets stamped PROP. OF THE DEPT. OF HOMELESS SERVICES.

"Your spot is on your bed," says Dasani. "So when you walk in the door, you put your stuff down, straighten up a little bit, you get a snack from the fridge, and you sit on your bed and do your homework. Or do whatever you gotta do. And you stay on that spot—you don't get up."

When the lights are off, Room 449 assumes a gray aura. Sometimes the children hear noises. Five-year-old Papa thinks he saw a ghost. None of the siblings will venture into the bathroom after dark. This is why they relieve themselves in what Dasani calls "the piss bucket."

Privacy is a luxury. Dasani carves out small, sacred spaces: an upturned crate by the window, a portion of the floor at mealtime, a stall in the scary bathroom. She sits here alone, the toilet lid closed beneath her. Sometimes she reads, or just closes her eyes. Her mind feels crowded elsewhere.

"It's like ten people trying to breathe in the same room and they only give you five windows," says Dasani.

The children keep growing, but not their room. Nothing stays in order. Everything is exposed—marital spats, frayed underwear, the onset of puberty. Supreme paces erratically. Chanel cannot check her temper. It has been this way for years.

Dasani is too young to remember the moment, nine years ago,

when her mother met Supreme at a homeless shelter in Harlem. Chanel was a recovering crack addict with two little girls—Dasani, then a toddler, and Avianna, still a baby. Supreme was a barber whose first wife had died of heart disease, leaving him with two small children of his own: Khaliq, who had trouble speaking, and Nana, who had trouble seeing.

These two single parents and their four children merged. After getting married, Chanel and Supreme had another four children, bringing their collective brood to eight. The sheer size of their family can make strangers stare in judgment.

Chanel imagines their thoughts: She is a "welfare mom," having children to profit from the system. She is careless with her body, hopping from man to man without contraception. She is financially reckless, producing more mouths than she can feed. To each of these judgments, Chanel has an answer. She'd like to meet the mother who endures childbirth, six times over, for some extra food stamps "that barely last the month." She is nobody's "baby mama." She is—unlike many women of higher stature and lighter skin—a stubbornly devoted wife, faithful to one man, with whom she is raising one family.

Chanel did not have her children by accident. She had them by design, planning for this small army of siblings, seeing strength in their bond. "This is a cruel world," she tells me. "I didn't want them to be hurt from the world. I wanted them to rely on each other. So they don't need to depend on people who aren't family—people on the street who call them 'sister' and 'brother' but really aren't their sisters and brothers.

"We didn't have family," she says of herself and Supreme, both of whom spent long stretches of childhood separated from their biological parents and siblings. Though Chanel had a doting godmother, she grew up longing to be with her birth mother, "longing to have love."

"That's why the street became our family," she says. "I didn't want the street to become their family too."

Sometimes Dasani can see that the street is still family—at least to her parents, whose livelihood depends on a network of near kin. Supreme hawks DVDs and cuts hair freelance at the shelter while

Chanel "boosts" clothes, stealing them from stores to sell on the street.

They also rely on public assistance, which can vary from month to month. Right now, in October 2012, Dasani's family is getting $182 in monthly welfare cash, $1,103 in food stamps, and $724 in survivors benefits for Supreme's first two children (due to the death of their mother, his first wife). This comes to about $65 a day, which, divided among a family of ten, amounts to $6.50 per person—the cost of a subway trip and a gallon of milk.

Still, this is more than many people get. Less than 2 percent of homeless families receive survivors benefits. Depending on the audience, Dasani's parents are either "working the system" or "making ends meet." Either way, they are living in a city where no poor family with eight children, supported by parents lacking college degrees, could easily get by.

New York, it often strikes Chanel, has no place for the poor. Her family survives because they live rent-free, in a shelter, and have access to three meals a day.

"How can I pull up any straps with no boots?" she says.

Over the years, Chanel and Supreme have occasionally landed in jail. Most of the offenses have been minor. They were caught stealing food or riding the subway without paying. The worst charges involved fights or drugs. Each time, they promised to do better. They talk of wanting real jobs, but many things get in the way—their criminal records, their periodic relapses, their daily attendance at the drug treatment clinics upon which custody of their children rests.

It has been six months since Chanel worked as a security guard at Duane Reade. Years before that, she was a park janitor in Staten Island, where Supreme worked at a barbershop. They bristled at any perceived slight, which tends to "trigger" them, Chanel has heard therapists say, reviving the childhood traumas that she numbs with drugs.

"You can't tell her nothing," Dasani says of her mother. "She needs to be her own boss."

Lately, Supreme has kept a tight hold of the family's welfare income and is now refusing to give Chanel cash for laundry, leading them to argue.

In moments like this, Dasani feels an anger toward Supreme that she cannot yet speak. She stares at him hard, her stomach knotting up. She has only known her stepfather to be erratic—a loving parent one moment, a tyrant the next. It is never clear which Supreme the family will get. Sometimes he vanishes altogether.

If Chanel pushes him too hard about the laundry, he could easily walk out. Instead she lets it go, and soon, Dasani's uniforms are stained. Her hair is also unbraided, inviting the dreaded insult of "nappy."

At school, rumors are circulating about where Dasani lives. Only six of the middle school's 157 students reside in shelters. When the secret of Dasani's homelessness is finally revealed, she does nothing to contradict it. She is a proud girl. She must find a way to turn the truth, like other unforeseeable calamities, in her favor.

She begins calling herself "ghetto." She challenges the boys to arm-wrestling matches. They watch slack-jawed as Dasani flexes her biceps, honed with pull-ups on the monkey bars.

Her teachers are flummoxed. When Dasani sheds her uniform, they assume it's because she is trying to act tough. In fact, the reverse is true: She is acting tough because she can no longer dress fly.

Dasani can count the white people she knows on four fingers: a court-appointed lawyer, a sidewalk preacher, an activist nun, and a computer science teacher. Adding to their ranks is the occasional social worker, beat cop, or city inspector.

White people divide into two categories: those who are paid to monitor Dasani's family, and those who are called to help. Sometimes the same people wear both hats. Rarely does the family trust them. They figure in Dasani's life because of the work they do. And on the afternoon of October 4, 2012, this small circle expands to include me, a staff writer at *The New York Times*.

I am standing in front of the Auburn shelter trying to talk to homeless mothers. For days, I've been looking for a way into this shelter, which is strictly off-limits to the public and the press. Conditions are said to be grim. A legendary local nun, Sister Georgianna Glose, had told me that a family of ten is crammed into one room.

The mothers look me up and down. I'm wearing the worn jeans of any street reporter—which could also, it turns out, be the attire of a social worker or, even worse, a snitch. Everyone on the outside tries to fit in.

"You should talk to her," says one mother, gesturing at a large freckly woman who is walking like a drill sergeant, trailed by seven children.

Chanel stops in her tracks and looks at me, unblinking (a practiced power move, she later explains). I introduce myself, handing her my card. She can see that I'm not a snitch, she will later admit, because I'm wearing a floppy, ill-fitting wool hat and I keep dropping my pen. I'm far too conspicuous to be in the narcotics squad.

Soon we are meeting in nearby parks, my notebook filling with the story of Chanel's life. Yet for every few lines I scribble down, another voice interrupts—the spunky eleven-year-old daughter by Chanel's side.

Again and again, Dasani steals my attention—doing cartwheels and backbends, reenacting her latest battle with Auburn's incorrigible mice. For all of her flair, Dasani is a careful listener. She absorbs the facts of my life as if holding her own recorder: that I am a thirty-nine-year-old mother of two little girls; that I work for the investigative team at the *Times*; that I take the 2 train from the Upper West Side, sipping green juice that makes Dasani stick out her tongue as if gagging.

Each revelation opens new lines of inquiry. She wants to know why I'm talking on the phone in Spanish (my mother is a Chilean immigrant). She wants to know my sign (Sagittarius) and my favorite musician (Prince). She wants to know how far I've traveled (I show her a magazine story I wrote from the slums of northern Morocco).

Dasani and Chanel have no reason to trust me. Eventually, Chanel will confess that if I weren't a mother, she would never have let me near her children. It also helps that I am not, in her words, "all white" because I am "Latin." My ethnicity delights Dasani, whose biological father is half Dominican. But to Chanel, race matters more. I am, at best, a white Latina with a graduate degree, making me the beneficiary of a privilege that she will observe and dissect for years to come.

My only other saving grace is the digital pen I use to record sound, which Dasani calls my "spy pen." Indeed, her family wants me to spy on Auburn. For this I need their help. The shelter is heavily guarded, which means I must report from the outside. So I ask them to document the condition of their room with video cameras provided by the *Times*. We also give Chanel a cellphone, to ensure solid communication, as Supreme always exhausts the minutes of his "Lifeline" phone (provided for free by the federal government).

Soon I am staring at footage of mice, roaches, and mold on the walls. Auburn's decay is no secret to city and state inspectors, who have cited Dasani's room for thirteen violations—including lead paint—since her family moved in. Elected officials and city administrators have also known of the shelter's problems for years, hounded by Fort Greene SNAP, the local nonprofit run by Sister Georgianna.

When Auburn's staff members visit Room 449, they seem more eager to scold than to help. They focus on the family's transgressions, finding the room "chaotic" and insufficiently clean. They give scant attention to Auburn's own obvious lapses—the absence of dividers for privacy, the presence of vermin.

Lately, it is the family sink that Auburn fails to fix. All night long, it drips and drips, keeping Dasani awake. She knows that her mother has pleaded with the staff to repair it.

Finally, Dasani gets fed up. She crouches down to examine the pipe.

"Nobody thought about pushing it in and twisting it," she says. A few quick jerks and she triumphs. Her siblings squeal.

It goes unremarked that here, in a shelter with a $9 million budget, operated by an agency with more than a hundred times those funds, the plumbing has fallen to an eleven-year-old girl.

chapter 3

DASANI CLOSES HER eyes and tilts her head toward the classroom ceiling. She has missed breakfast again—the free one at Auburn, with its long lines, and the free one at McKinney, with its strict curfew.

She tries to drift. She sees Florida. For a child who has never been to the beach, television ads are transporting. She is walking in the sand. She crashes into the waves.

"Da*saaa*ni!" her teacher cries out.

She opens her eyes.

There is Miss Hester, batting those lashes.

The teacher still does not know where Dasani lives, or how hungry she gets. She comes in late most mornings, never saying why. She seems sleepy, as if she just rolled out of bed. The truth is that Dasani has been up for hours. By the time other children are just waking, she has finished her chores and is scrambling to walk her siblings to their bus stop. This would alarm any teacher, prompting a call home or possibly to the authorities. So Dasani keeps it to herself.

Every morning, she slips into class quietly, tucking her coat and backpack into the closet, a precious ritual for a girl with no other closet. Her sixth-grade homeroom, true to its name, is becoming a substitute home—a cozy haven of book-lined shelves and inspirational phrases scrawled in chalk.

Dasani likes to recite them out loud. "Success does not come without sacrifice and struggle," she reads, after settling into her desk.

Miss Hester can see that Dasani lacks proper clothes and snacks, even basic school supplies. Yet she is keeping up in class, performing well enough to mask her troubles. She possesses, to Miss Hester's mind, an "intuitive" approach to learning, the kind that comes when rare smarts mix with extreme circumstances.

Others at McKinney are noting the same promise. Dasani's intelligence is "uncanny" and her "thought content far surpasses peers her age," writes a counselor at the school. Principal Holmes can also see it, calling Dasani a "precocious little button," the type of girl who could become anything—even a Supreme Court justice, if she harnesses her gifts in time.

"Dasani has something that hasn't even been unleashed yet," says the principal. "It's still being cultivated."

For now, Dasani's greatest skill might be one of obfuscation. She shrugs when teachers ask why she is late. She pretends not to notice when her classmates wear new Jordans. She stays quiet when they brag about their sleepovers, an invitation Dasani could never take, much less make. She comes to dance class without a leotard, sitting in the corner, stretching her legs across the wide wooden floor.

But as soon as the music starts, her body feels free. "When I'm happy, I dance fast," she says. "When I'm sad, I dance slow. When I'm upset, I dance both."

Dasani has been dancing for as long as she can remember. She burst into it as a little girl, showing such confidence that her mother took her to Times Square. Dasani remembers breakdancing for tourists, the family's boom box blaring, when a man walked up and handed her a dollar bill. She spent it on fries.

Every so often, Dasani and her siblings dance on the train for money. They arrange themselves behind her in the shape of a diamond, with Dasani at the tip. She is their choreographer—a word she will first hear at McKinney, though she has been doing it for years. "I don't listen to the beat," she says. "I listen to the words. The words tell you to do something."

Now it is Miss Harris, the dance teacher, who is telling Dasani what to do. She must learn to point her toes like a ballerina, and to fall back into a graceful bridge. Every night, Dasani practices in Auburn's communal bathroom, leaping and gliding across the floor as her siblings take turns showering.

Dance, she is starting to see, is more than spontaneity. It is a craft of discipline, a way of organizing the mind and body. Unlike the disorder at home—the missed welfare appointments, the piles of unsorted socks—McKinney's dance studio is a place where time is kept and routines are mapped.

The dancers are hard at work, rehearsing for the winter recital. Dasani has memorized each girl's part. From off to the side, she copies the other girls, moving her arms and legs in tandem. She is captivated by the star, a popular girl named Sahai.

Tall and limber, Sahai moves like a trained ballerina. There is nothing, it seems, she cannot do. She is the middle school's reigning valedictorian, carrying herself through the halls like a queen, her silky hair crowned by a giant bow.

You can be popular in one of three ways, her mother's words ring.

Dasani's frayed sneakers are no match for the trendy Dr. Martens boots flaunted by other students. So she applies herself to her studies.

By October, Dasani has made the honor roll.

Dasani often starts a sentence with "Mommy say" before reciting, verbatim, some new bit of learned wisdom, such as "peppermint tea cures a bad stomach" or "that lady is a dope fiend." She rarely wavers, or hints at doubt, even as her life is consumed by it.

She never talks about the biological father who vanished after she was born. The only person she calls Daddy is the one she can see: her thirty-five-year-old stepfather, Supreme, who has been around since she was two. She likes a mystery to be solved. She likes hard, cold facts, hence her obsession with the show *Criminal Minds*, followed by *Law & Order*, *Without a Trace*, *Cold Case*, and *The First 48* (in that exact order).

She watches these shows from a television propped on two milk crates. She hushes her siblings as the crime unfolds, guessing at the plot, mimicking the detectives. She could see herself as one of those hard-nosed prosecutors, pacing back and forth in a tailored suit. She would drill into witnesses with the same precision. Her jury would watch in awe as she holds "all those low-life thugs" to account.

Other times, Dasani pretends to be a newscaster she calls Dr. Coates. Holding an imaginary microphone, as if speaking to a live camera, she says, "Hello, my name is Dr. Coates, and I am here to report that Barack Obama has won the election. He is the first Black president to *win* the election."

Dasani never tires of saying that she shares her president's skin color.

"Yeah, but he lives in the *White* House," says Chanel. "It's for the whites. It's not for any of us."

Everyone knows Dasani's mother.

Chanel weighs 215 pounds and her face is a constellation of freckles lit by a gap-toothed smile. The street is her domain. When she walks, people often step to the side—in deference to her ample frame or her imperious air.

She has three names, each one taken from a different chapter of life. The old folks use her birth name, Chanel. By the time she was running the streets, she went by "Lady Red," owing to the copper-hued hair she got from her mother, who got it from her father—an inheritance Chanel traces to the white enslavers of her ancestors. On her right arm is the tattoo LADY RED, from her time running a crack house for the Bloods.

To new acquaintances, she introduces herself by a third name—Makeba—which she took when she left the Bloods to marry a man whose own three names follow the same arc: the "slave name" chosen by his parents (Eric), the "street name" chosen by gangbangers (Rat Face), and the "righteous name" chosen by himself (Godsupreme).

Supreme gives his wife the vaunted titles of "Earth" and "Queen." Yet "Chanel" is the word that comes first to her tongue. She sees no reason to shed one name for another. They all claim space within her kaleidoscopic self. When she is feeling up, she wraps her hair in a tubular scarf, in homage to her African roots. When she is down, she hides beneath a wool hat, the kind she hawks on the streets of Brooklyn. She cannot be bothered with the trappings of femininity, things like hair weaves or acrylic nails. Her uniform is a pair of men's sneakers, size nine, and her husband's extra-large coat.

She is often spoiling for a fight, and her brawls are legendary. Chanel was nineteen the first time she went to the jail on Rikers Island (for busting a cop in the head with a bottle at a corner store in Bedford-Stuyvesant after he struck her in the face with his walkie-talkie).

A five-minute trek through Brooklyn's Fulton Mall can take Chanel hours for all the greetings, gossip, recriminations, and nostalgia. She is in everyone's business, scoping out snitches, offering homeopathic remedies, tattling on a girl's first kiss. "I'ma keep my eyes on you this summer!" she warns a lanky teen named Cici.

Chanel is always on the move, plotting her next hustle, sweet-talking anyone she owes $10. While other people want the glamorous life of Jay-Z, Chanel would settle for being his pet. "Just let me be the dog. Shit, I don't care where you put me." When she laughs, she tilts her head back and unleashes a thunderous cackle.

These theatrics are something of a decoy. They distract from Chanel's most vulnerable parts, the way a car's shiny hood covers an intricate engine. Her mind is always turning, dipping into the past, guessing at the future, extracting wisdom from her current set of troubles. She ruminates on an endless supply of memory and longing. The scent of her newborn, before Lee-Lee was taken by caseworkers last year. The echo of her late mother's laugh.

Sometimes she will stop dead in her tracks, interrupting a crowded sidewalk to stare at a stranger. A woman's scrunched-up mouth means she hasn't had enough sex. A boy's swagger suggests a home without a father. She has what she calls a "bloodhound nose," sniffing out phoniness in seconds. Such inclinations have earned her the reputation of being nosy—a habit she does not deny.

"I want someone else's life," Chanel says. "That's why I always be watchin'." She can spend hours analyzing her interaction with anyone white—how the social worker's voice tightened, suggesting a hidden disdain; how the man in a suit brushed past her on the train, as if his body mattered more.

A person's face is a map. Those who look to the left are lying. Those who smile too much are wearing "a frown turned upside down." Chanel engages in endless wordplay, reciting lyrics, composing raps. An internal soundtrack accompanies her life. She switches from song to song like the dial on a radio—a bit of Luther Vandross, a smattering of Rihanna. She will hum a tender tune like "Mercy, Mercy Me," only to stop before it gets the best of her.

No one is allowed to see her cry. She would rather rage or go quiet, keeping the worst thoughts to herself. She is forever revisiting the facts of her life, trying to imagine it had the choices been different.

"I don't love myself," she says. "That's my biggest downfall."

A chilly November wind whips across Auburn Place, rustling the plastic cover of a soiled mattress in a trash bin.

Chanel and Supreme stand nearby, waiting for their children to return from school. They are short on cash. The children have tried to pitch in, raising $5.05 by collecting cans and bottles over the weekend.

Chanel inspects the mattress. Clean, it might reap $10. But it is stained with blood and feces. Janitors in masks and gloves had removed it from a squalid room at Auburn vacated by a mother with three small children. She rarely bathed them, and they had no shoes the day she gathered them in a hurry and left.

"You can smell it?" Chanel asks Supreme.

"No, I can see it," he says, curling his lip.

Chanel scrunches her nose.

"Nasty girl," she says.

A few minutes later, Dasani appears, lugging a bag of clothes donated by a security guard at school. She rummages through the bag, pulling out a white Nautica ski jacket. She holds it up to her shoulders. It is too wide, and somewhat dirty, but she knows that her parents are broke.

"Look, Mommy!" Dasani says, modeling her new coat.

"That fits you real nice," coos Chanel.

Now Dasani's sisters are picking through the bag. Avianna pauses as a gray Lexus SUV rounds the corner. The driver is Uncle Waverly, the brother of their maternal grandmother, Joanie.

Ten-year-old Avianna smiles and waves. Her uncle sees the child but keeps driving. She waves again as the car pulls off. He lives in the projects across from Auburn and works for the city's Parks Department. The children have never set foot in his apartment.

"Family sucks," Chanel says.

Avianna stares in the direction of the vanished Lexus. Just then, Supreme leaps into the air. His welfare benefits have arrived, announced by a recording on his prepaid phone. He sets off to reclaim his gold teeth from the pawnshop, at a 50 percent interest rate. He will then buy new boots for the children at Cookie's, a discount store in Fulton Mall. By week's end, the money will be gone.

Supreme and Chanel have been scolded about their lack of financial discipline in countless meetings with city agencies. But when that money arrives, they do not think about abstractions like "personal responsibility" and "self-reliance." They lose themselves in the delirium that a round of ice creams brings. They feel the sudden, exquisite rush born of wearing gold teeth again—of appearing like a person who has, rather than a person who lacks.

The next day, Dasani shows up to school wearing her new Cookie's boots. Feeling amped, she gets into a verbal spat with some boys during gym. She has also been disrupting Miss Hester's classroom. She must spend her lunch hour in the principal's office.

Miss Holmes glowers at Dasani, who tries to change the subject, bragging about her place on the honor roll. The principal is unmoved. Dasani has just a B average.

"I want the *highest* end of the honor roll," Miss Holmes says. "I want more. You have to want more, too."

After all, Miss Holmes was held to a high standard herself. Raised in nearby Clinton Hill, she was the daughter of Anna V. Jefferson, the second Black female elected to New York's state senate.

Dasani looks away.

"While we care for you, we're not going to take any crap," Miss Holmes says. "You understand?"

Trying not to cry, Dasani examines her meal—a slice of cheese pizza, chocolate milk, a red apple. She wrinkles her nose. Miss Holmes has seen it before, the child too proud to show hunger.

"Can you hurry up?" Miss Holmes says. "The drama with the pizza is not working for me."

Silence.

"I'll feed you," Miss Holmes says. "I will feed you. You don't think I'll feed you? Bring the tray."

Dasani slowly lifts the pizza slice to her mouth, her lips forming a smile.

Miss Holmes has seen plenty of distressed children, but few have both the depth of Dasani's troubles and the height of her promise. There is not much Miss Holmes can do about life outside school. She knows this is a child who needs exposure, who "needs to see *The Nutcracker*," who needs her own computer. There are many such children.

Here at school, Miss Holmes must work with what she has.

"Apples are very good for you," she says, smiling. "Bananas are, too."

"I don't like those," Dasani says.

"Pretend you like them."

When Dasani is finished, she brings her empty tray to Miss Holmes for inspection. The principal gestures at Dasani's milk-stained mouth.

"Fix it," she says. "Go."

On December 7, 2012, Dasani paces the dance studio. She checks the clock. Her performance is in less than two hours and she still has no leotard, which her mother promised to bring.

The other girls are dressed in matching leotards and tights, warming up for the winter show, the biggest event of the year. Dasani is stuck in a faded tank top and skinny jeans that manage to sag. She knows she cannot take the stage dressed like this. She distracts herself by watching a dance battle between two girls, who bump and grind in the mirror. Soon they usher Dasani to the center of the room.

The girls clap and whoop as Dasani tries to suggestively move her hips. Most of her classmates act older than their years. Dasani is the opposite. She still runs to the swings at the playground, and says "mommy" instead of "mom." Here in the studio, she is no match for her seductive rivals.

As night falls, parents walk into the school's auditorium, passing framed posters of Dizzy Gillespie, Billie Holiday, John Coltrane, and Josephine Baker. The theatergoers settle into squeaky seats as a teacher hands out flyers about the charter school that is trying to move in. Department of Education officials will soon vote on the matter. Tonight, after the recital, representatives of Success Academy have agreed to take the stage and answer questions. The place buzzes with talk of this impending collision.

Upstairs, the dancers are ready. Dasani has given up on her mother. She follows the group to the first floor, minutes before curtain call.

Suddenly Chanel comes charging through the school's entrance, her children in tow.

"You didn't think I was bringing your stuff, did you!" she says, holding out a bag of French fries and a leotard.

"No," says Dasani, devouring the fries, which Chanel had bought with her few remaining dollars. The leotard she swiped from Target.

"See? You didn't have any faith in me," says Chanel, who is now speed-braiding Dasani's hair. "If I don't pull through, who's gonna pull through?"

Dasani throws on the new leotard and races to catch up with the other dancers. Her siblings take their seats in the theater, where students hold cardboard signs protesting the charter school.

They hand a sign to Chanel that reads: FORCING SOMETHING WHERE IT'S NOT WANTED . . . SOUNDS PRETTY MUCH LIKE RAPE, DON'T YOU THINK?

Chanel shakes her head. "Who let them kids write that?"

She has never seen activism amount to anything. Her people always wind up with a bad deal. Why should this end differently? She puts the sign down.

The crowd goes quiet as the curtains rise to the Chris Brown song "Trumpet Lights."

Chanel searches for her daughter. There is Sahai, floating across the stage. Finally, Dasani leaps out with a terrified face. For all her bravado, she suffers from stage fright.

"Attitude! *Attitude!*" Chanel hollers.

Dasani makes a few more cameos, looking at the audience in search of her siblings. Avianna hoots and cheers. When the dance ends, they break into the kind of applause that has rattled this theater for decades.

"All *right* now!" Chanel yells, clapping hard. But she is already dissecting Dasani's performance with stage-mother focus. Minutes later, Dasani appears, smiling and out of breath.

"Listen, man," says Chanel. "You messed up on like two or three of your parts."

"That's what I was supposed to do."

"No, I seen you skip out of turn when you're spinning to get to the back and put your leg up in the air."

"That's what we was *supposed* to do!"

"Listen to me," Chanel says. She softens her tone. "Listen to me. You did good. But when you out there, you keep your focus on what you gotta do. Don't look at us."

Dasani turns away and reaches for Lee-Lee.

"Please do not drop her," Chanel quips.

Dasani is no longer listening. She nuzzles the baby, looking around for potential admirers.

"Mr. Heyward!" Dasani squeals out to the school's parenting coordinator.

Dasani holds up Lee-Lee like a trophy.

"This my baby!"

"It's not *your* baby," corrects Avianna.

"Shut up," says Dasani, turning back to Mr. Heyward. "When there's a doo-doo," she continues, gesturing at Avianna, "*she* don't even change it."

As the night wears on, the charter school representatives fail to show. Chanel signals for her children to leave. They head to the door as a teenage boy tries to stop them.

"They're late because they're waiting for their people," he says.

"Time don't wait for nobody," Chanel replies.

It is raining outside. The children dash under the Brooklyn-

Queens Expressway, pushing Lee-Lee's stroller as their mother falls behind. Her right knee is swelling and she is in a foul mood. Christmas is just weeks away. She must produce eight gifts, one per child, requiring a hustle that falls on the wrong side of the month, when the family's cash has run dry. She walks in silence as the children fall behind, crowding her part of the sidewalk. Finally, she snaps.

"Somebody get behind me again I'ma knock you out," she shouts as they scurry ahead. She knows she is being harsh, which sinks her mood further.

By the time they reach Auburn, the storm has passed. The children run up and down the rain-slicked street, under lamps that spew a yellowish light. Chanel remarks that other neighborhoods are lit more brightly. "If you keep the area dim, you can keep the minds of the people dim," she says.

Her mood is lifting. She is back in the mode of spectator, forgetting her own troubles as she turns to her surroundings. This is Chanel's own private bait and switch, pulling her from any funk. She could be critiquing her daughter's winter recital, observing a lovers' quarrel, or cataloging the infrastructure of her block like a tour guide. What matters is the distraction. She now turns to Fort Greene Park, just south of the shelter.

"You know what this is?" she says, waving a hand at the park. "This used to be an old war zone."

Chanel's mother, Joanie, had told her the story. Fort Greene, as the name suggests, was once a fort in the Revolutionary War. This was hallowed ground—the site of America's first major battle, in 1776, after declaring independence from the British crown. There is nothing to announce this in Fort Greene's topography, aside from an aging plaque under a 149-foot tower. History fades quickly, with only the most obvious facts, like the tip of that tower, standing out: Singular narratives take hold, casting the North as the symbol of abolition and freedom and the South as the land of the enslaved.

It is a less-known fact that Brooklyn was built on the backs of slaves, brought here by the Dutch in 1626 to clear land, build roads, and work the tobacco plantations. When the British took the colony nearly four decades later, renaming it for the Duke of York, the importation of slaves began in earnest. The colony's enslaved population swelled to 13,500, making it the largest slaveholding territory in the North. And nowhere in New York was the concentration of slaves higher than in Brooklyn—one-third of the population.

Thousands of enslaved Blacks took up arms in the Revolutionary War—some for the British, who promised them freedom, and some for the rebels (after George Washington reluctantly allowed them to fight). The biggest battle unfolded in Brooklyn, when the British took control of New York's port. They captured tens of thousands of Continental troops, including an estimated three thousand Black soldiers who languished on jail ships in New York's Wallabout Bay—the same waters that their African forebears had crossed in slave vessels. A prisoner's best chance at survival—white or Black—was to denounce the rebels and join the British. The corpses of as many as 11,500 prisoners, wasted from hunger and disease, were tossed overboard, their bones washing up along Brooklyn's shores.

The prisoners' remains are now interred in Fort Greene Park, beneath the granite Prison Ship Martyrs Monument, topped by an eight-ton urn. A sandstone slab honors those who "perished in the cause of liberty," proclaiming them "the spirits of the departed free."

Chanel has been hearing about these spirits since she was a child—how they cause doors to slam and windows to open. She calls them "old energy," the ghosts who haunted the hospital where her mother was born and where Baby Lee-Lee's life has just begun.

"Even in the shelter, the kids will tell you they don't like to use the bathroom cuz you hear the doors open," Chanel says. "You do!"

She is now standing near Auburn's gate. She gestures to the children to head inside.

"They built these projects on top of all this death," she says.

A light drizzle falls, dimming the streets.

The monument is lit like a rocket.

chapter 4

THE TREE BLINKS with Christmas lights, masking the lack of ornaments. Gifts are scarce: some coloring books, a train set, stick-on tattoos, a doll for each girl.

The children have gathered here, on December 24, 2012, in the row house of Chanel's sixty-five-year-old godmother, Sherry Humbert. Situated on the far eastern edge of Brooklyn, this is the closest thing Dasani has to a real home.

Cracked linoleum steps lead to Sherry's dining room table, where unpaid bills spill over the daisy-print cloth. A couch encased in plastic sits beneath a Roman-numeral clock that is permanently stopped at 2:47. The bank is threatening to take possession of Sherry's home. Her electricity has been cut, but the tree remains lit, and the heat stays on, via a cable illicitly connected to a neighbor's power supply.

Supreme stands at the stove, basting his honey barbecue wings as the collard greens start to steam. This is the family at its most peaceful—the father cooking, the mother braiding hair, the children playing with new toys.

At night they fall asleep on foldout cots. One floor below is the now-empty daycare center that Sherry once ran. Fading Bambi decals share space with empty liquor bottles left by Dasani's uncles, twenty-two-year-old Josh and thirty-nine-year-old Lamont, both of whom are jobless and living in Sherry's basement.

A few nights after Christmas, a loud crash wakes the children.

Uncle Josh has punched his hand through a window, threatening to kill Uncle Lamont. Josh pulls out a knife and lunges at Lamont. The men tumble to the floor as Chanel throws herself between them. Upstairs, Dasani calls out orders: "Nobody move! Let the adults handle it!"

Sirens sound. The police arrive. The children watch from the window as Uncle Josh is arrested and led away in handcuffs. An ambulance takes Lamont to the hospital with a battered eye.

They had been fighting over a teenage girl.

January brings relief.

This is the start of "tax season," when everyone Chanel knows rushes to file for their "refund"—the special tax breaks given to low-income families. The largest of these is the Earned Income Tax Credit, which can bring a cash subsidy of thousands of dollars to a family like Dasani's. Administered by the Internal Revenue Service, this is one of the largest antipoverty programs in the country, helping more than 27 million families.

It has been years since Chanel filed for a tax refund, given that she mostly works off the books. But this year, Auburn's administrators have another plan.

IT'S TAX TIME: GO GET YOUR REFUND reads a flyer at the shelter, where Chanel and Supreme must sign a "10 Day Contract" with Auburn, agreeing to file their tax return and bring proof of the filing. If they violate this contract, they may be forced out. They can stay, according to state law, only if they meet the shelter's requirements, which include searching for an apartment and saving enough money to move. The goal is to find permanent housing, as the city's shelters are meant to be "temporary" (a word that occurs thirty-four times in the state's three-page regulation on shelter eligibility).

In order to leave Auburn and rent an apartment, Dasani's family needs a minimum of $4,800, between the broker's fee, the security deposit, and the first and last month's rent (for the median cost of a three-bedroom apartment—about $1,000 in early 2013). This does not include moving costs, furniture, or the task of convincing a landlord that the family will continue to pay rent.

Chanel plans to seek out the storefront accountants who do business with the poor, angling for the highest possible tax refund. On January 7, the family heads to Manhattan, taking the Q train, which barrels high across the East River.

The city's lights glimmer, putting Chanel in a dreamy mood. Their tax refund might be enough to put down a rent deposit on an apartment—or even a house in the rolling hills of Pennsylvania. She announces to the children that they will start looking for a home.

"I wanna go somewhere where it's quiet," says Dasani.

"I wanna go somewhere where there's trees," says Chanel. "I just wanna see a bunch of trees and grass."

"Daddy say that he gonna buy this house with a lot of land with grass," Dasani says, "so that each of us would get a part, so that you can do whatever you want with that part of the land."

Supreme sits far off, his ears blocked by headphones. Baby Lee-Lee wails.

Suddenly, Chanel spots Chinatown. The children squeal. Dasani mentions a book she read about the Great Wall of China.

"That's not this town," Chanel says.

"It's a big wall, though," Dasani says.

"That's the real Chinatown," Chanel says. "This is the New York Chinatown, where they got Chinese people in Popeyes."

Dasani presses her forehead against the window. She cups her hands around her eyes, as if preserving the view for herself.

There are many ways to map a city. Geographers rely on the standard compass of north, south, east, west.

Dasani charts her city in a different way. It is a parallel map, seen only by certain people. Each borough corresponds to a particular code. The Bronx is DHS (the Department of Homeless Services). Queens is HRA (the Human Resources Administration). Brooklyn is ACS (the Administration for Children's Services).

These three agencies form the triumvirate of Dasani's life. They are part of a sprawling social service system known intimately to the poor. Their acronyms entered Dasani's vocabulary when she was still learning to spell. She says "ACS" (child protection) or "DHS" (homeless services) the way a migrant child knows of "ICE" (immigration enforcement).

Each agency represents a separate pillar of power, with its own offices, workers, and labyrinthine lines, its own shade of fluorescent lighting. But to Dasani's mother, they are one and the same. They are limbs of a monolithic body called "the government"—a system that profits off the poor, says Chanel, while punishing them for that very condition. It is also one of the nation's most generous systems. This stems from a Depression-era amendment to New York's constitution, declaring that the "aid, care and support of the needy are public concerns and shall be provided by the state."

By almost any measure, the system is vast.

The broadest limb belongs to the Human Resources Administration, better known as "welfare"—the provider of public assistance to the poor. With an annual budget of $9.4 billion, drawn from federal, state, and city funds, HRA offers help ranging from cash grants and food stamps to Medicaid, the government's health insurance program for the poor. Right now, in the fall of 2012, more than 3 million New Yorkers (roughly 38 percent of the city's population) are getting Medicaid, 1.8 million people are on food stamps, and 357,000 are receiving cash welfare.

Then there is housing. Over half a million New Yorkers live in the city's 334 public housing developments—including the Whitman and Ingersoll projects by Auburn—or rent private apartments with federal subsidies. The demand for cheap housing far exceeds the supply. More than 80,000 schoolchildren have been homeless at some point this year (a number that will surpass 100,000 by 2016). Many are doubled up with relatives; others, like Dasani, are living in shelters.

With a budget of nearly $1 billion, the Department of Homeless Services—the agency Dasani knows as DHS—manages nine city-run shelters, including Auburn, and more than two hundred nonprofit shelters, providing 43,000 beds to homeless people every night. Thousands more sleep on the street or stay in shelters for domestic violence survivors, homeless youth, and other groups.

And finally, there is child protection—better known as ACS—the weightiest acronym in Dasani's life. This agency investigates about 55,000 reports of child abuse or neglect every year. In 2012 alone, ACS will remove 4,072 children from their homes, placing them in a foster care system with more than 13,000 children—the vast majority of them Black or Latino. Almost half of New York City's residents (and a quarter of its children) are white. Nearly all of the city's foster children are people of color.

Don't become a statistic is something Dasani hears all the time—from the teachers at McKinney to the preachers on the street. There is little that Dasani can do to become, or un-become, the statistics that mark her life. She is among the 83 percent of students who qualify for free lunch at her school, the 16 million children growing up poor nationwide, and the 47 million Americans on food stamps.

She does not need the proof of abstract research. She can see with her own eyes where the numbers lead. "I want to get a job—not be on the street like other people. 'Can you spare some change?' I don't get that. Because then I'm gonna either get drunk, get arrested, go to jail, be there for a year, wait to get bailed out. Mmm-mmm," she says, shaking her head.

Like other poor children, Dasani knows the precise date when her family's food stamps replenish: the ninth of each month. Back when her grandmother Joanie first got food stamps, they came as coupons. Today, Chanel carries an electronic benefits card, which works like a debit card. She can use it in most bodegas to buy groceries (but not cigarettes, alcohol, hot food, or diapers, though cashiers often make exceptions).

The family's noncash benefits include Medicaid, the prepaid cellphone used by Supreme, and free meals at the Auburn shelter. The children can also eat for free at their schools, thanks to the federal government's meal programs, which feed Dasani and her siblings during the summer as well.

More money would come if the family got Supplemental Security Income, the disability benefit known as SSI. Two of the children show signs of a learning disability. Plenty of people rely on their SSI checks, but Chanel refuses to apply for the benefit, as evinced by her records.

This may seem contradictory for a woman who routinely steals, but Chanel's moral compass is mysteriously complex. She believes that "special needs" children internalize the label, accruing a school record that "marks them for life." As proof, she points to another family at Auburn, whose children get "like four checks, and they all mad slow."

She would rather get out and hustle.

A few weeks after Dasani's subway trip through Chinatown, Miss Hester opens a letter from ACS.

The teacher reads in silence. The letter is about one of her students.

"Okay, that's good," Miss Hester finally tells me, without sharing the letter's contents. "Sometimes they do overkill. Watch the wrong people. But not here . . . It's like, 'Watch. You've got the right person. Watch.'"

Child protection workers have been watching Dasani's family, on and off, since 2004, when the agency got an anonymous report that Supreme and Chanel had physically disciplined the children. ACS investigated but found no bruises or marks.

There are two categories of child maltreatment: abuse and neglect. Abuse, according to New York law, occurs when a parent inflicts or allows serious "physical injury" to the child. The most extreme cases make headlines that rile the public and shake up the agency. In 2006, two years after ACS began tracking Dasani's family, seven-year-old Nixzmary Brown was beaten to death by her stepfather in Bed-Stuy. Reports of abuse surged, and a new law was passed in her name.

Yet only 7 percent of ACS investigations involve findings of abuse. The vast majority of families—including Dasani's—face charges of "neglect," which is more about failure. A neglectful parent has failed to exercise "a minimum degree of care," according to the law, by not supplying food, clothing, education, supervision, or shelter. It is no surprise that the vast majority of these parents are poor. Many use alcohol or drugs, which is another form of failure: Their addiction has caused them to lose "self-control" of their "actions."

Over the last decade, from May 2004 until January 2013, ACS has conducted sixteen investigations of Dasani's parents. Six of the allegations were declared "unfounded." The other ten involved drug use, lack of supervision, or educational neglect. Only once, in 2011, did Chanel temporarily lose custody after leaving her children unattended at Auburn. Like other families surveilled by ACS, Dasani, her siblings and parents meet regularly with the caseworker assigned to monitor them. Sometimes this woman drops by unannounced, questioning the children privately and inspecting their bodies for signs of abuse.

Dasani's homeroom teacher, Miss Hester, knows plenty of families who are being monitored by ACS. She also knows that watching is not the same as helping. A child like Dasani could be watched for years while her poverty deepens and her prospects narrow. She is an eleven-year-old on the cusp of adolescence. She needs help now.

Yet McKinney's guidance counselor is overwhelmed, and the staff psychologist shuttles between three different schools. They jump from crisis to crisis, like ER doctors in triage, treating problems that have become acute or irreversible.

Prevention is a luxury reserved for schools with multiple counselors. In their absence, Miss Hester has one option: a nonprofit called Partnership with Children, which offers counseling to poor children around the city. The group's budget was recently cut, causing the Partnership office at McKinney to lose two social workers. Student interns are filling the void.

This is how Dasani finds herself sitting across from Roxanne, a blond student from Fordham University's Graduate School of Social Service. While Dasani has never had a counselor, she already intuits the rules governing this arrangement—the fact that Roxanne is a "mandated reporter," a person legally obliged to report abuse or neglect to the authorities. The warmth of her smile makes no difference. Just the words "How is your day going?" are enough to keep Dasani quiet.

All it takes to enter the child protection system is one phone call.

Anyone can make this call, from a professional like Roxanne to a jilted lover phoning anonymously. They dial a toll-free number, reaching an operator with the state's child abuse hotline. The call is screened, and if it seems credible, an investigation begins.

This makes Dasani so nervous that she googles "ACS questions" on the shelter's recreational computer. "Just to know what they would ask and what answers I would have next."

Say the wrong thing and catastrophe awaits. "They can use that in a court of law against the parent," says Dasani, who has heard the story of Supreme as a child, torn from his brothers without warning. Dasani would survive, she thinks, but not her youngest sister, Lee-Lee. Only Dasani speaks the baby's language, discerning a wet diaper in her cries. What would happen to Lee-Lee in the hands of strangers? "Some people don't know how to take care of babies," Dasani says. This is where her mind goes when social workers ask questions.

"I'm fine," Dasani tells Roxanne.

The counselor has only a few details at her disposal. Dasani has been referred to Partnership because of "aggressive and disruptive classroom behavior," according to her intake form.

Roxanne reaches for Mancala, a game in which glass beads are moved across a wooden board. Whoever captures the most beads wins. Dasani takes quickly to the game, eager to beat her counselor. "Student is reserved," Roxanne writes in her notes, adding that Dasani "holds herself in a confident manner."

Dasani has never met anyone like this Minnesota native, who ends her sentences with "sweetie," tipping her head back in silky laughter. She could be a movie star were she not dressed in rumpled shirts and distressed boots. Nothing Roxanne wears seems to match, suggesting a familiar chaos. Dasani knows how it feels to hunt in vain for a missing sock.

Yet Roxanne's outfits are free of stains, which means she has access to a washing machine. As the weeks pass, Dasani decides that her counselor's mismatched outfits are deliberate. She must be living in a clean suburban home, the kind where detectives search for clues on the TV show *Criminal Minds*. It is not the murders that intrigue Dasani so much as the orderly closets of the crime scenes—closets big enough to live in.

"After initial sessions student has opened up," Roxanne writes, "and while playing games will release all emotional tension."

Miss Hester wonders about these counseling sessions. There is no question that Roxanne is devoted. The problem comes down to experience. None of these interns has enough training, by Miss Hester's lights, to meet the challenge of children who carry generations of trauma. It does not matter that Roxanne is warm, or that Dasani now runs to her in the hallway for hugs. Her sweetness is undeniable.

"I don't need 'sweet,'" Miss Hester says. "I need a Ph.D."

Chanel, on the other hand, sees no need for help.

Just the word "counseling" makes her stomach turn. She has enough outsiders meddling, none of whom are trying to raise eight children while homeless. The only way to keep a child in line is to be strict.

In Chanel's book, this is called discipline—the occasional belt smack or being told to stand in the corner. Everyone she knows was "raised by the belt" because "it saves a kid's life." Proper discipline is a form of control. The unruly child grows up to join a gang or land in prison, which is just someone else's system of control. "My husband told me if you don't instill the fear of God in them when they babies," Chanel says, "there's nothing you gonna be able to do when they get a certain age."

Chanel has already made up her mind when she heads to the school on January 17. She is removing Dasani from counseling. Chanel walks into the Partnership office, finding Roxanne with her supervisor, whom the children call Miss Moya. She is tall and elegant—the kind of Black woman who exudes, to Chanel's mind, an air of condescension.

"So let me explain exactly what it is that we do," says Miss Moya, making steady eye contact with Chanel. "We are social workers placed in the school to work with the kids."

Chanel's worst suspicions are now confirmed.

"So, you're social workers?" Chanel asks.

"Yes, we're social workers."

The next few minutes are spent in a careful volley between Miss Moya, who must balance the needs of her students against the fears of their parents, and Chanel, a hardened veteran of the child protection system.

"So, anything in this session that's disclosed—that she says—where does it go?" asks Chanel.

"What do you mean?"

"I mean like if something's bothering her, where does it go? Like does it stay in the building? Or if it was something alarming to you, would you have to disclose it to someone else?"

Roxanne is silent.

"So, you're talking about ACS," says Miss Moya, naming the elephant in the room.

"No, not so much ACS," Chanel says unconvincingly. "Even if you didn't call ACS, but you shared this problem with the guidance counselor—"

"So, there are three things that we are mandated to tell because we are mandated to report it," says Miss Moya.

"That's what I'm trying to say—"

"There are three things—"

Chanel interrupts again.

"Listen!" Miss Moya says. "I'm trying to cut the fear."

"It's not *fear*," Chanel shoots back. "Go ahead."

Miss Moya pauses.

"If she plans on hurting herself, I have to report it," says Miss Moya. "If someone is hurting her, I have to report it. And if she plans on hurting someone else, I have to report it."

With that, Chanel poses a hypothetical question: What if her daughter says, "Oh, my mother beat my ass because I did something wrong?"

Miss Moya explains that her job is to "gauge" each situation. The law, after all, permits physical discipline within limits. "If she told that to me," says Miss Moya, "then there's an assessment process and I speak to her about it. I'm not seeing a bruise on her. I'm not seeing her mouth busted open. I'm not seeing her head open wide."

Chanel is not buying it. As if sensing this, the social worker goes out on a limb.

"I beat my kids," says Miss Moya. "I have no problem saying that. I don't *abuse* my kids, but—"

"Right!" Chanel says. "You don't *abuse* them, but—"

"But I do that to *discipline* my kids," Miss Moya continues. "There's a difference."

Chanel relaxes her jaw.

"I can see if a child is being abused or if they're not being abused," Miss Moya says. "You understand? There's a difference. . . . You can't just call them with your suspicions. You have to be sure."

"People do it every day," Chanel says, referring to the anonymous calls.

"People do it every day," Miss Moya says. "I agree. People do it every day. But I'm just letting you know that it's a process."

The social worker's strategy seems to work. Chanel backs off, allowing Dasani to stay in counseling. "I don't wanna stop her from coming here," Chanel says in a chipper tone, "because I don't want her to feel like she's limited. I want her to feel like any opportunity and open doors are for her and she can take 'em all if she wants, if she can handle them, you know?"

Chanel gathers her things.

Roxanne and Miss Moya trade a look of relief.

"I'm cool with it," Chanel says, heading for the door. "I understand what's going on. If any problems, just call me, you know? Talk to me before you talk to the Man, because the Man ain't no friend of ours."

chapter 5

THE HEAT IS off again at Auburn shelter.

It is 25 degrees outside, but Dasani thrums with energy. In a few more hours, she will try her luck at the Colgate Women's Games, a track competition known for plucking talent from the projects.

Dasani has never met an athletic recruiter, or even set foot on a racetrack. She heard about the Colgate races from her mother, who is always talking up Dasani's talents. And if street lore is any indication, Dasani has the goods to win. Everyone in her small corner of Brooklyn, from the crossing guards to the preachers, knows that Dasani can run.

The same cannot be said for her sister Avianna, who has the portly build of Chanel and would rather kick back and watch *America's Got Talent* than bolt toward any finish line. Her little sisters Maya and Hada are more athletic, so they decide to tag along on this January morning of 2013.

"Black is beautiful. Black is me," Dasani sings under her breath as she walks outdoors with her two sisters and Chanel.

Three blocks later, they have crossed into another New York: the shaded, graceful enclave of Fort Greene's brownstones. Dasani stops for a moment, puzzling at the pavement. It is clearly superior on this side of Myrtle Avenue.

"Worlds change real fast, don't it?" Chanel says.

They walk a mile before reaching the manicured grounds of the Pratt Institute, which is hosting the amateur track and field series in a campus stadium.

"She got shorts to put on?" asks one of the organizers.

Dasani reaches for her leggings, slipping her bare feet into a pair of Converse knockoffs.

"Those are the sneakers?" says the woman, pursing her lips.

Dasani ties the rainbow laces and walks to the track, where she will compete in the 200-meter dash. When her number is called, she takes her place among four other girls, all of them taller than she is.

The blank fires and she is off, ahead of the pack.

Win, Dasani tells herself.

At the first bend, she trips and falls behind.

By the second turn, Dasani has caught up with the lead runner.

"Run, Dasani!" Chanel screams. *"RUN!"*

Fort Greene occupies less than one square mile of Brooklyn.

On the map, its boundaries form the shape of a pitcher tilting west. The neighborhood divides along Myrtle Avenue, from Ashland Place to Vanderbilt Avenue.

Just north of Myrtle, Fort Greene's poorest Black residents are concentrated in two housing projects that surround Dasani's shelter. South of Myrtle is everything else: the lush thirty-acre Fort Greene Park, the Brooklyn Academy of Music, the historic Queen Anne and Second Empire townhouses famously built by Walt Whitman (whose poetry would eclipse his carpentry career). Also here, south of Myrtle, live the majority of Fort Greene's whites.

If one thing distinguishes Dasani's birthplace from the Brooklyn of her antecedents, it is a striking proximity to wealth. She regularly passes a boutique on Lafayette Avenue where calfskin boots command $845. Heading north, she sees French bulldogs on leashes and infants riding in elevated strollers with shock-absorbing wheels. Three blocks farther is an ice cream parlor where $6 buys two salted-caramel scoops.

Like most children, Dasani is oblivious to the cost of such extravagances. She just knows they are beyond her reach. On her favorite block of Myrtle, a fancy wine shop advertises "Que sera, Syrah" next to a rug shop with the sign "Buy now, pay later"—opposite a bike repair store selling kale chips, near the Chinese Fried Chicken that gives fries to hungry kids.

Fort Greene's two economies are an experiment born of gentrification—a term derived from the *gentry*, which means "people of high social status, nobility." To say that an area has been "gentrified" is to invoke the racially coded language of an "urban" neighborhood where muggings are down and espresso beans are roasted—a place that has been "discovered," as though no one had been living there.

Dasani's Fort Greene reaches deep into history.

Take 81 Adelphi Street, two blocks east of Fort Greene Park. Long before this property came under renovation (selling for $2.1 million in 2017), it was the nineteenth-century home of Charles A. Dorsey, a legendary figure of Fort Greene's long-lost Black elite. His name adorns the elementary school that Dasani once attended—a place that matters, she will tell you, because it was Brooklyn's first school for Black children.

Originally named the African Free School, it opened in 1827—the same year that slavery in New York ended under the state's "gradual abolition" laws. This is not to say that white northerners were tolerant. Contrary to New York City's image as a progressive beacon, it was a Manhattan-born minstrel named Thomas Dartmouth Rice who in the 1830s invented the slave caricature Jim Crow—a mockery, performed in blackface, that came to personify segregation.

If Brooklyn's Black children wanted an education, the African Free School was their only option. Another eighteen years passed—the lifespan of a childhood—before the Board of Education, in 1845, admitted the free school into the public system, renaming it Colored School No. 1 and moving it to Willoughby Street, facing what is now Fort Greene Park.

Racial tensions had long been simmering when, in 1863, Irish immigrants in Manhattan mounted one of the most violent anti-Black insurrections in American history. Angered by a law drafting them to fight in the Civil War—ostensibly to free slaves who might then take their jobs—rioters filled the streets, lynching Black people and burning down the Colored Orphan Asylum on Fifth Avenue as 233 children escaped out the back.

Brooklyn, by comparison, was a haven. Fleeing the draft riots, thousands of Black families left Manhattan for Brooklyn, finding an anchor in the Fort Greene school. This prominent tide included African American scholars, entrepreneurs, doctors, and an inventor. They launched businesses, started newspapers, formed literary clubs, and organized politically, transforming the area into the so-called Black Belt. "WEALTHY NEGRO CITIZENS," announced *The New York Times* in 1895, noting that "most of the wealthy negroes" live in Brooklyn—some with white servants and horse-drawn carriages. As many as seventy-one African Americans bought homes, forming the base of Fort Greene's Black intelligentsia, spiritual leadership, and civil rights vanguard.

These currents combined to spectacular effect on November 23, 1883, when the "Colored School" moved into a new building on North Elliott Place. As people crammed the street, trying to hear the six-hour opening ceremony, Brooklyn's white mayor, Seth Low, took a seat inside, along with the school's Black principal, Charles A. Dorsey, and other luminaries (Booker T. Washington would later visit the school). The most rousing words came from the keynote speaker, Richard T. Greener, the first Black graduate of Harvard.

"Why retain the word 'colored'?" demanded Greener, a legal scholar. If he could, Greener told the audience, he would "chisel" out the word from the building's facade.

"It shall be chiseled out!" called a person from the crowd to rapturous applause. By the time Mayor Low rose to speak, it was a fait accompli. The mayor had already curried favor with Black Brooklyn by appointing the first African American, Philip A. White, to the Board of Education. And now, with White sitting in the audience, Mayor Low seconded the call to erase "Colored" from the name of the building. A few weeks later, White proposed a resolution to desegregate Brooklyn's schools. In December 1883, the resolution passed, sealing Fort Greene's place—and Dasani's future school—as a staging ground for civil rights.

It took four more years for the word "Colored" to disappear from the school's name, in 1887, replaced by P.S. 67, and eventually the Charles A. Dorsey School. Nearly two centuries after the school opened, and five decades after Dasani's grandmother Joanie attended P.S. 67, Dasani enrolled in 2010, stepping through the same limestone entrance. By then, the building had moldy ceilings and no functioning water fountain. A charter school had moved in, calling itself Community Roots. Forty-one percent of the Roots students were white, whereas 95 percent of Dorsey's were children of color.

This meant that here, in Brooklyn's first school for Black children, Community Roots was giving Dasani her most frequent glimpse of white children. She passed them in the halls, never talking to them. By the time she graduated from Dorsey, moving on to McKinney, the Department of Education had targeted P.S. 67 for potential closure. To outsiders, this might seem like the destiny of a failing school. To locals, it constituted an act of historical erasure.

Like Dorsey, Dasani's new school is known by the name of another local legend: Dr. Susan S. McKinney, who in 1870 became the first female African American doctor in New York State, and the third in the nation. To understand the magnitude of this achievement, consider that Dr. McKinney went to medical school four years after the Emancipation Proclamation, as the only Black student in her all-female school. She then graduated as valedictorian. When Dr. McKinney died in 1918, W.E.B. Du Bois gave the eulogy at her funeral.

Today, one must dig to uncover the history of Black Fort Greene, whose pioneers seem in danger of being forgotten. Dr. McKinney's former brownstone at 205 DeKalb Avenue—the site of her thriving medical practice—would be listed for sale in 2016 for nearly $2.7 million, without any mention of its history.

Instead, the names of Brooklyn's slave-holding families dominate the terrain. Boerum Hill (named for Simon Boerum, a man with three slaves). Wyckoff Street (Peter Wyckoff, enslaver of seven). Ditmas Park (four slaves). Luquer Street (thirteen). Van Brunt Street (seven). Cortelyou Road (two).

Both Van Dam and Bayard streets are named for the owners of slave ships, while Stuyvesant Heights is named for the man who governed the New Netherland colony of the Dutch West India Company, which shipped tens of thousands of slaves. Even the McKinney school began with a slave-owning name. Back when Dasani's grandmother was a student, this was still the Sands Junior High School, named for Joshua Sands (enslaver of six) and his brother Comfort Sands (three).

None of this is known to Dasani, whose parents only talk about the slavery of their Southern ancestors. The North is where they came to be free.

"Run, Dasani!" Chanel hollers as her daughter sprints toward the finish line at the Colgate races. All five runners are in a dead heat.

Dasani comes in second. Her time is insufficient to make it past the preliminaries. Still, she leaves the stadium feeling euphoric.

"My baby's going to the Olympics," Chanel crows as they walk along Willoughby Avenue. They talk of finding a trainer. At times like this, Chanel thinks of her mother—how proud she would have been, how she always saw Dasani's gifts. They all start singing Joanie's favorite Luther Vandross song, "A House Is Not a Home."

> *A chair is still a chair*
> *Even when there's no one sittin' there*
> *But a chair is not a house*
> *And a house is not a home*
> *When there's no one there*

They turn north on Carlton Avenue, passing a renovated brick townhouse with metallic window frames. A young white mother is unloading her Volkswagen. At the sight of Dasani's family, she stops. She smiles nervously and moves slowly to her car, unbuckling an infant.

The mood shifts.

"She thinks we gonna jump her," says Chanel. "Why do they feel like they're so apart? She's just two steps away from us. If you got jumped out here, a Black man would be the first to save your ass. That's what I feel like telling her. A Black man would be the *first* to save your ass."

When they reach Myrtle, Chanel goes searching for a beer at her favorite corner store. Dasani is right behind her. Inside, the short-order cook, a Mexican girl, stares at Chanel a moment too long.

"Don't look at me," Chanel says.

The girl's face sours.

"You so *nice*, that's why I see you," the girl replies.

"You better watch that grill," Chanel says. "I don't want to scare you."

"You think you scare me?"

"Let's fight right now!"

"Wait for me outside!"

Chanel reaches for a mop.

"Mommy!" Dasani screams.

The owner, Salim, rushes toward Chanel.

"I'll crack her with a stick!" Chanel yells as Salim holds her back. Dasani freezes.

"I'ma wait for your ass when you come out," Chanel tells the girl. "What time she get off?"

"You run your mouth," says Salim, gently pulling Chanel away, as he has done before.

They turn to leave when Dasani looks back at the cook. Their eyes meet.

"She gonna knock you stupid, Chinese lady," Dasani says.

"Don't use those words," says Salim. "You're not supposed to turn out like your mother."

Dasani and Avianna look nothing alike. But inside, they could be twins.

Born eleven months apart, they are "full blood" sisters. They share the same biological father, Ramel, who vanished before they can re-member. They share the same fragile link to their stepdad, Supreme, who fathered all the children except for them: first Khaliq and Nana with his first wife, then Maya, Hada, Papa, and Lee-Lee with Chanel.

Only Dasani and Avianna have names like their mother's, evoking liquids that are bottled and sold. The two sisters function as a unit, sharing the same dresser and mattress, even the same pillow. They claim to read each other's thoughts. Silent jokes pass between them, bringing bursts of laughter.

They both hate surprises, but in different ways. "I don't like *sad* surprises," says Dasani. "I can take a good surprise, like a birthday surprise, but a sad surprise I can't take. It's sad. Avianna can take both surprises: I'm like, 'Really?' She takes sad ones."

A few weeks ago, in early January, the sisters were returning to Auburn when Avianna began to wheeze. She suffers from asthma, as do nearly seventy thousand public school children in New York City under the age of fifteen. She rarely complains, so her siblings fail to notice when an attack is coming. But this time, Dasani could feel it.

"Avianna, you'd better slow down," she said. "Something's gonna happen, I'm telling you so. You know I see things before they happen."

"Shut up," Avianna said. "You don't see nothing."

As they passed through Auburn's entrance, Avianna started to gasp. She clutched her chest. Her eyes got distant. She needed to get upstairs to her mother.

Unaccompanied children are banned from riding the elevator at Auburn, so Dasani began pleading with the guards. "We gotta ride the elevator!"

They refused.

Dasani glanced at her sister, and then the stairs. She tried to grab hold of Avianna, who is twice her girth. They stumbled up the first flight. Finally, Dasani managed to hoist Avianna to her back, telling herself *I got this heffa.*

Dasani attributes her strength to her genes. She is the descendant of her late grandmother Joanie, who never took an elevator. She would climb fourteen flights every time she visited her closest sister. Dasani was still a toddler back then, taking the lift with her mother, who would stop on every floor to check on Joanie.

"You sure, Ma?" Chanel would call out.

"I ain't takin' no damn elevator," Joanie would huff.

To Dasani, this was a sign of her grandmother's power. No one told her that Joanie had a phobia. Or that it began half a century earlier, when Joanie was a teenage girl. Or that the triggering event happened here, at Auburn, when Joanie was trapped in the same elevator that her granddaughters would later be denied.

Dasani knew even less about her great-grandparents, Joanie's mother, Margaret, and her father, June. They were said to have come to Brooklyn from down south. They had passed away, as had Joanie, taking their stories with them.

English is Dasani's favorite subject. She can get lost in a good novel.

Her class is reading *The Glory Field* by Walter Dean Myers, which follows five generations of one Black family from West Africa to the plantations of South Carolina and then north to Harlem.

Dasani's homework assignment is to write a "found poem," mixing lines from the book with her own words. She writes:

> *Taken from our homes*
> *"Beat to death"*
> *Trying to fight back*
> *Too weak*
> *Getting hurt*
> *They don't care*
> *Us colored people prayed*
> *"He prayed"*
> *Beat up so bad looks like a pothole*
> *In a street*
> *The bottom of the ship smells so bad*
> *Like rotten food*
> *Their fish bowl eyes*
> *filled with sorrow.*

She calls this poem "Pain." Her teacher tapes it up in the hallway for everyone to see.

chapter 6

ON A FREEZING February morning, Dasani zips up her white ski jacket, tucking her braids under a cheap fuchsia hat. Her mother insists on neon-colored hats so she can track her children from a distance.

Function over fashion. This mattered less in elementary school, but Dasani is now a sixth grader. She has the wrong sneakers, no earrings, and her forehead shows the first trace of pimples. She is dreading adolescence. Among girls of means—those who don't have to worry about the cost of tampons—menstruation is a celebrated milestone. Here in the projects, a girl can live in fear of blood-stained jeans. Her period is one more thing to outmaneuver.

"I don't plan on having one," Dasani says. "I'd rather kill myself."

If Dasani could design her own video game, she would call it "Live or Die." The protagonist would be an eleven-year-old girl fighting for her salvation. In the first round, Dasani says, she would confront the easy villains—her chores—scrambling to bathe, dress, and feed her siblings. She cannot find Baby Lee-Lee, who is crying and crying. The baby's tears turn into lethal rocks that fall from the sky.

If Dasani dodges the rocks, she makes it to the next round.

Here she sees social workers in the guise of angry pirates, battling her father and mother. Chanel tosses magical powers to Dasani, who defeats the pirates, melting them to the floor. In the third round, she goes to school, finding danger and deliverance. Her math teacher is a "supervillain" whose weapon is numbers. The numeral 10 turns into ten charging porcupines. Now Dasani must rescue her favorite teacher, Miss Hester, from giant rolling cans.

"If she dies, all the kids die, too."

Finally, Dasani faces off against her ultimate rival, Star. In the video game, Star turns into a giant "purple hulk" picking up cars and hurling them. If Dasani circumvents the hulk, she reaches "the queen"—Principal Holmes—who decides her future.

Winning brings the prize of a new house. Losing means returning to the Auburn shelter, "which is death."

"My goal is to make it to the end, but I keep dying," Dasani says.

She finds it easier to see Auburn as the worst possible outcome because the alternative—winding up on the street—is unthinkable.

She arrives at school that morning with frozen hands and wind-chapped lips, catching the notice of her principal, Miss Holmes. Four months have passed since Dasani made the honor roll.

The principal is sitting in her office, surrounded by scented candles and cranky computers. Soothing spa music spills from a portable speaker, drawing students to the door. They never know whether Miss Holmes is talking to them or to her Bluetooth, a purposeful confusion that keeps everyone on edge. They watch as she swivels about in her rolling chair, calling out orders and interrupting fights with a thunderous *"HEY!"* She will gladly end a romance with one phone call home.

"We're a school. We're not a dating service."

Yet McKinney is far more than a school.

The principal's office has become a makeshift Goodwill. And right now Dasani needs help. The child never makes it to school in time for free breakfast. Today she has a big field trip. What are the chances that her mother has packed a snack?

Miss Holmes knows better than to ask. She begins rooting around her desk, like a grandmother in search of a treat.

If Dasani's grandmother Joanie were still alive, she and Miss Holmes would be Brooklyn contemporaries. They were born two years apart—within two miles of each other—to African American mothers who had come north from the Carolinas. But in every other way, Miss Holmes fared better than Joanie. She was an only child surrounded by doting relatives, living in a comfortable three-story house in Clinton Hill owned by her grandparents.

Everyone worked to pay the bills so that Miss Holmes could attend Catholic school and take piano lessons. "Family was family— they really hung together," said her cousin Benjamin Bailey, adding that the grandparents had never gone to college but "were always pushing us forward." Their daughter, Anna V. Jefferson, got a master's degree from New York University before she became the second Black female elected to the state senate. Her own daughter, Miss Holmes, would also thrive.

Today, the principal lives in a high-rise in Jersey City, driving to Brooklyn in a leather-interior Nissan. The school in Fort Greene is her life; the students, her children. Long after they have gone home for the day, she is still in her office, writing grant proposals or calling to check on the graduates she still mentors.

Late at night, Miss Holmes can be found at the school's piano, playing traditional Negro spirituals, born of a time when the children of slaves were ripped from their parents and sold off. Miss Holmes's second-in-command, Michael Walker, also works late. He stands next to her at the piano, his baritone voice filling the empty school.

> Sometimes I feel like a motherless child
> A long ways from home . . .

Miss Holmes is now looking at Dasani's hands. This child has spent so much time washing clothes and bleaching floors that her fingers are creased like those of an old woman. Back when Miss Holmes was a child, she never left home without mittens or breakfast.

She hands Dasani a pair of white knitted gloves, chosen to match her jacket. Then Miss Holmes fishes two dollars from her wallet, pressing the bills into Dasani's palm. That should be enough for a snack.

Dasani skips down the hall, leaving one matriarch for another.

"Okey dokey pokey!" Miss Hester sings out. These three words, with enough repetition, can settle the room. Sometimes, for extra flair, she adds the word "shmokey": "Okey dokey pokey *shmokey!*" The teacher's voice is a balm, like other routine comforts—the heat, for example—that get noticed only in absentia.

The children are studying a handout in preparation for their field trip to Gracie Mansion, the city's mayoral residence.

"Are we gonna see the mayor?" a student asks.

For most of Dasani's life, New York has had one mayor: the billionaire media mogul Michael R. Bloomberg.

"Do you *wanna* see the mayor?" Miss Hester replies, batting those long lashes.

Laughter ripples through the room. Teachers are known to gripe about Bloomberg, who took "mayoral control" of the city's sprawling public school system, declaring it "a disgrace."

It is also true that under Bloomberg's long reign, New York City has been remade. More than three hundred miles of fresh bike lanes connect commuters to high-tech jobs, passing upgraded parks and futurist projects like the High Line. Real estate has boomed, jackhammering the ground as glassy roofs reach skyward.

Among Bloomberg's crown jewels is the charter school movement. His administration will ultimately close 157 public schools while investing mightily in charters (opening 174 in that same period). This is an especially sore topic at McKinney, where parents and teachers protested Success Academy Fort Greene, comparing the proposed charter to "apartheid."

Their objections went nowhere.

Success Academy will be moving into McKinney, this summer of 2013. Meanwhile, due to budget cuts, teachers are being eliminated with each passing year. Nobody's job is safe. The children are still laughing at Miss Hester's off-the-cuff jab at the mayor when she hushes them.

"Excuse me," she says. "I shouldn't have said that."

The mayor, like it or not, is the boss of her school. It's not safe to talk this way. It's also unhelpful to goad her students with lines like *Do you* wanna *see the mayor?* What should stop them from seeking an audience with their mayor?

She looks around her classroom, at the sea of little faces. They are just as entitled to visit Gracie Mansion as the private school kids who arrive on chartered buses. Entitlement is born of self-worth. Some kids have it naturally. Others must develop it against the proof of their experience.

Never mind that McKinney's students are unlikely to meet the mayor. They should not be robbed of the belief that they could, that the world belongs to them and not the other way around.

Miss Hester wants them to learn this, just as she did. The more they see, the farther they will reach. She is already planning a visit to the White House.

Each trip is a step forward.

There is no bus for today's excursion. The children must walk a mile to the subway, turning their cheeks from the icy wind.

By the time they reach the Upper East Side, Dasani is jousting with a boy in her class. He tells her that his grandmother's glasses cost more than Dasani's shoes. A torrent of foul language rushes from Dasani's mouth before Mr. Jenkins, a classroom aide, intervenes.

"He say something stupid!" Dasani grouses. "I got something to say!"

"So you can't help it?"

"Sometimes I can, sometimes I can't."

"You can't control it?" Mr. Jenkins asks.

Dasani's chest is heaving.

"I try to not let those words come out, but they wind up comin' out."

"That's good to know," says Mr. Jenkins. "Maybe you need some help with that."

"I been trying to keep them in. But every time I keep them in, somebody come and say something and they come out," Dasani says. "Cuz I'm tiny, they think I got no words. I have *words.*"

The students have reached their destination: a pale yellow eighteenth-century estate overlooking the East River. "I thought it was gonna be like a mansion," Dasani says. "That's not a mansion. That's a house. That's a house a person lives in."

Gracie Mansion is something of an oddity. In a city with a 2 percent vacancy rate and a shortage of public housing, the mayoral residence has been sitting uninhabited on eleven pristine acres of the Upper East Side. It has been more than a decade since Bloomberg, unlike other mayors, chose to remain in his townhouse, relegating Gracie Mansion to the status of a museum.

Dasani wants to see the mayor up close, this mysterious Wizard of Oz who makes decisions from behind a curtain of power. It never occurs to Dasani that the mayor does not live here. Who would have a mansion and not live in it?

"Look at that fireplace!" Dasani marvels as they step into the parlor where Mayor Bloomberg holds press conferences.

A woman in gold clasp earrings and tangerine lipstick introduces herself as the tour guide. She moves the children along, reminding them not to touch anything. They shuffle into the library. Still no mayor. Dasani scans for clues like the agents of her favorite television show, *Criminal Minds*. She inspects a telephone.

"His last call was at eleven-fifteen," she whispers.

The guide opens a pair of French doors onto the veranda where New York's mayors have entertained dignitaries from around the world. "It's a very gracious way of living," the guide says. "Very elegant." What impresses Dasani are not the architectural details or the gold-bound volumes of Chaucer and Tolstoy, but the astonishing lack of dust. She runs her hand lightly over the top of a Steinway piano.

"I tell you," she says. "This house is clean."

Dasani is well versed in city politics, not because she follows the news. She is simply forced to notice what other children miss.

When Mayor Bloomberg tried to ban the sale of large sugary drinks, Dasani calculated what two sodas would cost instead of the supersize cup that, in her family, is typically passed among eight small mouths. Lately, a citywide bus strike has caught Dasani's attention. She must now walk three of her siblings to school.

The word "billionaire," to Dasani's mind, conjures a sky full of dollars—too many to count. She has never known a mayor other than Bloomberg, who pushed to rewrite the law so he could serve a third term.

Even in small ways, Bloomberg has distinguished himself from his predecessors, starting with his refusal to move into Gracie Mansion. He sidestepped the tradition elegantly, declaring Gracie "the people's house" and directing $7 million in private donations (much of it his own money) to rehabilitate the mansion. In came new plumbing, floors, lighting, and ventilation, along with exquisite touches like a chandelier from the 1820s and a mahogany four-poster bed.

Gracie's renovation brought a glitzy spread in *Architectural Digest* and busloads of tourists, while just six miles away, another city-run home drew no such attention. There are few signs that children live at Auburn. Locked gates prevent them from setting foot on the lawn. In a city that has invested millions of dollars in "green spaces," Auburn's is overrun with weeds.

Since Bloomberg took office, the number of homeless families has risen by 80 percent. They are now staying in shelters for the longest period on record. When asked about this in August 2012, Bloomberg replied that the city's shelters offered "a much more pleasurable experience than they ever had before."

Years from now, one of Bloomberg's senior advisors, Howard Wolfson, would tell me that he and other aides had failed to convey "how much Mike actually cared about reducing poverty and homelessness. I wish in retrospect we had done a better job of it. I break it into three buckets: our intentions, our record, and our rhetoric. Our intentions were good, our record was better than we got credit for, and our rhetoric was lousy."

Just three days before the mayor described shelter conditions as "more pleasurable," an inspector at Auburn had stopped by Dasani's room, noting that a mouse was "running around and going into the walls," which had "many holes."

"Please assist," the inspector wrote. "There is infant in room."

Over the last decade, city and state inspectors have cited the Auburn shelter for more than four hundred violations, among them broken elevators, nonfunctioning bathrooms, faulty fire alarms, insufficient heat, spoiled food, sexual misconduct by staff, inadequate childcare, and the presence of mice, roaches, mold, bedbugs, lead, and asbestos. In interviews, the mayor's staff told me that Auburn's aging infrastructure was mostly to blame, and that the city had spent nearly $10 million on repairs and renovations at the shelter. They declined to comment on the reports of sexual abuse.

Just three months before Dasani's field trip to Gracie, a twelve-year-old boy at Auburn complained in writing that a woman at the shelter had molested him. The police were never notified. Nor did they hear about the fifteen-year-old girl who said that a security guard sexually assaulted her, the same month that a male resident exposed his genitals to a different girl in the bathroom. "I am still scared that someone will come in," the girl wrote in a complaint.

It may stand to reason that the complaints of children would go ignored when the warnings of adults carried so little weight. There was the parent who asked a janitor to remove a dead mouse from the cafeteria. The next day, the mouse was still there. "A child could have touched it," the parent said. The janitor laughed.

"Well, then, you should have cleaned it up," the janitor replied.

chapter 7

I T IS ALMOST noon. The tour at Gracie is coming to an end, as is the mayor's time in office.

After twelve years, Bloomberg will finally be stepping down. Miss Hester has taught her students about the mayor's three "consecutive" terms—a word she says with panache, breaking up each syllable.

Con-SEH-cu-tive.

When Miss Hester says a new word, Dasani watches her teacher's lips. She mouths the word quietly, storing it "in my memory." Later, she tries it out, usually on her siblings. Sometimes, it comes out scrambled, but eventually she gets it right. This is how, bit by bit, Miss Hester tries to close the "vocabulary gap" between children of different classes—a gap that can leave the poorest child exposed to fewer words.

The growing chasm between rich and poor has energized city politics. Just last week, New York's public advocate, Bill de Blasio, entered the race for mayor, pledging to leave "no New Yorker behind."

If Bloomberg personifies the new Gilded Age, de Blasio sees himself as the panacea—the modern urban leader of a new Progressive Era. Raised by left-leaning intellectuals in Cambridge, Massachusetts, de Blasio was seven years old when his parents' marriage ended. His father, a Harvard-trained economist and World War II veteran, fell to alcoholism, taking his own life when de Blasio was eighteen. By his midtwenties, de Blasio had become a radical leftist, aligning himself with the Sandinistas in Nicaragua before entering New York City politics in 1990 as an aide to Mayor David Dinkins, the first African American elected to the office.

More than two decades later, de Blasio still manages to project the image of an outsider. The fifty-one-year-old politician announced his long-shot bid for mayor in front of his Park Slope home—a pointed contrast to Bloomberg's opulent Manhattan townhouse.

"Let's be honest about where we are today," said de Blasio, standing next to his African American wife and their teenage son, Dante. "A city that, in too many ways, has become a tale of two cities, a place where City Hall has too often catered to the interests of the elite rather than the needs of everyday New Yorkers."

Over the next few months of 2013, as de Blasio drums up support, the homeless crisis continues to hound the current mayor. More than fifty-five thousand people are now sleeping in city shelters.

Lately, Bloomberg seems irritated by questions about the crisis, giving answers tinged with sarcasm. New York City, the seventy-two-year-old mayor will soon tell listeners on his Friday radio show, is the only city in America where "you can arrive in your private jet at Kennedy Airport, take a private limousine and go straight to the shelter system and walk in the door and we've got to give you shelter."

Dasani has never been in a plane or a limousine, or even a Greyhound bus, for that matter. She has certainly never seen a billionaire (as far as she knows) or a mayor. She is still looking for Bloomberg as the students head to Gracie Mansion's exit. She wants just one glimpse. What is he like?

The class now gathers on Gracie's steps to pose for a photograph. The children shiver. Miss Hester waves them toward the exit. They have a long trip back to Brooklyn.

Dasani refastens her neon-pink snow hat and puts on her new gloves. She feels for her two dollars. She is getting hungry. She has given up on the mayor.

"He lives somewhere else," Dasani says, waving an arm along East End Avenue.

On a blustery winter morning, Dasani bolts out of Auburn chasing after her siblings. It is no small feat to corral Papa, Hada, and Maya, a gaggle of untied shoelaces and candy-stained lips.

"They're annoying and they're hard-headed," Dasani says. "They don't listen. I don't know why!"

"Because I listen in *school*," Maya says.

Dasani rolls her eyes. She must walk them to their elementary school because the bus drivers are still on strike. To sweeten the deal, Chanel is paying Dasani $3 per week for as long as the strike lasts.

So far, Bloomberg has refused to negotiate with the bus drivers' union, making this one of the most bitter battles of his leadership. Dasani wonders why the drivers won't bend a little, though she imagines that any driver would welcome a break from this trio of miscreants.

Dasani is sure her siblings are to blame for what happened at the Walt Whitman Library. The tiny brick building was their sanctuary, filling the hours between when school lets out and night falls. But last month, Dasani and her siblings arrived to find the doors locked.

"Closed for repairs," read the sign.

The staff got fed up, Dasani guesses, "because all the kids, they don't read books there or do their homework." She is already behind on hers. She needs to research Plato, Socrates, and Aristotle in order to decide "which one you agree with." But she has no computer. With the library closed, Dasani's only other option is Auburn's recreation room, which is crammed with children and overseen by a man they call Mr. Rogers (who is known to surf the Internet for knives and guns).

"If I can't type it, the teacher said write it down really neat—like you never wrote that way before. And then I have to write down their whole history, how they got married, where was they born, and their whole life story," she says of the Greek philosophers. "And their life stories is *long*."

The little ones wander off the sidewalk.

"How many times I tell you to stay on the inside?" Dasani yells.

Like yo-yos, they snap back to Dasani. Their bond is automatic.

"Double up!" Dasani yells.

The children go silent, linking hands. They wait for the traffic to pause. Then, like spirits, they dash across six lanes under the Brooklyn-Queens Expressway.

Dasani scans the options before settling on an iced honey bun, a bag of nacho-flavored sunflower seeds, and some red gummy bears— a rare $3 breakfast earned as part of her allowance.

She glides into class on February 22, just a few minutes late. Her class has been preparing for the upcoming state exams. It bothers Miss Hester that McKinney lacks the sophisticated equipment found in other public schools. She shelled out more than $1,000 of her own money to give her classroom a projector and camera. On test days, she brings bagels, hard-boiled eggs, and yogurt, beating back her students' hunger so they perform well enough.

"High scores reflect the parents, not the kids," Miss Hester says, referring to homes plentiful in food, where studying is not a luxury.

Dasani's grades have plummeted. On her wrist is a bite mark left by a classmate Dasani had fought after the girl called her "musty." Two days after that incident, Dasani lunged at a different girl in gym class.

Miss Hester has had enough. "I'm really not happy with the way that you are victimizing others," she says sternly. "I need it to stop immediately. Do you understand me?"

The child nods at Miss Hester, her eyes dropping. For Dasani, school and life are entwined. When school goes well, she is whole. When it goes poorly, she cannot compartmentalize. It is a place to love or leave.

Miss Hester wants Dasani to stay in school and thrive. But she is among dozens of students whom Miss Hester must guide. "Dasani feels her life is not what it should be," the teacher says. "She's absolutely correct. The part she's incorrect about is that the rest of us have to pay."

Minutes later, Dasani is seated in McKinney's packed auditorium for an assembly on Black History Month. She hates Black History Month. "It's always the same poems."

The new honor roll is called out. Dasani's name is missing. *It must be a mistake,* she tells herself. She slumps down in her chair. She looks at the floor.

Right then, a group of boys takes the stage to recite Langston Hughes.

> *What happens to a dream deferred?*
> *Does it dry up*
> *like a raisin in the sun?*

Dasani knows this poem. They read it every year. She stares blankly at the stage.

> *Maybe it just sags*
> *Like a heavy load*
> *Or does it explode?*

chapter 8

CHANEL SPREADS THE cash across her bed, all $2,800 of her tax refund.

The children stare in awe.

"I don't know why I feel so happy," says Avianna.

New dollar bills have a fresh smell. It's almost like grass, says Dasani, or the Poconos, where her parents have promised to move. Once Supreme's refund arrives, they could have enough to leave Auburn.

The children are floating. Suddenly Chanel scoops up the cash and puts it away.

"Once you start to break them bills, that's it, they're gone."

The next morning, on February 14, Chanel heads through the projects, the cash bulging from her pocket. She cannot think of where to put it. She has no bank account, and Auburn is a den of thieves. For now, she will keep it pressed to her body.

She pushes Lee-Lee's stroller toward the Ingersoll Houses where Chanel's mother, Joanie, grew up, and then downtown, where the street names evoke riches. Gold. Tillary. Bond.

Bond Street is her favorite. *Word is bond*, she likes to say. There is no promissory note worth more than one's word.

Chanel takes an inventory of the things she could—but won't—

buy: a new stroller, new sneakers, a hair-braiding session for the girls. She makes a bond with herself not to cave like other people, blowing it all on a few pairs of Jordans. "It's about assets and liabilities," Chanel tells me. "You want something that will bring you something, not take from you."

Anyone can spend "like there's no tomorrow." But in the projects, Chanel says, the phrase rings true. Tomorrow brings disappointment. Sometimes she thinks of easy escapes. Maybe she'll get hit by loose scaffolding or struck by a crane—with just enough force to bring a large settlement while keeping her brain intact. For $1 million, she might part with a limb.

She keeps feeling for the bulge in her pocket, just to make sure. If she were still getting high, she points out, the money would be gone. Candy is another temptation. It provides the greatest thrill for the least amount of money. Chanel might refuse to buy her children Timberland boots, but she stuffs their mouths with Ring Pops and Twizzlers, bubble gum and Hershey's Kisses. Candy is a trick. It distracts from all that is missing. "It's a blinding thing," she says.

For a real treat, she takes them to Dylan's Candy Bar on Third Avenue, hoping the security guards won't notice when they leave without paying. She sometimes wonders if candy is like a drug, bringing a cheap thrill at the cost of long-term damage. Cavities tore through Chanel's mouth long before she ever smoked crack. Lately the children are complaining of toothaches.

She is now on Fulton Mall, passing a jewelry store. Years ago, she and Supreme came here to buy the gold caps known as "fronts" or "grills." There are cheaper ways to cover holes left by rotting teeth. Gold fronts can cost $1,000. This is how they spent their money, not thinking past the moment.

Chanel shakes her head. Fronts are liabilities. Now she wants assets. She heads back to Auburn, her bills unbroken.

If only life imitated Monopoly, Supreme's favorite board game.

"I like building up property and collecting rent," he says of Monopoly, which he plays with his children on a mattress in their room.

Supreme knows that becoming a real renter is harder than claiming Park Place on a cardboard square. He is reminded of this twice a month, when he and Chanel must sign and date their "independent living plan" with Auburn shelter, which requires them to save money, look for a job, and search for housing.

By early March, Supreme learns that the State of New York has seized his tax refund. He owes child support for the two children he had before meeting Chanel. The Tax Refund Offset Program will give Supreme's tax money either to these mothers or to the state, as repayment for cash assistance previously paid to the two mothers.

Dasani knows before her mother says a word.

They will not be leaving Auburn.

Dasani has learned to let disappointments pass in silence. Objecting does nothing to change the facts. But she reveals herself with the questions she asks.

"Mommy, if these projects was your only choice, would you take it?" Dasani asks as they pass the Whitman Houses. Chanel nods reluctantly.

It is now spring—a season to show off new wardrobes. In Dasani's family, spring is a time of scrambling. Appearances are more easily kept up when a winter coat is all that people see. Out on the street, a child in dirty clothes can occasion calls to ACS.

At school, Dasani's peers have been mocking her favorite pink sweat suit, calling it "pajamas." There are three ways to be popular, as her mother always says.

Dress fly. Do good in school. Fight.

On March 19, Dasani agrees to fight a girl named Elena. A crowd gathers in Commodore Barry Park, where the rules are set: No one can film the fight or tell a parent. The girls pull back their hair. Dasani takes the first swing and they tumble to the ground. A man walking his dog breaks it up.

That evening, in the bathroom at Auburn, Chanel inspects her daughter's busted lip. It will heal quickly, she says, dismissing the incident as "kitty-cat fighting." Back in Chanel's day, girls got cracked on the head with bottles.

Dasani is worried that her longtime rival, Star, will be the next girl to challenge her. Since the start of the school year, Star has been a thorn in Dasani's side, telling everyone at McKinney that Dasani lives at Auburn.

"You gotta keep your hood credit up," Chanel tells her daughter. "You take the biggest, baddest one down first and the rest of 'em will back up off of you. That's just how it works."

The next day, Chanel and Dasani walk up their favorite block of Myrtle, past China's barbershop, the fancy wine store, the bike repair shop selling vegan cookies. They stop at a juice store, where Chanel spots an old flame. He wears a long leather jacket and dark shades.

"Whassup, Red?" says the man, using Chanel's onetime street name.

"I'm good now, see?" says Chanel, waving a hand over herself like a magic wand: drug-free, married, mother of eight. She nods proudly at her children. It is Dasani's belief that she and her siblings are the cause of her mother's ruin. It never occurs to her that for Chanel, the children represent her only accomplishment.

Outside, the sidewalk is jammed with after-school traffic. Dasani and her siblings follow their mother along Myrtle.

"Mommy!" Dasani squeals. "These little kids over there are cursing up a storm!"

"Mind your business," Chanel says, in a voice loud enough to blanket the block. "They live right there."

Dasani stays quiet.

"And why you being a snitch?" Chanel continues. "People don't like snitches. Learn to hear and see things, but learn to mind your business."

To Chanel's mind, Dasani must survive the street just long enough to escape it. How she escapes is beyond Chanel's reckoning. Maybe it happens at school, though Chanel has little faith in school. Maybe it comes through some bolt of fortune. A talent scout could spot Dasani dancing on the train. A track coach might see her sprinting at the park. The train, the park, the school, the shelter. These are the cornerstones of Dasani's life. But only the street paves the way between them, and Chanel must teach Dasani its ways.

Chanel escorts her daughter to school the next morning. She wants to make sure that Dasani does not get jumped. If the girls see

Dasani with her mother, they will accuse her of being "punk," the opposite of brave. Chanel has already thought this through, and she is ready when Elena appears in the hallway.

"You can fight my kid," Chanel says hotly. "I'm with that."

They are standing near the principal's office. Elena looks surprised and runs off. This is Chanel's version of reverse psychology. Grant permission to do the forbidden, and a child will think twice.

This is not the principal's approach. A few minutes later, Dasani sits down in Miss Holmes's office.

"I believe you can change, but you're not showing me that," Miss Holmes says.

Dasani seems revved up and distracted. Nothing the principal says is getting through. It is her mother's permission—not Miss Holmes's prohibition—that propels Dasani. She returns to class, telling another girl, "I'ma fight you. My mother said she'll let me fight."

With that, Dasani is suspended.

Miss Holmes knows this is a risky move, but nothing else has worked. Dasani needs to be shocked out of her behavior. The alternative is to fail, in school and beyond.

"Get your things and leave," Miss Holmes tells her.

Dasani will be out of school for two weeks, as her suspension overlaps with spring break.

She cannot speak.

To be suspended is to be truly homeless.

part 2

THE
SYKES FAMILY

1835–2003

Jim Crow was there
Blocking their way.
Causing them grief
Day after day.

These men fought evil
That enveloped the land.
They battled for freedom
With one tied hand.

—IVAN J. HOUSTON,
veteran of World War II

chapter 9

DASANI WAS AWAKE to the world, even as a newborn.

Her eyes darted about the room, eager for exploration. She moved her tiny limbs in proud, restless jerks, as if fighting to leave the crib. Everything about her smacked of Dasani's forty-seven-year-old grandmother—the powerful hands, the caramel skin, even her name, Dasani Joanie-Lashawn Coates.

In the Sykes family, feisty babies were always a sign of strength.

Half a century earlier, on November 14, 1953, the mischievous, Luther Vandross–loving girl who would become Dasani's grandmother was born at 5:30 P.M. in the maternity ward of Cumberland Hospital. Joan Joanne Sykes took her first breaths in a sterile setting where swaddled newborns cried out from a third-floor nursery. Another thirty years would pass before the hospital closed, becoming Auburn, the city-run homeless shelter where Dasani came to live.

Back in 1953, the hospital at 39 Auburn Place was still a place of order, with nurses dressed in starchy cotton and corridors swept clean of dust. The neighborhood's new mothers carried their infants out the front door of Cumberland, returning by foot to the nearby projects.

All around them, Brooklyn was changing. The borough's Black

population had recently doubled to 208,000 as southerners kept arriving in search of work—just like Joanie's parents, June and Margaret Sykes, had come seven years earlier, leaving Goldsboro, North Carolina.

Brooklyn was a land of promise. It was still an industrial center, a place where Joanie's father, a trained mechanic, was sure to find work. But the city's master builder, Robert Moses, had another vision: He wanted to transform Brooklyn into a cultural and civic hub, which required clearing land. For this, Moses took aim at the manufacturing industry, closing hundreds of worksites between 1945 and 1955, at the cost of 8,200 jobs.

All of this happened by the time Joanie Sykes was two. The lost jobs were within walking distance of the projects where her family lived—a collection of thirty-five brick buildings that opened in 1942, the same year Moses joined the city's planning commission, broadening the reach of his well-established power. Moses had little regard for the poor and a particular loathing for Black people, whom he considered "inherently 'dirty,'" according to interviews conducted by his biographer, Robert Caro. Of the 255 playgrounds Moses built in New York City in the 1930s, only two were in Black neighborhoods.

Joanie would grow up in an island of urban poverty. By the time she was three, only a quarter of her neighbors were white. The Fort Greene Houses fell to disrepair made worse by vandalism and crime. In 1957, the *Daily News*—citing the cost of the Fort Greene Houses—dubbed it a "rotting $20,000,000 slum." The city tightened its control, dividing the projects in half: East of St. Edwards Street, they became the Walt Whitman Houses; to the west they were now the Raymond V. Ingersoll Houses.

The Sykes family lived at Ingersoll, in a fifth-floor corner unit at 29 Fleet Walk. Drawing on Southern tradition, June Sykes wanted a large family. He had been raised in a home where everyone helped. More children ensured a family's survival.

His daughter Joanie was the fifth of nine siblings, a tight-knit flock. With no decent playground, they gathered "down by the courts"— a stretch of asphalt anchored by benches and two basketball hoops. In the absence of swings, they played with their hands and feet.

Hot Peas and Butter. Johnny on the Pony. Cocoa Livia.

They took to roaming a dirt hill behind the projects, roasting potatoes over an open fire. They longed for fresh air, going by ferry to Staten Island's Clove Lake, where their parents brought a picnic of fried chicken and potato salad as the children scattered across "a big, huge forest," recalled Joanie's little sister, Margo.

Mostly, though, the Sykes family stayed home. On Friday evenings, June and his neighbors—all of them married, working fathers—welcomed the weekend with cups of syrupy Thunderbird wine. They played poker and danced with their wives to the Temptations and Smokey Robinson, as the children mimicked their moves.

After a few drinks, June sometimes talked about "the war." His stories were graphic. He had watched his comrade step on a bomb, blowing the man "to smithereens," recalled Margo.

The children stopped believing him.

"I thought it was the alcohol talking," said Joanie's sister Linda. "What they say? A drunk person always speaks a sober mind? He was speakin' a sober mind. But I didn't wanna hear it."

On the morning of July 15, 1944, just a few miles from the Virginia shore where America's first slaves landed, Dasani's great-grandfather staggered up the gangplank of a ship bound for Africa.

Wesley Junior Sykes was twenty-three years old—a newly minted Army private with the 92nd Infantry, an all-Black division summoned to fight in World War II. Shouldering his pack, he set foot on the SS *Mariposa*, joining thirty-five hundred other African American troops. Their combat regiment, the 370th, was the first to be called to duty—later making history as part of the only Black division to fight in Europe during the war.

The men were quiet, their faces drawn. Many had never been on a ship. Most were from the rural South, where venturing into unknown territory could end a Black man's life. The very notion that African Americans were joining the military—training to fight and carrying arms—met resistance. A Black serviceman could be lynched for wearing a uniform in public.

Back in Goldsboro, North Carolina, Wesley had gone by "June," short for Junior. Three years before he was born, his father—the senior Wesley Sykes—had registered for the draft in World War I, despite the racial terror visited upon Black recruits. Just seventy miles away, near Raleigh, an angry mob had attacked a Black veteran named Powell Green on December 27, 1919. They removed him from a police car, dragging him by rope for half a mile before hanging him from a pine sapling. The dead veteran's bullet-ridden body drew "souvenir hunters" who tore buttons from Green's clothing, according to *The News and Observer*, taking his "cheap watch and chain," even chips from the tree.

June was still a baby when the local *Goldsboro Daily Argus* ran an editorial musing that lynchings, and the practice of tarring and feathering African Americans, "breaks the monotony" of Southern life because it "gives people something to talk about."

The Sykes surname traces back to a white slave owner whose probable British ancestors came to America, via Virginia, by the early 1700s. A century later, that man—Kedar Sykes—had purchased a slave in Duplin County, North Carolina, creating in 1813 what may be the first record of Dasani's own ancestors. By 1835, the Sykes estate's documented "property" included six slaves. Among them was a little boy, around age five, whose name was David. He was valued at $100.

David was the great-great-great-great-grandfather of Dasani.

Little is known about David's first years, except that he lived with three other enslaved children—presumably his sisters, including a girl named Charity. For a time, they remained together. In the North Carolina of the 1830s, slave owners routinely broke up Black families—taking children from their parents and siblings to be sold to plantations farther south. This happened when David was only five: His presumptive sister, eleven-year-old Charity, was sold off to another enslaver. Seven years later, David (now valued at $450) became the property of Kedar Sykes's son, Holloway.

David's life would cross the expanse from slavery to Reconstruction. By 1870, he was no longer a slave, but a forty-year-old farmer living next door to his former enslaver, Holloway Sykes. That same year, David took part in the first federal census to include Black Americans, identifying himself as David Sykes, married with seven children, among them a boy named Albert—the future grandfather of June Sykes.

By the time June was born in 1920, his grandfather had been murdered by gunshot while working on a plantation near Goldsboro. A local newspaper described the suspect as a "colored man of notorious character" who "has not been captured."

The young June was soon working the fields, quitting grade school by age twelve. But unlike his forebears—from David to Albert to Wesley—Dasani's great-grandfather would leave that life. His chance came at age twenty, when he joined the Civilian Conservation Corps, a New Deal program that employed millions of men to plant trees, construct trails, and work on other outdoor projects. June began sending $15 to his mother every month while putting another $7 into a savings account. In November 1942, at the height of World War II, June enlisted in the Army at Fort Bragg, North Carolina.

Twenty months later, he boarded the SS *Mariposa*.

A light rain fell as the ship unmoored. Soldiers crammed the rails. They watched as the Virginia shoreline thinned into water. Until then, no Black infantry had been allowed into combat in Europe during the Second World War. The military—while fighting Nazi and Fascist totalitarianism abroad—hewed to the Jim Crow laws of white supremacy at home.

Army bases, buses, even blood banks remained segregated as more than 1.2 million African Americans served during the war. Their rallying cry was the Double V, an early civil rights campaign calling for "victory over our enemies at home and victory over our enemies on the battlefields abroad." Black recruits found themselves under the command of white southerners, with General George C. Marshall reasoning that officers must show an "ability to handle negroes." Most Black troops were relegated to service positions, including June, who joined the 370th as an auto mechanic.

It made no difference that Black soldiers had been fighting for America since the Revolutionary War, segregated into their own regiments after the Civil War. They had been sent west in 1867 to exert control over Native Americans, who referred to the Black troops as Buffalo Soldiers because—depending on the source—their curly hair resembled the buffalo's hide or because their bravery and strength mirrored this mighty animal. The name stuck, becoming an emblem of the military's Black infantries—a mascot in the form of a Buffalo patch that was sewn onto June's uniform. As World War II brought more casualties (the recent invasion of Normandy had claimed 2,501 Americans on the first day alone), June and his fellow Buffalo Soldiers were finally called in.

After eight days at sea, the *Mariposa* reached the coast of Algeria, a temporary stop en route to Europe. On board that day was Private First Class Ivan J. Houston, a nineteen-year-old California native who still remembers the moment someone cried out, "Land!"

Setting down their books and musical instruments, the men stared out. "Most of us were looking for jungle since the only perception we had of that continent came from Tarzan movies," Ivan later wrote. "We were aware, all of us, that our forebears had been brought from here to America forcibly in chains and that because of slavery we remained second-class citizens. Yet, despite that bitter history, we were committed to fight for America against the evil of Nazi Germany."

The Allied forces had invaded mainland Italy the previous September, and after heavy losses, had finally liberated Rome on June 4, 1944. The Nazis retreated north, into the rugged terrain of the Apennine Mountains, where they had constructed—using the forced labor of fifteen thousand captives—a wall of fortifications called the Gothic Line. Stretching two hundred miles from the Ligurian Sea to the Adriatic, this was the Nazis' last major line of defense. The goal for the Allies, as communicated to June's regiment, was to break through the Gothic Line.

On July 30, June and his fellow troops disembarked in the shell-torn port of Naples.

"We were under fire from the time we got in line until the war ended, I always say," Ivan told me by phone, at age ninety-four. His father had also been a Buffalo Soldier, serving with the 92nd in France during World War I. The artillery fire sounded just the way his father described it: "like a freight train."

June and his fellow Buffalo Soldiers advanced north through minefields, maneuvering around destroyed Italian bridges. They passed an abandoned Tuscan villa, catching stray chickens to fry in bacon grease using the Army's Ten-in-One ration packs.

Over the next year, June, Ivan, and most of their regiment survived three major battles. June remained a serviceman, tending to the convoys as a mechanic. But like all troops, June carried a rifle, and the attacks were relentless. He would later tell his grandchildren that he saw "heads roll." More than five hundred of his comrades were killed, another fifty-four were missing in action, and 2,280 were injured.

By the end of the war, June's regiment had liberated two cities from the Nazis. "The Italians knew we were going to fight the dreaded Germans and that some of us would not come back," Ivan wrote. "They threw flowers at our vehicles. They handed flowers and wine to those of us riding in the vehicles. They threw kisses at us." For decades to come, the Buffalo Soldiers' heroics would be taught in Italian grade schools and reenacted by Italian civilians, while going largely ignored in America.

There would be no hero's welcome home. If anything, the return to America brought a sense of dread, as laid bare by Langston Hughes's poem, "Will V-Day Be Me-Day Too?":

> When I take off my uniform,
> Will I be safe from harm—
> Or will you do me
> As the Germans did the Jews?

Nearly seventy-five years later, Ivan had retired as the CEO of a large corporation and was living in California. He told me that it was the Italians—not his fellow Americans—who made him proud to be a Buffalo Soldier.

No one in Dasani's immediate family knew that June Sykes had served in this historic infantry. By the time Dasani heard this from me, her only association with "Buffalo Soldier" had come from a Jamaican reggae song.

The lyrics of Bob Marley's ballad held new meaning.

"There was a Buffalo Soldier, in the heart of America," Dasani sang along, bopping her head. "Fighting on arrival. Fighting for survival."

After the Allies triumphed and the war wound down, Dasani's great-grandfather returned to Fort Bragg, and on November 14, 1945, he was honorably discharged. June left the military with three Bronze Service Stars, an American Campaign Medal, and a Victory Medal.

None of these medals brought victory at home. Congress had recently passed the monumental GI Bill, allowing millions of veterans to go to college with scholarships and stipends, to start businesses with generous loans and job training, to buy homes with government-backed mortgages. The GI Bill drove the creation of middle-class America while giving rise to its suburbs—both of which were strikingly white.

For Black veterans like June, a different life awaited. They were largely denied the GI Bill supports that lifted their white comrades into the middle class. Job training programs catered overwhelmingly to whites, as did universities and financial institutions. There was little that a scholarship or a mortgage could do for an African American veteran when colleges and banks turned down his applications. The GI Bill, like the military, answered to a Jim Crow South.

But the North brimmed with possibility.

June set his sights on Brooklyn, joining the six million African Americans who—in the span of five and a half decades—would leave the South for industrial cities in the West and North.

By the summer of 1946, June had married Margaret McIver, the daughter of a widowed laundress from his hometown. Together, they left Goldsboro, settling in Bedford-Stuyvesant, Brooklyn's largest Black enclave. With a baby on the way, June took whatever work he could find. Labor unions tended to exclude Black workers. For veterans with high-skill training, this was an especially bitter fate. Carpenters became dishwashers. Electrical aides worked as porters. Mechanics turned into janitors.

Dasani's great-grandfather—a triple Bronze Star veteran who had repaired military vehicles under Nazi fire—was by any measure a skillful mechanic. But June came to Brooklyn at a time when 94 percent of the profession was white. Instead, he cobbled together a living by working many jobs at once—sweeping floors, digging ditches, changing oil. Within seven years of moving to Brooklyn, June had worked for seventeen companies, including a bowling alley, a meat processor, and a service station.

In 1953 alone—the year that his daughter Joanie was born—June had five different employers, bringing him a total income of $2,900 (nearly $29,000 in 2021 dollars). Eventually, he found steadier work as a janitor, mopping floors and cleaning toilets at a private school for disabled children. He worked the night shift.

This was not just a professional loss, but a financial one. Black janitors earned 41 percent less than white mechanics. The gap between these incomes, over the next twenty years of June's working life, would come to $192,000 of lost earnings in today's dollars.

If June wanted to buy a home, he had one advantage over other African Americans: as a veteran, he qualified for a GI Bill–backed mortgage. But he also lived in Bed-Stuy, where a policy of racial exclusion was well under way. Back in 1904, a *New York Times* editorial had warned that renting or selling property to Black buyers would "depress real estate values." With nativism on the rise, the Ku Klux Klan (which had 150,000 members in New York City) visited a church in Bed-Stuy in 1929 to endorse the minister's exclusion of Black parishioners.

As more Black people moved to Bed-Stuy, the city withheld sufficient policing and other services. The neighborhood's fate was sealed in 1935, when the federal Home Owners' Loan Corporation began color-coding American cities, using race as a criterion to identify risky investment areas on the map. African American hubs like Bed-Stuy were marked in red for "hazardous." If you lived in a redlined zone, it was almost impossible to get a mortgage.

Brooklyn fell into decline as whites left for the nascent suburbs. Even with a veteran's loan, June had little chance of following them. In places like Levittown, restrictive covenants prevented Blacks from buying homes. Out of nearly 71,000 mortgages insured by the GI Bill in New York and northeastern New Jersey in 1950, less than 1 percent went to nonwhite veterans.

Yet home ownership was key to accruing wealth. White American families would eventually amass a median net worth nearly ten times that of Black families. Put another way, the exclusion of African Americans from real estate—not to mention college, white-collar jobs, and the ability to vote—laid the foundations of a lasting poverty that Dasani would inherit.

Renting was her great-grandfather's only option, and in this way, June got lucky. In 1952, he and Margaret landed a subsidized apartment in the Fort Greene Houses, a sprawling complex that had opened to great fanfare. This was the largest of the nation's so-called "projects," created with the New Deal purpose of aiding "the forgotten man at the bottom of the economic pyramid." That forgotten man, at first, tended to be white. Back when Fort Greene Houses debuted in 1942, most of the apartments went to white defense workers of the neighboring Brooklyn Navy Yard.

But the Navy Yard had also been redlined, along with part of Fort Greene. And by the time June's family moved in, Brooklyn was on its way to becoming the largest ghetto in America.

If June had been traumatized by the war, he numbed it with alcohol. By 1954, he was laying bricks and pouring concrete for Peter Liuzzo, a general contractor in Brooklyn.

June impressed his boss as a hardworking war veteran, "one of the best laborers" at the company, recalled Liuzzo's son, John. The job lasted eight years, but June's wages were not enough to support a large family, leading his wife to apply for welfare. This meant that June would have to leave home, he told his boss, because the government denied public aid to families with "a man in the house."

Instead, June's wife began to vanish. Word circulated that Margaret had a boyfriend. In her absence, June stayed home, drinking by night and working by day as his children looked after one another.

"All my life, I remember raising myself," said Joanie's sister Margo. "I don't remember a mother there."

Margo and Joanie became inseparable. Joanie's reddish hair and light, freckled skin drew a higher status than Margo's mahogany skin and jet-black braids. Their personalities also stretched in opposite directions. Joanie was the ringleader, the glue of the family—another trait that her granddaughter Dasani would inherit. "She was the house," said Margo, who marveled at her sister's charisma. Wherever Joanie went, Margo followed, scaling fences, jumping rope, trotting to P.S. 67, Brooklyn's first all-Black school.

By the time Joanie was ten, her father was mopping floors on the night shift. She and Margo tagged along with him to work, gliding up and down the school hallways that June cleaned. At home, the pantry went empty. To quash their hunger, the sisters stole bread and bottled milk from nearby stoops, racing off before the Italian deliveryman could catch them. For dinner, they improvised, sometimes at their own peril. They once dipped raw chicken in cement powder, mistaking it for flour.

Summers brought merciless heat. The closest public pool was forty blocks away, in Red Hook. Joanie and Margo cooled themselves by opening a hydrant near their building, prompting a cat-and-mouse game with the police, who would turn off the hydrant, only for the children to turn it back on.

Joanie's adolescence collided with the civil rights movement, which had found a northern base in Brooklyn. Local activists waged historic battles against school segregation, welfare and work discrimination, racist housing practices, and police brutality. It was in Manhattan, in 1964, that a white off-duty policeman shot and killed James Powell, a fifteen-year-old Black boy, setting off the first major uprising of the civil rights era. Four years later, when an assassin took the life of Martin Luther King, Jr., riots swept through Brooklyn and cities across America, leaving forty-three dead.

"A riot," in King's words, "is the language of the unheard."

Joanie hated authority. One afternoon, she was caught throwing bricks at a fire truck from an overpass. When a police officer chased her, she ran so fast that her skirt fell. Another day, she scored a bicycle from the Church of the Open Door, located across a dangerous highway. Margo watched in horror as Joanie mounted the bike, which was missing a pedal, then careened back home through oncoming trucks and cars.

The most daring feat came when Joanie jumped from the family's fifth-floor window to a mattress on the ground below. "She was floating down to the mattress," said Margo, who believed the projects were filled with ghosts. "Something must have been holding her because she didn't just drop down. . . . She bounced off the mattress like Charmin tissue."

Nothing seemed to scare Joanie, which made it all the stranger when she began to scream one day, from inside the elevator at Cumberland Hospital. She was about fourteen years old and had been riding with Margo when suddenly the lift froze.

Joanie pounded her fists against the metal door.

"We gonna *die* in here," Margo teased. About twenty minutes passed before the elevator door opened, releasing the sisters as suddenly as they'd been trapped.

From that day forward, Joanie avoided small, dark spaces. If a room got too crowded, she headed for the door. She'd rather climb ten flights of stairs than spend one second in an elevator.

She could control the stairs, even if they slowed her down or kept her from climbing at all.

chapter 10

JOANIE'S STOMACH SWELLED. It was 1977. She now had two children with a man called Sonny Boy. She needed a name for her third baby.

For a twenty-four-year-old unwed mother, the task of finding a name was lonely. She was leafing through a magazine when she noticed an ad for a French perfume.

Chanel.

The name had a certain elegance, the way it landed on the tongue. The scent remained a mystery, and who even knew the cost? Such details were found in the department stores of Manhattan. Here in eastern Brooklyn, the bodega offered simpler brands like "Baby Soft" and "Charlie."

A decade had passed since Joanie's rocky adolescence sent her roaming the Fort Greene projects, throwing rocks at cars and running from cops. Then came her little brother Junior's own rebellions. In 1968, after he was caught climbing walls and roofs, the Housing Authority evicted the Sykes family from 29 Fleet Walk. They relocated to Brownsville, one of the poorest parts of a city in decline.

Here and across the nation, factories were closing to make way for a service-based economy—a seismic shift that would hit African Americans especially hard. Six million Black southerners had resettled in cities north and west, finding low-skill work in the automobile, rubber, and steel industries—the very plants that were now shuttering. As unemployment soared in America's inner cities, another sea change occurred: Black middle-class families were migrating to the suburbs, empowered by civil rights legislation, which had opened jobs and neighborhoods to those with college degrees. Left behind in places like Brownsville was a deeply poor Black population that the sociologist William Julius Wilson controversially termed "the underclass."

The exodus of stable, norm-setting Black families, combined with the chronic joblessness left in their wake, led to social isolation and what Wilson called "maladaptive behaviors." Teenage pregnancy, single-mother households, welfare dependency, drug trafficking, and violent crime had reached striking new heights by the mid-1970s. While his critics challenged the concept of ghetto "culture," Wilson (who is African American) wrote that "culture is a response to social structural constraints and opportunities."

By 1975, New York City was on the brink of bankruptcy, with no federal bailout (FORD TO CITY: DROP DEAD read the legendary *Daily News* headline). As the crisis wore on, a new mayor, Ed Koch, slashed municipal services and eventually closed public hospitals including Cumberland, where Joanie had been born. Her family was now living in a wasteland of burned-out buildings and uncollected garbage.

Joanie had been looking for love. Still a teen, she fell for Samuel Humbert, a smooth-talking construction worker who went by the nickname Sonny Boy. He was twice her age and a playboy—still married to a woman from South Carolina, while in Brooklyn he lived with Sherry, his partner of more than a decade. Joanie became Sonny Boy's girl on the side.

"She was crazy in love with him," said her sister Margo. "Anything Sonny Boy wanted to do, Joanie let him do."

This included having babies. Joanie knew that Sherry had borne no children. So at age seventeen, Joanie gave birth to a son, dropping out of high school. Her little sister, Margo, followed suit, quitting the eleventh grade also to have a baby (also with an older man, a friend of her father's). By now, the sisters were living with their parents in a dilapidated building on Tapscott Street. As teenage mothers, Joanie and Margo qualified for welfare, so their own mother, Margaret, began charging them $50 each in rent. When the electricity and water were cut off, Margaret and June moved out, leaving their teenage daughters and two baby grandchildren to fend for themselves.

For a time, Joanie and Margo took jobs assembling foosball figurines at the Tudor Games factory in Brooklyn. Margo also found work as a barmaid at a nightclub in Brownsville, where she spied Sonny Boy leaving with other women. Joanie never wanted to hear it. By nineteen, she had two babies with Sonny Boy. He doted on them, providing clothes, food, a new apartment, and $75 in cash every week. He even took Joanie on a two-week vacation down south.

But he refused to leave Sherry.

The two women vied for Sonny Boy—Joanie by having his children and Sherry by forgiving him. "It hurt me," Sherry later told me. "But, you know . . . different strokes for different folks."

Sherry was the opposite of Joanie: sober, churchgoing, methodically ambitious. She owned a profitable business, running a daycare center from the basement of her home. She was responsible to the point of prim, or, in Margo's summation, "snotty." Raised by southerners, Sherry would be nobody's girlfriend. She called herself Sonny Boy's "common-law wife."

Elaborate church hats filled Sherry's closet, stored in shiny boxes. Each Sunday brought a new look—a feather on the side, a lace veil down the front. On Lincoln Avenue, Sherry held the stature of matriarch, caring for other people's children while pining for her own.

At twenty-three, Joanie got pregnant with her third child, the girl she would name Chanel. Joanie knew that Sonny Boy wanted a daughter. She also knew by now that he would never leave Sherry. Sonny Boy and Sherry owned a comfortable home nearby, in the Brooklyn neighborhood of East New York—a more suitable place for children.

This compelled Joanie to do the unthinkable. She gave her baby girl to Sonny Boy. This meant that Joanie's longtime rival—the same woman who had kept her man—would now raise her daughter, Chanel.

Sherry would never forget the moment when Sonny Boy handed her the six-month-old baby. Chanel had no socks on. Her feet were cold to the touch. In came a new wardrobe and a bedroom decorated with stuffed animals. From the ceiling hung a chandelier shaped like a carousel, with porcelain horses and glass poles that beamed rays of light. While Sherry fussed over the baby's hair and dresses, Sonny Boy showered her with affection.

Chanel had all the makings of a stable childhood. Then came the morning of December 5, 1980. She was two years old when her father walked out the door to work. Sonny Boy was earning about $400 a week operating a demolition machine for a Brooklyn construction company. He was always afraid of heights, which made his current assignment daunting: a seven-story teardown project at Bellevue Hospital's Building F. At around 10 A.M., the sound of falling debris shook the worksite.

What happened next is unclear. Possibly struck by debris, Sonny Boy plunged down a five-story shaft, suffering "irreparable damage to nervous system, heart and lungs," according to a lawsuit. At age forty-five, Sonny Boy was dead. The complaint listed as his dependents five children and two mothers: Sherry and Joanie.

The women made peace after Sonny Boy's death. But his little girl remained Sherry's to raise—as the official godmother of Chanel—along with a handful of other children who came to live with Sherry on Lincoln Avenue. They had been abandoned by mothers too young or troubled to parent. "We were all kids of kids," Chanel said.

Sherry made sure they lacked for nothing, working long hours to run her business while others tended to her flock. Miss Dorris came to clean and iron and Miss Mary to cook. Every two weeks, Miss Francine washed, pressed, and curled Chanel's hair at the salon.

"We was sharp," Chanel said. "Velour and lace dresses. I was one of the sharpest tools in the shed."

Chanel's red hair drew the notice of neighbors. Then came her freckles, just a few at first. By the time she started kindergarten, they covered her face in a swirl. Almost no one in the neighborhood looked like Chanel, least of all Sherry, the woman she called Mommy. But Sherry didn't care. She fussed over the child, getting her to school on time, her Buster Browns polished, her shirts ironed to a crisp. This was the way to succeed, Sherry said, looking like the life you wanted. And from the outside, Chanel looked complete.

Except for the freckles. When she gazed in the mirror, they greeted her, as if winking. Only one other person had those freckles.

"It was always a question in the back of my mind," Chanel said. "Where my mother at?"

By now, Joanie was living three miles west, in a chaotic two-bedroom apartment on a blighted stretch of Brownsville. She was a thirty-year-old unemployed single mother with two boys (the brothers of Chanel)—ten-year-old Lamont and twelve-year-old Shamell. Their bathroom floor had caved in and the landlord refused to fix it. She survived on welfare checks and cash from an unexpected source: Sherry.

Perhaps Sherry felt a duty to help Sonny Boy's survivors. She was always saving people. But to save her longtime rival, the woman who had competed for Sonny Boy? "I couldn't understand it," said Joanie's older sister, Linda. "But it was the relationship that they had."

Sherry began leaving Chanel with her birth mother on weekends. Chanel's earliest memories of this period are like scenes from two different movies: Joanie's apartment thumping with music, Sherry's house humming with order. Joanie watching *Soul Train* on an ordinary television, Sherry beaming in Jimmy Stewart westerns on cable TV.

During meals at IHOP and Red Lobster, Sherry coached Chanel to leave a bit of food on her plate—just like the white diners, who "don't show their hunger." She took pains to enroll Chanel at a predominantly white school in neighboring Howard Beach. "She thought she was white," Chanel later said of Sherry.

Christmas brought a stream of coveted toys, from Cabbage Patch dolls to shiny bicycles. No one told Chanel about the donated bike that her mother Joanie used to ride. But Chanel guessed that she was luckier than most children.

Her own neighborhood was succumbing to a desperate poverty, just as a lethal new drug hit the streets.

Chanel was eight years old when she opened her mother's jewelry box to find a brown glass object. She held it up to the light.

She had never seen a crack pipe.

"We gonna toss it," said her brother Shamell, now in his teens.

They leaned out the fifth-floor window of Joanie's apartment and watched as the pipe soared through the air, crashing onto the sidewalk. Joanie's habit was still hidden. Only later would Chanel hear the crackling of her mother's pipe, the sound that gave this drug its name.

Crack was the poor man's cocaine—smoked rather than snorted, at a fraction of the cost. It came in the form of a crystal rock, made by dissolving powder cocaine in hot water with baking soda. The rock was then heated through a pipe and inhaled. Crack had surfaced in America by the early 1980s, first in Miami and Los Angeles before spreading to New York. Unlike its pricier cousin, powder cocaine, crack brought an instant high. While coke remained a glamour drug, selling for $100 per gram, crack wound its way through the ghetto at $3 a rock.

By 1985, the crack market was exploding. Some addicts forgot themselves entirely, wandering the streets as their children went hungry. Joanie showed more control. She planned around each high, as if preparing for a storm: laundering her clothes, sorting through bills, making sure something was in the fridge.

Joanie's sister Margo had less discipline. Now a single mother, she lived a few blocks away with her two daughters, ages eleven and thirteen. Margo had always followed the lead of others, and crack was a ruthless boss.

"All I thought about was crack," she later said.

The drug's immediate, euphoric high and very low cost combined to devastating effect. Crack brought a surge of dopamine, a neurotransmitter connected to the brain's reward system. The high ended within twenty minutes, followed by a crash that left users craving more. In time, Margo needed the drug just to feel normal.

The government's response to crack could be encapsulated in three words: "Just Say No." Nancy Reagan's mantra, like the war on drugs, emphasized deterrence rather than treatment—an irony that the comedian Dave Chappelle would bitterly mock decades later, when the opioid crisis hit. "Hang in there, whites. Just say no! What's so hard about that?"

In 1986—the same year that Chanel discovered her mother's crack pipe—Congress approved a new law making punishment for crack possession (common among the poor) one hundred times more harsh than for powder cocaine (common among the wealthy). Even first-time crack offenders landed mandatory minimum sentences of five to ten years, contributing to the explosion of America's prison population—a disproportionately Black and Latino group that came to include Chanel's two brothers, an uncle, and four cousins. Within a decade, this population would surpass a million. The United States had claimed the highest incarceration rate in the world.

Joanie's apartment on Tapscott was the base of activity.

All of the children—Chanel and her brothers, Margo's two daughters, and a fifteen-year-old boy named Joe Robinson—watched as their mothers descended into Joanie's basement for strobe-lit disco parties that melded into dawn. Joanie never seemed to lose control. "You could tell when she was high because her mouth was dry, but it was more subtle than with other addicts," recalled Joe. "She seemed very centered. . . . Kind of like an alpha female." But when the high wore off, Joanie became irritable and detached, talking to her daughter in a way that made Chanel wince.

Bitch, turn on my TV.

By now, nine-year-old Chanel was spending her weekends with Joanie and the rest of her time with Sherry, who had never taken a drug or even a sip of alcohol.

"It was like two different people trying to raise the same kid," Chanel says.

Chanel's weeks with Sherry left her wistful. Her weekends with Joanie left her hungry. Neither mother could meet every need. For Chanel, something was always missing, like a car without a steering wheel or a kitchen without a sink.

She learned to adapt, staying quiet when terrible things happened. It was at Sherry's house that Chanel experienced her greatest trauma. She was still in elementary school when a male cousin lured her into a basement bathroom. He was in his twenties.

"He'd turn off all the lights so it was dark. So I couldn't see him. I guess that was what was in his mind. Like he wasn't there."

The cousin removed Chanel's trousers and began rubbing his penis against her backside. It happened four or five times. She learned to make her mind go blank. "If you tell, you'll get into big trouble," he would say before leaving.

She told nobody.

Chanel also stayed silent about her mother's drug problem. But Sherry had caught on and was getting worried. She decided that the only way to save Chanel was to send her away. "I think she saw what was gonna happen to me," Chanel said of Sherry. "She saw that I was gonna get tangled up and not know right from wrong."

At age ten, Chanel went to live in Pittsburgh with Sherry's sister—a registered nurse and married mother. The sister enrolled Chanel in a private Catholic school, where she tried to adapt. But the more time that passed, the lonelier Chanel felt.

She started to act out. The final straw came when Chanel stole a teacher's wallet. She was expelled and Sherry's sister gave up, sending Chanel back to Sherry in New York. This was the third time that eleven-year-old Chanel had been displaced—first by Joanie, then by Sherry, and now by Sherry's sister.

Things unwound quickly from there.

Chanel's return to New York sparked in Joanie a new rivalry with Sherry.

"I could do everything she do for you," Joanie told her daughter.

Chanel knew this to be untrue. But she wanted to believe it.

All her life, she had imagined the day when her mother would reclaim her. It was like a trick her mind played: Joanie's arms opening, Chanel crashing in. Against all available evidence, she came to believe her mother's promise. Then Chanel did what her father could never do.

She left Sherry for Joanie.

This was such a bold act that the whiplash did not seem to matter. Chanel went from living in a clean, food-stocked home to having no home at all. Joanie had fallen behind on the rent and been evicted.

On April 30, 1990, she took her daughter to the Emergency Assistance Unit, the grim entry point for the city's family shelters. Chanel and Joanie were officially homeless.

A century had passed since the first Gilded Age, when homeless children roamed the streets—selling newspapers, picking pockets, polishing boots, scavenging trash. The Great Depression had brought another wave of homelessness, as shantytowns and breadlines riddled the city. It was then that Mayor Fiorello La Guardia pushed the historic 1938 amendment to New York's constitution, declaring that aid to the poor "shall be provided by the state." Eventually, New Yorkers' right to shelter would rest on these words, but not without a court fight.

Starting in the mid-1970s, New York's streets filled with a new kind of vagabond—the so-called "bums," "panhandlers," and "shopping bag ladies" (known as SBLs among aides to Mayor Ed Koch). A third of this population, by some estimates, had been released from state mental institutions with nowhere to go. The city's cheapest housing, its notorious Single Room Occupancy hotels, were closing to make way for luxury buildings.

The homeless were "sleeping rough," as it was known, on park benches and sidewalk grates—most notably, for men, on a mile-long stretch of the Lower East Side called the Bowery. Among them was Robert Callahan, an Irish cook who had lost his job, becoming an alcoholic. In his name, advocates for the homeless filed a class-action lawsuit that established New York's constitutional right to shelter. In 1980, a year before the landmark court order went into effect, Callahan died on the streets of the Lower East Side.

This was the dawn of "modern homelessness," a phenomenon driven by Reagan-era cutbacks, stagnating wages, and the soaring cost of homes. To own a house remained the symbol of American triumph. The ultimate loss, then, was to be "homeless," a word that entered popular discourse in the 1980s. One population was disproportionately hit: African Americans. The musician Tracy Chapman alluded to this in her 1988 hit song, "Fast Car," singing "We'll move out of the shelter."

Chanel and Joanie spent their first homeless nights in 1990 sleeping on chairs at the city's intake office in downtown Brooklyn. Finally, they were assigned to the annex of the Hotel Allerton, the infamous Chelsea flophouse where Patti Smith and Robert Mapplethorpe had stayed in 1969, surrounded by half-naked junkies and wallpaper, Smith later wrote, that was "peeling like dead skin in summer."

Joanie tolerated the Allerton for two weeks before taking Chanel back to Brooklyn in search of help. Joanie's father, June, had died three years earlier, at the age of sixty-six. He was buried with military honors at Calverton National Cemetery on Long Island. His wife, Margaret, was now living in Canarsie—the same neighborhood where Joanie's closest sister, Margo, had landed a unit in the Breukelen Houses (which took its name from the Dutch enslavers who in 1645 settled the land that would become Brooklyn).

To Margo's doorstep Joanie went. Five people were already crammed in the two-bedroom apartment: Margo, her two teenage daughters, her newborn grandson, and the baby's father, Joe (the boy whose mother used to get high with Joanie and Margo on Tapscott). Joe was now in love with Margo's oldest daughter, Sherelle. To support their baby son, Joe had dropped out of community college and was dealing crack.

Joanie and Chanel, now twelve, were offered the floor. They slept on laundry bags filled with clothes. For breakfast, Chanel poured water into her cereal. In time, she realized that they were living in a crack den.

Every few weeks, a new cache of drugs arrived with Joanie's little brother, known to Chanel as Uncle Junior. He would rob drug dealers by posing as an undercover cop, flashing a stolen badge from an unmarked car. Whenever Uncle Junior scored, usually around 3 A.M., he came banging on Margo's door, bellowing a deep "Ha! Ha! *Haaa!*"

"They would get twisted and bring his liquor up and then the sun is up and then there's no school for us because they were hangin' up all night makin' all kind of noise," said Chanel. She was now in the sixth grade at P.S. 260, a chaotic school bearing no resemblance to the private Catholic school she had attended in Pennsylvania. The parties lasted for days.

Chanel became glued to Margo's fifteen-year-old daughter, whose name was Sharvelle. She had all the feistiness of her absent father,

Speedy, and moved like him as well—in fast, jerky motions resembling the Roto-Rooter trucks that came to clean sewer drains, causing roaches to scatter. Everyone called her Roto-Rooter, which morphed into the nickname Roach.

Margo began paying Chanel and Roach $3 apiece to clean up after parties. They sifted through crack vials and reassembled them, matching red, yellow, and green caps to the same-colored bottles. Margo would then resell the vials to dealers, turning a small profit.

Crack had reordered the local economy, making fortunes and destroying lives. By the end of that year, in 1990, more than twenty-two hundred people had been killed, including 75 children—39 of them hit by bullets. It was the bloodiest year in modern New York history, unsurpassed until the attacks of September 11, 2001.

Chanel learned to keep her head down. She was on the brink of adolescence when she rolled her first pretend joint, smoking the contents of a Lipton tea bag and calling it reefer. Occasionally, she took drags of her mother's Kool cigarettes, which Joanie ordered her to fetch and light.

Bitch, light my cigarette off the stove.

Chanel knew that Joanie said this to the women she loved. A bitch was a sister. But Chanel wanted a mother. And the more time that passed, the less possible this outcome seemed.

"I always got the sense that Chanel didn't know her place in the family," said Joe.

From time to time, Chanel turned up at Sherry's door, angling to come home. But Sherry had taken in three new children, including the baby of a crack addict. And she was still hurt that Chanel had left her for Joanie.

"No one gave her more chances than me," Sherry later said. "Chanel was on the road to becoming a real good student, but her mother ruined it. She was on drugs and didn't want her to do the right thing."

Sherry had raised Chanel to say please and thank you, and to share rather than take. Joanie and Margo were different.

"Because they never had anything, so they were . . . selfish people. And I just didn't get with that. I couldn't understand that," Chanel said of her mother and aunt. "We was like strangers. And so that's how I met the streets."

Chanel and Roach began to play hooky. They rode the subway, swiping candy from vendors as the trains pulled in. This gave Chanel a rush, as if she were winning at a secret game.

The cousins stuck together while their mothers bickered. In April 1991, Joanie grabbed Chanel and left. For the next two years, they drifted in and out of homelessness. At a shelter in Queens, they contracted tuberculosis. They stayed in three other shelters, including the former hospital where Joanie was born—the place that became Auburn. By age fifteen, Chanel had attended seven different schools.

Money was so tight that the following year, in 1994, Chanel agreed to have some teeth pulled. A dentist in East New York was offering a subway token, worth $1.25, for each tooth. Working from a dingy office on Pennsylvania Avenue, he billed Medicaid for this scam. None of that mattered to Chanel, Roach, Margo, or Joanie, all of whom had teeth pulled. Chanel remembers her body thrashing in pain as strangers held her down in the chair. The dental office charged Medicaid $235 for pulling four of Chanel's teeth. She left with a few subway tokens.

Chanel clung to Roach and her sister, Sherelle, who was now living in a Bronx homeless shelter with her three-year-old son. The boy's father, Joe, had gone to prison for killing a man in the upstate city of Utica.

It was around this time that Chanel noticed the odd grape-colored marks on her cousin Sherelle's face.

"I'm allergic to chocolate," Sherelle said.

She was dating a new man and had gotten pregnant. A few months later, the man enlisted in the Army, where a medical exam revealed HIV in his blood.

"Mommy, I got AIDS," Sherelle told her mother, Margo, on the phone.

"Oh, you ain't got no AIDS."

"Yes, I do. You'll see when you have to bury me."

Margo raced up to the Bronx, where her daughter showed her the test results. Sherelle's body began to shut down, but she wanted to live long enough for the infant to be born. She spent her final weeks at Presbyterian Hospital in Upper Manhattan. Chanel sat by her cousin's bed as the room filled with family—Sherelle's aunt Joanie, her cousin Lamont, her mother, Margo, her aunt Linda, and her only sister, Roach.

"Don't be cryin' over me," Sherelle told them. "When y'all come here, I want y'all laughin' and jokin'."

A pall hung over them. They had recently lost Junior, the uncle who used to rob dealers with a stolen police badge. He had died in a car accident. Then Joanie saw her brother in a dream. Junior was driving the same car that killed him. When Joanie tried to get in the car, he snapped, "It ain't your time! Get out!"

In the Sykes family, it was common to dream of the dead. They brought messages of comfort or caution. Another night, Uncle Junior appeared in his niece Sherelle's dream. He was coming for her, he said.

The doctors kept Sherelle alive on a respirator until her baby girl was born, via C-section. Sherelle died that same day, April 12, 1994—five months after AIDS became the leading cause of death for young Black men in America.

Sherelle's baby survived and, thanks to an antiretroviral drug, was spared the virus. Everyone began calling the baby Little Sherelle. Now she needed a home, as did Sherelle's older child, the boy named after his father, Joe.

Still in prison, Joe learned about all of this—the illness, Sherelle's death, the new baby by a different man—in a phone call. He asked Sherelle's sister, Roach, to take care of his boy. She agreed, despite her own burdens. Roach also had a new baby, by the best friend of the man who had infected her sister. The whole neighborhood seemed to be falling to AIDS.

Chanel had sworn off men before learning that Roach, too, was sick with AIDS. Sex led to misery. Chanel stopped wearing dresses or makeup. She avoided men by acting like them, by "being the aggressor." She trained herself to show less emotion. She responded coolly to the decline of Roach, who had a needier way of dying than her sister.

"Come over to the house, help me watch the kids," Roach pleaded by phone. She was now caring for four children—her own three girls and her late sister's boy (while the baby known as Little Sherelle had gone to live with her father's mother).

A sore began to fester on Roach's chin.

"There ain't nothing wrong with you," said Chanel, now nineteen. She did not know, she would later tell herself, that Roach would "die hard and horrible," or even die at all. They were at the start of their lives.

But the apparitions continued. One night in Roach's sleep, her late sister Sherelle came to say that Roach's time was up.

By the summer of 1998, Roach looked gaunt, "almost ghostlike," said Joe, who saw her for the last time while he was in prison. She'd made the trip to show him his son. She died that September.

Months later, it was Chanel who saw Roach in a dream. They were little again, riding the swings. Roach wore a white dress that whooshed up and down as Chanel swung alongside her.

"I'm so sorry I didn't come," Chanel told her. "I didn't know."

They kept swinging.

"I forgive you," said Roach. Then she vanished, leaving Chanel alone on the swings.

chapter 11

CHANEL'S MOTHER GOT clean.

It happened so fast that people spoke of a miracle. From one day to the next, Joanie had quit smoking crack. Chanel saw this in practical terms: "The AIDS deaths woke her up."

There was no time to dally. Joanie's late nieces had left behind five motherless children. Two were living with their paternal grandmothers. The other three children—five-year-old Jazmen, seven-year-old Justina, and eight-year-old Joe—had nowhere to go. Their grandmother Margo was still on crack, which meant they could wind up in foster care.

Back in the 1950s, when Joanie and Margo were still children, they had never heard of "foster care." Poor families—Black, brown, and white—relied on kinship networks to help raise their children. The alternative was a child welfare system that segregated by skin color. This practice had its roots in the orphan train era, when charitable organizations became the primary caretakers of poor children. They had monopolized the system, using taxpayer funds while discriminating on religious grounds. Jewish and Catholic children, the majority of them white, went to faith-based agencies offering foster homes, while Black children—the majority of them Protestant—

tended to land in the city's reformatories, correctional facilities, and other decrepit institutions.

For Joanie and Margo, that system was still a world away—reserved only for the unluckiest children. Poor families had yet to experience the surveillance of child protection workers. There was no family court, and the Administration for Children's Services had yet to be created. "If there was an ACS case, we would have had one," Margo later told me. The term "child abuse" had surfaced in the 1960s, after Dr. C. Henry Kempe, a Colorado-based pediatrician, launched a study of unexplained injuries among hospitalized children. The resulting paper he co-published, titled "The Battered-Child Syndrome," sparked a national outcry, leading to mandatory child abuse reporting laws and federal funding for investigations.

Margo and Joanie first noticed child protection workers in the 1970s, when their own children were small. They came to distrust a system that so blatantly discriminated by skin color, sending Black children to the worst institutions. One such child was Shirley Wilder, an abused runaway who became the plaintiff, in 1973, of a landmark class-action lawsuit seeking to reform foster care on behalf of Black protestant children. The case dragged on for fifteen years before settling in 1988, just as the crack epidemic brought a new problem.

Children were flooding the city's foster care system, including thousands of babies born to mothers who used drugs. News outlets sounded the alarm of America's "crack babies," who were said to carry serious physical and behavioral defects. These reports stemmed from a single medical study, based on twenty-three babies, which has since been debunked. Long-term research shows that prenatal exposure to crack causes subtle—if any—differences in adult outcomes.

But back in the 1980s, pregnant drug users became the target of law enforcement. As more mothers went to prison, the number of foster children in New York City reached a record high, in 1992, of nearly fifty thousand, overwhelming a child protection system that was already strained.

Then came the ghastly murder of six-year-old Elisa Izquierdo—a child with roots at the Auburn shelter. Her father had been working there, serving meals and distributing linens, when he met Elisa's mother, a twenty-two-year-old addict living at the shelter. From this tryst came Elisa, whose mother had gotten high while pregnant. The father took custody of the infant, learning from his Auburn co-workers how to change Elisa's diapers and comb her hair. Four years later, when he died of lung cancer, Elisa went to live with her mother on the Lower East Side.

For the next year and a half, Elisa was tortured by her mother as the authorities ignored multiple warnings. Right before Thanksgiving, in 1995, emergency responders found Elisa dead at home, her body so battered and violated that the authorities called it the worst case of child abuse they had ever seen.

A SHAMEFUL DEATH read the cover of *Time*, below a photo of Elisa's delicate face. "Let down by the system, murdered by her mom, a little girl symbolizes America's failure to protect its children."

Vowing to reform the system, Mayor Rudolph. Giuliani placed child protection under the control of a new, independent agency overseen by him, calling it the Administration for Children's Services (the very agency that Joanie's descendents would refer to as ACS). Children continued to stream into foster care, with 13,207 admissions in 1997 alone. When Roach died the following year, everyone assumed her children would get taken by ACS.

So Joanie stepped in.

She went off crack "from one day to the next," recalled Margo. By then, Joanie and nineteen-year-old Chanel were living in a one-bedroom apartment on Gates Avenue in Bed-Stuy. Their $657 rent was covered by the city's Housing Authority and a grant from welfare, which also paid Joanie's utilities while giving her $277.82 in monthly cash assistance and $340 in food stamps. This was still not enough to cover the cost of three more children, so Joanie asked for more help. With that, the welfare agency made a request of its own: Joanie would need to train for a job.

President Bill Clinton's welfare reform act had passed three years earlier, in 1996, sending hundreds of thousands of single mothers back to work across America. "Welfare is time limited," read a letter to Joanie on March 18, 1999. "A job is your future!"

Joanie entered a work training program and was hired, in the fall of 2000, as a janitor for the city's subway system. She would clean the A train, on the night shift, with a starting salary of $22,816—an income that far surpassed her welfare cash, which ceased the following spring.

On November 14, Joanie posed for her employee identification card, smiling like her cheeks hurt. She was on her way to a real job. It happened to be her forty-seventh birthday.

"This is the happiest day of my life," Joanie told Chanel.

The apartment on Gates teemed with life.

Joanie, Chanel, her brother Lamont, and the three motherless children of Chanel's late cousins, Roach and Sherelle, shared space with two iguanas, a litter of hamsters, a boa constrictor, a pit bull named Bruno, and the dog's mother, Jazz.

The snake grew several feet long before vanishing. As word spread through the six-story building, tenants started screaming. "It was some crazy shit," said Clarence Greenwood, a flaxen-haired musician who went by the stage name Citizen Cope.

Cope was the only white renter in the building. He sat on the front stoop strumming his guitar. Just the sight of this fair-skinned man in dreadlocks made Joanie gasp.

"You scared me!" she said one day, holding tight to her pit bull's leash.

"I scared *you?*" said Cope, gesturing at the angry dog.

Whites were still a rarity in the neighborhood known as "Bed-Stuy, Do or Die." In Chanel's experience, white people came with calamity: They drove fire trucks. They pushed gurneys. They frisked the bodies of teenage boys. They knocked, clipboard in hand, to inspect busted pipes. They brought legal papers that occasioned screams. A tenant was being evicted. A child was going into foster care. Almost always, the appearance of a white person meant that something had gone wrong.

This even applied to the weather. One day, a blizzard swept through the streets, bringing traffic to a halt. Suddenly, two white cross-country skiers appeared on Gates Avenue moving "like a pair of aliens," said Chanel. She had never seen people on skis. She watched as they coasted by, carving a trail through virgin snow.

By age twenty, Chanel seemed adrift. She had dropped out of high school and was selling pot to Cope. She often lingered outside the building, swarmed by teens dressed in red. She called them "baby Bloods," as if they were being groomed for the notorious gang.

Cope was intrigued. "It was new to me because I came from DC and I thought that shit was in California," he said.

Chanel's path into the Bloods had started a year earlier, in 1998, at the McDonald's in Bed-Stuy. She had been working there as a cashier when one night a group of men gathered in the back. They spoke in a manner that scared the other customers. Never one to mind her own business, Chanel walked over to the group.

"Just be quiet," she remembers telling them, "and I'll give you some food."

Back then, Chanel's only knowledge of the Bloods came from pop culture. They were famous for their red bandannas and their murderous rivalry with the blue-clad Crips. The two gangs vied for power on the streets of South Central Los Angeles, as memorialized in the 1991 film *Boyz N the Hood*, which Chanel saw as a girl. Only later would she learn how the Bloods came east: a New Yorker named Omar Portee had spent time with the gang in LA, absorbing their rituals, coded language, and intricate hand signals. By 1993, he had returned to New York, landing at Rikers on an attempted murder charge. There, Portee and another inmate created the United Blood Nation, aiming to break the dominance of the prison's Latino gangs.

By the time Chanel met the Bloods in Bed-Stuy, they were the most violent gang in New York City, trafficking in drugs and committing armed robberies and other crimes. To earn a few extra bucks, Chanel agreed to deliver stolen McDonald's food to the gang's trap houses, the condemned buildings said to "trap" people in a downward spiral.

Half a century after Chanel's grandfather June had come here from North Carolina, Bed-Stuy was a place of boarded-up doors and broken windows. Chanel moved in a hurry, leaving burgers and fries on each stoop in exchange for cash. One evening, a man invited her inside, offering a drink. They started to talk. His friends had been abandoned as children, surviving what they described as America's systems of control—foster care, prison, parole. Now they had their own system, built of Black solidarity and resistance to white authority. Their organization's name, they told her, stood for "Brotherly Love Overrides Oppression and Destruction."

"It was like family," she said.

On the street, the Bloods could be ruthless. Male recruits had to "cut" their way in, slashing the faces of people, while most females were "sexed in"—though Chanel's boyish affect spared her that tradition. She wore baggy shirts and Kris Kross jeans, smoothing her hair back and spitting with attitude. "I was like a guy in a girl's body."

Chanel learned the gang's coded language, passed down by Portee from prison. Known to his followers as O.G. ("original gangsta") Mack, he had a network consisting of fourteen divisions, known as "sets." One handled the money. Another taught lessons. Chanel belonged to the bounty hunters, known as Gangsta Killa Bloods; their mission was to hunt down anyone who owed money or drugs to the Bloods, forcing them to pay in ways Chanel would not describe. She went from bookkeeper to treasurer to trap house manager. As her stature rose, Portee sent her a "kite" (a secret letter) thanking her for her service in "the jungle" (Brooklyn) and deputizing her as the first female to "blood in" men (the right to brand their flesh with an iron shaped like a dog paw).

Chanel says that she never killed anyone, though "we all had our violent moments." She tried to keep her gang life a secret, but Joanie could sense that Chanel was in trouble—as could Sherry. The two women were friends again, venting on the phone about Chanel's descent. One day, both Joanie and Sherry got the same jarring phone call. Chanel was on the line, saying that a man was going to kill her if they did not give him $200. The man came on the phone to repeat the message.

"Please don't hurt her," pleaded Sherry, who drove with Joanie to the man's address, paying him cash to release Chanel.

By now, Chanel was also moonlighting as a madam for some of the neighborhood's prostitutes. "You are degrading another woman to make a profit," Chanel later said. "But my way of dealing with it was making sure they get a decent cut . . . and they respected that because they didn't have anything else to respect."

This landed Chanel the name "Lady Red," which she tattooed into her arm from a cell at Rikers, while serving time for theft and assault charges.

Every so often, Chanel took to the microphone at Bed-Stuy's clubs.

> It's Lady Red on the track
> I'm shootin' bitches
> Like rat-a-tat-tat

She was never going to be a rap star, this much she knew. She watched town cars pull up to her curb, taking the white musician, Cope, to record labels. He would soon sign a deal with DreamWorks, leaving Bed-Stuy for good.

Chanel found her own escape when she finally fell in love.

The man who would become Dasani's father went by Prince Ramel Natural Born Great Love Allah, though everyone called him Ramel. He was a thirty-two-year-old Brooklynite with fine, chiseled features—half Dominican and fully Blood, belonging to Chanel's same set. He was also a crack addict who, to support his habit, had robbed two convenience stores and twenty-seven people in the span of three months, landing a felony conviction in 1997. Two years later, on March 1, 1999, Ramel was released on parole; he met Chanel the next day.

None of that scared Chanel, who was larger than Ramel. If anything, the feisty "Lady Red" scared him. "She was a brawler," Ramel later told me. He was drawn to her freckles and her "spitfire red" hair. They had a world in common, despite their twelve-year age gap. Ramel had been born in the Fort Greene projects, in the same hospital as Chanel's mother. He had the smooth charms of Chanel's late father, Sonny Boy. A more seasoned girl would have pegged Ramel as a player. But Chanel was as blind to his flaws as Joanie had been to Sonny Boy's.

It was Ramel who got Chanel hooked on crack, she later said. She was in her early twenties when they joined forces to manage a trap house on Madison Street, two blocks from Joanie's home. On a busy day, they earned more than $1,000 in commissions, feeding their own drug habit (which cost Chanel $300 per day).

Back on Gates Avenue, Joanie spent her days watching the children of her late nieces and her nights cleaning the A train, wiping off graffiti and removing gum from the seats. She came home smelling like ammonia, her hands creased, her face tired.

When word of Chanel's exploits reached Joanie, she stormed over to the trap house. She banged on the plexiglass door, calling up to Chanel from the street.

"Why you livin' like this!" Joanie yelled. "Why you wanna be a gangbanger?"

Chanel did not answer.

"I didn't want to tell her, 'Cuz you was never around.'"

Dasani was a wisp of a baby, weighing just over five pounds.

"Baby girl delivered alive," wrote the nurse on May 26, 2001, seventeen hours after severe stomach cramps sent Chanel to the emergency room of the Brooklyn Hospital Center in Fort Greene. Chanel was twenty-three years old. For the duration of her pregnancy, she had never seen a doctor.

All that Chanel had was a name for her baby girl. She had spotted it on the shelf of her local bodega, with a label that read PURIFIED WATER, ENHANCED WITH MINERALS FOR A PURE, FRESH TASTE.

The nurse found Dasani to be "alert" and in possession of a "vigorous cry." A doctor examined the infant under a heat lamp. She was then wrapped in a blanket and "shown to mother to initiate maternal bonding." Due to her low birth weight, Dasani spent two days in the neonatal intensive care unit.

Chanel was in a funk. The father of her child was still running the streets. This was no place for a newborn child, so Chanel brought Dasani to her mother's apartment.

Joanie had never struck anyone as maternal. But from the moment she laid eyes on Dasani, she turned into a gushing, syrupy, helplessly tender woman the likes of whom Chanel had never seen.

Babies made life bright again. They were a salve, a chance to try out wisdom gleaned from past mistakes. One might not live long enough to watch them grow up. Better to spoil them now. Joanie reached for her granddaughter Dasani, and from that day forward, everyone else disappeared.

"That was her girl," said Joanie's sister Margo. "That was her baby girl."

A few days later, Chanel vanished.

chapter 12

J OANIE BEGAN CALLING Dasani "Muka."

They spent their days together on Gates Avenue, and at night, when Joanie left for work, her twenty-eight-year-old son, Lamont, took over. He was trying to stay off the streets and out of prison, where his older brother, Shamell, was now serving time for dealing crack.

Dasani's parents "were nonstop, nonstop running the streets," her father, Ramel, later told me. He and Chanel tried to escape by entering the shelter system, taking Dasani with them. "That was the fastest way for any single, young Black parent who wants to get out of their mama's house," Chanel said.

Dasani was three months old when she and her parents became officially homeless, landing a room at Concourse House, a shelter in the Bronx. They were there on September 11, 2001, when the first plane hit the World Trade Center.

Chanel grabbed Dasani, who was still in her pajamas, and ran out to the street. They looked up to the sky, seeing "a big ball cloud of dust, movin' in the air."

Nine days later, Ramel took off. Feeling alone and bereft, Chanel packed her bags, put Dasani in her stroller, and returned to Joanie's door. Soon enough, Chanel was back on the street.

"You can't just pop in, pop out," Joanie scolded her daughter when she visited.

Chanel swung from crack-induced highs to deep depression. One morning, back at the trap house on Madison, she was emerging from a binge when Maxwell came on the radio singing about childbirth.

I know you have a little life in you yet.

Something about his voice—the way he soared high like a woman, then dipped low like a man—carried Chanel back to Gates Avenue. She wanted her baby.

Chanel's brother was standing over Dasani's crib. He told Chanel to wash her hands. A moment later, Chanel lifted Dasani to her face and breathed in. She felt a swirl of jealousy and relief—that her daughter had a mother in Joanie, and that her mother finally had a daughter she could keep.

At nine months, Dasani learned to walk. "She wasn't even walking—she was running," recalled Snow, a cousin who often visited with her little sister Kalinda. They doted on Dasani, who tumbled about like an acrobat. As soon as she could talk, she was calling her grandmother "Nana."

By then, Chanel was back with Ramel and expecting a second child, a daughter. They tried again to get clean, entering residential treatment. After Avianna was born in April 2002, Chanel remained with her at Odyssey House, a Manhattan facility for new mothers in recovery. But in June, Chanel quit the program, asking her mother to take Avianna.

With two babies in her charge, Joanie wore down. She had sent the other three children (whose mothers had died of AIDS) to live with their grandmother Margo, who was now clean and in a welfare-to-work program. Chanel kept saying that she, too, would "pull it together," making the same hollow promises that Joanie had also made.

Joanie was in no position to judge her daughter. If anything, she felt guilty. She had turned her life around too late. She was now earning more than $34,000 a year cleaning the A train and was accruing a pension. She performed well enough to leave the night shift. But she had crippling migraines, stomach cramps, and back pain. "Swollen feet, could not put shoes," read her work log.

She still refused to take an elevator, decades after being trapped as a teenager in the lift at Cumberland Hospital. Even with her ailments, Joanie insisted on climbing three flights to reach her apartment. By the end of September, in 2003, she had called in sick twenty-four times. The following month, Joanie and Chanel argued so forcefully that the police came. Joanie told them that Chanel was constantly "disrespecting" her.

A few days later, Chanel walked into Joanie's apartment to find her little girls dressed as if ready to leave. Their belongings were packed, even their toys.

"You can't stay here no more," Joanie told Chanel. "I'm tired of this."

To be found "eligible" by the city's homeless services meant that you had been found ineligible by your closest kin. The shelter was only open because your family had shut the door.

"When God closes a door, he opens a window," Chanel told herself.

Toting her toddler girls, Chanel got in line at the South Bronx intake office for homeless families. While New Yorkers have the legal right to shelter, Chanel still had to pass "eligibility review." This meant proving a negative: that she had nowhere else to go. The burden of proof rested on the applicants, who in the best-case scenario could produce a piece of paper, like an eviction notice or a restraining order, to show why they had no home.

But Chanel had never been a tenant, and her brawls with Ramel did not cause her to flee. She was here at the intake office because her children needed shelter. Their father was gone. And Chanel, like other single mothers struggling with addiction, arrived in a state of chaos. There was no paper trail. She chased after her toddlers as the line crept forward. Only Joanie knew how to wrangle Dasani, who would soon be wailing for her "Nana."

The cries of children rattled this building day and night, much like when Chanel had become homeless as a child. That was thirteen years earlier, in 1990, when the city sheltered more than 6,700 homeless children. Now the figure had more than doubled: Dasani and her sister were joining the ranks of more than 16,700 children in New York City shelters.

The city's new mayor, Michael R. Bloomberg, was promising to tackle the crisis. He had taken office the previous year, in 2002, as one of the richest men in the world, generating skepticism among homeless advocates. What could a billionaire know about the poor? Yet solutions were needed, and Bloomberg had built his fortune on the strength of his innovations.

After coming to New York in 1966, fresh out of Harvard Business School, Bloomberg took a low-ranking job at Salomon Brothers. The Boston native rented a studio apartment that he divided with a curtain, calling it a one-bedroom. After rising through the ranks, making partner at the firm and then getting fired, Bloomberg parlayed his $10 million severance package into a global media empire, famously inventing a digital information system that became indispensable to bond traders. Bloomberg ran for mayor on a Republican ticket (after leaving the Democratic Party) and in the fractured political environment following the September 11 attacks, he won by a small margin, inheriting a ravaged city.

The raspy-voiced mayor brought a swift corporate efficiency to office. He broke down the arcane silos of City Hall to re-create the open bullpen of his Wall Street days. Everyone would sit in a regular cubicle, including the mayor, who paid himself a salary of $1 per year. By turns gruff and pragmatic, he drew quick applause for the creation of 311, a phone number that New Yorkers could call for any reason, from complaints about potholes to questions about the tax code.

Early in Bloomberg's tenure, as the shelter system filled to capacity, the mayor considered placing families on retired cruise ships. He sent aides to the Bahamas, on his private jet, to inspect three ships for sale. "We would have to remove bars and discos which are inappropriate for shelter," the homeless commissioner, Linda I. Gibbs, said at the time. In another headline-grabbing move, Bloomberg sent homeless families to the vacant, lead-ridden Bronx House of Detention for Men.

These short-lived experiments drew ridicule. But the ships came to symbolize Bloomberg's position: Shelters should be a temporary vessel on the way to self-sufficiency, not a destination. "Our own policies needlessly encourage entry and prolong dependence on shelters," the mayor said in 2004, taking aim at one policy in particular. For decades, the city had helped homeless families jump the waitlist for public housing. Only a small fraction of those families returned to shelters. But from Bloomberg's perspective, this policy gave families an incentive to enter the shelter system: They were becoming homeless to gain access to the projects or to Section-8 vouchers, the federal rent subsidy program.

With the economy growing, Bloomberg adopted a new set of policies intended to make the homeless more self-reliant. They would no longer get priority access to public housing. Instead, they would receive short-term help with the rent.

Promising to make "chronic homelessness effectively extinct," Bloomberg revamped the shelter system with a sophisticated database to track this population and a program offering job training, legal assistance, and other supports. He also created the Center for Economic Opportunity, a city-run "innovation lab" that would spend $662 million on poverty prevention programs emphasizing jobs and education. Poor people would be empowered, the mayor told his aides, and homelessness would decline.

As Chanel stood in line at the intake office, she braced herself for the questions to come. She would be asked for the names and phone numbers of all local relatives, and for every address where she had spent even one night in the last two years. This list would then be given to the "fraud investigators" to determine if she qualified for shelter.

The question driving the agency's investigation was whether an applicant had exhausted all options, every cousin's couch, each grandmother's last bit of patience. The investigators paid house visits. If all bedrooms were full, they could propose a new "sleeping arrangement." In one case handled by the nonprofit law firm the Legal Aid Society, an applicant was told to sleep in a relative's bathtub.

During this process, the city required all family members to wait at the intake office, forcing children to skip school and parents to miss work, welfare appointments, even court hearings. Three days passed as Chanel waited for a verdict, shuttling her daughters back and forth between an overnight shelter and the intake office.

Finally, on October 27, 2003, Chanel's name was called. She and her two little girls had passed inspection. They would be living at a shelter in Harlem.

It was after midnight when Chanel carried her daughters—eighteen-month-old Avianna and Dasani, two and a half—into the six-story shelter at 30 Hamilton Place. They were shown to a small, tidy room with a queen-sized bed, a crib, and a kitchenette.

Outside, the scent of fried plantains mingled with Spanish words unknown to Chanel. She did not speak the language of this Dominican neighborhood. Dasani kept crying for Grandma Joanie.

Even in her room, Chanel felt like a stranger.

part 3

ROOT
SHOCK

2003–2013

chapter 13

CHANEL WAS TRYING to stay off drugs. With Ramel gone, she was lonely at the Harlem shelter. By sheer luck Joanie worked nearby, cleaning the A train on 207th Street. Once a week, when her shift ended, Joanie stopped by with cigarettes for Chanel and Cheez Doodles for the girls.

On occasion, Chanel piled the babies into a stroller and headed to the heart of Harlem. She walked along 125th Street, passing the grand Apollo Theater and, a few blocks away, Malcolm X's former mosque. She liked to linger on the sidewalk, by the pan-African flags and burning incense, the bottled oils of kush and myrrh. This aroma stayed in her clothes for hours. "It made me think of my ancestors. The original people."

She had whiffed the same scent back at the shelter, coming from the room of a twenty-six-year-old barber named Supreme. He was the lone parent of two small children: two-year-old Khaliq and a baby girl he called Nana. She suffered from a hereditary eye disease that would slowly cause her retina to detach, leading to blindness.

People gossiped that Supreme was a widower, stoking sympathies and flirtations. Chanel had been watching him for days—how he sat, hunched over a book, his head bobbing as he read. He had large, tender eyes that blinked slowly, as if tired. He finally noticed Chanel when they stepped into the same elevator. He leaned in, saying, "I got bud." That evening, she came to his room, where they rolled a joint and watched Ice Cube's "Friday" trilogy, which Supreme had spliced onto one VHS tape.

Despite his name, Supreme seemed shrunken. He was a man of few words, as befits those with the longest stories. It would take weeks for Chanel to unwind the basic details—how Supreme had been raised in the same neighborhood as Chanel, just blocks from Sherry's home in East New York; how they had gone to the same playgrounds and bodegas but somehow never met. Supreme was sure of this. He would have remembered those freckles. The greatest coincidence involved their toddlers: Dasani and Khaliq had been born in the same hospital, the same week of May 2001.

Yet this is where their stories diverged. The more Chanel listened, the stranger the sensation. Here she was, stuck in a homeless shelter. But compared to Supreme, she was lucky. In almost every way, she had landed the better odds, starting with the drug that ruled their respective childhoods. Chanel's mother, Joanie, had chosen crack. Supreme's parents had fallen to heroin. Both habits could be catastrophic, but given the choice, crack was a better bet. A crack addict could learn to function between highs. Heroin left people flattened.

When asked about his childhood, Supreme went quiet.

He had gone from foster care to group homes, dropping out of high school to join the crack trade. By seventeen, Supreme had a felony drug conviction and was serving time at a maximum security facility in Massachusetts. He left prison in 1997 with a high school equivalency diploma, but struggled to adjust to life on parole. In quick succession, he got two women pregnant, absconding from his role as a father. It was only when Supreme fell for a twenty-year-old named Kylia that he wanted to get married and settle down.

Seeking a new city, they moved to Washington, D.C., where Supreme found work as a barber. They were living at a homeless shelter on August 26, 2003, when his wife—now pregnant with their third child—fell down a flight of stairs to her death. In an autopsy, the district's deputy medical examiner found that twenty-five-year-old Kylia had an enlarged heart and had died of hypertensive cardiovascular disease. Supreme returned to New York a widower with two young children.

In lieu of family, he had the shelter system.

Dasani watched her mother's new crush with intrigue.

She watched everyone. She would lean out of the stroller, staring at passersby with such intensity that Chanel called her Batman Eyes. Her favorite place to go was the Alexander Hamilton Playground, one block north of their Harlem shelter.

Supreme and his children started tagging along. Chanel found a double stroller so that all four kids—Chanel's and Supreme's—could ride together. Supreme would proudly lead the way, his boom box thumping as Chanel pushed the stroller behind him. With the playground in sight, Dasani raced off screeching while Khaliq followed in silence.

He had been trapped with his mother's lifeless body after she fell down the stairs. No one knows how much time had passed. Ever since that day, Khaliq had struggled to speak.

In his father, Supreme, Chanel saw a broken man. His children's hair was a matted mess that she could fix in a few minutes. She could also hustle for clothes, produce meals in a flash, and go nose to nose with any belligerent drunk. She possessed charms that Supreme lacked, covering his awkward silence with easy chatter. She had never felt more needed by a man.

"If I suck my teeth, he'd worry about me," she said.

In Chanel, Supreme saw a lost soul. As she talked on and on, he envisioned himself reaching inside her, to a field of untilled soil. She was open and curious. She had a fertile mind. But she had been fed all the wrong influences, from the hypocrisy of the Bloods to the "trickery" of white people and their "Greco-Roman European establishment called America."

This was a country, Supreme told Chanel, with an educational system, a government, a police force, and a job market that kept people of color trapped in "the false hope of an American Dream."

"It's all a trick, not real," he said. "It's all been built up to destroy us systematically, on all levels. . . . To empower others, at the expense of crushing the Black man, father, and husband—to render him totally ineffective and stagnant."

One day, Supreme stopped by Chanel's room to find her cooking pork. "You know, I don't mean to be rude, but I'm from the Nation of the Five Percenters," said Supreme. "You ever heard of them?"

It was in prison that Supreme had joined the Five Percent Nation, founded by Clarence Smith, a veteran of the Korean War who had defected from the Nation of Islam, the Black separatist group advanced by Malcolm X. In the early 1960s, Smith—now calling himself Allah—started a movement whose followers considered themselves the enlightened "five percent" of humanity. They were living a righteous life, guided by a divine "truth" that they must strive to teach others. They believed that God existed in human form, hence "the Black man is God." This doctrine spread like wildfire through the nation's prisons.

Supreme had tried church, but it left him empty. "You can't tell me to believe in something and then say I can't see it, touch it, feel it," he said. But his own hands he could touch. And God, according to the Five Percent, dwelled within those hands. Knowing this filled him with a sense of power.

He dropped his birth name, Eric, to become "Godsupreme," joining the culture of "the Gods," whose ranks were said to include Busta Rhymes, Mobb Deep, members of the Wu-Tang Clan, Rakim, Erykah Badu, and Jay-Z. The Five Percent had reshaped urban culture and hip-hop, birthing phrases like "break it down," "word is bond," and "drop knowledge" (as later immortalized by Lin-Manuel Miranda in *Hamilton*).

Supreme began studying the Five Percent's doctrine, which drew on Islamic and Christian scripture. By the time he met Chanel in Harlem, Supreme could recite verses from the Quran in Arabic.

"I fell in love with his brains," Chanel said.

.   .   .

To keep up, Chanel began reading.

She learned that she was doing everything wrong, from how she ate and dressed to the way she parented. Even the names of her daughters bowed to a white, material world.

Among the Five Percenters, women were "earths" and "queens," while words like "bitch" and "ho" were frowned upon. Chanel felt pure again. How had she gone from scorning the word "bitch" as a child to deploying it with her own daughters?

"Things become hereditary. Not even hereditary, just systematic. You know, like just a system," she said.

Chanel had been seeking a new system for years. This drew her to the Bloods, but she was disappointed. The lesson that they were all "brothers" contradicted the way they acted when it came to drugs and money. One could only "blood out" by dying or converting to "another religion." Now Chanel had found this religion. It was enough to chase away her occasional doubts about Supreme, who still smoked marijuana and sipped beers at the playground. Nobody was perfect. At least he was trying. Perhaps he needed Chanel to realize his potential as a provider. They fantasized about having many children— "one full family," to heal a history of broken homes.

Supreme chose Chanel's new name: Makeba, for "maker of babies." Their calling would begin with the four children in their midst: Dasani, Avianna, Khaliq, and Nana. Each of them, Supreme thought, carried a certain "vibe." Khaliq was holy. Avianna was buck wild. Nana was a little devil. Dasani was an angel.

To be an angel is to be incorruptible—to "think for herself" rather than being swayed by others. Dasani would grow up to be a leader, he predicted. And in the meantime, her parents "were going to break the chain of slavery," Chanel said. "We were gonna change their food. We were gonna change the way they think. Cuz what you put in is what you get out."

Chanel began wrapping her head in a scarf and stopped eating pork. She promised to stay off drugs. Over the next year, two incomplete families fused into one. They took the train to Bed-Stuy so that Supreme could meet Joanie. She seemed pleased with Chanel's reformation, and cautiously approved of Supreme.

On February 4, Chanel, Supreme, and their four children went to the city clerk's office to get married. There was no wedding ceremony, no dress or cake. None of that mattered to Chanel, for the act alone represented a victory.

No one she knew got married anymore.

chapter 14

DASANI REMEMBERS HERSELF, as a little girl, riding the train.

She was too small to touch the floor with her feet. They dangled from the plastic seats that her grandmother cleaned for a living. Some trains went so fast that Dasani felt she was flying. She would cover her ears when the brakes screeched. She watched as the doors opened like mouths, spitting out a dozen people before swallowing a new batch. Then back into the tunnel they went.

She called this "traveling with Mommy." Or just "traveling." They were always traveling, it seemed, while never arriving. They moved from Harlem to Brooklyn, living in back-to-back shelters as the family expanded. A few days shy of Dasani's fourth birthday, her mother and Supreme had their first baby, calling her Maya. A year later, in June 2006, came another girl they named Hada.

Dasani was her mother's chief helper, and her stepfather's star student—precociously reciting his Five Percent code of "supreme mathematics." Number one was "knowledge." Number two was "wisdom." Together they made three: "understanding."

From this code, anything could be divined. If Dasani wanted to know what a particular morning might bring, she did "today's mathematics" by looking at the date. February 23, for example, would be 2 + 3.

2 (wisdom) + 3 (understanding) = 5 (power)

A good day to visit the welfare office.

By kindergarten, Dasani had also memorized the "supreme alphabet," learning to break down the hidden meaning of words. This was an alternate form of knowledge, her stepfather said, a way of tackling the white establishment. The library was where the "lies are buried." A television was "telling a lie vision." Sometimes the two codes worked in tandem. The number 7 meant "God," which was interchangeable with "Allah," the meaning of the letter A. This meant that Dasani's grandmother Joanie was cleaning the Allah train, the train of God.

Five-year-old Dasani clung to Joanie, whose apartment in Bed-Stuy became a weekend haven. They would sit for hours, Dasani in her grandma's lap as Joanie combed "the mess out of my hair." They went to church and to Fulton Mall, where Joanie splurged on dolls and fussy outfits for Dasani. She knew all of the child's likes and dislikes, fixing her favorite BLT sandwich (despite Chanel's prohibition of bacon) and taking Dasani for double chocolate chip pancakes at the IHOP on Livingston Street.

"Don't be the same, like your mother and me," Joanie told Dasani. "Go to school and graduate." By night's end, they would be drifting to sleep under Joanie's covers, the television blinking with Beyoncé.

Chanel and Supreme had a temperamental love, which their children tracked like the weather. They knew a storm was brewing when Supreme stopped talking. He would act like Chanel no longer existed. Then her anger would rise until it burst like thunder. Supreme cowered from her, at least in the early years.

Over time, he lost all decorum, fighting back as if Chanel were a man. They went blind in such moments. Their words flew, their bodies crashed. Dasani learned to hustle the children into a corner. Some fights ended with Supreme packing his clothes and grabbing the two children from his first marriage—four-year-old Nana and five-year-old Khaliq.

"Mommy!" they would shriek to Chanel as their father whisked them away, snarling that Chanel was not their "real" mother. Chanel's retort was to say that Khaliq and Nana were "his income." Without them, Supreme would lose the monthly cash stipend known as survivors benefits, which provided for the care of Nana and Khaliq.

It became clear, in such moments, that the children divided along bloodlines. Chanel's two stepchildren, Khaliq and Nana, would remain with their father; Supreme's two stepchildren, Dasani and Avianna, would stay with their mother. Maya and Hada went without comment. They were babies, after all. They needed their mother.

The separations never lasted. "Peace, Queen," Supreme would say, invoking the Five Percent greeting. "Peace, God," Chanel would gamely reply. This was their pattern, to fight and make up.

A fresh start came in the summer of 2006, when Chanel signed up for a new program created by the Bloomberg administration offering time-limited help with the rent. The family moved into their first real apartment, a two-bedroom unit in East New York. For the next twelve months, the city would pay the family's $1,176 monthly rent in full, giving Chanel and Supreme a chance to land on their feet.

Yet they kept failing—to hold down a job, to resist getting high. The following year, in 2007, Chanel was pregnant again. After having four girls in a row—first Dasani, then Avianna, followed by their half sisters, Maya and Hada—Chanel hoped for a boy. In early June, her wish came true.

From the maternity ward of Brooklyn University Hospital and Medical Center, Chanel gazed at her newborn son—the boy she would nickname Papa. He was cherubic, the picture of health. But in Papa's blood the hospital had found traces of marijuana, signaling that Chanel had used drugs while pregnant.

The practice of drug-screening newborns and their mothers—often without informed consent—had become common in public hospitals. With Papa's test results in hand, the staff alerted the city's child protection agency.

Chanel and Supreme were summoned to the agency's office in Bedford-Stuyvesant—the same brick building where Supreme had been brought as a child. As he stood there in the lobby, the memory came rushing back. He was nine years old. His sister had just died. His parents were under investigation and he was about to be separated from his three brothers—the very thing Supreme had always feared.

Twenty years later, the same fear would pass to Supreme and Chanel's children. Six-year-old Dasani grew accustomed to knocks at the door. In walked caseworkers for the agency known as ACS. They came asking questions, looking through the fridge. They were searching for signs of neglect (not enough food) or abuse (bruises or welts). They inspected each child, one by one, from head to toe.

This trained Dasani to do the same in reverse: She studied the caseworkers. She could spot one just by the size of the lady's bag, which had to be large enough to hold files. Dasani took on the psychic task of managing strangers—of knowing when to say the right thing or avoid the wrong one. She learned to interpret facial expressions and vocal intonations. None of these skills were captured on her report card at P.S. 158, in East New York.

By the first grade, Dasani had the top mark, E for "excellent," in the categories of reading and written language. But under "personal-social development," she was judged by her ability to show respect, carry out responsibilities, exhibit self-control, and obey rules. The school found her "satisfactory" in all areas but one.

When asked whether she "gets along well with others," she was given an N for "needs improvement."

chapter 15

A LIGHT SNOW FELL on December 2, 2007. The temperature dipped below freezing.

Joanie's body ached in weather like this. But she kept such things to herself. It was still morning, too early to take a break from her shift.

A few minutes after 9 A.M., she set down her bucket and went to the crew room to drink some hot tea. A supervisor noticed the absence and filed a disciplinary complaint, reporting that Joanie had taken a twenty-minute "unauthorized break, lounging in the lunchroom." Specifically, she had broken Transit Rules & Regulations 2A, 2B, 4A, 4B, 10A, and 11E—a total of six violations for one cup of tea.

Joanie was asked to explain.

"I was cold," she wrote.

Christmas drew near. Her apartment remained the family's anchor. Joanie kept up appearances, wearing a Santa hat and playing R&B holiday tracks. She said nothing of her ailments, though her legs looked weak.

"Ma, why you walking so slow?" Chanel asked as they trekked through downtown Brooklyn.

"You wanna go ahead, bitch?" Joanie snapped. "You go ahead."

Clues to her condition were hidden in her work file. On February 7, 2008, she requested a three-day sick leave, complaining of lower back pain. Her superiors warned that she could be placed on the "sick control list." With that, Joanie stopped going to work.

She said nothing to Chanel, who faced her own crisis. For the last eighteen months, she had been paying rent with the city's time-limited subsidy—the program designed to encourage financial independence. As the subsidy decreased, the renter was expected to bridge the gap. By February, Chanel had defaulted.

The family was once again homeless, moving to a shelter in Flatbush. Dasani and her siblings would be switching schools midyear. For this they needed uniforms in a different color. As usual, Chanel was broke.

On February 29, she stopped by her mother's apartment. Joanie was sitting in her chair, watching television. She gestured to the bedroom, where Chanel found new school uniforms for each child, in all the correct sizes.

Chanel never knew what to say at times like this. She felt ashamed of herself, and proud of Joanie. She kissed her mother on her forehead, gathered the bags, and left.

By the next evening, Joanie could hardly breathe. She called 911.

Emergency responders carried her out on a stretcher, "gasping for breath & unable to speak in complete sentences," wrote a paramedic. She was rushed to the Brooklyn Hospital Center, where doctors tried to save her.

Forty minutes later, Joanie lost her pulse.

"Code Blue initiated," wrote a worker.

At 1:15 A.M., Joanie was pronounced dead. She was fifty-four years old.

She took her last breath at the same hospital where Dasani, six years earlier, had come into the world.

Dasani stared at the open casket.

Her grandmother looked different. Joanie's eyes were closed, her head resting on a satin pillow. Someone had swept her hair into a clip that matched the cream color of her pantsuit. The blush on her cheeks was a shade too dark. Even her lips looked wrong. They were pursed together, as if straining for breath.

Joanie's death hit the family like a car wreck. No one got to say goodbye, not even Chanel, who raced to the hospital after hearing the news. Her mother had "expired," Chanel recalled the doctor saying, as if she was "a piece of meat gone bad."

Joanie had died of cardiac arrest brought on by atherosclerosis. Her years of crack use had made her vulnerable to this heart disease, though it is unclear whether Joanie knew about her condition. She left no will or instructions for her next of kin. Her employer, the MTA, would not release Joanie's unclaimed paychecks or pension without a death certificate and surrogacy papers, all of which required time. And without this money, Chanel could not pay for the funeral.

So Sherry stepped in.

The only reason they were all at Funeraria Juan–John's Funeral Home in East New York was because Joanie's onetime rival had paid for the whole thing (as a loan to Chanel). Every last detail had been the work of Sherry, from the flowers to the dress chosen for Dasani, in the same shade of cream as her grandmother's pantsuit.

Six-year-old Dasani had never been to a funeral. She watched as her relatives filled the room. Some of them irritated her mother. Others opened Chanel like a faucet. She buried herself in Aunt Margo's bosom, remembering the scent of her own mother. They were so lost in their grief that Dasani's next move went undetected.

Chanel looked up to see her daughter running toward the casket.

Memories of this come in fragments: Dasani's body pitching forward. Her tiny hands reaching the coffin. Her legs trying to climb inside. Someone grabbing Dasani while she kicked and screamed, calling her grandmother's name, as if to wake her.

Nana!

After Joanie was cremated, her ashes went into a black and silver urn. There was no discussion of burying her. Joanie had spent a lifetime avoiding dark, enclosed spaces, and Chanel would keep it that way. She carried her mother's urn home and placed it on a shelf.

The children got used to the urn. They brought it to picnics and baby showers, raising the occasional brow. It was not Chanel's way to care what others thought. She knew that Joanie was happiest in motion, traveling with her family.

In June 2008, Chanel completed the paperwork required to claim her mother's pension.

"How long have you known the deceased?" read the last question on the form.

In careful script, Chanel wrote three words.

"All my life."

Joanie's death brought a rebirth.

She had left behind a small fortune, saved from eight years of cleaning subway trains, for which she had earned a total of $280,752. Her combined pension, death benefits, and unclaimed pay would be divided among her three surviving children: Chanel, Lamont, and Shamell.

Chanel's portion of the inheritance came to $49,000. She had never touched so much money. Her mind flooded with ideas. She and Supreme would open a Five Percent youth center, or perhaps a barbershop. They could finally quit the shelter system.

By sheer luck, the city was offering a new subsidy to homeless families. Called Advantage, it worked like the last program Chanel had tried, giving temporary help with the rent. But this time, she brought her own advantage: her inheritance.

They could leave Brooklyn, going anywhere in the city. Yet each place had its ghosts. There was only one borough left, one unexplored terrain.

Staten Island, as the name suggests, is no easy place to reach. On the map, it looks like a reluctant fifth borough, severed from Brooklyn's western shore. There is no subway line connecting to the island, which spans sixty square miles. The only way to get there is by crossing the water, either by ferry or car, on the Verrazzano-Narrows Bridge. After it opened in 1964, some realtors steered African Americans to the economically depressed North Shore, where housing projects overlooked abandoned factories and destitute streets.

The island remains New York City's most segregated borough, a suburban Republican outpost in a Democratic metropolis. In 1993, Staten Islanders voted by a 65 percent margin to secede from the city. An expressway divides the island's racial geography so bluntly that locals call it the Mason-Dixon Line. Just south are the white enclaves that, in 2016 and 2020, would vote resoundingly for Donald J. Trump. To the north are six housing projects forming the bedrock of the Black community. And from this tiny hub comes Staten Island's most famous export: the hip-hop sensation Wu-Tang Clan—the soundtrack of Dasani's childhood.

Wu-Tang was always thumping through Dasani's home, warning of revolution and apocalypse. Time and again, Dasani went to the Five Percent meetings known as "parliaments," watching Supreme hobnob with Wu-Tang's members. Their leader, Robert Diggs, known as RZA, had left Brooklyn as a teen to live on Staten Island, where the isolation worked in his favor. "You had breathing space," he said of the island, which they renamed Shaolin Land, after an ancient branch of Kung Fu.

To Shaolin Land the family would now go.

chapter 16

DASANI HAD NEVER been on a boat, much less a ferry. She raced to the back and leaned over the rails as the propellers hummed into gear, releasing a salty mist. She stuck out her tongue to taste the water. She watched as Manhattan receded, the skyscrapers shrinking until they fit in her palm, like toys. Twenty minutes later, the ferry docked in Staten Island.

Everything here felt different. There was more grass and less noise. The family set off on foot, lugging bags of clothes and groceries. Soon they were standing before their first real home—a two-story brick duplex on North Burgher Avenue. They had their own doorbell, their own balcony, even a backyard. For the next year, thanks to the city's new housing subsidy, the family's $1,481 rent would be paid in full.

The children zipped around the grass while Supreme and Chanel toured the apartment, talking in a giddy rush. Dasani had never seen her parents so happy.

"When they're happy, I'm happy. When they're sad, I'm sad. It's like I have a connection, like I'm stuck to them like glue."

Dasani and her siblings rolled around on the wall-to-wall carpet. There they lay, as night fell, in one exhausted heap. They could not sleep. It was too quiet. They weren't accustomed to this much space.

Supreme landed a job at Heavenly Cuts, a local barbershop favored by Wu-Tang members. Chanel drew from her savings to buy a used cherry-red Dodge Durango and a rolling kitchen island from Home Depot. She decorated the girls' room with pink Barbie curtains and matching TVs. She bought a Slip 'n Slide for the yard, which the children slid across barefoot as Supreme grilled burgers.

In the living room, Joanie's urn occupied a place of honor. This was, without question, the high point of their lives. It would take years for Chanel to understand why things fell apart.

It was not obvious, in that blinding moment, that money could be useful only if they knew how to spend it. To think it would bring salvation was like asking a set of keys to drive a car. Money could not erase the past. When customers took a seat in Supreme's chair at the barbershop, they saw a pair of hands expertly at work. They did not see the boy who, at age seven, had learned that very skill by cutting his brothers' hair while his parents were high.

What money brought was an escape from all of that.

The first time Chanel took a Percocet, she felt her body go calm.

She was a patient at Staten Island University Hospital, where she had come by ambulance on May 9, 2009, barely able to breathe. A lung biopsy showed that Chanel had pulmonary tuberculosis—likely a recurrence of the illness she had contracted as a child, at a homeless shelter in Queens. Here in Staten Island, a doctor gave Chanel the Percocet, saying it would relieve her pain. After three weeks in the hospital, she was discharged with a prescription for OxyContin—120 pills per month.

As Chanel got hooked on Oxy, she kept telling herself that a doctor had prescribed it. This was "medicine." How could it be "unhealthy"? Soon, Supreme was also addicted to opioids, joining the tide of white Americans who had fallen to the same fate. When Dasani's parents could no longer buy pills on the street, they turned to heroin, keeping their habit below the radar of ACS.

Supreme and Chanel bobbed and weaved through a fog of addiction. In their best moments, they held jobs—Supreme as a barber and Chanel as a park maintenance employee, earning $3,038 in 2009. But no job lasted, and Chanel's inheritance was soon spent.

Dasani, now eight, began to fall behind in school. She was in the third grade but scoring below grade level. She lost focus even when reading and writing, her two best subjects. In an essay about the painter Georgia O'Keeffe, Dasani wrote, "She looked deeply in the sky. She had picked up her paint brushes and her paint and painted what she saw. As you can see, Georgia O'Keeffe's way of looking at the world—"

The essay dropped off midsentence.

By the summer of 2010, bedbugs had infested the house, just as the family's rent subsidy expired. Mayor Bloomberg's plan to end homelessness had also collapsed. The following year, in 2011, Bloomberg would end Advantage after the state withdrew its funding. More than a quarter of the families who signed up for Advantage became homeless again, returning to a shelter system that spends roughly $3,000 per month on each family—more than double Supreme and Chanel's rent subsidy.

In late August, Dasani's family boarded the ferry and left Staten Island, drifting across the water to the southern tip of the Financial District. The children got off, slowed by the weight of bags. They were headed to the Bronx intake center for homeless families.

Nearly seven years had passed since they first made this trek, leaving Joanie for the shelter system. This time, Joanie's urn had come along, stashed in the few bags the family could carry.

They rode the subway for about an hour, resurfacing in the South Bronx. They were looking for the new family intake center, a hallmark of Mayor Bloomberg's homeless program. The modern seven-story Prevention Assistance and Temporary Housing office—known as PATH—had cost $65.5 million to build. It faced the corner of a blighted block, standing out like a Tesla in a used car lot.

Children shuffled up the ramp, pulling suitcases and holding toys. Forbidden objects were left on the pavement—including two baby turtles, abandoned in a cardboard box. Chanel loved reptiles. When no one was looking, she slipped them in her pockets and walked through security.

For six days, the family shuttled between an emergency shelter and the intake office, where cartoons danced across flat-screen televisions.

Dasani hated to wait.

Finally her family's number flashed across a screen. A space had opened up at Auburn Family Residence, a shelter in the northern Brooklyn neighborhood of Fort Greene.

Of the city's 152 family shelters, Dasani was being sent to live in the place where her grandmother had been born.

In the neighborhood, Auburn's children stood out. They wore the numb expressions of transplants to new soil—the so-called "root shock" of the serially displaced.

Of the nine addresses where Dasani had lived, Auburn felt the most like a prison. Nobody called the shelter by its full name, just as nobody said "Rikers Island jail." Both places were known for knife fights, rat droppings, cold meals, and unheated quarters. Each offered its own mix of shelter and purgatory, with the same offenders cycling through.

At Auburn, the offense was chronic homelessness. And among the offenders were hundreds of children whose families had been identified as "the longest-term stayers" in need of "intensive case management" to find jobs and apartments. It did not help that Auburn's only housing specialist had died a year earlier, never to be replaced—just as Brooklyn was becoming one of the most expensive rental markets in America.

Dasani adapted to Auburn's dehumanizing rituals.

She learned to wait in line for the shelter's prepackaged "Swedish meatballs," ignoring the roaches in the water dispenser and the mouse pellets on the ground. She learned to keep time, nudging her mother to meet the shelter's 10 P.M. curfew. If Chanel missed it, they would be "logged out," which meant that the entire family would have to travel to the Bronx intake center to get "logged back in," while the children missed school.

She watched in silence as Auburn's guards rifled through her family's bags, tossing out glass bottles and canned food in the name of "security"—even as drugs, guns, and lovers came in through the fire escape. She found ways to verbally trick herself. She called her living arrangement "the house," even after her family was moved into one cramped room.

She choreographed her own privacy, taking turns with her siblings to undress while the others looked away. They maneuvered around the shelter's rules as well. Residents were banned from bringing in bleach, yet the janitors refused to clean the bathrooms. So the children swiped the janitors' bleach and scrubbed the floors themselves.

On the outside, Dasani seemed steady. She kept a poker face when the staff scolded her thirty-three-year-old mother as if Chanel were a cheeky adolescent. Yet these episodes left their mark.

"Sometimes it feels like, 'Why you guys messin' with my mom?'"

To mess with Chanel was to mess with Dasani. There was no separating mother from daughter. They felt the same anger, the same humiliation. Feelings passed between them like oxygen.

Still, Chanel tried to shield Dasani from the worst things.

Each family was given an "independent living plan," meant to keep them on track to move out. The shelter's caseworkers supervised these plans. "Failure to comply will result in involuntary transfer" read a form signed by Chanel's caseworker in July 2011—the same summer that this man touched Chanel's breast. He was taken off her case after she complained about the incident to Auburn's staff. Yet he kept his job and soon got a raise.

Smaller degradations were a part of daily life. The shelter's rule against irons meant that residents went to job interviews wearing wrinkled clothes.

"They want me to work, but I look like a freeze-dried piece of coffee," said Jenedra Binyard, a forty-one-year-old home health aide.

In September 2010, Dasani enrolled at Dorsey, the same historic elementary school that her grandmother once attended. But unlike Joanie, Dasani came as an outsider. This would be her fifth school in five years. She was now a "shelter boogie"—the bottom rung, the butt of jokes.

Lording over the shelter boogies was nine-year-old Staraisa, known to her peers as Star. She lived in Whitman, one of two public housing developments surrounding the school.

In every measurable way, Star was better off than Dasani. She had spent her childhood in the same apartment, anchored to one place. She had only one sibling, and though her father was an alcoholic, her mother, Bonita, worked a string of jobs to cover the family's $619 rent.

Bonita fussed over each child's graduations, starting in kindergarten. She believed that these mini ceremonies paved the way forward. From time to time, the family relied on food stamps. But they had a fridge and a stove, which helped them plan meals, stretching groceries to the end of the month. In Dasani's family, food stamps could vanish with a few rounds of store-bought fried chicken.

None of these granular differences needed airing when Star and Dasani met. The equation was simple: Star had a home, so she was the winner. Perhaps this explains Dasani's first act of aggression. She grabbed Star's apartment keys and dangled them provocatively.

Star watched in disbelief as Dasani flung the keys to Star's apartment at the sewer. This was a brazen act for any child, not to mention a homeless girl. When Star returned home, she told her mother about the new girl.

"You know what to do," Bonita said. "She hit you, you hit her back."

At the shelter, Dasani tried to focus on the things she could control. One of her pet turtles had died, but the other one was growing nicely. The children named him Turtle. When the inspectors made their rounds, Dasani hid Turtle under a bed, taking him out again after they left. The children had a similar system with food: They kept perishable takeout from spoiling by rotating each carton in and out of the small fridge.

They had, in Chanel's words, "become the place." She even had a verb for it: *sheltemized*. The only antidote to *shelternization* was a real home. And the only home open to them was Sherry's in East New York—the same home where Chanel had spent her first twelve years, before taking off with her mother, Joanie.

Sherry was now sixty-four years old, with a soft, jowly face and a mouth that crinkled. She walked as though she were decades older, leaning on a cane, her body taken by diabetes. It had been years since she ran a bustling daycare center in the basement, making enough money to send her adopted children to private schools.

Sherry's home, like her health, was falling apart. Homeless service investigators had visited, finding the house overcrowded and unsuitable for the children. But Dasani and her siblings could still visit on weekends.

With Joanie gone, they were getting close to Sherry. They noticed how Chanel called her Ma, so they started calling her Gramma. They plied her for candy and birthday dollars, knowing that Sherry had spoiled Chanel as a child.

Sherry's hands wobbled, but her eyes were still lively, and her voice a forceful smack to the ears. She had no time for "wishy-washy, half-steppin' people," she liked to say, invoking the Jimmy Stewart westerns she never tired of watching.

She was prone to lecturing, in long-winded paragraphs, about the ravages of liquor and drugs, addressing one person in words so loud they were clearly intended for other ears. Her target audience was usually Chanel.

At the urging of ACS, Chanel had enrolled in a new drug treatment program. She was taking methadone, a legal synthetic opioid that was pioneered to treat heroin addicts in New York City in the 1960s. A daily dose of methadone could block the euphoric effects of heroin, oxycodone, and other opioids while relieving the craving for these drugs. Yet Chanel questioned the logic of trading one drug for another. Was methadone that much better? It left her light-headed and sluggish. No one seemed to leave the program.

"It's an all-your-life thing," she said.

She and Supreme were on another downward spiral, shoplifting when their food stamps ran out and fighting with little provocation. During the worst fight, on March 14, 2011, Supreme punched his wife in the face. By late August, they had separated.

On Labor Day weekend, Chanel brought the children to Sherry's. Then they lost track of time, missing the shelter's curfew. Chanel and the children trekked to the Bronx to get logged back in, returning to Auburn the following night.

When they walked into Room 449 on September 7, they found most of their possessions gone: their clothes, shoes, photographs, books, a television, journals—the traces of their existence. In a panic, Chanel searched for her mother's urn. She raced down to the security guards as Dasani chased after her.

"Where are my mother's ashes?" Chanel screamed.

The truth unfolded in spurts. A staff member had paid a resident $10 to empty the room, perhaps thinking that Chanel was gone for good. Some families get logged out and never come back. Within hours, residents had looted the room, stealing valuables and other items. Nearly everything else was tossed in the garbage.

Chanel bolted out the back of the shelter, setting off a fire alarm. There, a large metal incinerator held Auburn's rotting trash. She waded in as the garbage rose to her stomach. She plunged her hands through soiled diapers and rotting food, feeling for the smooth curves of her mother's urn.

She felt her mother trapped, everything closing in. This could not be Joanie's final resting place, she told herself. The stench made her gag. The trash sank beneath her feet. This dumpster was, unbeknownst to Chanel, a few feet from the former morgue of Cumberland Hospital.

She cursed and wept. She heard someone calling. She flailed her arms, throwing trash in all directions.

Finally she stopped.

She stood there in the dark. She could do nothing to reverse the fact that fifty-seven years after her mother was born, right here in this building, her remains had been lost in the garbage.

chapter 17

UPSTAIRS AT AUBURN, the room felt cursed.

Joanie had always protected the family, in life and in death. Even after the inheritance she left was spent, her ashes had been a talisman. They fended off evil. This is what the children believed.

Chanel paced the room. She was broke. Her children were due to start school the next day. She expected no help from Supreme, who was staying with his cousin in Staten Island.

Nor did she think the Auburn staff would care. Still, she went to the trouble of filing a complaint, summarizing her grievance at the top of the form with "All of my belongs went in garbbage." She then wrote, in hurried print, "I don't know what to do my kid start school tomarrow and I have nothing." She added, almost tangentially, that her caseworker had recently "groped" her—a problem so common that she never thought to file a separate complaint. She ended on a conciliatory note: "Peace."

The next day, on September 8, Chanel left the children alone in the room and hit the streets in search of cash. A man approached her on Myrtle Avenue asking where he could buy drugs. He didn't seem like a snitch, so Chanel steered him to a dealer in the projects. She was soon in handcuffs and charged—wrongfully, she says—with drug possession. No drugs or money were ever admitted into evidence, and the court later dropped the most serious charges.

When Chanel failed to return to Auburn that night, Dasani sensed that something was wrong. There was a knock at the door. She hushed the kids, but the knocking continued and finally the door flew open. An Auburn supervisor and a homeless services officer told the children to get dressed. They were escorted to an office to wait for their father, who returned to Auburn at 10:20 P.M.

By now, ACS had been monitoring the family, off and on, for seven years. Following Chanel's arrest, the agency ordered new drug screenings. When Chanel and Supreme refused, ACS went to court seeking to remove the children from their parents.

For child maltreatment cases in New York's family court, the poor have a right to free counsel. A judge assigned lawyers to each of the parties: one for Chanel, one for Supreme, and one for all seven children. In court on September 20, 2011, the children's lawyer, Marty Feinman, objected to removing the children. He was "not convinced," he told the judge, "that it's in the children's best interest—seven children—to take them out of this environment where they are living together . . . and have them wind up in foster homes, who knows where in the city and going to school or daycare or getting assistance who knows where."

To divide Dasani and her siblings would, Feinman argued, "present a greater imminent risk to the children than remaining where they are."

The judge struck a compromise: The children could stay with Supreme, provided he was monitored by ACS. But Chanel had to leave. She would be allowed supervised visits with her children, and if she met the court's requirements, she could eventually regain her parental rights.

Chanel broke the news to the children on a bench in Fort Greene Park. "Take care of each other," she instructed her firstborn child.

Dasani was silent.

She did not know the details: the fact that her mother had relapsed or that ACS was now watching Supreme; that with one more mistake, the family could be dismantled; and that on top of every-thing, Chanel was pregnant again. All Dasani could hear was that her mother was leaving. Her parting words echoed for days:

Take care of each other.

This meant many things. It meant staying out of trouble, for Su-preme ruled by fear. If the children laughed too loud, he yelled "Shut up!" and they froze, a silent dread passing among them. If they broke the rules, they would surely get the belt. Chanel had softened Su-preme, just as Joanie's urn had tempered Chanel. In the absence of these matriarchs, a new order would come. Supreme summed it up in two words, writing in black marker on the wall near Dasani's bed: "King Me!"

Chanel entered residential rehab at Mount Sinai Hospital in the Bronx, living in a sterile room. Everything felt empty. She could not imagine life without the clamor of her children, the mess of their sounds and scents.

They could only visit with a caseworker present. They nuzzled their faces into Chanel's belly, where a new baby grew.

"You want to bring another child into this world?" Supreme asked his wife.

After completing twenty-eight days of rehab, Chanel went to the place where her life had begun. Sherry's door was still open. They sat in silence most nights, sharing plates of Chinese noodles and fried chicken.

Chanel decided to keep the baby. She took a job as a security guard for the Duane Reade pharmacy chain, earning her first in-come in years—$1,098 per month. As her pregnancy progressed, she was reluctant to go back on methadone, thinking it would harm her baby. But the people paid to monitor Chanel's life—the caseworkers, the drug counselors—all seemed unfazed. Methadone babies were born, they were "weaned," and they adjusted.

For two and a half weeks after Lee-Lee's birth, she stayed in the neonatal intensive care unit of Kings County Hospital Center. A nurse instructed Supreme in "methadone taper down," the task of gradually reducing Lee-Lee's methadone dose until she was weaned. She suffered from a crush of symptoms—tremors, diarrhea, fever, "mottled skin," sleeplessness, loss of appetite. She was constantly "irritable with a high pitched cry," wrote a hospital worker.

On April 3, Supreme carried Lee-Lee out of the hospital and returned to Room 449. Day and night, the baby cried as Dasani raced to the cafeteria to heat her bottle. On weekends, the children visited their mother under Sherry's supervision. They raced up the steps calling out "Mommy!" Dasani always got there first, burying her head in Chanel's bosom. They could stand like this for minutes.

Dasani knew how her mother was doing from her girth. If Dasani could reach all the way around Chanel, this meant that her appetite was gone. If Chanel was eating, there was no circling her plumpness.

"Hi, Muka," Chanel would purr as Dasani closed her eyes, breathing in her mother's peppermint-soap scent.

They all had funny nicknames.

Muka, Mama, Papa, God, Nana, Hada, Maya, Lee-Lee.

They did not know the origins of these names, which had come as fast as Chanel now braided their hair, starting in the morning so she could finish by sundown. The girls winced as Chanel brushed out their tresses, parting them into sections. Her fingers flew in a blur, leaving row after row of tightly wound perfection. No one would be calling her girls "nappy," especially when she wasn't around to set the matter straight. By the time she finished the last of her girls' crowns, her hands were numb.

Sherry braided the children in her own way, trying to keep them in line. Were they doing their homework and making decent grades? No one, to her mind, had more potential than Dasani. She had been born with a lucky mix of intelligence and willpower. But she also had her mother's temper, pouncing at any slight. Such radioactivity could be her ruin.

"Dasani's a fighter," Sherry told me one afternoon. "Ooo-weee. She will fight anyone . . . anyone outside. Dasani will tear 'em up. You can see how small Dasani is. And she don't care how big you are. She will tackle you. If you bother her, look out."

This was certainly true when it came to Star, who had yanked

Dasani's hair while the students were watching *The Cat in the Hat* in the school auditorium. With that, Dasani threw her first punch, right at Star's face. They were now sworn enemies.

But to Sherry, this was middle school noise. Dasani still had time. Unlike her mother, she could be saved from the traps of early pregnancy and addiction. In fact, she was more than salvageable. She could keep rising, which meant not only getting into college but making it all the way to graduate school.

Sherry rested on the example of Dasani's cousin Sheena, one of the many children raised by Sherry. Sheena had made good enough grades to be accepted into Kents Hill, a boarding school in central Maine. From there she had gone to Bates College on a scholarship, and she was now finishing a master's degree in teaching.

Sheena had risen.

To tempt Dasani's imagination, Sherry dug up a glossy brochure from Sheena's boarding school. The rolling lawns, tennis courts, and library could all belong to Dasani. She only needed to focus in class and stay out of trouble.

Focus in class. Stay out of trouble.

When Dasani returned to Auburn, she tucked the brochure in her dresser drawer.

As the summer of 2012 neared, Dasani flunked out of the fifth grade.

Her school was also flunking. The city's Department of Education had given Dorsey a D rating. Brooklyn's first school for Black children was in danger of being closed.

At graduation, Dasani held a flag as her peers got their diplomas. She was forced to attend summer school. If she passed, she could leave Dorsey for McKinney, just two blocks away.

Something about the challenge excited Dasani. A summer could fly by. It was like seeing the finish line at a race. "I'ma do it, Mommy," she said.

Chanel was distracted by her own tests, the ones administered by ACS. The caseworker assigned to Chanel had noted progress of late: She was reporting daily to her methadone program and showing up to family team meetings. Even her urine samples were clean.

On August 2, after ten months away, Chanel was allowed to return to her family, at Auburn, under the supervision of ACS.

Chanel left Sherry's. Dasani graduated from Dorsey.

Mother and daughter were back together, in the sweltering heat of Room 449.

chapter 18

I T   I S   N O W the morning of April 3, 2013, less than two months
before Dasani's twelfth birthday. She has been attending the
McKinney school since September but was recently suspended
by the principal, Miss Holmes.

Dasani climbs the school steps wearing her best cardigan. She is
eager to try out the script that her mother has drilled into her.

How was your spring break, Miss Holmes?

(Pause, wait for Miss Holmes to ask the same question.)

Oh, it was good. I'm staying out of trouble!

(Wait for Miss Holmes to laugh and then walk away, showing new
resolve.)

Gotta get to class!

Dasani lingers at the principal's door. Too many students are vying
for Miss Holmes's attention, so Dasani heads to her homeroom. For
the next few days, she stays focused in class and quiet in the hall.

"It's a new Dasani," says Officer Andrews, the school security
guard, his brow dubiously cocked. Dasani's teacher, Miss Hester, is
also skeptical. Just two weeks ago, this girl was challenging students
to fight. Miss Hester wonders how long Dasani's reformation will
last.

Dasani has her own doubts as well. Fighting makes her feel powerful. It distracts from other feelings—from what she will learn, years from now, to call "being vulnerable."

"Cuz I don't like to be nice, cuz then kids take advantage," she tells me during a lunch break. Some feelings, she reserves for her poems, most recently, one she calls "Alone":

> I cry all day
> Couldn't find land
> Nowhere to stand
> On a boat without a friend
> Sharks trying to eat me
> I'm dead again

Dasani continues to see her counselor at school, Roxanne. They meet to play Mancala and to talk about "anger management"—a concept that Dasani finds odd. She does not consider her anger a thing to be "managed"—especially if this interferes with her ability to fight. Anger is critical to winning a fight. And only if Dasani wins does she keep her reputation—and her body—safe.

By this equation, anger + fighting = triumph = survival.

No adult at McKinney is going to tell Dasani to stop surviving. The trick is to nudge her toward another form of self-preservation: avoiding the fight altogether.

Roxanne asks Dasani to recount a typical fight, describing each move in slow motion. This is easy: The fight always begins with a taunt. This makes Dasani's heart beat faster and her breath come shorter. She stops hearing her thoughts.

"It's like my body just get hyped. And my body ends up hitting."

Roxanne offers a strategy: As soon as Dasani hears the first taunt, she must breathe in for ten seconds through her nose and then breathe out for ten seconds through her mouth.

Dasani gives it a try. For the next week, she keeps practicing.

"First, you close your eyes. And then you breathe in, and then you breathe out," she tells me while demonstrating. "You breathe in through your nose, and you breathe out through your mouth."

This gives her unseen power.

"Like when I want to hurt somebody, like when I want to fight, or when I feel really sad, I just breathe in and out," she tells me. "It works."

The two blocks separating Dasani's school from her shelter can be a minefield of drunks, sex workers, dealers, and cops. The local precinct will investigate six murders by the end of this summer.

Dasani knows to walk quickly. She can slip past the adults, but she remains a target among her peers—especially her longtime rival.

Star is now a foot taller than Dasani and easily twice her seventy pounds. She walks with a forceful step, tilting her head forward as if ready for battle. Her glasses distract from her beauty, covering hazel eyes and long lashes. Most of the time she appears sullen, her lips closed in the manner of a person who stews.

The long-simmering tension between Star and Dasani is close to boiling over. Rumors are circulating that they will fight. The following Tuesday, when school lets out, Dasani is swarmed by girls.

"You gonna fight her?" one of them asks.

Star hovers.

"No!" says Dasani. "Miss Holmes says if I get in another fight, I get suspended."

With that, Star walks up and slaps Dasani hard across her left cheek.

The crowd is silent.

Breathe in for ten seconds.

"You think that hurt?" Dasani says. "I eat those."

Star glares at Dasani.

Suddenly Avianna appears, jumping in between the girls.

"You better back up off my sister's face," Avianna yells at Star. "Before I hurt you."

The crowd disperses as the two sisters trot off. They are late for church—which they attend despite their parents' Five Percent religion. This is the same mobile church that their grandmother Joanie knew as a child, calling it "Yogi Bear" for the van's cartoon logo. The preachers still park in the same spot, opposite the Walt Whitman Library.

They are like a spiritual Pied Piper, offering candy in exchange for souls. This can be an awkward transaction, the white preachers stiffly breakdancing while the children pretend to pray. A less scrappy outfit might avoid such displays, but there is no competition. It is just Yogi Bear. And that's why Dasani likes them, in the same way she likes Miss Hester and Miss Holmes. Nothing counts like the people who show up.

Following the preacher's lead, Dasani and Avianna are soon chanting, "Jesus died for me!"

The next morning, the sisters wake to shouting.

Supreme shoves Chanel in the back. The children start to cry as their father packs.

Dasani's stepsiblings—Nana and Khaliq—go quiet when this happens, as if their silence might erase them from view. They know that if Supreme leaves, he will take them along. The last time they left, Nana was just five years old, and Khaliq six.

Supreme stops packing.

"I'm staying," he says.

On the Brooklyn block that is Dasani's dominion, shoppers can buy a $3 malt liquor in an airless deli where food stamps are traded for cigarettes. Or they can cross the street for a $740 megabottle of chardonnay at an industrial-chic wine shop decorated with modern art.

A sign outside that locale, Gnarly Vines, catches Dasani's notice one April afternoon: WINE TASTING TONIGHT 5–8.

Dasani is hardly conversant in the subject of libations, but this much she knows: A little drink will soften her mother's edge. Dasani points out the sign, and without further ado, Chanel heads into the wine shop on Myrtle Avenue trailed by four of her children. They are lugging two greasy boxes of pizza and a jumbo pack of diapers from Target.

The cashier pauses. The sommelier smiles.

"Wanna try a little rosé?" she asks brightly, pouring from a 2012 bottle of Mas de Gourgonnier. "I would describe it as definitely fruit forward at the beginning."

Chanel polishes it off.

"But really crisp, dry, refreshing—"

"Not refreshing," Chanel says. "I just think . . . dry."

"No, it's *very* dry," says the sommelier, a peppy blonde in wire-rimmed glasses. "It's high acid, a little citrusy."

Chanel sticks out her tongue. She finds the woman's choice of words unappetizing. As if sensing the distance, the lady sweetens her tone.

"You can try anything you want," she says. "I'm just letting you know."

"I'ma try 'em all!" Chanel replies.

"This is a Greek white," says the sommelier.

To the side of the wine display is a large silver vase, which looks strikingly similar to Joanie's lost urn. Khaliq stares at the vase. "This is for putting people in, right?" he asks the sommelier.

Chanel rolls her eyes. "That is not an urn," she sniffs.

"Oh my gosh, for cremation?" the sommelier asks, shaking her head. "We just use it for spitting in."

"For *spitting?*" Chanel says with horror.

"Yeah, it's got rejected wine in it," the sommelier says.

Chanel scoffs. She might not like the wine, but she sees no reason to "reject" it. She moves on to a Tuscan Sangiovese.

Ignoring the spectacle, Dasani scans the room. She frowns at a sign on the wall for LIQUEUR.

"They got 'liquor' spelled wrong!" Dasani yelps triumphantly.

Actually, the sommelier interjects, that is a French word for the delicate liquid spirits derived from fruits such as pomegranates and raspberries. "But you're very right," she offers. "That is not how you spell 'liquor.'"

"Not the hood liquor," Chanel says.

Sometimes Dasani wanders to the other side of Fort Greene Park, finding a sweeping lawn where, on sunny days, light-skinned women sunbathe or play tennis near a water fountain retrofitted for dogs.

She never sees those ladies at the Bravo Supermarket for Values, just a few steps north on Myrtle, where Polaroids of thieves fill the store's "Wall of Shame." Wearing naked expressions, they are forced to pose with their stolen items—things like Goya beans and Kraft cheese. A woman named Mary holds a can of tuna in a photograph titled "Catch of the Day."

Dasani reasons that wealth belongs to "the whites" because "they save their money and don't spend it on drinking and smoking." Fort Greene's demography may feed such perceptions: The top 5 percent of residents earn 76 times the income of the bottom quintile, making this one of the most unequal pockets in the city.

Exposure to the moneyed classes has its upsides. A growing tax base can improve public schools and parks while beefing up services like garbage collection. Ideally, gentrification also changes what scholars call "the geography of opportunity," by expanding the social networks of the poor and making some children more likely to attend college.

"Would we prefer a city in which the wealthy and the poor lived in entirely separate neighborhoods, rather than one in which they live side by side?" says Ingrid Gould Ellen, a professor of urban planning at New York University.

The early pioneers of Fort Greene's gentrification were, in fact, African American. In the 1960s—long after the neighborhood was redlined, allowing banks to disinvest—Black middle-class families took ownership of Fort Greene's brownstones.

The 1980s and 1990s brought a cultural revival that is likened to the Harlem Renaissance, with Black writers, musicians, and actors planting roots in Fort Greene—among them Chris Rock, Erykah Badu, and Branford Marsalis. Their de facto mayor was Spike Lee, whose homegrown 1986 film *She's Gotta Have It* takes place in the neighborhood.

By the time Dasani was born here, in 2001, Fort Greene was the beating heart of what *Essence* magazine called Brooklyn's "Black Mecca," a neighborhood that Black families had dominated for half a century. It was on a bench in Fort Greene Park that Richard Wright had written passages of his landmark 1940 novel, *Native Son*.

Then came a seismic change.

Much of it began in 2003, with Mayor Bloomberg's plan to remake downtown Brooklyn. Through aggressive rezoning and generous subsidies, developers broke ground on nineteen luxury buildings in Fort Greene, all in the span of three years. Within a decade, the neighborhood's real estate prices had doubled and its portion of white residents had jumped by 80 percent—while an estimated three-quarters of Fort Greene's Black-owned businesses closed.

Brooklyn was seeing the opposite of white flight—a white landing of sorts. This was coded in the language of class: the arrival of "educated" professionals who were lifting a community of "low-income" renters. Yet the color line persists: The very boundaries of neighborhoods that were once marked in red, excluding Black people from buying homes, now contain some of the hottest real estate.

In 2014—one year after Dasani competed in a track competition at the Pratt Institute—Spike Lee stood onstage there during Black History Month, delivering a rant against gentrification.

"Then comes motherfuckin' Christopher Columbus Syndrome," fumed Lee. "You can't discover this! We been here." He went on to compare Fort Greene Park to the Westminster Dog Show, "with twenty thousand dogs running around," while lamenting how his father, a jazz musician who had purchased his home in 1968, was playing acoustic bass when his new neighbors, in 2013, called the police. "You just can't come in where people have a culture that's been laid down for generations and you come in and now shit gotta change because you're here?"

The same forces are reshaping Bed-Stuy, the historic neighborhood where Dasani's great-grandfather June first landed and where her teacher, Miss Hester, still lives. Around the corner from her basement rental, a trendy café now sells $4 espressos. Miss Hester resents the neighborhood's white transplants, walking around "as if I am the outsider, and I'm like, 'Excuse me I was *born* here!'"

Dasani's mother sometimes wonders what would happen if Brooklyn's newcomers spent some time with the borough's older self. On Myrtle, opposite the wine shop, they would find a barber named China whose chairs are always full. A din of chatter fills the barbershop, where a tank of swimming turtles sits at the window. Dasani loves to watch them glide through the water. Her favorite turtle is missing its toes.

China's clippers fly over the skulls of men who were boys back when Myrtle was known as "Murder Avenue." Some of them came of age when Chanel's favorite Marvin Gaye song, "Inner City Blues (Make Me Wanna Holler)," first hit the airwaves in 1971—the same year that Dasani's grandmother Joanie fell in love with Sonny Boy.

Three generations later, Dasani's "inner city" is a place on the outside.

In every direction, the new Brooklyn screams—with jackhammers, bulldozers, and the endless *beep beep* of trucks in reverse. Two years from now, China's barbershop will vanish, along with its toeless turtle.

Just blocks away stand the Ingersoll and Whitman projects, which surround Dasani's shelter and have fallen into disrepair. For the arriviste investor, the projects present a rude visual interruption, an inconvenient thing to walk around, but never through.

For Dasani and her siblings, the projects are Brooklyn's last piece of sky. There are no forklifts here (despite the dire need for repairs). Some of these 1940s buildings were capped at six stories, which means you can still see the moon. "That won't last long," Chanel says. A new high-rise looms over Joanie's birthplace, as if claiming the sky itself.

Fort Greene is now a marker. For one set of people, arriving signals triumph. For another, remaining means defeat. Dasani will do better, she tells herself.

"People don't go nowhere in Brooklyn," she says.

"If I'm the choreographer, you all have to work these moves!" Dasani hollers at her sisters on March 9, 2013.

They are in Sherry's basement, practicing for their biggest performance of the year—a family event of unparalleled power.

Nearly fifteen years after Chanel's cousin Roach died of AIDS, her daughter Justina is having a baby. This is the same girl that Dasani's grandmother Joanie had taken in, along with two other children left motherless. They had stayed with Joanie until their grandmother Margo got clean, landing a job as a medical receptionist.

And now Margo will be a great-grandmother—something she could never have fathomed when her daughters, Sherelle and

Roach, fell ill. Everyone still remembers when Sherelle died, after doctors worked to save her unborn child. The family had rejoiced when the infant tested negative for HIV. She is now eighteen.

Tonight's celebration is less a baby shower than a testament to the family's staying power. Not since Joanie's funeral have the Sykeses rallied like this. Chanel is giving $107 of her tax refund to the event. Her husband's task is to make enough chicken wings to feed eighty people. He glides around Sherry's kitchen, where a washing machine sticks out between the stove and the sink, and a smoke detector beeps under the blast of Snoop Dogg's "Sensual Seduction."

Everyone in the family knows that Chanel is the baker (cornbread is her specialty) while Supreme is the cook—though he prefers the title "chef." Today, he is making his "secret sauce." He closes his eyes, breathing in the scent. Only amateurs rely on taste. A chef can smell when the dish is ready.

Supreme has spent hours watching *Diners, Drive-Ins and Dives*, hosted by the bleach-capped Guy Fieri. The show visits restaurants across America, celebrating chefs who can improvise—a skill that Supreme was forced to learn at age seven, making meals out of random ingredients. His favorite invention was "wish" sandwiches, as in "I wish there was something for me in there." He would pour sugar between two slices of bread, imagining another taste.

People say that a true chef can make a meal from anything in the fridge, but Supreme begs to differ. Were this true, the projects would explode with celebrity chefs. Hunger forces people to cook, but a chef must possess talent. And talent is revealed through choices—the ability to choose the freshest ingredients in the store, combining them to perfection.

"You gotta be focused," Supreme says. "There's an order to cooking, you know? Everything has an order. . . . I like law and order. I don't like disorganization."

This may sound odd coming from a man with no wallet. But when Supreme cooks, everything falls into place.

At tonight's baby shower, the Sykes family will be treated to Supreme's signature dish: "honey barbecue chicken wings with crushed pineapple." He places an emphasis on the word "crushed"—not sliced nor diced. He adds "a little hint" of vanilla and "a pinch" of nutmeg in order "to mess with the people's palate."

Therein lies the secret of the sauce.

Downstairs, in Sherry's basement, Dasani cues up Beyoncé. She has been rehearsing for days, gliding across Auburn's bathroom floor as Chanel muttered, "You crazy."

Tonight, Dasani's sisters have agreed to be her backup dancers. Avianna shuffles to keep up, gasping asthmatically for air. Nana is tall and limber by comparison, but lacks rhythm. She stumbles about, colliding with Avianna as they try to follow Dasani's lead.

The more they rehearse, the greater Dasani's frustration. She yells. They recoil. She orders them to start over as they roll their eyes.

In the sibling pecking order, no one questions Dasani's supremacy. Even she forgets that Khaliq is technically older. He was born four days before her—in the same Brooklyn hospital, back when Chanel and Supreme were strangers. By chance, Supreme's then wife, Kylia, and his future wife, Chanel, were both giving birth for the first time. They might have passed each other in the hall, in matching maternity gowns.

Chanel can still picture it—the two of them standing at the same window, peering at their newborns as Dasani's cries mixed with Khaliq's. Who would have guessed that these two random children would later join the same family, sharing one mother after the other passed away?

Upstairs, in Sherry's kitchen, eleven-year-old Khaliq sweeps the floor. He no longer remembers his mother's face. But he dreams about her. Just the other night, she reappeared, saying, "It's me."

Khaliq now attends a public school in Coney Island for children with behavioral problems or disabilities. He wakes at 5 A.M. to catch the first of two buses, often arriving before school opens. Last December, three days after the Newtown, Connecticut, massacre, he came to school saying, "I want to be killed like those kids in that shooting." The police took him to the emergency room of Lutheran Medical Center.

Most of the time, Khaliq is quiet. Nothing frustrates him like the room at Auburn. Everywhere he looks, he is surrounded by girls—their gossip, braids, catfights, vanity, and, worst of all, their prying. "I want my own house and my own room because I need my own privacy."

Khaliq recedes into video games, imagining himself as a warrior. He wants to become a cop "to protect myself" while "saving other people." His father proposes a loftier goal: Khaliq could join the Navy SEALs. The military would allow Khaliq to supplant his annoying sisters with a brotherhood of his own choosing.

For now, he has only his little brother—five-year-old Papa. Khaliq's little brother is so used to hearing his name ("Papa, get down from there! Papa, put that back!") that he responds with an irreverent cackle. He is forever scaling walls, chasing cats, shoving his sisters into puddles. Even his teachers have thrown up their hands. Papa "disrupts the entire class with noises he makes. He rolls on the floor, lies across the chair," his kindergarten teacher writes in a letter home. "No amount of threatening him works!"

Sherry is tired of getting calls from Papa's school, where she is listed as the emergency contact. When is he going to learn to behave? Because "there's no crappin' with me, young man." Papa scoots away before she can finish the scolding. He hunts around the house, venturing out the back, where weeds trickle up a gray cement wall, amid rusted cars and stray garbage.

Papa does not see these things as bad or ugly. They are the topography of his childhood. An empty beer can is to be crushed and kicked until something else catches his eye. Papa is fond of things that move of their own accord, like spiders, cats, roaches, and worms. By the time he resurfaces with sludge on his shoes and stones in his pockets, everyone is tired of calling his name.

If each child has a role, seven-year-old Maya is the family diva, six-year-old Hada the bookworm, and Baby Lee-Lee the clown. She is starting to walk. Her legs wobble as she waves her arms, tumbling forward. She gets back up, howling with delight. Strangers melt at the sight of Lee-Lee's plump cheeks and soft curls. She has her father's intense gaze, watching people like she knows their secrets. She can stare so hard that she frowns, leading Dasani to call her "Mean Baby."

But to Chanel, Lee-Lee's frown is a sign of intelligence. She has been teaching the baby to recite the alphabet. Lee-Lee can now say "Turtle" for the family pet, and "Sani" for Dasani, whom she also calls "Mommy." No one else is as quick to change her diaper, or as unperturbed by its contents.

By 5 P.M., Dasani is rallying her siblings. It is time to leave Sherry's for the baby shower.

"Let's get a pep in our step!" Chanel calls out, pushing a cart stacked with chicken wings.

The sun is setting. Almost an hour later, they reach the banquet hall in Bed-Stuy, where Chanel gathers the children in a tight circle.

"Let me tell you something," she says. "If you get in this place and you start running around like you don't got no sense, I'ma take you in that bathroom and I'ma *skin* you. You understand me?"

chapter 19

CHANEL KNOWS HOW to make an entrance. The children are her opening act, crashing into the room like lightning. She follows at an elegant pace, her chin held high, as if to say, "I'm raising eight kids. What have you done lately?"

There is Aunt Margo, arms flung wide. She is unquestionably Chanel's favorite aunt. At fifty-six, Margo still looks like a doll, with thick lashes, cherry lipstick, and flowing ringlets. It used to be Joanie who greeted guests with a booming "Hellooo!" but since her death, Margo is filling in.

Her pregnant granddaughter, Justina, circles the room in red flats and a smart blazer. She is joined by her sister Destiny and her cousin Little Sherelle. All of them had lost their mothers to AIDS. The young women hug Dasani as Biggie Smalls and Puff Daddy rattle the speakers:

> *I'ma always want you*
> *When nobody wants you*
> *If I die now*
> *My love'll still haunt you*

Biggie was raised here in Bed-Stuy. The song came out in 1996, a year before he was murdered, back when Justina was five and her mother, Roach, was still alive. Tonight, the deejay will spin many songs from that time.

Balloons cover the room in a swirl of red, black, and white, above a wicker loveseat where Justina and the baby's father will open gifts before cutting a sheet cake. Everything about the event recalls a wedding, from Justina's bridal white to the sparkling Moscato Rosé and the party favors. Few people get married anymore. A baby shower is the next best thing.

Dasani removes her coat, disappointed to be wearing her pink sweat suit. But stashed in Lee-Lee's stroller is Dasani's secret weapon: a spotless pair of Jordans. Chanel had finally caved, buying them with her dwindling tax money—one pair for Dasani and one for Avianna, as well as an outfit for Supreme. Tonight he makes the obligatory appearance, setting out his chicken wings before taking off.

"What kind of man bounces and then leaves his family to find their way home?" says Chanel.

Standing nearby is Margo's ex-husband, Speedy. Long after the death of their daughters, Speedy and Margo still pull together for family events. They glance sadly at their granddaughter's belly. Trying to keep the mood light, Justina jokes that the baby had better not inherit the red hair of her great-grandfather June.

"Grandfather had the good genes," says Speedy. "Went to high school, went to the military."

Minutes later, Chanel motions for Justina to take a seat, because Dasani has "a tribute for you." The crowd hushes. People lift their cellphones to record. Dasani bows her head, her hair braided into a Mohawk. She has decided to perform without her clumsy sisters. She waits for the music while staring at her feet. She is still wearing the old sneakers, opting to save her Jordans for school.

Dasani begins cautiously, as though she is still on Auburn's bathroom floor. She dips into a split, nearly stumbling. But soon her body takes over and she is breakdancing, doing backflips and one-handed cartwheels while thrashing her head to Willow Smith's "Whip My Hair."

She goes for broke, balancing on her head while moving her feet in scissor chops. The crowd gives Dasani a standing ovation. She takes a victory lap around the room, collecting praise while catching her breath. "I did so good," she says, looking toward Justina.

Chanel walks up smiling.

"That was good," she says. "You should have had your sneakers on though—changed into your new sneakers—you wouldn't have been sliding around."

The party now revs up, with Aunt Margo doing the electric slide as dance battles brew between the young and the old. Justina's sister takes the microphone to complain that her cellphone is missing.

"No worries!" a man calls out. "It's in the family!"

The children leave that night with twenty balloons, skipping along Fulton Street toward the subway. They dip into the station, hopping on the train. Suddenly, as if by magic, a ventriloquist appears.

"Look at him!" squeals Maya. The performer and his puppet begin their act, sending the children into spasms of laughter. Chanel can't recall the last time they were so happy. She fishes through her pockets, handing the ventriloquist her last two dollars before exiting at Sherry's stop.

As the children step into the cold, Dasani grabs Nana's balloons.

"No!" Nana yells. "Give it back!"

"You supposed to make a wish and let it go up to heaven," Dasani teases.

The balloons follow the children home to Sherry's, bobbing under streetlamps. On a whim, Papa lets go of his red balloon.

The children look up.

"It went to heaven," Papa says.

They stand together, watching as the sky swallows his balloon.

A few weeks later, Miss Hester stands up in class and takes a risk.

"I was different, and I don't regret it."

She rarely talks about her childhood. She prefers to think about the future. But her students are growing up in the kind of place that she escaped, and she wants them to hear her story. "I knew I didn't want to stay there," she continues. "And I wasn't making any sacrifices to stay. I was making sacrifices to *leave*. To exit, okay?"

The classroom falls to a hush.

For Dasani, it is strange to hear a teacher talking about Bed-Stuy. "The Stuy" is where her mother came of age, where her grandmother came to rest, and where Dasani still goes to ACS appointments—in the very building where Supreme had been separated, at age nine, from his siblings.

Teachers are supposed to be from some other place. It was like hearing that the crossing guard had gone to prom with Dasani's mother. Miss Hester grew up in *the Stuy*.

The teacher's story begins with her mother, Mary, who had dropped out of grade school in North Carolina—just like Dasani's great-grandfather June—leaving the South for Bed-Stuy, Brooklyn. There Mary found work as a seamstress, falling for an unavailable man. She raised six children on her own, among them Althea Faith Hester.

Miss Hester would do better, her mother kept saying. She would graduate from high school, earning the lifestyle enjoyed by whites. *You have to be better than them*, her mother insisted. *You have to work harder than them.*

Pride ruled Mary's home, a spotless three-bedroom apartment in the Marcy projects. She made her children's clothes, from sheets at first. No one dared sit on the family's golden couch, to keep it looking new. Mary never left the apartment without fixing her hair and makeup.

"People all thought we were privileged," says Miss Hester, who had no friends. She spent most of her time indoors, away from the neighborhood's violence. On Sundays, she watched her father preach from the pulpit of a storefront church. He was so gifted that Mary referred to him as "the Big B" for bishop, holding him in high regard despite the fact that he had abandoned her. His voice boomed as he preached about morality, his charisma eclipsing his hypocrisy.

Miss Hester was eleven years old when Brooklyn's schools began to desegregate. She enrolled in one of the first school busing programs, leaving Bed-Stuy every morning for the Brooklyn neighborhood of Midwood, where white boys chased after her, spitting and yelling.

Get out of our neighborhood!

Miss Hester took refuge in her studies. Her favorite class in high school was advanced literature, taught by a school legend, Phyllis Jaffe. "I loved her vocabulary," Miss Hester said. "She was so *aggravated* about everything you wrote. Everything was imperfect. . . . I felt like I could never measure up. But it wasn't because I was Black. It was because she was a great teacher."

By the time Miss Hester was sixteen, she had performed well enough to apply to college, winning a scholarship to SUNY Cortland. If Miss Hester had been a boy, this would have landed as good news. Her brothers were the proof. One would become a lawyer and another a psychologist. But girls, according to her mother, did not leave home for college. They "married their way out" of the projects.

Stubbornly, Miss Hester packed a large orange suitcase. When her mother refused to take her to the bus station, she left alone, dragging her suitcase along Park Avenue. She would clean houses to support herself in college, where she earned a bachelor's degree in English followed by two master's degrees from Touro College in 2004.

Back in the projects, people sneered that Miss Hester was trying to "be white." None of it mattered, she says. She can hold her own anywhere she goes. Her diction has range. She switches back and forth, from "ain't" to "isn't," ignoring anyone who considers this a betrayal.

"It takes a lot of courage to be different," she now tells her students at McKinney.

Dasani is listening carefully.

"Sometimes you have to be alone," says Miss Hester, looking around the classroom.

"I don't regret it for one second," she says, slamming her hand on a desk. "That was the *path*!"

The class is motionless.

"Do you understand what I'm saying?" says Miss Hester, her voice trembling. "There are going to be some places in your life where you feel bizarre. You feel outstanding. And remain that way. Stay just as you are."

Dasani stares at her teacher.

"Never apologize for who you are," Miss Hester says. "Never!"

When Dasani looks into the future, she sees who she won't be. She won't be a dropout. She won't do drugs or smoke or drink. She won't join a gang.

A few blocks away, the same month Dasani moved to the Auburn shelter, her cousin once removed, Cakes, was shot dead. Seven years before that, Cakes's sister Shakesha was raped and smothered by her boyfriend.

Dasani won't get married unless she finds "a gentle man, not a harsh man." She won't have children unless she can support them. She won't end up on the street.

It is harder for Dasani to see the person she might become. She has been told she must reach for college if she wants a life of choices, but who will pay? "Ain't nobody gonna pay for that college," she says, mimicking her mother. Chanel is quick to say this whenever Sherry brags about Sheena, who graduated from Bates.

Dasani's schoolmates talk of becoming rap stars or athletes, escaping their world with one good break. She also subscribes to this logic. Her life is defined by extremes. In order to leave extreme poverty, it follows that she must become extremely rich or extremely something. Precisely what, she is unsure. Even to dream is an act of faith.

"I don't dream at all," Dasani says. "Even when I try."

She believes in what she can see, and Miss Hester is real. She left the projects for a place that Dasani cannot yet conjure. And she did it by working hard enough to win a scholarship to college.

But even Miss Hester knows that her example is hard to match, especially for a girl like Dasani. "She has what I didn't have—all those young siblings," the teacher says. "She has allegiance to them and that's a problem, if any of them don't see leaving as important."

Dasani is the typical "parentified child," though her penchant for self-sacrifice runs especially deep. She is the kind of girl, Miss Hester says, who "will put the mask on everyone else and the oxygen runs out."

Still only eleven, Dasani has little interest in boys. But her teacher has seen it time and again—how girls like Dasani get pregnant just to free themselves. It is easier to care for one baby than seven. "It's like an escape," Miss Hester says.

For now, the teacher keeps these thoughts to herself.

The story of Miss Hester's suitcase has lifted Dasani. That afternoon, she walks home with her classmate Dawn. They are discussing an upcoming history project on ancient Egypt. Dasani does not see Star coming.

"I'm gonna fight you!" Star calls out from the underpass, shedding her sweatshirt.

Dasani pivots, walking against the traffic along Tillary Street. This time there are no siblings to rescue her. *Get back on school property*, she tells herself. She crosses over toward McKinney.

Star charges up behind her.

"Move before I punch you!" Dasani says. "You touch me, I'm gonna punch you!"

Star grabs Dasani's shirt and Dasani takes a roundhouse swing. They fall to the ground, biting and scratching. Another girl piles on, kicking Dasani in the face and laughing while Star holds her down. Somehow Dasani manages to throw Star off balance, scrambling on top and pummeling her face before they pull apart, bleeding and crying.

"I'm saying it right in front of your face," Dasani yells, her chest heaving. "You wanna fight me some more—"

"I'm ready!" Star yells.

"I will jump you in your face!"

"I want you to! I want you to!"

Star's brother appears with their pit bull, Sugar. "Take your ass in the house!" he yells. Star turns toward the Whitman projects as Dasani races into Auburn looking for Chanel.

The fights of girls often migrate to their mothers. A few minutes later, Chanel storms out of the shelter and heads into the projects, looking for Star's mother. "I told you, when they run up on you like that, bite one of them bitches," Chanel says.

Dasani's siblings surround her, watching Chanel. She will wait all night if needed—a fact that she broadcasts to the courtyard. She paces as people come and go, eventually cooling down. "The adrenaline goes and the thinking sets in," she says.

The next morning, Chanel escorts Dasani to McKinney. There, at the office, they find Star and her mother, Bonita. The women exchange a nod as Karen Best, an assistant principal, leads the group into a conference room. Miss Best wastes no time.

"Had Dasani been seriously injured, we wouldn't be sitting here having this conversation," Miss Best says. "Children as young as you go to jail. Okay? Real simple."

Chanel eyes Bonita. It seems strange they have never met, given their daughters' endless rivalry. Forty-one-year-old Bonita is nothing like Chanel expected. She looks shrunken and tired, as if short on sleep. There is no belligerence in her eyes. Chanel cannot fathom fighting such a small woman. She might have sent Bonita to the hospital, landing another assault charge.

Dasani and Star squirm in their seats. Out on the street, Star projects privilege, parading her pit bull puppy like a trophy. No one sees her life at home, where Star's alcoholic father lies bedridden and dying.

And out on the street, Dasani exudes strength, beating the boys at pull-ups in the park. No one sees how tired she gets from waking up with Lee-Lee, or how much Dasani longs for a dog of her own. These are the things that neither girl would dare disclose. To be vulnerable is to be punk.

"She could have had a concussion," Miss Best says looking at Dasani. "You want to do something? Prove how *smart* you are."

"There you go," says Chanel, nodding in approval.

"Everyone knows the negativity," Miss Best says. "You got that down pat. Show the brains."

chapter 20

SUMMER IS FAST approaching.

There is a lakeside camp in Upstate New York where homeless children go for free, sleeping in tents and roasting marshmallows. The application deadline is about to pass.

Dasani is holding the camp's forms on May 3, 2013. All she needs is her mother's attention. They're standing at the entrance of Auburn, where Chanel smokes a cigarette as Supreme storms off, grumbling that his welfare-to-work program is "making too many demands."

Right then, Dasani looks up to see a little Pekingese strutting on a leash. The dog's owner is equally peppy—a sixty-five-year-old retired accountant who lives across the street, in the Whitman Houses. Among the ironies of gentrification, Chanel likes to point out, is that lap dogs have become fashionable in the projects, while rescued pit bulls are en vogue among whites.

This dainty dog, the owner explains, has two identities: Princess Belle (her official name) and Killa (her street name).

Dasani crouches nervously. She is afraid of being bitten. As if sensing her fear, the lady instructs Dasani to hold out her hand. A dog must sniff in order to establish trust.

Dasani offers Killa her palm. The camp enrollment forms are now on the ground.

"You live here?" asks the woman, tilting her head at Auburn.

Dasani nods.

"I'll bring her every day," says the woman, her headphones pulsing with Luther Vandross. "You want to walk her?"

Dasani's eyes widen.

"What time you get out of school?" asks the woman.

Just like that, a homeless girl can get stitched to a neighborhood. Dasani is now beaming. She does not notice that the woman's breath reeks of alcohol.

"She ain't never walked a dog in her life," says Chanel, shaking her head.

Ignoring her mother, Dasani recites her entire schedule, from Monday to Friday. The woman chuckles at Dasani's earnestness. They settle on a meeting time. Dasani bids farewell to Killa, running off to tell her siblings.

The woman puts on her headphones, teetering with the tug of her dog. A few days later, when she reappears looking sober, she will breeze past Dasani as if the conversation never happened.

By then, Dasani will have missed the deadline for camp.

Dasani is learning to hide her feelings. She shrugs them away, as if swatting flies. Her face goes blank. Her eyes drift.

Sometimes she avoids the sadness altogether, preempting it the way detectives do with crime. She knows, for example, that when the school year ends, a cascade of goodbyes will come. She must part with the most reliable adults in her life—the teachers, the security guards, the cafeteria staff, the nurses. So Dasani pulls away first, acting distant or hurried.

This year, the losses mount. Dasani's counselor, Roxanne, won't be returning to McKinney. "You the only person I can talk to," Dasani tells Roxanne.

In early May, Roxanne's supervisor invites Dasani to be a host at the school's Career Day, a formal event requiring a special outfit and timely arrival.

That morning, Dasani leaves the shelter looking like a different child. She is dressed in a pleated navy skirt, black flats, and a white cotton blouse buttoned to the top. She could not find tights, so she wears a pair of Hello Kitty leggings that leave her ankles bare. Her bangs have been straightened and glossed, secured by two aqua clips that resemble earrings. In her hand, she carries a comb.

She walks slowly into McKinney, as if balancing a plate on her head.

"Beautiful!" exclaims Miss Hester.

Roxanne beams at Dasani, whose first task is to register the guests. They are professionals from every field. Up on stage is Sahai, the school's star dancer. She won't be returning to McKinney next year: She has been accepted into LaGuardia, the famous performing arts high school.

Dasani stares at Sahai with a tired face. Roxanne leans in.

"I think *you* are very talented," she whispers.

Four days later, Roxanne is gone.

There is only $190 left on Chanel's debit card, the balance of a $2,800 tax refund that was supposed to rescue them from homelessness. At times like these, Chanel sees fit to shoplift.

"You stealin'!" five-year-old Papa squeals as Chanel makes off with two prepackaged burgers from Target. "You crazy!"

"Shut up, man!" Chanel says.

"Look," she tries more softly. "It's not right to steal. But God knows when it's for a good reason."

Every year, the children's birthdays come in a mad springtime rush: Lee-Lee's in March, Avianna's in April, and the remaining six in the span of three and a half weeks. Expectations are calibrated based on where a birthday falls in the monthly cash flow. Those at the start of the month have high hopes, while those at the end of the month are luckless. So it goes for Avianna.

Supreme hands her $11, a dollar for each year of her life. The next day, he asks for $5 back. She waits for a cake that never comes. Finally the children light two small candles. Like carolers, they hold the candles beneath Avianna's face and sing. A week later, she takes her last dollar bill and folds it delicately, like a Japanese fan. She then places it inside a homemade card that Chanel opens on Mother's Day.

This year, birthday season collides with four of the children's graduations. They need new outfits, and money for class photos. "Do you know how much time and thought goes into the hustle?" Chanel tells me. "You have to think it through."

By the time Dasani's twelfth birthday comes, she tries to ignore it. She has already asked her mother to pay for a school trip to Washington. She will hold out for that, letting the birthday pass quietly.

Over the weekend, the family retreats to Sherry's. The children skip about as Supreme stands over the stove, tending to his wings. In walks Sheena, the cousin who graduated from Bates. She hands Dasani a bag from Old Navy containing new shorts, a skirt, two tank tops, and flip-flops. This is the first, and possibly last, gift of the day. Dasani squeals with the kind of delight that suggests zero expectations. "To plan is to fail," as her mother says.

Yet today, Chanel has a plan. She gathers the children around, gently lifting a vanilla sheet cake from its plastic casing. Dasani stares in wonder. The top of the cake is blank. Chanel covers it with candles and dims the lights.

The time has come to sing.

Dasani closes her eyes.

If I could grant you three wishes, what would they be? her counselor, Roxanne, had asked.

A *house of our own, a lot of money, and three more wishes* was Dasani's answer.

She blows out the candles as the children clap. Chanel fetches a long serrated knife. "Let me show you how to cut a cake," she says, gingerly placing her hand over Dasani's. Together, they move the knife through the buttercream frosting.

"Doesn't have to be perfect," Chanel says.

Putting her siblings first, Dasani bestows a flower-edged slice on each of their plates. She takes a plain piece for herself.

They race to the basement, where their uncles are blasting the Black Eyed Peas. Screaming with joy, Dasani and her sisters leap onto a rickety wooden platform and dance beneath a disco ball to the song "I Gotta Feeling." Papa bounces around them. They barely register the hard-faced men shuffling through the basement, exchanging elaborate handshakes, their heads hung low. Some play video games. Others mill about with girls in their teens wearing too much makeup and too little clothing.

One of these girls is a baby-faced Dominican who works at the supermarket across the street. She hangs on Uncle Josh, flashing braces when she smiles. To curry his favor, she hands Dasani a $20 bill for her birthday. The gift represents a chunk of the girl's paycheck. Dasani could not have predicted such luck. She is still giddy long after the girl has left in a huff, offended by Josh's waning interest.

Josh retires to the stoop. The sun is setting. A police car turns up the block, slowing in front of Sherry's house. Two white officers stare menacingly at Josh. He stares right back, his face cold and angry.

"Hey, cops!" he calls out bitterly. "Are you proud to be an American?"

The car pulls away. It is getting late. The children have collapsed on a sagging couch, but Dasani is still dancing.

> *She's living in a world and it's on fire*
> *Filled with catastrophe*
> *But she knows she can fly away*

Dasani reaches up, her arms bathed in lights, as if saluting Alicia Keys's audience.

> *Oh, she got her head in the clouds*
> *And she's not backing down*
> *This girl is on fire*

Dasani has never had a better birthday. It feels like perfection. It hardly matters that the cake was stolen from Pathmark.

A few days later, the children spill out of Sherry's house and down the rain-slicked steps. They are hungry and short on sleep.

In theory, they are heading to the thing they most need: psycho-therapy. Chanel signed them up after learning that she can reap $10 per child in carfare through Medicaid, from a clinic in the Kensington section of Brooklyn.

Chanel needs the cash. She is still hoping to find a way to send Dasani on her school trip to Washington. The $75 deposit is due to-morrow. So despite the pelting rain, Chanel instructs the children to meet her at a subway station.

Only Hada is wearing a raincoat. Papa's hoodie slips off as he tilts back to catch raindrops on his tongue. The children cross Lincoln Avenue holding hands. Dasani is in a foul mood. There is no telling how her anger will reveal itself. Sometimes it comes quietly. She will stare at an indefinite point, her eyes blinking, her mouth set. Other times, it bursts like thunder.

"Move it!" she screams at her ten-year-old stepsister.

Nana trails behind, her glasses fogging over. She has always been the orchid in this bunch of daisies, the most delicate and sensitive child. With each passing year, Nana's blindness advances, though she can still make out vague shapes and colors. She copes by getting "lost in a wonder world," Chanel says. "She separates herself a lot."

She can play with her doll for hours. She loves fantasy books like *The Wreck of the Zephyr* by Chris Van Allsburg, whose name Nana says with precocious reverence. Among her siblings, she tries to fit in. She calls her stepmother "Mommy." She tries to mask her blindness, resting a hand on Lee-Lee's stroller so as not to stumble. But today, Lee-Lee has been left at Sherry's.

"I said move it!" Dasani yells at Nana.

She starts shoving Nana, knocking her into a metal fence. Then she punches her in the arm. "You stupid!" Dasani screams. "You think you smart, but you stupid! Now keep walking!"

Nana begins to sob as twelve-year-old Khaliq yells, "Double up!"

In pairs, they sprint across a six-lane highway and into the Grant Avenue subway station, ducking under the turnstile to meet their mother. After they board the A train, she hands them a bag of luke-warm Popeyes chicken furnished by a stranger.

By the time they get off at Jay Street, their stomachs are full and their moods lifted. Dasani spots an umbrella on the ground. It still works, opening to reveal an intricate pattern of white and black flecks. She twirls it around and, when the 103 bus pulls up, carefully closes it.

Dasani and Nana race to the back of the bus, where the motor keeps the seats warm. They sit pressed together, newly reconciled. Dasani is soon asleep. The little ones watch, thumbs in mouths, as their mother closes her eyes. Every time the bus slows, she snaps awake. On the train, she can doze off completely without missing her stop. How she does this remains a mystery. She lives entirely in the present, wearing no watch and following no calendar.

Yet the important things she remembers—the date of her next welfare appointment, the anniversary of her mother's death. An internal alarm will sound, disrupting an otherwise unplanned life. The rest of her days are lived minute to minute. Mealtime is signaled by the yank of hunger, bedtime by drooping lids. It takes an emergency to jolt this pattern. Just the other day, Supreme began coughing uncontrollably. For the first time, Chanel thought, "What would I do if he died? We have no money to cremate him."

The bus slows to a halt on Church Avenue. The children pile off as Chanel looks around, trying to get her bearings.

"We got off at the wrong stop," Dasani announces. As soon as the words leave her mouth, she regrets it. Chanel is in no mood to be challenged. She fixes her gaze on Dasani.

"Shut the fuck up," Chanel says. "You know, that's one thing I don't like about you—your negativity. You always talkin' about the problem. You got a solution?"

Dasani freezes. Once her mother gets angry, the vitriol is hard to stop. And nothing triggers Chanel like the provocations of her firstborn daughter. She has vested enormous authority in Dasani, making her the family's second-in-command. This is both a privilege and a burden. Dasani's strength, competence, and agility—the very attributes that could lift her into a better life—also make her indispensable, threatening to keep her mired in the problems Chanel cannot meet alone.

Lately, Chanel seems taunted by her dependence on Dasani. It's as if her daughter is holding up a mirror, showing Chanel her own failures.

As the children walk single file toward Coney Island Avenue, Dasani tries to recover.

"It's this way, Mommy," she says, gesturing brightly toward a flower shop. They take a few steps before Chanel turns on her heel, choosing a different route.

"If you want to go somewhere, don't listen to Dasani," she sniffs.

Dasani cowers under her new umbrella. She can feel it coming.

"I'm sick of your attitude," Chanel unloads. "There's only like fifteen kids going on this trip because people can't pay. And me, who got *nothing*, is trying to send you and you gonna give me attitude?"

Dasani keeps walking as her mother's fury mounts. Chanel reaches for the same words every time. They will echo for days.

Dasani always gotta have the answer.

Dasani think she special.

She think she some-fucking-body.

She nobody.

Dasani is frozen. The tears fall down her face, like rain on a statue.

"I don't give a shit if she's crying," Chanel says as they approach a small house with a gold-embossed sign: ADVANCED PSYCHOTHER-APY & BEHAVIORAL HEALTH SERVICES.

"It's only one goddamn chief," Chanel says. "I'm the only chief."

Inside, the children file into their fourth "group therapy" session with a woman who asks vague questions like "What are your hobbies?" She sounds more like a distant aunt than a counselor.

Khaliq knows the difference. Earlier this year, ACS had sent him to a therapist who asked questions like "Do you want to kill yourself?" Those sessions felt like they never ended; these last only twenty minutes—roughly two and a half minutes per child. At the door, Chanel collects her $80 in carfare and heads back into the rain. The cash instantly settles the family, leaving the children calm and Chanel introspective.

By the time they reach the bus stop, Chanel's gray T-shirt is soaked. She is thinking about Supreme, who could not get out of bed this morning.

"What gets me down is the responsibility," she says. "They got shoes on, but no socks. I come all this way, on the bus, in the rain, to get the money so she can go on her trip."

She is shivering now.

"Those are the things you are supposed to provide," she scolds her absent husband. "You are the man. You made this family, but you don't provide."

Papa is jumping in puddles. The smaller children squeal, ignoring their mother.

"If you all don't start listening to me I'm gonna have a nervous breakdown," Chanel says.

"I don't even know what that is," Dasani says.

"I keep thinking I'm gonna leave," Chanel says.

"No," Dasani says.

"I'm serious. I'ma check myself into a program."

"I'm serious, too," Dasani says. "No."

"I'm gonna go away for eighteen months and leave you all with Daddy. You visit me on weekends. You want that again?"

The children are silent. They shake their heads.

Dasani feels empty. The day's weight has passed from her blind sister to herself, and now to their mother, who is weeping in the rain.

chapter 21

CHANEL AND THE children slosh through the rain to get back to Auburn after therapy. They arrive too late. The 10 P.M. curfew has passed. The guard on duty, Mr. Chris, refuses to let them through. The children plead to use the bathroom, but even that is not allowed.

They are turned away in the rain.

Chanel thinks through their options. They ride the train until morning, staying warm and dry, or they could trek to the Bronx family intake center, to be assigned an overnight emergency shelter. Either way, they will have to spend tomorrow trying to get "logged back in" to Auburn.

Luckily, they have a third option: Sherry. After spending the night at her house on May 28, the children skip school (as required by homeless services) to accompany their mother to the intake office. There, a worker assigns them a case number—A05—to identify their place in line. Dasani watches as other numbers race across the screen, each one signaling an unseen world. For Dasani, A05 is her turtle, her view of the Empire State Building, her journal, stashed in the second drawer of her dresser.

All across the city, from homeless services to welfare, mothers and children can be found waiting in line. There is often the same sign, warning that to assault the workers "is a felony." Chanel has come nose to nose with them on more than one occasion. She finds them disrespectful.

To Dasani, they seem more like robots, delivering verdicts in a monotone voice—how the family's "public assistance case" has been "denied" or "turned back on," how they have "violated" their latest "independent living plan" or fallen "out of compliance" with a work requirement.

These verdicts are a part of Dasani's vocabulary. She knows what they mean in material terms, filling the fridge again or leaving it empty. Today, at homeless services, the verdict finally comes: the family's case—A05—has been "rolled over," which means they can return to Auburn.

But other days bring harsher verdicts. The family's welfare income ebbs and flows. Sometimes it expands to include carfare or shrinks with fewer food stamps. Sometimes it grinds to a halt. Whenever that happens, Chanel is back on the train to the welfare office in Queens—an ironic destination, given the trope of "welfare queen."

Whether Chanel is a "victim" or a "queen" depends on the observer. To conservatives, welfare harms the work ethic, making people dependent on the government. To progressives, welfare marginalizes the poor while failing to meet their needs.

Lost in the vernacular of "welfare" is the word itself. It was enshrined in the 1787 preamble to the Constitution, commanding "the People of the United States" to "promote the general Welfare, and secure the Blessings of Liberty to ourselves and our Posterity."

It is no accident that the Constitution connects welfare to posterity, which means all future generations. For posterity relies on the existence of children, and it was children who gave rise to America's modern welfare program.

They were not just any children. They were an early version of Dasani—homeless, in New York City more than 130 years ago, at the height of the first Gilded Age.

American welfare began, like the country itself, with a British colonial model.

Guided by the English poor laws of the 1600s, America's colonists divided the downtrodden into two classes: the "worthy" and the "unworthy." The worthy included widows, the blind, the elderly—none of whom could be blamed for their plight and thus deserved public aid. The unworthy poor, on the other hand, were seen to have chosen their condition—among them, beggars, drunks, and other undesirables who were banished to the poorhouse.

Children in America migrated between these classes. Some landed in the draconian confines of the poorhouse, trading their labor for shelter and food. Others were placed with strangers, indentured as servants or apprenticed to tradesmen. Their fates, however grim, hardly compared with the horrors inflicted upon enslaved Black children. By the nineteenth century, a new system emerged to rescue the children of whites, and eventually of Blacks, placing them in orphanages, reformatories, and other institutions.

It all originated in New York City, where a staggering 3.6 million immigrants, mostly Irish and German, had landed between 1820 and 1860. Many found themselves at the mercy of an industrial economy. With inhumane work conditions and paltry wages, they were consigned to live in the city's "tenant houses"—a term that morphed into "tenements"—dark, sooty, airless spaces crammed with hungry families.

The Dickensian conditions of Manhattan's tenements were an eerie precursor to Dasani's life at Auburn. "One young immigrant described how his family of eight managed in a one-room residence," writes the scholar Karen M. Staller. "Five children—two boys and three girls—shared a single mattress stuffed with 'chaff' by sleeping three 'at the head and two at the foot' of the bed."

Thousands of girls and boys spilled outdoors, forming a children's world of hucksters, newspaper boys, pickpockets, scavengers, shoeshiners, beggars, and child prostitutes. By 1870, as many as thirty thousand homeless children wandered the city—a wayward tribe of "street Arabs," "waifs," and "gutter snipes" who belonged to the so-called "dangerous classes."

This was the dawn of the first Gilded Age, a phrase coined by Mark Twain in a popular 1873 book, co-written with his friend Charles Dudley Warner, that satirized the greed and corruption of post–Civil War America. Industry had boomed, with half of the nation's wealth concentrated in the hands of the one percent. America's tycoons lived lavishly in the "seat of the empire," as President George Washington once described New York—making this the Empire State (for which Dasani's favorite building is named).

New York's street children had drawn the notice of Charles Loring Brace, a twenty-six-year-old Protestant minister, educated at Yale, who came to be known as the father of American foster care. Brace believed that even a temporary home, in a rural setting, was better than the street. In Manhattan, he founded the Children's Aid Society, launching a movement to "place out" New York's street children by sending them on "orphan trains" to live with families in the Midwest. As many as two hundred thousand children boarded these trains for a new life.

America's first foster children were leaving white "ignorant Roman-Catholic" families, in Brace's words, to live with Protestant farmers who could offer "a good home in the West." Yet many of these children worked in arrangements reeking of indentured servitude. By Brace's lights, the orphan train movement was "emigration as a cure for pauperism." Most of these children were not even orphans. They had been taken from, or handed over by, parents too poor to feed them.

Society's answer to poverty, time and again, was to separate children from their families. By the early twentieth century, about 93,000 children were living in orphanages and as many as 75,000 more in foster homes or facilities for juvenile delinquents. Considering this a crisis, President Theodore Roosevelt called a meeting that would lay the foundations of America's modern welfare system. On January 25, 1909, some two hundred charity workers, academics, juvenile court judges, and other child welfare experts gathered for the first White House Conference on the Care of Dependent Children.

"There can be no more important subject from the standpoint of the nation," President Roosevelt told his guests. "Because when you take care of the children, you are taking care of the nation of tomorrow."

Most of the nation's Black children still lived in the South—a fact cited by Booker T. Washington, one of only two African Americans included at the conference. Black families, he told the white audience, had long practiced the ideals being touted at Roosevelt's meeting.

"The negro, in some way, has inherited and has had trained into him the idea that he must take care of his own dependents, and he does it to a greater degree than is true perhaps of any other race," said Washington, who hoped that Black Americans would stay in the rural South, where strong family ties kept children safe and where placing a child in an institution was seen as "a disgrace."

The audience burst into applause.

Across the lines of race, Americans shared the problem of child labor. For centuries, children had been treated like miniature adults, expected to earn their keep. But a new idea was making the rounds, advanced by G. Stanley Hall, a pioneer in the budding field of child psychology. Hall argued that childhood was a distinct phase of human development, which meant that children needed to act like children in order to become healthy adults. Rather than being forced to work, a child required nourishment and education. The "work" of young children was to play.

Children became the driver of America's future, making the 1900s the "Century of the Child"—the calling of the Progressive Era, whose reformers pushed to end child labor and tackle child poverty. The poorest families were headed by single mothers who had been widowed or "deserted," forcing them to work while their children were left stranded.

The homes of these children, President Roosevelt's conferees concluded, "should not be broken up for reasons of poverty." Roosevelt's meeting spurred a national movement to create "mother's pensions," distributed state by state to women deemed "worthy" or "deserving." America's first welfare mothers were overwhelmingly white. In 1931, of the 93,000 families who received these cash stipends, only 3 percent were Black.

All of that had changed by 1971, when Dasani's grandmother Joanie walked into a welfare office in Brooklyn. In the intervening decades, the mother's pension movement had launched the first federal welfare program, Aid to Dependent Children—created by President Franklin D. Roosevelt in 1935 as part of the New Deal, and greatly expanded three decades later by the Great Society legislation of President Lyndon B. Johnson. America's public safety net came to include Medicaid, food stamps, disability assistance, and new housing supports.

Black women had to fight to join welfare's rolls. Drawn north by the Great Migration, millions of African Americans had resettled in New York City, which became the base for a national welfare rights movement. By 1975, 11 million Americans were receiving welfare cash, most of them children and single mothers. Black families made up 44 percent of this group while representing less than 10 percent of the nation's population.

The words "welfare queen" caught fire the following year, in 1976, when presidential hopeful Ronald Reagan took the stage at a campaign rally. "In Chicago, they found a woman who holds the record," Reagan declared. "She used eighty names, thirty addresses, fifteen telephone numbers to collect food stamps, Social Security, veterans' benefits for four nonexistent deceased veterans husbands, as well as welfare. Her tax-free cash income alone has been running a hundred fifty thousand dollars a year."

It did not matter that Reagan had chosen an extreme outlier to represent the masses (she was identified as Linda Taylor, a con artist in Chicago, investigated for homicides, baby trafficking, and kidnapping). She bore no resemblance to women like Grandma Joanie, whose own welfare assistance would peak at $650 monthly—scarcely enough to cover clothing, meals, school supplies, and the other needs of her two dependent children.

Children were no longer at the center of the national discourse. Instead, the public's gaze was fixed on their mothers, whose poverty had deepened with the epidemics of crack and AIDS. By 1991, New York's welfare rolls were approaching one million, a number that now included Dasani's mother, Chanel.

That same year, a little-known Arkansas governor announced he was running for president. When Bill Clinton hit the campaign trail, welfare was costing taxpayers an estimated $13 billion a year in federal dollars alone.

Clinton would make good on his vow to "end welfare as we know it."

Welfare—as Dasani knows it—is less a program than an experience.

First there is the line. Then there is the wait. In Dasani's dictionary, welfare means "waiting a long time, impatiently, to be seen."

Some Americans can afford to skip the lines of bureaucracy. They
hire private agents to secure a new passport or a marriage certificate.
The poor pay with their time.

As Dasani's mother inches forward, her children fight boredom
with the card games "I Declare War" and "Go Fish!" When they
forget to bring cards, they play with their hands—Pat-a-Cake, Miss
Mary Mack—or with their feet—Red Light, Green Light, 1-2-3. Anything to pass the time.

Dasani has heard that things used to be different. Fewer women
worked, including her grandmother Joanie, who was still on welfare in
1996 when President Clinton signed the Personal Responsibility and
Work Opportunity Reconciliation Act. Out went the old system—the
one originating with the child advocates of the early twentieth century. In came a new program centered on the adults. The goal was to
move them off welfare and into the workforce. If you needed money,
you now applied for Temporary Assistance for Needy Families, facing
time limits on cash and a mandate to look for work.

The word "jobs" filled this new landscape, with Mayor Giuliani
renaming the city's welfare offices from "Income Support Centers" to
"Job Centers." He was eager to trim the caseloads, declaring the welfare system too "user friendly." Here, and across the country, new
sanctions created a culture of deterrence, with some welfare workers
cutting off aid for one or two missed appointments.

By the time Dasani was born in 2001, more than 6 million
Americans—mostly women and children—had left welfare's rolls.
Many of these single mothers found work, while others stayed unemployed. In New York City, the rolls had dropped by more than half
(from 1.1 million recipients in 1995 to under half a million in
2001)—a group that included Dasani and her twenty-three-year-old
mother, Chanel.

When it comes to being poor, there are less generous places than

New York, one of the nation's archetypal "safety net" states. New Yorkers have greater access to public healthcare, food stamps, and state-administered welfare cash, which comes with fewer restrictions than federal welfare and no time limits. New York City is the only American metropolis that guarantees the legal right to shelter, year-round, for both families and single adults, including non-pregnant women. But in practice, shelter gets denied and food stamps cut off with the vagaries of each city administration.

By late May 2013, Chanel has once again run out of cash. This might explain why, in Dasani's words, Mommy goes "loco."

There is a knock at the door. Chanel lets in the inspector, who promptly demands that she surrender the family's forbidden microwave. Chanel refuses. She cannot afford to buy a new one, nor can she fathom having to wait in line every night to reheat ten dinner trays in one of the shelter's two microwaves. The inspector leaves, and by the time two security officers arrive to confiscate the microwave, Chanel has hidden it in a friend's room.

As for the inspector, Chanel offers to "punch that bitch in the face."

Dasani thinks that her mother's biggest problem is her mouth. She reflects on this as Miss Hester begins a lesson on personal responsibility.

"I don't ever wanna hear, 'Well, my mother told me to do this,' unless you know that that's the right thing," Miss Hester tells the class.

The teacher has shimmied into an empty desk next to Dasani.

"I am telling you, as sure as I'm sitting here," Miss Hester says, her arm resting across Dasani's desk, "you're gonna be held responsible for the choices you make."

Miss Hester invites questions. Hands shoot up in the air.

"Yes, Miss Dasani?"

Dasani decides to talk about her longtime rival, recounting the day when Star slapped her as a taunt. Dasani's mother, she tells the class, "is a violent parent, so you can't tell her anything about fights because then she gonna want to get a stick and tell you to knock the chick out."

Miss Hester arches both brows.

"Okay," she says. "Now, let me ask you: Do you think that was the right thing to do?"

The room fills with chatter.

"Okay, okay!" Miss Hester yells. "I'ma tell you what I would have told my kid."

The children fall silent.

"Not everybody has something to lose," Miss Hester says.

"You care about your life," she continues. "There are people out there who are so hurt they don't care about leaving here. . . . They are looking for an opportunity to do something crazy and ridiculous. They have nothing to live for."

Dasani ponders this.

"I am telling you to listen to your internal barometer," Miss Hester says. "*Think* about your next move before you *make* your next move."

Dasani is still in bed the next morning when her mother rises from a fitful sleep. She heads to the corner store with Avianna. All around, men are leaving the projects to report to work. Chanel stands in the cold, watching them.

"Your father should be doing that," she says.

Just this week she had stopped a flag waver at a construction site. It seemed like a job that Chanel could perform perfectly. The woman told her about an organization that helps people with a GED find work.

For Chanel, words like "GED" can end a conversation. It has been twenty years since she sat in a high school classroom. She feels like a foreigner in her own country, unable to speak the language of bank accounts and loan applications. When filling out medical forms, she stops at the box requiring a work number, staring at its blankness.

"I want my kids to be able to come see me at my job, pick up my paycheck," she tells me that afternoon. She is standing with Dasani outside Au Bon Pain, where the day's pastries will soon sell at a discount. "Just be reliant on my money, you know what I'm sayin'?"

Dasani stares at her mother anxiously.

"I'm tired of my kids seeing me dull," Chanel says. "It's my time to shine."

"I don't see you dull," Dasani says. "I see you shine."

part 4

"THAT FIRE
GONNA BURN!"

2013–2015

chapter 22

DASANI CANNOT SLEEP.

It is June 9, 2013. For the first time in her life, she can see a path to something else. People say that spring and fall are the seasons of change. But for Dasani, it has always been summer. Every marker of her life—her first months in the care of Grandma Joanie, the day her family moved into their first real home, the loss of that home two years later, when they landed at the Auburn shelter—these all came in summertime.

Until earlier today, there was no telling what Dasani's twelfth summer would bring, aside from the usual heat. The sixth grade was still winding down when Dasani and her family headed to Harlem to attend the Five Percent's annual gathering.

People swarmed the entrance of the Harriet Tubman Learning Center, pushing past security guards and a vendor selling I ❤ BEING GOD pins. Supreme milled about, greeting friends with tight hugs. Chanel followed him, her chin held high, her daughters' hair freshly braided.

It was a rare moment of belonging in a year of rootlessness. Harlem is where Chanel and Supreme found each other. And to Harlem they have returned, time and again, to be reminded of their promise.

After the sun set, Dasani and her family stepped outside for some fresh air. A man walked by, his hoodie pulled low over his face.

"I seen your videos," Chanel said, stopping him in his tracks.

For years, Dasani's family had watched the DVDs of this former convict turned fitness guru who calls himself Giant.

Giant's team, Bartendaz, does acrobatic pull-ups and other "calisthenics," a form of exercise relying on the weight of a person's body. All you need is a prison courtyard, or a playground with some metal bars, and you can be as ripped as Giant—who is famously intolerant of drugs and alcohol, steering his followers to "the bars of health."

Giant looked Chanel up and down, noting the open can of beer she held in a paper bag.

"Bud don't make you wiser," he said, flashing a row of perfect teeth.

Chanel ignored the comment. She was already imagining, she would later tell me, the possibilities presented by this chance encounter. She quickly steered Dasani to the pull-up bars at a playground across the street.

"Show him what ya got!" she called out.

Giant accepted this impromptu audition the way Martin Scorsese might take a waiter's latest screenplay. People were always asking Giant to look at their children's moves.

Dasani sprang to the bars and began an impressive set of pull-ups, her shoulders popping with the muscles of an action figure. Giant was still chatting with Chanel when he looked over and paused.

"Whoa," he said.

Chanel was on to something. She continued her pitch, saying that Dasani had been doing pull-ups in Fort Greene Park for years. She could also dance, do gymnastics, run track. All she lacked was training.

Now it was Giant who raced through the possibilities. He could see that this twelve-year-old girl was uncommonly strong. She had a telegenic smile. She was spunky. "She seems like just the kind of girl we could use on our team," he said, grinning at Dasani, who grinned back.

Giant explained how his team works: It has a limited partnership with Nike that will hopefully lead to bigger things. In the meantime, the team earns modest pay by holding training clinics and performing at events. At the very least, he concluded, Dasani merited a proper tryout.

"Meet me at the park next Saturday," he said, leaving his number before disappearing.

Dasani has no idea if she will make Giant's team. But she cannot stop herself from dreaming a little.

"I'ma save all my money so we can get a house," she tells her mother.

"Use your money for you," Chanel says. "We'll be okay."

"No," Dasani insists. "I'ma save all my money."

She spends the next week in focused preparation, training on the fitness bars next to the basketball court in Fort Greene Park. At night, she plays the team's DVDs over and over, studying each member closely. Her greatest challenge will be getting to Harlem on time.

Punctuality is a miracle in her family.

On Saturday morning, there is no sign of Dasani as Giant's team starts to warm up. Their base—at Malcolm X Boulevard and 144th Street—is a playground named for Colonel Charles Young, a legendary Buffalo Soldier who was the first African American to hold the rank of colonel.

Just the sight of the Bartendaz team can slow traffic. One by one, they fly onto the bars, whipping through moves that seem to defy gravity. Their logo shows a man bending a metal bar, his brain lit by a bulb. "Salute that mind!" Giant calls out to his followers: Cinderblock, Honey Bee, Sky, Earth, Blaq Ninja, Water, Salubrious, and Mel Matrix. Giant's deputy is Dr. Good Body, a self-described athletic alchemist ("The library is my alma mater") who transforms the "base metal" of a person's character into "gold."

Giant orbits around his team, issuing commands in a lyrical code that is impenetrable to outsiders. He is especially fond of abbreviations. His favorite is CAP, which stands for "character, attitude, and personality." His chosen name, Giant, stands for "Growing Is a Noble Thing."

This is a bold name for a man who stands only five foot seven.

Born Warren Hassan Bradley, he grew up in the Baruch projects on the Lower East Side. In his teens, he gained a following as a deejay and street fighter, skilled at hiding razors in his mouth and spitting them out in combat. As the crack trade boomed, Giant went to prison in 1989 on two felony convictions, for selling drugs and for possession of stolen property. By the time he was released four years later, he had a high school equivalency diploma and a plan: He would capitalize on the pull-up routines that he had taught himself in prison yards.

Practice is winding down when Dasani finally shows up, accompanied by her mother, Nana, and Lee-Lee.

"What's your name again?" Giant says.

"Dasani."

"Dasani with a D?"

"Like the water," Chanel says.

Giant turns to the group.

"Everyone say, 'Peace, Queen.'"

"Peace, Queen!" they shout, using the Five Percent greeting that is now commonplace even among nonbelievers (Giant abhors the teachings of the Five Percent).

Dressed in bright pink shorts and flip-flops, Dasani is a dwarf among titans. The tryout begins with a set of pull-ups, demonstrated by Blaq Ninja and Sky. Dasani coasts through the exercise. "Damn!" says a team member as the others whistle.

"Stay there, breathe," instructs Giant as Dasani pedals her feet in the air while holding her head level with the bar.

Her next test comes on the parallel bars, where she knocks out a set of dips in good form, pedaling again as Giant counts aloud. He shakes his head incredulously.

"Do some diamonds!" Chanel calls out as Dasani dives into a set of push-ups. Then she goes for broke, clapping her hands behind her back mid-push-up. Honey Bee captures the image on the team's iPad before Dasani comes crashing to the ground, promptly dusting herself off. By now, her entire family has arrived, including Supreme.

"Look at this! Look at this!" Giant says, running over to show Dasani the photo. "You tellin' me I can't sell this poster for a hundred dollars?"

He turns to Chanel: "She's in."

The family is ecstatic. Giant treats them to lunch at a local bodega, where they are joined by Malcolm X's grandson, Malik, who congratulates Dasani, handing her a bottle of mango-flavored Snapple. She is so afraid to drop it, she carries the bottle home with both hands.

Back at Auburn, Dasani writes "Malcolm X grandson" on the label before stashing it in her dresser.

Chanel is unsure about Giant. She finds him charming, but vague when it comes to details like payment. Giant, too, can spot a hustler, and he is wary of Chanel.

When Dasani returns with her siblings to practice, Giant feels pressured by Chanel to feed them all. This time, he offers no meal, but tells Chanel that her daughter, like his other team members, will be compensated for events. The first one is a training clinic. All Chanel needs to do is bring Dasani. The rest is Dasani's job.

"That's why we got the word 'responsibility,'" Giant tells Dasani in front of Chanel. He holds up his right hand—"Response"—then his left hand—"Ability." "So respond to what? *Your* ability. Not your mom's ability."

On the day of the clinic, Dasani asks if her mother has heard from Giant, who has been calling Chanel repeatedly.

Perhaps Chanel is feeling jealous of her daughter. Sometimes Dasani suspects this, though her mother would never admit it.

"He never called," Chanel lies. (She later tells me she had felt humiliated when Giant refused to feed her children.)

Dasani goes to bed crushed.

She wakes at 5 A.M. for the long-awaited school trip to Washington. Still glum, she boards the bus on an empty stomach, sitting alone with a thin blanket. Five hours later, as they approach the Capitol, Dasani presses her face to the window.

It looks different here. There is space all around—trees, monuments, water. She can see well into the distance, her view unobstructed by skyscrapers. She is paying close attention, at the request of eleven-year-old Nana.

"Remember every single detail," Nana had asked, as if her life depended on it. Not only was she going blind, which meant that her siblings were becoming her eyes. But she longed to see Washington, D.C.—the city where she was born in 2002, back when Supreme was still married to her mother, Kylia, who died there.

Dasani's eyes are Nana's only link.

Every single detail.

Near the White House, Dasani gets off the bus and runs to the tall wrought iron gate. She has always wanted to touch President Obama's hair. She presses her face between two bars. A few minutes pass. She looks over at a group of protesters wearing orange suits and black hoods.

"Obama, close Guantánamo!"

Dasani has never heard of Guantánamo, but she knows what a prison uniform looks like. The protesters, she concludes, are pretending to be detained, and they want President Obama to close their jail. I DIE WAITING FOR JUSTICE, reads one of the signs.

Dasani shakes her head.

"I don't know why they protesting in front of Obama's house like he gonna be in here," she says, still disappointed by her trip to Gracie Mansion.

She walks over to her friend Dawn, who is staring at the protesters, her face ashen.

"It's *pretend*," Dasani says as she reaches for Dawn's earphones. "They're pretending."

Dasani waits to hear from Giant.

"It's all right," she finally tells her mother. "I didn't get attached."

Detachment is as much a rite of summer as sunbaked afternoons in the park. She will soon bid farewell to Miss Hester and Miss Holmes. But at least she gets to see Sherry more often. Once school lets out, the children can visit Chanel's godmother daily, riding their bikes up and down Sherry's block of Lincoln Avenue.

They have yet to hear the news: Sherry's house is in foreclosure. If she is not gone by the end of July, a city marshal will see her out. She can enter the city's shelter system, joining Dasani's family and well over fifty thousand other people—the highest number yet. Or she can return to Pittsburgh, living with the same sister who once took in Chanel. She opts for the latter, telling Chanel by phone.

"The Lord will take care of you," Sherry says.

Chanel stops taking Sherry's calls. This is Chanel's way of leaving before she is left. She does not want to say goodbye, much less tell the children they are losing their only true home.

In the meantime, Dasani keeps hoping that Giant will return. After a month passes, she decides to report to practice, acting as though nothing has changed. But Supreme stops Dasani when she tries to leave. "Not before this place is straightened up," he says.

By the time Dasani finishes cleaning, practice is over.

The next morning, she wakes up feeling defiant. She looks at Supreme, who is still asleep. *How you gonna take my destiny away from me?* she thinks. Dasani turns to Chanel, who waves at her to leave.

Dasani jumps the stile of the subway and hops the train to Harlem.

"Long time no see!" says Giant, who smiles, then gets serious. "If you know you're not gonna be consistent, then I need to know so I can invest in someone else."

Dasani is confused. Her mother said he never called, while Giant's version of events is the opposite. Dasani does not know whom to believe, so Giant decides to keep things simple. "There must have been a miscommunication," he says. With that, Dasani rejoins the team. She starts training every weekend, accompanied by her twin in all things, Avianna.

They are in Harlem on July 21 when a moving truck pulls up to Sherry's house on Lincoln Avenue. Chanel arrives with her youngest daughters just in time. The children cling to Sherry. "I'ma hide in the truck," says eight-year-old Maya.

Chanel walks through the house she has known since she was a baby. The electricity has been cut, and the windows will soon be boarded.

She pauses at the wooden door of the bathroom, which reminds Chanel of her father, Sonny Boy. He is there at that door, some flicker of a memory. These are the things one loses with a home.

Out on the stoop, Sherry and Chanel hold each other, shaking.

Dasani never gets to say goodbye.

Rap stars circle. The cameras roll. The crowd chants her name.

Da-Sa-Neee!

Her heart is racing. She looks up at the sky, extending her fingers. She is too small to reach the metal bar, so Giant lifts her by the waist. She is now in midair, twisting acrobatically as the audience gasps.

Dasani blinks.

"I thought it was a dream—make-believe—like this wasn't happening," she later says. "You know, like in movies, people pinch themselves like, 'This ain't real.'"

Today's performance marks Dasani's public debut with Bartendaz, filmed to appear in the opening sequence of Giant's forthcoming DVD.

"This is Dasani!" Giant yells into his bullhorn. "She is a *star.*"

Dasani skips about, mugging for photographs with the rappers Jadakiss and Styles P. At day's end, Giant hands Dasani $70—her first real earnings. She is too excited to think twice when Supreme asks to borrow the money. He spends $8 on pizza for the children, and disappears with the rest. (Supreme will later deny that this happened.)

Giant knows nothing about the loan when, a few days later, he calls Supreme with a proposal: Would he like to train with Dasani? After all, "movement is medicine."

On the phone, Giant tells Supreme to stop acting like "the all-knowing God" and humbly become a "student" like Dasani. Chanel is napping during the conversation. She wakes to hear Supreme saying "Peace" and hanging up.

At home, Supreme has been irritable, even cruel. Much of his wrath is reserved for six-year-old Papa, the most rebellious of the children. Supreme's latest tactic is to make Papa stand for hours in the corner of their room, holding a book. This is better than beating him, by Supreme's logic. But Dasani thinks it's wrong.

"If Daddy's so righteous and notices so many mistakes, how come he doesn't notice his?" Dasani tells me. "He said he was gonna stop smoking. He promised. But what he do? He still smoking. He told us to change our habits, cuz he said now we're responsible, so he said,

'Y'all gotta change your habits.' So everybody changed they habits, but he didn't change his."

Habits are the lifeblood of Giant's team. The next day, he summons Dasani to a basketball clinic for boys. He wants her to "mentor" them—despite the fact that she was suspended from school earlier this year. Dasani needs to act like a mentor before she can feel like one.

She takes to the task, guiding boys several inches taller as they struggle into pull-ups. When she orders them to line up, one of the boys smirks, saying, "You not staff."

"Oh *yes I am*," Dasani shoots back.

She is bonding with her teammate Sky, a nursing student, and Earth, who just got a bachelor's degree in psychology at Queens College. "I'ma take all of Sky's moves," Dasani says as she hits the low bars. They laugh and laugh, never ceasing to delight in their newest member. But when Chanel strides up, offering unsolicited tips, the team goes quiet.

After the clinic ends, Giant pulls Dasani aside for a quiet word. Then she tells him about the money she loaned Supreme.

Giant is livid. He storms up to Chanel and says that from now on, he will find other ways to pay Dasani. Perhaps he can give her sneakers and clothes, but the cash "is over."

Long after they leave, Giant is still fuming. Can this even work?

"You're fixing a child to send back to broken parents," he tells me.

chapter 23

SUPREME'S FIRST MEMORIES are of dark spaces, like the alcove where he hid when his parents fought. He recalls needles and crack vials scattered on the floor, and countertops crowded with liquor bottles.

If his childhood could be reenacted, the stage would be monochromatic—a setting of gray shaded rooms with clothing piled in corners. The protagonists would all be children, with the occasional adult dipping into view, like the time Supreme's father fell to the bathroom floor, his mouth foaming from an overdose.

"All I remember is violence," Supreme says. "Violence and being hungry and having to steal food to eat."

Supreme's mother and father were still teenagers when he was born in August 1977. They lived in an apartment in Crown Heights. His father was schizophrenic, and neither parent worked. They became what Supreme describes as "champion welfare recipients," paying for heroin by converting food stamps to cash.

As a small boy, Supreme would visit his grandmother in the nearby projects of East New York. He was five years old when an assailant burst into her home and shot her seven times. She died sitting in a rocking chair. News of the death in February 1983 sparked rumors that she was a loan shark and that the murder was a hit job. Others claimed that her son, Supreme's father, had stolen from a dealer and that this was payback. The police never found the killer. That year alone, 514 people were murdered in Brooklyn.

The grandmother's death left a vacancy in the Cypress Hills projects, where apartments were in high demand. The Housing Authority gave preference to next of kin, so Supreme's parents claimed the apartment and kept all the furniture—even the rocking chair. By then, Supreme had one younger brother and a second on the way. He began kindergarten at P.S. 202, in East New York, where a guidance counselor summarized the boy in three words: "Can be temperamental."

At home, there was no radio or television. Supreme fought his boredom by roaming the projects. "I always been a loner," he later said. "I can be by myself for days and I can entertain myself. I have an imaginative mind."

Solitude was better than being with adults. At home, Supreme learned to retrieve used needles off the floor, tossing them into the garbage. He watched as partygoers took swigs from shiny bottles. This made them dance and laugh, piquing the boy's curiosity.

Sometimes he wandered into the bathroom to find people shooting up. "Go to your room!" the adults barked. It was best to disappear, so Supreme and his oldest brother stayed outside, sleeping on benches. They could be found there at any hour, dozing off in the middle of the night, napping under the noon sun.

"Time didn't matter," he says.

If Supreme returned to an empty apartment, this meant that his parents were out of drugs and "running the streets." They could be gone for days, leaving the fridge empty. By age seven, Supreme learned to cook with stolen groceries, and to cut his siblings' hair. That year, he missed fifty-six days of school—nearly a third of the second grade.

He knew to collect his mother's food stamps at the start of every month; otherwise she would cash them in and squander the money on drugs. Supreme also did the shopping, which included waiting in the "free food line" outside the projects' community center. Every family received the same staples, which Supreme can still list without pause: a block of butter, a block of cheese, rice, grits, oatmeal, and a can of peanut butter (but no jelly).

Other groceries were so rare that no one threw them out, even when they spoiled. Supreme got so sick from bad mayonnaise that he never ate anything soft and white again, not even pizza. The phobia migrated, many years later, from Supreme to his daughter Nana, who would swear off all "white food."

Supreme does not recall seeing a dentist as a child, and he rarely went to the doctor, despite having asthma. At the time, this seemed like an ordinary life.

"For a child, you take it with a grain of salt. You just move with it. You go with it."

Supreme's father routinely beat the children and was ferocious with his wife. He once hoisted her from their sixth-story window, holding her by the legs as she dangled and screamed. Only when Supreme charged at his father with a broom did he pull his wife back inside.

The family first came to the attention of child protection workers when Supreme was nine years old. By then he had four siblings, including a baby sister. She was named for the month of her birth, April, but everyone called her Precious. On March 1, 1987, the city's Office of Special Services for Children—a precursor to ACS—opened an investigation into suspected neglect by Supreme's parents, based on a report made to the agency by an undisclosed person.

"Children constantly left alone for about four hours during the day," read the report. "Child appear very filthy. Parent may be on drugs."

More than three weeks passed. A caseworker made several failed attempts to see the family. "Investigation still in progress," the worker wrote. The following month, on May 9—just a few weeks after Precious's first birthday—Supreme went out walking. He did this often, to clear his head. At around 5:30 P.M., he returned to his building.

There, by the entrance, lay a baby girl. Her eyes were closed and she was wrapped in a blanket, as if sleeping.

Supreme drew closer. It was his sister, Precious. She was still warm to the touch, but the color had left her face. He gently picked her up, holding his sister for what felt like twenty seconds. He kissed her head and said her name.

"There was no life in her."

Suddenly, Supreme's mother burst out of the building.

"Take your ass upstairs!" she screamed, grabbing Precious as fire trucks and an ambulance arrived.

Supreme raced up six flights and ran to the window, forgetting that it faced the wrong side of the building. He wanted one more glimpse of his sister. By now, the ambulance was gone.

Precious was pronounced dead on arrival at the hospital. Her mother told investigators that she had left the baby with her husband that afternoon. When she returned fifteen minutes later, he was gone and Precious was "on the floor blue and unconscious, lying next to an open" vial "of medication," according to the case notes, which identified the medication as sleeping pills. Panicking, the mother took Precious downstairs and left her there for help.

Police officers removed nine-year-old Supreme and his surviving siblings—ages two, three, and six—from the home. All four were taken to the child protection office in Bed-Stuy. It was now evening.

They tried to stay together.

Supreme has no memory of what happened next. He does not recall being pulled apart from his brothers, who were assigned to different foster homes. The staff had to restrain him. At 2:08 A.M., a caseworker updated the file.

"All children have been placed," read the report. "Father has been arrested and is in custody of the police."

An autopsy revealed that Precious had not swallowed medication. She had died of sudden infant death syndrome. Nonetheless, both parents lost custody of the children.

For a year, Supreme stopped speaking at all.

He drifted from one group home to another, first in the tiny village of Nanuet, New York, thirty miles north of Manhattan, then in Staten Island. "All I remember is going from place to place to place to place." He rarely saw his mother. In her absence, he got violent. On one occasion, he tried to slit his wrists.

Supreme's teachers saw a troubled but intelligent boy—one who, at age eleven, "is very motivated to learn and do well but his lack of self control often hampers this," wrote a guidance counselor. Supreme was living with an aunt in Brooklyn when his mother regained custody of the children. They would all be reunited under one roof, this time in the Marcy Houses—the same projects in Bed-Stuy that Dasani's teacher, Miss Hester, had escaped.

Supreme landed at Marcy in 1990, when shootings were routine, and drugs ubiquitous. The first time Supreme tried marijuana, at age thirteen, he got so high that he couldn't move, right as gunshots sounded. "A lot of people ran right past me and nope, wasn't thinking nothing but why the hell I can't get up."

Supreme's brothers felt like strangers, their faces no longer matching his memory. Four years of separation had left a permanent wedge. Supreme began to pull away, sleeping on trains. In the ninth grade, he joined a gang called Face Heads. By age seventeen he had fallen into the crack trade, hopping into the red BMW of a dealer he'd met at Marcy. They drove to Charlotte, North Carolina, where Supreme sold crack from a motel room opposite a McDonald's.

Six months later, in December 1994, Supreme was arrested for trafficking cocaine, landing a prison sentence of up to four years.

"I didn't have, you know, a proper role model," Supreme says. "You know, you always tell your child, 'Don't put your hand in that fire. That fire'll burn you.' I didn't have nobody tell me, 'That fire gonna burn!'"

Supreme stands with the crowd on July 27, 2013, watching Dasani's new mentor, Giant.

"I am Trayvon!" Giant shouts into his bullhorn.

"I am Trayvon!" the crowd chants back.

Two weeks earlier, a jury had acquitted the Florida man who fatally shot Trayvon Martin, an unarmed African American teenager whose hoodie had become an emblem of national protest and whose death would spark the Black Lives Matter movement.

Supreme moves his lips to the words *I am Trayvon*.

Over the years, Supreme has had plenty of racially charged encounters with New York City police, whose practice of targeting Black and Latino people would become a signature legacy of Mayor Bloomberg. In the previous twelve years, officers had stopped and frisked more than 5 million New Yorkers—most of them people of color from the city's poorest neighborhoods. The majority of these stops yielded no weapons or arrests.

A few weeks from now, on August 12, a federal court will rule that the city's stop-and-frisk practice is racially targeted and unconstitutional. As Bloomberg vows to appeal the ruling, Bill de Blasio ratchets up his own mayoral candidacy with a video starring his biracial son, Dante. sporting his now famous giant Afro. In the video, which goes viral, the fifteen-year-old Dante echoes his father's promise to "end a stop-and-frisk era that unfairly targets people of color."

Back at the shelter, Supreme announces to Chanel that he will be leaving for a while. He is entering rehab once again. This coincides with the third anniversary of the family's arrival at 39 Auburn Place.

Three years—a quarter of Dasani's life—most of it spent in one room. She is relieved that Supreme will be gone. She suspects that he is back on drugs.

"If you look, his eyes be red," Dasani says.

Her hunch is confirmed at the detox center in Queens: Supreme tests positive for cocaine, opioids, and marijuana and admits to using heroin and drinking too much. A nurse notes that he is "neatly groomed," with a thought process that is "linear, logical, and coherent." He also seems agitated, like "people are out to get him."

Twelve days later, a van takes Supreme through the rolling hills of Putnam County, sixty miles north of Brooklyn. He is going to Arms Acres, a residential treatment facility paid for by Medicaid. This is the first time that Supreme is leaving his family to go to rehab.

Does he have any allergies? asks the nurse.

Supreme is system-savvy. He knows that if he says mayonnaise is his lifelong phobia, or that pork is "religiously prohibited," he could still get stuck with a mayo-slathered ham sandwich for lunch. His food preferences matter little to bureaucrats. But no one wants a lawsuit.

Next to allergies, the nurse writes mayonnaise and pork. From here, Supreme goes to the intake counselor.

"What would it be like for you to not use alcohol or drugs?" she asks.

"Boring," he says.

Supreme knows that it irks people to hear a homeless, unemployed, drug-addicted father complaining of boredom. Nor do they expect Supreme to be inspired, buried in a book, or feverishly writing. "The worst death is not a physical death," Supreme says, "but a mental death." He succumbs to the drudgery of welfare appointments and job-training programs until he snaps, his boredom giving way to the pursuit of revelation. He reads, he writes, he gets high. When he has a kitchen, he cooks. He can expound for hours on the teachings of the Five Percent.

This rarely works in his favor, especially when the person tasked with helping Supreme has never heard of the Five Percent.

Today, the counselor observes that the "patient" is making "grandiose" statements "such as 'I am God' and refers to himself as 'God Supreme' which he reports is part of his cultural beliefs as is his belief that 'Black men are God.'"

The staff concludes that Supreme needs a psychiatric assessment.

"Please evaluate," counselor writes.

chapter 24

A HIGH-PITCHED SCREAM RATTLES the Auburn shelter, yanking Dasani from her sleep.

"My baby's not breathing!" yells a mother down the hall. It is the early morning of August 27, 2013. The woman's infant had, months earlier, been diagnosed with respiratory distress syndrome. The baby was so sick that a social worker had asked homeless services to transfer the family to a shelter specializing in medical needs.

No transfer came. Instead, Auburn's staff gave the baby a damaged crib with a loose-fitting sheet, while assigning the family to a room that reached 102 degrees.

Dasani listens as the mother howls. A few hours later, her baby is pronounced dead. Soon, state investigators are combing the building. They find that Auburn's fire safety system is virtually inoperable. There is also no childcare, as legally mandated, nor does Auburn have the certificate of occupancy required to operate as a shelter. Black mold is spreading in the shelter's bathrooms.

The investigators release a devastating internal report: No young child with chronic breathing problems or serious medical conditions should be placed at the shelter, and no one under age two should live there at all. In other words, Dasani's family—with a one-year-old (Lee-Lee), two asthmatic children (Papa and Avianna), and another child (Nana) who is legally blind—should never have been at Auburn in the first place.

The exodus of Auburn's families begins in October 2013.

Chanel is summoned to Auburn's office and told the news: A space has opened up at another shelter—an apartment with a kitchen. The staff will not give her the address, or even the borough. Dozens of families are departing Auburn in vans arranged by homeless services. They have a few hours to pack.

Chanel has longed for this moment, but now that it's here, she feels wholly unprepared. Supreme is still in rehab. Her food stamps are low and she has $9 in cash. How will she produce three meals a day for eight children? She has no frying pans, dishes, utensils, or toilet paper. She returns to Room 449 to tell the children.

They must hustle to therapy, because Chanel needs the cash. It is drizzling out. The children walk in a daze. All Dasani can think about is having to leave her beloved school.

The sun has set by the time they return to Auburn.

It is strange, this feeling of heading toward an address they don't have while saying goodbye—in the span of a few hours—to their longtime home. They pack whatever they can fit into twenty clear plastic bags. At 9:26 P.M. on October 17, 2013—more than three years after moving into Auburn—Chanel and her children board the last van. Turtle is still in the room.

An hour later, they pull up to their new residence. Of all the shelters where Dasani's family could have landed, they have somehow wound up on West 145th Street in Harlem—one block from the Bartendaz base.

"I am right next to the park," Dasani tells Giant on the phone, enunciating each word. "I'm here! I'm in Harlem!"

Chanel grabs the phone, eager to hear his reaction.

"You see?" Giant tells Chanel. "The Lord sent you right here next to me."

It is a real apartment, with clean beige walls and hardwood floors. There are two bedrooms, a full bathroom, and a kitchen joined to a living room.

Fresh, home-cooked meals again, Dasani thinks as the children race about. Chanel opens the refrigerator, looks at the stove and sink, and then turns toward the living room, clasping her hands in prayer.

"I thank God for this," she says, her eyes shining. "Thank you."

The next day, Supreme drops out of rehab and rejoins the family. They are broke, so Chanel heads downtown to Macy's, accompanied by Nana, Avianna, and Baby Lee-Lee. In the store, Chanel tries to steal a stack of men's Polo briefs and undershirts, planning to sell them on the street.

"No!" Avianna whispers to her mother. "Put that back, we gonna get caught."

A security guard intervenes, leading Chanel and her children into the store's private jail. Avianna looks terrified as Lee-Lee waddles about the small, enclosed cell, saying, "Out, out."

The guard allows Chanel one phone call.

Supreme picks up his phone and is soon headed to Macy's, along with Dasani and the other children. Only after they arrive will Macy's release Lee-Lee, Nana, and Avianna from the store's jail—but not their mother.

Instead, the police take Chanel into custody, transferring her from Macy's to a city jail. When she comes home the next day, Supreme declares that the stealing is over. If they have to, they can beg.

"Better to ask than take," Supreme says.

It doesn't quite feel like "begging" to Dasani, the way she has seen it in the movies, with peasants holding out hands. It is a little more dignified, how Supreme stands near the local Pathmark, his children lined up next to him.

As shoppers enter the store, Supreme asks them to buy a few extra groceries "so I can feed my babies." Dasani runs in with a woman who pays for Froot Loops and Corn Flakes. And so it goes, until a particularly generous man tells them to just "get what you need," and they fill up the cart.

At the time, Dasani thought this was normal. She did not question her parents' judgment. "When you're a kid," she will later say, "all those questions—Is this wrong? Should I be begging? Do other kids do this?—those questions weren't in my mind."

Yet her mother's arrest at Macy's had nagged at Dasani from the moment it happened. She knew about Chanel's shoplifting habit, but this was the incident that "opened my eyes," Dasani later tells me. "That's when it hit me, that I knew there was something wrong."

Back in their new apartment, the family's spirits start to lift. Supreme hovers at the stove, making popcorn shrimp and glazed turkey bacon. He has joined a new methadone program in Harlem. Chanel is baking cornbread again. Turtle is now in the bathtub, after Chanel returned to Auburn to fetch him.

This could be a fresh start.

Principal Holmes is worried.

In theory, federal law gives homeless children the right to stay in one school even as their families move around. But in practice, there are no guarantees. Dasani and her sisters have been absent from McKinney for days. The commute from Harlem to McKinney takes at least an hour by subway, and the girls are not old enough to ride alone. When Chanel requests a bus pickup, only Nana is approved, because of her disability.

Chanel has transferred the younger children to schools in Harlem. She thinks it best that Dasani and her sisters stay in Harlem as well.

"No, Mommy," Dasani says.

Her sisters are learning to play an instrument at McKinney. If they make enough progress, Avianna can keep her trombone and Nana her clarinet. Near blindness has not stopped Nana from learning how to march for the school band. She demonstrates, holding her invisible clarinet aloft as she stomps her feet.

Finally, on the morning of November 4, Chanel relents. She and the girls board the No. 2 train, hurtling back to Brooklyn. They walk along North Portland Avenue, passing Auburn and the projects, where Dasani used to be known as a "shelter boogie."

See? Dasani thinks. *I'm gone and you are still in the projects.*

Minutes later, they enter the warm corridors of McKinney. Dasani races to Miss Holmes's office, flying into her arms.

"Hi, Miss Holmes," Chanel purrs.

The principal is stunned. She never thought the sisters would make it here without a school bus. She reminds Chanel that she must return to pick up the girls every afternoon until a bus is assigned.

In the presence of Miss Holmes, Chanel never feels like an adult. She regresses into an errant schoolgirl—a perception that is shared. Miss Holmes is hard-pressed to think of a less mature, more reckless parent at McKinney.

Despite this, she decides to make Chanel an offer: She can work as an unpaid volunteer while her daughters are in class. This will give Chanel a purpose and a form of shelter between drop-off and pick-up.

"We always need plenty of help." The principal smiles, adding that Baby Lee-Lee is also welcome.

Chanel's face brightens.

"But you can't make a whole lot of noise," Miss Holmes adds.

The day passes quickly and soon the bell rings. The three sisters—Dasani, Avianna, and Nana—return to the principal's office to wait for their mother.

"You have come home," Miss Holmes tells the sisters. "Everybody here is fighting to get you girls back here. There are certain things you have to do. *Home*work."

Soon Chanel is standing there, chiming in. No more bad behavior, she tells her daughters. "We not gonna have that, you understand?" she says. "Because soon I'm about to be volunteering here."

The girls go silent.

A few blocks away, poll workers are preparing for the next day's mayoral election, which Bill de Blasio will win by a landslide, restoring Democratic Party rule to New York City for the first time in two decades. He is vowing to tax the rich, lift the poor, and fix public education, all of which puts Miss Holmes in a good mood.

She waves Dasani and her sisters off with a smile. A moment later, Dasani returns for another hug.

"Goodbye, Dasani," Miss Holmes calls out. "And do your homework!"

"Yes!" Dasani shouts over her shoulder.

She skips down the hallway toward her mother and sisters. The front door swings open, bringing a rush of air. Together they step into the cold.

Four weeks later, on December 9, 2013, *The New York Times* publishes the first installment of a five-part series about Dasani, written by me and photographed by Ruth Fremson.

GIRL IN THE SHADOWS: DASANI'S HOMELESS LIFE reads the headline. And for five consecutive days, Dasani's story remains on the front page.

The series draws a fierce reaction. At a press conference, Mayor-elect Bill de Blasio blasts the city's treatment of the homeless and promises to "get to work on this right away" because "we can't let children of this city like Dasani down." By contrast, Mayor Bloomberg makes few public appearances, while privately expressing fury that the *Times* has tarnished his legacy. He finally speaks about Dasani at a press conference on December 17.

"This kid was dealt a bad hand," Bloomberg says. "I don't know quite why. That's just the way God works. Sometimes, some of us are lucky and some of us are not."

That same day, two of his deputy mayors publish a rebuttal to the series in *The Wall Street Journal*, claiming that the poverty rate remained flat during Bloomberg's twelve-year tenure (in fact, it dropped and then rose again after 2008), and that nine hundred thousand New Yorkers had left the welfare rolls—without mentioning that a million people had joined the city's food-stamp rolls in that same period.

Far from the fray of politics, Dasani is on the street, watching people read her story. This is as thrilling to her as it would be to any child. She relishes being the center of attention. Every morning, Dasani trots to the nearest Starbucks to look at the print edition. She can read the series on Supreme's phone, but holding the paper in her hands makes it real.

Strangers are recognizing Dasani and her mother, whose freckles are a giveaway. On the train, a man walks up and hands Chanel a $100 bill. Readers are offering donations. To avoid a conflict of interest, the *Times* sends all queries to an attorney with the Legal Aid Society, which has created a trust for the children. Similar calls are pouring into Dasani's school, with pledges of iPads, leotards, laptops, and a revamped theater paid for by Bette Midler's foundation and other donors.

If the pressure is too much, Dasani does not show it. Even when her classmates call her "homeless kid of the year," she laughs it off. Yet the nickname bothers her. Every time she hears it, she is reminded that her formerly hidden life has been exposed in detail—at the very school where she was afraid to be labeled a shelter boogie.

"Take it as a compliment," says Principal Holmes, who is guarding Dasani like a baby cub. The school has taken heat from education officials, furious that the *Times* spent a year inside McKinney without their knowledge. The same goes for Homeless Services, which had no knowledge of my reporting until after Dasani's family left the Auburn shelter.

On television, the newly elected public advocate, Letitia James, announces that she played a key role in the series, putting "the face of poverty" on the "front page of *The New York Times.*" I had never spoken to James—nor had Dasani until after the series ran, when James called to make an offer: Would Dasani participate in the mayoral inauguration?

Dasani would be back in the public eye—on live television—just nineteen days after the series ran. She would share the stage with Bill and Hillary Clinton, Harry Belafonte, and Governor Andrew M. Cuomo, among other notables. Her stomach flutters at the thought. She still has stage fright. Her only job would be to hold the Bible for the public advocate's swearing in, but what if she drops it? She tries not to think about that.

On the freezing morning of January 1, 2014, Dasani bounces up the steps of City Hall in a new winter coat and silver flats, gifts from James. Chanel leads the way to their seats, one row behind Mayor-elect de Blasio. Until now, Dasani's full identity has remained a secret. The *Times* never published her last name. But James has other plans. The first indication comes on Dasani's chair, which is marked by a placard, in full view of the press, that reads DASANI COATES.

She sits down as the ceremony begins, seeing an ocean of faces and cameras.

Don't look at the people, Dasani tells herself.

To stay calm, she chews on a piece of Wrigley's Winterfresh gum. She will count each time she chews. Counting settles her mind. Yet whenever she gazes at the seventy guests on stage, she sees someone famous—including Bloomberg in the front row.

Trumpets sound as crowds cheer for the new mayor. Soon Dasani is summoned to the pulpit with David Dinkins, the city's first African American mayor, who says, "Hi, Dasani," as James pats the child's ponytail. A minister introduces them, saying he wants "to acknowledge the heroic contributions of this young woman, Dasani Coates, who has captured the imagination and won the respect of the citizens of New York, who now holds the Bible."

Dasani smacks her gum. A news helicopter hovers. On the tips of her pink gloves, she holds the Bible steady. She is counting each chew of her gum. *Don't look at the people.*

After James is sworn in, the public advocate asks Dasani's family to rise. Chanel holds her chin high, standing with Avianna, Nana, and Khaliq. They are all chewing gum.

"This is Dasani Coates," says James, squeezing the child's hand. "You see, you all read about her in *The New York Times.* And this is my new BFF."

Dasani's eyes widen.

"If our government isn't securing the reforms New Yorkers were promised, you better believe Dasani and I will stand up," says James, lifting Dasani's right arm into the air. She offers Dasani a fist bump before they walk off, arm in arm, to Chaka Khan's "I'm Every Woman."

By now, Dasani's full name has blasted across the Internet. As she mills about backstage, everyone wants to meet her. Hillary Clinton, who will soon run for president, shakes Dasani's hand, saying, "When I'm in the White House, I'll give you your own office!"

Suddenly, there is Bloomberg, gently offering his own hand. Dasani is finally meeting the man she searched for at Gracie Mansion. He smiles at her warmly, saying, "Nice to meet you, Dasani."

To each politician in this room, Dasani represents a particular triumph or defeat. She carries the imprimatur of the *Times* and the blessing of a new administration. Among cynics, she is seen as a pawn to be used for hidden agendas. But Dasani does not see it this way.

Years from now, she will continue to regard the events of today more simply: "I was inspiring people."

For a while, the inspiration holds.

Mayor de Blasio announces that the city will remove more than four hundred children from Auburn and another decrepit city-run shelter, Catherine Street, permanently closing both facilities to all children. The two buildings will be renovated into shelters for adults. With the city's homeless population approaching a record sixty thousand, de Blasio will also reinstate a rent subsidy program similar to the one that ended under Bloomberg. No more families will be turned away from emergency shelter in freezing temperatures. And children will no longer be forced to miss school, trekking to the Bronx intake office, when their families are logged out from shelters.

Dasani's life resumes its former grind. Her family remains at the Harlem shelter. Once again they are short on cash.

Chanel complains that she cannot access the children's trust. But donors have expressed concern to Legal Aid about cash going into the hands of an addict. And even if Chanel's expenditures were monitored, the money would still count as income, causing the family to lose its food stamps and other public assistance. Should it be saved for major expenses such as college tuition or spent on more immediate needs—things like furniture or clothing? These are questions for the trustee.

By January 19, the children are eating peanut butter on waffles for dinner, and their soiled laundry is piling up. The *Times*'s readers press for updates on Dasani, imagining salvation—as if the problems of poverty might be solved through one girl.

chapter 25

FOUR MONTHS LATER, Papa follows his mother down a stoop.

It is the spring of 2014, and Dasani's six-year-old brother has just been suspended from P.S. 200, the school in Harlem where he recently transferred. Papa's principal sent a letter home complaining of his "extremely aggressive behavior."

Papa can only return to school after Chanel attends a meeting with his principal. But today, she has more pressing concerns. The welfare office has rejected her latest application for cash assistance on the grounds that she missed an "employment-related appointment"—although she was never notified of any such requirement. So she heads to the welfare office with Papa and Lee-Lee in tow.

Hidden inside Papa's hat are some of his favorite possessions, including an Ace card—"it's the biggest number of all the cards"—and two pages ripped from Dasani's diary. No one knows about these treasures, which he carries around the city.

"The house is full of stuff," he tells me. "Everything gets lost. I put my secret stuff in the hat."

On the R train, Papa removes his hat and carefully unfolds Dasani's diary entry. He will not say what compelled him to take these pages from her journal, but he is not the only sibling who reads it. In the entry Papa stole, Dasani complains that Hada has been "snooping," trying to read what she writes. Dasani is worried about her future with the Bartendaz team and its leader, Giant.

"I hope Giant is not upset about Thursday, because I did not go because he didn't pick up his phone when I called him," Dasani had written in crayon. The entry is dated January 3, more than three months ago.

A tall man wearing a do-rag stands nearby, talking to himself.

"When I get mad, I have to *break* something," the man says loudly.

Chanel eyes the man with a neutral expression. He belongs to the bottom rung. She is forever drawing a line between herself and them. She would rather go hungry than visit a soup kitchen. She would never make an announcement on the subway that begins, "Ladies and gentlemen, I am sorry to bother you." This man is beyond that. He is too high to ask. In Chanel's view, he is a "bum."

The train pulls into the Thirty-sixth Street Station, a short walk from the eight-story brick building in Queens known as "welfare." Chanel, Papa, and Lee-Lee take their place in a line that barely moves. Papa has been here so many times he can recite the drill that follows: His family will get a ticket and head to another floor, each line ending with a stranger telling his mother where to go next, or what she has done wrong.

The city's new mayor is promising a sea change. De Blasio has cleared the way for universal prekindergarten while drafting plans to create more affordable housing, increase low-skill wages, and stem the rising tide of homelessness. He has even recruited to his ranks a former political rival, Steven Banks, the head lawyer for Legal Aid and the city's most prominent critic of homeless policy. (Banks had run against de Blasio in 2001 for City Council.) Now Banks is agreeing to take the helm—this very month, in April 2014—of the city's Human Resources Administration, the agency overseeing the office where Papa and Chanel are standing in line. Banks will eventually assume responsibility for the city's shelter system as well. He has vowed to "make our government work for New Yorkers who need a helping hand—not against them."

In the meantime, the line at welfare moves at a glacial pace.

"Well, hey, girl!" Chanel sings out to a single mother she knows.

Each trip to a city agency brings a surprise reunion. Sometimes Chanel finds this depressing. The same people seem trapped in the same buildings all their lives. But at least they have one another.

Chanel and her friend waste no time trading gossip. Chanel's big news is that Supreme left last week, following an epic fight in which he broke the television and pulled out a knife. The argument was over money. If Chanel doesn't hustle, they go hungry. She is starting to question the Five Percent's influence.

"Reading all those books made him a racist," she later says. "He can't function because he's too worried about what the white man gonna do. What are *you* gonna do?"

She is once again talking to a man who is absent.

The police took two incident reports, one filed by Chanel (identifying herself as the victim) and one filed by Supreme (identifying himself as the victim).

"I don't want to go, Mommy," Nana had wept before leaving with Khaliq and Supreme.

Here at welfare, Papa stares out the window. His brother and father could be anywhere in the city. He wishes they had taken him along. He is the only male left, in a household full of girls.

Dasani's daily pilgrimage to McKinney starts at dawn, when she boards a yellow bus that winds around the city.

"You must fight for your education," Principal Holmes keeps saying. "Other kids don't have to."

It calms Dasani to crochet. She has one ball of yarn and a hook, left behind by Nana. The bus escort has been teaching Dasani how to make a scarf and a bracelet. Her other refuge is a cramped public library in Harlem, where she speed-reads her way through the *Dork Diaries* series. At home, the television is broken. The children keep asking about Nana and Khaliq, whose whereabouts remain a mystery until April 28, when they turn up at the Harlem shelter.

The siblings squeal, jumping up and down as Lee-Lee rushes into Nana's arms. She and Khaliq bring a fresh container of juice, sent by Supreme as a peace offering. They are now living at Genesis, a shelter in the Bronx.

Chanel is unimpressed by the juice. She wants a man who can provide. But in the absence of such a person, she must rely on herself—at least according to Giant. The fitness guru has resurfaced, finding opportunity in Supreme's departure. Giant is now calling Chanel every morning.

"Get up!" he says. "Get up! Go earn money!"

She smiles at this. Nearly a decade has passed since Chanel left the Bloods, and she misses the bond. Giant is another brother. She prefers a brother to a sister, because men are "straight up." There is less drama, less fuss.

A Black man like Giant is Chanel's first pick, but even a white man (with the exception of a cop) can occasionally earn her favor. Usually this man is a lawyer, assigned to represent Chanel—the kind of attorney who has bypassed a lucrative career to serve the public interest, though Chanel thinks that all lawyers are driven by status. Still, she is predisposed to like anyone who takes her side, and forty-six-year-old Joshua Goldfein is no exception.

A pale, curly-haired man of slight build, Goldfein is a staff attorney at Legal Aid, the nation's oldest law firm serving the poor. He was hired at age twenty-five, fresh out of New York University's law school after graduating from Princeton. Goldfein is best known for his work on homeless rights, helping to bring ten class-action lawsuits against the city. In his off hours, he devotes himself to the death row case of Derrick DeBruce, a Black inmate in Alabama who was wrongfully convicted, says Goldfein, in a 1991 fatal shooting at an auto parts store in Talladega. For seventeen years, Goldfein has worked with other lawyers to get DeBruce off death row. Six weeks from now, in July 2014, they will score a victory when the U.S. Court of Appeals for the Eleventh Circuit in Atlanta rules that DeBruce should be re-sentenced.

Chanel became Goldfein's client in the summer of 2013, after I interviewed him about the Auburn shelter. Legal Aid had threatened to sue the city about conditions at Auburn before the *Times* series ran, and planned to represent Dasani's family should the shelter evict them for granting us access to their room. Nowadays, Goldfein offers Chanel counsel on all manner of things, from housing and public benefits to criminal matters. Whenever she gets arrested for fighting or stealing, Goldfein is the first person she calls. This happened most recently on February 5, at the shelter, when Chanel punched her caseworker in the face, "causing pain and swelling," according to the police. She was charged with assault in the third degree.

If Chanel had passed Goldfein on the street, she'd size him up as one of Brooklyn's white transplants. He cycles to work from Park Slope, wearing Robert Marc glasses, crumpled suits, and earphones that pulse with a mix of indie, jazz, and rap (he used to moonlight as a music critic for *The Village Voice*). But to his face, Chanel calls Goldfein her "brother from another mother." This is not to say that they always get along.

It was Goldfein who laid the groundwork for the children's trust fund, recruiting the lawyers who created the trust and making recommendations on how the money should be spent. This is a constant source of tension: Chanel wants access to the money, which the trust does not allow. Only the children are beneficiaries. And besides, Goldfein reminds her, the donations could never meet all of the family's needs, nor can they pay for anything that is already covered by public assistance.

For now, Chanel is peddling candy from a cart while researching GED courses. She hears about a Catholic organization that offers a high school diploma by mail—provided you pay $100, take a test, and "write an essay about Jesus."

Dasani is heartened by Giant's return and vows to get back on his team. But she fails to make practice for the same reason that she misses school: "Babysitting and doing things for their mother," grumbles Miss Holmes on June 18.

The principal is looking at Dasani's report card. She is failing math and science and barely passing her strongest subjects. Most puzzling is her grade in gym class: She has a 65 average, despite being one of McKinney's most athletic kids. She should be coasting through gym.

"Look at this!" Miss Holmes tells the guidance counselor. "She went from a one hundred to a sixty-five?"

The principal is in detective mode. She turns to Dasani's attendance record. This year alone, she has missed fifty-two days of school—nearly a third of the academic calendar. Avianna has missed forty-one days and is failing two classes. Miss Holmes knows that absenteeism is high among the homeless. Two-thirds of all children living in city shelters are chronically absent. But she also suspects that Chanel is keeping the girls home from school. Today, a teacher heard one of the sisters complaining about childcare duties.

Almost nothing upsets Miss Holmes more than the "baby machine" mother who leaves the task of raising her children to others. The burden usually falls to the oldest girl.

"She's short-fused," Miss Holmes says of Dasani. "But her anger is really not at anybody here. Her anger is about this unnecessary baggage that's been imposed on this kid. She's not a caretaker. And that's always my biggest argument when I hear that 'I gotta go pick somebody up.' No, you didn't give birth to them. You know?"

Adults must have "accountability" for their choices, the principal says. "That's just how I was raised, and that's how I see it. You wanna have two? You take care of two. You wanna have ten? You take care of ten, okay? A school can only do but so much."

Several times a year, the staff at McKinney calls the child abuse hotline to make a report. The decision to make this call is carefully weighed. Miss Holmes is done looking at the girls' records. She hands them to the counselor. "The girls are going to tell the truth and you're going to report it," Miss Holmes instructs the counselor, who nods with grim familiarity.

A few minutes later, Dasani and Avianna walk into the office.

"Hi, Miss Holmes," they crow, taking a seat at the table.

The principal poses a simple question: Why have they missed school?

Avianna looks at Dasani.

"Tell her," Avianna says,

"Why I gotta do it? You tell her cuz she love you."

"Okay," Avianna says. "We haven't been in school cuz we been oversleepin'."

"You mean *you*," Dasani says.

"All of us!"

The sisters start to bicker. "We've been oversleeping," Avianna insists. "And goin' with Mommy."

"Where have you been going?" Miss Holmes asks.

The girls exchange glances.

"Her doctor's appointment," Dasani says in a hushed voice.

"Yeah, her doctor's appointment," Avianna says. "And where else we went with her? We went two places."

Avianna's voice trails off.

"Give it up," Miss Holmes says, turning to Dasani. "Why you haven't been in school?"

Dasani becomes defensive. Avianna starts to laugh. Dasani piles on, laughing louder. The laughter comes in spurts, as if they are watching a stand-up comic that no one else can hear. Melodramatic laughter, in the principal's experience, is "camouflage for tears, for neglect."

"I'm not laughin'," Miss Holmes says. "Not coming to school is costing you big-time."

The situation is serious; the girls' poor attendance and failing grades mean they might flunk, Miss Holmes says. The girls go silent. Sometimes a child must be angry enough to tell the truth.

Their absence, Miss Holmes adds, is not their fault. But when they are at school, they need to be giving "one hundred percent."

"Then when they get home, they have to fight," Miss Holmes continues, as the counselor watches. "Didn't I tell you that, Dasani? You've got to fight to do your schoolwork. Fight to do your homework. This ain't no joke."

Dasani looks stricken.

"So now I'm gonna ask the question again: Why weren't you all at school?"

The truth trickles out: Dasani and Avianna have been helping their mother with errands and retrieving the younger children from school—even taking them to get physicals for summer camp.

"How many times have you had to do that?" Miss Holmes asks. "Once a week? Twice a week? More than that sometimes?"

Dasani nods.

"Yeah, more than that," Miss Holmes says. "Who helps you with your homework?"

A moment passes.

"Nobody," Avianna whispers.

After the girls leave, Miss Holmes looks at the counselor.

"Do you have enough?"

The counselor returns to her office, picks up the phone, and dials the child abuse hotline.

chapter 26

DASANI RACES UP the steps of the Harlem shelter, hurrying after the little ones.

Suddenly they pause. An ACS worker is standing at the door. Three days have passed since Dasani's school called the hotline.

"Where's your mother?" the caseworker asks.

"I don't know," Dasani says. "She told us to go to the park."

The caseworker dials Chanel's phone.

"You can't send four kids up to the house on their own," the caseworker says. "Every other week I'm getting calls from the school saying Avianna and Dasani are missing school."

She hands Dasani the phone.

"Hurry up and get to the park," Chanel says.

The children take off.

There was a time in Principal Holmes's career when she might have expected more from the child protection system. She was young and idealistic. Now she knows better. She reports negligent parents because it is the law—not because she thinks that children are better off in foster care. Usually it is the opposite. A child does better at home, even under the stress of ACS monitoring.

For a child to truly thrive, says Holmes, her parents would be more than monitored. They would be given material help to fight housing instability, unemployment, food scarcity, segregated schools, and other afflictions common to the poor. Rarely does this happen. A child like Dasani is either surveilled by ACS and stays with her family, or she lands in the thicket of foster care.

But is there a third option?

Principal Holmes sits at her desk, pondering this question.

Then a word pops into her head.

"Hershey."

Most people associate Hershey with chocolate, or the theme park named for the chocolate, located in a Pennsylvania town by the same name. All three things—the chocolate, the park, the town—are owed to one person: Milton Hershey, the candy magnate, who died in 1945. He left behind a fourth institution that also bears his name. A clue can be found in small print on the wrapping of Hershey chocolate bars, stating that every candy sold "helps educate children in need through Milton Hershey School."

Miss Holmes knew nothing about the school when she visited Hershey's theme park in the early 1980s. At the time, she was a teacher at P.S. 307 in Brooklyn. Most of her students were poor and had never left the city. So she took them on trips, to show them new topographies and unfamiliar settings. She wanted them to know what it felt like, for instance, to walk through a college campus.

"It's exposure. How do kids think out of the box when they haven't seen anything out of the box?" she says. "It was almost like taking them beyond the walls of the boroughs. I'm not saying they went to college. I'm saying they *saw*."

On trips to Hershey, they rode roller coasters and toured the chocolate factory, their lips stained with Kisses. One day, Miss Holmes was standing in the park when she spotted a distant and majestic building with sweeping lawns. "I was nosy," she says. "I wanted to know what that building was." She led her students to the edge of this property. They stood there, looking at the manicured grass, which no one dared touch.

Miss Holmes returned to New York and did some research. She

learned that Hershey was a boarding school for poor children. Starting at age four, they can attend for free and all of their needs are
met—medical care, meals, clothing, even piano lessons. If they perform well enough, they can graduate with an $80,000 college schol-
arship.

"Hershey's one of a kind," Miss Holmes tells me one afternoon in
June. Six months have passed since the series on Dasani was published, and I've continued to follow her life as a reporter. I had never
heard of the Hershey school. I ask Miss Holmes if she knows anyone
who has attended. She says that she has tried to get students in, but
none were accepted. The last candidate wound up leaving New York
City for a boarding school down south.

Dasani might have a better shot, the principal says: She is athletic,
bright, and already on the public radar. Her sister Avianna would
have a harder time getting in. She failed the recent state exams for
sixth graders.

But both sisters must apply, Miss Holmes decides. Nothing could
be worse than separating them. Either they go together or they don't
go at all.

On June 23, the principal summons Dasani and Avianna to her
office.

"We found a school that can give you an opportunity . . . some
opportunities . . . that I don't think New York City can give you,"
Miss Holmes tells them.

It pains her to say these words. But after seventeen years at McKinney, Miss Holmes knows the limits of the public school system. Arguably no year has been as hard as this one. McKinney wound up losing
its top floor to the Success Academy charter school, whose founder
and CEO, Eva Moskowitz, is at war with the new mayor.

In March, Moskowitz closed her twenty-two charter schools—
including the one at McKinney—busing eleven thousand students,
teachers, and their families to the state capital to protest de Blasio's
policies. His rival, Governor Cuomo, had taken her side. A few weeks
later, Cuomo announced a deal on the state budget, giving de Blasio
$300 million for universal prekindergarten but requiring the city to
find space for charter schools or to cover the cost of housing them.

For Moskowitz, this was a coup. In six more years, her first large crop of seniors would graduate with a 100 percent acceptance rate at four-year colleges, including Yale, Columbia, Dartmouth, Duke, Tufts, and Cornell.

Miss Holmes, now sixty-three, had watched the Albany showdown with a sinking feeling. She is certain it comes down to money. Moskowitz has the backing of hedge fund investors.

This will be Miss Holmes's last year as principal. She is retiring after thirty-four years of service in the public school system. And now she is scrambling to leave things in order.

She looks at Dasani and her sister.

"It's a beautiful place," Miss Holmes says. "I know you've heard of Hersheypark. And Hershey candy. Yummy."

The girls nod.

Their first step, Miss Holmes explains, is to fill out the applications. She will do her part by pulling together the records. She has already secured their mother's permission and asked Miss Hester to write an evaluation.

"Do you have any questions?" Miss Holmes asks.

"Is the rooms . . . cabins?" asks Avianna, for whom rural Pennsylvania conjures the deep woods.

"I didn't say you goin' to a freakin' camp," Miss Holmes says.

Dasani is less naive. She has studied the brochures of boarding schools like the one attended by her cousin Sheena. Dasani imagines Hershey to be more like that—big buildings and generous lawns.

Suddenly Dasani winces. Her jaw is in pain. The principal walks over and peers inside Dasani's mouth, seeing a broken tooth. There is a second hole among her bottom molars. It has been years since she saw a dentist. That would all change at a place like Hershey.

"I need for both of you to think this through," Miss Holmes says. "And please keep your fingers crossed. This is a long shot."

Dasani crosses one set of fingers, then the other. She holds up both hands.

One for her, one for Avianna.

Dasani is the first sister to reach adolescence. She is now thirteen, and the boys are noticing. She ricochets from liking them to wanting to beat them up. She is back to training with Giant down the block.

When Chanel's food stamps run out in late June, she tells Dasani to ask Giant for $10. He has not given Dasani a penny since Supreme took her earnings. Dasani decides to halve the amount to $5 so as not "to go overboard." She just needs to ask.

Other people are better at this. No matter how hungry Dasani gets, her pride is greater. If Chanel and Supreme were the same way as children, they no longer show it. *A closed mouth don't get fed.* About halfway through practice, Dasani works up the courage, telling Giant that she needs $5.

"Tomorrow," he says.

Dasani blinks. Food is needed before tomorrow. "He acted like he didn't hear me," she says.

With Supreme no longer around, Dasani is talking back to her mother and coming home late from the local pool. "She's acting grown," Chanel complains. A boy named Jay Jay has caught Dasani's eye. He is also thirteen and living at the shelter, where the children pass their afternoons crowding the stoop. When the guard appears, they scatter like pigeons. Then they return to their former spots.

By mid-July, all eight siblings are together again, walking beneath a gray Harlem sky. Chanel is weighing whether to take Supreme back.

I miss you, baby, he purrs. *I want to be with you.*

She has heard this before. They pass a pawnshop containing the family's Xbox. It sits among watches, gold chains, and televisions swapped for cash, a shimmering collection of desperate acts.

The children step onto the 145th Street Bridge, where cars spit up a gravelly exhaust. Their flip-flops slap the ground. The route home is so familiar, they no longer look up. No one notices the Empire State Building off in the hazy distance.

After crossing the bridge, they head toward the Harlem shelter. At the bodega, Papa spots his father.

Supreme has stitches in his left brow, a bandage on his forearm, and a sprained ankle—all from fighting with another homeless man.

"Daddy got a cane!" Papa says.

He also smells of antiseptic, like the hospital he just left.

"I'm too old for this fighting shit," he says.

Chanel walks to the shelter, with the children—and now Supreme—trailing behind.

Nearly eleven years have passed since they met, here in Harlem. It is Chanel's pattern to take him back.

Giant is looking for Supreme.

Dasani makes the mistake of telling him the truth: Her stepfather is upstairs, at the shelter on West 145th Street.

Chanel frowns.

"That's why I always tell you: In the hood, you don't know where a person's at, you ask, 'Why you want to know?' If he wants money, you say, 'He's not here.'"

Giant does not want money. He wants to face off with Supreme. "You know what your husband put on Facebook?" Giant hollers at Chanel from his car. The feud began, according to Chanel, when Giant told her to bring water to an event. If she failed to do so, he would "shit on her." (Giant denies this.)

In retaliation, Supreme went on Facebook July 14, posting that "Brooklyn Gods" were coming to shoot Giant in the park with "big guns." YOU DONT KNOW WHO YOU FUCKED WIT PUSSY MAN, Supreme posted. NIGGAZ IS COMING FOR YOU.

Texts fly in all directions, from Giant's phone to Chanel's, from Chanel's phone to Supreme's. Anyone could have seen this coming. It was only a matter of time before the two men clashed. In Supreme's family, there is only one "King Me!" as he had written, years ago, on the wall of Auburn shelter.

Dasani sees no choice but to take her stepfather's side. She officially parts with Giant and his Bartendaz team. In her last text to the fitness guru, she writes, "When people say Bartendaz they think of me, not you."

Still, Dasani has reservations about Supreme, who continues to court her mother but has yet to move back in. She wonders if something is "a little off" in Supreme's "brain."

When Supreme was recently evaluated at Bellevue Hospital Center's methadone program, the doctor concluded that he suffers from a mood disorder and a panic disorder "with agoraphobia." His panic attacks last up to ten minutes, "primarily triggered in crowded areas such as the subway," wrote the doctor, adding that Supreme's paranoia rises in public.

Supreme refuses to seek psychological treatment. His anxiety deepens three days after the clash with Giant, on July 17, 2014, when a Black man in Staten Island is killed. A video of the incident goes viral. Supreme pulls it up, watching a white police officer choke the man, who gasps again and again, "I can't breathe."

Supreme stares at the victim's grainy image. He is stunned.

"That's my man E."

Over the years, Eric Garner had sold Supreme the untaxed cigarettes known as "loosies" because they are pulled loose from the pack. This underground trade, ironically, had been fueled by Mayor Bloomberg's antismoking campaign, which raised the minimum price of a pack of cigarettes to $10.50. Few of Supreme's peers could pay that much to smoke, so they began buying individual cigarettes, smuggled from Virginia.

This had given Garner, the father of five children and two stepchildren, his livelihood. On a noisy stretch of Staten Island's North Shore, Supreme would pay Garner a dollar for two loosies—preferably Newports or Kools. Garner had a soft spot for his regulars.

"I could be short, and he'd still give me a cigarette."

Supreme plays the video over and over, staring at the officer's white hands on Garner's brown neck.

Soon after their first kiss, Jay Jay lures Dasani into his apartment. He shows her to the bedroom and asks her to sit on the mattress. Then he asks her to lie down and take off her shirt.

This is how girls get pregnant, Dasani tells herself.

She gets up to leave. He pulls her hair.

"You do that one more time and I'll knock your teeth out," she says before running off.

Avianna's version of the story is less cinematic.

"He dumped Dasani for another girl. She wasn't fresh enough," says Avianna, referring to Dasani's chastity.

Soon, Chanel gets into a heated argument with another resident at the shelter and requests a transfer. Thirteen days later, on August 11, 2014, Chanel and her six biological children move to a shelter in the impoverished Hunts Point section of the Bronx. Nana and Khaliq are still living with Supreme.

A metal fence topped with chicken wire surrounds Dasani's new home, overlooking a drab stretch of the aptly named Faile Street. Dasani wonders if she has flunked out of McKinney. She and Avianna have not seen their report cards, nor have they heard from their principal. *Failure is not an option*, Miss Holmes always said. Dasani wonders if the principal is sick. Just before the summer break, she had said something ominous: "I'm not going to be around forever. So you need to do right and do what you gotta do."

Early on September 4, 2014, the sisters rise for the first day of school. They are now old enough—Dasani at thirteen and Avianna at twelve—to travel by themselves. They dress in fresh polos and khakis, carrying backpacks donated by the shelter. Dasani's three-ring binder is already organized by subject, each one labeled in careful script: "math," "social studies," "science."

They bolt across a highway, boarding the first of two trains and then walking a mile before reaching McKinney. The trip takes well over an hour. They race inside. The principal's door is wide open.

She is gone.

"Good morning, how are you?" says Michael Walker, the administrator who used to sing, late at night, as Miss Holmes played the school's piano. She had carefully groomed him to replace her as principal. And even now, from her retirement in Palm Coast, Florida, she continues to call Walker daily, guiding him. She has also been badgering the Hershey school's admissions office, imploring them to take both Dasani and Avianna. She knows the odds are slim. The school has a 10 percent acceptance rate.

Here at McKinney, the sisters still don't know if they have passed into the next grade. They stare at Walker, who directs them to the cafeteria, where dozens of students are waiting to learn their fate. Among them is Dasani's longtime enemy, Star.

"I am so confused," says Star, her voice shaking.

On one list, she has passed. On another list, she has flunked.

Star knows how it feels to be left back. She had to repeat the fourth grade. If it happens again, she will be two years older than her classmates. Avianna goes with Star to look at the first list. "Maybe you didn't pass. At least we gonna be left back in the same grade," Avianna says with a nervous cackle.

"No the hell we not," says Star.

The word "we" creates an instant bond between the girls. Dasani is also determined not to flunk. "I never got left back in my life," she says. Together, the three girls walk to the guidance counselor's office, where they are instructed to wait. They huddle around Star's phone, listening to Rich Gang as Star taps an acrylic nail to the beat. An hour passes before a staff member comes to announce the news.

Dasani has passed into the eighth grade.

She and Avianna cover their mouths in twin-like astonishment.

Star is next.

"You're going to 701," the administrator says.

Star's face falls. Everyone knows that 701 is a seventh-grade classroom, which means that she flunked.

Now it is Avianna's turn. The man locates her name. She has also flunked.

Each announcement lands like a life sentence. Avianna says nothing. Star is motionless, almost dreamlike. She reaches for Dasani's braids, gently sweeping them into a ponytail. One of Star's acrylic nails falls off.

Avianna picks up the green nail and walks to her new classroom. She stands outside the door, leaning her forehead against the wall. Her mouth quivers. Her eyes fill. She stares at the nail, trying to press it onto her fingertip. The classroom door opens.

There is Miss Hester.

"Sometimes you just have to turn the channel," the teacher tells her new students, after seating Avianna and handing her a box of tissues. "Where are we?"

"School!" the students reply.

Miss Hester lets the word sink in.

School. Not home.

There is no home for Miss Hester right now.

Two months ago, she was evicted by her landlord in Bed-Stuy, who was clearing the building for renovation. It will sell one week from now, on September 11, 2014, for $1.2 million (nearly double its value the previous year). Miss Hester packed up her life, putting most things in storage. Then, with a few suitcases, she took her fifteen-year-old daughter to the Bronx homeless intake office, joining more than sixty-four thousand New Yorkers now in city shelters.

Miss Hester knows it would devastate her students if she told them this. She has always been their beacon, the one who made it out of the projects and into the professional class. But Miss Hester also knows that in today's shelter system, she is no exception. Plenty of working New Yorkers have been uprooted by eviction. The city's lack of affordable housing is the primary reason that families enter the shelter system.

Earlier this morning, Miss Hester had walked out of her Manhattan shelter dressed in a prim suit, looking as put together as always.

"I feel like I'm a visitor in my own life right now," she tells me in a whisper.

Avianna has settled into her desk and is now staring at the teacher, unaware that they are both homeless.

Everyone has "situations at home," Miss Hester tells her students. But when you are in school, you must focus and "pay attention."

"You could have all these supplies and not be here," Miss Hester says. "And I need you here."

"We're moving to Staten Island," Chanel tells the children a month later.

She has landed a Section 8 voucher, the coveted federal housing subsidy, which helps pay the rent. A voucher is like a ticket to any part of the city. Chanel has only to pick a neighborhood and start looking for rentals.

For years, she has lived in places chosen by others—bureaucrats in crowded offices, administrators of the shelter system. She was like a pawn on a chess board, moved around by unseen hands. The randomness made it easier for Chanel to disown the failures that followed. This was always the pattern, to blame her troubles on someone else.

But now the hands on the chessboard are gone, leaving Chanel to make her own next move. She wants to choose wisely.

When she closes her eyes and thinks of a home, only one place comes to mind: Staten Island—the same place where she found her first home, six years earlier, after Joanie's death left an inheritance that Chanel eventually spent down. This time she wants to get it right.

She soon finds a rental on the island's North Shore, not far from where her family moved six years ago. The apartment is smaller and more expensive, at $2,044 per month. But most of the rent will be covered by the voucher.

It is raining on October 16 as the children gather on the sidewalk.

"I've moved plenty of times before," says Dasani, who is in a foul mood. She has been up all night with Lee-Lee, who has a cold, and none of the children have eaten since yesterday.

"I'ma choose my room first," says Avianna.

The sisters rarely get choices, so the act of choosing thrills them. They don't, for example, get to choose their school.

"You not going to McKinney," says Chanel.

Dasani ignores this. If she can get to McKinney from the Bronx, she can find her way from Staten Island. She has been mapping it in her head, the ferry-to-train routes.

By the time a homeless services van collects the children, to drive them across the Verrazzano-Narrows Bridge to Staten Island, Dasani is fast asleep.

chapter 27

D ASANI WAKES TO the chirping of birds. The sun is out, and trees shade the block.

Her new home is a boxy white duplex on Laurel Avenue, in the Stapleton neighborhood of Staten Island's North Shore. Concrete steps reach the front door, where a patch of plywood covers a hole by the mailbox. The door opens into a dark hallway, prompting the angry barks of dogs. More steps lead to the second floor, where Chanel is now searching for the keys. She does not know where she put them. The children are pressing in. They could explode from excitement.

Chanel gives up and throws her body against the locked door. She tries again, slamming the full weight of herself against the door. One more try and it busts open. The children race inside, scattering in all directions. There is a living room, a kitchen, a bathroom, and four bedrooms.

Everyone is shrieking. "This is my room!" "This house is *big*!" "Get out of my room!" Lee-Lee toddles about, saying something that sounds like "eboo." Dasani claims a bedroom facing the street. Papa explores every closet, each crevice. Avianna reaches for the only music she can find—a CD of the Temptations' greatest hits. She plugs an old stereo system into a socket in the living room.

She presses play, lying on the cool wooden floor as the song "Just My Imagination (Running Away with Me)" coasts through the apartment. She stares at the ceiling, mouthing the words.

Chanel surveys all the clothes packed in a hurry. She is overwhelmed.

Just then, "Papa Was a Rollin' Stone" comes on. Avianna turns up the volume. She knows that this song will make her mother weep. The children have heard it so many times they know every fragment — that first pluck of bass, the high hat, the swelling of violins and horns giving way to the pearly voice of Dennis Edwards.

> It was the third of September
> That day I'll always remember, yes I will
> Cuz that was the day that my daddy died

Avianna and Dasani are crooning every line as their mother walks over, locking her arms with theirs. Chanel could listen to this song again and again, thinking of her father, Sonny Boy, every time.

> I never got a chance to see him
> Never heard nothing but bad things about him
> Mama, I'm depending on you to tell me the truth

Now everyone is singing — including Papa, who belts out his own name.

> Papa was a rollin' stone
> Wherever he laid his hat was his home
> And when he died, all he left us was alone

There is no father here today. Supreme is still gone, along with Nana and Khaliq. The only male in attendance is seven-year-old Papa, who zips about the apartment. He longs to open the front door and step onto the grass. For most of his life, Papa has lived in shelters where metal detectors and guards stand between him and the world. Now he can just walk outside.

The sun is still out as the children rush down the stoop. Their new neighborhood is a mix of cozy homes and dilapidated lots. STOP DROWNING IN FORECLOSURE reads a sign stapled to a paint-chipped porch. The heart of the block is a bodega at Laurel and Gordon, where an intricate mural bears the words RIP FRANKIE FINGERS. Nearly half of the neighborhood's residents live below the poverty line.

Dasani leads the children north, keeping track of the street signs. Papa chases a butterfly and searches for worms. He races from door to door, ringing each bell. "I got a camera!" barks an older woman from her window. The children pass a busy highway, stopping into a grocery store where Papa steals an apple. Other kids might steal candy, but for Papa, apples are a luxury. For nine-year-old Maya, it is watermelons. For Dasani, it is grapes. But she cannot bring herself to steal.

"He gonna wind up in a crack den," she says of Papa.

As the day ends, the boy comes undone—cursing, punching his sisters, throwing rocks at passing cars. Nothing subdues him until they reach upper New York Bay, where a fisherman stands near some craggy rocks.

The children jump into the water, fully clothed. They splash and squeal. This is better than any city pool. The water tastes salty and warm. Papa dives in again and again.

"Freedom!" Dasani calls out as Papa swims toward the Manhattan skyline.

Seagulls circle the ferry on November 17. Dasani has no raincoat. A trash bag covers her head and shoulders. Her eyelids are thick with sleep. By the time she reaches McKinney, she will have taken a bus, a boat, and a train.

A month has passed since Dasani moved to Staten Island. Her mother insisted that she switch to the local school, so Dasani enrolled at I.S. 49, up the block, along with Avianna and Nana. Then, ten days ago, Dasani got suspended after fighting some girls who were making fun of Nana's thick glasses. Now Dasani wants to return to McKinney.

She looks at the water, misty and gray. She already knows that this commute is unsustainable. But she had to try it. Only McKinney feels like home.

Back on Laurel Avenue, Supreme has moved in, taking the rear bedroom, where he spends hours researching police brutality. He is closely tracking the Black Lives Matter movement. For years, he has been waiting for this clarion call, reading books like *The Assassination of Fred Hampton: How the FBI and the Chicago Police Murdered a Black Panther*.

A few days before Thanksgiving, a grand jury declines to indict the white officer who fatally shot an unarmed Black teenager in Ferguson, Missouri. The following week, here in Staten Island, the same thing happens. The officer charged in Eric Garner's death is spared indictment, even keeping his desk job. Hundreds take to the streets, marching to the Barclays Center in Brooklyn, where they shut down a Nets game with Prince William and the former Kate Middleton in attendance.

Supreme pays his respects to Garner more quietly. He stands on Bay Street by the flickering candles of a makeshift memorial. It was here, in front of the beauty supply shop, that Garner once sold loosies to Supreme. And where, last summer, Garner resisted arrest, falling to his knees as a white officer placed him in a chokehold. A list of chants is duct-taped to the wall, among them: FIGHT, FIGHT, FIGHT, SO WE CAN LIVE ANOTHER NIGHT!

Five blocks south, at the Western Beef supermarket, Chanel runs into Garner's stepfather, Benjamin Carr. She had seen him on television, asking people not to riot after the grand jury's decision. He is kind enough to give Chanel a lift home. When they pull up to the house on Laurel, Chanel hands him a few dollars for the ride. He smiles but his eyes are sad. She takes the groceries inside.

"Plenty of food for all family members," writes the family's new ACS caseworker in her notes on December 16. Supreme and Chanel thought they'd finally escaped the monitoring of this agency, but its tentacles are ever present. Today the caseworker tries to inspect the children. When she asks to see Avianna's legs and back, the twelve-year-old starts dancing around the room, saying, "I don't get hit by my parents so I'm not gonna have marks."

The caseworker takes note of which bed belongs to which child, writing that they share three bedrooms. But they don't really sleep this way. Every night, a different ritual unfolds.

"Bring me my *cup*!" Lee-Lee calls out to Dasani, signaling bedtime. As Dasani fills the cup (preferably with milk, but in its absence, juice), the other sisters drag their mattresses into the living room, forming one sprawling bed.

"We could have a mansion and they'd all wind up in one room," laughs Chanel.

They snore with their limbs tangled, one child's foot in another's face. Lee-Lee can only fall asleep while holding Dasani's right earlobe. No one tries to fool the baby. The ear must belong to Dasani.

One day, as I am sitting in the living room, Lee-Lee looks at me and says, "Every time I see you, you in my *house*!" Her siblings burst into laughter. The toddler has a point. I am constantly in her house, watching television, eating Supreme's wings, playing with Turtle. I have just spent the night on their floor, sleeping in a blanket.

"This is how I work," I say, trying not to sound crazy.

Since entering Dasani's life as a newspaper reporter, I have slowly morphed into "Drea," the person who "hangs out," taking notes with the pen that also records sound. Dasani knows that I am now writing a book, which requires spending large swaths of time with her family. This makes me less of a traditional reporter and more of an "immersionist"—a journalistic label that means little to most people. Lee-Lee calls it like it is: I am in her house.

This does not mean that I am always welcome. Chanel is tired of hearing me explain the rules of my profession when I decline to give her cash. (In the years to come, I will sometimes cave, bringing groceries or helping in other ways—especially at Christmas. I am, after all, human.)

But I am also a reporter. If I start asking too many questions, Chanel tells me I am "being nosy." If I stay quiet, my face is the problem. It always shows too much.

"On the street, you need a stiff face," Chanel instructs me in vain.

She loves poking fun at my "white-girl" voice while deploying it to her advantage. She will put me on the phone with ConEd, or with any city bureaucrat who is giving her a hard time—provided I am not reporting on the conversation. She then watches as I demand the name of the person's supervisor, before pausing and inevitably having to explain that "No, I am not Ms. Sykes's social worker"—by which point Chanel is in stitches.

She has forced me to memorize the part of the high-pitched robber in The Notorious B.I.G.'s "Gimme the Loot." Sometimes we drive around Stapleton blasting Biggie in my car. If we get lost, I enlist the GPS, which has the whitest voice of all. Chanel supplants it with her own improvised GPS, reengineering each set of directions into phrases like "Yo, bitch, I said hang a right on Roosevelt" or "Ah shit, you missed it again, now we gotta *reroute* this motherfucker." She wants to launch an app called Hood GPS, to spare drivers from the robotic white voices in their cars.

She is forever an entrepreneur, spinning with ideas that I rush to jot down. And while I am observing Chanel, she is observing me. She can catalog my many quirks, telling me to stop picking my cuticles and that I suffer from "worryation." She has seen my face taken by grief on more than one occasion. She is constantly dispensing advice—on how to stay married and, when my marriage ends, on how to stay strong as a single mother. She watches my own crucibles closely, noting that some things cross the lines of race and class. For decades, my brother has struggled with severe alcoholism. He keeps getting arrested or landing in the hospital.

"In sobriety, you have to want it," Chanel tells me. "Mad people can come to you and talk to you, but if you don't want it, it ain't gonna happen. You have to be sick and tired of being sick and tired."

Dasani leaves McKinney without saying goodbye.

She had tried to reenroll, on that rainy November day, but there was no point. The staff at McKinney already knew that Dasani had landed a two-month "superintendent's suspension" in Staten Island, after fighting the girls who were bullying Nana. This meant that Dasani would have to report to a "suspension site."

There are thirty-seven such schools in New York City, with around eight thousand students passing through this academic year—the majority of them Black, consigned to a system known as the "school-to-prison pipeline." The setting of Dasani's suspension site, Mount Loretto in Staten Island, has its origins in the first Gilded Age, when a Catholic priest took up the cause of homeless children, opening one of the nation's largest orphanages.

Every morning, Dasani settles into her desk at Mount Loretto, where students stare at computers. "It's just kids watching movies," she says. She is giving up on school. Both Dasani and Avianna have stopped talking about Hershey. They assume that neither of them made it in.

On January 6, 2015, Dasani is finally discharged from Mount Loretto, returning to her school in Stapleton. Two days later, her mother's phone rings.

"Yes, I have a couple of minutes," Chanel tells the caller.

She listens, nodding her head. She starts to cry. She hangs up, waving Dasani into her bedroom.

"You'll be going to Hershey starting the twenty-fifth," Chanel says.

"*Yeah!*" Dasani screams, jumping up and down. "*Wooohooo!*"

Chanel wipes her face.

"I want something better for you," Chanel says. "It's like sad but happy, right? It feels sad but it feels happy, right?"

Dasani tries not to cry.

"Your baby's gonna be something," Dasani tells her mother.

Avianna sits in another room. She already knows that she didn't make it. Chanel explains that the admissions office wants Avianna to take another round of tests. Some siblings must reapply several times before getting in. Others never make it.

Over the next two weeks, Dasani and Avianna are inseparable. They tread lightly, each sister reading the other's mind. A welcome packet from Hershey soon arrives, showing a young girl learning how to floss and a boy in a suit playing the trumpet.

In the school's brochure, Dasani sees the words "Golf Club" next to a Black boy standing on a hill. Wearing white trousers, his club flung over his shoulder, he looks into the horizon, toward a stream of photoshopped words. Courtesy. Sportsmanship. Confidence.

Dasani hides her excitement. Avianna feigns happiness.

They go dancing in the subway to make some money. Lee-Lee bounces her knees as their boom box blasts "Never Too Much." Commuters toss quarters and bills into a shopping bag, totaling $62. The siblings won't be dancing after Dasani leaves. They cannot imagine their lives without her.

Dasani's departure hangs over them like a silent clock.

Three nights to go.

Dasani and Avianna are cleaning the kitchen in silence. Chanel stands at the counter. The Beyoncé song "Listen" comes on the speaker.

Avianna's face bunches up. Chanel rushes to her, followed by Dasani. They stand there, in a huddle, pressing their salty wet cheeks together. They slow dance. Chanel cracks a joke and soon they are laughing.

This is how they chase off the sadness.

part 5

DASANI'S
DEPARTURE

2015

chapter 28

T HE CITY SHRINKS from view. Cars pass along the highway. Dasani looks out the window, seeing trees and snowy
banks, and then a sign:

Pennsylvania
Welcomes You
STATE OF INDEPENDENCE

All her life, she has been hearing about Pennsylvania. This is the
place where people go to be free. Her mother did it as a child, leaving
Brooklyn on a bus for Pittsburgh. Sherry made the pilgrimage in
2013 to live with a sister. Chanel still talks of moving to the Poconos,
though no one believes her.

Dasani, now thirteen, watches the highway.

She had tried to leave quietly. "You know Sani leavin', right?"
Chanel told Lee-Lee. The toddler pushed her tiny nose into Dasani's
face, mumbling "No, no, no, no." Then she poked Dasani in the eye
with a piece of Bazooka bubblegum.

"She don't understand," Dasani whispers. "Yet."

Neither did Papa. He had zipped around the apartment, waving a
certificate in Dasani's name with the words "Congratulations on your

acceptance to the Milton Hershey School." It had come in the mail with a school T-shirt, which Dasani is now wearing.

To avoid saying goodbye, Dasani had distracted Lee-Lee with the cartoon show *Peg + Cat*, slipping away before the toddler noticed. On the stoop, Supreme was standing in the snow, his eyes wet. He hugged Dasani hard, saying "I love you," which he never says. Then he watched her step away.

"I'm mad jealous," he said softly. "Wish I could do it all over again."

She carries no suitcase, only a stack of family photographs, a bottle of perfume, and a small black purse filled with dozens of coins. Chanel, Avianna, and Nana have come along for the ride. They watch as Route 78 gives way to a country road, cutting through vast fields of corn. Dasani sees farmhouses and silos pointing to the sky. She can look all the way to the horizon, finding nothing but hills, even when she squints. The cows make her shriek, the way that city rats might alarm a country child. Everything looks different.

Soon there are houses, and then a town so quirky, so appealing, that Dasani starts to giggle.

Even to a world traveler, Hershey might seem strange. Situated in south central Pennsylvania, with a population of 14,500, it is less a town than a chocolate fairyland. The first thing Dasani notices are the streetlamps, in the shape of Hershey's Kisses. They adorn the intersection of Chocolate and Cocoa avenues, where the air itself smells sweet. The scent of roasted cocoa beans drifts from the local factory, in keeping with the town's motto: "The Sweetest Place on Earth."

Dasani's eyes light up. She has been raised on candy, at the expense of several teeth. Nothing else brings the same instant joy.

And here it is, all around. Shoppers can buy cocoa-infused shampoo, s'mores-scented candles, Reese's Peanut Butter hot chocolate, and cocoa-filled jewelry. They are told, without irony, to "have a sweet day." They can sip chocolate martinis or chocolate Manhattans before dining at the Chocolate Avenue Grill, not to be confused with Chocolate World or the Chocolate Spa, where treatments include a "whipped cocoa bath" and a "chocolate fondue wrap."

The town's marquee attraction is a chocolate-themed amusement park that draws more than 3 million visitors yearly. The tallest roller coasters crank to their peak just over the shops. A Ferris wheel turns like a giant lollipop opposite two looming smokestacks bearing the name "Hershey." It is impossible to pass through this town without noticing its dependence on chocolate, or its reverence for the man who made this empire.

Everywhere you look, Milton Hershey is staring back—from a bronze statue, from a water fountain, from the facade of the Rite Aid pharmacy. His ultimate shrine is Founders Hall, the soaring epicenter of his school.

Dasani will soon stand there, waiting to be matriculated. She will see a portrait of the man, dressed in a tailored suit and high hat. She will assume him to be rich, almost kingly. No one would think that Milton was ever poor. Or that he, like Dasani, grew up craving candy.

Milton Hershey had a troubled childhood.

It began in the stone farmhouse built by his Swiss Mennonite great-grandparents, in the velvety fields of central Pennsylvania, where he was born a few years before the Civil War. His parents, Fanny and Henry, made an odd couple. She was the daughter of a Reformed Mennonite bishop, steeped in the values of frugality and self-denial. He was a bon vivant with a weakness for silk clothing. Fancying himself a writer, Henry lacked the discipline to make a living. They got so poor that Fanny took to "stripping" the neighbors' cows for any remaining drops of milk.

As a boy, Milton loved the taste of anything sweet. Caramels, peppermints, sourballs. Candy—known as "tzooker" in Milton's Pennsylvania Dutch dialect—was a rarity for children of little means. He attended seven different schools as his family moved from town to town, pulled by his father's desire to strike it rich. Henry tried selling farm equipment, planting fruit trees, harvesting trout. As each scheme failed, Milton went hungry at times, or lacked proper shoes.

The event that broke the Hersheys came in 1867, when Milton's only sister, four-year-old Sarena, contracted scarlet fever and died. His parents eventually separated, and by age thirteen, Milton had quit school to work. He soon took an apprenticeship at Royer's Ice

Cream Garden in Lancaster, Pennsylvania, where he learned to make taffy. Four years later, Milton moved to Philadelphia to try his luck as a confectioner. In 1883, he landed in New York City.

There was no more thrilling place for a twenty-six-year-old entrepreneur than Manhattan at the height of the Gilded Age. It was a city of stunning contrasts, of squalid tenements and lavish mansions. A handful of tycoons had amassed great wealth—the oil magnate John D. Rockefeller, the steel mogul Andrew Carnegie, the banking giant J. Pierpont Morgan, the shipping and railroad titan Cornelius Vanderbilt. Few might have guessed that Milton Hershey—a rural candy maker with a fourth-grade education—would join their ranks, becoming the nation's premier chocolate magnate.

Nearly broke, Milton opened a candy shop near Hell's Kitchen, coming into frequent contact with the poor. Little was known about this other New York, where ragged children worked long hours in sweatshops or roamed the streets in vagrant packs, beset by disease. Their small corpses filled the city's morgues.

There were no federal laws protecting the rights of children. This was still the era of "Spare the rod, spoil the child." A turning point had come in 1874, with the Manhattan case of nine-year-old Mary Ellen. For years, she had been sadistically beaten by a guardian. A local missionary wanted to help, but there was no government office tasked with preventing child abuse. So the missionary turned to the American Society for the Prevention of Cruelty to Animals, whose founder helped bring Mary Ellen's case before the state supreme court. A blitz of news coverage followed, resulting in the child's rescue and leading to the creation of the first nongovernmental organization devoted to protecting children from "cruelty."

By then, New York's child savers had planted the seeds of American foster care (with the orphan trains) and its child protection system (with the case of Mary Ellen). She had lived in Hell's Kitchen—just a few blocks from where Milton was now selling candy, and where the muckraking Danish-born journalist Jacob A. Riis was working on his first book. They witnessed the same abject poverty in the same pivotal decade, shaping each man for years to come.

Riis's book *How the Other Half Lives* would spark a public outcry, fueling the Progressive Era—a period of social activism and political reform that counted Milton among its recruits. Progressives wanted to better the world, fixing the problems brought by modernity, of rapid industrialization, mass immigration, political corruption, and urban life.

The city, Milton thought, was a poor fit for humanity, "especially for children." After three years, he packed up and returned to his roots, opening the Lancaster Caramel Company.

"If you want to make money," his father, Henry, had told him, "you have got to do things in a big way."

Chocolate was still a luxury product, imported from Europe and sold in fancy packages. The most coveted chocolates had a smooth, creamy finish, suggesting the presence of milk. No one knew how to make this delicacy affordable. The shelf life of milk chocolate was too short to survive freight train rides.

The problem came down to chemistry. To make milk chocolate required binding two incompatible ingredients: the water in milk and the oil in cacao butter. Only one company in Switzerland had mastered the secret, while confectioners in the United States fumbled.

Relishing the chance to experiment, Milton purchased German chocolate-making machines at the 1893 Chicago World's Fair. He began toying with formulas at his Lancaster factory but wanted a more private location. He found it twenty-nine miles away, in the stone farmhouse built by his great-grandparents, which was up for auction. In 1897, Milton bought the property for $10,311, adding a dairy farm, a milk-condensing plant, and a chocolate production facility.

Milton's birthplace became his laboratory. Night after night, he tinkered for the right formula, boiling milk in kettles and grinding cocoa into powder. His breakthrough came in 1900—the same year Milton sold his caramel company for $1 million to make way for the Hershey Chocolate Company. From a new factory near the farmhouse, individually wrapped bars came off assembly lines, selling for five cents apiece. With that, America had its first mass-produced milk chocolate. Milton had popularized a luxury commodity, making him "the Henry Ford of chocolate."

By age forty, Milton had settled down, marrying Catherine "Kitty" Sweeney, a twenty-five-year-old Irish Catholic known to be theatrical, chatty, and fond of furs. As Milton's chocolate empire grew, he designed a new town in his name, modeled after the village built by the Cadbury chocolate family near Birmingham, England. Hershey's town would feature a library, a theater, a pool, a trolley, even a zoo. Milton wanted his workers and executives to live in harmony, upholding the same progressive values while abstaining from any "offensive purpose or occupation."

It soon became clear that Milton and Kitty could not have children. To fill their void, Milton's birthplace—the stone farmhouse where he had invented his milk chocolate—would become a new kind of laboratory: the site of an innovative school for orphans. This would be Milton's ultimate experiment and proudest legacy—a place where poor boys could transcend their origins.

Milton had done it himself, and wanted the same for his recruits, whom he identified in his own image as "poor, healthy, white, male orphans." He began this project much like his chocolate venture, with no expert knowledge. But he had an innate sense of what his orphans needed. "Those boys must grow up with the feeling that they have a real home," he told *The Brooklyn Daily Eagle* in 1929. They would, according to the school's deed, be "fed with plain, wholesome food" and "neatly, and comfortably clothed, without distinctive dress." The school's ultimate purpose was to train young men to "earn their own livelihood."

When the school opened in 1910, the first crop of orphans, ages four to eight, spent their weekdays learning arithmetic, reading, and other subjects. Their home life resembled Milton's early years on the farm, with exposure to Christian scripture and the Golden Rule. They did chores, milked cows, said grace before dinner. Milton and Kitty built a mansion nearby, leaving another couple to serve as the boys' "houseparents."

This couple-for-hire, in Milton's untested vision, would re-create the family that these boys had lost. After Kitty passed away in 1915 of a mysterious disease, Milton never remarried. His wealth grew, along with the town. In a move that made the front page of *The New York Times* in 1923, Milton gave $60 million worth of his company's shares to the school, and eventually his entire fortune.

"It's a sin for a man to die rich," he told his friends.

Dasani presses a button to hear Milton's voice.

"Good evening, ladies and gentlemen," he says softly.

This is the only known recording of the man, taken from a radio interview in 1938, when he was eighty years old. His voice quivers as he talks about the "character building" of orphans, next to a glass-encased exhibit of his antiques.

Dasani examines each of Milton's things—his blue velvet chair, his mahogany radio—as Chanel stands nearby, wearing a pin that reads THE BLACKMAN IS GOD. She is staring intensely at a painting of Kitty, who sits in elegant repose, clutching a fur in long satin gloves. Chanel cannot imagine being spoiled in this fashion. She loves the name Kitty.

Behind them is a corridor lined with photographs of each graduating class—a long procession of white faces that begins to include African Americans starting in 1968, followed by women nearly a decade later.

More than a century has passed since the school's founding. More than nine thousand children have graduated. Many things are different. The word "industrial" is gone from the school's name, much the way manufacturing has left the Pennsylvania rust belt. The school's own fortunes have skyrocketed. The trust that funds the school owns a controlling share of the Hershey Chocolate Company. This endowment, which can be spent only on the school, was valued at $12.2 billion in 2015 (and surpassed $17.6 billion by 2020). This makes the Milton Hershey School wealthier than all but a few American universities.

Unlike institutions that rely on state funds, the Milton Hershey School has little regulatory oversight and, for most of its existence, has stayed under the public radar. In the 1980s, the school's academic program weakened and enrollment declined. A new crop of leaders updated the curriculum (students would no longer be milking cows) and spent more than $250 million revamping the campus. But the school's most devoted watchdogs—its alumni—grew concerned that the trust was lining the pockets of board members and local developers rather than helping needy children. This criticism came to a head in 2006, when the trust bought a $12 million golf course, at two to three times its appraised value, benefiting a board member who had once invested in the losing property. A probe by the state attorney general found no criminal misconduct but forced new limits on board members' compensation and tenure.

Set on a sprawling campus, the Hershey school could pass for a modern utopia. More than two thousand children live in suburban-looking villages owned and maintained by the school. Each home is the domain of one married couple, hired to oversee eight to twelve children. The oldest homes surround the original farmhouse where Milton was born. The newest ones resemble McMansions, with basketball courts and spacious garages.

Children as young as four can board here year-round, entering in preschool and staying until the twelfth grade. Their "houseparents" act as surrogate mothers and fathers, driving the students to soccer games and dentist appointments and helping them with homework. The children are groomed at the school's salon. They get a fresh uniform for each day of the week, as well as swimsuits, Crocs, nightgowns, socks, slippers, and dresses or suits and ties. If their teeth are crooked, they will soon be wearing braces—all of this covered by the trust.

Hershey's students are a cross-section of poor America. Nearly 44 percent are white, 33 percent Black, and 9 percent Latino. Only low-income families can apply; the average student's family earns $17,207, well below the federal poverty line. Most come from Pennsylvania, per the deed of trust, while a quarter have crossed state lines from as far away as Iowa, Texas, California, and Puerto Rico.

Among these children, Dasani's struggles are not unusual. About one in five of Hershey's students has been homeless, nearly a third have had a parent incarcerated, and half have witnessed drug or alcohol abuse. Hundreds of students have avoided foster care by enrolling at Hershey as part of agreements made between their families and child protection workers. They are leaving homes of scarcity to attend the richest private school for children in America.

Here Dasani can do things she never thought of, like play field hockey. Just the name of it sounds exclusive: a sport requiring a field. The school's amenities rival those of a top university: eight tennis courts, two indoor pools, a seven-thousand-seat football stadium, an ice skating rink, and a sports complex with an indoor track. Its medical services include staff pediatricians and a twenty-four-hour health clinic with forty beds. The school dentists are also busy. This year, Dasani is among the 326 new students bringing 1,532 cavities to be filled. (Dasani has two.)

Near Founders Hall, a clock tower overlooks the quad, where students mill about in polo shirts and starchy khakis. Their after-school enrichment includes tutoring and piano lessons. By the time they graduate, they will have learned to swim, drive a car, and manage a bank account. Those who have kept up their grades and followed the school's rules will leave with a college scholarship.

The annual cost of this experience, paid for by the trust, comes to $84,886 per child. By comparison, the tuition at Phillips Exeter Academy is 45 percent less, but does not include things like orthodontia or birthday presents. Such expenses fall to the parents of America's elite schools, where contributing to the endowment can keep a family's legacy going.

Hershey wants to be the opposite of a "legacy school." After all, a child must be poor to apply. If the descendants of Hershey's alumni do not qualify for admission, then the school has done its job.

"Your family's income does not have to determine your outcome!" bellows the school president, Peter Gurt, from the stage of an auditorium where Dasani and sixty-seven other students are matriculating on January 27, 2015.

A Philadelphia native, Gurt grew up at the Hershey school after enrolling at age five. "Being here is not easy," he says, scanning the audience. "And we don't want it to be. In fact, we take pride in the fact that we are going to make you stretch, struggle, and grow."

From her seat, Dasani rifles through a yellow Hershey welcome tote. She finds a list of expected chores, with one daily task, such as sweeping or cleaning windows. Dasani looks amused. Back home, she could complete this entire list in one morning.

Minutes later, President Gurt mills about the crowd, greeting new students.

"It's all good from here," he says, smiling at Dasani. "You have to trust us on that."

"I do," Chanel says.

"All of us would prefer different circumstances," Gurt continues. "I tell students that all the time. The next best thing is Milton Hershey School."

"She's gonna love it here," Chanel says. "She's not gonna worry about nobody else but *her* and her schoolwork—"

"She wants me to be a gymnast!" Dasani blurts out.

President Gurt looks at Dasani.

"What do *you* wanna be?" he asks.

Walking toward them is a thirty-seven-year-old white woman in a long plaid skirt. Blond highlights streak her hair. She introduces herself as Tabitha McQuiddy. She will be Dasani's housemother.

Chanel smiles, looking Tabitha up and down.

It is time to go.

"Do you see your coat?" Chanel asks her daughter, handing her the missing coat. "If *mom's* not here, Dasani, it would be lost, okay?"

Tabitha turns to Chanel.

"I assure you I say the same things. '*Do you have your coat?*' Even with twelve!"

Dasani pulls away to explore the auditorium with her sisters. Chanel and Tabitha watch as they race around, giddy with excitement. Dasani is now standing on a brick walkway.

"Mommy, look! It's real brick!" Dasani squeals. "It needs to be painted yellow!"

Dasani has seen mansions in the foothills of Staten Island, high above the projects. Her new house, Student Home Sienna, would fit right in. Spanning 10,365 square feet, the stone-facade structure was designed to be "neo-eclectic with farm home elements"—a modern and sprawling version of Milton's farmhouse.

A smooth driveway winds past the formal entrance, where guests ring a doorbell that sounds like an organ. Tabitha parks the van near the garage, leading Dasani, her sisters, and Chanel through the side door. All students are made to enter this way, stopping in the mudroom to remove their day shoes. A hallway leads to the "guest powder room," a gleaming kitchen, and a dining room.

Dasani has never lived in a home like this, with central air-conditioning and a game room featuring a giant TV, a pool table, and a ping-pong table. A wooden stair rail leads up to the second floor, where the words TOGETHER WE MAKE A FAMILY adorn the wall. Framed photos of Sienna's girls fill a glass-encased cabinet, near a prominent etching of the Ten Commandments. While the school describes itself as nondenominational, Christian scripture is all around. The children attend a mandatory chapel service every Sunday and say grace before dinner.

Dasani, her sisters, and Chanel are now following Tabitha to a large supply closet filled with brand-name toiletries such as Nivea cream, ACT mouthwash, and Prell shampoo. Nana spots a clear box containing what might be dollar bills.

"You have money in there?" she asks.

"It's fake money," says Tabitha, explaining that she runs the closet "like a store," teaching the girls how to "manage themselves so that they don't overspend."

"Mommy!" Avianna calls out. "She teach them how to budget their money!"

Chanel strides up.

"She needs Secret deodorant," says Chanel, enunciating the *t* at the end of each word. "She needs everything high standard because Dasani likes to work out. Dasani's very athletic."

"I see Secret right there," says Tabitha. "She will get it."

Chanel has read the parent handbook, which advises her to have "a positive relationship" with the houseparents and to "always remember we're on the same team." Chanel periodically flashes Tabitha a smile.

Down the hall is Dasani's new bedroom, which she will share with another girl. She walks inside, spotting her bed on the left and a stack of clean sheets. Dasani has her own dresser and a tall wooden armoire. She opens it and stares inside, her mouth dropping.

"See how big they closet is?" she says to her mother.

"Stop saying 'they,'" Chanel says. "You're *here* now."

"Yeah, *my* closet," chimes in Tabitha. "Look how big *my* closet is!"

"Yeah," says Chanel, who is standing by the window, looking at the woods behind the house. Snow covers the hills where Dasani will learn to sled.

"Wow," Chanel says quietly. "You have a beautiful view."

"I have a new light, Mommy!" yelps Dasani, turning on the lamp. Chanel is still staring out the window.

"You get to see the roosters," she says, almost to herself. She imagines all kinds of animals passing below this window.

A few minutes later, Chanel steps outside. She circles the house, peering through a ground-floor window into what she assumes is the McQuiddys' bedroom (in fact it's the guest room). The bed is unmade. This gives Chanel a secret lift. They are hardly the example of "neat."

Chanel resurfaces with a grin.

Everyone is gathered in the living room. It is time to say goodbye. Tabitha is standing near her forty-two-year-old husband, Jason. Their sons—eleven-year-old Tristan and eight-year-old Carter—will soon be home from school, along with a gaggle of Hershey girls.

Tabitha holds Leo, the family's new puppy. He is a hybrid "Mal-Shi," a cross between a Maltese and a Shih Tzu. Like other designer dogs, Leo is an affable, hypoallergenic, and largely non-shedding specimen of canine perfection.

Chanel nuzzles the tiny creature.

"Look over my baby now, okay?" she tells the dog. "You smell so good."

She turns to Tabitha, adding, "You, too," although it is unclear whether Chanel means that Tabitha should also take care of Dasani or that Tabitha smells as good as her dog.

The two mothers hug. They have already discussed Dasani's "four-week adjustment plan." Chanel is allowed one weekly phone call to Dasani, at a predesignated time. There are no visits for an entire month—a separation that is designed to help incoming students form new bonds, particularly with their houseparents.

This can bring a swell of emotions: sadness, guilt, confusion, rage.

Some children rebel, hoping their transgressions will send them home. But the longer they can endure this separation, the better they will do. The ultimate goal is for Hershey's students to become independent and "lead fulfilling and productive lives."

The unspoken message is clear. In order to leave poverty, Dasani must also leave her family—at least for a while.

The sun is setting as the McQuiddys walk Chanel to the door. Dasani bolts outside with her sisters. They fan out across the lawn, throwing snowballs with vicious precision. It is always easier to fight than to cry.

On the ride home, Avianna stares at the highway.

"I don't miss Dasani," says Nana. "Do you miss her, Mommy?"

"No, Nana. I know she all right."

"She havin' dinner right now," Avianna says.

They try to imagine it.

chapter 29

DASANI LIES AWAKE.

She has never slept alone, with a mattress to herself. She keeps reaching for Lee-Lee. "I don't know how to sleep with nobody."

Outside, the sky is wide and dark, the snow almost silver. Hershey is so quiet that any noise is jarring—the rustling of branches, the thrum of a truck. Everything feels different, even the air. A few feet away, Dasani's thirteen-year-old roommate, Helena, is fast asleep. She, too, is a city girl. But Helena came from Trenton, New Jersey, eight years ago, which is long enough to learn how to sleep through the quiet.

It's not just Lee-Lee's absence that keeps Dasani awake. She is feeling the pressure that Hershey represents. "I believe I can achieve my dreams in this school," she writes in her journal on January 27, 2015. "I believe I can make good and new friends if I just keep fighting and all that New York stuff where it came from."

She makes no mention of Helena or her ten other housemates, for fear they might read the diary and turn against her. They had greeted Dasani warmly at dinner, bowing their heads for grace. She had stayed quiet, eating quickly, as if the food might vanish.

This much the McQuiddys expected. The new students are not

used to second helpings or side dishes. Sometimes they guard their plates, hunching over each meal. Or they try to ration it, hoarding food in their napkins.

"Every year we go through it," says Dasani's new housefather, Jason. "You have to set it up like it's a classroom when they first come." He and Tabitha give a tutorial in table etiquette, showing the children how to use a fork and knife. "You don't have to hide your food," Jason tells them. "You don't have to protect it."

Each girl brings her own idiosyncrasies. The McQuiddys notice that Dasani cuts her food with a knife, then picks it up with her hand, placing it in her mouth. She is accustomed to eating street food in a rush. No one uses a fork with French fries or chicken wings, especially when the meal is shared by eight siblings.

The McQuiddys need no explanation. They have houseparented more than eighty children, from the streetwise to the rural. They expect Dasani to bring the "survival skill set" of a city child. She is unafraid of strangers. She can adjust to crowds. She can make quick decisions, undistracted by the honking of cars or the shoving of hands. She will do fine on the upcoming field trip to Philadelphia.

But the woods behind their house are another matter. For Dasani, this is unfamiliar terrain. The McQuiddys are not surprised when she announces "I don't do bugs" and is never going camping "so don't even try it." They expect Dasani to stay close to the house, unlike their country kids.

A girl from Appalachia sees the woods as opportunity. She might have been raised trapping animals. Trees and berries are not "nature" so much as a canvas upon which to roam. "You're talking backwoods rural deliverance," says Jason, who has found himself nearly yodeling to locate his young wanderers.

Some habits are "a rural thing" and some are an "urban thing." When asked whether hoarding food is rural or urban, Jason and Tabitha say the same words, at the exact same time:

"It's a poverty thing."

The McQuiddys not only finish each other's sentences, they often share the same sentence.

Tabitha will say, "There was this time—"

Jason: "When we were driving up to Maine—"

Tabitha: "And the road was so curvy."

The story will continue in this fashion until they pause and look at each other, the way other people might check the mirror. They are constantly locking eyes, fourteen years into their marriage. They have disagreements like any married couple, but for years they kept this behind closed doors. They felt it was their duty, as "professional parents," to project the image that "everything is fine."

"We were so guarded," Tabitha says.

Then one day the guard dropped. The McQuiddys were in the dining room, in the presence of their middle school girls, when they had a few words. The disagreement was so minor that neither of them recalls the details. It "wasn't an argument," Tabitha adds, so much as "we weren't in favor of each other's opinion at that moment." There might have been a silence, perhaps an eye roll. Usually, when this happens, the McQuiddys take a moment to collect themselves, and then "talk it out." But they did not get that far.

The room had gone still. The girls "just stopped and stared at us," Tabitha recalls.

For many of Hershey's children, a parental quarrel brings catastrophe. Nearly 40 percent of the students have been exposed to domestic violence. They have seen verbal disputes lead to slug matches, calls to 911, even death. The school's most recent valedictorian, Kayvon Asemani, came to Hershey in 2006 after his father tried to kill his mother while Kayvon was in the house. She was left in a coma.

"Does it always appear like we get along?" Tabitha asked the girls, who nodded. They had assumed that the McQuiddys were "perfect," which—to them—meant free of conflict. By pretending to always agree, the McQuiddys were presenting an impossible ideal.

The girls needed to see the real McQuiddys.

Jason is a stout, bearded man who wears wire-rimmed glasses and plaid flannel shirts. He seems to relish suburban fatherhood, mowing the lawn, firing up the grill, driving a 35-foot Sprinter on camping trips. His musical tastes run from Dave Matthews to Michael Bublé's Christmas hits, which Jason belts out with operatic precision. He tends toward the theatrical, from the zest with which he serves his "famous chicken" to the bellow of his laugh. He does not need the intercom to be heard.

Tabitha prefers to listen. She can be found knitting in a quiet corner of the house, or making cookies in the kitchen. A teacher by training, she is the modern iteration of her Pennsylvania Dutch ancestry. A fan of Christian rock, she wears Birkenstocks and jeans, rarely bothering with makeup. She almost never raises her voice. The girls know they have crossed a line if Tabitha ceases to speak at all. "When I get very, very quiet . . . that's more trouble than when I'm talking."

"Don't ever try to lie to this woman, ever," says Jason. "Ever, ever, ever, ever, ever. She remembers every detail."

Tabitha was born in the quiet town of Honesdale, in northeastern Pennsylvania, where "everybody knows everybody." She grew up camping by a lake and baking "peanut butter blossom" cookies that burst with a Hershey's Kiss. Her parents were teachers and money was tight, "but we didn't really want a lot either, so we just learned to deal with what we had." Almost everyone in her family attended Lebanon Valley College, a short drive from Hershey. By October 1999, Tabitha was working as a second-grade teacher when her best friend got married.

Tabitha was the maid of honor. Jason was the wedding singer. He stood before the crowd, microphone in hand, belting out a rock ballad by Barenaked Ladies:

> I think it's getting to the point
> where I can be myself again

Jason's parents had split up before he was born. Raised in Fairfield, Connecticut, by a single mother who worked as a paralegal, Jason rarely saw his father. As a boy, he was quick to anger. "I was kind of a loner as a kid," he says. This changed when he discovered, by age ten, that he could sing. Theater became his outlet, and more than two decades later he was living in Los Angeles, trying to make it as an actor while singing at weddings on the side.

> If you call, I will answer

Tabitha smiled at Jason. This was one of her favorite songs. Soon they were chatting and, after the wedding, Jason reluctantly flew home. Four days later, he was back on a plane to see Tabitha, and three months later, they were engaged. Jason moved to Lancaster, where Tabitha was living, and took a job in set construction for a local opera company. They searched for a wedding venue, driving through the town of Hershey.

"What is that place?" asked Jason, pointing at the Hershey school.

Tabitha knew about the school because her father had briefly taught here. The students, she explained, lived in homes with married couples who were paid to be their "houseparents."

Jason and Tabitha looked at each other.

"Yeah, we'll *never* do that!" they both recall saying. They thought it was "nuts."

Six years later, in 2006, Tabitha went on Craigslist to search for jobs in Pennsylvania. By then, she and Jason were living in Seattle, where he worked in theatrical set design while she homeschooled their two boys. With no family nearby, they missed home. Under "education" she saw an ad seeking houseparents for the Milton Hershey School. Candidates had to be married, with no more than two dependent children.

At first, the McQuiddys chuckled. This was the very job they had written off. But the more they learned, the less they laughed. They could earn a combined starting income of about $81,000 while living a low-cost existence. Everything would be covered by the school: their move from Seattle, their housing in Hershey, their food and utilities. The school had its own gas pumps to fill the van they would drive. And while their children could not attend the Milton Hershey School, the local public schools had high ratings.

Those perks were only a part of the draw. For the McQuiddys, who are Christian, the idea of devoting themselves to poor children held power. There is a strong evangelical presence among the houseparents, some of whom have done missionary work in Africa. Absent faith or some other set of altruistic values, the job at Hershey can lead to burnout. A typical day starts as early as 5 A.M. and ends after 10 P.M. Most couples work twelve-day shifts, with three days off in between. Roughly 11 percent of the school's houseparents quit during any given year.

The McQuiddys applied for the job and were flown to Hershey for the first round of interviews. After clearing an extensive background check, they were hired, arriving on campus on October 1, 2007.

"We'll give it our all," Jason told Tabitha. "And if it's not right for us, then we'll move on."

Seven years later, the McQuiddys still shudder at what happened.

Like all new houseparents, they had completed the school's one-month training, assuming the entry-level position of "flex parents," akin to a substitute teacher role. They would learn on the job, rotating in and out of student homes to fill in for parents on their days off. After one to two years of "flexing," most couples graduate to running their own student home.

The McQuiddys' first weekend assignment was to watch the home of middle school girls. Tabitha and Jason introduced themselves, smiling brightly. The girls traded glances. New houseparents, like untested babysitters, were an invitation to rebel.

"We were like fresh meat," Jason says.

The girls refused to listen or clean up after themselves. By Saturday night, the McQuiddys were exhausted. Then came Sunday. After the group returned from chapel, four of the girls ran away.

When a child at Hershey disappears, the school issues an internal Amber alert, setting off the phones of Hershey's staff. Rarely does the child wander far. A few hours later, the four missing girls resurfaced.

"I thought they were gonna fire us," Jason says.

This was hardly the greatest trial of their houseparenting career. Two years ago, in May 2013, a girl in their home—fourteen-year-old Abbie Bartels—threatened to hurt herself. She had been at Hershey since kindergarten. As her depression deepened, the school sent Abbie for mental health treatment at two different facilities off campus, then placed her on leave, citing Abbie's "high level of need currently beyond our programming."

Despite Hershey's commitment to serving children from poor families—many of whom carry traumas—the school does not accept students with what it calls "serious emotional and behavioral problems." Only a third of the students are in psychotherapy, and 14 percent take psychotropic medications. On June 19, a psychiatric hospital released Abbie to her family. She still wanted to attend her middle school graduation, but Hershey's administrators said no (even warning Abbie's mother that security would escort them off campus if they tried to come).

On Abbie's behalf, the McQuiddys and their two sons drove to her house in Steelton, Pennsylvania, and reenacted her graduation, calling out her name and handing her a diploma. A week later—after missing several days of medication while in her family's care—Abbie hanged herself in a closet. Her suicide drew outrage, a lawsuit by her family, and a segment on CNN. Abbie is now buried at Hershey's cemetery, in a plot maintained by the school, near Milton Hershey's own grave.

Critics of the school find its rules draconian, but administrators consider discipline essential to Hershey's "safe and structured environment." All newcomers must learn the rules, which are designed to "aid students in recognizing the necessity for controlling both their emotions and behaviors," reads the student handbook.

Misbehavior falls into one of five categories, known as "levels." The lightest offense in Hershey's system is a Level 1, given for minor infractions such as lying or talking back. Repeat offenders get a Level 2, which can result in a ten-day detention. A Level 3 is reserved for "serious acts of aggression" or "insubordination" as well as fights that cause injuries. This brings a longer detention or the grueling work known as "restitution"—things like shoveling snow or cleaning the school's barns. A Level 4 goes to more serious offenses, such as sexual assault or the possession of drugs or weapons. Consequences include the loss of a student's college scholarship, a twenty-day detention, and enrollment "review," the process by which a student can be expelled. A Level 5 brings automatic expulsion.

Every year, an unknown number of students leave Hershey. The school would not disclose its average graduation rate, but said that in 2015—the year Dasani enrolled—one in ten children was either expelled or dropped out. The reasons for voluntary departure range from homesickness to the whims of unstable parents.

At elite boarding schools, holidays are usually a time to rest and reconnect. At Hershey, returning home can explode a child's life. Students are swapping safe, predictable routines for the uncertainty that attends poverty. To help, the staff sends each child home with a box of groceries. Every year, a small number of these children don't make it back.

Staying at Hershey requires a mix of effort and luck. The most promising students can get waylaid by family dramas, such as an eviction notice or a prison sentence. The school tries to act as a buffer. "We ask parents," reads the handbook, to "share your love, encouragement *and* happy news from home." Even when the students graduate, there are no guarantees that they will get through college.

For Jason and Tabitha, the goal is more immediate.

"When you leave our house, you need to be able to stand on those two feet by yourself, take care of yourself, clean yourself, wash yourself, organize yourself . . . cook for yourself, keep yourself alive and . . . be your own person," Jason says.

"Then you can go off. It doesn't matter where you go. Even if, God forbid, you dropped out of here and you didn't come back here—I'd hate for that to happen—but if you did, and you had to go back to the hood, to high school, you would have the skills to survive."

Dasani's first days at Hershey are carefully plotted. She holds a printout of her schedule.

On January 27, she has a psychiatric evaluation at 9 A.M., then a computer orientation at 10:15 A.M., then lunch. Her first week also brings a medical exam, academic testing, "more speeches," and two excursions to Chocolate World, where she takes a trolley ride to learn "how they make" Hershey chocolate, Dasani writes in her journal. Soon she will see a dentist, who will give her two fillings and eventually a root canal.

But first, Dasani needs a wardrobe.

WELCOME TO THE CLOTHING CENTER reads the sign on January 28.

The school's Clothing Center spans more than 17,000 square feet, with floor-to-ceiling shelves, two fitting rooms, and an alterations department. Dasani's eyes travel the room. There are crisply folded shirts and sweaters in every size, followed by rows of blazers and suits. There is an entire wall devoted just to socks.

Dasani must first choose two leather belts — one in brown and one in black. She wraps each belt around her waist as a woman checks her measurements. From there, she builds her school uniform, selecting polos in pink, orange, yellow, and red, and a pair of khakis for each weekday. Formal clothes are next, as required for chapel: dress shirts and trousers, a pleated skirt and matching blazer. She completes the look with tights, flats, and a charcoal coat with faux fur trim. For "leisure" time, she gets Levi's jeans and sweat suits, polkadot shorts and shiny black Crocs. In the sleepwear section, she finds pajamas with a candy motif.

Dasani zips in and out of the dressing room, roaming the store in a bright pink Speedo swimsuit. She is like a child at Christmas. She wants everything in pink — a pink bathrobe, a pink winter coat, pink Saucony sneakers, pink slippers.

"Ohhh, look at my coat!" She beams at Tabitha, back at the house, as she cuts off the tags and puts things away.

"That's *mine,*" Dasani says with each new item. "That's mine! That's mine!"

"Yes, it is," Tabitha replies. "Yep. Yep."

Dasani cannot believe these things belong to her. The moment recalls a scene in the musical *Annie,* when Grace, the secretary of Daddy Warbucks, shows the orphan her new home. In the 1982 film version, Grace gestures to the maid, singing, "Cecille will pick out all your clothes!" Annie grins at the staff, belting out, "I think I'm gonna like it here!"

Just last month, a new *Annie* premiered. Dasani has not seen this version, starring eleven-year-old Quvenzhané Wallis, the so-called "Black Annie." Bootlegs of the film have hit the streets of New York City, where Supreme is still peddling DVDs.

While Dasani unpacks her new clothes, the pirated *Annie* sits in her former living room, back in Staten Island.

Her little brother Papa reaches for the DVD. He presses Play. He watches the spunky orphan, who reminds him of Dasani and also of himself.

Annie hates her life and plots her escape. She winds up in the care of a wealthy mayoral candidate, the film's version of Daddy Warbucks (played by Jamie Foxx). As Annie tours her new home—a penthouse with sweeping views of Manhattan—she sings, "I think I'm gonna like it here!"

Three days later, Papa runs away.

The only person to see Papa leave on January 31 is Baby Lee-Lee. She waves, mouthing the words "I love you." He says it back.

Outside it is 18 degrees, one of the coldest days of the year. Seven-year-old Papa is without a coat, underwear, or even socks. He left the house dressed in a long-sleeved cotton shirt, gray trousers, and sneakers.

The cold bites at his face as he starts to run, passing the corner store and turning north. His destination is unclear, although he will later tell an ACS caseworker, "I watched the movie *Annie* and I want to go to a foster home, too."

He seems not to distinguish between Daddy Warbucks's penthouse and the foster care system. What he knows is his apartment, where the fridge is bare and the heat is off. The children have been warming themselves in the kitchen, where four stove burners fire at full blast. Dasani left five days ago. It feels different without her. Even ACS has noted this, asking Chanel how she is "dealing" without Dasani, to which Chanel "sighed" and said, "It's the best for her."

But it's not best for Papa, in his opinion. Dasani looked out for him. "She protect everybody in the house," he later tells me. In Dasani's absence, Papa feels bullied. Earlier that morning, Khaliq had locked Papa out of their bedroom, complaining that it was a mess. With that, Papa had grabbed his shoes and left.

Out on the street, Papa runs to keep himself warm. He moves in a playful zigzag, passing piles of gray snow. He falls and scrapes a knuckle. On Gordon Street, he jumps a fence, cutting through a littered yard and across the projects to a bus stop near Tompkins Avenue. He boards the bus, getting off at Bay Street, where he walks into Family Dollar.

In the store, Papa asks a white lady for money. She gives him $20, some of which he spends on a giant pack of Takis Fuego rolled tortilla chips. Toting his Takis, Papa leaves the store and walks along Boyd Street, stopping at a brick stairway. Nothing looks familiar, least of all the stranger who pulls up in a van to ask, "Where's your parents?"

By 11 A.M., Chanel is awake. The children tell her that Papa is gone. She thinks he is playing a game. They search under the beds and along the stairwell. Chanel tells Khaliq to check the basement, where the neighbor's pit bulls growl from the dark. "He's not there," Khaliq reports back.

Chanel's stomach tightens. She looks out the window, spotting a police car.

More than a mile away, Papa is lost. He keeps running in circles. He wants to reach the ferry, the only place he knows is warm. Before he can find it, another stranger finds him. It is 11:26 A.M. when a person later described by ACS as a "good Samaritan" calls the police to report that a seven-year-old boy is wandering the streets "without proper winter attire."

Papa knows that the police are "lookin' for me" by the time they find him, crouched on a stoop along a desolate stretch of Union Place. He is sitting on his fingers, near a notice that reads $600-DOLLAR FINE GRAFFITI WILL BE PROSECUTED and another sign advertising WE BUY GOLD.

"Who are you with?" asks an officer from the 120th Precinct.

"I'm lost," Papa says.

The police ask for his address. He pauses. It has been over three months since Papa's family moved to Stapleton. This is his seventh address—one for each year of his life. He is now attending the local elementary school, P.S. 78, where he recently came to the attention of his principal, Lou Bruschi. Papa was showing up too early for breakfast and roaming the halls, looking hungry. On two recent occasions, he tried to run away.

Some schools would hand the matter to ACS, but Bruschi, forty-three, has seen too many things go wrong. He is the rare principal who, as a boy, attended the inner-city school he now runs. The son of a cop, Bruschi (who is white) grew up in Stapleton when much of the neighborhood was Italian American, becoming the first person in his family to graduate from college.

Today, most of the neighborhood's whites are gone, while the vast majority of Bruschi's students are from poor Black or Latino families. Many have a parent in prison. Their needs are so great that Bruschi pushed to hire two full-time guidance counselors and four social workers—for an elementary school with 668 students.

"It's nine layers of complexity, every single time," Bruschi says.

The children lack socks, which may seem like a minor problem. But their sneakers begin to stink, making them vulnerable to reports of "poor hygiene," which can prompt an ACS investigation. So Bruschi does what he can: He hands out clean socks. For Papa, he came up with a morning plan, giving him an office "job" to occupy his vibrant mind. "He has a remarkable social intelligence," says Bruschi. "He knows that he's suffering."

In December, Papa showed up with a nickel-sized wound in his scalp, saying that his father had struck him with a belt. The school notified ACS, and Papa recanted the story. More recently, his behavior became so destructive that Bruschi suspended him. Papa was due to return to school this Monday.

Papa gives the police officer the name of his school: "P.S. 78."

Bruschi is at home when he gets the call. He hops into his car and starts driving to Richmond University Medical Center, where an ambulance is now taking Papa (still clutching his Takis). The dean of the school is already at the hospital. They have been through this enough times to know what might happen. If Papa's parents don't show up, ACS could take custody of the boy.

At P.S. 78, visits by ACS caseworkers are so frequent that the staff keeps a daily roster: about fifty students at any given time are being monitored by the agency, says Bruschi. The school's North Shore neighborhood has 2,062 children enrolled in ACS-contracted services to prevent child abuse or neglect—the second-highest number of children citywide. Caseworkers come and go, with 20 percent quitting ACS after their first year. They often leave due to "burnout," a condition that is never applied to the children, as if they run on eternal flames.

The children cannot quit, though sometimes they run away.

"No coat, no socks, and no underwear," writes the nurse at 12:06 P.M., noting that Papa has scraped knuckles and dry skin. She gives him an ice pack, a blanket, socks, and some food while a police officer watches over him in the emergency room. Then the nurse calls ACS and Papa becomes combative. He starts spitting, throwing objects, ripping the sheets off his bed and trying to hide under it.

Back on Laurel Avenue, Chanel is now talking to the police. They have good news: Papa is safe. Chanel asks them to retrieve him from the hospital, as she cannot leave her other children unattended. The officers agree. But when they get to the hospital, they learn that ACS has been called. The nurse writes "mother and father are both refusing to come to ER as per NYPD." Then she updates the log, writing ACS "will send worker to claim child." With that, Papa explodes, screaming and "threatening to harm staff."

At home, Chanel is starting to panic. Anytime something major happens, she alerts me so I can report on it. Today, when I arrive, she asks me to drive her and Khaliq to the hospital. By the time we walk into the emergency room at 3:27 P.M., Papa is handcuffed to the bed.

He has been sedated with Benadryl. His eyes are hollow and sad. Chanel begins yelling at the staff. Principal Bruschi is standing nearby, along with an ACS caseworker who turns to Chanel, remarking that she smells like "weed."

Chanel shoots the man a deathly look. Marijuana, she replies, is "not even" her "drug of choice"—words that the agency will later use against Chanel. "I am in a program for methadone," she adds. "I don't smoke marijuana."

Papa watches as his mother argues with his doctor, while his principal tries to mediate. Bruschi has been to the ER so many times that he knows this particular doctor, finding her condescending and overly eager to report suspicions to ACS.

Chanel is now weeping. The ACS caseworker has left the hospital, en route to Laurel Avenue, where he will find five of the children unattended. He will inspect their bodies for signs of harm, interviewing them, one by one, to ask if they have been abused. The older children deny it. Baby Lee-Lee offers a different response to the question "What happens if you do something bad?"

"My daddy beat me," she says, motioning with an open hand. "He puts me on the bed."

"What happens next?" asks the caseworker.

Lee-Lee says nothing.

The next day, Chanel picks up the phone to call Dasani at Hershey. They have not spoken since they parted. Chanel has tried calling, only to get the answering machine, which sounds like a sunny commercial: "Hi, you've reached Mr. and Mrs. McQuiddy and the ladies of Sienna!"

Ladies.

Chanel likes that word. She redials the number, putting it on speaker. The phone rings.

"Yeah?" answers Dasani.

Chanel no longer recognizes her daughter's voice.

"Hi . . . um . . . may I speak to Dasani?"

"Hi," Dasani says softly.

"Hi, Pumpkin!!!"

"Hi, Mommy!"

"Hiii," Chanel purrs. "How you doin'?"

"Good."

"Are you okay?"

"Yeah."

"What's been goin' on?"

"Nothin' really. I was playing chess."

"You was playin' what?"

Dasani repeats the word: "Chess, Mommy. The game chess."

"Oh, chess. *Chess,*" Chanel says. "Oh, that's good you learnin' that."

Chanel mentions that Dasani's uncle Shamell, the brother of Chanel and Lamont, had come to visit. Dasani feels a pang of sadness. She then asks for Lee-Lee. Chanel explains that she is calling from the street, and Lee-Lee is at home.

"I was waitin' for your call," Chanel says.

"Oh . . . I was playin' the game," says Dasani, having dropped the word "chess."

"Yeah, so you wasn't even thinkin' about me," Chanel says.

Dasani's voice tightens. She explains that she had asked permission to call a few days ago, but Mr. McQuiddy reminded her of the transition schedule, which allows for one weekly call.

"Did he tell you I called?" Chanel asks.

"Yeah, and he told me that you said you loved me," Dasani says. Chanel pauses.

"Do you know that Papa ran away yesterday?" says Chanel, forgetting the rule against sharing bad news.

"Papa ran away?" Dasani asks.

Chanel tells the story—how Papa went missing for two hours, how she had to pick him up from the hospital.

Dasani asks if he got in "trouble."

"No, he didn't get in trouble," Chanel says haltingly. "But you know tomorrow's gonna be a lot of trouble for me because of him. . . . So ACS will be there tomorrow."

Dasani already knows what this means. The child protection agency will launch another investigation to determine whether her parents are neglecting the children. This will bring impromptu visits by caseworkers and other forms of scrutiny, at least for a few months.

Dasani pivots to lighter matters, saying that she went to the movies and now gets an allowance of $3 per week.

"Gosh, that's it?" says Chanel.

Dasani repeats the amount. Chanel replies that she will be sending care packages, including an iPad. Dasani changes the topic, telling her mother that some of the students are from New York, including a girl who is "mad ghetto. More ghetto than me—"

"She's like bully ghetto?" Chanel asks.

"She curses more than I do," says Dasani. "She curses like crazy."

"Well, you wanna stay away from her, then," Chanel says. "You wanna stay away from her. Cuz you don't wanna pick up any of her bad habits."

Chanel now takes command of the conversation, asking if Dasani is sleeping well (yes), if she is avoiding pork (yes), if she likes her houseparents (yes) and her roommate (yes), and if she has new clothes (yes).

Dasani begins to describe each item of clothing.

"Did they give you underwear?" Chanel asks.

"Yeah, underwear and bras and socks."

"Deodorant? Lotion? Shampoo?"

"Yes."

As if sensing her mother's need to mother, Dasani thinks of something missing: chapstick. The climate in Hershey is different, and her lips are chapped. Chanel leaps at the chance to offer an easy remedy: Vaseline. Now Dasani is back in the role of daughter.

"Mommy, would you mind if a girl pierced my ear?"

"Yes, I do mind."

They begin to argue.

"Listen to me," Chanel says. "Don't let nobody pierce your ear or I'm gonna kill you when you get back here. I'm gonna pierce your ears myself. If you want piercings we'll do 'em. Do not let her stick stuff in your ears, you understand?"

Chanel has never been in the position of having to rein in her daughter by phone.

"Do the McQuiddys know?"

As soon as the words leave her mouth, she realizes that she has shown her hand. The McQuiddys have all the power. What can Chanel do from Staten Island? All she has is a phone, and one call per week.

She collects herself.

"Are you a freak for pain?" Chanel asks, already knowing the answer.

"No!" Dasani says.

"Then don't let her give you that type of pain, cuz that hurts."

Dasani finally relents. There is only one person on the planet who has mothered her for thirteen years. No one else knows her the same way.

"I love you," Chanel says.

"Love you, too," Dasani says.

"Lee-Lee was cryin' over you today."

"Oh."

"Lee-Lee was looking at your pictures. She like 'I miss Sani.'"

Dasani says nothing.

"Yeah, everybody's good," Chanel says. "And we're all rootin' for you to do your best out there."

chapter 30

ERSHEY IS NO longer a man. It is a town.

But what if the place could be reverse engineered, back into human form? Who would Hershey be as a teenage girl? Dasani pictures her as prim and blond, a follower of rules.

No one would say that about Dasani. She is the embodiment of New York City—charming, fearless, tactical, brash. She has been steeped in the culture of her African American matriarchs, from the elegant poetry of Maya Angelou (learned in school, recited on the street) to the fierce lyrics of Nicki Minaj (learned on the street, recited in school).

Dasani finds Hershey's people, like the town itself, "boring" and "mad white." They drink Starbucks "white girl" lattes and listen to Bing Crosby's "White Christmas." They go on early-morning jogs, while driving to the most minor errands. Each of these things Dasani attributes to being white, which is not just a skin color but a destination. She grew up hearing her mother say it was "luckier to be white," while Supreme dismissed all whites as "devils."

Dasani's only previous exposure to white suburbia came through TV. She can imagine a laugh track when the McQuiddys say goofy things, or a collective "awww" when they hug.

"They look like a sitcom together," Dasani says. They seem like caricatures, and this much the McQuiddys expect. It will take time for Dasani to understand them, much like the McQuiddys have tried with students of color. The learning curve continues.

The first time Tabitha heard "bae" in place of "babe," she thought the word was being mispronounced.

"I'm like, 'bae'?"

"Yeah," said the girls, rolling their eyes.

"Oh, that is not a *word!*" Tabitha insisted. "Let's just talk this through."

In some ways, the McQuiddys remind Dasani of her own parents. The dad cooks and the mom bakes. They are religious. They favor vegetables. They tell their children to study the dictionary. Their marriages are a yin-yang of extrovert (Chanel, Jason) and introvert (Supreme, Tabitha).

But in other ways, the McQuiddys are different. They call each other "honey" rather than "baby." They don't smoke or do drugs. Dasani never sees them reading, while Supreme is always in a book. He and Chanel are proud of being "self-taught." The McQuiddys went to college. They are more controlled, less spontaneous. There is no Wu-Tang bursting from the speakers at midnight, no dance battles in the living room.

In her new home, Dasani hears songs like "Cowboy Take Me Away" by the Dixie Chicks mixed with "All of Me" by John Legend. Tabitha and Jason make a fresh playlist every year, which is occasionally played in shuffle mode.

The rest of the house remains unshuffled, as perfect as the lobby of a small-town Marriott. The pillows are in place, the shelves dusted. Night after night, the same ritual unfolds. Tabitha sits in the corner, knitting a scarf for each girl. On rainy days, she reaches into her mother's recipe box.

She loves to watch a child tasting a meringue for the first time. Dasani is her latest recruit. She places the delicacy in her mouth. Before she can bite, it melts like a cloud. Dasani's eyes widen.

The meringues are always a surprise, but not the McQuiddys. They are as predictable as Dasani's schedule: The girls rise by 5:30 A.M., unless they are being tutored, which brings an earlier start. Then they dress, make their beds, tidy their rooms, and at

6 A.M. their "team chores" begin. Jason rates each task on a "daily performance tracking sheet." At 6:30 A.M., they have breakfast and Christian devotions. At 6:50 A.M., they brush their teeth. For the next half hour, they are free to read or play chess, and at 7:35 A.M. they are off to school.

The weekends are equally scheduled, with things like "snack" at 1 P.M. on Saturday and "ironing for the week" at 10:30 A.M. Sunday.

"We lean, *leeean* on the schedule, on the routine," says Jason. "It is like clockwork."

"This is how we do it at Hershey!" says Tabitha.

"This is what we do!" says Jason. "You know the drill, girls. Here we go! It's written on the board. Go down the list. One, two, three, four—" He thumps his hand on the desk with each count. "They know dinner's at six." *Thump!* "They know they're gonna have a whole plate of food." *Thump!* "They know they're going to bed at eight-thirty." *Thump!*

This thumping routine is the pulse of Hershey. Dasani will absorb it by sheer repetition, until she is sleeping properly and eating healthfully and feeling physically safe. Only when such needs are met can she be expected to thrive. This theory is at the core of Hershey's approach. Milton's original deed of trust provides for food and shelter before any mention of studies. The same logic came to inform the groundbreaking work of psychologist Abraham Maslow, who in 1943 created the "Hierarchy of Needs."

Maslow's hierarchy is often taught as a pyramid. At its base are the things needed for survival: air, food, water, shelter, clothing, and sleep. Without these things, a person struggles to rise to the next level: "physical safety." After that comes "belongingness and love," satisfied by friends and family. Then comes "esteem," which allows for self-respect and the respect of others.

Finally, at the top of the pyramid is "self-actualization"—the ability to reach one's full potential, to be moral, to lead a life of purpose. One cannot reach the top of the pyramid without possessing the things at its base.

Dasani has seen this with her mother. Even when Chanel is sober, she is so preoccupied with feeding her children or staying sheltered that she is always on high alert. Her brain is consumed by the project of survival. Chanel cannot thrive like this any more than a race car could win on an empty tank. Only at the top of this pyramid of needs would she find things like "confidence" and "creativity," which keep a person believing that the base will hold. Chanel cannot see the top of her pyramid, she is so consumed with its crumbling bottom.

The first goal at Hershey is to re-create this lost pyramid, giving Dasani the structure her mother lacks.

Dasani is nervous about her first day of school. More than two years have passed since that morning in Brooklyn when Chanel had to push her up the steps of McKinney. Now Dasani must push herself.

She knows she is smart, but she bristles at anything hard. Math is her worst subject. She tries not to think about that. Instead, she plans her outfit. For the first time in her life, she has five brand-new options. She settles on a pink polo and beige khakis, smoothing her braids back with gel. Then she makes her bed, does her chores, eats breakfast, and hops into the van, riding up a long, curvy road to Hershey's middle school campus.

At the top of this hill stands the town's landmark—the majestic Catherine Hall.

Named for Milton's wife, it was built during the Great Depression, when chocolate sales had slipped and Hershey's employees needed work. Up went an Art Deco castle made of steel and sand-covered brick. Catherine Hall overlooks the theme park, high above the town.

This is the place that, years ago, had caught the eye of Dasani's Brooklyn principal, Miss Holmes. She had been standing in the theme park below, squinting up, saying, "What is that?" Now Dasani stands at the top of that hill, gazing down at the park. She sees a tangle of roller coasters and other rides, a view that leaves her awestruck. It is hard to know which sight holds more power—a theme park in the eyes of a poor child, or a palatial school in the eyes of a Brooklyn principal.

By now, Dasani has attended eight schools. She has never set foot in one like this, with long hallways of shiny lockers. Hundreds of students move quickly to class, where teachers distribute apples and granola bars at snack time.

The school feels safe, even "peaceful," says Dasani. Everything is more quiet, including her own mind. She is no longer consumed by the usual worries—of Lee-Lee's bottle or Supreme's temper. Each part of her day is now decided by other people. This could make a girl feel caged, but for Dasani, it has the opposite effect.

She feels free.

Even the fact that her "free time" is scheduled does not seem to register. "At Hershey, free time is everywhere," Dasani writes.

Most new students experience some kind of honeymoon. They have left behind the pangs of hunger, the sound of gunfire. In the absence of such threats comes a temporary peace.

It is not coincidental that Dasani can think more clearly. There is no part of her body as critical to defeating poverty, or as vulnerable to its effects, as the brain.

To be poor is to be stressed—a condition that all children experience, to some degree. A young girl might dread getting a shot at the doctor's office. She sees the needle, and her stress response system is activated: Her heart beats faster, her adrenaline surges, and her body is energized for "fight or flight." Once the threat passes, she returns to her physiological baseline, ideally with the help of a nurturing adult.

But what if the threat continues, day after day? Poor children tend to live with chronic stress. They have greater exposure to violence, hunger, sleep deprivation, and illness.

A child like Dasani can get stuck in "fight or flight" mode, leading to an overproduction of cortisol and a surge in blood sugar. This can make her resistant to insulin, causing diabetes or obesity. It can accelerate atherosclerosis, the heart disease that killed Dasani's grandmother at age fifty-four. And it can leave lasting "wear and tear" effects on a growing brain.

When poor children fall behind in school, with low test scores or behavioral setbacks, they are presumed to lack character, or to suffer from "bad genes." A new frontier of research, known as the "neuroscience of poverty," tells another story.

In 2013, Seth Pollak, a child psychologist at the University of Wisconsin at Madison, examined the brain scans of seventy-seven infants from a range of economic backgrounds, following them for three years. He focused on the parts of the brain that are less hereditary and more influenced by the child's environment. At first, the scans were identical. But by age four, the poor children had developed less "gray matter," the areas of the brain responsible for impulse control, emotional behavior, problem solving, memory, and other skills critical to learning.

Chronic stress also produces higher amounts of cortisol, the hormone that promotes survival. To be "soaked in cortisol," says Pollak, changes the brain's architecture. The child becomes overly sensitive and hyperreactive. Small slights can seem like grave insults. Once the child escalates, it takes much longer to cool down.

Pollak does not see these behaviors as irreversible, and neither does Hershey. The school has aligned itself with the work of Carol Dweck, a Stanford psychologist known for pioneering the "growth mindset"—a theory that the brain is malleable; that a person can get smarter with effort, good strategies, and the help of mentors.

Children commonly come to Hershey with the opposite view, which Dweck calls a "fixed mindset." They assume that intelligence is a preordained trait, as immutable as the color of one's eyes. They believe they are stuck being "bad" at math, or that they were born "dumb." This is their perceived destiny, which flows from another belief: that the poor are to blame for their condition. Poverty is the proof of deficiencies, including an intellect that is "fixed."

Dweck's research challenges this belief. She shows that when children think that their intellectual abilities can improve, they are more likely to work hard. And working hard allows the brain to "grow," by strengthening its neural connections. If they labor over a math problem, even with frustration, their brains are getting "stronger," says Dweck. This makes struggle a good thing—not a sign of stupidity but a path to intellect.

At Hershey, the growth mindset can be reduced to one word: "yet."

The school wants its children to go from saying "I'm not good at math" to saying "I'm not good at math *yet*." The "yet" places them on a continuum where mistakes are embraced rather than shunned. Students are taught about the "growth mindset," using it as a crutch when they stumble.

In math class, they can be heard telling one other: "Wait! Don't get frustrated. We can feel our brains growing!"

Dasani pines for her sisters. In their absence, she latches on to Kali, a thirteen-year-old who lives down the hall. Kali has golden skin, brown curls, and twinkly eyes. She is—like Dasani—part Dominican.

It also helps that they are both new to Hershey. Kali grew up on the outskirts of Philadelphia, in a neighborhood so violent that she and her five siblings rarely went outside. Kali's single mother works two jobs—one stocking shelves at Walmart and another bartending.

Kali first learned about Hershey at her public school, from a classmate who had failed to get in. "They said that it was pretty, and that it had big houses that twelve girls lived in, and that they had a house mom and a house dad," she says, pausing on the word "dad." Kali does not know her father.

Dasani finds Kali "real" as opposed to "fake," which is the worst thing that Dasani can say about a person. Kali listens more than she talks, which makes her nonthreatening. Yet she is no pushover, which would bore Dasani. She has a quick mind and a generous laugh. She loves being around anyone funny.

The first thing Kali noticed about Dasani was "that she was short and she was feisty. And she was different. She wasn't like the other girls in our student home. . . . She didn't complain about everything."

Instead of complaining, Dasani cracks jokes. Kali giggles at almost anything Dasani says. "I think we have the same mindset," says Kali. "She's just more blunt about it than I am."

Together, Kali and Dasani ride the roller coasters at Hershey's park, which divide children by height. Only the tallest—the so-called "Jolly Ranchers"—are allowed on the scariest rides. Dasani barely makes the cutoff, hovering at just five feet.

Below Dasani's height are the smaller children: the "Twizzlers," followed by the "Hershey's Milk Chocolates," then the "Reese's" kids and the "Hershey's Kisses." The toddlers are relegated to "Hershey's Miniatures."

It takes no time for Dasani and Kali to create their own Hershey-inspired system, categorizing skin color by chocolate type.

Hershey's lightest kids are "white chocolate." The brown students are "milk chocolate." Anyone of a deeper shade is "dark chocolate." "Caramel" is reserved for Latinos.

"I'm basically a Rolo," Dasani tells me. "It's a candy that's milk chocolate with caramel on the inside."

Avianna beams from a photograph above Dasani's bed. Below that, a cubby holds her other possessions: the purse she brought from home, her journal, and a couple of books, next to an alarm clock.

"They showed me how to organize my drawers," Dasani tells me in February. She stands next to her armoire, opening the doors to reveal her bathrobe (always on the left), her sweatshirts (always on the right), and her formal clothes (always carefully hung).

Tabitha and Jason are teaching Dasani other things as well.

Whenever a guest comes, the girls must stand up. Dasani demonstrates the ritual: You "look them in the eye," offer "a sturdy handshake," and say in a clear and confident voice, "Hello, my name is . . ." This comes naturally to Dasani, who seems eager to please the McQuiddys. She makes her bed with military precision. She leaves no chore undone.

Other things are more difficult. A candy empire may have spawned the Hershey school, but nutrition here is strict. New students are weaned off junk food and their sugar intake is policed. Dasani has never eaten this way. She finds herself craving Oreo cookies and Chicken McNuggets with sweet and sour sauce.

Language is also a challenge. WORDS HAVE A LIFE OF THEIR OWN, warns a poster in the home. THINK BEFORE YOU SPEAK.

Some words the McQuiddys have learned to leave alone. (Long ago, Tabitha submitted to "bae.") Other words require an adjustment. No swearing is allowed, so in place of the F word, Dasani learns to say "fudge" or "fiddlesticks." "Damn" becomes "dang," and "hell" becomes "heck."

Then there is grammar.

"Me, Kali and—" says Dasani one evening.

"Who?" says Jason.

"Me and Kali and Angie is doing this—"

"Who?"

"Dasani, Kali, and Angie!" she says.

"*Whooo?*" he presses.

"Kali, Angie, and I."

"Ahhh, okay. That's what I thought you meant."

By now, all the girls are laughing.

"You go last," says Tabitha, making sure the point sticks.

This exercise is not just about diction; it's about reversing what the McQuiddys call the "me first" psyche. "It's an ego problem," they both say. This may sound odd, the notion that poor kids are prone to egotism. Society tends to cast them as helpless victims. What Dasani knows is that she and her siblings are neither "selfish" nor "selfless" when handed a plate of fries to be divided by eight. They grab for what they can.

Here at Hershey, there is more than enough food, which Dasani can see and taste. But getting her to think differently, by putting herself last in a sentence, is another challenge entirely—especially when she is not in the mood.

The McQuiddys find Dasani unpredictable and, in some ways, outspoken. "She makes no excuses about who she is," says Jason. But it would be a mistake, he says, to confuse this bravado with transparency.

"She still has layers that she covers up and keeps hidden."

Dasani does not tell the McQuiddys that she likes them. She is never one to gush. But when Jason and Tabitha take the weekend off, Dasani's mood sours.

Her "flex parents" (the backup couple) are pleasant. But they don't cook like Jason. Their food tastes different. Dasani keeps thinking of the McQuiddys and their two boys, off somewhere else, eating

Jason's homemade meals. It will never be Jason's "job" to cook for his own family.

Dasani watches this new couple, Mr. and Mrs. Marshall. They seem to know all the rules. But do they know everything? Dasani doubts that the McQuiddys told them about the arrangement governing her hair.

Dasani had come to Hershey with perfect rows of braids, the kind that usually last for weeks. Her mother was doubtful that Hershey's salon could do the same intricate work. So the McQuiddys had promised to consult Chanel before changing her daughter's hairstyle. They know that parents need to feel in control of something.

Now, in the McQuiddys' absence, comes Dasani's first act of defiance: She pulls out her braids. Two days later, when the McQuiddys return, they are stunned.

"Mom said don't do that!" Tabitha says. "Why would you pull it out? It looked beautiful."

Dasani shrugs, saying that her mother had given permission by phone. This sounds dubious to the McQuiddys. As they press for more details, Dasani's explanation shifts. She is now saying that she pulled out her braids because "I wanted to."

"You've explained it four different ways. Obviously I'm not getting the truth," says Tabitha. "Can we just go back to square one? If we start with the truth, I'm not angry."

Finally, Dasani admits that some girls had ridiculed her hair, saying the braids looked "old."

"I'm being made fun of," Dasani says, tearing up.

Tabitha softens.

"That's hard to say, right?" she replies.

The conversation shifts to the opinions of others, and what it means to "fit in," and how it feels to be rejected. "Why does that hurt?" Tabitha prods. This sounds silly to Dasani. Obviously, opinions matter.

But Tabitha is prevailing in one important way. She is getting Dasani to talk. And the more she talks, the clearer it all becomes. Dasani had been feeling out of control, so she reclaimed control. Her hair belongs to her alone—not to her mother nor to the McQuiddys nor to any salon.

But is she happy with her hair now? Tabitha asks. Dasani shakes her head. She had acted without thinking about the "consequences," says Tabitha, using a word Dasani will hear many times. Now her hair looks worse, and Chanel is not around to fix it. Meanwhile, the Hershey salon can book up weeks in advance.

"Here's how we're gonna do it next time," Tabitha says. "Before you go just yankin' it all out, we talk. It's not that we're gonna say no. But it helps us to communicate."

Tabitha gets on the phone with the school's Spartan Beauty Salon, booking the first available appointment.

Most of the salon's stylists are Black, which brings comfort to Dasani. But they must work quickly, churning through sixty-two children a day.

Back in New York, Chanel would spend hours braiding Dasani's hair. On special occasions, she went to a salon in Harlem, where a stylist named Fatima could devote an entire day to Dasani's head. The longer the session, the finer the braids—as many as twenty rivulets from ear to ear.

Here at Hershey, Dasani is done in an hour. Seven thick braids crown her face. She smiles politely, saying nothing.

Soon Dasani is sitting in a rocking chair opposite Julie Williams, a forty-one-year-old therapist with a cozy office on Hershey's campus. Next to Dasani is a table of crayons, the game Uno, and "feelings" cards that students can thumb through, selecting the face that matches their current mood.

Like most children, Dasani brings to therapy a psychological barrier—a wall that Julie must try to break through. WHAT'S YOUR WALL? reads a sign near Julie's desk. SILENCE? LAUGHTER? JOKES? SMALL VOICE? MEAN WORDS?

Words have always mattered to Dasani. She is incapable of hearing a song without absorbing the lyrics, line by line. She writes as carefully as she reads. (English remains her favorite class.) She also knows that words can hurt, especially those of her mother. Dasani hates it when people say that "actions speak louder," as if words were not an action. It is usually a person's words, in Dasani's experience, that cause a fight. Almost nothing has the power of language.

Use your words, Julie will tell Dasani, again and again. These therapy sessions remind Dasani of her time with Roxanne, the blond counselor at her Brooklyn school. Julie also has a sunny smile. She talks about the same techniques, like breathing and "anger management." The difference is that Julie is Black. And in a white town, it helps to know one adult who can say "I gotchu" without sounding ridiculous.

Dasani likes the calm, unhurried way that Julie listens. Even when they are standing in the hallway, outside their private sessions, it is clear that Julie puts Dasani at ease. They lock eyes and Julie nods with a smile that says *I know*.

As a therapist, Julie avoids talking about her past, preferring to keep the focus on Hershey's students. But every so often, she will hint at a shared experience, saying, "I have been through some things" or "I know it's possible to transcend."

Julie spent her childhood in Chambersburg, a former mill town in south central Pennsylvania, living with a drug-addicted father and witnessing things that she "shouldn't have been seeing." At age eleven, she moved in with her single mother, who worked such long hours that Julie and her two siblings were left to "raise ourselves." In her teens, Julie showed talent as a runner. She dreamed of going to college and competing in track. By her senior year, she had made it into Spelman College, the prestigious historically Black school in Atlanta, Georgia. Even if she could have afforded the tuition, Julie had another impediment: She was pregnant.

At age seventeen, Julie moved out of her mother's home and went to live with the paternal grandparents of her soon-to-be-born son. They offered to help raise him so that Julie could get through college—provided she had no more children. For the next ten years, Julie worked to put herself through college and graduate school—at one point, going straight from her all-night shift at a homeless shelter to her morning class. She graduated from Marywood University with a master's degree in social work, and in 2004 she joined Hershey's staff as a therapist.

In Dasani, Julie sees "a very engaging and outgoing young lady"—a girl who "wants to be successful" and who is "highly resilient." While resilience is celebrated in children, it can complicate therapy. In order to survive, Dasani has learned to suppress her feelings, downplaying traumatic events. Her psychological "wall" presents itself in the mode of "I'm fine." She says this often, whether she is talking about herself, or her family, or the hardship they have suffered. She carries the "lens," writes Julie, "that her trauma history is normal."

Julie's goals for Dasani are rooted in the present: To help Dasani build "positive peer relationships," resolve conflicts, and achieve academic success. She is two grade levels behind in math, so Hershey assigns her a tutor.

In class, Dasani moves with purpose, sharpening her pencil, shuffling through her books. When the bell rings, she glides to the hallway, reaching for an apple. She stays close to Kali, who is taking the same class—technology education.

Their latest assignment is to make a movie. Dasani plots out the scenes, then places a Canon digital camera on a tripod, pressing the zoom button.

The campus is her set, and Kali her star. They are wearing matching T-shirts with the school's hashtag and the words PERSEVERANCE and ADVERSITY.

"Action!" Dasani yells.

In the editing suite, Kali takes over, cutting her scenes out. The film opens with the words DASANI FILMS.

"Why am I all in it?" Dasani asks.

"Because you're the special star person," Kali says.

Dasani knows that people see her this way. She has always been the star (she can still hear Chanel telling her, at age nine, "You my favorite, but shhh"). She takes to this role naturally. In the school's gym, Dasani draws crowds to a dance battle, spinning on her head.

But being a star is work. Sometimes Dasani wants to recede from view, slipping into a quiet space. "Built a fort & a snow castle," she writes in a journal entry. "Finished my essay for does religion cause war? And come to find out it does. I thought war was fought over land & not religion (wow)."

On February 20, students venture to Philadelphia's Franklin Institute, where Dasani stares at the anatomy of a giant bull. This is part of the "Animal Inside Out" exhibit, which uses a technique called plastination to remove the skin of animals while preserving their muscles, organs, and tendons in microscopic detail. Dasani is mesmerized. She moves on to the giraffe, then the ostrich, then the mountain goat.

Dasani's weekends bring dinner outings at Red Robin and ice hockey games at the Hershey sports arena. Her housemates move like an amoeba—twelve girls, two boys, and their parents, the McQuiddys—a total of sixteen. They are a distant version of Dasani's own family, with Tabitha counting heads before the children hop into the van, just as Chanel counted her children on the train.

Five days after the museum trip to Philadelphia, Dasani writes a poem called "Dear Mama":

> You raised me and seven other kids
> We love you for that
> You may be strict and mean
> But we love you all in between

A few nights later, Dasani sits in the audience as the McQuiddys' eleven-year-old son, Tristan, performs a piece he composed on his clarinet.

She cheers, just as she did for her siblings. They pop into her head—Lee-Lee bumping her hips to Rihanna, Avianna's belly-aching laugh. Once upon a time, Dasani hid her journal from her siblings. Now she writes as if they are reading it.

"Just want to say Happy Valentine's Day. Miss you guys so much."

In shop class, Dasani gets to work making a candy dispenser for her siblings. She smooths the wooden edges with sandpaper, planning to fill the glass jar with Skittles. She needs no reminder of the birthdays she is missing. Each one is noted in her journal, right on time.

"I love you with all my heart," she writes on her mother's birthday. A few days later, Lee-Lee turns three.

"Happy birthday my little sweet pumpkin pie," Dasani writes.

She feels the urge to reach beyond her journal. She sends a post-card home that begins, "To my beautiful family. I miss you guys."

Hershey is "fun," Dasani writes, especially Chocolate World, where she saw "how they make chocolate. You must come and see me / visit." She asks everyone to give Lee-Lee "a kiss for me and tell her I love her sooo much." She ends with a message for Supreme.

"And Daddy I always knew you loved me even if you didn't say."

Two weeks later, a letter arrives from Supreme.

"Peace my most beautiful, strong and wise young Earth Dasani," he begins, in careful script. "I truly hope this missive reaches you in the best of health mentally as well as physically. How's everything? How's the food? The people? The staff? The facilities? Your living quarters? So on and so forth."

Dasani has never been in the position of receiving a letter from Supreme. She is reading words that he does not say.

"You know I love you and miss you, but I know you are up there doing your thing so that you can have a successful future. Always keep your head up, and stay focused!! LEAVE them boys alone! Girl, I mean it you will have enough time for that after you graduate and get out of school. First things first."

Supreme's four-page letter is accompanied by a copy of the Quran and two books on Islam.

"Remember Islam is our culture," writes Supreme, "our natural way of life."

He concludes with "I love you Dasani," signing off as "your father and daddy Godsupreme."

Dasani folds the letter and tucks it away.

Your father and daddy.

She still wonders about her biological father, Ramel. She has heard that he is sober and working at a shoe store. He briefly resurfaced in 2013, taking Dasani and Avianna to his apartment in New Jersey, where he lives with his girlfriend and their baby. The visit stirred up old feelings, and then he vanished again.

It would be as hard for Ramel to compete with Supreme as it is for

Supreme to now compete with Jason McQuiddy. Nothing beats being present.

Jason stands at the stove making Sloppy Joes. He cooks almost as well as Supreme, maybe even better. They don't make the same things, so it is hard to tell. The girls scarf down dinner, clear their plates, and head upstairs to shower. They reemerge in matching pajamas, robes, and slippers. Jason looks over his son's homework as the girls begin the card game Spit.

Sometimes these games lead to arguments. Dasani's tendency is to meddle even if the dispute has nothing to do with her. Jason has noticed this pattern and wants Dasani to resist "always being in charge."

Left to her own devices, Dasani would settle every fight. Her family chalks this up to Dasani's "bossy" personality. But she sees it the other way around. She was given too many responsibilities at too young an age, and this shaped her personality.

She is, in the parlance of experts (including her former teacher, Miss Hester), the "parentified" child. In chaotic, trauma-prone families—rich or poor—firstborn children tend to take on parental duties. This can make them self-sufficient, quick on their feet, and adept at survival. But once they assume a parental role, they have trouble transitioning back to childlike behavior. They are more resistant to authority and less trusting of people. They often struggle to develop lasting emotional bonds, having learned to care for themselves rather than leaving the task to anyone else.

The McQuiddys know that if they push Dasani too hard or too quickly, she might snap and rebel. They must gently nudge her toward a more age-appropriate set of behaviors. Her bossiness is a kind of cover.

Dasani is now gazing at the puppy, Leo.

"Mr. McQuiddy, is Leo gonna get any bigger than that?" she asks.

"A little bit, but not much," he replies.

Jason nods when he answers a question, as if to say "everything is okay." Even when he does not know the answer, he sounds reassuring.

Yet some things Dasani cannot bring herself to ask.

She notices that the other girls shave their legs. She would seek instruction from her mother, but Chanel is not here. So Dasani decides to teach herself. The razor slips. Blood trickles from both shins. She goes to find Tabitha, who calmly dresses the wounds and then shows Dasani how to shave.

This is Tabitha's way, to let things happen naturally. Sometimes a girl must flounder before she comes for help. Soon enough, all the girls seek Tabitha out. They need a bra fitting. They get their period. Tabitha is ready. She hosts an "Eighth Grade Talks" night, lighting candles, filling flutes with cider, and laying out a rose for each girl. She then listens for "whatever they want to ask," from questions about their anatomy to their latest boy drama.

Until high school, dating at Hershey is forbidden. But crushes are a part of life, and when a girl catches one, the McQuiddys want to know. They vet these young suitors the way any parent would. "We'd like to meet him when we're at a football game together," says Tabitha, who occasionally allows a boy to dinner at Student Home Sienna. "It's that open level of respect. I'm not shutting you off because you like someone. I'm not shutting you down from being a teenage kid."

Dasani has other things on her mind, like making the track team. Tryouts are coming up.

"I want to be a sprinter," she writes in her journal in March.

A few days later, she tries out for the team. Hershey is full of athletes. Some of these girls have been training for years.

"Hope I make it," she writes that evening. "(Praying.)"

chapter 31

A LIGHT RAIN FALLS on the Staten Island Family Court. Perched on a grassy knoll overlooking New York Harbor, this neoclassical building is a proud, if fading, relic. Originally built in 1931 as a "children's court," 100 Richmond Terrace is now the domain of a child protection system that spans the city. Through these metal doors walk judges, therapists, lawyers, social workers, foster parents, security guards, juvenile escorts, and others whose careers have flowed from broken families.

Cast stone steps lead to the terra-cotta entrance, where a sign reads NIGHT COURT IS SUSPENDED DUE TO FISCAL CONSTRAINTS. Every morning, mothers and fathers climb these steps in various states of distress—frazzled, silent, red-eyed, sobbing. No one comes here unless something has gone wrong. And for Chanel, today is no exception. She takes her seat on March 27, 2015, rising when the judge appears.

"Madam," says the judge, "the Administration for Children's Services has filed a neglect petition against you involving your children."

Nearly two months have passed since Papa ran away, setting off an investigation that has culminated here, in the family courthouse, with ACS accusing Chanel and Supreme of parental neglect.

Today marks the family's reentry into a system so complex that even lawyers struggle to understand it. The system, Chanel has learned, has three major players: the "investigator" (working for ACS); the "judge" (presiding over the state's family court); and the "provider" (a pool of private agencies contracted for services ranging from therapy and parenting classes to foster care and adoption).

Families can enter this system with one anonymous tip. The caller dials a twenty-four-hour hotline in Albany, New York, managed by the Office of Children and Family Services, which oversees all child protection agencies in the state, including ACS. Sometimes the person calling is an unnamed neighbor or ex-boyfriend. Other times the call comes from an identified professional who is legally obligated to report suspected abuse or neglect. This could be a teacher, a therapist, or, in Papa's case, the nurse at the Staten Island hospital where he landed after running away.

The hotline's operator logs the complaint and screens it. If the allegation could "reasonably constitute" child abuse or neglect, per the state's social services law, the operator alerts the child protection agency working in that child's zip code. Within twenty-four hours of receiving a screened complaint, the agency must investigate, taking no longer than sixty days to make a finding.

At ACS, the person investigating is called a "child protective specialist," commonly known as a caseworker. Either the allegation is "unfounded" or there is enough proof to declare it "indicated." What happens next depends on the severity of the case. If ACS determines that a child's safety is at risk, the agency files a complaint, known as a "petition," seeking court-ordered supervision of the family. Eventually, the case goes before a family judge. If there is a "preponderance" of evidence—what amounts to, mathematically, more than a 50 percent chance that the allegation is true—the judge can make a finding of neglect or abuse.

Of 54,302 investigations opened by the agency in 2015, the vast majority—72 percent—involve allegations of neglect, which is strongly correlated to poverty. The parent has failed to provide adequate shelter, or to properly dress, feed, and get the children to school, or has turned to drugs or alcohol—a common form of self-medication in a world of untreated traumas. Nearly all of these parents are people of color. This year alone, ACS will remove 3,232 children from their parents, more than 94 percent of whom are Black, Hispanic, Asian, or "other."

This is not unique to New York. Over half of all Black children in America are subjected to at least one child protection probe before turning eighteen. They are 2.4 times more likely than whites to be permanently separated from their parents, entering a foster care population of more than 427,000 children nationally. So prevalent is the view that Black parents are being criminalized—many of them mothers like Chanel—that advocates have nicknamed this practice Jane Crow.

Chanel looks around the courtroom, seeing strangers in suits. She is trying to figure out who represents ACS. Since February, the agency has visited her home eight times, searching her kitchen for food and inspecting her children for marks or bruises. "Children appeared to be very close with their parents," observed a caseworker in the agency's "investigation progress notes."

Papa tried his best to make the investigation go away. He blamed himself for the presence of ACS. Had he not run away, his mother kept saying, none of this would have happened.

"Don't be mad at me," Papa told the caseworker, putting his head down.

"Is he the targeted child?" she wrote. In the vernacular of ACS, the "targeted" child is the scapegoat, the focus of parental wrath. Sometimes a child is singled out for being hyperactive or disabled. In other cases, he or she reminds the parent of a past trauma.

It was seven years ago, after Papa was born with marijuana in his blood, that ACS filed the first petition of neglect against Chanel and Supreme.

Back then, in 2007, Chanel answered to Brooklyn's family court, which ordered the family to be supervised for a while. The judge presiding over that case—Arnold Lim—was reassigned to Staten Island. And here is Judge Lim, staring at Chanel once again.

"I can assign to you an attorney free of charge here today, or you can get your own attorney," says the judge. He does not seem to recognize Chanel, one of thousands of parents to come through his court.

She has no memory of him either. Too many years have passed, bringing countless judges but always the same room, as cold and stale as a forgotten library.

Judge Lim speaks with a quick monotony born of having more cases than time. A sixty-six-year-old native of Manhattan, raised by Chinese immigrants, he was the first Asian American to be appointed to family court in New York City. He came to the job in 2000 with a well-rounded résumé—first as a psychiatric social worker and later as an assistant attorney for the city's Law Department, prosecuting juvenile delinquency cases, before taking the bench in Brooklyn's family court.

Today, Chanel would be better off in Brooklyn, where a public interest law firm represents the majority of poor parents. Such lawyers tend to be driven by ideals more than salaries. They work in every borough except Staten Island, where the only free option is an "18-B" lawyer, named for the law that established New York's system of assigning counsel to the poor. These lawyers—paid by the city at $75 per hour—are notoriously undermotivated.

Judge Lim is now recommending that Chanel accept an 18-B, "since all the attorneys who appear before me are quite competent and know what they're doing and quite frankly, you may not get the expertise in a privately retained attorney. All right?"

Chanel stares at the judge.

The very notion that a "privately retained attorney" would lack "expertise" strikes Chanel as absurd. She has watched *Law & Order*. She wants to meet the well-off white mother who would take a public lawyer over a private one.

But Judge Lim is repeating the standard script, which presumes Chanel to be a person with choices.

Chanel plays along.

"Okay," she says, agreeing to "choose" the lawyer assigned to her case—a tall, silver-haired man named Glenn Yost.

"Mr. Yost?" the judge says.

"Yes, judge," says Yost, who must now recite his client's name.

"Accepting service for, uh . . ."

While Yost has barely registered Chanel, she has been watching this white lawyer since he barreled into the courtroom, saying, "Who's payin' me? Cuz I should be playing golf right now."

Chanel could imagine herself making the same entrance. She would tell that kind of joke, were the tables turned. *I should be playing golf right now.* She is just as brash, without the law degree or country club membership. She loves an audience, and this fifty-one-year-old litigator seems no different. He is wearing her favorite kind of jewelry, a thick gold ring and watch that suggest words like "solid" and "24-carat." Chanel's eyes travel to his belt, where he often carries a concealed Glock pistol, leaving it with the guards at the courthouse entrance.

Weeks from now, when Chanel finally sees the gun, her face will light up.

"Mr. Yost, why you got a boom boom?"

His answer reveals a shared history.

For twenty years, Yost served with the New York Police Department, working in the mid-1980s as a deep undercover operative in east Brooklyn. He cruised the same neighborhoods where Chanel and Supreme played as children, back when they were nine and ten years old. It was around this time that Supreme found his baby sister dead on the steps of the Cypress Hills Houses. The crack economy had exploded, and Yost was there to make busts. He had grown his hair long, posing as a narcotics dealer who purchased large quantities of cocaine, heroin, and guns.

By the time Supreme got swept up in the crack trade, landing in prison with tens of thousands of other African Americans, Yost had made enough arrests to be promoted out of Brooklyn, becoming a detective in Staten Island. He then went to law school and started a private practice while "paying the bills" as a court-assigned attorney.

Chanel does not know a thing about this man—the fact that he dabbled in Republican politics, or that he owns a house in an exclusive part of Staten Island, or that he moonlights as the singer for a rock band called the Straps. She just knows that he is like her: theatrical to the point of vain.

Chanel is so busy sizing up Yost that she seems to forget why they are here.

ACS is requesting court-ordered supervision of Chanel and Supreme, citing Chanel's "long history" of drug use, her inconsistent attendance at a treatment program, and her lack of parental supervision when Papa ran away. Supreme is also a neglectful parent, according to the petition, because he was aware of Chanel's addiction (having given her doses of his methadone supply) but still left the children alone with her.

For now, ACS wants the children to be "paroled" to their parents, a word that does little to hide the criminal feel of family court. "Paroling" the children means they can remain at home if their parents comply with the court's orders—more visits by caseworkers, mandatory drug screenings, and other forms of scrutiny.

"The bottom line is whether the mother is using or not," Judge Lim says. "A hair follicle test will dispel any problems, okay? So, the mother should take it within twenty-four hours."

Back at home, Chanel stays quiet about the latest developments. She wants her children to stop worrying—most of all Dasani, who is off to a promising start at Hershey.

Within a month of arriving, Dasani is excelling in school, with the help of tutors and the daily discipline of homework. She now has 80s on her report card, surpassing all expectations, even her own.

She cannot believe she has a B in math, and A's for conduct and effort.

"I was always a D or an F," she says. "I never did my homework."

She still remembers "Live or Die," the video game that Dasani had thought up as a Brooklyn sixth grader. Her math teacher was a "super-villain" whose numbers became porcupines and the social workers were disguised as pirates. Today, those impediments are gone—including the bully at school named Star.

Dasani is now the star. She has even made Hershey's track team. When she finds out, Dasani jumps up and down, screaming and laughing.

Still, what she wants most—what is driving her performance at school—is the reward of returning home. Spring break is around the corner.

"I just miss being there," she says. "I miss my siblings."

On April 1, Dasani boards a fleet of buses chartered by Hershey and bound for New York City.

She takes her seat among 104 students. In her backpack, she carries her long-planned gift—the candy dispenser she made in shop class. It is polished to perfection.

The city flashes in the distance. Dasani is almost home. The calendar says she has been gone from January 26 to April 1—a total of sixty-five days.

Yet time cannot always be measured this way. It is less a number of days than a series of lost moments. Lee-Lee may have new words, and Papa new teeth. Will they forgive Dasani for being gone?

She is dressed in her old clothes, as if passing for poor. She still remembers the story of her sixth-grade teacher, Miss Hester, pulling her orange suitcase out of the projects. When she came home from college, the neighbors sneered that she was "acting white." The teacher's words have stayed with Dasani.

There are going to be some places in your life where you feel bizarre. You feel outstanding. And remain that way. Stay just as you are.

Dasani wonders what Miss Hester meant by "stay just as you are." Trying to be like anyone else is what Dasani considers "two-faced." And she definitely won't "act white." But Chanel has already noticed a change on the phone. Dasani went from saying "This is lit" to saying "This is *amazing*" and "*awesome*," words that Chanel mimics with a flat, nasal *a*.

"She never even knew that word 'ah-MAY-zing,'" Chanel says. "She went from talkin' hood to talkin' with some class."

Dasani searches for her mother from the window. She is desperate to hug her, to feel the folds of Chanel's warmth. But the return home also brings worry. Dasani knows that her mother's pattern is to one-up her firstborn child, to reassert control of Dasani whenever she strays too far.

Chanel waits for the bus to pull into the Port Authority. If Dasani can make A's, Chanel can be punctual (even without a watch). She looks at the other parents, who seem nervous, even afraid.

She must keep her daughter in check. Dasani's pride could be her downfall. There is nothing more dangerous, in Chanel's estimation, than an arrogant girl, one who walks with her chin so high she can no longer see the ground. The savvy girl, the survivor, keeps her head level and her eyes open. Chanel will remind Dasani of the rules. To think of herself as separate—or better—is to beg for trouble.

The bus pulls in. The doors open.

Children slam into their parents. They hop in tandem. They laugh and weep. Dasani pushes through the mayhem and into her mother's arms. She reaches around Chanel's waist to check if she is still fat, which means she is okay. Chanel lifts her chin above her daughter's head, which means Dasani is still a child.

Dasani pulls out the candy dispenser.

"I made the wood. I routed it. I cut it. I scraped it. I sawed it," she says, demonstrating how the candy will spill from the jar down a slide. Soon they are riding the train as Dasani munches on a Hershey chocolate bar.

She watches as her mother inspects the jar.

"Candy for life, Mommy. Candy for life."

On the ferry, they step-dance together, slapping their thighs and stomping their sneakers. They get off, and then, one block from home, Dasani runs into the corner store. The bodega boss, Santoine, is so thrilled to see Dasani that he flings his body under the counter's bulletproof divider to give her a hug.

"This one! I missed her too much!" he says, smiling. "What's up? How's life there? You like it?"

"Not really."

"Not really?" Santoine asks.

"It's good," she corrects herself. "It's good."

Chanel grabs a Colt 45 from the fridge, and then shows Santoine the candy dispenser.

"You see she made that? Look, Santoine! She made this on her own," says Chanel. "This is Dasani's first creation."

Chanel helps Dasani fill the candy jar with Skittles, and Santoine tests the dispenser. Then Dasani walks up Laurel Avenue, toward the steps of her duplex, and (hoping to surprise her siblings) rings the buzzer. She gets no farther than the front door.

"Dasani! Dasani! Oh my God, Dasani!"

A stampede of little feet rumbles down the stairs. The children tackle Dasani as three-year-old Lee-Lee runs up in a diaper.

"Oh my God, you look so *fat!*" Dasani squeals, hurling Lee-Lee into the air. "What are they *feeding* you!"

She tickles Lee-Lee, who bursts with laughter.

Dasani wipes her eyes. She feels happier than she can ever recall. Avianna reaches for Dasani's gift. Dasani hugs Avianna hard, then pulls away. They stare at each other.

The children have their own homemade gift for Dasani — a poster with drawings and quotes: "We love how funny you are." "I miss dancing with you and the song 'Never Too Much.'"

By Lee-Lee's name on the poster are the words "Hi sani I love u."

Khaliq writes, "what you doing."

Papa writes, "Best sister."

Near the bottom of the card is Avianna.

"I hope I get in with you."

The first night, they stay up for hours, floating on adrenaline. Everyone is talking and no one seems to listen, except Avianna. She can hear the change in her sister. The first hint had come as soon as Dasani walked in the door, asking Lee-Lee, "What are they feeding you?"

A few months ago, Dasani would have said this another way, without the word "are" and without the "g" at the end of "feeding."

What they feedin' you?

The new phrasing would be fine with Avianna had her sister left it at that. But Dasani is not just talking differently. She is correcting those who talk the old way.

"You don't gotta do that," Avianna says.

"You don't *have* to do that," Dasani replies.

The siblings let this slide at first. It is Dasani's way to boss everyone around. They are excited to have their leader back, regardless of her current fixation on words. But their excitement wanes at mealtime, when Dasani insists on using a fork. She makes a face at Avianna, who likes to eat with her hands. Adding to the insult is Dasani's refusal to do the dishes. The old Dasani did everything. She made the house run.

"She used to pick up after us," Avianna tells me. "Now she only care about herself and that's it."

The new Dasani hews to the rules of another home, where each child must clean up after herself. Her siblings watch as she takes her own plate to the sink, rinses it off, puts it away, and sits back down.

"This is what we do at Hershey," she says.

She wants them to learn what she is learning. "This is how we make our bed," she says. "You gotta wrap the pillow inside the blanket." The lesson continues with cleaning. "You gotta wash the floor on your hands and knees and dry it on your hands and knees." Their clothing is yet another focal point. It sits on the floor in heaps. Dasani shows her siblings how to fold, just like Tabitha showed her. Shirts go in one stack, pants in another. Avianna tries the exercise. "That's not how you fold your clothes!" Dasani quips.

Avianna cannot believe her sister.

"You changed!" she tells Dasani. "You actin' real white."

Most of the time, Avianna absorbs friction. But twelve-year-old Nana is another story. It has never been her style to accept defeat. Even as her vision worsens, she never calls herself "blind." Just a few weeks ago, when the children ran outside to play in the snow, Nana stayed behind. "I don't like the snow when it hits my glasses," she told an ACS caseworker, who had just dropped by. "It's hard to see."

The worker noted that Lee-Lee now sleeps with Nana, who has replaced Dasani as a primary attachment. Nana is competitive by nature and resents Dasani's luck. In school, Nana has become "withdrawn and slow to engage," according to education records. She routinely arrives late. These changes began, according to the report, "when her sister went to another school."

Nana also wants to go to Hershey, but Supreme is insisting on a school for the visually impaired. He keeps promising to look into it.

Late one morning, the sisters gather in the living room as Lee-Lee scrambles onto Dasani's lap. Lee-Lee holds her cup and reaches for Dasani's ear. Nana cannot contain her bitterness. It is one thing for Dasani to escape home. But for her to come back and reclaim Lee-

Lee is too much. Nana mutters something, inaudible to others. Dasani fires back, exaggerating her recent strides at Hershey:

"I'm doing twelfth-grade work!"

Nana goes quiet. She knows that her intelligence is threatening to Dasani.

"So how smart are you now?" Dasani says. "How *you* feel?"

To Avianna, this last question—which omits the verb "do"—sounds like the old Dasani. Her sister is back. She is once again dropping F-bombs, sleeping late, and scarfing Takis Fuego hot chili pepper and lime tortilla chips.

It took no time at all.

Nearly a week has passed since Dasani returned. On April 6, she is getting ready for bed. Then comes a scream.

"Are you dying?" Chanel yells. "Lee-Lee! *Lee-Lee!*"

What happens next feels fast and slow. Dasani is running to another room. Chanel is holding Lee-Lee's stiff body. Blood is seeping from the toddler's mouth. She is covered in urine. She cannot breathe. Supreme is calling 911. Dasani is rushing to fetch a towel. An ambulance is pulling up. Dasani is racing to get inside the ambulance, along with her mother. The doors close.

Lee-Lee has had a seizure.

The toddler is conscious by the time the ambulance pulls into Staten Island University Hospital, but the doctors decide to keep her under observation. Dasani spends the night in Lee-Lee's bed, next to Chanel, who sleeps in a chair. The next morning, Chanel heads to her drug treatment program as Dasani watches Lee-Lee.

Wires protrude from the toddler's skull, reaching a machine that sends squiggly lines across a screen. Lee-Lee munches on a chicken strip, watching the television.

There are voices outside. Lee-Lee turns to listen, her ears permanently perked.

"Turn this Mickey Mouse off!" Lee-Lee says.

"Why?" asks Dasani.

"It's loud."

"So you want me to turn it down?"

"Yeah," says Lee-Lee, looking at the door. "I can't hear Mommy talkin'."

"Mommy's not talkin'," Dasani says.

Chanel is gone. Another day passes, then another night. The doctors think that Lee-Lee may have a seizure disorder, requiring more tests. As Chanel comes and goes, Dasani stays by her sister's side.

She would rather sleep on this chair than return to Laurel Avenue, she tells me. She does not say why, only that the apartment is "boring"—a word Dasani tends to use when she is angry.

She will soon be on the bus back to Hershey, which she calls by another name.

"In three days, I go home," Dasani says.

Dasani's definition of "home" is more fluid than fixed.

At Hershey, she had missed the aroma of Supreme's cooking, the plants Chanel hangs in the bathroom, the scuffling of Turtle in his bin. But now that Dasani is back in Staten Island, other things stand out. Her bedroom door hangs off its hinge. The front door is still broken.

Gone from Supreme is the tenderness of his recent letter. He walks about looking glum, while Chanel is always tired. They fight loudly about money. Every month, they run out of food.

Before Dasani leaves, she choreographs a new dance routine to help her siblings earn some cash. They lug their boom box to the busy train station below the Barclays Center in Brooklyn, following Dasani's moves to the Beyoncé song "Love on Top."

People toss coins and bills into a shopping bag. By night's end, the children have more than $60. Chanel decides that Dasani needs a professional braiding session and new cleats for track. It does not matter that Dasani attends Hershey, where such things are provided for free. All of Chanel's dollars are now vested in her firstborn child.

On April 10, two days before Dasani departs, she and Avianna head out the door. They take the bus, then the ferry, then the train. With enough moving around, a child can belong to the city itself. No neighborhood is off-limits. Dasani can always find an anchor, a familiar Burger King or playground. In Harlem, Dasani's anchor is a hair salon on 125th Street.

This is the same bustling corridor where Chanel had once pushed a stroller carrying Dasani and Avianna. Back then, they held on tight, staring at the crowds. Twelve years later, they walk with a quick, confident step. Dasani wants to get braids in the shape of a Mohawk. There is not enough money for Avianna's hair, but she seems unbothered. Just tagging along feels like a gift, like she is on Dasani's path.

It is almost 3 P.M. when Dasani spots the unmarked entrance of Fatima Hair Braiding, tucked in the basement of a beauty shop. The salon is just a few blocks from an underpass where homeless addicts live. Mayor de Blasio will soon announce that he wants this encampment and seventy-nine others cleared—his latest attempt at quelling the homeless crisis, which has dogged him since he took office.

The sisters scurry down the steps to a windowless room, where the Senegalese owner, Fatima, is braiding the hair of a twelve-year-old Nigerian girl.

Fatima nods at Dasani and Avianna, her fingers still in motion. No one braids like Fatima—certainly no one at the Hershey school. Dasani smiles and takes a seat. She must choose among several shades of synthetic hair, which will be braided into her scalp. The session can take five hours.

The Nigerian girl turns to Avianna.

"What grade you in?"

"Sixth," says Avianna, sounding embarrassed. "I'm so funny, right? To be in the sixth grade when I should be in the seventh, like, you think they should move me up, right?"

"You supposed to be in the seventh," Dasani says. "But you know what happened to you."

Avianna had missed class too many times. She now goes into the mode of performer. She stands on an imaginary toilet, pretending Miss Hester is searching for her.

"She's gone?" Avianna says, feigning relief that the teacher has left.

Dasani giggles. The Nigerian girl is not amused. "That's not something to laugh about," she says.

"But it was funny how I was doin' it," Avianna says. "I know I got left back. That's what is not funny."

Dasani rises to her feet.

"Told your dumbass to go to summer school!" Dasani says, wagging a plastic spoon. "You ain't wanna listen to me!"

"You should have been listenin' in school from the beginning," the Nigerian piles on.

"I was!" says Avianna, explaining that she flunked "because I missed a lot of days."

"No, cuz you failed math class," Dasani says.

"*And* missed a lot of days, right?"

"Yeah, and I tried to convince you to go to summer school," says Dasani. "But you know what? You didn't wanna listen."

"You know where I was at?" Avianna says. "You know where we lived at?!"

The room is silent.

"Harlem! Harlem! Harlem!" yells Avianna, her face flushed. "You dummy! And do you know where that summer school's at? Brooklyn, Brooklyn, Brooklyn! And Mommy says she doesn't want me travelin' six o'clock in the morning every morning . . . raped and cut up into pieces and put into a box. You shut up!"

"You just mad," says Dasani, walking over to her sister. She leans in to Avianna's ear. "They brung up your past and they gonna show you your future. You gonna be fifteen and what?"

Avianna is on the verge of tears.

"But aren't you supposed to be fifteen in ninth grade?" the Nigerian asks unhelpfully.

Avianna will soon turn thirteen, making her among the oldest sixth graders in her crowded Staten Island school. She cannot think of one teacher she likes. She is barely passing and will soon be taking the Regents, a set of statewide standardized tests. She flatly recites the dates: April 14, 15, and 16.

Dasani tries to correct her sister, saying that Avianna will not be taking "a *state* test."

"I'm takin' the state test!" Avianna snaps. "This is not Milton Hershey!"

The return to Hershey is never easy.

Jason tries to soften the landing by making his homiest dish—

lasagna. "Many of them haven't eaten in the last five days and haven't slept in the last five days," he says.

Some of the girls look relieved to be back. Others look numb. Dasani is among those who cry the first few nights, walking around with heavy eyes. Whatever happened at home tends to stay there. "We don't talk about our business," Dasani says.

Then the sadness starts to lift.

"Back at school," Dasani writes in her journal on April 13. "Feel confident."

That morning, she wakes for breakfast, gets dressed, does her chores, and is on her way to class—all by 7:35 A.M.

The same morning, back in Staten Island, her siblings are late to rise. Chanel starts to flat-iron Avianna's hair, which is not the same as salon braids but better than nothing. Nana heads out first, walking in a manner that suggests her shoes are too small. Avianna catches up near the entrance of the school. It is now 10:30 A.M. They have missed free breakfast and their first two classes.

"You go to the store?" Avianna asks.

"Yeah, but I already ate what I got," says Nana, her shoelaces coming undone.

The sisters had marveled over Dasani's new Nike cleats, gifted by Chanel. They now sit untouched in her closet at Hershey. Dasani tells herself she cannot use the cleats because they are the wrong kind. Over the next few weeks, she makes no mention of her siblings in her journal.

She is focused on a new tribe. Her track team consists of 135 girls and boys who meet five times a week to train and compete. The team is divided into six groups: hurdlers, jumpers, throwers, pole vaulters, sprinters, and long-distance runners. Dasani has no doubt where she belongs. Her coaches had immediately noticed her speed, selecting her to train for the 100-meter dash, four-by-100-meter relay, and shot put. She begins recording her times in her journal, writing entries like "For my 100 meter I got 13 flat."

Dasani believes that her speed came from Grandma Joanie, who learned to sprint in Fort Greene's projects. But Joanie never got to train, much less compete. Even Dasani hasn't competed since the Colgate competition two years earlier, when she ran without socks.

Now she has a track suit, a plush bag, and a bright yellow uniform. She is among eight female sprinters.

"So, are you the fastest?" Jason asks her.

She nods.

"Are you really?" he prods with a smile.

"Well, there's one girl that's faster," says Dasani. "But I'm this close." She holds up two fingers pressed together.

Dasani's coaches avoid flattery. They want their sprinters to work hard rather than relying on their natural speed.

Easy victories are the enemy of growth. A child must learn to reach beyond her comfort zone, ignoring immediate urges (to stop running when it hurts) in service of a long-term goal (to become a professional sprinter). This kind of exchange comes with "grit," another buzzword making the rounds at Hershey.

Grit, at its essence, is perseverance. The word itself has persevered through the ages, informing American politics, sports, film, and literature. In the 1977 children's book *Bridge to Terabithia*, the protagonist is Jess Aarons, a farm boy who wants to be the fastest runner in his class: "He had never learned to run properly, but he was long-legged for a ten-year-old, and no one had more grit than he."

In popular culture, grit is understood as innate. Jess was born gritty. But among educators, the word has taken on a new meaning. This largely began in 2013, when Angela Duckworth, a psychology professor at the University of Pennsylvania, gave a TED Talk originally titled "The Key to Success? Grit." It drew more than 22 million views, spurring a movement among education reformers.

Success, according to Duckworth, hinges not solely on talent or IQ but also on "grit," which she defines as the "passion" for a goal combined with the "perseverance" to meet that goal. Absent the passion, perseverance wanes. Absent perseverance, passion is fleeting. When a person possesses both attributes, long-term goals can be met.

People can learn to become "grittier," says Duckworth, who measures this quality with a "Grit Scale." The grittiest people are not discouraged by setbacks or distracted by new ideas. Her most famous subjects include West Point cadets, spelling bee contestants, and powerful CEOs, including Amazon's founder, Jeff Bezos.

Duckworth has also conducted research on a less well known group—the students here at Hershey. For a pilot study on "strategic self-control," she briefly collected data on the study habits of Hershey's high school students. In August 2014, five months before Dasani enrolled, the school invited Duckworth to give a lecture to the staff.

Before Duckworth took the stage, the school's president addressed the crowd, saying, "Mr. Hershey, in my view, was the true founder of the word 'grit,' long before anyone knew what the word meant."

There are some uncanny parallels between Duckworth's research and the early views of Milton Hershey, who in 1924 said, "If a man does not like the work he does, he is not a success; if he loves his work, he does good work and lots of it." Three years later, Milton told the aptly named *Success* magazine: "When you tackle a job, stick to it until you have won the battle."

Milton called this "character building." Duckworth calls it "building grit." She advises choosing one thing and learning it well—precisely what Milton demanded in his original deed of trust. If a student is deemed "incompetent" to "master a trade," reads the trust, this is grounds for expulsion.

But how to teach such mastery? Duckworth gave some pointers. Hershey's houseparents should try to create "optimal conditions," instilling in these children the discipline of "deliberate practice." This is how Olympic athletes and professional musicians hone their skills. Children can do the same. They must set "stretch goals," which are things they cannot yet do. They need instant feedback and constant repetition. When the goal is conquered, a new "stretch goal" is set.

"How much deliberate practice do kids at this school get?" Duckworth asked the crowd.

For the McQuiddys, just getting the girls from breakfast to dinner can feel like a "stretch goal." There are no virtuoso violinists or Olympic skiers in Student Home Sienna. This is not to say that such heights are beyond reach. One of the school's star alumni, Garry Gilliam, is now an offensive tackle for the Seattle Seahawks, another team that Duckworth has studied.

Yet Gilliam came to Hershey when he was seven. Dasani arrived here at thirteen, which turns out to be a pivotal age. In 1994, the federal government began a social experiment known as Moving to Opportunity, gathering research on more than 4,600 families from five major cities—860 of whom were given housing vouchers to leave the projects for lower-poverty neighborhoods. Nearly twenty years later, researchers returned to see how the children of these families had fared.

Those who had moved before age thirteen did better: They were significantly more likely to attend college, earn more money, and avoid becoming single parents. Those who left the projects after age thirteen fared less well. Perhaps the disruption to their former lives was too great, or the influence of their early years had already left its mark.

"The start has a tremendous influence on a boy's later life," Milton Hershey once said.

Dasani brings to Hershey a skill set not measured by the Grit Scale. It is in many ways the opposite of what Duckworth teaches.

On Brooklyn's streets, a high "grit score" comes with managing the unknown, with improvising and shifting, with daring to try new things—absent any practice at all. It does not consider the future. It is moored in the present, where distraction is a tool, not a vice: Dasani's brand of grit keeps her alert, guarding survival. It does not concern itself with things "going well." It requires being so attuned to the moment that nothing can go wrong.

All of this contradicts one of Duckworth's favorite lines: "Grit is living life like it's a marathon, not a sprint."

Dasani wants to run, but in a different kind of way. She says the same three words, writing them down.

I'm a sprinter.

chapter 32

"SPRINT ALL THE way to Destiny!" says the coach.

She is not being poetic. She is pointing to a girl named Destiny, who stands off in the distance.

Dasani stares at Destiny. They are at Palmyra Area High School, about twenty minutes from Hershey. The sun is out and a light breeze rustles the grass. Long-legged girls stretch and jog. Everyone looks taller than Dasani.

She gets into position. This is her first time competing in the 4-by-100 relay, a race involving four team members, a gold baton, and one lap of track. Each runner must sprint 100 meters before passing the baton to the next runner. The team's performance relies on the starting sprinter, chosen for her speed.

Today, the starter is Dasani. She looks at the baton. Whatever happens, she cannot drop it. "I'm so scared," she tells her coach.

"You're okay," says the coach, looking surprised. Dasani rarely shows her feelings. "You're okay."

Nearby, a man in a yellow jacket holds the starter pistol. A voice blares from speakers, summoning the attention of all officials.

"I'm so scared," Dasani says again.

"Shhh," says her coach. "Focus."

The whistle blows. The blank fires. Dasani is off.

"There you go!" the coach yells. "There you—"

She pauses.

"Oh my *God*."

Dasani is flying ahead of the other girls, rounding the bend. She is in the lead.

"Go, Dasani!" yells a teammate.

"Come on, Dasani!" cries another girl.

She makes it to Destiny before all the other runners. Now comes her moment of truth, the transition they have practiced again and again. Dasani must yell the team's code word—"Hoyt!"—signaling to Destiny that the baton is coming. Then Destiny must sprint, looking forward while extending her left arm backward so that Dasani can place the baton between her thumb and index finger. If it falls, they are disqualified.

"*Hoyt!*" Dasani screams as she lunges toward Destiny's outstretched hand. The baton is successfully passed, and Destiny takes off.

As the race continues, Dasani walks to the middle of the field, holding her side in pain.

"If I come in first place, my whole team wins," she says out of breath, smiling wide as ever.

She is winning and wincing, all at once. Running has this effect. It mixes pleasure with pain. Winners cross the finish line looking tortured and ecstatic, not unlike mothers after birth. Dasani is so excited by the prospect of winning that the ache in her side feels almost sweet. It is easy to ignore pain at a competition, with people watching and cheering.

But training is another story. During practice, Dasani makes faces and complains. She loses focus, chatting too much. For the warm-up jog, her coaches move Dasani to the front of the team so she can lead without distraction. But this brings other challenges. She runs too fast, pulling away from the group.

"Slow it down, Dasani!" one coach yells.

Sometimes she quits altogether. Another of her coaches, thirty-one-year-old Fonati Ward, has seen this before—the child for whom track is two different things. On a bad day, it is an obstacle; on a good day, a passage.

"This track was that to me," says Ward, who was seven when she left her home in Trenton to attend the Milton Hershey School, becoming a sprinter and middle distance runner. She now works as a home life administrator at Hershey while also teaching track as one of the team's three Black coaches.

"It hurts!" Dasani says during another drill.

"Everyone's hurting," one of the coaches shouts.

They always say the same things.

Everyone's hurting. Push through the pain.

Coach Ward finds the "grit" craze curious, having been taught these things as a child. She breaks it down for Dasani the way Duckworth might: "When it starts to get uncomfortable, you know you're getting better," says Coach Ward. "When you back off, someone else is pushing through and others are getting better than you are."

There are times when Dasani seems numb to pain. In the middle of a fight, someone could tear out her braids and she wouldn't notice. But on other occasions, she cowers. She hates needles and dreads the doctor's office. Her mother knows this, which is why she told Dasani that piercing her ears would hurt.

Dasani would never choose to be in pain. For most of her life, pain has chosen her. She had no control over when she was fed, how warm she stayed, whether she slept through the night. She woke to toothaches, bellyaches, headaches. Pain came without notice, like Supreme's temper, which brought the belt.

Adults can escape pain with pills. Children find other ways. Dasani's method is to think of something else. She remembers doing this in Fort Greene Park while practicing pull-ups. "I used to black out," she says. She would fix her gaze on something in the distance, putting her thoughts there.

"You can feel your body feeling it but your mind is not thinkin' it," she says. "That's what I do."

Dasani's recent trip home to Staten Island has left its mark.

She seems unfocused, drawing the notice of her track coaches. They had given the team a checklist of exercises to complete over the break. Dasani's list returned blank. She is back to swearing, as if looking for trouble. She finds it on April 22, ten days after returning to Hershey.

That afternoon, on the bus home from track, Dasani leans past a girl to holler out the window. The girl complains that Dasani is yelling in her ear. They begin arguing, calling each other "ho" and "bitch."

Dasani lunges at the girl. She feels arms on her body. Students yank Dasani to the front of the bus where the driver, who has pulled over, is radioing for help. Campus administrators notify Dasani's housefather, Jason, who walks up the hill to where the bus is parked.

"We've got a real problem here," the driver tells Jason. Dasani stands with her arms folded, listening to the driver's account. When she jumps in to correct him, Jason orders her to "be quiet." With that, Dasani walks off.

"You need to come back here!" Jason says.

Everyone watches as Dasani ignores him, storming off to her student home. By the time Jason catches up, she is sitting on the back porch swing, staring at the yard. Jason can see that Dasani is too upset to talk. He was the same way as a teenager. His temper got the best of him.

Jason lets some time pass before trying again.

"You wanna tell me what's going on?" he says.

"You're not gonna believe what I have to say, so . . . ."

"I've never shown you anything but respect the entire time you've been here," he says. "I expect nothing less."

Jason waits for Dasani to talk. He knows that "if she feels like she's been heard, she'll settle down." He wants Dasani to exhaust her side of the story, which means hearing "how she saw it" and "the flavor" and as many "facts as I could get." She needs to "use her words," as her therapist keeps saying.

Jason also wants Dasani to think about her role, and how she could have handled the conflict differently.

"What do you mean?" she asks. "Be fake?"

"Fake" is a word that Dasani uses all the time. Politeness is "fake" if it hides a person's true feelings. Restraint is also "fake," whereas giving someone the middle finger is "real." Dasani will only be real. She is fond of saying, "This is who I am. Love me or hate me."

As Jason listens, he has a revelation.

Dasani loves to blast other people for being "fake." But this time, she is talking about herself. She is arguing that to follow Hershey's rules of conduct is to be "fake."

Jason looks at her.

"Do you know what code-switching is?" he asks.

Everyone at Hershey hears about "code-switching": the ability to switch between one linguistic or behavioral "code" and another. For new students like Dasani, the switch from an urban place to a rural one can feel extreme. They are like "immigrants to a different society," in the words of one Hershey administrator. They are taught a different way of speaking (what Dasani calls "talking white") and a different way of acting (what Dasani calls "being fake").

Among the first code-switchers studied by linguists were Mexican Americans whose mix of languages resulted in "Spanglish." But everyone switches to a degree. Teenagers do it on social media, texting in one language and speaking in another. The same can be said for lawyers or bankers, who may sound different on business calls than on the phone with their children. Or even Miss Hester, Dasani's former Brooklyn teacher, who learned to toggle between "ain't" and "isn't."

"You have a big thing about being fake," Jason tells Dasani. "But I'll tell you right now you're doing things that *you're* even calling fake." He offers an example: "You're one kind of person when you're home, because you know exactly what's gonna set your dad off."

Dasani can see his point. Back at home, she talks to Supreme in a respectful manner. But with her sisters, she is bolder, more provocative. Now she needs to learn to code-switch on "this scale, and in this environment," Jason says. "When you're here you have to be, in a sense, a different person. It doesn't take away from who you are. But it is just a different representation of who you are."

This representation, Jason says, could be described as more "ladylike."

To Dasani, that sounds like code for being white, which would require her to be "two-faced." She wonders how much Jason really knows about switching between white America and Black America.

Dasani's therapist, Julie, seems better suited to address this. She is not just any African American. She is a Black woman working in a predominantly white town. She has been seeing Dasani twice a week, and they have grown close.

"I can't be two different people," Dasani tells Julie. "That's just me and you have to accept me for who I am."

Julie responds in a way that makes sense to Dasani: You remain the same person, with the same feelings and urges. But you are choosing not to act on every urge. "That's not being two-faced," says Julie.

Dasani thinks about this. It sounds more like editing, which she is learning in film class. Some scenes get cut to make the movie better. She can do this with her thoughts, cutting some out so they never reach the audience.

But inside her, they will stay.

Two days after Dasani's argument on the bus, her siblings are nervously watching as an ACS supervisor inspects their Staten Island apartment.

A month has passed since Judge Lim ordered Chanel to take a drug test. She never showed up, hoping the matter would be forgotten. For a while, it seemed to work. The agency's "progress notes" show little progress with either parent.

"When was their last drug test?" the ACS supervisor writes. "What were the results?"

Supreme stands in the living room as the supervisor questions the children, noting that they have no "marks/bruises on their face, hands, etc." She asks to see Papa, but he is sleeping. The supervisor checks his room "to ensure that the child was alive and he appeared to be," she writes, adding, "The family is in need of beds."

ACS has visited the apartment six times in the last month. Chanel is never home. But the caseworker assigned to the family, Marisol Quintero, has found the children in good spirits, with Maya and Hada doing their homework, Avianna sweeping, Lee-Lee playing with toys, Nana watching television, and Papa bragging that he is "behaving much better in school."

Supreme is also in reform mode. He has made a flyer advertising his freelance barber hours, and he has near-perfect attendance at his methadone maintenance program, testing negative for drugs. But his wife is another story.

Chanel comes and goes at odd hours, telling Supreme that she is "downtown," which is code for Brooklyn—specifically, the back entrance of a Burger King on the corner of Fulton and Pearl. This small stretch of pavement is the province of addicts, beggars, boosters, dealers, sex workers, pimps, and other people cycling between jail and the street.

When Supreme hears the word "downtown," he assumes that Chanel is getting high. Her pattern is to deny it. Only later, when she is clean again, will Chanel acknowledge the truth—usually as an act of reflection, worded in the past tense. *Yeah, I was getting high.* Supreme no longer bothers to ask. He simply tells Chanel to "turn yourself in," by entering rehab.

"You're starting off with a clean slate, you know what I mean? A fresh new track. A fresh new piece of paper and everything you do from then on is what they gonna document. So now you can write your own story. . . . Get a job. I get a job. We do what we gotta do. And then we move out of New York like we planned to do."

Sometimes Chanel listens. She enrolled last month in an outpatient opioid-dependency program at Mount Sinai Beth Israel in Manhattan, where she admitted to recent "opiate use," telling the intake counselor that she supported her habit by selling candy. A few weeks later, Lee-Lee had her seizure. The next morning, Chanel left the hospital to attend her drug program. By the following morning, April 8, she had dropped out.

That same day, ACS referred the family to "preventive services," adding a new form of scrutiny. When Chanel thinks about child protection as a trio of characters—first "the investigator" (ACS), then "the judge" (family court)—this is the third: "the provider" of services. Filling this role, on contract with ACS, are sixty-three nonprofit organizations.

Their services trace the human arc of the system, from parenting classes and therapy—for families that are still intact—to foster care and adoption for children who have been removed. Most parents begin services when they still have custody. Like Chanel and Supreme, they start as "prevention" cases, though precisely what is being prevented is open to interpretation. One read is that ACS is preventing the breakup of a family, working with parents to keep their children at home. Another take is that ACS is preventing child abuse or neglect. A third view is that the agency is preventing all of the above, while staving off the public backlash that comes when horror stories make the news.

The vast majority of families complete services, avoiding foster care. (In 2015—the year that Dasani's family began prevention—less than 2 percent of families who completed services had a child removed in the following twelve months.) While New York City's foster care numbers have dropped significantly over the last twenty years, ACS's preventive spending has nearly tripled. The agency's investment in these programs has been touted as a national model.

But if the goal of prevention, per the ACS website, is to "stabilize families at risk of a crisis," the federal government makes this difficult. ACS is currently spending, in 2015, about $532 million on foster care—more than twice what it spends on prevention. Around 44 percent of ACS's budget depends on federal funds, of which the lion's share goes to foster care and adoption services—not prevention.

Put another way: More than a century after President Theodore Roosevelt's landmark conference concluded that America's homes "should not be broken up for reasons of poverty," the federal government is giving ten times as much money to programs that separate families (most of them poor) as to programs that might preserve them.

"Saving Children. Preserving Families . . . Since 1869" reads the letterhead of the New York Foundling, the agency now assigned to preserve Chanel's family.

Foundling traces its roots to the first Gilded Age, when orphans were called "foundlings" because they were found on the streets. Eager to save them were three Roman Catholic nuns who opened Foundling's doors as an orphan asylum on East Twelfth Street. For newborns, they left a wicker cradle at the entrance. Some babies came with handwritten notes.

"Guard this little one," wrote one mother, "and if things turn out as I hope I shall repay you for your trouble."

Over the next 150 years, Foundling followed the path of American child welfare, creating a Catholic offshoot of the orphan train movement and becoming a powerful foster care and adoption agency—while contributing to the racist policies that kept Black children institutionalized. When the *Wilder* case challenged this practice, some damning evidence came to light. A Foundling administrator testified that in the 1960s, the nursery's nuns brought babies of "indeterminate race" to the American Museum of Natural History, where an anthropologist examined their skin tone, skull size, and other features to identify each infant's race. A Black baby was far less likely to be adopted.

Foundling has since evolved into a twenty-first-century operation, promising on its website "that all children, adults, and families can have the opportunity to reach their full potential." Headquartered in a gleaming sixteen-story building near Gramercy Park, Foundling is the second-largest foster care provider in the city, with a $133 million annual budget drawn mostly from government contracts.

To create a service plan for Dasani's family, Foundling collaborates with ACS, which has identified three major goals: substance abuse treatment for both parents, mental health and "emotional stability" for Chanel, and help with "parenting, decision making." Following that guidance, Foundling enrolls the family in a therapy-focused program, pairing them with an African American "prevention worker" named John.

John's own goals for the family are to "increase hope, build alliance, build trust and maintain engagement and motivation." He will do this, he writes, by "meeting the family where they are," through humor, tone of voice, sympathy, and praise.

Prevention workers have cycled in and out of Chanel's life for years. Ideally, they act as a buffer between the family and ACS, building trust with the parents while addressing the agency's concerns. But to Chanel's mind, there is no difference between these two entities—the private agency where John works (Foundling) and the public one where Marisol works (ACS). They both make home visits, asking questions and doing inspections.

Nonetheless, John makes a good impression. He is a tall, soft-spoken man with brown skin like Avianna's, and "pretty white teeth," she says. During "therapeutic visits" to the home, John tries to draw the children out. He listens with a look of kindness as they describe how Papa ran away. They wonder what they could have done differently to prevent this mess.

"I can see how hurt you guys all are," John tells the children. "But I believe under all that pain is that you guys now feel responsible."

As John walks around the family's apartment, he takes note of needed repairs. He can see, he later writes, that "this is a tight-knit family."

"I can't imagine how difficult this entire thing is," he says to Chanel. "Having people come into your home."

Khaliq sweeps and scrubs. He takes out the trash. It happens every time Chanel and Supreme fight. The thirteen-year-old boy is not cleaning so much as walking an impossible line—as the loyal son from Supreme's first marriage, and as the stepson who is now Chanel's "man of the house," long after Khaliq's own mother died on the stairs in front of him.

Sometimes Khaliq dreams of building Chanel a mansion. There would be a grand staircase and a chandelier, like in the movie *Home Alone*. Except his staircase would spiral "around and around," and there would also be an elevator. "If you want to take the elevator, you take the elevator. If you wanna take the stairs, you take the stairs."

His voice has grown deeper. He wears a rhinestone earring and a baseball jacket emblazoned with BROOKLYN, provoking stares on Staten Island. He stares back, steady and hard. But his face still shows the boy inside. His eyes will occasionally brighten, his mouth lifting into a toothy smile.

Khaliq should be in the eighth grade, but he has stayed back a year and is still reading and writing at a fifth-grade level. He is best at math, according to his "individualized education program" assessment. An IEP allows a child to be designated with "special needs," which can bring benefits but also stigma. Until recently, Chanel had refused to have eight-year-old Papa evaluated.

Khaliq's IEP summarizes his disability as "emotional disturbance." As such, he has been sent to a "District 75" school in Staten Island for children with cognitive delays, severe emotional problems, and other challenges.

It is hard to envision the "grit" agenda guiding Khaliq's school, much less assigning him "character scores." According to his IEP, Khaliq gets "very frustrated if work becomes too difficult," may "revert to sleeping," and "doubts his abilities even in situations whereby he seems to be thriving." He would "benefit from learning ways to control his emotions and behaviors when provoked by others."

One afternoon this spring, Khaliq gets upset following an argument with a classmate. When he tries to leave the room, he is stopped by a teacher, "wrestled to the ground," and placed in an ambulance. In the emergency room of Staten Island University Hospital, a physician's assistant diagnoses Khaliq as "worried well." This means he can be discharged, avoiding psychiatric intervention.

Khaliq is handed his discharge papers.

"You have been seen for a grief reaction (grieving)."

This reaction is "a natural response" to "something tragic or sad." Among the examples given are "losing a pet," "getting a divorce," and the loss of "personal property."

If Khaliq feels "sadness," according to the hospital's discharge instructions, he should talk to a "psychiatrist, counselor or support group." He should seek medical attention "immediately" if his "grief reaction" does not "get better as fast as you think it should."

Khaliq leaves by himself, taking the bus home.

Dasani is still on detention following her outburst on the bus. She must stay behind while her housemates go hiking for the weekend. She tells herself it doesn't matter.

"I don't do bugs and I don't do woods. Rocks, dirty water, shorts. Nah."

On Sunday morning, she picks up the phone. Chanel has summoned all the children to join the call, except Baby Lee-Lee, who is sleeping.

"Say hi to Dasani!" Chanel says.

Upon hearing Dasani's name, Lee-Lee's eyes open. She asks for the phone.

"Hi Sani," she says. "Why you leave me?"

Dasani tries to answer.

"But you left," Lee-Lee presses. "You didn't make my cup."

A moment passes.

"I hate you," says Lee-Lee.

Four days later, birthday season begins. Dasani notes this in her journal. She is no longer writing to "you," as if her siblings are reading. Instead, she writes about them in the third person. Today is Avi-anna's birthday. "She'll be 13. Wish I can see her now but tomorrow is the first day of May and it's a student home buddies birthday."

Spring launches Dasani forward. She wins first place at three track events. She tries new things, like canoeing ("never again"), archery ("I shot a red"), a Tuesday spent "reading many books," rock climb-ing, a live performance of West Side Story ("too much singing for me"), a Cub Scout picnic, and homemade ice cream. She works up the courage to ride the Skyrush, Hershey's scariest roller coaster. "I felt like I was gonna die because my feet didn't touch the ground." Track season ends on May 14 with a pizza party that Dasani declares "awesome," using the word her mother mocks.

She is gearing herself up for high school. She has been imagining this moment ever since she can remember. She wants to feel "ac-cepted." She wants to go to homecoming in the perfect dress. She is trying out for a spot on the cheerleading team, which would seal her popularity.

But high school also means another round of changes. Dasani will have to find her way around a new campus, two miles from her current one. And she will be assigned to a new student home specifi-cally for high school girls. She had gotten used to the McQuiddys.

"I don't want to go," she says.

This feeling usually passes, just like the anger she is learning to squeeze into her Play-Doh. She carries two containers in her back-pack. The idea came from Julie, who "motivates me to do things I don't wanna do." When Dasani has the impulse to curse, she is learn-ing to slow down and ask herself, "How much trouble would I get in if I say this?"

She must not only "use her words." She must use the right ones. Or she can stay quiet, reaching into her backpack and pressing her fingers into the Play-Doh. She does not consider this code-switching, because the word "switch" suggests something deceptive. Julie calls it "changing the channel," which feels better to Dasani. It's like TV.

If Dasani could "change the channel" back to Staten Island three days later, she would see police cars pulling up to the family's home. She would see her siblings huddled by the window, ducking in and out of view.

"I own you, bitch!" screams the neighbor downstairs after smashing his son's bicycle through a window. All morning long, the man has been breaking furniture. A wrecked dresser and two flat-screen televisions are now tossed on the front yard. Avianna and her siblings listen for signs that the boys downstairs are safe. "He put all his anger on the kids," says eight-year-old Hada.

Out on the stoop, Chanel smokes a cigarette beneath a tree filled with house sparrows. The birds are trilling loudly. The police are here.

"You know it's over when they start breaking TVs," Chanel says as the officers inspect the wreckage. She glances over at the man's wife, who is talking to a cop.

"And he grabbed you, right?" the officer asks.

"Yeah, we was fightin' and I got cut," replies the wife, holding her injured arm.

"And then he just got on the motorcycle and he left?"

The wife nods, describing the bike as "all black."

"Mommy, it was black and *gold*," says her smallest boy. With that, two officers hop into a car and take off searching for the boy's father.

Dasani's siblings grab a basketball and head out the door. Papa smacks the ball on the ground as they pass a gray-bearded man in a T-shirt that reads I'M NOT DEAD YET. He is smoking a blunt. He smiles at the children with a faraway look. An hour later, they return to the house. The two boys are standing next to their broken televisions.

"Look, Papa, I can climb a tree!" one of the boys says.

"What happened with your father?" asks Papa.

"He threw all the glass at us. And then he punched the TV. Both. You hear that glass? That's what he did."

One of the boys lifts up his leg to show Papa a cut.

"That's how I got this."

"Damn," Papa says, sounding older than usual. He tries to give the boy a look of reassurance, as if to say, "It'll be okay." But as Papa walks away, he shakes his head. Some families have it worse. "I feel bad for him," he tells me.

Soon the broken televisions are gone and the window is boarded up. By the end of May, more than half the siblings' birthdays have passed. Khaliq is now fourteen. Next up is Dasani.

Dasani has never been away on a birthday. Her last party was two years ago, at Sherry's. Everything had come together like magic—the home-cooked food; the barefooted children dancing; the stolen cake from Pathmark.

She still remembers how her siblings circled round as she blew out the candles; how Chanel showed her to cut each slice, saying, *Doesn't have to be perfect.*

At Hershey, the bakery produces about fifty cakes a week. For Dasani's fourteenth birthday, she must choose the flavor, along with a "wish list" of presents. She has never had such choices, so she keeps her list short: She would like vanilla cake, along with a coloring book, pencils, and a bracelet-making kit.

For dinner, she requests Chef Boyardee, which she misses eating from the can. Tabitha orders the closest thing: a vat of tortellini with meat sauce. On May 26, streamers and balloons adorn the dining room as the girls sing on cue. Dasani blows out all fourteen candles, taking a breath between each one.

"All right," Tabitha says. "Do you want a corner piece? Do you want a middle piece?"

"Uh, a corner piece, please," Dasani says. "Thank you."

Tabitha slices the cake as her eleven-year-old son, Tristan, announces four choices of ice cream: moose tracks, cookie dough, coffee bean, and a flavor called Bronx Bombers Sundae. Dasani goes with "the Bronx one," fidgeting in her seat.

She stares at the pile of gifts. She will start with the cards. One is from the President's Office, featuring Mr. Gurt's computer-printed signature. Another card has been signed by ten of the girls, with hearts, smiley faces, and five versions of "I love you."

"Happy B-day Best friend," writes Kali.

The gifts match Dasani's list, with added flair—a deluxe bracelet maker, packs of metallic pencils and SuperTips markers, and a "Techellations" adult coloring book featuring geometric designs and 3-D glasses.

At 7:50 P.M., Chanel calls.

"Guess what?" Dasani tells her mother. "They got me a bracelet maker, like with the yarn and the beads so you can make your own bracelet. . . ." She continues to list the gifts, slowing down at one point as if troubled by a thought.

She is now listening as her mother talks and talks.

Two weeks later, Khaliq's body crashes to the ground. Blood bursts from his nose. His father runs to him. The boy's eyes are closed.

"What's wrong with you?" Supreme yells, holding his son.

Khaliq begins to stir, muttering that he "smoked K2," the synthetic marijuana that Supreme rolls into his cigarettes. Unlike weed, K2 tends not to show up on drug tests, providing a high that escapes the scrutiny of ACS. The drug is also cheaper than marijuana, making it popular on the street.

Khaliq had spotted the discarded blunt on the kitchen floor, next to the stove. He then sneaked into the bathroom to smoke it and passed out. Now Khaliq is shaking.

"He's dying!" Supreme screams.

"No he not," Chanel says. "He just high."

She throws water on Khaliq's face after calling 911. She then lays the boy on her chest and begins to recite the Fatiha, the one Muslim prayer she knows in Arabic. Supreme is yelling at his son, "I'ma fuck you up! I'ma beat the shit out of you! What the fuck you doin' smoking that stuff?"

The paramedics arrive and Chanel climbs into the ambulance, escorting Khaliq to Richmond University Medical Center. This will be the fourth time since January that one of her children has been hospitalized. As Chanel sits in the ER, her eyelids droop. Medical staff, observing her to be "under the influence" and "out of it," report this to ACS.

At around 3 A.M., Chanel goes home, telling Supreme that she will return to the hospital in a few hours. Instead she disappears, leaving Supreme alone with the children and Khaliq alone at the hospital.

Khaliq wakes to what feels like a nightmare. He is covered in a sheet. His eyes dart about the emergency room, which is crowded and airless. A psychotic woman lies on a bed nearby, screaming "Get off of me!" She flails her arms.

By now I have arrived at the hospital, after getting a text from Chanel. Wires connect Khaliq's body to a machine that beeps. He watches the monitor, where three electronic lines skip up and down in different colors. They are tracking "his pulse and his oxygen level and blood pressure," says the medical aide assigned to watch Khaliq. Minors cannot be left alone, so she has been stationed here since 7 A.M.

An ACS worker had also come by, noting Chanel's absence and questioning Khaliq about what happened. He said he had taken "three pulls" of a cigarette rolled with K2, given to him by a friend. When the caseworker pushed for details, Khaliq said that "Durk from Park Hill" had given him the K2. In her notes, the caseworker spelled the name D-E-R-K, seemingly unaware that Khaliq has no such friend (while Lil Durk is one of his favorite rappers).

Khaliq refuses to eat. He tries calling Chanel, but her phone is off. The medical aide stares tenderly at Khaliq.

"I can't resist this," the woman says. "Because this is the mother in me: Every decision you make is gonna affect your mother in one way or another."

Khaliq glances at the woman. She is forty-one years old, with bronze skin and short-cropped hair. She has a soothing voice and gold triangular earrings that sway as she speaks.

"I only have two children. I—I can't imagine having eight," she begins. "And it takes a strong person to be able to do that, and someone with a lot of patience. And you're testing her patience every time you get yourself into trouble. I grew up in the hood, so I'm not like one of these people that's obsolete, you know? Don't really know what's goin' on. I *know* what's goin' on. But you know what? I made my choices. I made my choices. I wasn't gonna turn out like that. You know what I'm sayin'? And I did what I had to do to get where I'm at."

Khaliq's mouth scrunches to the left, which is the face he makes when skeptical.

"This is not a fairy tale," the aide continues. "I did everything backwards."

She had grown up in Staten Island's North Shore, dropping out of college after she got pregnant. She eventually turned her life around by going to a technical school for medical assistants.

"I still—kind of—don't believe I work here," she says, beaming.

Khaliq picks at his tray of food. The crazy lady is back to hollering. Khaliq recognizes her. He is certain. She has the same face, the same paranoid voice—"Let me out!"—as a woman who was admitted to the ER back in January, when Papa was hospitalized.

"Let me *out!*"

Khaliq tries to ignore her. The K2 is still leaving his system and he is irritable.

"You can turn this all around," says the aide. "Cuz you've had a lot of time to lay here and think!"

She grabs Khaliq's sheet to make her next point: Should he get arrested, "it's gonna affect the jobs that you get. . . . It's real! I know you lookin' at me like, 'Oh, this lady.' But it's so real. I—I would not lie to you. I would not lie to you at all."

A few feet away, another patient is now screaming. This man will soon turn violent, bringing police officers to the ER.

"You've got two strikes against you already," the aide continues. "You're a male and you're Black. Are you *kidding me*? Doors ain't just gonna magically open for you. You've gotta make them shits open."

Curtains are now drawn around the crazy woman, who is still wailing.

"It's all about choices," the aide says. "That's what I keep saying. We all have choices."

Khaliq has heard this word—"choices"—many times. It belongs to a familiar rhetoric. The right "choices" would allow Khaliq to "beat the odds" or "break the cycle" in order to "make a difference" so that others may follow in his "footsteps." These things sound good, in the abstract.

But Khaliq is not an abstract thinker. He responds best to concrete facts. He asks the woman for the name of her projects, adding that he is from Stapleton.

"I was too scared to go over there," the woman says.

From behind the curtain, the same voice wails.

"Get me *out*!"

Khaliq rolls his eyes. "Why she didn't take her meds?" he says.

No one can find Chanel. It is now 12:35 P.M., and ACS is at her door. Only Supreme is home, watching Lee-Lee. The other children are in school and Khaliq is still in the hospital.

Supreme looks at the ACS caseworker, Marisol. This time she is armed with information: the nurse's observations that Chanel was "out of it" at the hospital and recent test results showing that Supreme had smoked marijuana.

"This is my first mess up," pleads Supreme, whose medical records bear this out: Over eighteen consecutive months, he has been screened for drugs fifty-three times, always testing negative. He slipped up at a recent barbecue, he now tells Marisol, taking "a few pulls from a joint." He knows "it was wrong" and vows to "not do it again."

This does not seem to concern ACS as much as Chanel's transgressions—namely her refusal to get a drug test or to stay in a methadone program. After weighing the options, ACS workers decide that the children should remain solely with Supreme.

The agency files an emergency motion asking Judge Lim to temporarily exclude Chanel from the home—a repeat of what happened almost four years ago, in 2011, when she was forced to leave the Auburn shelter after being arrested on a drug charge.

Often in ACS cases there is only one parent in the home. But when there are two adults and only one of them presents safety concerns, the agency prefers to remove that person (in this case, Chanel) rather than taking the children out of the home. Excluding one parent is almost always less traumatic than breaking up a family.

If Supreme cooperates with ACS, he can keep his children. Today he must attend an emergency court conference. The agency already has a plan for the children: While Supreme is in court, the family's prevention worker, John, will be waiting for the children after school, "since they know him and they will not panic." A supervisor will then escort them to the ACS office, where Supreme can retrieve them after court.

Supreme tries to reach Chanel, but her phone is dead.

At around 3 P.M., she turns up at the hospital, where Khaliq is still under observation, with me by his side. The entrance is blocked. No one can get inside. In fact, the whole building is on lockdown because of the belligerent man near Khaliq's bed. A curtain is now drawn around that patient, but Khaliq can still hear him.

"They're attacking me!" screams the man. "You're fucking dead, cop. You're fucking dead!" He is accompanied by a woman who yells more obscenities. A crowd gathers. Someone restrains the man, who is white. "I have got heart problems!" he yells at the officers, one of whom is brown-skinned. "You're fuckin' dead, nigger."

Outside, Chanel waits and waits. She sees none of the frantic messages from Supreme.

chapter 33

SUPREME RISES BEFORE the judge.

"Do you understand that your—"

Judge Lim pauses, as if unsure whether to say "wife." No one presumes Chanel and Supreme to be married.

"The child's *mother*," the judge continues, "has basically blown it, all right?"

Supreme does not bother to inform the judge that Chanel is Khaliq's stepmother.

"So, until she is rehabilitated," says Judge Lim, "she is not going to be coming back to the home. All right?"

"I hear you."

Judge Lim explains that he is "releasing" the children to Supreme on the condition that he "enforces" the court's temporary order of protection against Chanel, keeping her "away from the children."

"If you fail to do so and you willfully disobey this order, I can hold you in contempt and I can put you in jail for up to six months," says the judge. "Additionally, the district attorney of Richmond County could also criminally prosecute you—separate and apart from my contempt order—and jail you for violating a family-court judge's order. Do you understand?"

"Yes, sir."

"So, if the child's mother comes knocking at your door, wants to see the children, you keep that door locked. And if she continues to knock on the door, you have the right to call 911 and—I am sorry—but she will be arrested."

Supreme listens in silence. His texts to Chanel have gone unanswered. The court's order, says Lim, "doesn't mean that you can't communicate with the mother. You just have to keep the mother away from the children."

"Do you understand?" the judge asks.

"Yes, Your Honor."

By the time Chanel reads Supreme's texts, it is too late.

"They got my babies," she tells me outside her Staten Island apartment. "They're gonna split 'em up. . . . They're gonna split them all up, man."

When Chanel gets to the courthouse, the conference is over. She spots her attorney, Yost, outside. He rifles through his briefcase, handing her the court order. She has five days to enroll in a drug treatment program and get tested. Chanel hurries to the ACS field office, where her children are being held in a playroom on the fifth floor.

She steps into the elevator, pressing the number five. Her pulse quickens. Five means "power" in the mathematics of the Five Percent. ACS has the power now. The elevator rides up, the doors open.

The children swarm their mother. Papa is quiet. Maya sucks on two fingers. Chanel fusses over them, smoothing their hair, telling Hada to "fix your pants." These are the things that any mother might say. She speaks the next words just as naturally.

"I can't take you all."

The children go quiet. In fact, she can take none of them. They must wait for their father.

A cartoon flashes on the television.

"But I'll talk to you all in a little bit," Chanel says with a brave face. "I'm not leavin'. I'll be in the area." Her voice is so steady, so reassuring that the little ones settle down.

But Avianna knows better. She is old enough to remember the first time that her mother was removed. She walks up to Chanel and leans in. They touch foreheads.

"It's gonna be like how it was," Chanel whispers.

"I know," says Avianna.

It is dark outside.

"This is gonna be the longest night ever in my life," Chanel says.

She has nowhere to go. She would have gone to Joanie's, were her mother still alive, or to Sherry's, had she not lost her home and left for Pittsburgh. Chanel's brothers, Lamont and Shamell, are still in Brooklyn. But for years, they have kept their distance.

She could ride the train all night. Instead, she finds herself walking the streets of Fort Greene. Chanel is broke, a word she rarely uses, though she has heard it spoken by white people. *I'm broke*, they will say, as if announcing a temporary condition. Chanel does not doubt that the gap between an artist's mouth and a $5 latte can feel impossibly wide. Plenty of New Yorkers have had occasion to feel "broke," uttering the word without considering its etymology: To be broke is to be broken.

She is now approaching Auburn Place, where the streetlamps cast a familiar glow. She stops at the shelter's iron gate. This is right where she stood, four years ago, the first time ACS separated Chanel from her family. She had come to the edge of the shelter, knowing her children were inside.

Today, there are no children living here. Since last year, the city has spent over $1 million renovating Auburn, which is now a shelter for adults. Chanel turns away, wandering into the projects. If people think she is in crisis, their doors will close. But if she shows up casually, she is more likely to be offered a couch. For a few nights, Chanel stays with a childhood friend of Joanie's, and then with a guy whose son was taken by ACS.

During the day, Chanel walks the streets. She cannot think. Her mind has lost precision. She keeps texting Supreme, but she gets no answer. Everything is numb, except her bad knee. The pain shoots upward, like an electric shock.

Relief comes in the form of a stolen Citi Bike. In the projects, few people use the celebrated bike-sharing program, which requires a $101 security deposit for a day pass. Today's bike has been "loaned" to Chanel by her late mother's friend.

"I forgot I knew how to ride!" Chanel says.

Now that she is mounted, the pain in her knee is gone.

She coasts down Atlantic Avenue, the wind in her face. As long as she is moving, there is less sadness. Out of nowhere, she sees one of her friends from downtown.

"Come on, Barbara!" hollers Chanel. "Get on the back of the bike!"

From a distance, Barbara could pass for a child. She is tiny and frail, with a high, staccato laugh. She lost her own children to foster care and now, at age fifty-three, is homeless and often high.

"I never rode a bike in my life!" Barbara huffs.

"Just shut the fuck up and get on the bike," Chanel says.

Barbara slowly climbs onto the seat with Chanel and they promptly crash to the ground.

Barbara is, unlike Chanel, a crier. She begins to weep so uncontrollably that people stop and stare.

"Yo, Barbara, get *up*," Chanel grouses.

The last thing Chanel wants is to be alone right now. In this way, Barbara is a balm. She knows how it feels to lose one's children. She also knows that it helps to keep moving. They will do this together.

Their first stop is the Brooklyn Hospital Center, where Dasani was born and where Joanie passed away. Chanel can no longer take the pain in her knee. She is admitted to the emergency room at 9:47 P.M., where a nurse notes that Chanel is accompanied by an "aunt."

"You on your feet a lot?" a resident asks, inspecting Chanel's knee. She has walked it to the bone, wearing out the cartilage. He diagnoses her with "crepitus suprapatellar effusions," and "most likely osteoarthritis." Her knee will have to be replaced, he says. This should land as bad news. But to Chanel, it feels irrelevant. It is like opening a letter after a tornado has flattened her house and reading that she needs a new roof.

The resident gives Chanel a shot of Toradol, an anti-inflammatory pain reliever, and she is discharged. When no one is looking, Chanel swipes two hospital bedsheets. Tonight she and Barbara will sleep outside. They walk to Fort Greene Park. They ache to lie down.

Suddenly, a bed appears.

It does not look like a bed to most people. Technically, it is a sculpture made of two plastic septic tanks forming the shape of an open heart. This is the creation of a Red Hook design studio called Stereotank, which is interested in "the activation of public space through the insertion of participatory objects that engage, entertain and educate the users." The "HeartSeat" had a former life as an "immersive" sound installation that made noise resembling a beating heart.

Luckily, the sculpture is now silent. Chanel wants to sleep.

Each chamber of this reconstructed heart covers a bench. This is described on the website of the Architectural League of New York, which collaborated on the project: "The 'opening' of the heart physically and conceptually embraces the public while providing shelter from the elements."

Chanel claims one half of the HeartSeat, and Barbara the other. They lie there, side by side, in separate chambers of the same heart. They cannot see each other, but they can still talk. Barbara prefers this to sleeping on cardboard. Chanel's eyes close.

It begins to rain.

"Well, come on this side," Chanel calls out to Barbara. "It's cold."

Barbara scurries over to Chanel's side of the HeartSeat. They curl up under a damp hospital sheet. Soon the two homeless mothers are fast asleep.

"I tried calling u guys but it wouldn't pick up," Dasani scribbles in her journal on June 4, 2015.

She is back to addressing her siblings directly, as if they are reading her dispatches. Today is Hada's birthday. She is nine. Then comes Nana, who will turn thirteen.

With summer around the bend, fourteen-year-old Dasani has

made the cheerleading team. Practice will soon begin, along with high school. On the morning of June 12, she jumps out of bed, getting dressed in her favorite blazer and skirt. She pulls her hair back into a white band.

In a few more hours, Dasani will graduate from Hershey's middle school. She tries not to think about all the parents who will come. Even Hershey's cash-strapped families exist within a hierarchy. There are those who can afford the bus ticket to attend graduations. Chanel cannot.

Dasani has yet to hear the news from home—that her mother was ousted by ACS. She just knows not to look for Chanel in the audience. At 1:27 P.M., Dasani crosses the stage, nervously smiling as other mothers cheer, among them Tabitha.

A camera flashes. Dasani reaches for her diploma.

Back in Staten Island, it is well past noon.

Khaliq is cleaning. Just yesterday, an ACS caseworker had picked him up from the hospital, bringing him to the field office. By then, Chanel had said goodbye to the children, who returned home from the ACS building with their father. They huddled in his bedroom, watching a basketball game between the Golden State Warriors and the Cleveland Cavaliers. Supreme waited for the right time to tell them about Chanel. No such time came. Finally he just said it.

"Mom's not allowed in the house no more. If she do, I get arrested."

The children stared at him, as if to say, *And then what?*

"And you all be taken away," Supreme continued, "and split up into different foster homes."

Supreme is not one to mince words. He wants his children to understand the gravity of the situation. There can be no more mistakes, including his own. He must stick with his treatment program. They must behave. The house must be clean at all times. And if Chanel tries to visit, they all know what will happen.

So Khaliq cleans and cleans. It is now almost 2 P.M. The house smells antiseptic. Lee-Lee toddles about, looking lost. Her mother's clothes sit in a pile. The sheets still have her scent.

To Supreme's mind, Chanel carries all the blame. She should

have "turned herself in" and gone to rehab. It's "her fault," he tells me. "And she's not ready to hear that. All this could have been prevented if she did what she was supposed to do."

Chanel sees it in reverse.

She was forced out of her home when Khaliq, Supreme's biological son (not hers), smoked Supreme's K2 blunt (not hers) after Supreme tested positive for marijuana (not her). For all ACS knows, Chanel could be drug-free. They still have no test results for her.

She had been ousted before, but that was after getting arrested on a drug charge. She is starting to wonder if Staten Island answers to a different code than Brooklyn. After all, ACS is as sprawling as the city it serves. Each field office is bound to reflect the character of that particular borough.

"They took my kids," Chanel tells the intake worker at a Staten Island methadone clinic on June 15.

"Welcome to Staten Island," replies the woman. "Welcome to this racist ass island."

Later that afternoon, Chanel stops by the apartment. She plans to grab some of her clothes and give the kids a furtive hug. She cannot fathom that Supreme would deny her this.

She rings the bell, violating the court's restraining order.

"The kids are here!" Supreme calls out from the window. "You can't come upstairs."

"You serious?" Chanel shouts. "You not gonna let me see the kids?"

"Oh, this wasn't ever supposed to happen!" he yells back, dipping out of view. Chanel stares at the window.

Supreme is now dialing 911.

Chanel is stunned. All she can think to say about Supreme are two words: "He's gone." She whispers it, again and again. "He's gone. He's gone."

She formulates a plan: She will regain custody and throw Supreme out of the house, along with "his kids"—Khaliq and Nana.

It is Nana's birthday tomorrow.

"I'm not bringin' her nothin'. Let him do it. Let him do it. Let him *feel* how it feel. That you gotta get the fuck out and hustle. Let him do it."

The next morning, Chanel walks into family court. She carries a document proving that she is now enrolled in a methadone treatment program. She has also taken a urine test, the results of which are pending.

"What about the hair follicle test, though?" asks Judge Lim.

Chanel sits next to her attorney, Yost, who seems at a loss. She leans in and whispers a prompt. He repeats her words out loud: "She'll do it today."

This ventriloquism continues, with Chanel guiding Yost on everything from the ages of her children to the holes in ACS's arguments. It's as if Chanel is representing herself from behind the suit of her white lawyer. Her strategy is to persuade the judge to allow her back home today. If her drug test comes back positive, she will immediately enroll in residential treatment.

Judge Lim is not convinced.

"I would like to get her back into the home, but I can't do it without the results of the hair follicle test and I can't do it without her being completely compliant to treatment and testing negative," says the judge. "That's the bottom line."

Hair tests can detect up to ninety days of drug use, a much longer window than a urine exam (which is also more prone to tampering). In a hair follicle exam, a small sample of hair is taken from close to the person's scalp and tested for metabolites, which are trace remnants of drugs that have been absorbed from the person's bloodstream.

Yet for African Americans, the test presents a serious flaw: what the federal government's researchers and other scientists call a "hair color bias." Black people tend to have more melanin in their hair, which absorbs a higher concentration of metabolites—sometimes just from the atmosphere. This means that a Black person who is drug-free could test positive simply from being in the same room as someone smoking crack.

Right now, Chanel's greatest concern is time. Even if she takes the hair test, her next court date is not until August 11. This means that her children will be without their mother for at least two more months. Yost asks the court to reconsider. Judge Lim balks, citing "the summer" and "vacation schedules."

Upon hearing the word "vacation," Chanel forgets her place. She is not supposed to address the judge directly, but the words come flying out.

"I have a three-year-old baby! I'm on the streets!"

She starts to cry.

Judge Lim asks the clerk to look for an earlier slot on the calendar. Things may be turning in Chanel's favor. Her lawyer seizes the moment, offering more details about Chanel's plight: "She has nowhere to go. Nobody's helpin' her. ACS isn't helpin' her—"

The ACS lawyer jumps in: "And with all due respect, Your Honor, ACS didn't create this situation!"

Chanel kicks the woman's chair, muttering, "You fuckin' fat bitch."

Her temper always flares too soon.

Only later, when she is calm again, will Chanel think of a more measured response to the question of who "created" this "situation"— the situation being too many things to name in a court conference lasting seven minutes and twelve seconds. The situation, according to ACS, is encapsulated in Article 10 of the Family Court Act, which identifies Chanel's children as "neglected" by virtue of her "failure" to "exercise a minimum degree of care" in supplying, among other things, "adequate food, clothing, shelter or education."

But to Chanel, the "situation" only ends with her own failure. Where does it begin? To answer this question takes her back in time, to the South of her ancestors and to the grandfather who fought in World War II before coming to Brooklyn. It takes her to the school he cleaned at night, keeping his war stories quiet. And to the hospital where his children were born, long before it became Auburn shelter. It takes her to Joanie's Brooklyn of the 1960s, throwing rocks at the cops and falling for Sonny Boy. And to the crack dens of the 1980s and to her cousins dying of AIDS, and then to Chanel's own kind of quitting—when she left high school for the Bloods, and for the drugs that make everything go quiet. Who created all of that?

"ACS did not create it," says Judge Lim, responding to the lawyer.

"The mother created it. I directed her on March twenty-seventh to take a hair follicle test. Three months ago. What happened?"

"Judge," Chanel begins.

"Stand up," Yost tells her.

She rises to speak.

"You know something?" says Judge Lim. "It doesn't matter. Three months' hiatus for you to take a hair follicle test. There's really no explanation for it. You created this situation, ma'am. And I regret this. Do you know who I regret this on? On behalf of your children. Because they do need you. But they don't need *you* using drugs. That's the bottom line."

"But Judge, can I say something? I have been in a program for years. I just—"

"I ordered you to take a hair follicle test!"

"Yes."

"You didn't do it," the judge says. "There's no explanation unless you were in a hospital, comatose. I'm sorry. That means that you had something to hide. You should have had nothing to hide. You should have taken the hair follicle test. We wouldn't be here today."

With that, the clerk sets a new court date for mid-July, four weeks from now.

Chanel leaves the courthouse in a daze. She walks to the ACS field office, looking for her caseworker.

If Chanel is an alpha, she has met her match in Marisol Quintero, a forty-five-year-old caseworker with ACS.

Marisol grew up in Queens, where her Colombian immigrant mother constantly reminded the family's six children of "how blessed we were to live in NYC and have the things we did." Marisol takes her privilege seriously, dressing sharply for work, her hair pulled into a sleek ponytail. After getting a master's degree from John Jay College of Criminal Justice, Marisol took a job with ACS's Staten Island field office in 1996.

She can come across as brusque, like the cop who has seen too much. This may be owed to the fact that for more than fifteen years,

Marisol has worked with the Instant Response Team, a specialized unit that rushes to hospitals to investigate serious crimes against children—the kind involving broken limbs, sex abuse, even fatalities.

"The safety of the children we serve is our main goal," Marisol later writes me. "And the outside world doesn't always see it that way."

Today, Chanel wants Marisol to explain why ACS has let Supreme off the hook, given his marijuana use.

"How do they not find him accountable?" Chanel fumes.

Marisol explains that Supreme is in a drug treatment program and has tested positive only for marijuana. "When you were in a program, you know that relapse is a part of recovery," she tells Chanel, who is secretly recording the conversation.

They continue to joust until Marisol changes the subject.

"What happens with Dasani when she finishes school?" the caseworker asks. "Is she staying here for the summer or—"

"I'm not sure where she's gonna be," Chanel snaps.

Chanel has yet to tell Dasani what happened. What would she say? The Hershey handbook encourages parents to "share happy news from home." Chanel is neither "happy" nor "home." She is spending her nights riding the train and the ferry.

"I'm homeless," Chanel tells Marisol, hoping the caseworker will take pity. Chanel has heard that ACS offers emergency financial assistance in situations like this.

"Okay, look. I know this is gonna sound heartless," says Marisol. "But you're an adult. You can figure it out."

Chanel spends her nights on the train.

Sometimes she takes the bus so she can see out the window. The nice drivers let her on without paying. She chooses the longest routes, like the M15, which goes from the southern tip of Manhattan all the way to Harlem, making sixty-six stops. Each mode of transportation fits a different shade of her mood. The train hurtles forward. The bus stops and starts. The ferry floats.

Chanel cannot shake Judge Lim's words.

You had something to hide.

It is true. She has failed, once again, to show up for the hair folli-cle test.

She does not say why, except that the test scares her. Chanel has dreadlocks, which take years to grow, and locked within them, she believes, is her entire drug history. It is in her hair, in her blood, and in her Medicaid files: Over the course of Chanel's life, starting at age twenty-three, she has attended twelve drug treatment programs, three of them residential, testing positive for drugs at least seventeen times—the last of which, per her records, was more than three years ago.

"They don't let me live down my past," she says.

Is it solely her "past," though? She can see that Judge Lim suspects otherwise, as does ACS. And surely, on the streets of downtown Brooklyn, Chanel's addiction is no secret. Why else would she steal so often? How else to pay for drugs? These are the kinds of questions she prefers to leave unanswered.

Perhaps she should just surrender, by entering residential rehab. She should "turn herself in," like Supreme said. Chanel has done this with criminal matters. Since 1997, when Chanel struck a cop in the head with a bottle, she has been arrested eight times on charges including theft, drug possession, harassment, and assault in the third degree. When she fails to appear in court, a warrant is issued.

Other people pay lawyers to get them out of trouble. Chanel has her personhood to offer, hence the phrase "turn your*self* in." She has gone to Rikers twice, serving the time she owes. She leaves feeling "spent" but free.

On June 19, Chanel reports to the detox center of Mount Sinai Beth Israel, on Manhattan's Lower East Side. In a few minutes, she will walk inside and tell the intake counselor, "I am trying to clean my life up from opiates." She will test positive for opioids, cocaine, and cannabis. She knows this is coming.

Chanel lingers by the entrance, wiping her forehead. She looks at her phone, then dials the number for Dasani's student home.

Dasani has just returned from a five-day vacation with the Mc-Quiddys in Virginia, where they toured caverns and went to a water park, coasting down slides in rubber tubes. She has also been hiking and climbing trees. A recent photograph shows Dasani clutching two branches, her sneakers planted on the trunk, her face triumphant.

If Dasani goes to Staten Island, she will spend the summer in a crowded, poorly ventilated, food-scarce apartment. Chanel will not be there to keep Supreme's temper in check. She has already talked to the McQuiddys about this. They agree that Dasani should stay at Hershey, where plenty of students live year-round.

By the time Dasani answers the phone, the plan is set.

Chanel begins with the facts: the ACS trouble, the temporary restraining order, the possibility that Chanel will not be allowed back home.

"I only want you to prepare for the worst. I'm not sayin' that this is what's gonna happen. You know? I'm waiting to go back to court," says Chanel, adding that she is about to enter a drug treatment program. She is just a few feet from the entrance. "So that way I can, you know, get them to see that I'm doin' something inside and then, that way, I can get back faster."

By "back," Chanel means "home," which is the same place Dasani wants to be.

Dasani is now weeping.

"I'm in crisis right now, Dasani," says her mother, who has been homeless for a week. "Come on! You gotta at least understand that and try to work with me. . . . I can't have you upset with me and I'm tryna do something. You know? You gotta understand that I only want what's the best for you."

Chanel's voice cracks.

"There's no reason to come home right now. There's nothing here to do, Dasani."

With that, Dasani unloads. She needs to be back home. She says Hershey is "boring" (the word she uses when angry).

"We don't go anywhere!" Dasani wails, unconvincingly.

"You just *came* from Virginia!" Chanel shouts back. "Don't start getting like those other kids! Cuz you know what you *had* before you got there . . . And this shit is a lot better than what you came from! And I don't know how you could be acting so ungrateful! Now it's pissin' me off. How dare you? You slept in a bed with six and seven fuckin' people and you in your own space and you're actin' so ungrateful."

Chanel's face is flushed.

"It's not fair," Chanel continues. "It's not fair to *me*."

There is silence.

"Dasani? Dasani!"

Her daughter has hung up. A few minutes later, Chanel heads into detox.

Phone calls are rarely private in Dasani's student home. The landline is stationed at the base of the stairs, making it easy to hear another girl's drama.

By the time Dasani hangs up, the whole house is listening.

"Are you okay?" Kali asks.

"I'm good," says Dasani.

Tabitha watches her closely. She knows that Dasani is not "good," but for now she seems okay. "Some kids, they'll get that call and it's a breakdown," she says. Dasani carries on as if little has changed. She does her chores and says grace and brings her dish to the sink. She plays cards. Her face reveals nothing, and neither does her journal.

Its pages are now blank.

Back in Staten Island, Supreme is starting to panic.

You gotta get the fuck out and hustle.

This was Chanel's bitter parting shot. She knows that hustling is her strength, not his. Everything is in her name: the apartment lease, the gas and electric bills for which Chanel gets public assistance, and all of the family's food stamps. Supreme has zero cash right now. There is scant food in the fridge. His phone has been shut off. He does not even know that his wife just entered detox.

In her absence, Supreme has the man he calls "my so-called prevention worker."

John has visited the home seven times, writing in his notes for the Foundling agency that there was "not enough food in the home" and that the front door was broken, so the family "barricades the door with a shopping cart to prevent anyone from entering."

When families of means are in crisis, friends and relatives tend to offer material help. They drop off casseroles or make phone calls to doctors. They see their primary purpose as one of stress reduction, because no family can properly function — much less attend therapy — when the electricity has been cut or the fridge is empty.

Yet when poor families enter the child protection system, the opposite tends to happen. Parents must attend therapy or parenting classes. This approach, writes the scholar Dorothy Roberts, "hides the systemic reasons for poor families' hardships by primarily attributing them to parental deficits and pathologies that require therapeutic remedies rather than social change."

John has no casserole to offer Supreme. Instead, on June 18, the caseworker makes his way to Laurel Avenue with a list of local food pantries and a referral for family counseling. By now, John has interacted with Supreme enough times to know that the man is mercurial. Catch Supreme in the wrong mood and he will curse John out the door. One must tread lightly.

Supreme examines John's list. Most of these food pantries are too far to reach by foot. Supreme has no MetroCard and seven children to haul. He looks at John, whose easy smile hints of privileges that Supreme can scarcely conjure, things like dental care and a college degree. In John's world, a man can feed his children without considering it a victory.

The longer Supreme stares at the list of pantries, the angrier he feels. His impulse is to lash out, but he catches himself. He invites John to come inside. Nearly two months ago, ACS had conducted a "home assessment," finding that two doors were "hanging from the hinges." Mold is now spreading across the ceiling, and a washing machine routinely floods the kitchen floor.

John follows Supreme inside, noting that the apartment is "in need of some repairs." But the most urgent problem is the children's hunger. There are no food stamps, because the welfare office has not transferred the children's public assistance benefits to Supreme. The family is down to one carton of milk, a pack of ramen noodles, a few eggs, some strips of turkey bacon, and a little pancake mix.

Supreme imagines Foundling to be a well-stocked institution, one that can offer groceries in a pinch. The local office does little to contradict this image. Just two blocks away, Foundling's modern five-story building sits on a manicured hilltop overlooking the faded projects. The $14.5 million facility offers a meditation room, basketball courts, and twenty-four bedrooms for pregnant teenagers, young mothers, runaways, and other modern foundlings.

It is never easy for Supreme to ask for help, especially from another man. He would rather go hungry.

"I need some help here," Supreme says.

John can see that Supreme is "upset," he writes in his notes. John is also a father. He can only "imagine," he tells Supreme, what it must be like "to have to worry about how the kids are going to eat."

The caseworker promises to return the next day with two gift cards—a $10 card for Subway and a $10 card for McDonald's. The following afternoon, Supreme waits and waits. He cannot check his phone, which is still off. He has no way of knowing that John has called in sick.

Time crawls slowly, as if mocking Supreme. He concludes that John was bluffing all along. There is no worse offense, in Supreme's view, than for a man not to keep his word.

"John not coming back to the house no more," Supreme tells Khaliq.

Hours later, Khaliq posts a photograph of himself on Instagram holding a small pistol. He is pointing the gun's barrel at the camera. His caption reads, "Fuck with me iii smoke you."

By the next morning, the milk has run out. Supreme rises early, gathering his things.

"I'm gonna rob somebody," he tells Khaliq.

The boy tries to think of an appropriate response.

"I didn't know what to say cuz there was no food. I said, 'Okay,'" Khaliq later tells me. "I said, 'Be safe.'"

Before Supreme walks out, he grabs an unopened package of diapers and some paper towels. A few minutes later, at 7:52 A.M., Supreme enters the Island Food Market on Broad Street holding the diapers and paper towels.

In his mind, Supreme is weighing two choices. He could rob the store, which fills him with shame. Or he could ask the storekeeper to buy his items, which risks rejection. Somehow, these two options combine into one.

"I will kill you if you don't buy these paper towels," Supreme tells the clerk, pointing what looks like a "black firearm," the clerk later tells the police. A clumsy argument follows, captured on the store's security camera. Supreme gives up and flees. Soon he hears sirens. Four police cars come screeching up. The officers jump out.

Supreme knows to stand completely still.

He is a short walk from Bay Street, where Eric Garner died the previous summer, choked by an officer who still has a job. Supreme's survival right now hinges on his ability to manage these cops, to "control them."

"Get against the wall!" an officer yells.

Supreme drops his bags and slowly raises his hands.

They ask if he has a gun. He says no. They search his body and find nothing.

Supreme is handcuffed, shackled, and led to a police car. He takes small, chain-laden steps. He tries not to fall. Supreme has never understood the purpose of shackles. What handcuffed Black man, here on Garner's turf, would try to run from a bunch of white cops with guns? The only point of shackles, it seems, is to make a man feel enslaved.

The car door opens. Supreme knows that his best chance is to lobby the officer at the wheel. It is not too late. The cop controls the car. He could turn south, toward Laurel Avenue, instead of north, toward the precinct. Perhaps the officer has his own children. Tomorrow is Father's Day.

"I got children at home alone, man," Supreme tries. "They home alone. If you lock me up, who's gonna look after my children, man? And this is not over no serious matter. I didn't hurt nobody. I didn't *do* nothing."

The officer pulls up to the 120th Precinct. The handcuffs are so tight that Supreme's wrists begin to chafe. Charged with menacing, harassment, and criminal possession of a weapon (though none was recovered), he will spend the night in jail. He is allowed one phone call. He cannot alert his children because they have no phone. And Chanel's phone has been taken by the detox center.

Supreme pleads with the sergeant, but his words go unanswered. Only his body seems to matter—his hands for fingerprints, his face for the mug shot. He is led to a light-brown cell crowded with four men. Urine pools on the floor. Random names are tagged on the wall. From there, Supreme is moved to another cell downstairs. He lies down on the cold cement, trying to ignore the smear of feces. His hands are still tingling from the cuffs.

The same thoughts keep returning.

I didn't do nothing to be sittin' in no cell. Just a little misunderstanding. A little argument. You know, I gotta control my emotions. But still! I got children to take care of, and certain things is just not right.

The same word comes to his tongue.

None of that would have happened if I had some simple humanity *around me.*

As night falls, the children wait. They are restless with hunger. Avianna has rationed out the last of the waffles. Khaliq has polished off the ramen noodles. His sisters find this selfish. But as the oldest child, Khaliq is in charge. If ACS comes, he reminds the children, they must run to the back bedroom and close the door.

They know how to be invisible.

Lee-Lee starts to cry.

"Just be quiet," Khaliq keeps saying. "Cuz we can't be in the house by ourselves."

By themselves they remain. They watch the front door. Whatever happens next depends on who walks through that door. If the door opens to Supreme, the children will have him back for Father's Day. There is still some pancake mix in the cupboard.

If the door opens to ACS, the family ends.

They listen and wait.

Like this, the seven siblings fall asleep. They do not know that just two miles away, Supreme sits in a jail cell, trying to close his eyes. Or that their mother is another eight miles away, also in a strange room. She tosses and turns with the hot-cold flashes of opioid withdrawal.

Completing this scattered circle, 170 miles west, is Dasani.

She, too, must sleep alone. Her roommate has gone home for the summer.

chapter 34

ASANI SLEEPS UNDER a moonless sky. She could get
lost in the depths of Hershey's nightfall, when the woods
roll into darkness.

Morning brings light, but not clarity. Dasani has no idea that her
stepfather was arrested for trying to hold up a bodega, or that a judge
released him the next morning, dropping the weapon charges and
allowing Supreme to safely reach his children before ACS caught on.
Nor does Dasani know that her mother will leave detox in two more
days, landing back on the street without a home or a phone.

In the dark Dasani remains, just like the theater where she sits in
late June. It is movie night, and the McQuiddys have chosen the new
Pixar animation *Inside Out*. Dasani never expects to like anything.
She'd rather reject a movie outright, lest she wind up looking foolish.
The same thing happens with food. She'll crinkle her nose at any
foreign dish, proclaiming it "disgusting" before she even tries it. This
does not apply to General Tso's chicken or shrimp fried rice, which
Dasani considers as American as fried chicken. Those things she
misses.

Only five months have passed since Dasani left home, but she is
starting to talk about her childhood in a different way. She knows that
she grew up too fast. She wonders why her parents don't follow their

own Five Percent dogma, which prohibits alcohol and drugs. She used to say that Chanel was just "tired" when her eyes closed and her mouth went slack.

But from Hershey, Dasani is starting to acknowledge that her mother was "smoking," which is code for getting high. She is also talking more freely about Supreme's violence. The passage of time has not erased the memory. This is another reason that Dasani shrinks from new movies. They show what she has already seen—and not because she chose to see it.

"I've already seen half the world that I shouldn't have seen," she says.

The movie begins. The film's protagonist is Riley, an eleven-year-old girl whose life has been disrupted when her family moves to a new city. The audience travels into Riley's brain, where her primary emotions—joy, sadness, anger, fear, and disgust—are presented as characters, each one vying for control of Riley. Ultimately she prevails by allowing her emotions to coexist, with the help of two devoted parents and a stable home.

"Really great movie," Dasani writes in her journal. "Still wish to go home."

The wish hovers like a bird, circling over Dasani as she steps into summer. She has never known a summer like this one. Her days unfold at Hershey's camp, which features an Olympic-sized pool and water slides. She will take dance and art classes. She will sample Thai cuisine and Tex-Mex. Every Friday, she will find herself at a pool party, where children splash about, working up an appetite for pizza and ice cream. At Hershey, hunger is occasion for excitement.

In Staten Island, hunger is a thing to outsmart.

There are several ways to do this. The children can linger at the corner store, making hangdog faces at Santoine in exchange for candy or chips. But now that school is over, they will need more than snacks. Two of their daily meals—breakfast and lunch—are offered at school on summer weekdays. The siblings refer to this as "free free," dashing to the nearest school cafeteria to beat the line. That leaves dinner, which, in the best of times, Supreme makes.

But these days, the kitchen is bare.

More than two weeks have passed since Supreme spent the night in jail. ACS appears to be unaware of the arrest. It took four more days for the family's prevention worker, John, to bring the promised gift cards, along with some groceries. When he returned the following week to discuss a therapy referral, Supreme blew up, yelling, "Get the fuck out of my house!" Fearing for his safety, John quit the case.

Now, on July 8, Supreme heads to the crowded welfare office to apply for emergency assistance. He stares at form LDSS-2921, which reduces to a small rectangle all the afflictions his life might contain. "Do any of these apply to you?" asks the form, with a list that includes "victim of domestic violence," "no place to stay," "fire or other disaster," and "pending eviction." Supreme checks the boxes for no job, no food, and no childcare. At the risk of repeating himself, Supreme also chooses "other." Next to this box is a blank line, the length of one inch.

"Single father with 8 children in need of food!" writes Supreme in his most careful script, the words spilling over the allotted inch. These aforementioned children are not new to the system. They have been receiving food stamps since they were born. The problem is that their food stamps are now going to a parent who is absent. The immediate solution, then, seems simple: The welfare agency should issue an emergency food grant—as required by law—until Supreme can get access to food stamps for all the children. Today he brings a court order proving that he has sole custody of them.

Incredibly, his request is denied.

A computer spits out Supreme's verdict on form LDSS-3938, which shows a checkmark next to the box "ineligible," followed by the words "due to program rules." Supreme has broken no rules. If anything, the welfare agency has failed to keep pace. The children's food stamps for this month have already gone to Chanel. Supreme's only option is to track down Chanel (who is missing), make amends (for calling 911 after she violated the court order by coming to the house), and arrange to meet her at a local supermarket to buy food together (while persuading her not to follow him home).

Supreme cannot even call Chanel to begin this obstacle course. Her phone has been stolen.

One could imagine, at this juncture, an ACS caseworker intervening on the children's behalf by explaining the situation to the welfare office and asking for mercy. This does not happen. "I'm not going to the public assistance office," the ACS caseworker, Marisol, had said to Chanel, recounting her recent conversation with Supreme. "I told him, 'I'll write you a letter. You go down to public assistance.' He's not a dummy. He knows how to walk. He knows how to read."

Today Supreme will leave the welfare office empty-handed, with the exception of $131.15 in rental arrears, sent directly to his landlord. He has given up on Foundling and ACS.

When it comes to caseworkers, Chanel is more strategic.

Two weeks have passed since she left detox and reentered the shelter system in eastern Brooklyn. She is trying to do everything right in advance of her next court appearance. She took the hair follicle test and began a new drug treatment program. In early July, she walks into the ACS office in Staten Island, looking for Marisol. "I don't wanna get to the fuckin' courthouse and the bitch has got some tricks up her sleeve," Chanel tells me. "You can't say that I didn't come and see you before."

A receptionist rings for Marisol. Heels click in Chanel's direction. A door swings open. Chanel asks Marisol how she is doing. "I'm-good-how-are-you," replies the caseworker, sounding irritated.

Chanel's true answer to the question "How are you?"—were it posed as an actual question—would include the following facts: She is living in a homeless shelter, in the same neighborhood where her life began, a short walk from Sherry's now shuttered home. Every night, Chanel falls asleep in the worn brick building that used to be Public School 63. Had Chanel chosen to stay with Sherry fifteen years ago, she might have graduated from this high school.

Instead, Chanel became someone she never intended to be, much like this school, which is now a homeless shelter. Some of the guards there used to work at Auburn. They recognized Chanel the night she walked in, as if to say, *You're back?* She is always back, never forward.

"Well," says Marisol, "at least you're not sleeping on the ferry, right?"

Chanel resists the urge to punch the caseworker. Instead, Chanel reminds Marisol of their upcoming court date.

"July seventeenth?" asks Marisol.

Perhaps Marisol is overwhelmed, juggling far too many cases to remember each date. The average ACS caseworker oversees nearly ten families at any one time. This year alone, Marisol will work an estimated 252 hours in overtime, for an agency that will spend more than $29 million just in overtime pay.

But Chanel, too, is overwhelmed. She is hungry, anguished, short on sleep, dehydrated, and living in a shelter so dangerous that she hides a razor in her hair. She is without a phone, a pen, or even a reminder scrawled on her palm, but nothing will erase the court date in her head.

In seven more days, she is sure to be home. In the meantime, she will not see her children on ACS's terms—in a sterile setting with strangers watching over. She thinks such visits undermine the parent, while upsetting the children with each departure.

"It looks bad for you that you don't see them," says the caseworker, adding that she recently gave Supreme some canned goods, rice, and dried milk.

This was not to be mistaken for an ongoing gift but simply "to hold him *over*, right?" Marisol adds. "Because if you starting to show us that you can't take care of these kids, that's how the system works. Understand it, right? That now we're gonna take your kids. We're not gonna do everything so that you can take care of them. You have to fend for *yourself*, right?"

"Right," says Chanel.

Marisol seems satisfied that she has done her part. She went the extra mile of having to "beg" a local food pantry to give groceries to Supreme. At this, Chanel stiffens. She wonders why ACS or Foundling lack "petty cash" for emergencies, to which Marisol replies that "a lot has changed," that budgets have been slashed. But at whose expense? Chanel wonders. She does not even know the figures involved—the fact that the president and CEO of Foundling will earn $572,902 this year alone.

Regardless, Chanel would never hoard her food stamps. No matter how furious she is with Supreme, "I'm a mother no matter what."

In three more days, when her food stamps come, she will go shopping at Western Beef, paying a cab driver to take the groceries to Laurel Avenue.

The children will look for her out the window.

Sometimes they pretend that Chanel is still home.

Hada puts on her mother's clothes and sashays her hips, as if coming "from work."

"Hello guys," she singsongs.

Lee-Lee says it differently: "*Hey* y'all."

Avianna does it even better: "Y'all want a *snack*?"

Chanel never came home empty-handed. She always brought a treat—trail mix, candy, granola bars, cookies. But now she is gone, along with Dasani. The family keeps shrinking.

This might explain Supreme's urge to bring home a stray pit bull. By his lights, the pit is far more tender than its reputation, a misunderstood creature much like himself.

Supreme names his new dog Akeelah, for the movie *Akeelah and the Bee*—about a poor eleven-year-old Black girl who becomes a spelling bee star. The children had seen this movie with Sherry, tending to the fantasy that they, too, could escape. And now Dasani had done it. Who will the family's next Akeelah be? Every time they say the dog's name, Supreme hopes that this question will reignite.

On the street, Akeelah wears a spiked collar, lumbering down the sidewalk in the shadow of her master. Upstairs, she crashes about the apartment like a love bomb, nuzzling Lee-Lee and playing fetch with Khaliq. At night, she scrambles into Chanel's empty bed. (Upon hearing about the new pet, Chanel rolls her eyes, saying, "You can't feed your children but you gonna get a *dog*?")

"Beware," Supreme writes on the front door. "Do Not Enter. 'DOG' Will Bite!"

On the other side of the door, Supreme has doodled an intricate ode to the Wu-Tang Clan in black marker. He has been going to food pantries while trying to look for work, designing a résumé that describes him as "extremely motivated." He wants to set an example for his sons. He still talks of Khaliq's plan to become a Navy SEAL.

This is not to say that Supreme disavows street life. He sees the Marines as a legal kind of gang. They storm into foreign places, murdering in the name of brotherhood. They pose with war loot, brandishing their guns. In a photograph Khaliq will soon post on Instagram, his father is holding two small pistols. Supreme's face looks distant, his eyes inscrutable. A blunt hangs from his closed mouth. In the caption, Khaliq writes "Real G," short for gangsta. Supreme will later say that he was "young in the mind" to let Khaliq take such a picture. But Supreme also finds pride in the image.

"It's like a warrior spirit," Supreme tells me. "Warriors have to fight."

Being a warrior means you are "not a coward" because you would "rather die on your feet than live on your knees." Smoking reefer "makes you 'refer' to the mind." It keeps you "cool," which is not just a social status but a temperature gauge—the antidote to a heated argument, a hot temper, a childhood spent under fire.

It is now July 2015, the midpoint of a summer that feels like no other in Supreme's memory. Two weeks earlier, a white supremacist had gunned down nine Black worshippers at a historic church in Charleston. The country seems ripe for another civil war, with a cohort of white Americans defending their Confederate flags while Black activists mount a movement that has enshrined Eric Garner's name. In Texas public schools, new social studies textbooks have minimized the role of slavery in the Civil War, while a geography book depicts slaves as "workers" who came by way of "immigration" from Africa.

Supreme tells his own children the unsparing narrative, recounting slavery's sociopathic horrors in detail: "To cut a pregnant woman open and stomp on the baby. To tie a person to four different horses and then beat them so the horses will rip the person apart in four different pieces. To bury a person, head deep in dirt, and put molasses on their head and watch the ants eat him alive. Castrations."

Soon Supreme will post a cartoon image of a gun firing into the head of a police officer (shown as a pig). In the caption, he will write what sounds like a call to arms: "rush police stations in every state at the same time awesome." This last word, "awesome," Supreme never used before Dasani came home from Hershey.

In the absence of Chanel and Dasani, the role of mother has passed to Avianna and Nana. They hold a meeting to create a schedule. Khaliq and Maya must attend summer school. The others will follow a strict routine. On Mondays and Wednesdays, they will swim at the local pool. On Tuesdays and Thursdays, they will go to the local library. On Fridays, they will play on the parched front lawn. On Saturdays, they will watch television. On Sundays, they will do their chores, scrubbing the entire house.

Week after week, the children hew to this ritual. Seventeen library books are stacked on the radiator. Their laundry dries over a broken window, near a wall where John's phone number is scribbled in marker. The apartment is so hot that the children open the freezer "and let the cool air hit us," says Nana. They know not to bother Supreme, who is more irritable than ever. If he blows a fuse, Lee-Lee starts to sing a song she learned on the cartoon show *Daniel Tiger's Neighborhood*.

"When you feel so mad that you want to roar, just take a deep breath"—Lee-Lee inhales, her eyes wide—"and count to four!" She exhales with gusto.

Avianna takes over dinner duty, coating the pan with vegetable oil and butter. She has memorized Supreme's moves, adding chopped onions and peppers, followed by salt, adobo, garlic powder, onion powder, and meat if she can find it.

Avianna thinks about Dasani.

Dasani thinks about Avianna.

They can go weeks without talking, but they remain connected. Dasani has started a new journal, filling two pages with the word "Love" and her sister's name. Below that, she writes "Don't let nothing hold you back sister" and "Family is everything" and "May ♥ hold us together forever."

At Hershey, Dasani says that her best friend is "me, myself, and I."

But if anyone is gaining ground, it is Kali, who knows how it feels to leave a sister behind. The first time Kali and two sisters applied to Hershey, no one made it in. Then Kali was accepted, and next fall, after a third try, one of her sisters will enroll.

Over the summer, Kali goes home. She and Dasani stay in touch through Facebook. They will soon be leaving the McQuiddys for high school, where each girl has been assigned to a different student home.

Dasani keeps thinking about the movie *Inside Out*. The character of "Anger" is a red man who literally explodes when his temper strikes. But if he controls that urge, he can be useful, pushing for things like justice.

Lately, when Dasani gets mad, her housefather has only to say, "Those who anger you . . ." and she finishes the sentence: ". . . control you." Or sometimes she just says, "Oh, Mr. McQuiddy," rolling her eyes like a practiced teen.

Even Dasani admits that something has changed. Five months have passed since her last physical altercation. This could be her all-time record.

Chanel gets to the courthouse on time, wearing a clean white shirt. Her last known drug test—a urine toxicology from a week ago—came back clean. No cocaine. No opioids. Not even marijuana. She can already picture her children's faces as she walks in the door.

She climbs the steps, the sun in her face. She stares at all the people in suits. Staten Island, she is reminded, is "about who you know." She spots an Asian man, mistaking him for Judge Lim.

"Hey, Judge Lim!" Chanel yells out. The man smiles awkwardly and keeps walking. Chanel's lawyer has yet to arrive. But just in case, she has summoned another to her side: Goldfein, the same Legal Aid attorney who helped set up the children's trust.

Whenever Chanel is in trouble, she dials his number. This makes Goldfein the recipient (depending on Chanel's mood) of gushing praise, four-letter-word tirades, or mockery of the "white devil" establishment, sometimes in the span of a single phone call.

Today she hopes that Goldfein's mere presence, as a white man in a suit, will send the court a message that she knows "the right people." Together they walk inside, joined by four ACS representatives and Chanel's court-assigned counsel, Yost, who is complaining that the place "smells like a dead dog."

Soon they are standing before the judge. What happens next feels, to Chanel, like it is not really happening. The judge's mouth is moving, but he is not saying that she can go home. He is saying that her hair follicle test shows traces of cocaine and morphine. Marisol says nothing of Chanel's clean urine test, or her efforts to meet and cooperate with ACS.

Instead, Marisol gives the opposite impression. She complains that Chanel's phone has been "out of service" and claims that Chanel has been absent from her new treatment program. Marisol has no records to prove this. Regardless, the judge rules against Chanel going home. She will need to wait until the next court date in August.

Chanel explodes. Curse words stream from her mouth. She kicks a garbage can. A security guard escorts her outside, where she comes undone. She is crying and heaving. A woman walks up, trying to steady her.

"This isn't forever," the woman says.

"No, it is for me! It feels like it to my kids! It mentally damages my fucking kids. It *is* fuckin' forever. When you separate, it is."

Chanel assumes that this woman—who is white—has never lost her kids.

"You ever go on a vacation from your *dog*?" Chanel asks. "And you know how you feel when you fuckin' leave your dog behind?"

"Yeah," the woman concedes.

"Imagine leaving your eight fucking kids."

Words are spilling out faster than Chanel can think. She wants to blow up the building. She feels "like knockin' Marisol's fucking face off." She wants the whole island to go up in smoke—the courts, the police—the whole racist system that brought Garner to his end. Today, the city will agree to pay Garner's family $5.9 million to settle a wrongful death claim. Yet the officer who choked him is still working. These two facts coexist awkwardly at best. To Chanel, they confirm a system conspired to protect whites at the expense of Blacks.

"Like, hey, you choked the motherfucker out, killed him!" she yells from the courthouse steps, to no one in particular. "You don't even consider it a death! But, hey, let's put you back on the payroll?"

An officer can kill a person. An ACS worker can mislead a judge. And they get away with it.

"Now you wanna tell a judge, *She don't got a working phone?* You ain't tell the judge I been coming to your office all week? You ain't tell the judge I been there? Like, if I'm such a fucking drug addict, I'm coming to your office, doing your job. You supposed to be finding me. I'm finding you. Chasing *you* around. Setting up dates with you! You supposed to be doing that shit with me!"

The door swings open to Marisol.

"Marisol, leave me alone!" Chanel tells her. "Cuz I'm ready to wring your neck. Leave me alone—"

"I'm trying to talk to you," the caseworker says.

"Cuz you didn't go and do none of your work, Marisol—"

"Listen, the one thing I'm not gonna have you do—"

"You didn't get no urines!"

Chanel tries to walk away, saying, "They fuckin' lie, man!"

"No! No! No! No!" says Marisol.

A crowd is gathering.

"This bitch ain't sign no release!" Chanel screams.

People are staring.

"She's calling me names!" Marisol says. "Stop calling me names—"

"No, leave me alone!"

The women are in each other's faces.

"Stop calling me names!"

"Stay away from me!"

"Stop calling me names!"

"Back up *off* of me!"

Chanel says this three more times, telling the caseworker to "back up off me." She does this instinctively, knowing her words might be recorded on the cellphone of a bystander. This is, to Chanel, a Black person's only protection.

Yost is nowhere to be found. Goldfein pulls Chanel away.

"She can do whatever," Marisol says. "But the one thing I'm not gonna allow her to do is call me out by name. I would not do that to *her*, so she's gonna do that to *me*. And I get that she's upset. She's supposed to be upset. Those are her kids." (In Marisol's case notes, filed the next day, she will say nothing of her own behavior, writing only that Chanel "proceeded to yell and curse at" her.)

Goldfein is now trying to calm Chanel, having the same conversation they've had before. Yes, the system sucks. No, they cannot ignore its power. "We gotta take this plan one day at a time," he says. "Do I need to give you my number again?"

Chanel angrily recites his number out loud. Her memory never ceases to amaze Goldfein, who smiles.

"There's this new kids' movie, *Inside Out* . . ." he begins.

She cannot hear him. She is fixated on Marisol, calling her a "stink ass."

"She's doing a bad job, all right?" says Goldfein.

"But nobody sees that!"

"But what's more important? Solving this? Or—"

"Whoopin' her *ass*," Chanel seethes.

"Okay," says Goldfein. "Can we make that number two?"

Chanel looks at him. Just the thought of this skinny man trying to whoop anyone's ass is enough to make her grin.

"Okay?" says Goldfein. "So let's make that number two. And as soon as we've resolved this, we'll start on that."

"Thank you for coming, Josh."

"You gotta help me," he says. "You gotta help me help you, all right?"

Dasani's mind wanders to her siblings. She shoos the thoughts away, like mosquitoes at dusk.

But the memories keep returning, of Avianna's hearty laugh and Lee-Lee's squishy face. Not calling might hurt more than just picking up the phone. Finally, on August 1, Dasani dials the number. She hears a voice she cannot place.

"Who is this?" she asks.

"*Khaliq*, dum-dum."

"Why you sound like a grown man, Khaliq?"

"I don't know."

Dasani makes a face.

"Just remember, Khaliq, I'm always older than you."

"No, you're not. You're not older than me."

"You're older than me by like five days," Dasani says. "But I'm always quicker than you."

The phone passes from child to child, as Dasani asks for each by name. Nana comments that Dasani "sounds white." Finally she gets to Papa.

"Why did you pick me last?" he says.

Just the sound of Papa's voice melts Dasani. She tells him, in her sweetest tone, that she saw a photograph of his new haircut. He wants to know when they will see her. She stumbles to answer as the phone passes to another small hand.

"Hi, Dasani," says Lee-Lee, sounding like a different child. She never used to say Dasani's full name. It was always "Sani." This is a sign either that Lee-Lee has matured, or that their bond has weakened.

"Do you miss me?" Dasani asks.

"Yeah."

"How old are you now?"

When Dasani hangs up, she is quiet.

She is leaving the McQuiddys for a new student home. When confronted with the unknown, it helps to reach for the familiar. Ideally, a call home would have anchored Dasani, reminding her of where she belongs.

Instead, she feels disconnected.

The sun is setting as Dasani approaches the entrance of Student Home Morgan, her new home. She lugs three bags, walking with a heavy step.

Her guard is up, her face empty of emotion.

"If you show your feelings, it's like you're showing you're weak," she says. "I don't show my feelings to nobody."

Most houseparents need training to manage a child like Dasani. They read manuals, attend conferences, and watch PowerPoints by experts in "early childhood adversity."

Jonathan and Melissa Akers draw from a deeper well of knowledge. They were born poor, in New York City's projects. They would have qualified to attend Hershey as children, had they known about it. They are, like Hershey's alumni, what they call "graduates of poverty."

There is no part of Dasani's New York that is unfamiliar to Jonathan. He has the same scattered roots, from Staten Island's North

Shore to the Spanish Harlem of his in-laws. But at his core, Jonathan is—like Dasani—Brooklyn-made.

Jonathan came of age in Grandma Joanie's time, back when the milkman visited and gangs like the Roman Lords wandered Brooklyn's projects. He and his five siblings grew up in Canarsie (the same public housing complex where Joanie and Chanel had slept on Margo's floor). Jonathan's father earned a living as a truck driver, but he liked to gamble, and got hooked on cocaine. His wife took refuge in her Catholic faith, enrolling Jonathan in a parochial school.

"My mother would try to keep it together, and my father was trying to pull it apart," says Jonathan, whose mother was bipolar.

Jonathan became "the glue" of the family. He remembers, at age eight, waking early every morning to make his parents coffee, even though he hated the smell. He would then scrub and wax the floors, trying to create perfect order. "I always wanted to please them."

At age ten, Jonathan took his first trip out of the city with the Fresh Air Fund. He remembers staying with a white family, somewhere peaceful, and that they took him to the Smithsonian Institution in Washington, D.C. His luck continued back in New York, where a Jewish couple sponsored him as a yo-yo competitor, driving him all over the city to tournaments.

After graduating from high school, Jonathan found another way out of Brooklyn, joining the Army and fighting in Vietnam. He came home with three shrapnel wounds and returned to the projects to live with his mother, who had split from his father. Jonathan took a job at a temp agency, where he laid eyes on a stunning Puerto Rican woman, Melissa. They were both working as recruiters.

Though Melissa was sixteen years younger, she and Jonathan had a world in common. They had both been raised Catholic. They were both living with their single mothers, amid the wreckage of alcoholism.

"I just remember, at a very young age, thinking there's gotta be more than this," Melissa said. "There just has to be more than this."

Jonathan took Melissa to see *Me and My Girl* and she took him to see *Cats*. They dined at the Marriott Marquis in Times Square and rode a horse-drawn carriage through Central Park.

Soon they married, leaving their two mothers behind—and eventually the city itself. They wanted a quiet life for their baby girl, whom they named Jamae (which stands for Jonathan Akers, Melissa Akers, "and an *e* for extra love"). By April 1999, they were living in a small town near Hershey, where the Akerses saw a full-page newspaper ad seeking houseparents for the Milton Hershey School.

Each couple brings its own lens to Hershey. The McQuiddys knew middle-class America but were strangers to urban poverty. The Akerses were survivors of urban poverty but knew nothing of its rural cousin. No sooner were they hired than the learning began.

To Jonathan, some of Hershey's students seemed spoiled. They needed to be taught the most basic chores. "I'm from Brooklyn!" he says. "I've been doing this ever since I was, like, eight. Ironing my own clothes, cooking my own meals."

More than sixteen years later, the Akerses hold iconic status at Hershey. Many recruits have trained under them—including the McQuiddys, who consider Jonathan and Melissa their role models. They bring a personal flourish to the job, with their own catchy slogans. They follow the three F's: "Firm, Fair, and Fun, in that order." Sundays are "Soul Sundays," with fried chicken and fireside chats. They are fond of saying, "If you don't like the results you're *getting*, then check out what you're *giving!*"

Melissa is "Mama Akers" and Jonathan is "Mister." Each of their girls has a nickname, like "Bumblebee" and "Petunia." Collectively, these girls are "the Morgan Mamas."

As Dasani approaches the front door, she sees a dry-erase board outside.

"Welcome to the home of the Morgan Mamas!"

Below it are thirteen names, written in curly letters.

Dasani locates her name.

"I'm a *daughter* of Morgan Mama," she says skeptically.

She rings the doorbell.

chapter 35

THE DOOR SWINGS open to Jonathan Akers.

Dasani smiles and he smiles back.

Now sixty-three, Jonathan has a trim gray mustache, a military crew cut, and soft brown eyes that crease at the corners. He is wearing his usual preppy attire—a striped polo and pleated trousers. Golf he picked up here, whereas bowling he learned in Brooklyn. The two places share space inside him. He will quote Nietzsche in one breath and say "the hood" in the next. This is less a matter of code-switching than of coexistence. To the Black people who think he is "acting white"—and to the white people who think he is "too urban"—Jonathan gives the same unapologetic message: "This is who I am."

Dasani warms to him right away, calling him Mister. She likes his calm aura. Mr. Akers's wife, by contrast, is a chatty, gushing Latina who doles out kisses and sugary words like "honey" and "sweetie pie."

Dasani watches how Mrs. Akers charms the room with her floating laugh, how she moves her hands as if tracing imaginary fireworks. She is a forty-seven-year-old beauty, with long tresses of shiny brown hair that she flips with a French-manicured hand. Today she is wearing a cream silk blouse, pressed denims, and white platform sandals.

Dasani has never lived with a "girly girl," as Melissa is prone to describe herself. In some ways, this New York housemother is more foreign to Dasani than her Pennsylvania Dutch predecessor, Tabitha, who rarely wore makeup. And there is no comparing Mrs. Akers to Chanel, who would rather go fishing than paint her nails or shave her legs. But Dasani misses her mother, so she welcomes the distraction of Mrs. Akers's dazzle.

"Hi, sweetie pie!" the housemother sings to Dasani. "Are you ready? All right? It's happening now! *Senior division!*"

For Dasani, the words "senior division" are as thrilling as candy. Hershey's high school students can walk to campus by themselves. Their good behavior is rewarded with up to $20,000 per year in college savings. The most unusual perk comes at the end of junior year, when students move to "transitional living." They live in homes free of houseparents (though an adult is on the premises) and are given a budget to follow and a bank account to balance, buying groceries, cooking for themselves, even sharing a car.

Mrs. Akers shows Dasani to her bedroom, which faces a cornfield. "That's a bougie look!" Dasani blurts out as Mrs. Akers smiles, opening the large closet where Dasani will hang her clothes. Her new roommate has already unpacked and stepped out, so Dasani gets to work, now confident in her organizational skills.

An hour later, Dasani takes a seat in the living room, joining her new housemates for their first meeting.

"How many of you know the reason why you're here?" asks Mr. Akers, standing next to his wife.

The girls are silent.

"You're gonna have some days—whether you've been here for a while or whether you're new—that you're gonna want to give up and say 'This ain't worth it.'"

Mr. Akers hands out blank index cards.

"And that's when you pull out your 'why' card," he says.

He got the idea from *Man's Search for Meaning*, the 1946 memoir by Viktor Frankl, a Holocaust survivor. "And in the book," Mr. Akers tells the girls, "it talked about how you can watch your whole family die and still have a reason for living."

This quiets the room.

"If you have a big enough *why*, then you can endure almost any *how*," says Mr. Akers, enunciating the key words of this classic quote.

Each girl must write the word "why" on her card.

Dasani writes, in all caps, WHY.

On the other side of her card, she must explain her "why"—her reason for being at Hershey. That way, on the "rough days," Mr. Akers says, she can reach for her "why" card and be reminded.

To endure almost any how.

This Dasani has always done. She is a doer. She knows her "hows" better than her "whys." Her parents taught her to decode the meaning of every word. The word "how" starts with the letter that has defined her path: homelessness, the hood, Hershey, and now high school. She has surpassed her own mother, who dropped out in the ninth grade.

Dasani's "why" spills from her pen.

"To get a good education. To make a difference in my family."

Chanel is the newcomer at 116 Williams Avenue, a "single women's shelter." They are not single so much as severed—from the children they have lost, many to foster care, and from the men they have lost, many to prison. One is the mother of a Rikers inmate who hanged himself. Another is a prostitute with a glass eye.

There is no air-conditioning and it is well over 90 degrees. Chanel complains to the guards, who are indifferent. She goes to bed naked. Still she cannot sleep. The next evening, she puts on her slippers and wraps a sheet around her nude body. Like this, Chanel walks into the lobby and stands there.

"Miss, you can't come down here like that!" snaps a guard, looking away. But technically, Chanel is clothed. She knows the rules well enough to push their limits. If the shelter is so hot that a woman must sleep naked, then here she will stand, shifting from foot to foot. Her words do not matter, but her body is hard to miss. She loves her sheer heft, how it crowds the sidewalk, how it gets in the way. She strolls to the recreation room, her curves undulating beneath the sheet.

The next day, a portable air conditioner appears in her room. This does nothing to lift Chanel's funk. She spends hours obsessing about ACS. She burns with hatred for her caseworker.

At least you're not sleeping on the ferry, right?

Marisol was not taunting Chanel so much as describing her. This is how she is seen by the professional class. She is the woman who sleeps on the ferry, with no clear origin or destination. She is someone to ignore, so the people look away, taking refuge in their phones and books.

Chanel wants Marisol removed from the case. But the women at the shelter tell her not to bother, for targeting a caseworker is a waste of time. You "can't play with these people," says the glass-eyed woman. If Chanel wants to go home, she must do what ACS demands. She must attend her children's "visitation," an exercise as institutional as it sounds.

"I think it creates unhealthy feelings, this 'visitation,'" Chanel tells me. "It riles them up and I don't want to do that. Right now, they're good. I can talk to them. They're peaceful because they haven't seen me. But then, if they see me, they start to feel things. And then Papa will start acting up and I don't wanna see Lee-Lee crying and I don't wanna feel all those things either."

She wants to feel nothing. She will numbly attend her meetings with ACS, blaming everyone but herself. She is beyond reproach, until she becomes depressed, at which point she swings in the opposite direction. She calls herself a "bum," a "loser," a "fool."

"What am I worth that I can't even keep my kids?"

She heads to her methadone program at Staten Island University Hospital, a commute that takes half the day. The bus dips under the Mason-Dixon Line. Chanel gets off in Dongan Hills, which borders the exclusive neighborhood of Todt Hill.

This is the highest point in all five boroughs, rising 404 feet skyward—the domain of a country club, a prep school, and the plush home of Chanel's court-assigned lawyer, Yost. With no sidewalks or streetlamps, Todt Hill is off-limits to pedestrians like Chanel. In the hill's shadow, she walks to her clinic, spotting colonial homes "built like plantation houses." She is always looking for America's past in its present.

At the next court conference, on August 11, ACS is busy with another matter, so the case is adjourned.

Chanel has given up. "You go to *hear* what they gotta say. That's why they call it a *hearing*." She stops attending her treatment program or returning anyone's calls. She has no appetite, causing her pants to sag from a shrunken waist. She talks of killing herself.

On August 29, the police come to the shelter. A woman has plunged to her death on the subway tracks of the nearby Broadway Junction station. They think Chanel may be the victim because her meal ticket was found among the woman's remains.

The police search Chanel's locker. Another resident offers to identify the victim's body, leaving with the police. When she returns, she announces that the victim was another woman who had just transferred to the shelter.

When Chanel walks in late that evening, the glass-eyed woman looks at her, saying, "We thought you was dead."

Dasani's desk is the portrait of order. Her alarm is set for 5:30 A.M. next to a container of sharpened pencils beneath her framed middle school diploma. A corkboard holds photographs of her family and two calendars—one for cheerleading and one for school. She is taking nine classes this semester, including exploratory electronic media, environmental science, and American cultures.

She marks each passing day with two pen strokes, scribbling her latest goals into the margins. First, she wants to exit "striving," the lowest conduct rank given to students. By early September, she is promoted to "achieving," earning the privilege of a later bedtime. She jots down her next goal: to make it to "excelling."

On the morning of September 29, she rises dutifully for breakfast, taking her seat next to Mr. Akers, whose coffee mug reads FAILURE IS NOT AN OPTION. Dasani recites the Lord's Prayer along with eleven other sleepy girls. They eat quietly as Mr. Akers reaches for his clipboard, peering at the day's schedule. Soccer. Marching band. Tutoring. Field hockey. Cheerleading.

Dasani has always been more a naysayer than a cheerleader, a provoker of discord rather than a promoter of "school spirit" and "a positive winning attitude," as outlined by the team's manual, which she has studied word for word.

The Spartan Cheerleaders are asked to maintain a feminine appearance at games. Dasani hates skirts and refers to her girlfriends as "sons." But ever since training began, she has thrown herself into it (ignoring her mother, who claims that cheerleading "is not a sport"). Dasani thrills at the acrobatics and can recite all the team rules: no gum, no tattoos, no piercings, no nail color, and "bows MUST be in, this is considered part of your uniform."

A cheerleader remains a cheerleader even off the field. She is expected to show "personal exemplary conduct" at all times. Dasani loves the sisterhood, the way they move together, chanting things like "Victory is sweet!" She relishes her chocolate-brown and gold uniform, with its matching pom-poms and bows.

Breakfast is over. It is now time for the "daily devotional." The blond girl known as Bumblebee reads Proverbs 12:18:

> The words of the reckless pierce like swords
> But the tongue of the wise brings healing.

Bumblebee pauses. Mr. Akers looks around.

"What did you girls get from it?"

Dasani speaks up.

"That the words we say should be used for healing and not to, um, put people down," she says softly.

"How about you, Ashley?"

Ashley is Dasani's new roommate. A white fourteen-year-old native of Royersford, a factory town northwest of Philadelphia, she had come to Hershey in the fifth grade. Now an honor roll student, she sings in the choir, plays field hockey, and runs track. When Ashley talks about home, she brings a hopeful spin: Her single mother is dating a doctor who promises to move them to a "big" house and "be settled." The plan has yet to materialize.

Like Dasani, Ashley keeps a neat desk and tracks her goals, pinning up notes like "Try to stay with it" and "The kindest hearts have felt the most pain."

Ashley thinks there is more to Dasani than she reveals.

"She says she does not believe in God but I think she does," Ashley tells me.

Three nights ago, they had primped for homecoming, applying bright shades of lipstick and mugging for the camera. Dasani wore a pink crepe gown, selected from hundreds of donated dresses in the school's "Cinderella Closet." The dress is now Dasani's, hanging in her room near the khakis she must iron for school.

It is nearly 7 A.M. when Dasani begins this task. Mr. Akers walks up and takes the iron, demonstrating the proper method. He sprays some steam to sharpen her pleat, proudly jutting out his chin.

"You really make it look all *professional*," Dasani teases.

"Look at the difference!" he says. "If you gonna do it, do it *right!*"

There is no denying that Dasani and Mr. Akers have a bond. When Dasani tells him that she wants to go home for Columbus Day weekend, he replies that the charter buses are full and the deadline has passed.

Still, like any New Yorker, he wants to know exactly where she lives.

"Staten Island," she says vaguely. "But we *not* in the projects."

Mr. Akers presses for details.

"Park Hill," she says, naming a different North Shore neighborhood.

"Oh, yeah? I used to hang out there," says Mr. Akers.

"Really?" says Dasani.

"Yep," he says. "And by the way? That's the projects."

Paint peels from the ceiling and walls. Rain drips from the roof. Supreme thinks through his options.

He never signed a lease. The apartment was rented to his wife, Chanel, who is gone. The rent is mostly paid by a Section 8 voucher—which is also in Chanel's name. Supreme has no idea how to reach the property manager, Natalya Trejos (whose LinkedIn profile lists, among her tasks, "coordinating evictions with local Marshal's office"), nor does Supreme have a phone number for the building's landlord, whose identity remains a mystery to him.

On Chanel's lease, the landlord is listed as "GRI 89 Laurel LLC." One of the company's founders is Alexander Gorokhovskiy, a Wall Street banker in his thirties who will soon build a $1 billion–plus portfolio of private credit assets, making him a "rising star in the world of private debt," according to an industry publication. Gorokhovskiy bought 91 Laurel (the property where Dasani's family is now living) in 2013 for $351,500—a market value that would rise by 70 percent over five years. He then transferred it to the LLC, for which he and Steven Rudgayzer, a corporate lawyer, are listed on Chanel's lease as "agents," along with two other people. Chanel would come to regard them as her "landlords."

A few weeks before the family moved in last October, city housing inspectors had cited the LLC for failing to install carbon monoxide detectors, as required by law, while allowing infestations of "roaches in the entire apartment." The landlords promptly fixed these problems. But now—nine months later, in July 2015—the family's unit has a moldy ceiling, a leaky roof, a busted door, and broken smoke detectors. Supreme is at a loss for what to do.

Both ACS and Foundling are aware of the apartment's condition, but their workers have transferred off the case—John because he quit the case, Marisol for standard reasons. Her job was to conduct the initial investigation, which normally ends after sixty days, when ACS makes a finding. In this case, neglect has been "indicated," which means that Dasani's family will move to a different caseworker.

"NO FOOD," writes Supreme's new Foundling worker on July 24.

It is becoming clear that ACS made an error: Dasani's family is in the wrong preventive program. Therapy is a mismatch. What they desperately need, the Foundling worker tells an ACS supervisor, is material help. The family cannot benefit from therapy without their "concrete needs met," the caseworker says—things like "daycare, food supply and food stamps, early intervention, household needs and more." On August 10, ACS agrees to transfer the family to a "general preventive program."

Seven days later, the same Foundling worker visits the home, noting that the children are "sleeping on broken mattresses" but "doing well despite all of the chaos. . . . Everyone is trying to hold it to-gether." A new ACS worker also comes, dropping off smoke detectors and groceries while promising to order new beds. Supreme tells her that he does not know how to contact the landlord. She advises him to call 311, the city helpline.

The events that follow will replay in Supreme's mind for years to come. He will memorize this sequence, as if watching a video on re-peat. He will slow it down, frame by frame, examining each moment in isolation. Were he to scramble these events into some different order, removing one or two crucial details, would the outcome have shifted?

The sequence begins on August 29, 2015, at the height of a swel-tering summer. It is Supreme's thirty-eighth birthday. He turns on the stove. There is no gas. He reaches for the faucet, feeling only cold water. This means that the children cannot bathe, and without gas, Supreme cannot cook. He tries using an old hot plate, but it takes two hours to boil water just to make spaghetti. The gas bill remains in Chanel's name, along with the family's welfare case—nearly two months after Supreme tried to rectify the error.

The children improvise. In order to bathe, they must fill the tub with cold water and then add some boiling water. Only two children can wash at a time before the water gets dirty. Supreme alerts ACS by text. A week later, the gas is still off. "He feels helpless," writes his Foundling worker. Still in the role of therapist, she uses "strength based statements to build hope."

For the next month, the children stay clean on rotation, each one bathing every three days. This hygiene holdup has the misfortune of colliding with the start of school, when guidance counselors will be watching for signs of neglect.

The children miss their first three days of school while Supreme scrambles to fix his mounting problems, which now include the bathroom sink. It has detached from a rusted pipe in the wall, crash-ing down by the toilet. The family's mattresses have also come apart, and mold is spreading on the ceiling, where a heavy leak persists.

On September 12, ACS caseworkers come with gift cards to buy the children clothes. But the home is still falling apart and the food stamps never came, despite fourteen weeks of pleading with the welfare office.

Supreme dials 311 and files seven complaints with the city's Housing and Preservation Department. He reports the collapsed sink, the presence of mold, the lack of a functioning carbon monoxide detector, the roof leak, and the broken window guard.

The next day, on September 14, Supreme returns to the welfare office to press his case, citing an "urgent" personal problem. This time, Supreme brings a letter from a Foundling supervisor stating that he has sole custody of the children and "requesting that you assist" by switching the children's benefits to his name. "Children are in need of food and other concrete needs," writes the supervisor below letterhead that reads THE NEW YORK FOUNDLING — ABANDON NO ONE. Again, the welfare agency refuses to assist him — a decision that Supreme goes to the trouble of appealing at the state level.

The following afternoon, on September 15, Avianna texts her mother from Supreme's phone: "mommy its me" and "can you come over and do our hair because school is tomorrow."

There is no reply. Again Avianna writes: "can you come over right now to do our hair because school . . . is tomorrow and we need our hair done."

Still no reply.

Four hours and thirty-eight minutes later Avianna sends a third text: "we can't go to school with some raggedy hairstyle like two ponytails we need a real hairstyle," followed by "mommy can you at least give daddy some money to do our hair," followed by a missive from Supreme himself: "For 3 days I've been trying to get you to come over here . . . your babies they desperately need you."

Chanel is in jail. She has fallen back into a life of hustling and was caught stealing $119.99 worth of merchandise from T.J. Maxx, which she planned to boost for cash. She sees the texts only after she is released. Worried that Supreme will not believe her, Chanel sends him a picture of her jail release form.

"I love u," she writes to her estranged husband. "I wish I had everything u ask for when u need it what man is going to take care of 8 children I love you for being the man the Maker the owner of the kids and me don't ever forget that I love you peace just getting a bed."

The children go to school trying to look their best—except for Papa, who has been transferred to a school for behaviorally challenged children and whose new commute requires a school bus, which has yet to appear. For now, both Papa and Lee-Lee are stuck at home.

That afternoon, Supreme searches for the website of his local councilwoman, Debi Rose, the first African American from Staten Island elected to the New York City Council. In an email to her, he writes:

> Peace miss Debi Rose I'm one of your constituents in from Staten Island . . . I have no hot water I have no gas I'm a single father taking care of seven children every day by myself and I can't seem to get no public assistance I'll go down to get public assistance and then and then I know no there's no hot water no gas for these children that I just need some help

Supreme gets no response. Two days later, on September 18, housing inspectors come to examine the apartment in response to Supreme's recent 311 complaints. There is no one home, so they leave a card at the door.

A week later, the gas remains out and the bathroom sink still sits on the floor. On the family's behalf, an ACS supervisor tries calling the landlord division of the agency that oversees Section 8 housing, but is "left on hold for over 20 minutes," she writes. (Chanel's landlords said they received no complaints about the property, from any city agency, for nearly a year.)

Every morning, Papa gets dressed, pours himself a bowl of cereal, and then eats while standing by the second-floor window. He wants to make sure that he does not miss his bus—which has yet to come.

Papa is still waiting for the bus on September 23 when the Foundling worker makes a final visit to the home to officially "close out" preventive services. She notes that Supreme "is about to explode." The next morning, Papa stands at the window. He is wearing a bright yellow T-shirt that reads IT'S GOOD TO BE RAD.

"There's a bus downstairs!" one of the siblings yells.

Papa looks outside. It is another child's bus.

chapter 36

S UPREME HAS NOW sounded dozens of alarms—by text, by email, by phone, and by foot, with long treks to the welfare office. He feels like a man lost in the city's wilderness, his voice unheard, his face unseen.

Only when a school counselor raises her own concerns does anyone start to pay attention. She reports to ACS that the children appear not to "be the cleanest," an account that is confirmed by another guidance counselor.

On October 1, ACS comes to the house to question the children. On October 2, housing inspectors visit the apartment, allowed in by Supreme. The next day, the gas is restored and, two days later, Supreme receives emergency funds from welfare, including a "retroactive" food stamp benefit totaling $3,812—for the allotments the children should have received since June, as if money could erase four months of hunger.

This sudden rash of fixes will be presented, by ACS in court, as evidence that the agency did its job. They will say that the children are in distress, but not because of inaction by ACS or the welfare office or Foundling or the landlords or the councilwoman or 311 or the housing department or the gas company. The culprit, they will say, is Supreme, who neglected the "hazardous" conditions of his home, and by extension his children, who are found to be "unkempt, dirty, smelly and having a foul odor."

It does not matter that Supreme has made perfect attendance at his drug treatment program. By October 6, his fate is sealed.

At 10 A.M., housing inspectors ring Supreme's buzzer. They have returned to assess the condition of the apartment.

The dog starts to bark. Supreme opens his eyes. All the children are in school except Lee-Lee, who is sleeping next to him. Only later will Supreme remember that the housing department had promised an inspection. An ACS caseworker is also outside. She takes note of Supreme's failure to answer the door and then heads to family court, where ACS is about to make an emergency request.

The inspectors leave a notice on Supreme's door that reads "a Housing Inspector came today to inspect your apartment." They list three complaint numbers corresponding to Supreme's 311 calls. The fact that he made these calls will go unmentioned in court. Instead, ACS will give the impression that the agency discovered, and is now preventing, a disaster in the making—a group of untended children, arriving late to school and returning home to a slum with "no window guards" and the sink "off the wall" and the ceiling "leaking all day," whose father could not be bothered to answer the door.

The agency wants the children removed.

Judge Lim asks ACS why Supreme and the children cannot enter the city's shelter system, given that their home is a "disaster." This should make them eligible for shelter. The ACS lawyer pushes back, saying that Supreme "*does* have housing right now that can be repaired." In other words, the problem is Supreme's neglect—of his home and therefore his children.

Judge Lim asks for Supreme's phone number, placing the call on speakerphone. It goes straight to voicemail.

"It is a safety issue at this point," the ACS lawyer tells Judge Lim. "These kids are going to school dirty. They don't have hot water at all. They don't have any lights in their bedroom. These are things that he could have remedied."

With that, Judge Lim grants ACS permission to take the children overnight.

At 1 P.M., two ACS caseworkers board a silver Ford Windstar.

They are soon driving through the North Shore, collecting the children one by one.

"What's going on?" Khaliq asks the caseworkers.

"We'll tell you later," one of the women replies. They turn on the radio, trying to make small talk. Khaliq hangs on every word, waiting for clues.

Avianna is in gym class when the van pulls up. Her teacher tells her to go to the principal's office. It is now 1:45 P.M., almost the end of the last period. Nana has already been pulled out of social studies and is sitting in the office, along with the school's principal, an assistant principal, and "the ACS lady."

Nana's first thought is that something has happened to her father. After Avianna sits down, the sisters start to giggle, which happens when they are nervous.

"Now, be serious," says the ACS lady.

"Okay," the sisters say.

"We are taking you to a place where you all will stay overnight," she says. Then tomorrow, the children will go to "court."

"Why?" the two sisters ask.

"I can't tell you that right now, but you all will not be seeing your parents tonight."

"Okay."

"Do you have any questions for me?"

"I do," says Avianna. "What about my clothes?" It is the only question she can think to ask. The caseworker replies that clothing is provided by the facility where the children are staying.

"Is all of us going?" Nana asks.

"Yes."

The sisters follow the caseworker out of the building and into the van, finding their oldest brother inside. Again, they start giggling. Khaliq shushes them.

"We about to go somewhere," he warns. Their next stop is P.S. 78, where they are joined by a thumb-sucking Maya and a stone-faced Hada. Papa has already been transported in another van.

Again the dog barks. Again Supreme opens his eyes. This time the pounding won't stop. From the other side of the door comes a voice of panic.

"They takin' the kids!" his wife screams.

Chanel has just come from the courthouse. She knows she should not be here, but Supreme's phone is off. He opens the door as she unloads a rapid-fire of disconnected words like "the house is filthy" and "you missed that appointment" and "the sink, the hot water."

Supreme grabs Lee-Lee and stumbles outside, where Chanel's list continues: how ACS had said "you been duckin' appointments," how the children arrive late to school, how Chanel is suspected of sneaking visits, how "the blind child is watchin' the kids," how they look "dirty," just like their house.

Supreme's eyes widen like those of a man who has been swindled. It is one thing for ACS to spend months virtually ignoring his decrepit house, his lack of daycare, his welfare debacle. But for the agency to go to court—after a last-minute series of fixes—and present the family as "dirty" sends him over the edge. It suggests that he has chosen a life of filth amid optimal conditions. If anything, the reverse is true.

While the children rotated baths, they still washed their clothes and a neighbor braided their hair. While the apartment was falling to pieces, they still kept it scrubbed, stepping around the collapsed sink. Even today, the floors are immaculate and the counters wiped.

"They lyin'! They straight *lyin'*!" he yells. "Every time they come to the house it's clean!"

"I know, Daddy," Chanel says softly. "I know, I know, I know."

She is trying to contain Supreme for the sake of Lee-Lee. A few minutes later, Supreme races up the courthouse steps. The case has been adjourned. He looks at Chanel. "Please, man. You cannot blame me, man. Cuz I got tired, man," he says, turning to Lee-Lee for corroboration: Weren't they napping when the inspectors came?

The toddler nods.

"I'm not blaming you," says Chanel, who is getting nervous. If ACS sees her with Lee-Lee, they will add this to their complaints. The safest course of action is to remain in a public place. Supreme chooses Tompkinsville Park, a well-worn stretch of Bay Street that feels like a second home. He paces up and down the block while his wife and daughter look on. His hands are shaking. He needs a cigarette. He happens to be standing right by the spot where Eric Garner died.

ACS will be calling any minute. Supreme's mind is racing. He still thinks he can persuade them to let Lee-Lee stay with him.

At 2:54 p.m., his phone rings.

"Yes," Supreme says, listening for a moment.

"So you have Khaliq and everybody?" he asks.

Silence.

"And where they supposed to be going tonight? . . . They all gonna be together or they getting separated?"

Supreme's face contorts. ACS is demanding immediate custody of Lee-Lee.

"You know, you know, you know—y'all hurting my heart, right?" he says, his voice breaking. "How am I supposed to do that? No, really! I can hear what you saying but how I'm supposed to do that? Talk to me, like, how am I supposed to do that?"

A moment passes.

"My baby's not gonna go with you! She loves her daddy! All she knows is her daddy! How you gonna take a baby from her daddy?"

Silence.

"You don't know how to answer my question!"

Two minutes later, Supreme hangs up. He must surrender Lee-Lee within the hour.

Lee-Lee watches her father in silence.

They are back on Laurel Avenue, standing by the front stoop. Chanel has already left and ACS has yet to arrive. It is unclear whether Lee-Lee understands what is happening. She is three years old, a girl of few words.

She still has the features of a baby doll, with plump cheeks and lips that purse in the shape of a heart. There is nothing about Lee-Lee to suggest the word "unkempt." She is dressed in a spotless pink jersey and laundered jeans, her face scented with lotion. She is the portrait of clean. Yet in the last few minutes, Lee-Lee has become preoccupied with getting cleaner. She wipes her forehead and cheeks with a damp tissue, dipping it again and again into a water bottle.

Supreme stares at Lee-Lee's fresh braids.

"Come on, man. Hair's done," he says, as if ACS is still listening. "Come on, man. I'm not—I'm not playin' no games! I'm trying to have them kids look appropriate!"

The three-year-old girl plunges her tissue back into the bottle and wrings it out. She dabs her right cheek.

"You see how quick they come and take the kids?" he grumbles. "That's how quick they should have had them people come and fix the hot water and gas!"

Lee-Lee tells her father to wipe his nose.

They are close like this. They even look alike, with the same melancholic eyes and feathery brows, the same sheepish smile. Their bond has deepened in Chanel's absence, which might explain why Lee-Lee remained calm as her mother bade farewell just now. Lee-Lee is accustomed to Chanel leaving, but not her father. They are rarely apart, sharing the same naps, the same meals, the same walks.

"They ask you any questions, you say 'I don't know. Ask my daddy,'" Supreme instructs Lee-Lee. He is certain that ACS will twist her words, just as they told the judge that his children are "dirty."

"Tell 'em like that. 'I'm a baby. Don't ask me *nothin'*,'" he reminds her. "'You don't talk to no baby.'"

Lee-Lee trots after her father as he heads to the corner store, holding Akeelah on her leash. He pulls out his welfare card, which now contains thousands of dollars in retroactive food stamps. He cannot believe this sudden bounty and the cruelty of its timing. He fills three grocery bags for his children, which he will send in the ACS van. For Lee-Lee, he selects two special treats: a pack of Cheetos and a bottle of Sunkist. She holds them to her chest, trailing her father as he returns to the stoop.

At 3:50 P.M., the silver van pulls up.

An ACS supervisor is at the wheel. Supreme has removed Akeelah's leash, commanding her to sit while Lee-Lee hovers in her father's shadow.

"Okay, you gotta get inside," Supreme finally says.

Lee-Lee freezes. Supreme places a hand on her tiny shoulder, as if to steady the child.

"Do you need anything clarified for tomorrow?" the caseworker asks.

Akeelah is now skulking toward Supreme. The dog presses her face into the back of his legs, while Supreme's hand remains on Lee-Lee's shoulder. Like this, the three of them stand, forming a canine-human triumvirate.

"No, I'ma clarify everything when I go to court! I'ma clarify *everything*. I got a whole can of whoop ass . . . cuz this should have never happened. For one time me missing? . . . I got something for you all. Weeks I've been without water and gas!"

Lee-Lee is motionless.

Supreme hoists his daughter and places her in the van. Her mouth is pressed shut. There is no car seat. The caseworker climbs in next to Lee-Lee, reaching for the child's seat belt. She then slides the door shut.

Supreme blinks. He pitches forward, as if knocked by an unseen hand. "Get the fuck out of here," he grumbles, catching his knees to balance himself.

The van idles for a moment. He looks inside.

Lee-Lee is clutching her Sunkist and Cheetos like a life vest.

"See you tomorrow, baby!" he says in his most manly voice. "I'll get you back tomorrow. ASAP!"

The van pulls away.

The children wait for Lee-Lee. They hear different things. The agency cannot locate her. The agency has found her. She is now on the way. Here she is, toddling into the room.

A while later, Supreme stops by the ACS office. He has more snacks for the children.

"Whatever happens, stay together," he says before leaving.

They rummage through the snacks.

"Are y'all hungry?" asks an ACS caseworker.

The children nod, and are soon eating McDonald's. After the sun sets, they board a van, riding across the bridge toward Manhattan's

Lower East Side. The van pulls up to 492 First Avenue, a terra-cotta building that will become known, among the siblings, as "the holding cell." Formerly the morgue of Bellevue Hospital, it is now the emergency intake center for children entering foster care—a child-only version of the Bronx intake point for homeless families.

From the outside, both places have the same modern gleam. And inside, a similar process unfolds. The four oldest children are told they must be "scanned." They step through a metal detector while their coats and bags are searched. Khaliq is made to relinquish his phone. The children must also surrender their father's snacks, so they rush to eat them instead. From here, they are led to what Nana calls "a big nursery," joining 364 children to pass through this month. By the end of the year, nearly four thousand will have stayed at the Nicholas Scoppetta Children's Center, named for a celebrated ACS commissioner.

Scoppetta had been a foster child in the 1930s, taken from his home in Manhattan's Little Italy when he was five years old. He spent that first night in a facility called the Children's Shelter, sleeping head to toe with his brother on a foldup cot. "One of the traumatic events for me," Scoppetta later told the *Observer*, "was when I was separated from my brothers, who are two and five years older. When we were reunited, it had been so long since I saw them, about a year, that my brother had to tell me who he was." Nearly sixty years later, Scoppetta became the first-ever commissioner of ACS, appointed by Mayor Giuliani in 1996 to bring reforms.

Yet the center bearing Scoppetta's name is now a dreaded place. Newcomers arrive at all hours, from infants to twenty-one-year-olds. The lights are always on, making it difficult to sleep. Many children stay only a few nights, until a foster home is located, while others— most commonly teenagers—can remain here for months. Those who act out are sometimes sent across the street to Bellevue Hospital for psychiatric intervention, receiving a shot of a sedative like Ativan or an antipsychotic such as Haldol. If the child runs away, ACS files a missing person report, enabling the police to return that child, sometimes in handcuffs. In the span of 13 months, children ran away from the center nearly sixteen hundred times. No one wants to stay in "the holding cell."

Lee-Lee clings to her siblings, who are waiting to be assigned beds. It is now 10:30 P.M. The children's fatigue is offset by the shock of leaving home. They are waiting quietly when, all of the sudden, a staff member separates Lee-Lee and Papa from the rest. They must sleep on a different floor.

"I got scared because I thought we was not going to see each other again," Avianna later writes to me in a seven-page account of these events, which closely matched a six-page description penned by her stepsister, Nana.

The two girls are relieved to be on the same floor as Hada and Maya, while Khaliq is sent to an all-boys landing. Soon the oldest children are being escorted to the nurse's office for a physical exam. Khaliq goes in first, emerging fifteen minutes later. Next up is Nana, whose height, weight, heartbeat, ears, and eyes are checked by the nurse. She then presses on Nana's stomach, asking if it hurts. Nana says it hurts a little. With that, the nurse makes Nana—who is thirteen years old—take a pregnancy test.

Nana is still a virgin. Nonetheless, she obliges, testing negative. Avianna goes in last, finishing around midnight. The sisters are then offered "food that looked like it was cooked 3 days ago," writes Nana, who sticks to pretzels and juice. They are led to their bedroom, where the staff gives them lockers, hygiene kits, and a duffel containing two jumpsuits and other clothes.

They finally fall asleep at 1 A.M., their bodies leaden. Five hours later, the staff wakes them. They must now go to court.

In a fog, the children put on their matching jumpsuits and board a van, riding toward the Staten Island courthouse. Once they arrive, an ACS caseworker takes them to a room to meet their new court-appointed attorney, Anthony Morisano.

A few steps away, in Judge Lim's courtroom, Supreme and Chanel take a seat next to their lawyers. Today, the family's housing debacle will go without mention. The judge's focus has shifted: He wants both parents to take a drug test—despite the fact that Supreme's last four urine exams came back negative (reports that none of the lawyers have in hand). The family's case will reconvene tomorrow, while the children remain in ACS custody.

"I don't take pride or joy in removing a child or children from any parent," Judge Lim tells Chanel and Supreme. "I understand the devastating consequences it has on the children. But as a parent you have an absolute obligation to make sure that your children are safe under your care. And if it means testing negative for drugs and going for services, then that's why you have to go. Because this is a court case."

The children are now at the ACS office, waiting "for the next move," says Avianna. They snack on chocolate chip cookies. Finally, a caseworker tells them they will be spending another night at the Manhattan facility. The children get up to leave. They head outside, passing the family court.

From the top of the steps, Supreme spots his children. They are all dressed in the same maroon jumpsuits—even Lee-Lee. As the children walk single file toward the van, Supreme stares in disbelief. To him, they look like prisoners.

From the street, Khaliq sees his father.

"They putting her in *jail*?" shouts the boy, referring to Chanel.

The van whisks the children away before Supreme can answer.

Supreme leaves to take his drug test, returning to court early the next morning. He will give ACS no more excuses to keep his children. Nothing will stop him from being on time.

If Supreme were to make a movie of his life, he would not think of a plot twist as conspiratorial as what follows. At around 10 A.M. on October 8, he is sitting on the family court steps. A white female guard approaches him. Supreme recognizes her from Judge Lim's court.

"Come on," she says. "Your case is ready."

She gestures for Supreme to follow her. But instead of walking him to the family court, the guard leads Supreme into the building next door—the criminal courthouse.

When Supreme steps inside, he is swarmed by police officers.

"You are under arrest," one of them says.

"What for?" he asks.

"Bench warrant," says the officer. At first, Supreme cannot recall having a warrant. He pleads with the officers to let him go or he will miss his family court proceeding. They ignore this, handcuffing him and taking him to the holding cell.

Sure enough, in the family court next door, Supreme's case is now being called.

ACS begins with an alarming update: Yesterday, the agency's "investigative consultants" conducted a "criminal background search," learning of Supreme's bodega incident, when he was arrested June 20 on "charges of criminal possession of a weapon in the fourth degree—a firearms weapon—menacing in the third degree, harassment in the second degree."

It barely matters what the lawyer says next: that Supreme was only arraigned for menacing and harassment, because the weapon charge was dropped.

The image is now sealed.

A *firearms weapon.*

And because Supreme failed to appear in court on August 12, a bench warrant was issued. The lawyer switches to the topic of Supreme's drug test, which has returned negative except for methadone (the legal medication he takes).

Suddenly, Judge Lim makes an announcement: "Um . . . I have information from my court officers that the respondent father has been taken into custody right now. So he's being processed. So this moots out the application for return of the children to the father. . . . He may be released on bond. He may not, depending on his history."

Next door, Supreme is taken from the holding cell to a judge. Supreme explains that he had come to family court to reclaim his children—only to be arrested on a warrant for failing to make a different hearing because he was so overwhelmed caring for these same children. The judge takes pity and releases Supreme without bond. But by the time he races back to the family court, the conference is over.

Judge Lim has granted ACS its request, allowing the agency to take custody of the children. They will go into foster care, joining nearly fifteen thousand other children to enter the system this year. The family's next court date is set for two months from now.

"Do we know anything about where the children are being placed?" Judge Lim asks before the conference ends. The ACS lawyer replies that they are "working to try to get them placed together, or as much of the siblings together as we can. That is our priority. We do really want to keep them intact."

Then the children's lawyer, Anthony Morisano, speaks up.

"I think these children have a very close bond," he says. "So I think it would be very devastating if these children are separated at this point."

Early the next morning, the children rise and get dressed. ACS escorts them from the Children's Center to their Staten Island schools. The teachers have been alerted.

"If there's anything you need, just tell us," says Avianna's teacher.

What Avianna most needs, her teacher cannot provide: permission to go home. Her house on Laurel Avenue is just one block away.

There the buzzer sounds, and this time Supreme answers the door. The city's housing inspectors have returned to conduct their first inspection since the family moved in almost a year ago. Today they find fourteen housing violations, including the ceiling leak, the broken bathroom sink, two damaged doors, and no working smoke detectors.

Later that afternoon, Avianna and her siblings return to "the holding cell," trying to do homework and eat dinner. Suddenly, they are ushered into a private room and told to sit down.

The children are silent.

Whatever happens, stay together.

A female worker announces that ACS has "found a home for all of us," recalls Avianna. She wants to dance and cry, so great is her relief. The words "all of us" can only mean one home for all.

But this is not the case. What the worker means is that all of the children will be in foster homes—not in "one home for all." The good news is that each sibling will live with at least one other sibling. They will be divided among three homes in Staten Island. The first home will be shared by Hada and Maya. The second home will be shared by Nana and Avianna, who—upon hearing her name—cuts the woman off.

"If I'm not with Lee-Lee, then I'm not going."

"Can I finish?" says the woman.

Avianna, Nana, and Lee-Lee will share the second home.

Papa and Khaliq will go to the third home.

Khaliq sucks his teeth. Hada and Maya start to cry.

"It's gonna be okay," Nana tells her little sisters, who are nine and ten years old. They have never been apart from their family. Nana cannot think of what else to say, so she keeps repeating the same four words, against all available evidence. "It's gonna be okay."

As Maya and Hada leave, their siblings ask to use the phone. They try calling their parents. Neither one answers. The only other number they know is mine. They call me at 9:45 P.M.

"They splittin' us all up," says Nana, her voice hushed and afraid. Papa and Khaliq are next. They have been told to pack their bags.

"I gotta go," Nana whispers. "They getting ready to leave."

The boys vanish before the last three siblings are led to a van. At around 1 A.M. they pull up to their new home in Staten Island.

Lee-Lee has heard the word "home" so many times, she thinks they are returning to Laurel Avenue. She expects to see her father again. Instead, a stranger is at the door. Lee-Lee starts to cry.

By now, two ACS caseworkers have gotten into a car, bound for Hershey. They have some questions for Dasani.

part 6

"TO ENDURE ANY HOW"

2015–2016

chapter 37

THE CAMPUS IS a ghost town. Almost everyone has left for Columbus Day weekend. Dasani is among the children with nowhere to go. Today they gather in the school's Memorial Hall to watch the film *Unbroken*.

It is the true story of Louis Zamperini, a troubled boy who ran track, making it to the 1936 Olympics before fighting in World War II as an army bombardier. Then his plane crashed, stranding him on a raft in the Pacific Ocean for forty-seven days before the Japanese Navy captured Louis as a prisoner of war.

If you have a big enough why, you can endure almost any how.

More than two months have passed since Mr. Akers said those words. Dasani stares at the screen. She has already seen *Unbroken*, so she knows what to expect. Heavy bomber planes whir through the sky, taking aim at the Japanese. They fire back, striking an American crew member. Louis dives to the floor to help his bleeding comrade.

Suddenly, Dasani's name is being called over the loudspeaker. She must report to the office immediately.

"Ooohhh, you in trouble," says a friend.

Dasani walks out as the bombing continues. In the hall, she is greeted by a Hershey staff receptionist.

"Some people are here to see you," the receptionist says, leading Dasani into a conference room where two women are waiting.

"Hi, Dasani."

"Hi."

"We're with the Administration for Children's Services."

Dasani looks at the women. One is an ACS caseworker, the other her supervisor. They begin with polite conversation, asking Dasani how she is doing in school. Then they move on to more difficult questions.

They want to know if Chanel and Supreme "beat" the children. Dasani has been interviewed by enough caseworkers to know that if she gives them something to write down, they are less likely to probe. She replies that "they take away our privileges" and "they smack us and stuff, but they don't beat us." She adds that Supreme picks favorites among the children and is unnecessarily harsh with Papa.

Supreme "really needs to get his life together," Dasani says.

What happens next will lodge itself in Dasani's memory like an accidental mosaic, made up of sentence fragments and random facts. She will hear words like "lost custody" and "foster care." That her siblings were "removed" because of the "poor condition" of the house. That "the pipes were broken" and "the wall was dirty." But the children are "okay." They will be divided up "in pairs."

Here Dasani's memory goes blank.

According to the agency's notes, "the child" begins "to cry." The ACS workers stop talking to give Dasani "a minute to release her feelings."

The next thing Dasani remembers saying is, "If anything—if you split them up—put the baby with one of them."

The baby, Dasani explains, has three mothers: Dasani, Avianna, and Nana. (The caseworker notes that Chanel is not listed "as a mother to them.") Dasani adds that before coming to Hershey, she had tried to show her sisters how to care for Lee-Lee. They must not be separated.

"The child stated that the children are all they have," writes the caseworker.

Dasani waits for the next question.

"Does your mom or dad have a job?"

Here at Hershey, Dasani has been learning about "career prepara-tion." A glossy poster in the hall shows students peering into the en-gine of a car. In high school, they can major in culinary arts, engineering, construction, law. They can "begin their journey to pro-ductive and fulfilling lives," which requires being "professional"— Mrs. Akers's word for the code switch. You don't disavow the past. You just sound more like the future.

To Dasani, these ACS workers sound professional. But the ques-tion "Do your parents work?" makes her queasy. The agency has been tracking her family for eleven years, cataloging every detail of their lives, from the contents of their pantry to their sleeping arrangements. Surely they know that Chanel and Supreme are unemployed. It is unclear why ACS needs Dasani to confirm the job status of parents she has not seen in six months. But by doing so, she is naming their failure out loud.

"No," she says quietly. "They don't work."

The women hand her a business card. On this card, they explain, is a phone number Dasani can dial to reach her siblings. They reas-sure her that the children are well. ACS even "took them shopping" and can help them all apply to Hershey.

"Are you all right?" one of the workers asks.

"Yeah," says Dasani.

"Are you sure you can go back to watching the movie?"

"Yeah."

Meetings like this are routine at Hershey, with child-protection workers, police officers, even detectives asking to see students. Such visits are prompted by any number of crises—the murder of a relative, the loss of parental custody. The school's social workers and thera-pists try to help the children cope, but they do not prevent these meetings, or even attend them sometimes. This morning, a Hershey social worker had reassured ACS that she would contact the Akerses and Dasani's therapist. But since it is a holiday, they are all gone.

The ACS workers get up to leave, telling Dasani to stay in touch and that everything will be "okay."

Dasani walks out of the room, drifting down the hall and back to the movie. She has no sense of time. She could have been gone for minutes, or hours. The only clue comes when she opens the door right as the actor playing Louie is brought before his fellow prisoners to be punched. This means that ninety-two minutes have passed.

She sits down as if nothing has happened.

She knows nothing will ever be the same.

Her friend leans over to ask what happened.

"My counselor," Dasani says, which is code for "private."

They stare at the screen.

Louie is now a prisoner at a camp near Tokyo run by a sadistic corporal. The camera pans out to dozens of American and British prisoners.

"This man must be taught respect!" growls the corporal. "Each prisoner will punch this man in his face."

The men are horrified. Louie is their brother in arms. They refuse, upon threat of torture, until Louie intervenes. "Come on," he says, offering his face to be punched. "Just get it over with."

One by one, the men swing, knocking Louie to the ground.

Dasani returns to her student home in a daze. Everyone she trusts is gone for the holiday weekend: the Akerses; her therapist, Julie; her best friend, Kali.

She could go to the health center and talk to a counselor she doesn't know. But this has never been Dasani's way. She looks at the number on the ACS card. She cannot bring herself to dial.

Instead, the phone rings. Dasani picks up, hearing her mother's voice.

Chanel is sitting in a TGI Fridays near Union Square. She is short on sleep, her eyes puffy from crying. She has just gotten word from Goldfein, the lawyer at Legal Aid, that ACS had gone to see Dasani.

"They told me everything, Mommy," Dasani says.

The word "everything" makes Chanel nauseous.

She had implored ACS not to contact Dasani, who was doing well at Hershey, with no plans to return to New York. Had Chanel known that the agency would ignore her wishes, she would have called Dasani herself.

Now Chanel is scrambling to catch up.

"What did they tell you about me?" Chanel asks. "Dasani?"

The call disconnects. At Dasani's student home, phone calls cut off after a few minutes—"like in jail," she says. This ensures that each girl has enough time to call home.

Chanel redials.

Dasani picks up, her voice shaky and distant. ACS took the children, Dasani says, because of the condition of the home. She speaks haltingly, as if someone is listening. She adds that ACS is planning to enroll all the siblings at Hershey.

Chanel is thunderstruck. She cannot fathom how ACS would make such plans, or even talk about this with the children absent their parents' consent. She would never agree to send her younger children to boarding school right now. She still plans to get them back. She wonders what else the caseworkers are telling them. *This is how they break the bond*, she thinks. She can hear it in Dasani's voice.

Chanel summons her best defense. She begins by explaining that ACS "tricked Daddy," arresting him outside the courthouse.

Again, the call cuts off.

Dasani is unsure whom to believe. She later plugs the ACS number into her cellphone, saving it under "Siblings."

Dasani keeps her news quiet. But over the next week, her behavior becomes loud.

She curses in class, flips someone the middle finger, and cuts the snack line. "We were here first!" says a boy. Dasani turns to him, drawing her fist. For this, she lands a Level 2, a serious disciplinary infraction that could imperil her scholarship money.

"You don't understand what I'm going through!" Dasani tells Mrs. Akers. "You've never been through anything that I've been through."

"Sweetheart," Mrs. Akers says, "you don't know my story either. If I told you, you'd probably have a box of tissues for me."

Dasani hates it when Mrs. Akers says "sweetheart."

"I've lost my brothers and sisters!" Dasani says. "I don't know where they are. They took them away."

Such news is not unusual at Student Home Morgan, where the phone is forever ringing with some family's drama. The Akerses are responsible for twelve girls, but each of those girls connects to many other lives, forming a constellation of crisis. On any given day, a child can be found weeping in this office, much as Dasani is now.

Mrs. Akers tries to comfort Dasani, as does her husband. When Dasani puts up the same wall—"You don't know what I've been through!"—Mr. Akers looks at her carefully.

"I don't know how you feel. One thing I do know? I can identify with the pain. Because I've been there," he says. "My dad died when he was fifty-five years old of drugs and alcohol. We all have stories. But what are we going to do with them? Are they going to allow us to grow, or bury us?"

Dasani's siblings are in survival mode.

Four nights have passed since the moment they were separated. They are now divided among three foster homes overseen by Foundling, the same agency that worked on "prevention" before ACS removed the children.

Hada and Maya have landed in the home of a matronly woman on Staten Island's North Shore. When a Foundling worker comes to visit, she finds the girls "nervous but very polite." They make their beds with hospital corners. They are following the advice of their siblings to "behave and be nice."

Avianna, Nana, and Lee-Lee are also minding their manners. Their foster home is a few miles east of their sisters' and just five blocks north of their brothers', where Khaliq's foster mother finds him "respectful" and unusually neat. He cleans and cleans while his little brother acts out.

On Papa's second day in the home, he digs a hole in the yard, fills it with water, and starts slinging mud at a neighbor's house. He wants to go home.

"You can feel them cryin' for you at night," says Chanel.

Nightmares crowd her sleep. Both she and Supreme have asked repeatedly to see their children. On October 13, Supreme tells the counselor at his methadone clinic that he is "losing it" and "walking the streets beating up people." When the counselor asks if he has seen his caseworkers from ACS and Foundling, he says, "I'm going to kill them both, I promise." The counselor reports Supreme's death threat to ACS.

Three days later, Chanel calls an ACS supervisor, the same woman who had gone to Hershey to see Dasani.

"You've got beautiful children," says the supervisor.

"Thank you," says Chanel, placing the call on speakerphone. "And I really work hard to get them like that."

They begin to debate the merits of the case. Chanel wants to know why ACS tipped off the criminal court to arrest Supreme.

"How could y'all do that?"

The supervisor demurs.

"Was it wrong?" Chanel asks.

"I can't—I can't do anything about that."

"But it was wrong. It was wrong. It was *dead* wrong . . . and you know that."

"Okay," says the supervisor. "I'm not disagreeing with you. But that's out of our control."

She advises Chanel to focus on herself, by getting back into drug treatment and complying with other requests. Just three days earlier, Chanel had tested positive for alcohol, and a few weeks ago for opioids.

"Let him handle him. You handle you," says the supervisor.

"But we are a *family*," says Chanel. "This is the divide and conquer. This is the Willie Lynch shit that I'm not gonna let happen to my family. . . . That's what this is and you know it better than I do because you're an African American woman like me."

When Chanel says "Willie Lynch," she is invoking a well-known code. Lynch was said to be a British enslaver who came to Virginia in 1712, giving a speech on his method for controlling slaves: They should be "broken" like horses—and their families divided—as a means of social control. Though historians have declared the speech a hoax, it continues to echo, from Louis Farrakhan's 1995 address at the Million Man March to Kendrick Lamar's 2015 album, *To Pimp a Butterfly*.

Chanel knows that to accuse a Black person of "Willie Lynching" is a grave insult, far worse than being called an Uncle Tom. And that is her point. ACS took her children, physically and mentally. She still cannot shake the sound of Dasani's voice on the phone.

"How could you go up there and tell Dasani all that stuff?" Chanel asks the supervisor.

"What do you think we told Dasani?"

"You told her that the kids were removed from the home. They're no longer in the house. . . . She's a baby! Why would you tell her that?"

"Because Dasani needed to know," says the supervisor. "She holds a lot of responsibility. She's very parentified for her siblings. She loves them like she was their mother."

"I know," says Chanel.

"Okay, so—"

"So, you don't think that that hurt her like a mother?"

"I know it did. That's why we went up there to tell her. And not make it impersonal. We didn't make it impersonal."

"So have you been checking on her behavior and on how she's been doing since you told her that?"

"Since Tuesday?"

"Since Tuesday. Have you checked to see how she's been since then?"

"No, I haven't personally. We talked to her. We asked her what she needs."

Chanel pushes for more details.

"She needed to know that her siblings gonna be all right," says the supervisor. "Who better than us to tell her that? Was us. That's the reason why we went up there. That's the reason why I felt and we felt it was important to tell your daughter personally. Not hear it from her lawyer—"

"Why she couldn't hear it from her *mother*?"

"Well, I don't know," says the supervisor. "Why didn't you call her and tell her?"

"You—you beat me up there to tell her! You beat me up there!" Chanel says. "I just don't understand how they can allow you to go up there and disturb the education of a fourteen-year-old child that's already in a situation. I don't understand that."

"Did she feel that we disturbed her?"

Chanel cannot believe she must now inform ACS of Dasani's current state—how Dasani has been fighting, accruing disciplinary points, getting sidelined as a cheerleader, losing her phone privilege, struggling to focus in class. She starts to sum this up, only to hear the supervisor say, "I think your daughter—if she's hurting for anything, it's probably because her siblings—"

"Probably because we've never been *separated*!" Chanel explodes. "We've—we've been a family all our life. That's—what is wrong wit' y'all?"

"More reason for you to get yourself together so you all can be reunited," says the ACS supervisor. "Except for Dasani. Because Dasani needs to stay where she is until she graduates."

"That's what she *is* gonna do," fumes Chanel.

"Okay."

"I got my kids' plans . . . in order. I got a plan for them."

Chanel hangs up feeling powerless.

The sky darkens over Hershey. Thunder rolls across the cornfields. Then comes the rain, crashing down with such force that traffic slows and sidewalks pool. The storm slams against the windows of Dasani's student home, rattling the frames.

Inside, the living room is toasty. A fire crackles beneath two porcelain angels and an acrylic painting of a French cottage. This is Dasani's calmest hour, after school has ended and while dinner has yet to begin. She sits in her favorite armchair, near seventeen-year-old Caché, who is working on an elaborate drawing of the pop star Lana Del Rey. A few feet off, fifteen-year-old Angel occupies her usual spot by the chessboard, her legs flung over the floral armrest.

The scent of lemon-marinated chicken signals dinner. Dasani carries her plate to the buffet, eyeing the roasted vegetables. She has yet to embrace Hershey's healthful diet. Can she get away with just a roll, some rice, and a serving of meat? As if reading her mind, Mr. Akers gestures to the salad.

Dasani crinkles her nose.

"You gotta straighten out your face," he says.

"I'm happy!" Dasani says brightly.

"Notify your face."

"My face is notified."

On the outside, Dasani seems fine. Foundling caseworkers have heard from the school that "Dasani is adjusting outwardly at least to the turbulence that her parents are undergoing."

She has gone nine days without a behavioral outburst. If she makes it to Friday, she will earn back the privilege to cheer at the last varsity game of the season. But on the inside, there is no cheering. She thinks about Lee-Lee crying at night. She has a mother's angst, absent the nightmares that hound Chanel.

"When I go to sleep, all I see is black," says Dasani. "I don't dream. What I dream about is blackness."

After ACS came to the school, Dasani pushed her therapist away. She was too upset to talk. She was also angry that the visit came on a weekend when Julie was gone, as were the Akerses. This felt like abandonment. So Dasani skipped her next two therapy sessions. Only when Julie came looking for Dasani, waiting outside her classroom, did the trust return.

Lately the therapist has tried to shift Dasani's focus to the things that she can control. She can run track and cheer. She can make good grades. She can succeed "for them," for her siblings. " 'To show them that even when you have a minor setback in life, you can still move forward,'" Dasani recalls Julie saying. "That was her main thing. To move forward and never look back."

Dasani finishes dinner, taking her plate to the sink.

The house is calm but for the periodic crash of thunder and the muffled violin strokes of Vivaldi's Concertino in D Major, which the Akerses' daughter is practicing for a recital. The other girls do their homework as Mrs. Akers makes her rounds, checking on their progress and passing out Welch's fruit snacks.

Dasani sits at a computer, researching the history of lynching. She grabs a snack, barely looking up. Not everyone is as focused.

"Our little Bumblebee was watching *Lost*," Mrs. Akers reports to her husband as the girl stands in the doorway, skulking.

"*She's* lost!" chuckles Mr. Akers.

They have a soft spot for Bumblebee, who came to Hershey speaking in a whisper and staring at the floor. She got her nickname the way everyone does: Mrs. Akers blurts it out—"Cupcake!" "Yaya!" "Cuddles!"—and the name sticks. Dasani is now "Nini."

These days, Bumblebee is no longer afraid of eye contact. She is staring directly at her houseparents, angling for sympathy.

"You wanna take this one?" Mrs. Akers asks her husband. "Get the paddle!"

Bumblebee is silent.

Then they all burst into laughter.

The next morning, Dasani wakes before sunrise. Every day, she walks more than two miles to school, passing cornfields and distant silos. She makes this pilgrimage with other students who carry the school's low rank of "striving." Their morning trek is meant to encourage better behavior, earning them a seat in Mr. Akers's van. But Dasani no longer cares to leave "striving." She has stopped thinking about goals or tracking them on her calendar.

She is living moment to moment.

The sun appears. She squints at the horizon. It looks like the African safaris that Dasani used to watch on her television at the Auburn shelter. Only two years have passed since that time, when her walk to school spanned a few Brooklyn blocks. She still recalls how quickly she moved, keeping her head down.

Here she looks up. She sees apple orchards and Canada geese and sugar maples in full bloom, throwing punches of fuchsia at the sky.

Hershey's high school is full of unfamiliar faces—947 students, most of them new to Dasani. She sticks close to her best friend, Kali, ready to protect her should anyone pose a threat.

"If ever a girl gets in your face, you gotta back her up," Dasani says.

Watching Dasani closely is the high school's assistant principal, Tara Valoczki, who works with Hershey's most challenging students. She invites them into her office, to vent or share stories—an invitation that Dasani accepts with particular relish.

Part of the reason Dasani warms to Tara—a white, thirty-six-year-old suburban mother—is that they are so different. Dasani may have nothing to teach Mr. Akers, but in Tara, Dasani has a ready student.

When Dasani uses the term "street cred," Tara looks intrigued.

"What's that?" the Hershey native asks.

Dasani explains that "street cred" is the good credit of one's name on the street, which must be defended at any cost.

When Tara listens, she rarely blinks. She seems to hang on every word, which pleases Dasani. "She needs to be heard," Tara later tells me. "She needs to know that I am listening to her. . . . I don't believe you can make an impact on a kid unless you have a trusting relationship."

By the end of the week, Dasani has earned back her right to cheer. She gets dressed for tonight's game, opposite a dry-erase board where she has written, "If cheerleading was easy, they'd call it football." She boards the bus to nearby Palmyra, where the Spartans will face off against the Cougars. Twenty minutes later, Hershey's football players and cheerleaders step into another America.

Palmyra is a small working-class town where football is sacred. Nearly all of the town's residents are white. The cheerleaders prance across the field, their blond tresses pinned with pink bows, waving pom-poms to the AC/DC song "Back in Black." As the temperature dips to 41 degrees, more than a thousand spectators fill the floodlit stadium. They huddle under blankets, sipping hot chocolate.

"Ladies and gentlemen, please rise," says the announcer, "and remain standing for the playing of our national anthem."

Dasani stands, lifting her right hand to her left shoulder. She is not just a cheerleader. She is now a "flyer," the girl lifted into the air during stunts. Tonight Dasani must perform a new extension she has barely mastered. It is so cold that the girls stay in their track suits, warming up with their standard cheers.

> We're awesome!
> So hot!
> MHS is gonna
> Rock it to the top!

The cheer holds true. By the third quarter, Hershey is well ahead and it is time for Dasani's stunt.

Focus, she tells herself.

Three girls hoist Dasani up, holding her feet. The trick is to look straight ahead, never down. The slightest loss of balance can send the whole group crashing. Dasani stares ahead, locking eyes with her coach. Slowly she lifts her arms to seal the move. Then she remembers to add a smile.

"She did it," says the coach.

Dasani leaps to the ground, her face victorious. She is so happy that she forgets herself, shedding all poise. She breaks into her own wild cheer, a cross between the air guitar and the funky chicken. The other cheerleaders have stopped to rest, leaving Dasani by herself, gyrating across the field.

"Look at her go now," says the coach.

Dasani's siblings are dressed in new clothes, their hair groomed, their skin scrubbed. Ten days have passed since they were separated. They will see their parents for the first time this afternoon at Foundling.

The children rush to one another, nervous and giddy.

"Y'all know your foster mom names?" asks Nana, sounding hyper.

"Miss Sherrie."

"Miss Walter."

"Miss Nanny."

A caseworker shows them to a room with toys, games, and art supplies. As the children settle down, they compare notes. Each of their homes has a computer and hot showers. They all have a weekly allowance. Khaliq has a new phone. Avianna's bathroom has heated floors.

"Y'all got a car?" asks Maya.

"Yesss, a big Mercedes," says Khaliq.

Upstairs, Chanel and Supreme take their seats in another conference room. Before they can see their children, they must have a "transition meeting" with the foster care staff at Foundling and two ACS workers, who have opted to join by phone due to Supreme's recent death threat (which he later withdraws, expressing remorse).

Running today's meeting is Linda Lowe, the family's new Foundling supervisor. A fifty-six-year-old native of the New Jersey suburbs,
Linda has been at the agency for five years. She is tall and thin, with
muscles honed by rock climbing. She dresses primly for work, in
blazers and leather loafers. Shiny golden curls bounce around her
face. Without even knowing Linda's pedigree—she is an Ivy League
graduate—Chanel is ready to dismiss the supervisor as "just another
white devil."

Then Linda opens her mouth. She speaks in a low, casual drawl, as
if chatting with friends. Chanel wonders if she smokes. She has met
Linda a handful of times. The woman is full of surprises, cursing with
abandon, cracking jokes at her own expense. "I'll listen to NPR but I'll
also listen to Howard Stern. Can you get any more extreme than that?"

Linda has been keeping tabs on Chanel's children, reporting back
with encouraging news: They are better behaved and more orderly
than most foster kids. Hada even "made her bed with hospital bed
corners, very surprising to see," wrote one of Linda's caseworkers.

Again and again, Linda tells Chanel, "Our goal is to reunify your
family."

Chanel has heard this before. At least a dozen caseworkers have
passed through her life. Yet something about Linda feels different.
Just the other day, the Foundling supervisor spotted Supreme on the
street. He looked hungry, so she reached into her wallet. Linda knows
that she shouldn't do this. She also knows that she should. There is
no right answer. Such is the paradox of "social work," two words that
merge awkwardly at best.

Linda follows her gut, handing Supreme $20.

This is the kind of rule-bending that wins Chanel's trust. She can
see that Linda has "a flexible mindset," which is key to survival.

"She looks like she had a hard life," says Chanel, whose instincts
prove correct.

Linda grew up on a golf course in Branchburg, New Jersey. Her father, a Wall Street broker, routinely beat his wife and five children,
leaving bruises and welts beneath their clothes. The more he drank,
the worse it got. When Linda was eight, he broke her sister's nose.

"If he was hitting somebody, I would go and try to stop him," Linda said. At one point he turned to her, saying, "I need help."

Help never came. The family's well-off neighbors knew of the abuse but kept it quiet. Back then, much like today, a white family was less likely to land in the system. Linda recalls an especially bad episode when she was in the seventh grade. "He threw me up and down the living room. My other sister and a couple of friends were sitting on the front porch. And I remember going right back out and pretending nothing happened."

To this day, Linda startles easily. She also knows that, given the option, she would never have chosen foster care over staying with her father. "Abuse has no boundaries in the sense of feelings. You forget pain. For some reason, that man was always held on a pedestal, forever. I want it to be known that to the very end I adored him. . . It's how every little kid thinks. They want to go home. They want their mom and dad. They want to be loved."

This makes Linda sympathetic to the parents she supervises, whose lapses rarely compare to those of her father. When people ask how she copes with her job, she shrugs.

"As horrible as it is, some of these kids you just fall in love with," Linda says. "I think when you're with them, you're not sad."

Downstairs, the children wait. Hada reaches for some paper and draws a red rose. Lee-Lee tumbles into the room with fresh braids.

Suddenly, in walks Chanel.

"Hi, booga butt!" she croons, lifting the toddler into the air. The children rush to their mother, pressing in. She inspects them, one by one. She is certain that Hada has an ear infection. She pops a pimple on Avianna's face. She shows Maya the proper technique for putting on a sweater. While Chanel is busy mothering, Supreme tries to provide. He hands the children bags of vitamins, toothbrushes, peppermint tea, and candy.

Supreme's face is pained. A few minutes later, he leaves, saying he is going to fetch everyone dinner.

As the children race to the basketball court, two caseworkers observe them. From now on, each visit will produce a computerized report. Today's will note that Chanel "appeared emotionally stable and coherent" and was "dressed appropriately" but that Supreme was "very quiet and detached" and "did not display emotions towards the children."

When the caseworkers are out of earshot, Chanel turns to Nana. "Watch what you say to these people. I'm telling you. Watch what you say."

Chanel is hurt that Nana was so excited about her new allowance and other perks.

"You seem like you happy here, I dunno," Chanel says. "You wanna be here?"

"No," says Nana. "I want to go home."

Shortly before the visit ends, Supreme returns with cheeseburgers and fries for the children. They scarf down dinner while Linda hands Chanel a stack of medical releases. This Chanel finds puzzling. If ACS has custody of her children, why do they need her permission for anything?

Linda refers Chanel to the parenting handbook, which explains her rights.

The children will be seeing new doctors, dentists, and therapists. Lee-Lee's front teeth have rotted. Nana's eyes must be checked. They need vaccinations. At this Chanel bristles. Both she and Supreme believe that vaccinations make children sick. She is certain that Supreme will refuse to sign. No, says Linda, he has already signed.

Linda watches Chanel's face, writing that "it is clear how nervous they are" and that Supreme "may have signed out of fear."

Chanel is now signing page after page. Below Avianna's name, she initials her consent for psychiatric and psychological evaluations as well as for psychotherapy. On another form, she writes "no pork."

Avianna wants her mother to stop signing. Chanel looks at her daughter, trying to soften the girl's frown. "We live for you, you know that?" Chanel says. "We fighting—all we can—to get you back."

It is time for the children to leave.

Papa whizzes toward his mother.

"You wanna meet my Nanny?" he says, using his foster mother's nickname. "It's that BMW right there!"

Three cars are idling along the circular driveway.

To Chanel, these women seem well off. She suspects that they are profiting off her children, though many foster parents would beg to differ. Rarely are the funds enough, and no amount of money makes fostering an easy job.

Foster children divide into three categories: those with "normal," "special," and "exceptional" needs.

These labels determine a foster parent's stipend, with "normal" bringing the smallest amount (around $23 per day for a seven-year-old child) and "exceptional" the largest (around $62). In order to care for a special or exceptional child—one with medical, behavioral, or mental health issues—the foster parent may need additional training to designate her home as "therapeutic."

All of Dasani's siblings have been placed in therapeutic homes, bringing the foster parents an average monthly income of up to $1,900 per child. For each day that these children remain in foster care, the Foundling agency receives another $93 for every child. In total, the care of Chanel and Supreme's children is costing more than $33,000 per month—a figure that will approach $400,000 per year.

The Foundling supervisor, Linda, often thinks about this math. It would cost far less to keep a poor family intact, sparing them the trauma of separation, by placing a full-time aide in the home to prevent the problems that lead to neglect. An aide could help to fill out medical forms, keep school appointments, draw baths.

There is no doubt, to Linda's mind, that Supreme loves his children but lost them because he became overwhelmed. Just the presence of another adult can make a difference, tweaking a parent's behavior.

"If I'm driving down the road and I see a police car, I'm gonna look at how fast I'm going, if I'm driving appropriately," Linda says. "I might put my foot on the brake."

ACS has a version of this program, called "preventive homemaking services." But only 470 families (less than 3 percent of the families entering prevention this year) are enrolled in the homemaking program, which allows an aide into their homes to "maintain normal household operations during periods of stress or crisis." To qualify for this help, a parent must have a disability or medical diagnosis.

By law, the burden is on ACS to inform parents of such a service. Why the agency did not offer this to Supreme, who has been diagnosed with panic and mood disorders—or to Chanel, who has a severely impaired knee—is unclear. (The agency would not discuss the family's case, citing confidentiality.) But to categorize a parent as "disabled" also brings a stigma. Dasani's parents are so opposed to the label that they won't even apply for disability benefits, forgoing hundreds of dollars a month in potential income.

"How you doin'?" Papa's foster mother asks Chanel.

"You look like my mother!" says Chanel, trying to curry favor with Miss Nanny.

"That's my boy!" says Nanny, looking at Khaliq. "That's my helper."

Chanel can only imagine all the cleaning that Khaliq has done for this woman. Foundling also takes note, reporting that Khaliq "loves to keep a clean kitchen." Chanel would tell it differently. He does not want "to keep" a clean kitchen. He wants the calm that a clean kitchen brings.

Chanel stands in the middle of the driveway as each car takes off—the van holding Lee-Lee, Avianna, and Nana; the black BMW containing Khaliq and Papa; the leather-interior Honda CR-V where Maya and Hada sit quietly.

Long after they are gone, Chanel is still standing there. As the sun sets, she and Supreme take their leave on foot.

"Concerns as to the children's hygiene . . ." reads Chanel's lawyer, Yost, from a court report filed by ACS. He pauses at a paragraph about Khaliq. The boy's school, Yost reads, "is concerned there is no reinforcement of behavioral correction at home."

"So what—we don't kick his ass?" Chanel says. "But if we do, they call ACS!"

Yost puts the report away. His conclusion is simple: Chanel must do whatever ACS asks. She has already left the shelter system, returning to Staten Island to live with Supreme.

But to comply with the demands of ACS means that she must take parenting and anger management classes, arrive on time to family visits, make repairs to her home, get a mental health evaluation, enroll in a new drug program, and test negative for prohibited substances. She has fifteen months to succeed. If she fails, the court may terminate her parental rights, placing the children up for adoption.

This is known as the "death sentence" of family court. It became a central part of child welfare law under President Clinton in 1997, the same era that brought tougher crime laws and other policies impacting people of color. While the crime bill would later haunt the presidential bids of Hillary Clinton and Joe Biden, the Adoption and Safe Families Act has received far less attention. Under this law, once a child has spent fifteen months in foster care, the state's child protection agency (with few exceptions) must move toward ending parental rights. Otherwise, the state cannot be federally reimbursed for the cost of foster care.

The push to end parental rights and speed up adoption came at a time when more than half a million children were languishing in foster care (a population that has since dropped by 24 percent). But the law signed by Clinton brought a new dimension to the problem: In 2015, more than sixty-two thousand children had been rendered orphans—the rights of their parents terminated—while they had yet to be adopted. "We now destroy families, disproportionately Black families, at an unprecedented rate," said Chris Gottlieb, co-director of New York University School of Law's Family Defense Clinic, adding that the system "celebrates as victories cases that end with the permanent severing of parent-child bonds."

Chanel has yet to learn this history, or how her family fits into it. What she knows is her own case, and the details infuriate her. Less than two weeks before ACS removed her children, the family's prevention worker had written "there does not appear to be abuse or neglect in the home."

If anything, Chanel now tells her lawyer, she should be suing ACS for unjustifiably taking her children.

Yost shakes his head.

"You can't sue ACS. No one wins."

He begins a short lecture on the law, explaining to Chanel that the standard is different in family court. It is not like criminal law, which requires proving a case "beyond a reasonable doubt." In family law, all ACS needs is to demonstrate "a preponderance of evidence," which he likens to "a feather or a paper clip" that "tilts in favor of the prosecution."

He offers her a visual. In almost every courtroom, there is a statue of the "scales of justice." Chanel nods. She has seen the scales many times.

It takes very little, Yost says, to tilt those scales.

Chanel glares at Yost.

"You all just fucking pussies, all you lawyers," she says. "You don't stick up for me. Get in the judge's face!"

"You've been watching too much TV."

Chanel blows her fuse.

"Stand up for me!" she shouts.

"Give me something to stand up for!" he shouts back.

chapter 38

DASANI HAS NOT spoken to her mother in weeks.

It is by mere coincidence that, shortly after Chanel's meeting with her lawyer, Dasani is also learning about the scales of justice. She sits in Hershey's mock courtroom, staring at a bronze rendering of Lady Justice.

Courtrooms around the world contain a version of this statue, which traces back to ancient Egypt, where she was known as Maat, and Greece, where she was Themis, the goddess of divine law and order. Here at Hershey, Lady Justice wears a blindfold for impartiality and carries a sword for swift action. Two scales hang from her hand, representing the opposing sides of each case.

Law is Dasani's new favorite class.

Her teacher, Dave Curry, has turned the room into a laboratory, with a foam-padded interrogation cubicle, an up-to-date FBI Most Wanted poster, and a full-blown crime scene. Dasani steps past police tape and is transported into a *Criminal Minds* of her own making—a ransacked apartment, a murder victim dummy, evidence markers. She will learn how to lift fingerprints and search for clues.

But first she must learn the basics: the difference between a misdemeanor and a felony, and between a defense attorney and a prosecutor. Dasani will be the latter. She likes playing offense. She is good at starting arguments and closing them. She wants to be on the right side of the law, as opposed to her mother, whose phone calls Dasani has stopped taking.

"What's the difference between probation and parole?" Curry asks one morning.

"Does probation go on your record?" asks Dasani, who sits in the front row.

"Absolutely," says Curry.

Often his students ask questions tinged with personal worry. Many have a parent or an older sibling in prison. A few minutes later, Dasani raises her hand again. She wants to know about house arrest, which leads to a discussion of ankle bracelets. The bracelet, Curry explains, has a GPS that allows the police to track the parolee.

"What if you take it off and slip it on someone else?" asks Dasani.

"That's very illegal," laughs Curry. A person can get arrested just for forgetting to charge the bracelet's battery. "People usually do it when they're asleep. . . . When they go to bed they'll plug themselves in."

The room explodes with laughter.

A white girl raises her hand.

"Can I share, like, a story?"

"Sure," says Curry.

"Okay. So my dad—he has that. Like, he had gotten out of jail and he was on parole and he wasn't supposed to be around me and my brother. But he came anyway. And I was like four. And he cut his ankle bracelet off. And then, like two minutes later, there was a bunch of cop cars all around the house. And people were running into the house. And I was like, 'What's going on?'"

"Pretty scary," says Curry.

"I was so scared. I hid under my bed with my brother."

Class ends and Dasani moves through her day. English. American Cultures. Algebra.

That same afternoon, in Staten Island, Avianna and Nana leave school, heading to their foster home. They are living in a three-story duplex with cedar shingles and aluminum siding. They have never had a house like this, with a swimming pool in the backyard. Their forty-eight-year-old foster mother, Sherrie Byrd, runs a daycare on the same property while looking after Lee-Lee.

The toddler and Mrs. Byrd have been bonding. But today, when the sisters arrive, they find Mrs. Byrd crying.

"Lee-Lee's leaving," says the foster mother.

Avianna goes numb.

Mrs. Byrd explains that an "aunt" has offered to take in Chanel's three youngest daughters, Hada, Maya, and Lee-Lee. This is known as a "kinship placement"—when a close friend or relative steps forward to foster a child, as Chanel's mother, Joanie, had done for her sister Margo's grandchildren.

Today, the family volunteer is Joan, the longtime girlfriend of Chanel's brother Shamell, with whom Joan has a son. Dasani's siblings have always known her as Auntie Joan. She is forty-two years old and works as a math teacher in Brooklyn.

Avianna wants to know exactly when Lee-Lee is leaving.

"Today?"

She cannot imagine that Lee-Lee would go before tomorrow.

"Yeah, right now, in a couple of minutes," says Mrs. Byrd.

Lee-Lee looks at her sisters and announces that she is going "home."

"You not going *home*," Avianna says.

This will be the fourth time in five weeks that Lee-Lee has been separated from a family member. First she was taken from her father, then from her sisters at the Children's Center. After that, she was separated from her brothers and two youngest sisters here in Staten Island. And now she is leaving for Brooklyn.

She is three years old.

"I *am* going home," Lee-Lee says. "I am."

Her face knots up.

"Don't cry, Lee-Lee," says Avianna.

Two Foundling workers appear at the door. They already have Maya and Hada, who look terrified. Mrs. Byrd invites everyone to sit in the living room, offering them pizza. As the adults chat, Nana and Avianna slip outside.

Whatever happens, stay together.

They climb into the back of the van, crouching to hide.

"Get out of the car," says one of the caseworkers.

Avianna and Nana watch as their sisters climb in.

They wave as the van pulls away.

Seven days later, Dasani arrives at Penn Station for Thanksgiving.

She takes the Q train to Midwood, Brooklyn, where her youngest sisters are now living with the woman they call Auntie Joan. Dasani has not seen her sisters in six months. No one was going to tell her to remain at Hershey for the break—not ACS, not the Akerses, not her mother. They didn't even try.

Chanel tracks her daughter's movements by text. She is prohibited from seeing the children without supervision. Auntie Joan knows this and has told Chanel that she must obey the rules.

At 9 P.M., Dasani gets off at Cortelyou Road station. She must now wait for Uncle Shamell. Dasani does not know this part of Brooklyn. She shivers. She sings along to a Beyoncé song on her phone. Half an hour passes.

Suddenly, there they are: Hada and Maya running in her direction. They fling themselves at Dasani. Together, the three sisters form a tent, their arms interwoven.

"You got glasses now!" says Maya.

"You so *big*!" says Shamell, pulling Dasani in for a hug. He explains that Lee-Lee is at home sleeping. Dasani looks at her sisters and then reaches into her backpack, pulling out her middle school diploma. The girls nod with approval. They, too, will be starting a new school in Brooklyn. All three sisters start dancing across the pavement, singing in tandem.

> *Betcha can't whip like me*
> *Can't Milly Rock like me*
> *Can't sexy walk like me*
> *Can't Hit the Quan like me*

Chanel watches her phone. The texts have stopped.

Three days later, Dasani and her three youngest sisters ride in Auntie Joan's car over the Verrazzano-Narrows Bridge. This will be Dasani's first visit with all seven siblings since they were removed. They pull off the island's expressway, heading into Stapleton and then up to Foundling's circular driveway. Dasani follows her sisters into the building. The siblings are already waiting as Dasani strides in with a casual "Hi, guys!"

A collective scream rocks the floor. The children jump and stomp and hug. Dasani is so excited that she scarcely notices the caseworker by the door. "You could hear nothing but the sounds of laughter of joy coming from the room," writes the worker.

Chanel arrives over an hour late "without any explanation," writes another worker, adding that she "did not bring any activities or snacks for the children." Chanel has not seen the case notes. She would need a lawyer to request them, and her court-appointed attorney, Yost, has yet to do that. Chanel is already looking for a private lawyer, someone who might take her case pro bono.

Here at Foundling, Chanel turns Dasani in the direction of the woman taking notes.

"This is your caseworker who I'm trying to get rid of," says Chanel.

The Foundling supervisor, Linda, pops in and out of the room. She congratulates Papa for making student of the month, and Khaliq for improving his grades. With Chanel, she treads carefully. No one can tell Chanel how to parent her kids. But when she yells at them during visits, Linda has a way of looking at Chanel, or taking Chanel's hand, to make a point. "No person big or small likes to be yelled at," Linda says. "It is *very* demeaning."

Chanel would normally bristle at such corrections, but she holds back with Linda. She must choose her battles.

The children buzz about, cracking jokes, combing hair, breaking into dance. They are still in the foster care version of a honeymoon, not unlike Dasani's first weeks at Hershey. The material novelty—of cars and clean clothes, of mold-free walls and full refrigerators—has yet to wear off.

Toward the end of the visit, a stranger appears at the door.

"That's my Mama Sherrie," says Nana, gesturing at her foster mother.

The room goes quiet. Ten days have passed since caseworkers removed Lee-Lee from Mrs. Byrd's house. They had been bonding. But now, when Mrs. Byrd reaches for Lee-Lee, the three-year-old crouches to the floor.

Lee-Lee presses her hands together, as if in midapplause. She continues to squat, her eyes moving nervously between her mother and Mrs. Byrd.

"Big girl!" gushes Mrs. Byrd. "Big girl! Look at you!"

Adding to the confusion is the fact that Lee-Lee's new foster mother, Auntie Joan, is also here.

Lee-Lee looks away from Mrs. Byrd.

"Don't act like you don't know who that is!" Chanel says. "Mama Sherrie was good to you."

Again and again, Chanel will try to ease her children's guilt, showing kindness to their foster mothers. Dasani is less diplomatic. She introduces herself to Mrs. Byrd with a cool "Hi-I'm-Dasani."

"How are you?" asks Mrs. Byrd.

"Good."

The foster mother turns back to Lee-Lee, and then to the sisters who remain in her care. She has taken to calling Nana "my beautiful butterfly."

"Those are my *girls!*" Mrs. Byrd beams at Nana and Avianna.

"My sisters?" Dasani coughs.

It is time to go.

The children gather at the Foundling entrance, roughhousing, screaming, pulling at one another's hair. This is how they say goodbye.

On the drive home, Dasani looks out the window.

"I don't wanna come back here no more," she says softly.

The next morning, the sun rises over a cloudy North Shore. At around noon, a sixty-three-year-old white woman is walking along Rhine Avenue. Dressed in a lilac blazer, she has a serene face, as if going about her day. She is passing a deli when a Black teenager in a hoodie approaches her from behind.

The boy strikes the woman, who lurches forward. This is captured on the store's surveillance camera. He has no intention, it seems, of robbing her. The sole purpose of this attack is the attack itself— a random act of violence known as the Knockout Game. The objective is to sucker-punch a stranger, knocking the person unconscious with one blow.

The attackers, as reported in the press, tend to be Black teenagers. The victims are often senior citizens, immigrants, or Jews. A spate of recent attacks prompted the Reverend Al Sharpton to condemn the game, while headlines have spurred a social panic.

Today's "Knockout" victim falls to the ground. She begins crying and shaking as the boy runs off with two of his friends, chased by a volunteer "auxiliary officer" with Staten Island's police. The man catches one of the boys, but the assailant escapes.

ASSAULT ON WOMAN PROMPTS "KNOCKOUT GAME" CONCERNS reads a headline in the *Staten Island Advance*, which posts the surveillance video on its website. Police are now searching for the perpetrator, whose face is shown on the video.

It is Dasani's stepbrother Khaliq.

He skips school the next day, hoping the police will lose interest. He has never done anything like this. He cannot explain it, except to say that he was broke and his friends dared him to punch someone for $50. He would have preferred to strike a man, but they steered him toward an elderly woman.

"I'm not knocking her out," Khaliq had told them.

"Knock her out," they said.

Khaliq thought about the money.

"In my head, I was not gonna knock her out, because she was a female," he later told me. So he struck her with his forearm, pushing her to make it "look like I knocked her out." Then "she just tumbled, like that."

Khaliq recalls what happened next with rat-a-tat-tat speed. He saw the officer grabbing his friend as police descended on the scene. He ducked behind a car, removing his jacket and shoving it down his sweatpants "so they didn't know it was me." He ran to a nearby park looking for members of his new crew.

"The cops comin'! Hide me!"

From hiding, Khaliq returned to his foster home, which doubles as a daycare run by Miss Nanny. In her home, Khaliq sheds his street persona. She finds him sweet, "very helpful, not disrespectful," the kind of boy who "listens to reason." She considers him "a blessing."

The only hitch is that Nanny recently found marijuana in the bedroom Khaliq shares with his little brother, Papa. She reports this to Foundling. If it happens again, Khaliq will need to attend a drug program for teens and could be forced out of Nanny's home.

This would mean leaving Papa. Just the thought causes Khaliq anguish. He promises to stay off drugs from now on.

Meanwhile, pressure is mounting for the police to make an arrest in the Knockout case. Readers of the *Staten Island Advance* are outraged by the video, sounding their alarm in the comments section of the website. The families of these three boys should lose their "STATE BENEFITS for 31 days," writes one reader. Others are furious that the newspaper did not emphasize the race of the victim and her assailant.

"How about 'Black 11 year old attacks elderly white woman!'" writes one reader. "SI Advance, keep watering down the black on white crimes and watch people begin to cancel their subscriptions." To this, someone replies, "They can't call it what it is because it goes against the 'white privlage' theory."

Below that, a third person writes, "The lil' colored boy needs vicious prison SODOMY on his tender butthole . . ."

A few days later, Dasani boards the bus at Penn Station. But she can only leave New York with her body. She cannot turn off her phone, which buzzes with texts and updates from Facebook.

She cannot, like Miss Hester, pull an orange suitcase out of the projects and walk into the future, undistracted by the past. Miss Hester grew up at a time when it was easy to disconnect, when the word "unplug" referred to electricity.

Dasani cannot unplug. She gets signal after signal that her siblings are in distress—Khaliq smokes a blunt on his Instagram page, Nana sends a text about being bullied at school. It is worse to be three hours away. All Dasani can do is watch from afar, like a girl who arrives late to the scene of her burning house.

None of this would have happened, Dasani thinks, had she remained in New York. The moment she chose Hershey, she was choosing herself—at the expense of her siblings.

"When I left the house, that's when everything started happening. Did it or did it not?" Dasani asks me one morning, at a diner near Hershey.

She picks at a plate of pancakes.

"When I was in the house, did the kids get taken away? No. When I was in the house, did my mom get kicked out of the house? No. When I left the house, this is what happened. This is why I did not want to come to this dumb school."

Dasani seems to forget that her mother was ousted from Auburn back in 2011, while Dasani was home. She is angry at Chanel for pushing her to come to Hershey. And she is angry at me for not opposing Chanel.

There is no reminding Dasani that she had wept with joy, eleven months ago, when she got into Hershey. There is no trace today of the girl who wrote in her application essay that she wanted to "be away from my family" and the "distractions" of home.

Then again, Dasani could not foresee the distractions that came, and would keep coming.

On December 7, 2015, a detective visits Khaliq's school in Staten Island with a copy of the Knockout video. Twelve days have passed since the assault. A school security guard looks at the footage and recognizes Khaliq's face.

For the first time in his life, the fourteen-year-old boy is arrested. In handcuffs, Khaliq is taken to the 120th Precinct—the same station where his father had landed six months earlier, after holding up the bodega. Detectives begin to question Khaliq. He denies striking the old woman. Then they tell him about the video. Still he shakes his head.

The police summon the Foundling supervisor, Linda, who walks into the precinct with Khaliq's caseworker. The two women watch the video, seeing clearly that Khaliq is the assailant. Absent such proof, they never would have believed it.

It is not lost on Linda that she shares the traits of the victim. She is an older white woman who can be found, on any given day, walking through the North Shore in a blazer.

She asks to see Khaliq. When an officer leads her to the boy, Linda finds him "chained to a pipe" by one arm.

"I'm never getting out of here," he tells her. "This is my future."

By now Khaliq has confessed to the crime, with no lawyer present. He faces an assault charge. He must spend the night in a detention facility. According to the police, he has shown "no remorse for his behavior." But what Khaliq shows is not necessarily what he feels. From jail that evening, he scolds himself in silence.

Stop knocking out old ladies. That's stupid. Cuz when you get locked up, you can't be in the Navy SEALs. . . . You gotta have a good record, goin' to school. . . . You can't be a Navy SEAL no more.

He sits with this realization. The door marked NAVY is now closed. He must find another way "out of here."

For Khaliq, "here" is not just jail or the surrounding North Shore, with its rival gangs and drugs. "Here" is a borderless territory determined by whites and lived by Blacks. It is the defeat he sees in his father's face, and even in his own. When a caseworker asks Khaliq how he wants to "be perceived," the answer is that it does not matter. Society already sees him as "a thief, a trouble maker, and angry."

"It's hard," he tells her, "for a Black youth to get any other perception."

There is little that Khaliq can do about "here"—except to leave it. He thinks about his options. With the right training, Khaliq might catch the notice of a football recruiter. He spends much of his time playing ball at a park in West Brighton. Or he could rap his way out. He grew up listening to Wu-Tang, the ultimate example of North Shore redemption. But Wu-Tang belongs to his father's time.

Khaliq's rapper of choice is Chief Keef, a teenager who grew up in Chicago, which Khaliq refers to as Chiraq. The nickname gained traction last year, after forty-five people were fatally shot over Easter weekend. Khaliq doesn't have to go to Chiraq, because Keef brings it here. In the song "Faneto," Keef "is ridin' through New York" with plans to "blow New Jersey up."

Khaliq will start by making a mixtape. He knows "some people," who will "make it come through." The following day, Khaliq appears in court. Because he is a first-time offender, the judge drops the charge. Khaliq must write a letter of apology to the victim and will be on probation for sixty days, with a strict curfew.

If he slips up again, he could be sent to a correctional facility—the juvenile version of jail.

As Christmas nears, all the siblings are struggling.

Good manners have given way to mood swings and tantrums. The children are less keen on following the rules, less eager to make beds with hospital corners. When they come together for visits at the Foundling agency in Staten Island, they are noted as "very hyper" and "very anxious." At night, they are sleepless. The little ones reach for their mother.

The truth is settling in. They could be in foster care for good.

It does not help that Chanel arrives late to visits, if she comes at all. When she fails to show up—the same day that Khaliq is arrested— Papa pulls the office blinds to the floor. At the same visit, his thirteen-year-old sister, Avianna, regresses into a small child. She keeps climbing on top of a table, over the objections of a caseworker, while Nana stews in anger.

"Everyone keeps saying it is going to be okay. But what does that mean?" Nana says. "I just want to be home."

If Nana can't be home, then she wants her sister Lee-Lee back in her "custody," she tells Foundling. Three weeks have passed since Lee-Lee was transferred to Brooklyn, where Auntie Joan has overseen a rocky transition. Nine-year-old Hada and ten-year-old Maya keep challenging the aunt's authority. They want to bathe, feed, and put Lee-Lee to bed, as if she "is their child," a caseworker writes. When the aunt objects, Hada stomps off. The aunt tells Hada to "concentrate on being a little girl."

Throughout Foundling's case notes, the children are observed as parenting one another. To address this, the caseworkers come up with behavioral goals. Khaliq's goal is "to allow" his foster mother to "take care of" his little brother. The siblings must begin the process of "de-parentification," which is the reverse of growing up. They must learn to be children again.

Instead, they rebel.

The following week, two electronic tablets disappear in Khaliq's home. His foster mother accuses him of stealing. If she reports this to the police, Khaliq's probation will be blown. Instead, Foundling offers to reimburse the foster mother for the missing tablets. She accepts a check for $280, agreeing not to call the police. But Khaliq must go.

On December 14, he packs his things. He says goodbye to his little brother. He is moving to another foster home—the one vacated by his sisters Maya and Hada before they left for Auntie Joan's in Brooklyn.

Each move, known as a "transfer" to a new "placement," takes the children back in time. They are reliving the first rupture, the moment their family broke.

Papa begins misbehaving in school, just like Nana, who has become "extremely disrespectful and dismissive of teachers," writes a caseworker.

Avianna holds to the familiar: She bakes. For years, she had followed her mother around the kitchen, learning how to mix the batter, watching the cornbread rise.

From her foster home, Avianna bakes the same cookies and cakes. Soon she has an idea: She will organize a bake sale at school. She wants to donate the proceeds to an animal shelter, because she remembers "being homeless and how difficult it was" and "feels bad for all the homeless dogs and cats that are out there."

The bake sale is a triumph, raising $902. The *Advance* runs a story with a photograph of Avianna beaming next to a rescued pit bull.

Two siblings—in the span of eight weeks—have drawn headlines in the same newspaper. One is a story of redemption, the other of destruction. No reader could possibly make this connection, as Khaliq's identity remains unpublished while Avianna's last name is incorrectly reported as Handler.

Still, this is her proudest achievement. She hopes it will impress the admissions team at Hershey as much as it does the Foundling supervisor, Linda, who composes a letter to a charity, on Avianna's behalf, seeking money for a tablet.

"If you know this family and all they have been through you would be so amazed at the strength of this young lady," writes Linda.

"For a child to want to give, as opposed to take," Linda adds, "is remarkable."

Dasani wakes on Christmas to a strange room. The Akerses are away, along with her roommate. She is spending the holidays in another student home.

She makes her way downstairs, finding a brightly lit tree. Unmarked stockings and plastic garlands hang from the fireplace. A ceramic Santa winks next to Mrs. Claus, their hands cupping their bellies. It looks as perfect as a window display—except for the missing gifts. They will soon be delivered prewrapped from a van.

It feels to Dasani as if she is visiting someone else's life. Her phone blinks with unanswered calls. On Christmas Eve, Nana kept trying to reach Dasani, texting: "Good night. I know you have to go to sleep. Merry Christmas."

Then Nana added: "You a ho."

Dasani scrolls through Nana's angry texts, seeing a photograph of thirteen-year-old Avianna holding a martini glass filled with frothy orange liquid. "Avianna is drinking an alcohol drink," Nana writes.

When Dasani gets on the phone with her sisters, they confirm that they have alcohol. They start cursing at Dasani, who demands to speak to their foster mother. "You need to watch them," Dasani tells Mrs. Byrd, "because they're speaking disrespectful to people."

Dasani and her sisters were raised to notice such behavior. No one could talk down to their mother without facing Chanel's wrath. Respect was a person's currency on the street.

Dasani is even less tolerant of the girls at Hershey, especially her new white roommate.

At first Ashley seemed relatable. She and Dasani had both come from fractured families, finding the same outlet, as sprinters on the track team. Then, one day, Ashley could not locate her Jolly Ranchers. Next her lipstick went missing. With that, she accused Dasani of stealing. The Akerses searched through Dasani's belongings. They found nothing. But after that, everything shifted.

It is now December 28, 2015. During cleanup duty, Dasani and Ashley begin arguing in the kitchen. Before things escalate, Dasani alerts Mrs. Akers, who pulls them into her office.

Dasani looks at Ashley.

"I know you've been through a lot," Dasani says. "But so have I. And I will let my anger out on you."

"You guys are not gonna let anger out on each other," says Mrs. Akers. "You guys are *sisters*."

Dasani is tired of hearing about the sisterhood at Hershey, especially when her real sister has yet to get in. And there is no giving the title of "sister" to a white girl who has called Dasani a thief.

"I already have too many sisters," Dasani says. "I don't need another one."

She refuses to hug Ashley but agrees to shake her hand.

To the Akerses, this is progress. Dasani has been at Hershey for almost a year. She has yet to throw a punch.

Dasani tries not to think about her siblings. She applies herself in school, earning an A in her law class. For English, she is learning about different types of language.

Colloquial language, Dasani writes in pencil, is "a regional dialect that is only spoken and understood by a group of people; includes slang."

Objective language, she continues, is "dealing with facts," whereas subjective language is "influenced by a person's emotions, prejudice, and opinion." She distinguishes between the "literal," which "means what is said," and the "figurative," which uses "devices to create an image in the reader's mind."

If Dasani were to describe—in a figurative way—what happens on January 8, 2016, she would say that her anger had been swelling like a giant cloud. If a cloud gets too big, it must rain.

This anger has its source in many things, going back many years. The absence of Dasani's biological father, Ramel. The drug addiction that stalks Chanel and Supreme. The violence between them. The degradation of growing up homeless. The burden of caring for seven siblings, who have now been separated. And because that separation happened while Dasani was away, her fury is felt by another set of people.

It is Hershey's staff and students who stand in Dasani's rain. "I tend to let out my anger on them, with my family in mind," she says. "It's more anger than it would have been."

The literal events of January 8 are as follows: Shortly after track practice, a girl named Innocence gets on Dasani's nerves. They begin to argue. Dasani loses control of her body. She charges at Innocence, pummeling her face before other students intervene.

Dasani is placed on probation, without access to a phone, and is barred from competing in track meets. Yet she continues to lash out, punching a boy in school, insulting her math teacher, talking back to the Akerses. Within a week, Dasani has landed five disciplinary levels, drawing the notice of the school's president, who walks up to her in Founders Hall.

"How's that working for you, insulting everyone?" says President Gurt.

While Dasani continues to meet with her therapist, Julie, and the assistant principal, Tara, no one seems to be getting through. The worst incident follows nine days later, when Dasani is cleaning up after dinner. She grabs a small steak knife, playfully jabbing it at her housemate.

"Come on, Dasani, cut it out," says another girl.

Dasani keeps poking the knife into the air. When her roommate, Ashley, alerts Mrs. Akers, Dasani starts slamming dishes around the kitchen.

There are times when Mrs. Akers helps Dasani, and times when they clash. They have equally strong personalities, hitting the same high notes of emotion. Dasani's impulse is to run from Mrs. Akers, but the rules prevent this. When Dasani is being reprimanded, she must stay in the Akerses' office, which makes her want to explode.

Dasani's therapist has offered a strategy: Anytime Dasani is stuck in the office, she can silently count backward by twos and her mind will settle. One hundred, ninety-eight, ninety-six. And she will feel in control. The Akerses can keep her in the office, but they "can't tell me I can't count numbers backwards in my head."

She can also pace back and forth while standing in the office.

They cannot tell her not to pace. Dasani's body and mind belong to her alone.

But tonight, all tactics vanish. Dasani bolts past the Akerses' office into her room. As Mrs. Akers follows behind, Dasani slams the door in her housemother's face.

Mrs. Akers barges in. They begin to argue, their voices rising. A security guard is summoned.

No matter what Dasani says, the fact remains that she has frightened her housemates. Whenever a student causes others to feel unsafe, that student must be mentally evaluated. Dasani will spend the night at the school's health clinic.

The Akerses explain this to Dasani.

She looks numb.

"Are you okay if we pray before you go?" asks Mrs. Akers.

Dasani gives a one-shoulder shrug.

Mr. and Mrs. Akers kneel before Dasani, taking her hand. They close their eyes. She listens in silence. Only when the Akerses finish the prayer and open their eyes do they see that Dasani is crying.

Dasani is now on behavioral "restitution," Hershey's version of detention.

She will be cleaning stables, raking leaves, and doing other "hard chores." This old-fashioned approach is the legacy of Milton Hershey, whose orphan boys were made to milk cows. Dasani is grateful to be spared that job. She finds it hard enough to shovel manure.

"It's gross!" she says.

Back in New York, Dasani's siblings are now divided among four addresses—three foster homes in Staten Island and Auntie Joan's in Brooklyn. Chanel is still living with Supreme on Laurel Avenue. Late at night, fourteen-year-old Khaliq turns up at their door.

He is often hungry or broke. They give him whatever they can find—a bag of chips, a few dollars. Sometimes he goes to the ferry, where other foster children seek refuge, riding back and forth across the harbor until dawn.

No one seems to be watching Khaliq.

"How you just snatch them and they have no supervision?" Chanel says of ACS.

Chanel has deteriorated. She cannot eat or sleep. She has lost twenty pounds. Her jeans droop and her lips are chapped. Both she and Supreme have been blunting their pain with drugs. Chanel will soon test positive for opioids.

ACS has ordered both parents to enroll in a program for the "mentally ill chemically addicted," known as MICA. Chanel and Supreme are refusing on the grounds that they are not mentally ill. "The ACS system is broken and people are going to pay the consequences," Supreme tells a Foundling caseworker.

Privately, Supreme admits that he and his wife are depressed. Who wouldn't be? Sometimes Chanel catches herself muttering like a bag lady. Memories intrude at inopportune times—a flash of Papa's smile, the sound of Lee-Lee's giggle.

The ache deepens when Chanel is still, so she passes her days in motion. On January 19, she wanders through downtown Brooklyn, wearing a thin coat covered in stains. She is shivering. She feels someone staring.

It is Miss Hester, the teacher from McKinney.

More than three years have passed since that first day of school, when Dasani settled into a metal desk in Miss Hester's classroom. Today, the teacher is heading to the D train because she no longer lives in Brooklyn.

After spending a year in the shelter system, Miss Hester had saved enough money for a down payment and bought a modest apartment near her church in the Bronx. She will never be someone's tenant again.

Miss Hester could easily have taken a teaching job in the Bronx, ending her cumbersome commute to McKinney (about ninety minutes each way). But she refused.

"This is my last connection to Brooklyn and I don't want to let go," she tells me.

Still, the train ride is wearing Miss Hester down. This may be her last year at the school.

None of this does she share with Chanel, for Miss Hester knows that her problems would sound enviable. Instead, the teacher says nothing at all. She wants to give Chanel the option to keep walking, in case she is embarrassed to be seen in this condition.

"Hey, Miss Hester!" howls Chanel.

An awkward hug follows.

"How are you?" Miss Hester asks.

"Not too good," Chanel replies.

Neither woman will say what she is really thinking. Miss Hester is horrified by Chanel's appearance and wonders if she is homeless, because "that situation is too awful to know about and not help." Chanel is certain that Miss Hester is judging her, as if to say, *See, dummy? Look what you did to yourself.*

Chanel refrains from telling Miss Hester about the children going to foster care. Instead, she asks for the teacher's number. She taps it into her phone, her hands trembling.

They hug once more.

chapter 39

D ASANI LOOKS OUT her window. It is January 25, 2016, and Hershey's trees are draped in white. A lethal blizzard has paralyzed the northeastern United States, burying roads, cars, homes, people.

Avianna wakes in Staten Island to the same deep snow. It covers her three-story foster home on Maple Parkway, and those of her siblings: Papa's doorstep five blocks south, Khaliq's lawn two miles west, the Brooklyn rooftop of Auntie Joan's building, where Lee-Lee, Hada, and Maya now live. The snow has blanketed all five boroughs, including the house on Laurel Avenue where Chanel and Supreme remain.

There Chanel reaches for a pair of shoes. She never has proper boots. When it snows, she tries to step in the footprints of other people to keep her feet from getting wet. "Poor people don't want a white Christmas," she says.

She walks outside, heading to her first job in years: as an emergency snow worker for the city. Chanel had cajoled Linda, the Foundling supervisor, into driving her to Walgreens and paying for the required $24.50 identification photo.

Men and women gather in the biting cold, waiting for a shovel. Some of them Chanel knows from jail. They pose for selfies, their faces giddy. A job is hard to find when you have a criminal record. Soon Chanel is hacking at the snow. She ignores the pain in her knee.

That same afternoon, Dasani is also shoveling. She must clear the periphery of her student home, digging her way out of detention. Lately, the Akerses have seen improvements in Dasani. She is learning to apologize and to express gratitude. Back in New York, she rarely did either. To say "I'm sorry" was to show weakness. To say "Thank you" meant you needed help.

Dasani's pride and self-sufficiency—the very things that enabled her to come this far—are now a detriment. They interfere with what Mr. Akers, a devout Christian, calls "that healing part of her life." He wants to see Dasani "allowing herself to become vulnerable and be able to really face some of those things that hurt her so much."

She will hear this phrase—"to become vulnerable"—again and again. It gives Dasani pause. Vulnerability is the opposite of what she learned on the streets, "where you keep your guard up." She must now unlearn that habit, says Mr. Akers, pointing to his own example. He is no longer beholden to the Brooklyn projects of his youth. He has "let go of the tribe."

In February, the Akerses release Dasani from detention just in time to watch the Super Bowl. On television, Lady Gaga sings the national anthem, dazzling the girls at Student Home Morgan. Dasani has little interest in football, but she lights up when the cheerleaders fill the screen, and when Beyoncé takes the stage at halftime.

On Staten Island, her sisters are also watching the game.

More than two months have passed since Foundling came for Lee-Lee, separating her from Avianna and Nana. In the toddler's absence, the sisters have tried to adapt. Their home on Maple Parkway is shared by a third foster child and two foster parents—Mrs. Byrd and her husband, Elvis—as well as two of their grown children and a girlfriend.

Avianna and Nana are fond of Mrs. Byrd, but they sense danger in the house. They do not know the details: that Mrs. Byrd's thirty-one-year-old son was arrested three weeks ago and charged with possession of cocaine, while Mrs. Byrd's husband, according to a complaint his wife will later file, has physically and emotionally abused her for "many years."

Nor do they know the most chilling secret of all—that eighteen months ago, a child drowned on the premises. The victim, a three-year-old boy, had been enrolled in Mrs. Byrd's on-site daycare center. Among Mrs. Byrd's employees was the boy's mother, who had found her baby son in the backyard pool, floating facedown.

Five days after the boy's death, state investigators revoked Mrs. Byrd's daycare license. Yet she continues to run another daycare from the same duplex. Among the children she recently enrolled at "Mother Byrd Daycare" was Lee-Lee.

When Avianna and Nana learn of this, it will not alter their attachment to Mrs. Byrd. In this way, they are loyal. They had come to her shattered. She had taken them in, soothing them with her Cayman Islands accent, her warm laugh, her homemade curry chicken and stewed peas. This was the woman who had wept when Lee-Lee left, so tender was their bond. The problem, the sisters say, is not Mrs. Byrd but the men in her midst.

Tonight, as the Super Bowl ends, Elvis Byrd walks into the house. He starts complaining that the garbage bin is in the wrong place and that the entrance is crowded with shoes.

The sisters flee to a second-floor bedroom, but Mr. Byrd comes charging in. Avianna mutters something, snickering.

"Do you have something to say to me, li'l bitch?" Avianna recalls Mr. Byrd saying.

He is now in Avianna's face, going "nose to nose, screaming" at the thirteen-year-old girl, according to Foundling's investigative notes. Avianna races up another flight of stairs, searching for her cellphone, as Nana chases behind. Then Mr. Byrd becomes violent. He shoves the nearly blind girl in the chest. He follows Avianna into the bedroom, opening the door with such force that it "came off the hinges," writes a Foundling investigator.

Mr. Byrd throws furniture around the room, punches a hole in the wall, and breaks a lamp. His oldest son has joined in, shoving Nana "mad hard," recalls Avianna, and calling them "ghetto children." They watch as Mr. Byrd throws their belongings on the floor, screaming that he no longer wants them there.

It is his wife who intervenes, grabbing her husband to stop him from striking Avianna. Mrs. Byrd rushes the sisters outside, into the freezing cold. The three of them start walking, with no clear destination. After a few blocks, Avianna calls Supreme, who tells her to dial 911. He also calls the police, giving them the address.

By the time the police arrive, Avianna is too afraid to talk. She "refused to answer any questions," writes an officer, who files a report of harassment. The police do not arrest Mr. Byrd because, according to Foundling's notes, both his wife and the foster children are found to be free of "marks and bruises."

Still, the girls feel unsafe, so Mrs. Byrd spends the night with them at a Hilton hotel. In the morning, she files for an order of protection against her husband, only to withdraw the filing two days later. By then Avianna and Nana are headed to a new foster home. The van pulls up to the projects near their former house on Laurel Avenue.

The sisters have "a very difficult time getting out of the van," observes a caseworker. They blame themselves for losing Mrs. Byrd, saying they wish they had never called the police.

The caseworker reassures the sisters that they did "the right thing." They proceed to the new apartment, where an ACS worker is waiting to ask them about the Byrd incident.

Every time the children are questioned, the past reemerges. They fear for Mrs. Byrd as they feared for their own mother. This new apartment is so crowded that the foster mother moves to a couch, giving her bed to Avianna and Nana.

"We know that she just wants the money," Avianna says.

A few days later, the sisters dial Dasani's number. Her phone is back on.

"You sound so white right now," says her stepsister, Nana.

A year has passed since Dasani came to Hershey. Nothing offends her fourteen-year-old ego like hearing that she sounds "white." She wants to tell her sisters that they sound "stupid" because "they don't know how to talk," though Dasani can feel that way at Hershey sometimes.

If Dasani says "'bout" instead of "about," she is corrected. "You gotta say every word—the correct word . . . the *whole* word." She keeps reminding herself of this while trying to improve her vocabulary.

Her favorite new word is "irk." Her sisters are irking her right now. She puts the call on speaker, rolling her eyes. Everyone is talking at once—laughing, teasing, swapping stories about boys.

"We need you to pop some girl," Avianna says.

"Why?" asks Dasani.

It turns out that Nana is being bullied at school.

"Wait, wait, wait," says Dasani. "You got jumped? . . . By who? . . . When? When was this? . . . All right, I gotchu. I'm not gonna . . . um . . . Am I coming home for Easter break?"

The plan is unclear.

"You better be comin'," says Avianna.

No one wants to tell Dasani about Mr. Byrd's violence. All she knows is that Nana and Avianna have moved to a new home. After they hang up, Dasani is glum. Maybe her sisters are right. "I'm gonna turn white at Hershey and I don't wanna be white," she tells me. "I wanna go home."

When she says this to her mother, Chanel replies that there is no more "home." If Dasani were to leave Hershey and move back to New York, she would enter foster care.

Yet for Dasani, "home" is more than a place.

"Home is the people. The people I hang out with. The people I grew up with. That, to be honest, is really home. Family who have had my back since day one. It doesn't have to be a roof over my head. . . . At Hershey, I feel like a stranger. Like I don't really belong. In New York, I feel proud. I feel good. I feel accepted when I'm in New York."

She wants to feel at home wherever she goes. And that means having the freedom to speak like her sisters—without hearing the voice of correction, nudging her from "ain't" to "isn't."

"I be having to correct myself. It just makes me feel like I can't really be myself. I always gotta be aware of how I talk, all the time."

Most of Dasani's mentors at Hershey are Black: Mr. Akers; her therapist, Julie; her cheerleading and track coaches. They have tried, in their own ways, to challenge the notion that one must "be white" to succeed.

Dasani is not sure she believes them. "I'm not saying I'm *not* gonna be successful, but I'm still gonna keep the streets in me."

She has the beginnings of a plan. She will major in business, starting a family-run music production company. Nana can draw, and Maya is good with colors. Hada is a natural writer. The three of them can design the ads, whereas Avianna is more of a performer. "She can fake it till she makes it." And their mother will promote this business far and wide, using her street smarts to find investors.

Dasani is waiting for the right moment to tell them her plan.

Hershey's theme park empties out every winter. There are no roller coasters cranking up the rails or dipping into free fall.

Skyrush. Fahrenheit. Great Bear. Dasani has ridden them all. She no longer screams like the other children, thrilled by each twist and turn. They know they can dismount at the end of the ride, catching their breath, regaining their balance.

The roller coaster of Dasani's life is one that never ends. On March 14, she gets into another serious fight, attacking a girl so ferociously that she lands a Level 3, for "serious acts of aggression," her worst disciplinary infraction yet. Over Easter, she must go to "intercession," a temporary residence for students who have misbehaved. She is so bitter that she tells the Akerses she wants to leave their home permanently.

She blames everyone but herself.

The girl she fought is to blame: "Don't disrespect me and you won't feel my fire."

The Akerses are to blame: "If they wanted to help me be successful, they should have done that by now."

Her parents are to blame: They "don't listen. And they're lazy. And they do nothing to help me."

The school sees it differently. In fact, the assistant principal, Tara, has recruited Dasani's mother to help create a new "behavioral plan" for Dasani. This is part of Hershey's "whole child" approach. Tara identifies all the most influential adults in a child's life—her teachers, athletic coaches, counselors, houseparents, and, when possible, her biological family. The goal is to get all these disparate adults to work together as one coordinated team.

In addition to Chanel and Tara, Dasani's team includes her counselor, her new track coach, and the Akerses. Right now, they are worried that Dasani will keep fighting the same girl. Dasani seems "very agitated," Tara writes, adding that she is "having difficulty making eye contact with me, shaking her legs and just very fidgety."

Tara looks at Dasani.

"Help me understand why you can't walk away," she asks.

Dasani is tired of this question. She grew up on the streets. Her instinct is to protect herself. She has explained this to Tara many times. "If someone walked up to your daughter and punched your daughter in the face," Dasani says, "what you gonna tell your daughter to do?"

"Tell the teacher," Tara replies.

"See, I'm not like that," Dasani says. "I'm gonna hit her back."

She knows that she sounds like her mother right now. But when it comes to fighting, Dasani trusts her mother: To protect yourself, Chanel says, is to protect your reputation. And just because Dasani left Brooklyn does not mean she has lost her "street cred," which she must "defend."

Tara mounts her best counterargument regarding how to "defend" one's street cred: "You end up being the bigger defender by walking away."

To Dasani, this sounds like a clueless if well-meaning trope, the kind spoken by a Hershey native. Dasani doubts that Tara has ever had to defend her life with her body.

Back in her student home, Dasani "gets really sad and, like, dreary and she doesn't want to do anything," says her roommate, Ashley. "She just sits there."

Dasani keeps thinking about her fourteen-year-old brother, Khaliq, punching the elderly woman in Staten Island. He seems destined for a life of trouble.

"I don't want anything to happen to him," Dasani tells Ashley.

"God puts everything in place," Ashley says.

Dasani wants to believe this. Sometimes she bows her head in prayer. She figures God is "somewhere around. We just can't find him." If she closes her eyes, he might show up.

You can trust he will take care of you is what the sidewalk preachers used to say, outside the Auburn shelter. To "trust" means to believe in things you cannot see. This has never worked for Dasani.

She trusts what she can see—her phone, her cheerleading team, her best friend, Kali. They are closer than ever despite living in separate homes. Kali, now fourteen, recently got braces, which she tried to hide on a recent trip home. She worried that people would be jealous. They told her to smile. Then they called her ugly.

"It was just because they were mad," Kali says softly.

She knows, because she carries the same anger. It binds her to Dasani, who is also "an angry person," says Kali.

"When you have two angry people, you don't talk about things that make you angry," Kali says. "You talk about things that make you happy. Because that's the one time you can be happy."

No one can explain Khaliq's violence.

He strikes victim after victim, with little or no provocation. His latest target is a sixty-six-year-old woman riding the S74 bus. She is talking on her cellphone when some teenagers head to the back.

"I can't even hear you because these kids are being so loud," she tells her daughter on the phone. "They're obnoxious."

The woman's "disrespectful" tone gets "under my skin," Khaliq later tells the police. After she hangs up, Khaliq strikes her in the eye, causing it to swell. A few weeks later, on February 7, he punches a woman outside a deli before robbing her. Soon after that, he gives a classmate "a bloody nose for no reason," says a teacher.

At a supervised visit, Chanel implores Khaliq to stop because "he wasn't raised in a violent home" and "if he were home he would not behave this way." His foster mother is also surprised. Khaliq is like two different boys, she tells his caseworker. He completes "chores and extra chores" at home while "acting out violently in the community."

Khaliq's street antics climax on the afternoon of February 25, in what appears to be a gang-related dare. Khaliq is accused of getting off a bus on Hylan Boulevard, sucker-punching an innocent man, and then getting back on the bus. When the police catch up with the bus, Khaliq tries to escape by crawling through a window.

By the time Khaliq is summoned to family court on March 18, he is living at Boys Town, a juvenile detention facility in Brooklyn. He faces three charges of assault and six robbery-related charges—a total of six felonies. He sits slumped in the waiting room, his face empty. Just two days earlier, the Boys Town staff had found a razor in his room.

Supreme and Chanel get to court early, joined by Khaliq's Foundling caseworker and his court-appointed lawyer, a white woman with heavy eyeliner who stands in a permanent shrug, clutching a stack of folders. She seems overwhelmed.

Chanel takes one look at the lawyer and begins delivering a set of instructions: "You have to establish and let them know that this was an *unbroken* home. This home got broken up, and *through* it being broken up, this child is going through peer pressure, and he's doing some things."

As Chanel continues to coach the lawyer, Supreme turns to his son.

"You should know better," Supreme hisses.

Khaliq stares at the ground.

"You not savage," his father says. "A savage is a person who has no knowledge of self and is living a beastly life. Meaning they have no conscience, you understand?"

"Yes."

"You say you understand but you not showing you understand. Meaning you know better than hitting a lady! . . . An old lady? Come on, brother. What's on your mind?"

"But she came toward me—"

"Still, you could walk away!" snaps Supreme. He looks at his son. Supreme has very little time to make an impact. He tries quizzing Khaliq on today's mathematics and other tenets of the Five Percent.

"Every action has a . . . what?" asks Supreme.

"A consequence," says Khaliq.

"A consequence," repeats his father. "A reward or a penalty."

A few days later, Supreme will meet his own consequence when he enrolls in a residential detox program, determined to become clean. On the following morning, March 22, Khaliq returns to the cramped courtroom to learn what will become of him.

The courtroom is silent.

Judge Helene Sacco glances at Khaliq, who looks terrified. Chanel leaps to her feet, forever in lawyer mode. "He was always a good boy," Chanel begins as Judge Sacco listens patiently, asking when these assaults occurred, to which an ACS lawyer replies, "A short period of time." This seems to sway the judge, who decides that Khaliq can return to foster care, under "intensive case management" with a strict curfew. Khaliq smiles with relief, promising Judge Sacco that he will "do better."

Chanel and Khaliq leave court accompanied by Khaliq's case-worker, whom Chanel calls J. Lo because of her curly golden locks and bronze skin. As they head to the probation office, Chanel is beaming. She has not had a court victory in a long time. J. Lo smiles at Chanel as Khaliq walks alongside them, a fresh bounce in his step.

They pass a Corvette.

"You should be drivin' one of those," says Chanel, who is wearing a T-shirt with the word BROOKLYN scrawled over a bleach-blond girl making a gangsta sign, the word HOMIE across her white chest.

"I don't like Corvettes," says Khaliq.

The conversation shifts to Khaliq's temper, and why he loses it. Perhaps he was traumatized "by the footprint," says J. Lo.

Years ago, when Khaliq was living at Auburn shelter, he became the target of bullies at school. They routinely teased him for being homeless and poor. One day, a boy wearing a coveted pair of Timberlands stomped Khaliq in the face. He returned to Auburn with his head hung low, the boy's footprint indented in Khaliq's cheek. It was the ultimate symbol of defeat.

The footprint disappeared, but only physically.

Khaliq nods at J. Lo. She is correct. He had been stomped to the ground and humiliated—yes, "traumatized"—because "I walked away," he says.

"So, I got to defend myself."

To change Dasani's behavior, the team at Hershey must identify her triggers—any thoughts, words, or actions that cause her to lose control.

It does not help that Dasani hates the word "trigger," which makes her think of gunfire. The word is, in and of itself, a trigger. It disrupts the peace of Hershey, where "you don't hear no gunshots." It takes Dasani back to Brooklyn's streets. Yet in both places, her "trigger" is the same.

Don't disrespect me and you won't feel my fire.

Here at Hershey, Dasani's team wants to disrupt this pattern. There is no controlling another girl's behavior. But Dasani must learn to contain her fire. They want her to "use her words" or—failing that—to "walk away."

With this in mind, the team drafts a "behavioral agreement" for Dasani to sign. This is a last-ditch strategy that the school tries with troubled students. Each agreement is different, reflecting the needs of that particular child. Some of them need to withdraw when they are angry. Dasani needs to vent.

Dasani's agreement outlines the following plan: When she starts to feel upset, she must remove herself physically, going to a "safe space" such as Tara's office at school. Dasani's trusted adults must then give her at least five minutes to talk. She needs to air her grievances. Only then is she able to listen.

A few days later, Dasani leaves Tara a note: "This is Dasani. Feeling agitated. Needed to talk to you. Took a few minutes. Went back to class."

Tara arranges for Dasani to call her mother, who has been briefed on the behavioral agreement, and the fact that Dasani will face consequences for good behavior and bad behavior. This is the message that Chanel must reinforce.

Sometimes involving a parent can backfire. But in this case Tara is willing to take a chance because she knows that Dasani listens to her mother.

Tara hands Dasani an iPad so she can FaceTime her mother. The call comes as Chanel is heading to her new methadone program in Harlem. She looks at the screen of her phone, seeing her daughter's luminous face.

"You look so much better than New York City," says Chanel.

Dasani chuckles. She holds the iPad close, staring back at her mother. There is no question that Chanel has lost weight. She seems tired, smiling only with effort.

"You look comfortable," says Chanel. "But you gotta learn to control your temper."

Dasani jumps to her own defense, telling her mother what she told Tara about the fight: "Don't hit me in my face if you don't want to get hit back."

Chanel's response is notably different from Tara's.

"How'd you even let her punch you in the face?"

Chanel listens as her daughter recounts the fight, play by play. Slowly, Chanel's lip curls into a smile. She never ceases to be impressed by her daughter's might.

"And so who got the trouble for it?" Chanel asks.

"Both of us! They gave me a Level 3 because I hit her back—"

"Because you hit like a *man*," Chanel says proudly. "That's why."

"That's not my problem! Don't hit me in the face!"

Chanel laughs.

"But you hit like a man, see? It's a different force."

"That's what all the boys say!" Dasani says. "They be like 'Damn, you hit like a man!'"

"It's a different force of hit," Chanel continues. "Cuz we stronger than the average woman. So you need to know that. And you need to know that we have strength like horses. And you need to know that and you have to control that because I'm tellin' you, we will *hurt* something. . . ."

Chanel has veered off script.

"But I don't wanna support that," she says, remembering Hershey's behavioral plan for Dasani. "If you do the right thing, I don't mind letting you come down for every holiday. But if you aren't doing the right thing, then why the fuck am I letting you come home?"

"So, I can do the right thing, take a break?" Dasani says in disbelief. "I think I need a trip home! I'm starting to sound white! I'm starting to talk with proper grammar!"

"I know, I know, boobie," her mother says softly. "That's why we comin' to steal you."

Every time Chanel betrays the Hershey script, she tries to recover. This is not how she likes to parent.

"Yo, I gotta go," Chanel finally says. "My program is gonna close at two-thirty."

"All right."

"So listen. I'm gonna call you every day at the student home, right? But our deal is you gonna behave from this point on and get in no fights and shit, man. Cuz I really need you to graduate from there and do what you gotta do. I really, really need you to do that for me . . . for you."

Dasani is silent.

"You understand? Didn't nobody else get this opportunity like you. You are blessed. I'm tellin' you. And use your blessings. Use them wisely. And it doesn't seem like it's gonna pay off now. But at the end, baby girl, it's gonna pay off. And you gonna be so glad that you did it. You gonna kiss my wrinkly-ass toes—"

Dasani starts laughing.

"No, I'm not!" she says.

"You gonna kiss the ground that I walk on with my wrinkly-ass old toes. Thanking God . . . that you don't have to eat from here."

Chanel points her phone at the "Relief Bus," a mobile food pantry parked near 125th Street. "See this bus?" she says. "I eat from this bus. . . . I eat from this bus, right here, every day. Soup and bread. You see? You see the people?"

"Yes."

"That's where I'm at," says Chanel. "You don't want to be there with me. All right?"

Dasani looks devastated.

"Do what you gotta do," Chanel says. "Get your education, girl. You hear me?"

"Yes."

"Cuz I didn't have it, and I want you to have it," says Chanel, her face twisting up. "I'm sheddin' blood and tears for you. . . . These are strong tears. These ain't tears of pain."

Dasani wipes her own cheek and nods.

"You hear me?" says Chanel. "I love you."

part 7

DASANI'S WAY

2016–2021

chapter 40

"HEY, BABY!" SAYS Mrs. Akers, pulling Dasani in for a hug. "You're so cold!"

She touches Dasani's cheeks. It is below freezing on this winter day in 2016. The weather never seems to faze Dasani, who has just come in without a coat on. After all, she grew up trudging through snow in tattered sneakers.

She lugs a heavy backpack with BROOKLYN written in silver across each strap. Mrs. Akers listens as Dasani delivers a report about her day, from the bad (she failed a test) to the good (she got into two honors classes: world cultures and science). She is talking at her usual high speed, switching from the Cold War to communism as Mrs. Akers nods, unable to get a word in.

Dasani is so chatty that her new track coach calls her Little Bit, because he can "only take a little bit of her at a time." Here at home, the Akerses continue to call her Nini. But to Dasani's ear, the only nickname that sounds right is Muka—the one spoken by her grandmother and carried on by her mother, who whispers it in their sweetest moments.

Even from 170 miles away, Chanel's force is felt. The other day, she called Mrs. Akers in a fury. She had been to Avianna's school to drop off the Hershey application, after signing the parental consents for a second time. (Avianna's school had lost the first batch of forms.) Upon seeing Chanel, the staff told her to leave, citing the order of protection that prevents Chanel from seeing her children without ACS supervision. It would be one thing if Chanel were sneaking a visit with her daughter. But she had come on urgent business, for the sake of Avianna's future.

Now, on the phone with Mrs. Akers, Chanel begins to vent. She believes that ACS is working against her children: subverting Avianna's application to Hershey while disrupting Dasani's education. Why, Chanel demands, did the Hershey school allow ACS—back in October—to visit Dasani right after her siblings were removed?

Mrs. Akers tries to explain the school's policy, saying that students need to be "made aware" of "certain things."

"Wait," Chanel says. "You agree?"

She lights into Mrs. Akers, saying she does not know how it feels to be "Black and poor in New York City."

To this Mrs. Akers replies that not only is she from New York City, but "my husband is African American." There is a lot more that Mrs. Akers could say—about her own childhood in the projects, about being a Puerto Rican with tan skin. But she knows when to hold her fire.

Angry mothers often call, for reasons as varied as their suffering. They have lost a job. They have relapsed. They have gone to jail, or come out of it. They have been evicted. They have landed in the hospital. They have run out of food stamps. They are having another baby. Any one of these events can make a mother pine for her missing child—especially if that child is the oldest, the strongest, the one capable enough to have left in the first place.

Mrs. Akers is trained to manage these phone calls, staying calm and diplomatic. Her goal is to help the parent "de-escalate." If the call goes well, the child is shielded. If it goes poorly, the child could wind up leaving. Sometimes there is no phone call. The parent shows up and takes the child away.

To outsiders, this might seem selfish. But to the parent, it can feel like reclamation. The school's own president, whose widowed mother sent him to Hershey, often tells parents that the most "selfless" thing they can do is to enroll their child at Hershey. Many of these adults have known only failure. Their sole accomplishment is the child they must give away, like a half-made sculpture to be finished by another artist.

On the phone, Chanel makes Mrs. Akers's job easier than expected.

"It's not you, Mrs. Akers. It's the system," she says. "They're trying to take away my role as a mother."

While the matriarchs in Dasani's life vie for power, it is Mr. Akers who holds the most sway. Dasani adores the man. Just the sight of him causes her to smile, bumping hips with him.

"Mister! I ain't cursed today!"

"Well, that's good. You're not supposed to."

"Ah-ka-ka-ka-ka!" trills Dasani, caricaturing the sound of laughter. Mr. Akers loves this particular quirk of hers, parroting it right back.

"I missed you, Mister!" she says another day, after a weeklong absence. She finds him hilarious and strange, how he shifts from one linguistic mode to another, bonding with her by "talkin' hood," while at formal events "he will start talkin' mad proper and using big-ass words."

This is not a betrayal of his roots, Mr. Akers tells Dasani, but a mark of cultural agility. He can access the worlds he wants. He is like an explorer, going from one place to the next, from east Brooklyn's projects to Hershey's golf course, sometimes in the same week. If there is discomfort in this, Mr. Akers does not speak of it. He belongs only to the group of his own choosing—his wife, his children, and their Christian faith. And in this, there is freedom.

"You're not everyone," Mr. Akers tells Dasani. "You're not your father. You're not your sisters. You are uniquely you."

To be unique is to stand apart, which Dasani does well. But she does it better with people watching. They could be as familiar as her sisters or as alien as the ladies at A Tea Affair, a fussy establishment where Mrs. Akers brings the girls for high tea on April 15, 2016.

The lavish shop is near Lancaster, where Milton's fortune began and where he and his bride, Kitty, hosted posh parties. Today Dasani walks in to find long tables covered in white cloth, set with dainty

cups and doilied treats: lemon raspberry scones, cucumber sandwiches, tiny pots of crème brûlée.

Each girl is handed a pearl necklace and a silk or lace flower for
her hair. Dasani is already wearing a thick black sports headband,
which she refuses to remove. Her compromise is to tuck a red flower
above the headband.

She cautiously takes her seat as a round of introductions begin.
Each girl's name must be preceded by "Lady."

"Lady Mimi!"

"Lady Tamaya!"

The group turns to Dasani.

"My name's not 'Lady.' It's Dasani."

Ruptura is the Latin origin of "rupture." It means the breaking of a
limb, the fracturing of a bone—a tearing, "a bursting." From the
same Latin root came other words suggesting the trauma of immediate impact. Abrupt. Erupt.

But the rupture of a family happens at a different pace. It only
begins with the event itself—the afternoon of October 6, the seven
children stepping into a van. Many months later, they are still pulling
apart. Their separation is not fixed in time. It is less an event than a
condition, festering without end.

Nightmares hound the children. Nine-year-old Maya keeps
dreaming of a unicorn, the gentle fixture of girlhood fantasies and
pink pajamas. But in this dream, the unicorn turns angry, charging at
her.

Eight-year-old Papa hears the voice of a stranger, threatening to
strangle him in his sleep. Twelve weeks have passed since his big
brother left their foster home after being accused of stealing two tablets. Papa's only glimpse of Khaliq is at supervised visits. On April 18,
Papa races to his brother.

"I love you!" squeals Papa, offering a hug.

Khaliq pushes him away. He no longer wants to see his family,
writes a caseworker, because "they do not want to see me." When the
caseworker tries to challenge Khaliq, he walks off, muttering, "No
one understands."

Avianna's face is registering a new distance. She neither smiles nor scowls. Her sister, Nana, is more transparent. She cries without warning. Everyone had always teased Nana about every little thing—her blindness, her crusty nose, her fanciful stories. They had called her "sneaky" and a "drama starter" and a "pathological liar." But no one questioned her bond with Baby Lee-Lee.

Nana still considers herself a second mother to Lee-Lee and can sense, during visits, that the toddler is out of sorts. One afternoon, Lee-Lee pees in her pants. As they search for a change of clothes, Nana leans in to comfort Lee-Lee, planting a peck on her mouth.

The adults exchange glances. A kiss on the lips, writes a case-worker, is "inappropriate affection." Auntie Joan begins to correct Nana, telling her to kiss her sister "on the cheek." Nana is stunned. She has always kissed Lee-Lee on the mouth, the same way she kisses her dolls.

"This is my *sister!*" Nana says.

She and Avianna have now moved to a third foster home: the apartment of a thirty-eight-year-old hairstylist in Brooklyn. She seems prickly, but at least her place is clean. Supreme reminds the girls to be on their best behavior. If this woman puts her hands on either girl, says Supreme, they "should break things in the home."

Both sisters want to leave foster care. With the help of Foundling, Nana applies to a boarding school for the blind, while Avianna awaits a decision from Hershey. Their new foster mother tells them she wants the weekends to herself, shuttling the girls between the homes of random relatives, sometimes to sleep on couches.

Every Sunday, the hairstylist takes them to church—over the religious objections of Chanel and Supreme. Another offense comes when Nana is accepted at the New York Institute for Special Education's school for the blind in the North Bronx. She wants to enroll after having retinal surgery in May 2016 (a surgery that Supreme attends to show his moral support). But a few weeks later, a letter arrives at Foundling, signed by a doctor who has examined Nana at the foster mother's behest. The doctor declares that Nana is "not legally blind and does not need to attend a school for the blind."

Upon hearing this, Supreme explodes. He can foresee what will happen: Nana's grades will tank while her vision worsens. (The doctor's diagnosis is later reversed.) Meanwhile, ACS will continue to cite Nana's eye condition as an example of Supreme's "inadequate guardianship" because he did not provide "appropriate glasses" for his daughter while she was in his care.

Supreme texts the Foundling supervisor, Linda, writing that he wants "the murder and slaughter of all you devils."

Each of Dasani's siblings must undergo psychiatric evaluations. As the process unfolds, their files grow thick with labels and codes. Among the children's diagnoses are V 61.20, "parent child relational problem," V 61.8, "sibling relational problem," and V 611.21, "victim of child neglect by parent."

Their diagnoses include "conduct disorder," "oppositional defiant disorder," "disruptive mood dysregulation disorder," "intermittent explosive disorder," "disinhibited social engagement disorder," and "adjustment disorder with anxious mood."

There is little doubt that the children need help. It is also true that a psychiatric diagnosis brings a financial boost to foster parents—as much as $1,200 more per month for each child.

The system's therapists adhere to a strict protocol, asking the same questions during intake. It is noted that Lee-Lee, who is barely four, has "never attempted suicide," "has no criminal charges," and "does not use alcohol, tobacco or illicit drugs." As with any bureaucratic system, some workers are excellent while others miss the mark.

Papa reports to his psychological evaluation "in a pleasant mood, saying hello and smiling," writes the clinician. The boy is asked to make some art. He loves to draw, setting about the task with great energy. Yet his renderings are described as "impulsively" made, "sketchy," and "poorly drawn with gross distortions."

One of Papa's drawings is of a person, the therapist writes, "with disproportioned facial features, outstretched wing like arms, with limbs that are uneven in length and thickness. The large head is resting on the torso without a neck." The person's mouth is open, and decorated with what the therapist believes to be a "grate like covering."

"This is bizarre in nature and may reflect some psychotic process," concludes the therapist.

Nowhere in the report is Papa's drawing explained by him. He has drawn this image again and again—a crayon version of his father. The boy renders Supreme proudly, to look like his name, with a head large enough to hold a great brain. His mouth is usually open, and covered in what might look like a grate to an outsider. But to Papa, this is clearly a depiction of Supreme's gold teeth—the "grills" that resemble braces—his most prized possession.

The portrait is one of dignity, not psychosis.

Birthday season brings a material bounty the children have never before seen. For Papa's ninth birthday, he gets a new bicycle and a trip to a water resort. When Nana turns fourteen, she is treated to a seafood buffet dinner, a braiding session, and a manicure. She and her siblings have enrolled in after-school enrichment classes like West African dance and boxing.

But nothing can fill the void left by absent parents. During a supervised visit, Lee-Lee scoots next to her mother. Chanel looks at her baby. For the last year, she has played the same Sam Smith song on her phone, again and again:

> Can I lay by your side, next to you
> You
> And make sure you're all right

They rest their faces on a long wooden table, touching their foreheads and closing their eyes. Chanel slowly breathes in, trying to retain Lee-Lee's scent.

"I miss you, Mommy," whispers Lee-Lee.

They stay there like that, pretending to sleep.

chapter 41

WHAT DOES A newborn baby need?

The question ricochets around the living room of Dasani's student home, where each girl must write down the answers that come—"diapers," "a safe home," "milk," "a father." They will scribble these words onto index cards before stacking them into "prioritization towers." Then they will see the towering needs of a newborn child.

Dasani is in a light mood.

"The baby needs everything because it's broke!" she howls.

Today's exercise is part of Hershey's character-building curriculum, taught by houseparents in every student home. They organize these monthly meetings around four themes: wellness, self-sufficiency, the growth mindset, and social intelligence, which the school defines as "the ability to negotiate diverse environments, manage complex relationships and be empathetic."

It is time to get to work. Dasani and her partner, a willowy brunette, head to the mudroom for privacy. "Lee-Lee's not even a baby anymore," says Dasani. "She was bald-headed when she was a baby. She needed some *hair* is what she needed. And some teeth. Bald-headed baby! She was always crying. Ugh."

The other girl seems at a loss, so Dasani takes charge, scribbling words on index cards. "High chair." "Baby bottles." Her partner writes, "Binkies."

"See now . . . this is why I'm not having kids," Dasani finally says. "They need too many things."

Mrs. Akers makes the rounds, checking on each team. The cards must be taped together to form a tower, a task that frustrates Dasani.

"I give up," she says.

"You can't give up," Mrs. Akers says. "That's your baby."

"It's too hard."

"You have to work as a team! Those are your baby's needs."

"I let the baby cry to sleep," says Dasani. "That's what I do with my sister. Otherwise she spoiled."

"You can't do that," says Mrs. Akers. "A baby has needs."

It will soon be six months since Dasani was home for Thanksgiving. Despite all the tumult, she has A's in five classes, including law and business. But her standardized test scores are low, so she must stay for summer school. Nor did she qualify for the district track competition. Her speed in the 200-meter race had fallen short by a fraction of a second.

"I played around on that track a lot, so I didn't focus," Dasani says. "When it was time to run, I would complain."

She is sounding older, more self-possessed. She seems eager to reflect, taking responsibility when bad things happen. She can feel herself changing. "I know I have potential," she tells me. "Everyone says it . . . I have my grandmother's genes. Grandma Joanie did sports. I have my mom's thinking and communicating. I can advocate for stuff."

On May 24, Dasani is in a peppy mood as she walks to school. In two more days, she will turn fifteen. After lunch, Dasani settles into one of her favorite classes, Habits of Success. She is editing a video project when the teacher interrupts her.

A social worker is here to see Dasani.

Dasani walks into a conference room to find Linda Lowe, the family's supervisor from Foundling.

Then something bizarre happens, almost like a dream. Dasani sees Barbara—the same homeless woman who, the previous summer, had spent the night with Chanel in the heart sculpture. Dasani knows that Barbara is her mother's friend from "downtown," the part of Brooklyn where homeless addicts find camaraderie.

All of a sudden, it comes together: Chanel must be here. Dasani races around the room, searching for her mother. Sure enough, she finds Chanel crouching behind a door.

"I tried to hide from you!" laughs Chanel as Dasani rushes into her arms. "Hi, baby! Hi, babeee."

"You got on makeup!" squeals Dasani. "Why?"

Her mother looks thinner and her hair is longer, swept up in delicate dreadlocks. Silver eye shadow covers her lids and oval earrings swing to her shoulders. She wears a long black dress and matching sandals. Dasani wonders if her mother is shoplifting again.

Chanel is equally struck by Dasani's appearance. She is taller, with fuller hips. She stands upright, hands in pockets, wearing a royal-blue polo. Her hair is pulled back into a polished bun. The child is gone.

Chanel gently runs her hand across Dasani's cheek.

"Look at your face all broken out, pimple-face Annie," says Chanel, wiping her tears. She wraps her arms around Dasani like a nest, holding her in place. A silence passes as Dasani looks at Barbara.

"Go give Barbara a hug and a kiss," says Chanel, who knew better than to ask Foundling if she could bring Barbara, as the answer would have been no. Instead, she sprang Barbara on the Foundling team that morning, introducing her as "moral support." Linda didn't feel like arguing.

Barbara is wearing huge aviator sunglasses in the style of Elvis Presley, shrouded by an Adidas hoodie. She gives Dasani a toothless smile. They used to be the same tiny size, but not anymore. "You could knock me out, right?" chuckles Barbara.

Linda sits nearby, in her standard Oxford shirt, trousers, and penny loafers. She is joined by a Foundling caseworker and Dasani's Hershey social worker. (I am also present, with the permission of Hershey's staff.) Linda has started taking notes when Chanel reaches over to Dasani and squeezes her left breast.

"What are you *doing*?" says Dasani, jumping back in embarrassment.

"You got boobies and everything!"

"What are you *doing*!"

"I'm just checkin' you out."

Dasani crosses her arms over her chest.

"Let me see your booty!" Chanel says.

They begin pawing at each other competitively. By now, Linda knows Chanel well enough to understand some of her behavior. Chanel expresses herself physically, whether she is showing love or anger. Sometimes she crosses boundaries, but Dasani is good at pushing back.

In her notes, Linda writes that Dasani is "thrilled" to see her mother, that they "couldn't keep off one another," and that Dasani "appeared very happy and healthy."

"Let me see if your booty grow, Judy!" sings Chanel (a nod to the movie *ATL*).

"Yes it did!" Dasani says. "It grew—"

Chanel takes her daughter's hands and twirls her around to survey Dasani's backside. They are both laughing.

"Yeah, and if you make another one of those—" Chanel says, moving her hips suggestively.

With that, Dasani knows that her mother has been on Facebook. Chanel is mimicking Dasani's most brazen videos, which show her twerking to no end. She feels free to post such things from Hershey because the Akerses cannot patrol the social media accounts of twelve girls hour by hour.

"I didn't do nothing!" Dasani protests.

"Yeah, yeah," says Chanel. "You make another one of those on the tape, I'ma get you."

She now reaches for a box containing Dasani's chocolate birthday cake. During the drive this morning, Linda had asked Chanel to hold the cake in her lap. Dasani peers into the box. The cake has caved in.

"You bust it," says Dasani.

"How bad?" asks Linda, afraid to look.

"Really bad," says Chanel, as Linda starts grumbling about her efforts to order the cake. Dasani can tell that her mother feels comfortable around the Foundling supervisor because they bicker like sisters.

Chanel puts the cake down and walks toward Dasani.

"Happy birthday to you," she sings. "Dance with your mother."

"I'm grown."

"Come on. You remember how we used to do it."

"Yeah, that was when I was like eight. I'm fifteen."

"Come on, dance with your mother," Chanel purrs.

She keeps reaching for Dasani.

"You're not a baby no more?" Chanel says.

"No!"

"You my baby. You always gonna be mine."

Barbara dozes off in the corner. Periodically, she opens her eyes and slips out of the room. Near the receptionist is a bowl filled with Hershey's Kisses. Barbara returns with fistfuls of white chocolate Kisses, whispering to me, "These are my *favorite*."

"Get out of my book bag!" Dasani says to her mother.

"Who you talkin' to?" says Chanel, lifting a heavy binder and plunking it on the table. There, on the cover, is a photo of Dasani and Avianna.

No one wants to break the news.

Since Avianna entered foster care, her grades have dropped. Today, a Hershey staff member informed the Foundling team that Avianna's application was rejected. She will not be coming to Hershey.

Linda solemnly keeps this to herself, not wanting to upset Dasani right before her birthday. "How is your report card?" Linda asks brightly.

"Where's your work?" says Chanel, cutting Linda off. Together, they survey the contents of Dasani's book bag. She has researched President Grover Cleveland for one debate, artificial intelligence for another.

Chanel leafs through a notebook of poems, handwritten by Dasani.

"This is not a poem," says Chanel.

"It is a poem," says Dasani. "It's a free-verse poem, which means it doesn't have to rhyme."

"Okay," says Chanel.

Dasani rolls her eyes.

Her mother starts to read each poem aloud. Haters "ain't worth my time so Ima walk away and not cry." Track is "life for me." Track is "better than running on the streets."

Chanel turns to a short poem, which Dasani explains is "a haiku."

> *Proud to be Living*
> *I enjoy it as I laugh*
> *Respect the breath given*

Chanel muddles the last line, saying "breathe." Softly, Dasani corrects her. Chanel moves on to a poem about the Hershey school, which Dasani describes as "the real struggle in life," and she would "rather live with wildlife."

Chanel pauses.

"Now let me tell you something, girl. There's a lot of children who would love to be in this place —"

"When I wrote this — is when I didn't want to be here," says Dasani.

"I know," says her mother. "But what I told you about this place and you?"

"That it's good for me."

"And what I told you? Ain't no what?"

"Turning back or going home."

"That's right," says Chanel. "There's no home for you. There's no turning back."

Chanel can stay for only a few hours. Each visit is supervised, per the court's orders, and the Foundling team must return to New York before nightfall.

"What is it about, *To Kill a Mockingbird*?" asks Chanel, holding the book that Dasani is almost done reading.

Chanel is proud to have recently finished two novels she found on the street: *The Adventures of Ghetto Sam* and *The Dopefiend*. She keeps this to herself as Dasani recounts Harper Lee's plot: how a white widower named Atticus helped a Black man named Tom Robinson who was wrongly accused of rape.

"I think we seen that movie," says Chanel.

It is clear that she is feeling left out. Chanel never made it past the ninth grade. And now she has been surpassed by her firstborn daughter—a fact that fills the room while going unremarked.

As if sensing her mother's insecurity, Dasani says that the book is "boring."

Linda arches a brow. Perhaps Dasani is trying to close the distance between herself and her mother.

"You think it's boring?" Linda asks incredulously.

"The only time I read this book is when it's time for me to go to bed," Dasani insists.

"Well, read it as an adult, then," Linda says. "You'll like it."

Dasani ignores Linda. It is her mother who dominates, especially in the absence of her siblings. Dasani keeps them in the room by saying their names. She remarks that Lee-Lee must be getting fat because Auntie Joan feeds her "outside food." And that Nana is being "hardheaded" again and that Khaliq blocked her on Facebook.

Chanel looks at her daughter.

"Khaliq's not on Facebook. Khaliq's in jail."

A few weeks earlier, on May 6, Khaliq had struck a court officer with a piece of metal ripped from a radiator in the holding cell of Staten Island's family courthouse. He was handcuffed and shackled so officers could "gain control" of Khaliq, according to Foundling's case notes. Two days ago, he spent his fifteenth birthday in a secure detention facility, and will remain behind bars for months to come.

This is the sort of news that Chanel is supposed to avoid sharing. Dasani shows no emotion.

Soon, she and Chanel are play fighting. Dasani may have outdone her mother in all kinds of ways, but Chanel is still the better fighter. When she presses her body against Dasani, the teenager pushes back.

"Mom, I'm stronger than you!"

With that, Chanel challenges her daughter to an arm-wrestling match.

Dasani balks. "You always want to start something that you can't finish!" she says, parroting one of her mother's lines.

"Ready?" says Chanel.

They take their seats, facing each other.

"One, two, three . . ." says Chanel. *"Go!"*

Dasani has no chance, and they both know it. Out of kindness, Chanel holds her daughter's fist aloft rather than crushing it down.

"You're kind of strong, though," Chanel sniffs. "But you'll never be stronger than me."

The visit is winding down by 2:40 P.M. when Mrs. Akers walks into the room. She has never met Dasani's mother.

"Hi!" Mrs. Akers beams.

Chanel looks her up and down, struck by her beauty. The lady's smile is enough to disarm Chanel, who wants to bond with Mrs. Akers—just as she wanted to bond with the foster mothers at Foundling. As Dasani steps out of the room, Chanel starts to talk.

"I'm walking around a lonely house," says Chanel, who is still living with her husband in Staten Island. They have managed to keep their Section 8 housing subsidy, hoping that their children will return.

"All the beds. Sometimes I might sleep in this room, I might sleep in that room."

The most jarring detail Chanel keeps to herself: Last month, on April 7, her landlords had served her with an eviction notice. While she has continued to pay the rent with her voucher, Chanel is now on a month-to-month lease, giving her landlords the right to push her out.

It does not help that Supreme and Chanel have repeatedly broken the building's rules, or that Supreme fights with the tenant downstairs, prompting calls to the police. In February, Chanel got into an argument with one of the landlords, leading him to file a complaint of harassment at the local precinct. (Chanel was not named or charged.)

Today, Chanel talks about other things—how no one understands the pain of losing her children, how they keep telling her to take this time "to think about myself."

"But I can't. Because myself is the kids."

"Yeah," says Mrs. Akers.

"I have no self. That *is* myself."

Mrs. Akers has learned to keep conversations light when a parent comes. She changes the subject, saying, "So your trip was good. You got to see your baby? Does she look *awesome?*"

Dasani walks back in.

"Hey, Nini!" Mrs. Akers blurts out. "How are you, love?"

"Good."

"Good! Are you *sure?*"

"Yeah."

"Good to see your mom?" Mrs. Akers presses.

"Yeah."

"Yeah?"

Chanel stiffens at Mrs. Akers's last "yeah?"

Dasani can feel the tension rising. She tries to lighten the mood by making fun of Mr. Akers (who is not here). "When we don't have our seat belts on, he'll be drivin'—he'll just stop the van!" says Dasani, demonstrating how Mr. Akers slams the brakes and the girls lurch forward.

"Well," says Chanel, "that's not as bad as when, back in the days, you would get arrested."

The room goes silent.

Chanel begins a tutorial on the police vans of her youth. "They didn't have any seats before. So they would just throw you in the back and then, if you be back there—talkin' junk—like, 'Oh hurry the hell up and get me to the goddamn bookings,' and then they'll, like, drive real fast and go *Eeeee*," she says, mimicking the sound of brakes. "And then everybody will go flyin' to the front—wham! boom!"

Mrs. Akers is speechless.

"So, it's a lot better now," says Chanel, dispelling any notion that these arrests are a thing of the past.

No one knows what to say.

"You still hit your head?" asks Dasani, trying to stay with her mother.

"No, now they have it like—it's like, one van. With a divider in it. And it's like—you're in a little . . ."

"Box," says Dasani.

Chanel nods. She has become self-conscious. "None of you probably ever been in there," she says, looking at Mrs. Akers and Linda. "You all probably would die."

Only Barbara knows what Chanel means. Last fall, they were arrested together for shoplifting at Sephora, riding the van side by side to Central Booking. Barbara nods, her chin resting in her hand. Dasani lowers her head and shakes it.

As nervous chatter fills the room, Linda's focus has shifted to Dasani's housemother. The job of the Foundling supervisor is to assess anyone in the role of parental caretaker, which includes Mrs. Akers.

Dasani has been complaining about her forty-five-minute walk to school.

"We were wondering about that," says Linda, looking at Mrs. Akers.

"It's a forty-five-min walk!" says Dasani.

"It's thirty," says Mrs. Akers.

"We gotta get you a bike or something," says Chanel.

"Yeah!" says Dasani, pointing at Mrs. Akers. "She crazy!"

Linda is not letting this go.

"From where they *sleep* . . . to *here* . . . is thirty *minutes*?" she asks.

"It's about, yeah, give and take," says Mrs. Akers. "Forty-five if they take their time and talk to their friends and they stroll."

Chanel announces that she will be buying Dasani a bicycle.

"But, Miss!" Dasani says to her mother, catching herself. She meant to say "Mommy."

Dasani looks at Mrs. Akers and then at her mother.

"See? I been at this school too long cuz I'm calling you 'Miss,'" Dasani says to Chanel.

Mrs. Akers laughs nervously.

"No," says Chanel, her voice faint. "That means you haven't been home enough to remember my name. You just called me 'Miss' like fifty times here."

It is time to go.

Chanel reaches for Dasani's backpack, putting it on. She is also wearing Dasani's visor.

"What are you *doing*?" Dasani asks.

"Well, I'm going to my next class," says Chanel, pretending to be her daughter. "I don't have time to waste time with you all."

She playfully saunters away.

"Class is over, though," says Dasani. "School is over. As of now, I would be heading to my student home. I would be halfway there."

Chanel removes the visor.

"Doin' what?" Chanel asks, pressing the visor to her nose.

She breathes in.

"Just layin' on the couch trying to sleep," says Dasani.

Gently, Chanel places the visor on her daughter's head. They head out the door, stopping at the front desk so Chanel can root through a box of granola bars.

"You wanna come home with me, baby?" Mrs. Akers asks Dasani.

Dasani nuzzles her housemother.

"You can come home with House Mama," Mrs. Akers says.

As the group heads outside, Dasani pushes ahead with a tour of the campus.

"This is south," she says. "Over there's north."

"That's west," says Chanel, pointing at "Founders Hall." Dasani is impressed that her mother still remembers the name. Sixteen months have passed since Chanel brought Dasani here to enroll.

"Bye!" shouts Chanel as Dasani trots away. "Love you!"

"Love you, too!" shouts Dasani, her voice echoing.

Chanel watches her daughter's silhouette.

"She looks good."

"She looks really good," says Linda.

"Yeah, she seems happy," says Chanel.

"She seems really happy to see you," says Linda.

"Yeah," chimes in Barbara. "She love her mommy."

"I think that'll help her out for the rest of the month," says Chanel. "Cuz I care about her. They just making me seem like a mean person, that I don't care."

"Who?" says Linda.

"The ACS," says Chanel. "But not you, Miss Lowe. You good to me. Miss Lowe is good to me."

The women walk through the parking lot toward the agency's silver van. A strong wind lashes at them, causing Linda to quicken her pace. Chanel is in less of a hurry. Soon they are driving by the sign that Dasani had passed two years earlier, on her way into Hershey.

The words have changed. Pennsylvania is no longer THE STATE OF INDEPENDENCE. It has a new motto:

PENNSYLVANIA: PURSUE YOUR HAPPINESS.

chapter 42

DASANI ZIGZAGS FROM happiness to emptiness to things she has never felt.

Three months have passed since her mother's visit. She is now a sophomore at Hershey. It will soon be a year since she was home. She pulls out her braids and heads to the gym.

She dances alone, across a spotless floor. She moves in a style of her own making—part street dancer, part ballerina—to a soundtrack of R&B. She films herself poppin' and lockin' it, then spinning into a hard-earned fouetté.

Gone is the little dancer who used to practice at Auburn shelter, gliding across the bathroom floor. Back then, Dasani idolized the sunny voice of Alicia Keys. Now she prefers the harder sound of Nicki Minaj.

"Why are you always so angry?" asks her best friend, Kali, one afternoon.

Dasani dodges the question. She prefers to reveal herself on social media, spewing venom about girls, talking trash about boys, laughing uproariously, even crying at times. It is here on Facebook that Dasani tells the world she is bisexual. She finds girls to be loyal, but exhaustingly dramatic; boys are simpler, though selfish and unreliable. She prefers being single, which means being alone.

"I think I might be the saddest happy person and the meanest nice person to ever exist," reads a post that Dasani shares on November 4.

It is the eve of the 2016 presidential election. The counties surrounding Hershey will vote overwhelmingly for Trump. Dasani's peers are too young to cast a ballot, but they take to social media, decrying the candidate as a racist. Dasani posts a message about Trump's anti-immigration stance. Until now, politics held little interest for her. But Trump's rise feels like something else.

She sees his slogan on the socks of her English teacher, Mr. Baker—the same white man who teaches code-switching in class. The students are aghast. When they challenge Baker, he cites the Trump mantra, which Dasani repeats coolly: "that he gonna make America *great* again."

Thanksgiving finally brings Dasani home, where nothing feels the same. Khaliq is gone, serving an eighteen-month sentence at a secure detention facility upstate. Papa no longer wants to attend sibling visits (he remains at his foster home in Staten Island). All of the sisters have moved to Brooklyn—Avianna and Nana, who are still with the hairstylist, and Hada, Maya, and Lee-Lee, who are still with Auntie Joan.

Gone is Linda, the family's trusted Foundling supervisor. She has taken a new job, running a foster care program in Pennsylvania. A few weeks before she left, Linda thought about writing the children notes because she never got to say goodbye.

"Weird how things are so personal and suddenly all impersonal and nobody blinks," Linda writes me in a text. "I can't get shit out of my head. I think of all those guys daily."

Dasani's siblings have detached—most notably Avianna and Nana. Their foster mother forces them to put Chanel on speakerphone whenever they talk. This so infuriates Chanel that she tells the foster mother, by text, that she is just a temporary "babysitter." With that, the foster mother draws new boundaries, refusing to open her home to anyone who is close to Chanel—including Dasani.

When Avianna and Nana finally arrange to meet Dasani at a Popeyes in Brooklyn, the foster mother insists on chaperoning. She orders a meal for herself. None of the girls are given anything to eat. They are in a hurry, the woman explains, because after this visit, they will be seeing a play at church. Dasani is not invited.

There are times when a loud restaurant has a way of going quiet. The people are still talking, but their voices do not register. Everything has stopped. Dasani is here, but she is not here. Her sisters are pulling away, as if tugged like puppets.

Dasani is blotted from view. Only when she hears Nana saying "stepmother" to describe Chanel—a word never used in all the years they were together—does Dasani lose her composure.

"She raised you!" Dasani says.

The foster mother ends the visit, whisking Dasani's two sisters out the door. Left alone on the pavement, Dasani calls her mother, who flies into a rage, texting the foster mother "threatening" messages, according to Foundling's notes. In response, the foster mother files an order of protection against Chanel.

In a few more months, the foster mother will treat Avianna and Nana to Red Lobster to "commemorate" their first anniversary together, telling the girls that she wants to adopt them.

Avianna has stopped talking to Dasani.

The fracturing of Dasani's family follows her back to Hershey.

Her grades drop. Her language is foul. She is threatening to leave. If she cannot exit voluntarily, she will fight her way out. On December 14, she goes on Facebook to announce, TERMINATION COMING.

Chanel watches this from afar.

Only two and a half years stand between her daughter and graduation. A blink of a girl's life. Chanel wishes Dasani could see how quickly the time will fly. Before she knows it, she will be stepping into the cap and gown that none of her matriarchs got to wear—not her mother, not her grandma Joanie, not her great-grandmother Margaret.

Dasani would be the first.

"You don't gotta like Hershey," Chanel keeps telling Dasani. "All you gotta do is smile until you walk across that stage."

But Dasani cannot see past this moment. Chanel knows this, because she was the same way. She had been exiled to Pennsylvania as a girl. She had acted out to come home.

She tries to scare Dasani: "You are on thin ice and it's gonna crack and you gonna drown." Dasani rolls her eyes, ignoring Chanel's argument that there is "no home" in New York, that "it's just weed and the projects and having babies."

Nor is Dasani swayed by Mr. Akers when he talks his best game: "I know you don't wanna be hangin' with all them drug-dealing boys, that ain't got no life and nothing to do but mess with girls' hearts."

Every plea falls flat. Dasani lashes out at students and teachers, racking up fifteen behavioral reprimands in the span of two months. By the end of January, she is on the brink of expulsion.

Two Foundling workers drive to Hershey to assess the situation, reporting back to the agency that Dasani "recognizes the privilege that she has been afforded but she sometimes misses her family."

That same day, Dasani goes on Facebook, warning that she is "bouta have a fight and be gone from the school."

It takes four more weeks. On the afternoon of February 28, Dasani and Kali are walking home from school when they see a fourteen-year-old student on the path. She is only in the eighth grade, but eager to be noticed. She and Dasani had clashed a few times, at basketball and hockey games.

"That's the girl I was gonna punch," Dasani says loudly.

The girl replies that she, too, was planning to "beat up" Dasani. Her friends laugh. Then Dasani hears the girl saying "dumb bitch."

Kali is getting nervous.

"Let's just go," Kali tells Dasani. "Let's just go."

The eighth grader takes off her belt, handing it to her friends and walking toward Dasani. "No! No! No!" says Kali.

As the girl charges at them, Kali grabs Dasani by the waist, trying to hold her back. Somehow, perhaps by accident, the eighth grader kicks Kali in the stomach. Dasani's best friend is now wincing in pain.

"When Kali got hit, I felt some type of way," says Dasani. "I just— I blacked out."

A cellphone video of the fight shows Dasani striking the fourteen-year-old girl. By the time Hershey's security guards intervene, the girl has a busted lip, a bloody nose, and a swelling eye. Dasani returns home, wearing a yellow polo stained with the girl's blood. As the school investigates, the video circulates on Facebook.

Hershey alerts the police that a minor has been injured. Dasani faces an assault charge (which is later dropped). She is moved to the health center and banned from campus. A few days later, a Hershey administrator contacts Foundling, asking the agency to find a foster home for Dasani in New York City.

Chanel hears the news from Foundling. This time she wants to reach Dasani before anyone else. She calls the health center. Dasani comes to the phone.

"Yo, baby," Chanel says. "I got something to tell you."

"What?"

"You're discharged from the school."

"What you mean, Ma?"

"They terminated you."

A silence passes.

"Well, there's one good thing about it," Dasani finally says. "I can see you more often."

Chanel tries to contain her anger. Dasani was the only child who remained safe, more than a hundred miles from the projects. "I was trying to shield you from the hard shit," Chanel says. "Now I gotta worry about a knife in your face."

Dasani searches for the right thing to say. She had tried, at least for a while, to succeed at Hershey.

"I was trying to do it for you," says Dasani.

"I guess that was the problem," says Chanel. "I wanted it more than you."

"I wanted it," says Dasani.

"Well, it's gone now, sweetie. It's gone."

chapter 43

A SILVER MINIVAN IS coming for Dasani.

She waits at the health center. A staff member has packed her personal belongings, removing most of Hershey's wardrobe.

At around noon, two Foundling workers exit the van and walk into the health center, where Dasani's longtime therapist, Julie, has come to say goodbye. She hugs Dasani long and hard.

"Remember what I taught you," Julie says.

Dasani nods, wiping her eyes. She will remember how to calm herself by counting in her head, by pacing her body, by knowing her triggers. Most of all, she will remember Julie's mantra: *Use your words*.

Dasani steps outside, squinting at the sun. She has been in seclusion for more than two weeks, unable to communicate with her peers. She is not allowed to say goodbye—not even to Kali. As the van pulls off, Dasani turns on her phone and announces her departure on Facebook.

"My girls Ima miss y'all," she writes.

Only later, when Dasani looks back on this moment, will she begin to understand what happened. She will see that she was "depressed," a word she uses with clinical savvy. Dasani had denied symptoms of depression while at Hershey. And even if the school had prescribed antidepressants, Dasani says that she would have refused them.

Her depression, she insists, was not the problem. It was a reaction to the problem, which nothing could fix. Her family was broken. And for this Dasani continues to blame herself. She chose to leave home. And by doing so, she not only left her siblings. She abandoned the person who needed her most: Chanel.

"I felt like I did something wrong," Dasani later tells me. "It was like I left her . . . I felt like I left her at the wrong time. Like, I left her too early. Like she wasn't—she wasn't ready for that leap."

She pauses.

"I was really disappointed, though, cuz I thought she could handle it. But then it was like she couldn't. Then it was like, soon as I leave, *this* is what happens. So I coulda—I shoulda just stayed. If I woulda stayed, we probably wouldn't be in this predicament, to be honest."

She repeats the same words.

I left her too early. She wasn't ready for that leap.

Dasani knows that her exit from Hershey will be seen as self-sabotage, as a form of educational suicide. But for Dasani, succeeding at Hershey required another kind of death. It meant losing, even killing off, a basic part of herself.

"It was like they wanted you to be someone that you wasn't," she says. "If I talk the way I naturally talk—to them—like, something's wrong with me."

She looks out the window, passing trees and barns and cows.

Again and again, she thinks of her mother. *She wasn't ready for that leap.* Perhaps Dasani wasn't ready either. But would she ever have been? To leap from her mother was to leap from herself.

As the van winds through town, she sees the words "Thank you for visiting Hershey."

Soon she is asleep.

The city wakes Dasani with its lurching traffic and bleating horns. She looks out the window as they pass through Staten Island's North Shore, pulling up to a three-story home with a landscaped lawn.

A soft-spoken woman comes to the door. She is Dasani's new foster mother, Denise, an African American teacher who works in special education. She has been fostering for two decades.

Denise shows Dasani to an orderly bedroom, which she will share with a fourteen-year-old girl named Charisma. Two other foster children—a teenage mother and her baby daughter—live down the hall. Also in the home is Denise's adult daughter, bringing this all-female household to a total of six.

Dasani looks around. She knows that foster care is a place of last resort. *There's no home to come back to*, her mother kept saying. She still thinks of her nearly blind sister running from Mr. Byrd.

Yet this home feels safe. It is peaceful and clean, with nutritious meals and structured chores. Framed photographs fill the living room, opposite a delicate china cabinet. The girls take turns making dinner, earning a weekly allowance of $20 each. Denise, who is fifty-six, would fit right in with the Akerses and the McQuiddys. She relishes her role as a foster parent, doling out hugs and reminders about the schedule.

"She wants us to obey the rules and be good kids and have a successful future," Dasani tells me.

A few days later, Denise takes Dasani shopping at the mall for clothes. She will be enrolling at Susan E. Wagner High School, more than three miles south.

If Hershey was a river, Wagner is the high seas. More than thirty-three hundred students attend the high school, exceeding the entire population of the Hershey school. Security is everywhere, with officers patrolling the halls to break up fights. Wagner has more repeat suspensions than any other public school in the city.

Dasani is among Wagner's minorities—the 11 percent of students who are Black. On March 28, she wanders the building, trying to find her first class. She feels lost and disoriented. The loud chaos of Wagner's hallways "makes my head hurt."

The next day, Dasani goes to a more familiar place: the Foundling agency. This time, she is not coming as a visitor. She is officially a foster child, just like her siblings. She waits impatiently for them to show up.

There is no sign of Avianna or Nana, who have stopped talking to Dasani since the visit to Popeyes. Dasani's younger sisters—Maya, Hada, and Lee-Lee—are also absent, while Chanel is running late, Khaliq is locked up, and Supreme has been banned from Foundling on the suspicion that he brought a gun to a visit (which he denies).

This leaves nine-year-old Papa, who walks in with a framed photograph of himself and a homemade card for Chanel's birthday. "I love you so much and I will call you every day," reads Papa's card. "I hope you will come next week to the visit so we can all love you up."

Eighteen months have passed since Papa and his siblings were taken. No amount of therapy seems to debunk the family narrative— that Papa is to blame for their ruin. He has heard this from his parents and siblings, time and again: Had he never run away, they would all still be together.

It does not matter that this story makes Papa the culprit, as if his parents had never used drugs. There is little that any trained professional can say to offset the source of Papa's guilt, which resembles Dasani's: They left home, and things fell apart.

Increasingly, Papa explodes in tantrums. He cries frequently and has trouble sleeping.

"I don't have a smile because I had a sad life," Papa tells a caseworker. Ten months ago, the Foundling agency began medicating Papa for ADHD, over his parents' objections. Chanel and Supreme don't believe that Papa has a problem; they think that ACS wants to control their son, "slowing his mind with pills," says Chanel. While Papa's focus has improved, he is often drowsy and irritable. When his parents don't answer his calls, he assumes they don't love him. When Chanel skips a visit, Papa is sure that she is avoiding him.

The truth has little to do with Papa.

Three weeks ago, on Chanel's thirty-ninth birthday, she and Supreme were evicted by their landlords after a long fight in housing court. Even before this happened, the couple had few reserves. They struggled to keep up with ACS's requirements—the parenting classes, counseling appointments, anger management instruction, and drug testing.

The morning they were evicted, Chanel and Supreme scrambled to pack whatever they could. Chanel left Turtle with a neighbor. Supreme left Akeelah with the bodega owner down the block. They were once again homeless.

Chanel finally walks in the door at Foundling, reaching for her first-born daughter and her youngest son.

Papa is "extremely excited" to see his mother, writes a Foundling caseworker who goes by the nickname Tea. She has been assigned to work with Papa, Khaliq, and now Dasani. Tea's observations will go into a computerized log of notes, to be shared with ACS. These notes are divided into categories such as the "social emotional presentation" of each child and Chanel's "progress in parenting skills."

Under "describe discussions," Tea notes tension. Chanel says she is disappointed that Dasani left Hershey, and fears she is "coming home to hang out with the wrong crowd." When mother and daughter start to argue, Tea intervenes, asking Chanel to "leave the subject alone," that "Dasani is here now and that's all that matters."

Dasani likes this caseworker. She seems unflappable. She does not try to "pass for white," which is among the worst things her mother can say about anyone Black. Tea can talk like Chanel, using words like "ratchet" and "punk." She is the same shade of brown as Dasani, with the same strong build. She carries herself proudly, like all the women Dasani admires.

Out the window, Dasani gazes at the Stapleton projects. She seems to be "daydreaming," writes Tea. Indeed, Dasani is reminiscing about some boys she used to know. She wonders if they are still there.

Just before the visit, Chanel had seen her daughter at the ferry, a meeting point for drifters, dealers, and foster kids. She thinks no one is parenting Dasani, much less protecting her. And protection—on the street—is what Chanel has always offered. Dasani needs "a curfew," Chanel remarks.

Dasani replies that her foster mother sets the curfew. Chanel is further stung when Tea takes Dasani's side, confirming that the foster mother sets the curfew.

As Chanel's fury mounts, Dasani puts "her hat in front of her face to cover up her feelings," writes Tea. When the visit ends, Chanel follows her daughter from a distance. The court order prohibits Chanel from seeing Dasani unchaperoned.

Half an hour later, Chanel calls Tea to report that Dasani is wandering the projects, possibly in danger. The caseworker drives through Stapleton, finding Dasani on the street with two boys. Dasani promises to take a bus home. With that, Tea drives away.

Forty-five minutes later, Tea's phone rings again. It is Chanel, calling to say that Dasani is "still in the projects."

"You should have taken her home in your car," Chanel snaps.

"That is against agency policy," replies Tea.

There is nothing more that Chanel can do. If she approaches her daughter, Chanel is violating the judge's order of protection. If she obeys the judge's order, she leaves Dasani unprotected.

In the absence of family, Dasani searches for new kin.

Thousands of teenagers swarm the hallways of Wagner, their cliques too fluid to track. It has been years since Dasani's mother explained the three paths to popularity. *Dress fly. Do good in school. Fight.*

Dasani is still short, just five feet. She has blazing brown eyes and a regal face, with the full lips of her mother, the high cheekbones of her father. She scoops her long braids into a slouchy bun, trying to look current. She knows she cannot dress fly when her nicest clothes remain at Hershey. To do "good in school" will also be hard. She has landed at Wagner more than halfway through her sophomore year, and all the classes are different.

But a fighter Dasani remains. She starts calling herself "Deedee," writing on Facebook that she is "a former Wide receiver at NFL" as well as a "dancer, bi, single." She adds a warning: "don't hurt me i won't hurt u." She joins the intramural sports team at school, playing flag football. Within days, Dasani has a new set of friends. She posts pictures of them with the labels "bestie" and "sis."

Dasani knows that her estranged sister, Avianna, might see this. They used to say they were twins, finishing each other's sentences. Now they don't even talk. All they have is Facebook. And in the secret language of twins, Dasani's message is clear. There is no bond like theirs, and no way to replace it.

Still, Dasani tries to extend a sister's loyalty to the new girls, offering herself as their protector. She seems eager to fight. For more than two years, she has lived in Hershey's controlled environment. The few times she fought, security guards intervened, followed by nurses with antiseptic wipes, Neosporin, and ice packs.

The street brings no such order. This is where Dasani finds herself on April 15, facing off against a hefty white girl near the Stapleton projects—a teenager who had just beaten up Dasani's new best friend. "For me it's all about loyalty," Dasani says.

A crowd has gathered to watch.

Dasani parades the pavement wearing a white Hershey sweatshirt that she managed to save, with her name emblazoned on the back. A scarf covers her braids to prevent them from being pulled. Her opponent is both taller and wider, which makes for an uneven match. But Dasani is undeterred, telling the crowd that this girl has been "talking mad shit," and they now need to settle their "beef."

"Come on, bitch," says Dasani, holding up her fists. The other girl swings. They tumble toward a fence. The girl yanks off Dasani's headscarf, grabbing at her hair.

"Let go of her hair! Let go of her hair!" yells the self-appointed referee, who is filming the match. "We don't pull hair, bro!"

It is too late. Dasani's braids have been ripped from her bleeding scalp. She is bashing the girl as others pry them apart. The referee demands a three-minute break. Like boxers in a ring, they cool down, their chests heaving, as their allies survey the damage.

Dasani's torn braids lie on the ground like a dead bird. A boy bends down to pick one up. The referee announces that neither girl is scratched. She seems impressed with Dasani, telling her, "You stood your ground." No sooner are the girls fighting again than someone yells, "Police!"

Dasani runs into the apartment of her new best friend—the girl she was fighting to defend. A throng of kids gather outside the door, threatening Dasani's friend. The two are vastly outnumbered, so Dasani calls her mother.

On the phone, Chanel orders Dasani to stay inside. Then Chanel calls Dasani's foster mother, asking her to fetch Dasani. Denise refuses, fearing for her own safety. From Brooklyn, Chanel heads to the ferry carrying a baseball bat and a container of bleach. By the time she gets to the Stapleton projects, the crowd is gone. Chanel and Dasani leave unharmed.

Two days later, Dasani logs on to Facebook, posting a video of the fight that draws nearly four thousand views. Her reputation is sealed. In the coming months, she will fight again and again, earning the nickname Deedee Unstoppable.

This makes her mother proud or angry, depending on the audience. In front of caseworkers, Chanel blasts Dasani, warning that she could get arrested or even murdered. But on Facebook, Chanel crows.

"You something else," Chanel writes below a video of the fight. She starts calling her daughter Little Mike, for the boxer Mike Tyson.

By contrast, Dasani's foster mother is appalled. She cannot understand why Dasani would risk her life on the street. Denise tries grounding Dasani, but she just gets more angry. She slams doors and curses. She refuses to do her chores, saying that kitchen work is a "trigger" because of her childhood.

"I don't know what to do with you," Denise tells Dasani late one evening while driving her home from the hospital after another fight.

"You act like I had a good role model," Dasani replies. "I never had a good role model. So what do you expect me to go on?"

This conversation will stay in Denise's mind for years to come. The words "role model" had replaced "mother," because Dasani could not say, *I never had a good mother.* She did not lack for role models, either—her grandmother Joanie; Chanel's godmother, Sherry; Dasani's teacher, Miss Hester; her therapist, Julie. But no one can replace her mother.

"Nobody knew her pain," Denise tells me. "I'm not saying I knew it. But they come here with so many problems, you just gotta listen. . . . She loves her mother. She never put her down. She was just saying, 'It is what it is. Don't expect more.'"

On March 30, 2017—just two weeks before Chanel had come to Staten Island to rescue her daughter with a baseball bat—Judge Lim made a finding of neglect against her and Supreme, closing the investigation that began with Papa running away. Chanel and Supreme had been recently evicted and missed the hearing, which included testimony by ACS that Chanel had been using heroin the previous year, based on records from her former drug program.

ACS will now change its "permanency goal" for the children from family reunification to adoption. This means that the agency will file a new case against the parents, seeking the termination of parental rights.

Dasani dodges therapy and anger management. She is "enjoying her freedom," she tells her caseworker. But Tea is worried that the "freedom of not being in boarding school" could derail Dasani's "educational goals."

Reluctantly, Dasani agrees to see a sociotherapist, who gives her a daunting exercise: She must write to her "future self" and to her "past self." Dasani meets him halfway, agreeing only to write to her future self.

She does not want to revisit the past.

Avianna is hitting a similar wall.

She wants to skip over the past. She had tried doing this with her first therapist, an African American man she came to adore. He was sophisticated enough to draw Avianna out, asking gentle questions while making her laugh. He knew when to push and when to back off. But then he backed off entirely, transferring to another job. Avianna was so upset that Foundling changed her treatment goal. She would now "process the loss of her former therapist."

It does not help that Avianna's new therapist is a white woman who says "I feel you." This sounds ridiculous to Avianna's ear. She has heard other phrases migrating to the mouths of white people, words like "I gotchu," "the bomb," and "fly."

But "I feel you" is different. It suggests the transmission of a particular experience—a plight known only to African Americans. When Avianna finally tells her white therapist to stop saying "I feel you," she explains it in literal terms: Avianna "does not think anyone can feel what she felt unless they went through what she went through," writes the therapist.

Avianna wants to feel nothing. Feelings make a girl vulnerable, and then she gets crushed. Avianna will do the opposite. If someone tells her she looks "angry," she says, "That's just my face." She answers to no one, calling herself the Boss. A boss holds the power.

"You need to be more like me," Avianna tells one of her sisters. "Feel nothing. No feelings. No one matters but me, myself, and I."

Yet every time someone leaves—a teacher moves, a therapist quits—the wound of loss reopens. Avianna is back in the place of her original sorrow. Every time ACS comes knocking, to inspect her latest foster home and check the bathroom for mold, she is reminded that the scrutiny never ends. It chases her from home to home. She tries not to worry, which means staying in the present. But every time she hears the word "adoption," she is hounded by the past and the future all at once. Her mind flashes forward to an uncertain home, and backward to the moment when her family broke.

Adoption would make it final.

In a few more months, when caseworkers raise the prospect of adoption, the children start to panic. Maya, Hada, and Lee-Lee remain in the care of Auntie Joan. They have bonded with her, but the word "adoption" repels them. The oldest of the three, eleven-year-old Maya, worries that "Mommy won't be Mommy anymore." Her ten-year-old sister, Hada, wants to know if she can still see her mother. A caseworker replies that this is "up to" the aunt. The sisters propose a compromise: They will be adopted by the aunt provided they can keep calling her "Auntie" while Chanel remains "Mommy."

Only Chanel birthed them. And only Chanel will be their mother until the day she dies. She knows that she will think of them when she takes her last breath, just as they will think of her when they take theirs.

Nothing can change that—not the passage of time, nor the word "adoption," which reduces Chanel's children to the status of orphans. To be orphaned is to be motherless.

Yet anyone who observes Baby Lee-Lee can see that she is no orphan. As soon as the five-year-old spots Chanel climbing up the hill to Foundling for a visit, Lee-Lee bolts through the door, flying toward her mother.

It makes no difference that Chanel comes late, or that she was not invited to Lee-Lee's graduation from kindergarten. The child runs with such abandon that a caseworker must chase after Lee-Lee to prevent her from being hit by a car.

Chanel was—and remains—the only mother here.

In early April, Papa comes to Foundling for a family visit. He has cuts on his face. Another boy had pushed him down the stairs at school.

Dasani begins to tease her nine-year-old brother, calling him a "punk" and "weak." The caseworker, Tea, tells her to back off, but Dasani presses on, saying that their "parents are fighters so all of them should know how to fight."

"Leave me alone!" Papa screams, hitting Dasani in the arm. She warns him to stop, but he hits her again, so she strikes him back.

Papa starts punching the walls. The staff summons his therapist and takes Papa to another room to de-escalate. The opposite happens. He gets "angrier and angrier," according to Foundling's notes. He bangs his head against the door until a knot forms on his skin. When a worker throws himself between Papa and the door, Papa punches him in the stomach.

"Just let me die!" the boy wails.

He is threatening to jump out the window. He throws furniture to break the glass. By now, an ambulance is on the way. When the staff removes the furniture, Papa smashes into the window with his head and fists.

Medics rush into the building, accompanied by four officers. They restrain Papa, strapping him to a stretcher. In the ambulance, he thrashes about, hitting his handcuffs against the glass. They tell Papa they will have to sedate him if he does not calm down.

Papa goes quiet, making "grunting noises," notes the medic. He is terrified of needles. That evening, Papa is released to his foster mother.

A few weeks later, it happens again. Papa's foster mother takes some time off, placing him in a temporary "respite home." Just before Papa can be transferred to the home, he tries to run into traffic.

The "patient was brought in on stretcher by EMS, began screaming at staff, kicking and jumping on furniture," according to a medical assessment of Papa, signed by a psychiatrist at the Richmond University Medical Center.

"Fuck the police!" Papa yells, banging his fists on metal and plexiglass. This time, the staff sedates him with Thorazine. "I don't care about my life," the boy tells them. "I don't want to live anymore." When asked why, he says, "Because life is worthless."

Papa is transferred to a residential facility that specializes in troubled foster children. He remains there for the next month and is placed on five medications. On May 25, Papa threatens to kill himself, landing back in a hospital psych ward.

It is the eve of Dasani's sixteenth birthday.

She has no desire to celebrate. She has not seen Papa since his first hospitalization, nor does she speak of it. "There comes a point where talking about it doesn't make you feel better anymore," reads Dasani's Facebook post, taken from a poetry website. "You just live with your mouth closed and your walls up and your heart hidden."

She has just been suspended from Wagner for using foul language. She seethes with resentment for all authority, including ACS. To Dasani's mind, there is no "order of protection," as commanded by family court. She and her mother will be undivided. To make this clear, they now leave family visits together, walking out side by side. When caseworkers object, Chanel knows exactly what to say: This is the only way to keep her daughter safe.

On the street, Dasani is now a target. Everyone wants to fight her, even the boys. One of them is the cousin of Bubbles, a longtime rival of Dasani's from Stapleton. Two summers ago, Bubbles had fought Dasani's sisters while she was at Hershey, unable to protect them.

Now that Dasani is back, Bubbles's cousin is stirring up trouble. He plans to attend the same party as Dasani on Saturday night, hosted by a local legend—the thirteen-year-old DJ Fussyman, who started spinning when he was ten, landing a gig at the White House. A forty-foot mural of the boy's face covers a brick wall in Stapleton.

Dasani knows the DJ as "Fussy." His Facebook page shows him in a preppy blazer and gold-rimmed glasses, smiling sweetly by the words "Straight Outta Staten." Fussy's manager is his mother ("He was a fussy baby"). She chaperones this monthly party on Broad Street, where children pay as little as $5 to hear Fussy spin. Everyone knows the rules: no drugs, alcohol, or weapons.

Rumors are already spreading that Dasani will be jumped after the show. There is talk of knives and possible "slicing," with Bubbles's cousin at the fore of these threats. If Dasani skips the party, her rivals will have won. But if she shows up, she needs a big enough crew to ward off danger. So she tells everyone she knows to come.

When Chanel hears this, she gets a bad feeling. It was only a few weeks ago that she had come to rescue her daughter, wielding a baseball bat and bleach.

This time, Chanel gets on the ferry with a more serious weapon. Tucked in her bag, on the evening of May 27, are the disassembled parts of a .38-millimeter revolver, on loan from an unnamed friend.

When the ferry docks on the North Shore, the air is charged. Chanel walks to Broad Street, where music thumps from behind closed doors. She lingers, making small talk with Fussy's mother, who is bragging about his gig at the White House. Several police cars have pulled up. At around 9 P.M., the music stops, the doors swing open, and the street fills with teenagers. Bubbles's cousin is goading Dasani. Then he spots her mother.

"Wait till I see you without your mom!" yells the boy after crossing the street.

Chanel ushers Dasani and her friends up the block, where they encounter another set of rivals. One of them threatens to spit in Chanel's face.

"You talkin' to my mother like that?" shouts Dasani.

"Yeah I'm talkin' to your mother—"

Dasani punches her, causing a nail clipper to fly out of the girl's pocket. Someone grabs the clipper, slicing another girl in the shoulder. As things spiral out of control, Chanel throws a glass bottle to the ground, shattering the air. Everyone freezes. She knows how to stop a fight.

"Listen, man," Chanel hisses at Dasani as they walk away. "I could go to jail for what's in my bag, so you should just try to get home."

At around 10:40 P.M., they are waiting at a bus stop when Bubbles's cousin reappears, flanked by dozens of kids. He claims to have a "toaster," which means gun.

"We *all* got toasters," snaps Chanel. "I got one on me right now."

Just then, a police car cruises up the block.

"She got a gun!" Bubbles's cousin shouts at the cops. "She got a gun!"

chapter 44

CHANEL IS LED from one jail to another. The local police station. The courthouse holding pen. The prison bus bound for Rikers Island.

Handcuffed and shackled, she moves slowly. Metal grates divide the bus into cells. A guard leads Chanel to hers, where bars cover the windows. The bus pulls away. Her body jerks with each stop. She can hear the murmurs of another passenger who has never been to Rikers. There is terror in his voice. When they reach the narrow bridge leading to the island jail, everyone is silent.

They cross over the East River like a ghost vessel, chains rattling, metal clanking. The bus pulls up to the women's facility of Rikers, where "everything is gates," Chanel says, "gates slamming and opening, slamming and opening." Inside, Chanel is told to strip naked. She must squat, cough, and spread her buttocks while a guard searches for drugs and weapons. Once cleared, she is given the usual items: a brown jumpsuit, some panties, a bra, a pair of shoes, a green plastic cup, a toothbrush, a blanket, and a sheet.

This marks Chanel's passage into the Rose M. Singer Center, better known as Rosie's. It was here, more than a decade earlier, that a cellmate had tattooed LADY RED on Chanel's biceps with a needle and ink. Tonight she will sleep on a cot near another homeless woman who was just arrested, making the front page of the *New York Post*: SUBWAY SLASHER: PSYCHO SLICES MOM AT GRAND CENTRAL.

Chanel is intrigued. She always wants to know "why they did it." The slasher's victim—a thirty-one-year-old mother with a baby—did not want to sit next to the homeless woman, who became enraged, according to the *Post*, leaving a gash in the mother's face requiring thirty stitches.

Chanel ignores all warnings to avoid the slasher, and soon they are chatting. The slasher is one of several high-profile inmates currently at the jail—among them Geraldine Perkins, who idly watched as her boyfriend beat her six-year-old son, Zymere, to death, and then waited hours to bring him to the hospital. Perkins (who had previously been the subject of five ACS investigations) pleaded guilty to manslaughter. In the wake of Zymere's death, the ACS commissioner had stepped down and three employees were fired. Also here is Tiona Rodriguez, who was caught carrying her dead newborn in a bag while shoplifting at Victoria's Secret. She will be convicted, early in 2018, of smothering her eight-pound baby.

These are the crimes that make headlines, causing ACS to tighten its reins. Chanel knows that she is a different class of mother, not to be lumped with sociopaths. Her latest crime is a pittance compared to theirs.

"I have a gun on me, it's in my bag," Chanel had told the police officer, according to his arrest report. "It's to stop these kids from fucking with my daughter." The officer had found no bullets, and—perhaps out of pity for Chanel—described the pistol (wrongly, she says) as a BB gun. She was ultimately charged with possession "of an imitation pistol."

If anything, Chanel had gone to Staten Island to take "possession" of her daughter. She wanted Dasani to feel "the power of a mother." And to see that "I was gonna hurt someone for her," that "I stood with her, against all her enemies, to let her know I'm your sister, I'm your mother, your keeper."

Now Rosie is the keeper of Chanel, for five long nights. She calls Dasani, again and again.

"I was praying for you, Mommy," Dasani says on the phone.

"Oh, now you prayin'? I'm on Rikers Island. If you keep going down the path you going down, you will end up here."

"No, I will not end up there!"

"Yes, you will!"

They argue like this, day after day. Chanel wants her daughter to stop fighting. She even threatens to call ACS to demand that Dasani be placed in a facility.

"If you lock me away then what child are you gonna see?" Dasani asks. "Cuz I'm the only one that can bend the rules. I'm the only one that can be defiant. The little ones cannot. The little ones have to follow the rules. They have to. I don't have to. I can see you when I want and they cannot tell me that I can't. And even if they do, they cannot stop me. So therefore, if you lock me away, what older child are you gonna see?"

Dasani reaches for what she knows will hurt: Avianna and Nana don't want to see their mother anymore. The little ones keep missing visits. The boys are locked up.

Who is left?

Chanel has no good answer.

"Didn't you drop out in the ninth grade?" Dasani piles on.

"What does my education have to do with you?" Chanel asks.

"I made it a grade ahead of you!" Dasani says. "A whole grade. You have street knowledge. Right, yeah. You have street cred. But the thing is, um, you're what—thirty-seven? And years change. Languages change. Everything changes."

Chanel thinks the opposite is true. Nothing ever changes.

"It's a cycle," she tells her daughter from the prison's phone. "It already happened. It's just coming back around."

Five weeks later, on July 1, Dasani gets a friend request on Facebook. It is her sister Avianna. They have not spoken in eight months.

"Sis," writes Dasani.

"Hey," replies Avianna.

They begin a careful exchange, with Avianna asking Dasani what she is doing. Even the basic facts of her life are a mystery—that Dasani is still in Staten Island, with the same foster mother. She has failed two classes since enrolling at Wagner and must attend summer school to avoid flunking the tenth grade.

Avianna prods Dasani to accept her friend request, to which Dasani replies, "I did, sissy."

At this, Avianna melts.

"When u gonna come and see me," Avianna asks.

Dasani tries for a cool response, using the shorthand for "I don't know u gotta let me know."

"Okay," writes Avianna.

She sees on Facebook that Dasani's braids were ripped out, leaving part of her scalp exposed. Avianna wants to know if her sister is still fighting because "I just seen your fight with some fat white bitch and why did u cut the side of your head."

Yes, Dasani replies, she still fights.

"Are u still a virgin," Avianna asks.

"Why u ask me that . . . ???"

"I can't ask"

"No wtf . . . R u a virgin"

"Yes," writes Avianna.

"Ok good for u."

"Good for u too."

Their conversation ends as quickly as it began, with Dasani writing the words "love u."

"love u too," replies Avianna.

On a misty September morning, the ferry docks in Staten Island. Dasani steps on board wearing a BROOKLYN T-shirt. Her scalp is half shaved, like that of a warrior, smoothing the skin where her braids were ripped out. Five months have passed since that first Staten Island fight.

She looks out at the water.

You must fight for your education.

These were the words of her beloved Brooklyn principal, Miss Holmes. She and Dasani had lost touch after the principal moved to Florida. Then, over the weekend, someone posted it on Facebook.

"RIP Ms. Holmes."

Dasani felt weightless, like when "your heart drops." At age sixty-five, Miss Holmes had been found dead in her home in Palm Coast, Florida, stricken by an apparent heart attack. She left no spouse or children, only the legacy of her school.

"I was one of her favorite students," Dasani tells me.

She had slipped out early this morning, planning to skip school. From the ferry, she would hop the train to Brooklyn and then walk to McKinney. This was the only way to pay her respects, because "I don't do funerals." Not since the age of six, when Dasani flung herself at Grandma Joanie's open casket, has she been to a funeral.

The water glimmers as barges pass in the distance, casting long silhouettes. To the east is the Statue of Liberty. A look of wonder crosses Dasani's face. It is the same expression she made as a small girl, gazing at the Empire State Building from the Auburn shelter. Whenever she sees a tower, she imagines herself on top. She wants to visit this statue, she says brightly. She has always wanted to "climb to the crown."

Dasani's phone is lighting up as Facebook floods with memories. Miss Holmes was a "warrior" and a "bulldog," but also a softie who made the best homemade brownies. She was a workaholic who sent her favorite students to fetch Chinese fried chicken with hot sauce. "She made middle school kids tremble in fear and still want to tell her everything," writes the drama teacher. These memories collect under hashtags like #ProudMcKinneyAlumnus and #YoureNot-FromMckinneyIf, which invariably leads to anecdotes about the school's other matriarch—Miss Hester.

Dasani reads these posts out loud. "You are not from McKinney if Miss Hester ain't tell you gunshots were her alarm clock in Marcy. . . . You are not from McKinney if you never heard Miss Hester say, 'Oh my gooney goo hoo!'"

A smile spreads across Dasani's face. She is back where she belongs. On her shoulders she carries the same backpack she wore at Hershey, with BROOKLYN written on the straps. She knows that her expulsion would have devastated Miss Holmes. Going to Hershey was the principal's idea, her way of sparing Dasani from foster care. Miss Holmes had predicted that Chanel would lose her children.

Three months after Chanel's stint at Rikers, she is still homeless, living with Supreme at a shelter in Brooklyn. Ten days ago, the family's ACS case took a critical turn: The agency filed its petition to terminate the parental rights of Chanel and Supreme. They could lose the right to see, or even talk to, their children. ACS is now preparing for trial. Should the judge rule in the agency's favor, the children will be put up for adoption.

That same day, Judge Lim received two court reports about Dasani. According to ACS, she is "not adjusting well in the home." According to Foundling, she "is adjusting fairly well in the home."

Dasani wants to quit foster care altogether. She would rather live "locked up" like her brothers, she says. Just last night, she got into a heated argument with her foster mother's daughter, who told Dasani, "You think you run the house and you don't even pay the bills," to which Dasani replied, "Your mother don't pay the bills either! *Foster care* does."

She is still fuming about this when the ferry docks in Manhattan. But as Dasani crosses into Brooklyn, her mood lifts. The sun is out, glinting off the high-rises. She finds these buildings impressive, despite her mother's rants. They are both keenly aware of gentrification, without using that word.

Chanel's latest gripe is the welfare building on Flatbush Avenue. Just two weeks ago, a white Brooklyn artist began a prominent mural, covering the facade with black-and-white images and names like "Biggie Smalls" and "Spike Lee." Chanel watched as this woman drew her designs, stopping to chat with welfare recipients.

"When we do that it's *graffiti*," Chanel says. "And when you all do it, it's a *mural*."

Dasani cuts through Fort Greene Park, passing the projects, and then Auburn.

"I don't live here no more," she says, crossing the sidewalk where Dasani and her enemy Star had fought. It all feels like "a gazillion years ago."

She walks into McKinney, finding her former teacher, Miss Hester, red-eyed. The new principal, Mr. Walker, has not slept. Teachers and students exchange long, somber hugs, speaking in hushed tones. People are wandering in and out of the principal's office as Dasani takes a seat at the same round table where Miss Holmes used to feed her.

Mr. Walker looks at Dasani. He wants to know why she is no longer at Hershey.

"I transferred schools," she lies.

He presses for more details.

"Cuz I didn't like it," she finally says. Coyly, she asks if she can "transfer" to McKinney.

She knows it will never happen. Mr. Walker's mind is elsewhere. The phone keeps ringing. After a while, Dasani reaches for a pen, scribbling something on a Post-it. When she gets up to leave, she places the note on her principal's wall.

It is her name, followed by a heart, followed by the word "McKinney."

Dasani pierces her tongue and wears a red bandanna, in homage to the Bloods.

At age sixteen, she is joining a Brooklyn set, just like her mother. She brags on Facebook about her sexual conquests. She gets suspended from school again and again, fighting so fiercely that a security guard injures Dasani's shoulder while trying to restrain her. In a video that draws more than sixty-five hundred views, she pounds a male teenager into the ground.

Nine months have passed since she left Hershey. She has repatriated herself to the city she lost. This should make her mother proud, Dasani thinks. But when she tries weed for the first time, Chanel comes undone.

"You were supposed to be the leader!" Chanel screams on the phone in December 2017.

Dasani hangs up. She stares at the ground. She tries to breathe. What follows is a torrent of fast and furious words, directed at the mother who is gone.

"What you *talkin'* about I am supposed to be the leader?" Dasani cries out, as if Chanel is listening. "I am their *mother*! How many years did I spend doing their hair, dressing them, taking them to school, making bottles? What did you expect me to do in high school? This is the first time I am free. . . . You not even they mother! They come to *me* with problems. Lee-Lee comes to me, not you. Papa calls me to say that a boy did something!"

She is weeping.

"I have been their mother all this time! Doing everything! All my childhood, taking care of them. While you out all night, on the street, *stealin'*. People stare at you on the train when your eyes roll back and you fall asleep and you are sitting next to me, your *kid*!"

Dasani still won't call her mother an addict. Certain things remain unspoken. Even the words Dasani now uses, she cannot say to her mother's face. She is railing at an imaginary Chanel, much as Chanel used to blast her absent husband, yelling into the air as if Supreme could hear.

It has taken a long time for Dasani to speak this way at all. At Hershey, she only hinted at her anger, logging Chanel into her cellphone as "Immature Mom." But to list her mother's failures, Dasani could not do. To look down on Chanel from the high perch of Hershey would have proven her siblings right: Dasani had left. She had chosen a better fate. She had broken their promise to "stay together" no matter what. To depart is the ultimate betrayal.

Coming home changed all that. It reconnected Dasani to her kin. It loosened her anger into words that she could speak.

This is the first time I am free.

Only now is Dasani starting to make sense of what happened at Hershey. When she tells people she "transferred," she is speaking her own truth. She took it upon herself to leave, fighting her way out. The choice was hers, whether or not it was the right one. She can see that her mother's predictions have come true. She is back in the projects, with no visible way out.

Instead, she burrows in, agreeing to "rep" the Bloods in Staten Island. If this brings danger, Dasani shrugs it off. She feels more protected by the Bloods than by any of the adults paid to look after her— the caseworker, the foster mother, the principal, the school counselor. They are, to Dasani's mind, a public version of Hershey, making the same demands without providing the same perks.

Gone is the plush campus of her former school, with its plentiful food and wardrobe, its steady rhythm and rigorous classes. Dasani no longer rants about Hershey, deriding its rules or mocking its staff. She no longer blames Mrs. Akers for the tension that came between them. With distance comes perspective. They clashed, Dasani has come to realize, because they shared an admirable trait.

"She told it like it is," says Dasani. "We was too much alike."

At times, Dasani swells with remorse. She considers how different her life would be had she chosen to stay at Hershey. She thinks back on her decision to fight the eighth grader, which led to expulsion.

"You know, sometimes I regret beatin' her up," she tells me. "Cuz I feel like my opportunity"—she pauses—"would have been better . . . But then again, it's like—it is what it is. I can't take it back. I can always just think about it and move forward and change my actions."

On Instagram, Dasani posts a photograph of herself, beaming as a Hershey cheerleader. "Wanna go back," Dasani writes, adding two pink hearts with wings. She misses her friend, Kali, who is now a junior at Hershey, on target to graduate. They text every day. Kali will soon be accepted at Temple University in Philadelphia, where she wants to major in construction engineering.

Dasani also feels the absence of Mr. Akers. "I dead miss him," she says. Everyone seems to leave. They are gone until they resurface—just when Dasani is forgetting them. So it went with Giant, the fitness guru from Harlem. He pulled away, then briefly returned, awakening the memories Dasani had laid to rest, all the familiar longings for a father who would stay.

It happens every time. She is back in the man's clutch, where all things are made right. She is under his spell, until he leaves again.

Lately, it is Dasani's biological father, Ramel, who has returned. Fifteen years have passed since he ran a crack house with Chanel, leaving their daughters in the care of Grandma Joanie. Ramel is now fifty-one and sober, working as a shoe salesman in Jersey City, where he lives with his girlfriend and their baby. He has been showing up in Staten Island's family court, saying he wants custody of Dasani and Avianna.

This is not the first time Ramel has resurfaced, trying to make up for the past. Dasani is wary. Yet whenever Ramel appears, their bond is undeniable. She is, without question, made from his body. They have the same bright smile, the same wiry build. They walk and talk at an equally quick pace, rapping in perfect sync to the same Meek Mill songs.

"I rapped to you in your mother's belly," Ramel laughs, and Dasani laughs back. They shadowbox and breakdance and hug each other hard. A current of electricity flows between them, binding them one moment and separating them the next.

"You left me!" Dasani screams during a visit in Brooklyn.

"My dad left me, too!" Ramel yells back.

"Then you should have known from his example," Dasani says.

She has already told the Foundling agency of her decision. She will not be "adopted" by her own father. He has shown up too late.

Dasani is learning the shorthand of incarceration. On Facebook, she posts two words—"Free Khaliq"—and everyone knows that her brother is behind bars.

Khaliq remains in juvenile detention, shuttling between places with utopian names. Sheltering Arms. Horizons. Boys Town. Children's Village. Last year, during a brief stint at Crossroads, Khaliq began cursing so loudly that a fitness instructor intervened. It was Giant, the former guru of Dasani. They exchanged high-fives and small talk.

"How's Dasani?" Giant asked Khaliq.

From Staten Island, Dasani tries to keep tabs on all of her siblings. She travels by train to see Papa at his Bronx facility. She visits her youngest sisters—Lee-Lee, Hada, and Maya—at Foundling, though they are prone to arriving late.

Avianna and Nana remain distant.

"They'll be back," Chanel keeps telling Dasani. She says the same of Supreme, who is gone in a different way. Eight months have passed since he last saw the children, when Foundling banned Supreme on the suspicion that he had brought a gun to a visit. His beard is now gray. He walks with a slower step. He is like a ghost in reverse— physically here, but vacant inside.

Chanel can hear him, late at night, crying like a baby. He tries to muffle the sound with his pillow. Sometimes he mutters or whimpers in his sleep. One night he wakes Chanel, shouting, "My babies! My babies!"

Supreme is certain that ACS will prevail, taking his children forever. It does not seem to matter that he and Chanel have completed their parenting and anger management classes. Or that Supreme went to residential rehab to treat his addiction. Among the reasons that ACS filed for a termination of parental rights last month was Chanel and Supreme's "inability to secure housing."

On the morning after Thanksgiving, they transfer to another homeless shelter, in Far Rockaway, Queens. Out on the street, Chanel keeps up appearances. She does so by smiling. She smiles until her cheeks hurt, like a "fool, a clown." She used to make fun of such people, saying they had "a frown upside down."

People try to lift her spirits, commenting on her sunny outlook, calling her "an inspiration."

She smiles when she hears this, too. She always has the same thought. "When I get my kids back, that's when you will see me frown."

Dasani wants to believe her mother's promise.

Everyone will "be back." The whole family will one day resume its former shape. But how long will that take? Dasani seeks comfort in what she knows.

She is the firstborn daughter of Chanel. She is the near twin of Avianna. Together, they are the original family from which Dasani sprang and to which she will return. Of this she is certain. She already has her mother back—and Avianna will soon follow.

Tensions in Avianna's foster home have escalated. Her foster mother, the Brooklyn hairstylist, tells Foundling that Avianna has "challenged her authority daily." In the fall of 2017, Avianna is transferred to a new home in Queens. Since then, her "mood and affect have stabilized," writes a Foundling caseworker, and she is "happier."

In court, the family's case is moving along. The children must declare their wishes. The three youngest sisters have agreed to be adopted by Auntie Joan. Nana is still considering adoption by the hairstylist. The oldest siblings—Dasani, Khaliq, and Avianna—all plan to "age out" of foster care, returning to their parents.

This leaves Papa. Three years have passed since he watched *Annie* and ran off without a coat. He was not just running away. He was running toward something as well. He imagined finding his own adoptive family—a real Daddy Warbucks, with the kind of happy home where the movie ends.

Instead, Papa landed in an institution. At age eleven, he has a psychiatric record that would repel many adoptive parents. No one has stepped forward to take him. The very boy who ran away after watching *Annie* is now the only child living like an orphan.

"Forever Family," writes Dasani on December 3, 2017, above a photograph on Facebook showing three new friends. They are throwing gang signs.

Dasani, now sixteen, knows that her estranged sister, Avianna, will be rankled by this.

To write "Forever Family" is Dasani's way of saying the opposite—that nothing is forever, not even family. That one's sister can be replaced as easily as one's own blood, which is not "thicker than water," as their mother used to say. In the photograph, Dasani wears a red bandanna in allegiance to the Bloods. One family is poised to take the place of another.

Dasani has not seen Avianna in over a year. They last exchanged texts five months ago. But Dasani knows how to break her sister's silence. Precisely two hours and thirty-five minutes after Dasani posts the "Forever Family" photo, Avianna appears on Facebook, clicking a digital hand. The hand waves at her sister.

Dasani waves back.

"Hey sis," writes fifteen-year-old Avianna.

A feverish correspondence follows. They agree to meet the following weekend, at a subway station in Queens. They are both nervous, so Avianna sends detailed instructions. Dasani must take the A train to Broadway Junction, then the J train to Queens, "to the last stop, get off, go upstairs and then meet me at the turnstile."

Queens is not Dasani's turf. She asks for the name of the station, which worries Avianna. Nothing can be left to chance. Instead, they settle on Broadway Junction, which is impossible to miss.

"Got u sis," Avianna writes.

On the afternoon of December 10, Avianna leaves her foster home in Queens and Dasani leaves her foster home in Staten Island. They check their phones.

"I'm on the train," writes Avianna.

"Me too," writes Dasani.

By 1:28 P.M., they are minutes apart. Both trains arrive and the sisters dismount. They cannot find each other.

Avianna writes that she is here. Dasani writes that she is coming upstairs. Avianna writes that she is coming down. No, Dasani writes, she is coming up. Where you at, Dasani asks. Avianna is at the turnstile. Come to the escalators, writes Dasani.

The thread stops. The station stops.

Two sisters are crashing into each other.

They have no words. They hold each other like refugees who have crossed an unseen border.

Everyone is watching.

"Mind your own damn business!" Dasani manages to shout from her sister's impossible clutch. She cannot breathe like this. No one hugs like this. "You're holding me too tight! Let me go! Let me go."

No one lets go.

They stand like this for minutes. They already know their next move. The A train will come, taking them to downtown Brooklyn, where Chanel is waiting.

The train is coming—the very train that their grandmother used to clean. It pulls into the station. The doors open.

chapter 45

NEVER AGAIN WILL Dasani and Avianna pull apart. This much they promise. *Whatever happens, stay together.*

Yet a vast body of water separates their two boroughs. They hop the ferry for occasional visits. They text every day. They plot their future, imagining the exile of Dasani from Staten Island and of Avianna from Queens, and the home they will recover in their Brooklyn birthplace.

For now, Dasani takes refuge in the house of fifteen-year-old Marie. She lives in a crowded subdivision in New Brighton, a short walk from the Staten Island street where Dasani once lived.

They had met the previous summer, through a friend of Dasani's from Hershey. The girl was home on break and getting into trouble. This led to a fight in Brooklyn, where Marie watched as Dasani rose to the Hershey student's defense. No one could defeat Dasani—not even Marie, who also liked to fight. Instead, they became inseparable.

Dasani cuts school to be with Marie, whose stepfather is a weed dealer and whose brother is a high-ranking member of the 400s, a local gang. Marie's mother passes the day playing video games and watching her two-year-old granddaughter. Violence occasionally erupts, bringing visits from ACS.

But the greatest threat is far less visible.

On the evening of April 4, 2018, Supreme's cellphone rings in Harlem, where he is now living in a shelter with Chanel. A close relative is calling from prison to say that Dasani's life is in danger.

"They got a hit on her head," the young man tells Supreme.

A photo of Dasani has appeared on Facebook, standing with Marie and her brother's friends. The boys are holding up four fingers—in solidarity with the 400s. Marie's brother is an "old head" of the gang, while Dasani's close relative—the inmate now calling Supreme—is a well-known member of a local rival gang.

This makes Dasani a possible snitch. The 400s have caught wind of her connection to the other gang, and they are planning to kill Dasani, the relative tells Supreme. She must leave New Brighton immediately.

Now Dasani's phone is ringing. She is sitting on Marie's bed. Dasani picks up to hear her mother's voice. She listens in silence. Until this moment, Dasani had naively thought that she was immune to local gang rivalries. She answered only to the Bloods of Brooklyn.

Following her mother's orders, Dasani hangs up and returns to her foster home. She hides in the basement, untagging herself from the Facebook post. She thinks about the day that the photograph was taken. Marie's brother had lost his temper.

"Ever since you came around, she been actin' different," the brother had snapped, telling Dasani to stay away from Marie or "I will put fear in your heart."

"My heart beats the same," Dasani had shot back. "It don't skip a beat for nobody."

The next day, Dasani walks out of her home, saying she will be gone for a while. Her foster mother, Denise, calls Marie's mother, who tells Denise about the death threat. Denise alerts the Foundling worker, Tea, who calls the police. More information is trickling in: Tea reports back to Foundling that "gang members staged fights in the community for Dasani with other peers to see if Dasani would win these fights." Her reputation as "Deedee Unstoppable" has made her a target.

That evening, Dasani hides out in my apartment in Harlem. She knows that she is putting me at risk, while I worry that her life is in danger. By the next morning, she is on the phone with Tea, who comes to collect her. She will go to the Good Shepherd group home on the eastern edge of Brooklyn. Tea tells Dasani that the move is temporary. She will stay there for a few days while Foundling locates a new foster home.

Chanel has forbidden Dasani to talk to Marie. The loss is so abrupt, the threat of murder so jarring, the move to Brooklyn so sudden, that it takes Dasani a few days to register her heartbreak.

The next few months pass in a blur.

Dasani remains at Good Shepherd as other girls come and go, returning to their families or moving on to foster care. She assumes that no one wants her because she is "too much to handle."

Fifteen-year-old Nana also feels unwanted. She recently left her foster home after a loud argument with the Brooklyn hairstylist, who had locked Nana outside in the rain. As Nana's vision worsens, she is shuttling between foster homes, lugging a trash bag filled with clothes.

One might assume that Nana is homeless. But to foster care veterans, the trash bag gives her away. Very few foster children have a suitcase.

Chanel is still searching for a new lawyer, determined to win back custody. She chats up random attorneys on the street, saving their business cards. They never call back. No one wants to take a pro bono case, involving eight children, all the way in Staten Island.

In the meantime, Nana is adrift, Papa and Khaliq are languishing in facilities, and no one can explain why Dasani is still at Good Shepherd. But at least she is back in Brooklyn.

Dasani can feel the roots beneath her feet. She is living in East New York, where her mother came of age. Chanel had been a student at Thomas Jefferson High School—the very building where Dasani now attends the High School for Civil Rights (everyone still calls it Jeff). A few miles west, at the corner of Gates and Franklin, is Grandma Joanie's apartment. And two blocks from there is the homeless shelter where Chanel, by sheer coincidence, has now landed.

She and Supreme are no longer together. The collapse of their marriage had come slowly. It began when their children were taken. "It starts from the home," Chanel tells me. "Nobody being there. That's how the anger starts to build up. They take all your children away and now you're just left with the shell. . . . We blamed each other for the removal of the kids. And we were just so angry at each other."

Then came a grief that nothing could contain. "My pain, his pain, the kids' pain . . . it destroyed us. The kids were the only thing that kept us sane. The kids kept us looking forward to something. We never accomplished anything or could be anything. That was our future."

Supreme is now living in a single men's shelter in Harlem, while Chanel finds herself back in the neighborhood where she first became a mother. By chance, Chanel's shelter has not only put her near Dasani, but also Avianna, who will soon return to Brooklyn, moving into her fifth foster home.

This geographical stroke of luck gives Chanel a boost. She is certain that her late mother, Joanie, is behind it, scheming with God to outmaneuver the city's agencies. They can try to block Chanel from regaining custody, but no one can stop her from mothering her girls. Only Chanel will meet them in a flash, doing their hair, taking them to McDonald's, shoving a few dollars into their hands.

Brooklyn is also home to Chanel's three youngest girls—Hada, Maya, and Lee-Lee—who see their mother on October 10, 2018, at a supervised visit.

"Mommy, when is court?" asks Lee-Lee. Chanel starts to answer the question when a Foundling caseworker interrupts. Chanel is not allowed to discuss her ACS case with the children.

Instead, Chanel waves them into a corner, saying that she wants to show them photos on her phone. As the girls gather round, Chanel opens her text thread and begins to type "court is Oct. 31. Tell them u don't want to be adopted. This is the last chance u got or u never gonna see me again." The girls follow their mother's cues, pretending to look at photos. But the Foundling caseworker is getting suspicious. She walks toward them and they disperse.

Eight days later, Avianna goes to see Dasani. It is dark outside as Avianna approaches the group home, where a crowd of teens have gathered. A fight is brewing. The two sisters are separated by a window. Dasani wants to protect her sister, but the staff at Good Shepherd refuses to let Dasani outside. She starts banging on the window and throwing furniture. As her temper explodes, the police are called.

Avianna watches as her sister is handcuffed and placed in an ambulance. The same thing had happened to Avianna earlier this month: She was sent to the ER following an argument with her foster mother.

Avianna is now screaming at the police, who threaten her with a Taser gun. An ambulance takes Dasani to Woodhull Hospital's emergency room, where she will spend the weekend under observation. The hospital is so crowded that Dasani is confined to a gurney in the hallway.

No one from Good Shepherd, ACS, or Foundling visits Dasani over the weekend. Only her mother comes, toting a bag from McDonald's.

Chanel knows without asking: Chicken McNuggets with sweet and sour sauce, Dasani's all-time favorite.

Together, Dasani and Avianna walk into a tattoo parlor in downtown Brooklyn on February 28, 2019.

Hours later, they emerge, their arms tingling. On Avianna's left forearm, encased in a heart, is the name CHANEL. On Dasani's left forearm, under a red rose, is the name JOANIE.

Almost a year has passed since Dasani fled Staten Island. She is now a senior at her east Brooklyn high school, one block from her group home. She might have dropped out if not for the man she calls Mr. E—the school's Haitian-born assistant principal, Jean Etienne, who has been at the school for nineteen years. At first, he had butted heads with Dasani, suspending her for bad behavior. But he also saw her promise.

"She has what we call the intrinsic motivation," says Etienne, fifty-seven, who began mentoring Dasani, carving out a space in his office for her to study.

This year, Dasani will turn eighteen, marking a milestone as the oldest sister. The youngest child, Baby Lee-Lee, is about to turn eight. Their fates may soon be decided. More than three years after they were separated, the ACS case has gone to trial as the agency moves to end the parental rights of Supreme and Chanel.

On March 13, Dasani and Avianna skip school and take the ferry to Staten Island. They hurry along Bay Street toward the family court steps. They have yet to miss a court appearance, and today's is about to begin.

Gone is Judge Lim, who retired in December. The family's case has been transferred to Judge Alison Hamanjian, who presides over a wood-paneled courtroom facing New York Harbor. She speaks in a soft, careful tone, taking her time with every detail. Chanel likes this judge, while Dasani is more guarded.

She carefully scans the courtroom, which is flanked by lawyers: five for the children, three for the city's agencies, and another three representing Chanel and Supreme. Among them is David Lansner, a prominent seventy-one-year-old lawyer who has agreed to take Chanel's case pro bono.

Of all the developments in this sprawling four-year case, nothing compares to the arrival of Lansner. By turns revered and hated, he has made a career of suing the child protection system, winning large settlements for poor parents on the grounds that their civil rights were denied. For forty-seven years he has specialized in family, matrimonial, and civil rights law, running a private practice since 1991 with his wife, Carolyn Kubitschek. Often working pro bono, they have argued cases before state and federal courts, bringing reforms that have changed ACS.

Lansner is known to be showy, argumentative, and a stickler for details that make other lawyers roll their eyes. He approaches a new case like a blank canvas, questioning every motion, every court order, every stated "fact."

To Chanel, the man can be summed up more plainly: "I found my pit," she says, naming her canine of choice.

The search had taken years. Chanel could never afford a private attorney, and although she lived in Brooklyn, her case was stuck in Staten Island—the only borough without a public-interest law firm representing poor parents. For a time, Chanel consulted with New

York University's Family Defense Clinic. She also relied on her Legal Aid lawyer, Goldfein, but child neglect was not his expertise.

Last October, as Chanel's trial drew near, she began to panic. Her court-appointed lawyer, Yost, had not spoken to her in three months, according to his pay logs. (Yost told me he had sent Chanel a standard monthly letter seeking "client-attorney contact," but he had the wrong address.) Chanel's mounting desperation led her to the Manhattan office of Nora McCarthy, the founder of Rise, a parent advocacy group. Rise publishes a magazine written by parents in the child protection system.

In person, Chanel struck McCarthy as "the classic parent at the mercy of the system because she doesn't bow down." On Chanel's behalf, McCarthy began contacting lawyers—among them, Lansner. She mentioned the *Times* series, which jogged his memory. Lansner wanted to help the family "because it was Dasani," he said. "She was a symbol of so much that was wrong with the system." But Lansner was semiretired and had been turning down new trial cases. So he waited to see if another lawyer stepped forward. No one did.

Today, Lansner has riled the courtroom with a motion to vacate prior orders, demanding that Dasani and her siblings be returned to their mother immediately. They have suffered needlessly in foster care, he says—all of which could have been avoided.

To begin with, the family was enrolled in the wrong preventive service—a therapy-based program that failed to meet their concrete needs, such as helping to restore the children's food stamps or arranging to replace the window guards. Then, after the children were taken, the court violated the law, Lansner says, by failing to take testimony from the parents and children, and by excluding them, at times, from the courtroom.

Regardless, Chanel has complied with most of ACS's demands: testing negative for drugs and completing all required classes. Lansner's strategy is to seek custody in phases, first by returning the two oldest daughters, Dasani and Avianna, to their mother.

The room is so crowded that there is no chair for Chanel's court-appointed lawyer, Yost—the same man who told her that "no one sues ACS" and that the scales of justice are stacked against her because "that's just the way it is." He is left standing, his face bewildered.

Chanel's Legal Aid lawyer, Goldfein, watches the scene with wary optimism. By chance, he had crossed paths with Lansner five months earlier, in what became an embarrassing day for City Hall.

On October 5, 2018, Mayor de Blasio had gone to his longtime gym, the Park Slope YMCA, to work out—a routine that requires transporting the mayor, by chauffeured SUV, some forty minutes from Gracie Mansion most mornings. He was stretching on a mat when a Black homeless woman named Nathylin Flowers Adesegun walked up and asked why his affordable housing plan gave so few units to the homeless.

"I'm in the middle of doing my workout," said the mayor. "I can't do this now."

"Can you look me in the eye and tell me why—"

"I'm in the middle of a workout," snapped the mayor.

This was the same mayor who had been elected in 2013 on a social justice platform, sharing his inaugural stage with Dasani, then twelve. Dressed in a new winter coat, she had held the Bible for the swearing-in of Tish James, the incoming public advocate, who had then lifted Dasani's arm high into the air.

Dasani was, for a moment, the city's most celebrated child— a beacon of "enduring hope" and "eternal optimism," James had told the crowd. Dasani personified the crisis that de Blasio vowed to fix, and James would hold him to it. If he failed, James warned the crowd, "you better believe Dasani and I will stand up."

Five years later, James has moved on, becoming the state's attorney general. Meanwhile, de Blasio's public approval ratings have dropped to 42 percent—down 18 points from two years prior.

Despite being reelected in 2017, the mayor has left a trail of disappointments: a still-segregated school system, a public housing system so broken it has required federal intervention, and a police department that is far from reformed. The mayor's own questionable fundraising practices have brought numerous legal probes, overshadowing his triumphs—universal prekindergarten, a raised minimum wage for city workers, free lunch for all public school students, access to free legal counsel for evicted tenants, and a paid sick-leave program.

While de Blasio presses on with plans to create or sustain three hundred thousand units of affordable housing, he has cut deals with developers at the expense of low-income New Yorkers. Most notably, he has failed to solve the homeless crisis. There are currently more than seventy-two thousand homeless New Yorkers (up from nearly sixty thousand when de Blasio took office).

Undeterred, de Blasio is now raising funds to run for president. In a few more weeks, a Brooklyn prankster will post a sign outside the mayor's gym that reads BY ENTERING THESE PREMISES YOU AGREE NOT TO RUN FOR PRESIDENT OF THE UNITED STATES IN 2020 . . .

The homeless woman's ambush of de Blasio last October had been carefully plotted, with protesters standing outside the gym, monitored by Goldfein. By coincidence, Chanel's new lawyer, David Lansner, had just finished his own workout. He joined in with the crowd, chanting for justice.

By the time de Blasio left the Park Slope Y, a video of the mayor's encounter with Adesegun had been posted on the Web. She was the new heroine of homelessness, a role that Dasani had long ago relinquished.

Dasani looks across the courtroom, from her mother to Lansner to the other lawyers. She has been watching them, one by one—their attire, their mannerisms, their vocal intonations. She finds the head lawyer for ACS "rude," but Dasani also knows that lawyers are paid to perform.

She still thinks of becoming a prosecutor, the kind worthy of *Criminal Minds*. She would certainly make a better impression than her own court-appointed lawyer—an overworked white woman with a sour expression. They have barely met, but now this lawyer will guide Dasani and Avianna through one of the most important questions of their lives: Do they want to return to their mother?

The sisters huddle with their lawyer, who lays out the options: Dasani and Avianna can stay in foster care, receiving a financial stipend, free housing, help with college, and other perks. Or they can part with all of that and go back to their mother, which means returning to poverty and homelessness.

"You'll go into a shelter," the lawyer says repeatedly. The sisters confer, then whisper to their lawyer, who stands to address the judge. "They theoretically would like to be returned home," the lawyer says. "But they need to know what home looks like. They need to know where they are gonna be going. They want to see the place that their mother's living in."

Dasani frowns. This lawyer is truncating her words and omitting key points. It is not "theoretical" that Dasani wants to go home. As if reading her mind, Lansner butts in, asking the judge if Dasani can speak for herself. This is a risky move, given that Lansner has not prepared Dasani. He represents only her mother.

It is Chanel who wants her daughter to speak. Chanel knows that this could backfire, as Dasani is unpredictable. But to Chanel's mind, no one in this courtroom—including the powerful white lawyer she calls "Mr. Lansner"—should carry more weight than her own child.

Before Dasani can open her mouth, her own lawyer interjects.

"There's no reason to hear from Dasani," the woman snaps. "I have spoken with Dasani."

If this lawyer had known Dasani, she might have avoided such a provocation. On the street, saying "There's no reason to hear from Dasani" would surely cause a fight. But here, in the courtroom, the rules are different.

Dasani breathes. She collects her thoughts. On her arm, the tattoo of her grandmother's name is still fresh. Joanie's was the first of many voices guiding Dasani forward, from Sherry to Miss Hester to Miss Holmes to Julie the therapist.

Use your words, Julie always said.

The Foundling lawyer is now talking about a "change of goal conference." With that, Lansner leaps to his feet.

"Your honor, the agency has screwed this case up from the very beginning!" he shouts. "And now they want to continue their bureaucratic ways. And nobody wants to hear from this child who's right here."

He gestures at Dasani, who stares at the judge. The judge defers to Dasani's lawyer. They have two choices: Either the lawyer can speak for Dasani, or Dasani can speak for herself.

To Dasani's mind, a lawyer is a paid speaker. This woman is here because of her job. Dasani is here because of her life. She wants the judge to see and hear the words "coming from me," she later says. "I'm saying it because I feel that. I feel those words."

It is doubtful that a lawyer who barely knows Dasani could have the same impact.

"She just gonna *tell* the judge how I feel?" Dasani later tells me. "I could tell the judge how I feel myself. I got a mouth for a reason."

Yet Dasani stays quiet as the conference wears on, with ACS making its position clear: It is unsafe to return the children to Chanel and Supreme because they failed to attend a program for mentally ill addicts. It does not matter that their lawyers have produced a recent record of clean tests. The agency suspects that Chanel is still getting high, based on how sleepy she seemed at the last court conference.

"Quite frankly, given the mother's appearance in court last week—" begins the ACS lawyer.

Now Dasani raises her hand.

Chaos erupts. People are yelling—even Yost, who objects to ACS's making "disparaging remarks about my client." He is defending Chanel like never before. As the bickering peaks, Dasani's lawyer stands and tells the judge that her seventeen-year-old client would like to speak.

Dasani rises.

"I just have one thing to say. The day—the day that my mom was asleep? She always did that, because she be up like—you feel me?—in the morning time, to make sure we go to school."

The room is motionless.

"She goes to sleep because she does *a lot* of stuff. She buys us food. She makes sure my hair is done. A lot of stuff. That's why she's asleep!"

Everybody here—the judge, Dasani's mother, the ACS lawyer, the court officer—is staring at this young woman dressed in a black hoodie, her hair pulled back, her eyes shining. As Dasani's voice rises, her body moves in sync. She jabs her right arm into the air, punctuating each sentence. She is a prosecutor of her own making, and the city—not her mother—is now on trial.

"That facility that I'm in? I'm not supposed to be in there for eleven months. That's supposed to be temporary placement, from what my caseworker told me. I'm supposed to be there two, three months. I've been there eleven months seeing different girls come in and out, in and out."

"I want to go home to my *mother.*"

The judge nods.

"I'm tired of—you feel me?—being in a *facility.* My school is across the street from my facility. On my facility," she says, repeating the word a third time, "it has a big sign that says 'Good Shepherd Services.' I have to leave my school early to *run* so people don't know that I live in a facility—in a group home—with a bunch of other females."

Judge Hamanjian looks at Dasani.

"I know that," the judge says. "And I hope you understand that the court is trying to, um—for lack of a better word—get to the bottom of what the case is about and what the right answers are for you and your siblings. What's not in dispute is that you love your mother. What's not in dispute is that your mother loves you. What's not in dispute is that long after we're out of your lives, you're still going to be a family."

"How can we be a family when we're all separated?" Dasani cries out. "How can we be a family and I couldn't even see my sister when she turned eight yesterday? That's not a family!"

Dasani still knows every line of "A House Is Not a Home," the Luther Vandross song held sacred by Grandma Joanie. For all of her struggles with crack and single motherhood, Joanie had finally found a home. It is still possible, Dasani thinks, for her own mother to do the same.

That evening, Dasani returns to Good Shepherd by herself. Two days later, without warning, the staff moves her to a facility in the North Bronx. She is more isolated than ever, with a two-hour train ride separating Dasani from the anchors in her life—her mother, her sister Avianna, and her high school mentor, Mr. E.

Dasani's graduation is now in peril. Outraged, Lansner files an emergency motion accusing the Foundling agency of retaliating against Dasani for speaking out in court (which Foundling denies).

Three days later, Chanel gets the phone call of her life.

ACS has backed down. The agency will release custody of Dasani and Avianna, returning them to their mother. No one expected things to move so quickly, except Lansner, who is accustomed to wearing out his opponents. ACS has agreed for the girls to be transferred to Chanel this week.

Dasani will leave her group home. Avianna will leave her foster home. Chanel will leave the shelter near Joanie's final home. Together, they will walk into the Bronx intake center—repeating the trek they made fifteen years earlier, the first time they were homeless. Back then, Dasani was a toddler, Avianna a baby, and Chanel a twenty-four-year-old mother.

Now they are resuming their original form, entering the shelter system as a family.

On March 27, 2019, the sun rises over a bright and cloudless sky.

Dasani is already packed for the intake center on East 151st Street. She knows from experience that the day will be long. She devours two biscuits before boarding a minivan. The driver lets her crank the radio as the van winds through the Bronx, blasting the Shawn Mendes song "There's Nothing Holdin' Me Back."

She looks out the window as the van approaches the seven-story building that opened under Mayor Bloomberg, promising a new era of efficiency. Dasani's stomach knots. She still has flashbacks to Auburn's dark corridors and predatory men. In her pocket she carries a sharp nail file for protection. She watches her phone, which pings with adoring texts from her boyfriend. He is one year younger, and crazy for Dasani. She rolls her eyes at his love, "like I be caring."

But Dasani is caring more these days. On her phone, Chanel has gone from "Immature Mom" to "Mama Bear." Her younger sister Avianna is now "Baby Blood." Dasani remains loyal to the gang, but only from afar. She wants to be different from her mother. She wants a crime-free life.

The temperature has risen to 44 degrees, signaling the start of spring. Dasani waits by the entrance as families drift up the ramp, passing the trash pile where, nine years earlier, Chanel had rescued

Turtle. The pet is still alive, in the care of a friend in Staten Island. Chanel plans to come for him once she has a home again.

At 11:04 A.M., Dasani spots her mother, pushing a rolling cart of clean clothes. Chanel is beaming despite her lack of sleep. She spent the morning near her Brooklyn shelter doing laundry, eager to start this new chapter free of stains.

She and her daughters climb the ramp, accompanied by a case-worker from Foundling. They join a long line inching toward the metal detectors. Although the building is off-limits to reporters, the guards are so hurried that they wave me through. But they are vigilant enough to catch Dasani's nail file, confiscating it as she scowls.

Thus begins a twelve-hour trek that will send Chanel and her daughters to five different floors, each one as familiar as the next. Their first stop is the lobby, where the family is assigned a code that Dasani commits to memory: L 382. She knows it will be called again and again, and if they miss it, everything stalls. Next, they are riding the elevator up to the ACS office—located on the fifth floor of the intake center.

Chanel takes a seat. She is so tired that today's anniversary goes unnoticed: It was four years ago, on March 27, 2015, that she was first summoned to Staten Island's family court. She had risen before Judge Lim, never imagining the calamities that would follow.

She glances at her two daughters—how grown they seem, and at the same time how innocent. Their bodies have taken the form of women, while their faces still look baby soft. Avianna slides into a chair next to her mother. Soon the girls are napping in the style of always—Avianna like a rock and Dasani like a leaf, her eyes fluttering with each announcement as she listens for their number.

"Now serving L 370 at the fourth-floor reception," goes the robotic voice.

Dasani pulls her hood over her head.

Next to her, a five-year-old girl is building an imaginary house. She holds a stuffed animal—a rainbow-colored owl she calls Owlie.

Long braids fall across the girl's face. Her eyes are full of wonder, resembling a younger Dasani. Owlie, she says, will be living in her pink jacket, which she places on the seat by Dasani. She fashions the sleeves into rooms: a kitchen, a bedroom, a basement.

"This is Owlie's nest!" she says, looking at her father, a thirty-eight-year-old Puerto Rican with tired eyes. This morning, they were evicted because their Bronx landlord no longer takes housing vouchers. They have never been homeless.

The dad smiles as his girl places an apple on top of Owlie.

"We're going home?" she asks when her father stands up.

"No, they're calling our number."

Dasani shuffles in her seat as the room fills with howling babies.

When "L 382" is finally called, she leaps up, grabbing her mother for the first round of interviews. They migrate from the third floor to the fourth, then back to the fifth—every stop a version of the same weary wait.

Janitors sweep as numbers flash on the screen, each one representing its own singular trauma. None of these children know where they will sleep tonight. "I've been here for three hours!" screams a woman everyone ignores.

Dasani and Avianna distract themselves, beatboxing and freestyling about boys. They watch as their mother hugs a woman named Precious, who goes back to Joanie's time.

"Bye, boo."

"Bye, stink. You be good now."

Most everyone is Black or brown. They stare in the direction of a skinny white mother. She chases her toddler around the room, frantically running her hand through her hair. The same word comes to both Dasani and Avianna, who say it aloud, at the exact same time.

"Crack."

They know all the signs. The unkempt hair. The darting eyes.

Dasani and Avianna have created a secret handshake for every time they think alike. They touch their own head, then wiggle their fingers up into the air, bringing their hands together. Back on the ACS floor, they are verbally jousting about Avianna's "fat girl" eating habits, a comedy routine that has the room in stitches.

"Are you sisters?" a woman asks.

"Sadly," says Dasani, to which Avianna bolts up, yelling, "I was *about to say that!*" They burst into cackles, exchanging the secret handshake.

Night falls as they head to the "departure lounge," still waiting to be assigned shelter. The room vibrates with delirium—toddlers wild from exhaustion, parents spent from screaming. Chanel scans the crowd, recognizing her younger self. Most of these mothers look hungry and distressed.

"I'ma spit in your face!" a woman yells at the staff after learning that her assigned shelter is too far from work.

Finally, at 9:17 P.M., Chanel is summoned to the counter. Her daughters surround her, pressing in to hear the verdict. They have been assigned a two-bedroom apartment at a family shelter in Brooklyn. The address is near Brownsville—seven blocks from where Chanel was born.

A look of relief passes among them. Dasani maps out the address on her phone. It is one train stop from her school, and one bus ride from Avianna's.

As the news sinks in, each family member reacts in a predictable way.

Avianna worries.

"Will we be able to cook?"

Dasani suspends judgment.

"We will have to see when we get there."

Chanel brims with optimism.

"Everything gonna work out. You'll see, everything gonna work out."

Ninety minutes pass as they wait for their ride, arranged for each family by homeless services. The families who came too late must board a yellow school bus outside, now idling in the cold. Small children stand there, shivering under blankets. They will be going to an overnight shelter.

Dasani did it many times as a child.

But tonight is different. When her family's ride finally comes at 10:51 P.M., she jumps to her feet. Chanel buttons up her coat. Avianna gathers her belongings.

Together, they walk through the door.

On August 5, 2020, a van pulls up to Papa's foster home in Brooklyn. Nearly five years have passed since the first van came, taking Papa and his siblings into ACS custody.

Papa is now thirteen years old. He climbs into the van, calmly strapping in. Today will be his last supervised family visit. Next week, if his mother tests negative for drugs, Papa can begin his transition home. They will start with weekend visits, paving the way for Chanel to regain full custody of Papa—just as she did with Avianna and Dasani.

Papa looks out the window as the van heads to Foundling. Both he and his caseworker are wearing masks, though the coronavirus no longer scares Papa. He managed to dodge it, even at the pandemic's peak last spring, while living at a state psychiatric hospital in Queens. There is nothing he wants more than to be home again.

Only after Dasani returned to her mother did her behavior begin to improve. She applied herself in school, rescuing her grades with summer classes and the mentoring of Mr. E, her assistant principal. "She wanted to graduate and that made it possible for me to help her," said Etienne, who has learned to distinguish between a child's potential and her traumas, which can flare unexpectedly—disrupting focus, revving up anger.

These traumas, Etienne says, are rooted in America's deep inequities, among them an education system that is "rigged" against children of color. Still, he believes that Dasani can succeed anywhere, provided she has the support of one person who cares. "That's all she needs," he said. "She needs love."

Three months after Dasani turned eighteen, she became the first person in her family to graduate from high school. On August 29, 2019, she crossed the stage in a white cap and gown and reached for her diploma. When she looked into the audience, she spotted her mother and Avianna, who was leaping like a lunatic.

"That's my *sister!*" Avianna screamed as people turned and stared.

Dasani floated for weeks. "Being the first to do it," she said, "I felt like I finally did something that meant something. . . . I know when Avianna graduate, I'm gonna act a fool. . . . They gonna have to say,

'She need to leave the auditorium!' Cuz I'ma be so loud. It's over. Cuz that's my little sister."

It would take another year for Dasani to get motivated enough to apply to college, asking for Etienne's help with the following text: "Good morning . . . This is Dasani Coates. I believe I am college ready and I know that I can buckle down and work hard to be as successful as I can."

She was still living at the Brooklyn shelter with her mother and Avianna, staying sequestered in their room as the virus exploded. Night after night, the sirens wailed as refrigerated trucks filled with corpses. Then, on May 25, came the killing of George Floyd, bringing a new sound to Brooklyn's streets.

"No Justice, No Peace! Fuck These Racist Ass Police!" chanted Dasani, who had turned nineteen the morning after Floyd's death. She, Avianna, and thousands of others protested at Barclays Center — the same place where people had marched six years earlier after the killing of Eric Garner.

Echoes of Garner's death could still be heard. Both he and Floyd had lost their lives in front of spectators, at the hands of white officers responding to minor offenses. Both men had died repeating the same three words: *I can't breathe.*

In the mathematics of Dasani's upbringing, three is a special number. It represents "understanding," which means to see all things clearly. And now the world was seeing another Black man die, in another viral video, saying the same three words. Yet this time it felt different — at least to Dasani.

Her mother was less sure. Chanel had watched the police react with brutal force as Mayor de Blasio stood back defending them, his failed presidential bid long over. One night in June, Chanel pulled away from the protests to stand at the Brooklyn family courthouse. She peered through a window at the lobby's electronic screen. It was flashing the docket numbers of child protection cases, next to hundreds of names — each one a different child. Who was marching for them?

In early May 2020, Chanel attended her first "Black Families Matter" meeting. It was led by Joyce McMillan, a Black mother and activist who, in 1999, lost custody of her children to ACS for two and a half years. McMillan is spearheading a movement to abolish the child protection system, which she calls the "family regulation system." Her posters carry the slogans

THEY SEPARATE CHILDREN AT THE BORDER
OF BROWNSVILLE TOO

SOME COPS ARE CALLED CASEWORKERS

FROM THE PLANTATION TO THE PRESENT, BREAKING
UP BLACK FAMILIES HAS ALWAYS MEANT PROFIT

When Chanel thinks about the breakup of her own family, she sees eight children trying to survive—not only "the system," as the public knows it, but the private rupture of a sacred bond. She sees the lines of her own sorrow in the faces of other mothers. "I see a lot of Black families like me."

It is her boys, Chanel says, who carry the deepest scars.

A few months from now, in September 2020, a surveillance video will show a young man approaching a white Mercedes Benz on Staten Island's North Shore. The assailant—his face obscured by a hoodie—will point a nine-millimeter semiautomatic pistol at two young men in the car, opening fire and killing one of the men in a gang-related hit.

It will take detectives another four and a half months to make an arrest, charging nineteen-year-old Khaliq with the murder.

Dasani will read about her stepbrother's arrest in the New York Post. When the news reaches Supreme, he tries to steady himself. Even if his son is innocent—Khaliq will plead not guilty—he is unlikely to be acquitted, says Supreme, because the system is unjust. Chanel has the same feeling. "The next time he sees the streets again, he'll be fifty-something," she says.

This is the very fate that Khaliq had imagined for himself as a fourteen-year-old boy, when he lashed out violently a month after entering foster care and went to jail for the first time. *I'm never getting out of here. This is my future.*

Khaliq's future would have been different—there is no question in his father's mind—had ACS kept the family together.

"When I was in the home, he was going to school," Supreme says. "He was working on a plan of going into the Navy SEALs, going into the Marines. He had little fights but he never got arrested. I had a control on him. I had an *influence* on him. You know what I'm saying? We went out. We talked a lot. And that, right there, is the most beneficial part of a boy's life: to be able, at the end of the day, to have a conversation with his *father*. So that he can know that what he's doing, as a boy, is right. You understand what I'm saying? That he's on the right path. That he's doing the right things. That's what helps his confidence. That's how kids fall victim to peer pressure, cuz their self-esteem and their confidence is down. And that comes from not having a father."

It was in foster care that Khaliq pulled away, losing all contact with his father.

"That's the most important part for the children—is my presence," says Supreme. "That's what they took away. My presence."

Baby Lee-Lee is now eight years old. More than half her life has passed in the care of Auntie Joan, who also continues to have custody of fourteen-year-old Hada and fifteen-year-old Maya.

Lee-Lee is writing her own songs, and wants to be a singer when she grows up, while Hada—the family bookworm—has blossomed into a sketch artist. Maya remains a diva: She is plotting a future in the nail-salon business, where she will "become an entrepreneur," she says with panache.

Their eighteen-year-old sister, Nana, remains in foster care, where she has not seen a doctor in thirteen months, a dentist in thirty months, or a therapist in years, according to an ACS court report.

"Such indifference," Chanel's lawyer, Lansner, writes to ACS, "would result in a finding of neglect against a parent."

Although Nana's eye disease has worsened, her life is pressing forward. She will soon graduate from high school and plans to enroll as a psychology major at Borough of Manhattan Community College. She wants to work with children of trauma.

"Unfortunately, I was a kid who had no one to advocate for me," says Nana, who has come to regard her childhood as dysfunctional. "I want to help children and teens who are a product of their environment. Why should other kids have to start way behind in the race of life because of things they couldn't control or never learned how to control?"

Chanel is focused on her own reform. She has found opportunity in the pandemic, making deliveries for the app service Postmates. She bought a used $600 moped to get around more easily. She tells everyone that she is drug-free, and on August 11, 2020, she proves it—testing negative, as the judge requested.

This opens the door to Papa's return. Four days later, on a Saturday morning, Chanel fetches her son by bus. In Papa's pocket, he carries a deck of cards to play Pitty Pat with his mother, just like old times. They hold hands, making their way back to the shelter.

Dasani and Avianna are waiting as Papa flies into their arms. Soon, they are all riding the train to Long Island City, where the Sykes family is gathering for a barbecue in Queensbridge Park.

The sun peeks through the clouds as Dasani leads Papa down a grassy slope, trailed by Avianna and Chanel. Behind them are the housing projects, and ahead, the glistening East River.

Everyone is coming: Aunt Margo, two of her grandchildren, her late sister Joanie's children and grandchildren, nieces and nephews. Aunt Linda cleans the grill as a portable speaker blasts the beats of Sleepy Hallow, a rising Brooklyn rapper.

Today's occasion is a "gender reveal" for Joanie's pregnant niece, twenty-five-year-old Kalinda, the daughter of Linda. This is the same cousin who used to visit Dasani and Avianna when they were babies living on Gates Avenue with Grandma Joanie.

Will Kalinda have a boy or a girl? Everyone must guess. For the Sykes clan, nothing compares to the thrill of an impending birth. Each new life expands the circle. Dasani takes a long look at Kalinda's stomach.

"It's a boy," Dasani declares.

Avianna disagrees, saying it is a girl. They start bickering over who is right.

Papa has stepped away.

The last time the Sykes family saw Papa, he was a mischievous five-year-old boy, chasing balloons at a baby shower. Now he is taller than Chanel, with a stocky build and a serious face. He wears the clothes of institutional life: a pair of burgundy pants and a matching T-shirt.

Looking lost, Papa wanders at the party's edge, his maroon figure standing out. The uncles greet him with open arms. They nod gently at Chanel. They have seen this before—the young man who exits the system and returns to the family's fold. It cannot be rushed.

As the sun sets and the music thumps, Papa starts to relax. He breaks into the occasional dance move, calling out "Mommy!" as Chanel works the grill. Her daughters remain consumed by the same burning question: Will Kalinda have a boy or a girl?

Sometimes at a "gender reveal" the couple will set off a confetti cannon or a smoke bomb to announce the answer. The Sykeses have opted for fireworks. If they explode pink, it is a girl. If they explode blue, it is a boy.

The time has come. The family gathers in a circle as the baby's father lights a match. Kalinda smiles. Dasani holds her breath.

The air crackles, then explodes. Everything is blue. Dasani leaps up, victorious. She was right all along. She screams the same three words over and over: *It's a boy!*

Torpedoes of light shoot into the horizon. Everyone can see this new child coming. The whole family is watching, their faces turned skyward. Chanel is beaming. Papa is laughing. Avianna is pouting that her sister must always win.

Dasani knows it does not matter. Boy or girl, a new child is here.

afterword

My path to Dasani began hundreds of miles from Brooklyn, on the bookshelf of my childhood home in Washington, D.C. It was January 2012 and I was visiting from New York with my two daughters—four-month-old Clara and three-year-old Ava—when one night I went looking for something to read.

Tucked among my high school yearbooks was a hardcover edition of Alex Kotlowitz's 1991 classic *There Are No Children Here*. It had been twenty years since I opened this book, which tells the story of two brothers, Pharoah and Lafeyette Rivers, growing up in a Chicago public housing complex that has since been torn down. America was in a new century.

But for children like Pharoah, how much had really changed?

This was the question I kept asking as I read back through Kotlowitz's book. A quick Internet search confirmed my hunch: One in five American children was living in poverty—the same rate as twenty years earlier, when Kotlowitz published his book. In fact, the United States had, in 2012, the highest child poverty rate of any wealthy country after Romania.

At *The New York Times*, my editors Christine Kay and Matt Purdy ran the investigative desk, where I had been stationed since 2007. By the time I pitched the idea that would eventually become this book,

America was in the midst of an awakening. Protesters had recently launched the Occupy Wall Street movement in the shadow of the Great Recession—a period that had also given rise to the Tea Party movement. We were entering an era of populist upheaval, which made poverty a timely subject.

Reporting on poverty had never been easy. Journalists faced the noise of partisan politics—the heated debates about "self-reliance" and the size of America's government. My editor Christine had left her working-class Pittsburgh roots to rise up through the *Times*'s ranks. She thought it was harder than ever to transcend readers' pre-conceived notions—that the poor, for example, lack "personal re-sponsibility."

"What if I just write about the kids?" I proposed.

Children are bystanders, after all—no more to blame for their pov-erty than for their very existence. It would be difficult to argue that America's poor children (numbering 16 million in 2012) are respon-sible for their own well-being, or that their destitution is the result of their own bad choices. Their struggles exist on the margins of Ameri-can politics. Children cannot vote. Their voices are rarely heard.

The first time Dasani spoke to me about being "invisible," she was eleven years old. She had taken something painful—the feeling of being unseen—and reimagined it in her favor, as a "superpower."

Dasani was not just articulating her own private experience. She was describing a public relationship: between herself and her city, be-tween the homeless and the housed, between Black disadvantage and white privilege. Her childhood was being shaped by the encounter of these two worlds—these two sets of people—the seen and the unseen.

There was never any question to which lot I belonged. People may wonder how I gained the family's "trust," a word that fails to cap-ture the complexity of the reporter-source bond. Trust is, at best, a work in progress. It ebbs and flows, depending on the day.

I was raised by a woman who taught me this. My mother, a Chil-ean immigrant, spent years of her life working as the mental health director of a free clinic for Latinos in Washington, D.C. One of her great gifts was her ability to listen.

Some of her patients were dying of AIDS. Others were refugees of El Salvador's civil war. They carried the scars of torture—something my own Chilean uncles were lucky enough to escape, having fled the brutal dictatorship of General Augusto Pinochet before resettling in America.

To speak up, in Chile, could cost one's life. But silence brought a different kind of death. Stories were the lifeblood of our exile community. They had to be heard. In one of my earliest memories, my mother is strumming her guitar late at night, singing Violeta Parra's "Gracias a la vida."

> *Thank you, life, for giving me so much*
> *You gave me my hearing, with all its power*

In one of my first interviews with Dasani, she gestured at her mother, saying of Chanel: "She be tellin' me that I talk too much! She said that when I get older, I'ma *know* why I talk too much because, right now, I don't know why."

Chanel corrected her: "You don't know why it's not *good* to talk so much. Cuz the best teacher is a listener."

All I wanted to say was "Dasani, please keep talking."

For months, I had been searching for a child like Dasani—a girl who could narrate her own experience of growing up poor. My earliest reporting had cast a wide net, taking me to places like Camden, New Jersey, Scranton, Pennsylvania, and Van Buren County, Michigan. Experts had encouraged me to find a "representative" child, one whose family reflected demographic trends—perhaps a single mother with two children (by different fathers), working a low-wage job, part time.

That checklist would never have led me to Dasani, whose parents were married, chronically unemployed, and raising many children. But by the time I landed at the Auburn shelter, what mattered more to me than any demographic profile was finding a child who could breathe life into this story. And on that sunny afternoon in October 2012, she was staring right at me.

Dasani crackled with energy. She was precocious, daring, full of adventure. Already, at age eleven, she could articulate what she was feeling in a profound and moving way. She was a keen observer of her life—a rare trait, even in adults. These attributes are not just admirable; they are instrumental to the work of any journalist.

Most of the people I write about have never spoken to a reporter. The burden is on us to explain what we do. One way of describing it is this: We go to an unfamiliar place. We spend a lot of time with people who regard us as outsiders. We watch, we listen, we try to understand.

The word "understand" comes from Old English—*understandan*. Literally, it means "to stand in the midst of." It does not mean we have reached some ultimate truth. It means, to my mind, that we have experienced enough of something new, something formerly unseen, to be provoked, humbled, awakened, or even changed by it. If I did anything in my eight years with Dasani, it was to stand in the midst of her life.

During our first weeks together in 2012, I explained my rules of engagement to Dasani's family: that I was writing a story for the *Times* and unless a person tells me something is "private," whatever I observe could be published in an article read by many people; that I record conversations to ensure accuracy; that no one I write about should be surprised by what is printed, because I vet every fact ahead of publication, giving the person time to respond; and that neither I nor the *Times* ever pays anyone for their story. I gave Chanel a stack of my published work, inviting her to call anyone I had written about, to ask if I had been fair.

From the start, Dasani seemed so eager to participate that I wondered: Was she doing this to please her mother? Would she regret it later on? What was my moral obligation to a child versus an adult, who possesses the wisdom and agency to make informed decisions?

And what if I witnessed things that made me want to intervene, stepping out of my role as a reporter?

Auburn was off-limits to the public, so I spent long stretches of time with Dasani's family on the street—listening to music, sitting in the park, lingering by the bodega. Chanel took the lead in explaining my presence to others. I did not object when she called me her "friend," but I encouraged her to tell anyone she trusted that I was there to write a story.

The relationship I was forging with Dasani's family had no clear road map. I certainly couldn't find it in the *Times*'s reporter handbook, which hewed to the traditional rules of beat reporting. Under the section titled "Personal Relations with Sources" is this gem from a bygone era: "A City Hall reporter who enjoys a weekly round of golf with a City Council member, for example, risks creating an appearance of coziness. . . ."

Per the rules of my profession, I could pay for meals with Dasani's family at restaurants, which also gave us a place to meet when the weather turned cold. With cameras provided by the *Times*, the family kept a video diary, describing the "high point" and "low point" of any given day (something my own family did around the dinner table, without a camera). I also asked Chanel and Supreme to document the condition of their room, while a local nonprofit, Fort Greene SNAP, filed freedom of information requests for city records on my behalf.

Working by my side was the veteran *Times* photographer Ruth Fremson. To stay under the city's radar, we spent large swaths of time at Dasani's school, McKinney, which required buy-in from Principal Paula Holmes. While she was reluctant at first, Miss Holmes believed in the power of journalism enough to give us access to McKinney for an entire year.

Eventually, Ruth and I snuck into the Auburn shelter through a fire escape, setting off the alarm and slipping past four security guards to reach the family's room. In advance of this, I had alerted the Legal Aid Society, which agreed to represent Dasani's family should they be evicted from the shelter for breaking its rules.

Luckily, our presence went undetected.

After the *Times* published my five-part series in December 2013, it was clear that I had only scratched the surface of Dasani's story. Over the next seven years, as I worked on this book, I relied on the brave and steady commitment of Dasani and her family. Our relationship took many turns—deepening at times, growing distant at others. What I could depend on was the respect I had for Dasani's family, and they for mine.

While they never questioned me on the rules of my profession, I imagined hearing these rules from their perspective: I am housed. They are homeless. I have food. They are often hungry. And yet here I am, writing about them—and their poverty—as my job.

Plenty of journalists have struggled with similar dilemmas. I found more clarity among academics, who had given great thought to the ethics of their work. For the ultimate example of this, look no further than the twenty-five-page "statement on method" in Mitchell Duneier's *Sidewalk*, an iconic ethnography of street vendors in Greenwich Village.

One of my guides was the late Lee Ann Fujii, an ethnographer who had studied Bosnian and Rwandan victims of genocide. Over many conversations, we compared notes on our relationship with sources—which, in Lee Ann's words, involved an "asymmetry of power." There were no clear solutions to this power imbalance.

"We must remind ourselves that to enter another's world as a researcher is a privilege, not a right," Lee Ann had written in 2012. "Wrestling with ethical dilemmas is the price we pay for the privileges we enjoy."

One way I have wrestled with it is to set up a charitable fund to benefit Dasani's family and others like them—something I only told them about after this book was finished. I am donating a portion of this book's proceeds to that fund. For more information, visit www.andrea-elliott.com.

In what ways did my presence impact Dasani's life? There is no question that being on the front page of the *Times* would be a formative event for any New Yorker, especially a poor child who had been living in obscurity.

It is also true that whatever power came from being in the *Times* was no match for the power of poverty in Dasani's life. If my editors and I were struck by anything, it was that so little actually changed.

As I continued to follow Dasani's life on the streets of New York City, I tried my best to fade into the background. Arguably no journalist would cease to be noticed, least of all a white person working in a predominantly Black community.

Chanel noted two patterns: On the street, my race could present a barrier, giving people pause or making them suspicious of my motives. (I had experienced the opposite in Miami while reporting on immigrant Latinos, who saw our shared culture as a sign I could be trusted.)

The second pattern Chanel noticed was that among white workers—in places like family court or the welfare office—my skin color might bring the family preferential treatment, perhaps because of the perception that another powerful person (me) was watching. While I don't doubt that this happened, my general observation in city agencies was of the family feeling powerless and ignored.

Did the *Times* series help Dasani get into Hershey? While the school may have seen a media opportunity in Dasani, it took weeks for me to convince administrators to grant me access. They had never allowed a reporter into the school for an extended period, which posed more risks than gains.

To never help a poor person—in the name of ethics—strikes me as a posture born of privilege. I have watched Chanel, on numerous occasions, giving her last dollar bill to another homeless person. During economic downturns, it is often the poorest Americans who are the most charitable.

After I began working on the book, I offered occasional assistance, bringing the family groceries or cash for things like diapers. I celebrated their birthdays with cake and gifts, just like they celebrated mine.

A cellphone is a necessary tool of reporting, which is why the *Times* provided phones to Dasani's family—an arrangement that I continued to support on my own. I sometimes drove Chanel or Supreme to appointments, which often dovetailed with my reporting. In a few instances, when they were homeless, I put them up in a modest hotel room. For every time I helped out, there were many more times when I did not.

Why, then, did Dasani's family keep me around for eight years? One possible answer is that they wanted their story told. It also helped that my work process was no longer a mystery. Dasani had seen how my questions had informed my writing in the *Times*.

Perhaps a simpler explanation is this: I kept showing up. Most people, in the family's experience, did the opposite. To this day, when Chanel is ending a phone call, she cannot bring herself to say "good-bye" (opting instead for "peace").

Almost nothing counts more than the person who shows up.

To be poor is to be surveilled. Government agencies keep countless records on a family like Dasani's—a paper trail that has filled more than a dozen boxes in my office.

The search for these records took years because each batch unlocked a new mystery. The same process could describe my time with Dasani's family. Whenever I thought that my reporting had ended, something else would happen, revealing a new layer.

This sequence of revelations filled the arc of the book. Dasani began as a homeless girl in the shelter system and wound up a foster kid in the child protection system. Each system carried a different label, corresponding to a different plight. But as I followed Dasani's path, I saw how these systems interacted and overlapped, how labels like "homeless" and "foster kid" were more synonymous than distinct.

The same children were cycling through these systems after being born into poor communities. Dasani's "poverty" was merely the point of departure for understanding her human condition. Every part of her life had been touched by poverty, from childcare and education to housing and medical care. And there was no separating poverty from race—from the family's constant encounter with individual and systemic racism.

Embedded in Dasani's story are the stories of her ancestors and the crucibles they endured, from slavery in North Carolina to racial segregation in Brooklyn. All of these stories are inextricably linked.

To write about a child is to reckon with other childhoods—the ones that formed Dasani's parents, the childhoods that still live inside them. Society does not see Chanel and Supreme as former children, which makes it easier to blame them for their problems.

That is the very reason, back in 2012, that I asked my *Times* editor, "What if I just write about the kids?"

acknowledgments

My deepest gratitude goes to Dasani and her immediate family—Chanel, Supreme, Avianna, Khaliq, Nana, Maya, Hada, Papa, and Lee-Lee—for granting me the honor of their trust, for the privilege of being among them, and for summoning the bravery to let me try to tell their story.

I am also indebted to Dasani's extended family for making this book possible: To Ramel, Lamont, Shamell, Sherry, Sheena, Justina, and Josh, for opening the door to me as I followed Dasani's life. To Margo, Linda, Snow, Kalinda, Waverly, and Joe, for helping me piece together the family's history.

And, in spirit, to the late Joan Joanne Sykes, may she rest in power.

To the heroic educators in Dasani's life, for believing in this project and for becoming my teachers as well: the late Principal Paula Holmes, for opening her school to me; the magnificent teacher Faith Hester and her daughter Victory, for gracing this book with their story; and to the staffs of P.S. 278, the High School for Civil Rights, P.S. 78, and above all McKinney, including Michael Walker, Karen Best, and the late Frank Heyward, for showing me the small miracles that unfold daily in New York City's public schools.

I offer my immense gratitude to the residents of the Auburn shelter who patiently sat through interviews and documented the conditions of their rooms; to the late Sister Georgianna Glose, who was critical to my early reporting; to the many New Yorkers who figured in Dasani's story, including Citizen Cope, Barbara, Staraisa, Bonita, Giant, Joan, and Dasani's foster mother, Denise; and to the late Ivan J. Houston, who gave hours of his precious time to help me reconstruct June Sykes's military history.

Guiding my research was a coterie of scholars I came to regard as my brain trust: Sheldon Danziger, Jane Waldfogel, Chris Gottlieb, Greg Duncan, and Karen Staller, each of whom read multiple drafts of this book. I also benefited from the scholarly direction of Irwin Garfinkel, Chris Wimer, Robert Doar, Arloc Sherman, and the late Lee Ann Fujii.

To Josh Goldfein of the Legal Aid Society, for helping my reporting in too many ways to enumerate and, above all, for his steadfast support of Dasani's family; and also to his former colleagues Steven Banks and Jane Sujen Bock of Legal Aid and Patrick Markee of Coalition for the Homeless.

To David Lansner, Carolyn Kubitschek, Nora McCarthy, Linda Lowe, David Tobis, and Richard Wexler, as well as Andrew White and Stephanie Gendell of ACS, for leading me to a deeper understanding of the child protection system. And to various officials at HRA, DHS, HPD, DOE, and NYCHA, whose cooperation and input improved my reporting.

This book would not have been possible without the dogged devotion and brilliant research of Craig Hughes, who stuck with this project for eight years and, in my darkest hours, kept me on the path. To Craig's wife, Catherine Trapani, bless you. To my phenomenal fact checkers, Jessica Corbett and Cashen Conroy, both of whom gave months of their lives to this book, I owe an eternal debt of gratitude. Any mistakes are mine alone.

My thanks also go to the indefatigable Lily Smith, who orbited around this project for five years, transcribing interviews, pulling court records, and conducting research, as did Eryn Mathewson in

2017. To Claire Gabriel and Katie Winograd of the Russell Sage Foundation, whose historical research proved invaluable; to Rachel Swarns, who advised me on the challenges of tracing African American ancestry; and to the genealogist Diane Richard, whose painstaking work helped me unearth the Sykes family's history.

To Sam Freedman, who read various drafts of this book, long after his epic journalism class put me on this path. To my legendary colleagues Jason DeParle and Nina Bernstein, both of whom offered crucial input on early drafts, and also to the following readers: Ricardo Nuila, Sara Olkon, Casey Parks, Mosi Secret, Aparna Sundaram (and her son Rohan), Mesmin Destin, Tim Golden, Tarima Levine, Laura Wides-Muñoz, and Maxim Loskutoff. Their imprint is on these pages.

To my beloved *Times* editor, the late Christine Kay, who launched the series that seeded this book, and whose spirit lives within it. And, also at the *Times*, to the intrepid photographer Ruth Fremson for soldiering by my side, to ace reporter Rebecca Ruiz for her early research, to Dean Baquet and Matt Purdy for their devotion to Dasani's story and the great patience they have shown during my book leave, and to Jill Abramson, under whose leadership the Dasani series was born.

To my stalwart agent, Tina Bennett, who shepherded this book from its inception, her faith in me unwavering, her gifts too many to name. To my superb editor, Kate Medina, a visionary who saw the book in Dasani's story long before I did. To my incredible team at Random House: Gina Centrello, Noa Shapiro, Matthew Martin, Andy Ward, and Avideh Bashirrad; in production, Evan Camfield, Benjamin Dreyer, Rebecca Berlant, and Maggie Hart; in design, Paolo Pepe and Jo Anne Metsch; in publicity, Maria Braeckel, Susan Corcoran, and London King; in marketing, Barbara Fillon and Ayelet Durantt. And to Dorian Karchmar at WME, my immense gratitude.

This book would not exist without the generous support of the following institutions: New America, Emerson Collective, the Russell Sage Foundation, the Columbia Population Research Center, the Whiting Foundation, Yaddo, MacDowell, the Logan Nonfiction Program, Marble House Project, and All Our Kids. To Richard Brand for his sage counsel over the years. And to the following individuals who championed this book: Amy Low, David Macy, Elaina Richardson, Lela Goren, my lifelong mentor Sig Gissler, and the inimitable Boykin Curry, whose generosity of spirit knows no bounds.

Dasani's story is a testament to the power of family. I would be nowhere without mine.

To my dear father, Robert, whose work in civil rights and passion for social justice left its mark on me early; to my mother, Maria Gloria, mi estrella del Norte (y del Sur); to Thomas, Pablo, Esther, and my nephews, for their unabating love; to Tim, with whom I am raising two phenomenal girls.

And to Ava and Clara: You are my why.

notes

Sources and Methods

This book draws on eight years of research, which began in 2012. Over the course of this project, I reported on the day-to-day life of Dasani's family and, with their permission and assistance, conducted a search for records detailing their multigenerational history and their encounters with government agencies. I also immersed myself in academic literature, relying on a brain trust of scholars to help me contextualize what I was learning.

In-person Reporting

As I followed Dasani's life, I took extensive notes, recorded most conversations, and shot cell-phone videos and photographs of many things I witnessed. Her family also helped me document their lives by taking their own videos, photographs, and audio recordings. This collection of recordings—132 hours of audio and 28 hours of video—improved my ability to depict events and capture dialogue and quotes exactly as they were spoken.

On the few occasions when I was not present for an event in this book, I reconstructed that scene by interviewing as many people as possible to corroborate the facts. When I describe someone's thoughts, I have done so with the person's collaboration and their review of the passage. Before publication, I read the book out loud to Dasani and Avianna so that we could check, passage by passage, for issues of tone, representation, and factual accuracy. I also reviewed portions of the book with Nana, Khaliq, Papa, Margo, and others, and gave the book to Supreme and Chanel to read. They found no factual errors but suggested some minor clarifications.

Naming Sources

Over the years, I have interviewed more than two hundred adults and dozens of children. In an attempt to protect the identity of these children, I have withheld their surnames. Only Dasani and Avianna are fully named, to which they consented as adults. Their half siblings and stepsiblings are identified by their nicknames, and several adults in this book are identified by their street names, including Dasani's biological father, Ramel; her uncle Shamell; and her great-uncle Speedy. While most people in Dasani's life understood that I was a reporter, not everyone wanted to be interviewed. In some instances, I have left out a person's name (including the ACS supervisor whose phone call in 2015 Chanel recorded).

Finding Records

To report this book, I obtained and reviewed 14,325 records from various government agencies and other sources. While a portion of these documents pertain to the history, policies, and oversight of city services (for example, the state's inspection reports of the Auburn shelter), the vast majority of records relate to Dasani's family.

The family's records include child protection case files, court transcripts, birth and death certificates, school report cards, housing and eviction records, 911 logs, criminal court and prison records, wage and employment documents, and Medicaid, hospital, and drug-treatment records. Chanel and Supreme were instrumental to this research, filing dozens of Freedom of Information Law (FOIL) requests for records to share with me.

To document the family's interactions with the city's welfare, homeless services, and child protection agencies, I relied on a combination of direct observation, interviews with the family, and records from the family's case files with these agencies. To trace the Sykes family's ancestry, I worked with the genealogist Diane L. Richard to analyze hundreds of records dating back to the 1700s. To piece together June Sykes's military history, my researcher Craig Hughes and I tracked down records from the U.S. Department of Veterans Affairs and other sources.

Greater detail about this research is in the notes that follow.

List of Abbreviations

ACS: Administration for Children's Services
DHS: Department of Homeless Services
DOC: Department of Correction
DOE: Department of Education
HPD: Department of Housing Preservation and Development
HRA: Human Resources Administration
IRS: Internal Revenue Service
MTA: Metropolitan Transportation Authority
NYCHA: New York City Housing Authority
NYPD: New York Police Department
OTDA: Office of Temporary and Disability Assistance
SSA: Social Security Administration

vii **"For these are all our children"**: Letter from James Baldwin, cited in Robert McParland, *From Native Son to King's Men: The Literary Landscape of 1940s America* (Lanham, Md.: Rowman and Littlefield, 2017), p. 74.

Prologue

xix **First they came for Papa**: This scene is based on interviews with the children and parents, direct observation by me, and case notes from the family's child protection files with two agencies: the Administration for Children's Services (ACS) and the New York Foundling. State laws prevent ACS and Foundling staff members from commenting on the family's case, but they answered general questions about their respective agencies.

xx **formerly the site of the Bellevue Hospital morgue**: Nina Bernstein, "New Center for Foster Children Echoes Changes in an Agency," *New York Times*, June 1, 2001.

Chapter 1

4 **"It makes me feel like there's something going on out there"**: All quotes by Dasani, unless otherwise noted, are either from interviews or from moments witnessed by me.

4 **the old Brooklyn was vanishing**: Themis Chronopoulos, "'What's Happened to the People?': Gentrification and Racial Segregation in Brooklyn," *Journal of African American Studies* 24, no. 4 (2020), pp. 549–72; Vivian Yee, "Gentrification in a Brooklyn Neighborhood Forces Residents to Move On," *New York Times*, Nov. 27, 2015; New

York University Furman Center, "Focus on Gentrification," *State of New York City's Housing and Neighborhoods in 2015* (New York: Furman Center, 2016), pp. 4–24.

4 **as prosperity rose . . . poverty deepened:** Yee, "Gentrification in a Brooklyn Neighborhood"; Jana Kasperkevic, "A Tale of Two Brooklyns: There's More to My Borough than Hipsters and Coffee," *The Guardian*, Aug. 27, 2014.

5 **more than twenty-two thousand homeless children:** Four agencies administer New York City's various municipal shelter systems: the Department of Homeless Services (DHS), which oversees the city's main shelter system; the Human Resources Administration (HRA), for domestic violence victims and people affected by HIV/AIDS; the Department of Youth and Community Development, for runaway and homeless youth; and the Department of Housing Preservation and Development (HPD), for individuals or families who have lost their homes as a result of a fire or city-issued vacate order.

There are different ways to count New York City's shelter population, but any tally is—at best—an approximation. DHS publishes a daily "shelter census" on its website that does not include individuals in shelters administered by other agencies, nor does it factor in some shelters overseen by DHS, including overnight drop-in sites, veterans in short-term housing, low-threshold shelters reserved for individuals coming in off the streets, and individuals who have applied for family shelter but are yet to be deemed "eligible." The other agencies providing shelter did not publicly report census data until they were required by law to do so, starting in 2011.

My estimated tally of the city's homeless population differs from DHS's official tally because I am including data from all four city agencies that administer shelter, based on monthly shelter reports published by the Mayor's Office. Neither my tally nor DHS's includes the number of homeless people living on the street or those who are "doubled up" in the homes of other people. Additional analysis was provided by Giselle Routhier, policy director at Coalition for the Homeless, and Joshua Goldfein, staff attorney at the Legal Aid Society.

5 **the most unequal metropolis in America:** Of the ten largest cities in America in 2012, New York ranked as the most unequal. Analysis of 2012 census data by Andrew Beveridge and Susan Weber-Stoger of Queens College's sociology department.

5 **Almost half of New York's 8.3 million residents are living near or below the poverty line:** The "poverty line" (also called the "poverty threshold") is the minimum income required for a person or family to meet their basic material needs. To fall below the poverty line means that your income is less than the cost of essential things like food, shelter, and clothing. Estimates of the poverty line vary, but most experts consider the federal government's "Official Poverty Measure" (OPM) to be outdated. It was developed in the 1960s by Mollie Orshansky, who determined the poverty line based on the cost of food and what portion of a family budget was spent on food (about one-third of household expenditures). This dollar amount was then multiplied by three to estimate the overall cost of basic needs. To this day, the OPM uses the same one-third budget portion for food, despite the fact that food costs have gone down while expenses like housing and childcare have risen.

Building on decades of research, the U.S. Census Bureau released a "Supplemental Poverty Measure" (SPM) in 2011 that takes into account family resources and expenses not included in the OPM, as well as noncash government benefits and geographic variations in the cost of living. Drawing from a similar methodology, New York City became the first to create its own poverty measure, in 2007, under Mayor Michael R. Bloomberg. According to this measure, in 2013, the city's poverty line for a family of four was an income of $31,156; New Yorkers who were living under 150 percent of this threshold were considered to be in "near poverty." This gave the city a near-poverty rate of 45.9 percent. (As of 2018, the last year the report came out, 41.3 percent of New Yorkers were still in near poverty.)

Analysis provided by Jane Waldfogel, co-director of the Columbia Population Research Center, and Christopher Wimer, co-director of Columbia University's Center on Poverty and Social Policy. Also see the *New York City Government Poverty Measure* reports for 2017 and 2018 from the Mayor's Office for Economic Opportunity; Gordon M. Fisher, "The Development and History of U.S. Poverty Thresholds—A Brief Overview" (U.S. Department of Health and Human Services, Jan. 1, 1997); Liana Fox, "What Is the Supplemental Poverty Measure and How Does It Differ from the Official Measure?" Economic Housing and Statistics Division, Census Bureau, Sept. 9, 2020.

6 **911 dispatchers will take some 350 calls from Auburn:** New York Police Department (NYPD).

6 **back when nurses tended to the dying in open wards:** "Undermanned Hospital Dismal and Crowded," *Daily News,* Nov. 18, 1951.

7 **more than a hundred families will soon stand in line:** DHS.

9 **a public hospital serving the poor:** Suzanne Spellen, "Past and Present: Decades of Change for Fort Greene's Cumberland Street Hospital," *Brownstoner,* July 14, 2015.

9 **She is among 432 homeless children and parents:** DHS.

Chapter 2

11 **More than five hundred students:** Unless otherwise noted, all facts about the McKinney school were provided by Principal Paula Holmes for the 2012–2013 academic year.

11 **a quarter million New Yorkers are currently on the public housing waitlist:** New York City Housing Authority (NYCHA).

13 **poor enough to qualify for free or reduced price meals:** Department of Education (DOE).

13 **the city has cut the school's budget by a quarter:** DOE.

14 **known to exclude children with learning disabilities:** *Charter Schools—Implications for Students with Disabilities* (Washington, D.C.: National Council on Disability, 2018), pp. 47–48.

14 **"shouldn't have to trek to other Brooklyn neighborhoods":** This was posted on the Success Academy website on Feb. 13, 2013, under "Success Academy Fort Greene."

14 **Whites were fleeing:** Craig Steven Wilder, *A Covenant with Color: Race and Social Power in Brooklyn* (New York: Columbia University Press, 2000), pp. 212–14.

14 **now the largest in the nation:** In 2012, New York City's public school system had 1.1 million students. "New York City Department of Education Teacher Incentive Fund Grant Program 2013–2018: Teacher Career Lattice," *Application for Grants Under the TIF General Competition* (Washington, D.C.: U.S. Department of Education, 2012), p. 18.

14 **is also among the most segregated:** Ford Fessenden, "A Portrait of Segregation in New York City's Schools," *New York Times,* May 11, 2012.

14 **seven thousand are enrolled in fourteen schools:** Success Academy spokesperson.

15 **Long after she gave up dreams of acting:** Interview with Faith Hester.

15 **"Where we call the cops the A-Team":** Jay-Z, "Where I'm From," *In My Lifetime, Vol. 1* (Roc-A-Fella, 1997).

15 **One of them was a boy named Angel:** Interview with Hester.

19 **Chanel imagines their thoughts:** Unless otherwise noted, all descriptions of Chanel Sykes, including her quotes and biographical facts, are from interviews with her or from my direct observation.

20 **They also rely on public assistance:** The family's cash assistance and food stamps are provided by HRA. Survivors benefits are provided by the federal government's Social Security Administration (SSA). HRA and DHS records.

20 **Less than 2 percent of homeless families:** HRA data.

20 **Chanel and Supreme have occasionally landed in jail:** All references to Chanel and Supreme's criminal history are based on their Department of Correction (DOC), criminal court, and ACS records, as well as on interviews with Chanel and Supreme.

20 **their daily attendance at the drug treatment clinics:** All references to Chanel and Supreme's drug treatment programs, including test results, are from their records with each program, as well as from their family court, Medicaid, HRA, and ACS records.

20 **It has been six months since Chanel worked:** All references to Chanel and Supreme's employment are from their DHS, ACS, HRA, or SSA records.

23 **his "Lifeline" phone (provided for free by the federal government):** A program of the Federal Communications Commission.

23 **Auburn's decay is no secret to city and state inspectors:** Inspection reports by DHS and the state's Office of Temporary and Disability Assistance (OTDA).

23 **who have cited Dasani's room for thirteen violations:** Family's DHS case file.

23 **in a shelter with a $9 million budget:** DHS data.

Chapter 3

30 **Anna V. Jefferson, the second Black female:** *Lawmakers: Women of the New York State Legislature* (New York: Legislative Women's Caucus of New York State, 2017), p. 53; "Constance Baker Motley: Judiciary's Unsung Rights Hero," United States Courts, Feb. 20, 2020.

34 **America's first major battle, in 1776:** John J. Gallagher, *The Battle of Brooklyn* (Boston: Da Capo Press, 1995).

34 **under a 149-foot tower:** New York City Department of Parks and Recreation website.

34 **Brooklyn was built on the backs of slaves:** This paragraph and the following one are based on multiple sources, primarily: Seth M. Scheiner, *Negro Mecca: A History of the Negro in New York City, 1865–1920* (New York: New York University Press, 1965), pp. 1, 4; and Roi Ottley and William J. Weatherby, eds., *The Negro in New York: An Informal Social History, 1626–1940* (New York: Praeger, 1969), p. 13.

34 **When the British took the colony nearly four decades later:** Ottley and Weatherby, *Negro in New York*, pp. 13–15, 19–22.

34 **The colony's enslaved population swelled to 13,500:** Edgar J. McManus, *Black Bondage in the North* (Syracuse: Syracuse University Press, 2001), p. 209.

35 **making it the largest slaveholding territory in the North:** McManus, *Black Bondage*, p. 16.

35 **And nowhere in New York was the concentration of slaves higher:** Wilder, *Covenant with Color*, pp. 19, 33.

35 **Thousands of enslaved Blacks took up arms:** Harry A. Ploski and James De Bois Williams, eds., *The Negro Almanac: A Reference Work on the Afro-American* (New York: Bellwether Publishing, 1983), p. 541.

35 **The biggest battle unfolded in Brooklyn:** Edwin G. Burrows, *Forgotten Patriots: The Untold Story of American Prisoners During the Revolutionary War* (New York: Basic Books, 2008), p. 203.

35 **The corpses of as many as 11,500 prisoners:** Benedict Cosgrove, "The Grisly History of Brooklyn's Revolutionary War Martyrs," *Smithsonian Magazine*, March 13, 2017.

35 **"perished in the cause of liberty," proclaiming them "the spirits of the departed free":** Art Commission of the City of New York, *Catalogue of the Works of Art Belonging to the City of New York*, vol. 2 (New York: Gilliss Press, 1920), p. 28. (This slab is no longer on the monument.)

Chapter 4

37 **punched his hand:** Police report and interviews with Josh, Lamont, Chanel, Dasani, and her siblings.

37 **the Earned Income Tax Credit . . . helping more than 27 million families:** Internal Revenue Service (IRS).

37 **The goal is to find permanent housing:** For shelter requirements, see New York Codes, Rules and Regulations, Title 18, Section 352.35: "Eligibility for temporary housing assistance for homeless persons."

37 **Dasani's family needs a minimum of $4,800:** Analysis by Community Service Society of New York; and by Zia O'Hara, sales agent, Douglas Elliman Real Estate.

39 **one of the nation's most generous systems:** Tracy Gordon, Richard C. Auxier, and John Iselin, *Assessing Fiscal Capacities of States: A Representative Revenue System — Representative Expenditure System Approach, Fiscal Year 2012* (Washington, D.C.: Urban Institute, 2016), pp. 44–45.

39 **The broadest limb belongs to the Human Resources Administration:** Unless otherwise noted, all data about the city's social services system are for the fall of 2012 and were provided by each of the agencies mentioned.

39 **more than 3 million New Yorkers:** Citywide HRA-Administered Medicaid Enrollees data for September–November 2012, accessed via New York City's "Open Data" website: opendata.cityofnewyork.us, April 8, 2021.

39 **roughly 38 percent of the city's population:** Vital Statistics of New York State, Department of Health: "Table 2: Population, Land Area, and Population Density by County, New York State — 2012."

39 **and 357,000 are receiving cash welfare:** Separately, the Social Security Administration pays Supplemental Security Income (SSI) benefits to another 426,000 New Yorkers who are disabled or sixty-five years old and over.

39 **More than 80,000 schoolchildren have been homeless:** Both DOE and DHS keep a tally of public school students who have experienced housing instability at any point during the school year. This population, known as "students in temporary housing," includes those who are doubled up in other homes or are living in temporary housing such as motels, as well as those in the city's shelters.

40 **This agency investigates about 55,000 reports of child abuse or neglect every year:** In addition to child protection, ACS is responsible for administering juvenile justice services and early childhood care and education.

40 **the vast majority of them Black or Latino:** In December 2012, New York City's foster child population was 53 percent Black, 30 percent Latino, 12 percent "other/unknown," 4 percent white, and 1 percent Asian. ACS data.

40 **Almost half of New York City's residents (and a quarter of its children) are white:** In 2012, 449,001 of New York City's 1,785,358 children were white. 2012 census data and analysis by the Citizens' Committee for Children of the Census Bureau's American Community Survey 1-Year Estimates, 2005–2019.

40 **16 million children growing up poor:** 2012 census data.

40 **47 million Americans on food stamps:** In 2012, a fiscal average of 46,609,000 Americans received food stamp benefits. U.S. Department of Agriculture.

40 **The children can also eat for free at their schools:** Ibid.

40 **Two of the children show signs of a learning disability:** ACS and DOE records.

41 **Child protection workers have been watching:** Family's ACS case file.

41 **Abuse, according to New York law:** New York Codes, Rules and Regulations 432.1(a) and Section 412 of the Social Services Law (for the definition of "child abuse"); Section 1012(f) of the New York Family Court Act (for the definition of "neglected child").

41 **seven-year-old Nixzmary Brown was beaten to death:** Kareem Fahim and Leslie

Kaufman, "Girl, 7, Found Beaten to Death in Brooklyn," *New York Times*, Jan. 12, 2006.

41 **Reports of abuse surged, and a new law was passed in her name:** Sewell Chan. "Rise in Child Abuse Reports Has Family Court Reeling," *New York Times*, Jan. 12, 2007; Glenn Blain, "Gov. Paterson Signs Nixzmary's Law," *Daily News*, Oct. 9, 2009.

41 **Yet only 7 percent of ACS investigations involve findings of abuse:** In 2012, ACS conducted 54,952 investigations, finding "abuse only" allegations indicated in only 1 percent (554) of those cases. During the same period, ACS found both abuse and neglect indicated in 5.8 percent (3,168) of all cases. ACS data.

42 **the vast majority of these parents are poor:** Michele Cortese and Tehra Coles, "Poor and at Risk of Losing Their Kids: Moms and Dads Under ACS Investigation Deserve More Legal Help," *Daily News*, Dec. 14, 2019; Kathryn Joyce, "The Crime of Parenting While Poor," *New Republic*, Feb. 25, 2019.

44 **"After initial sessions student has opened up":** Records kept by the Partnership for Children and provided to me by Dasani's family.

Chapter 5

48 **Just north of Myrtle, Fort Greene's poorest Black residents:** Jan Rosenberg, "Chapter 9: Fort Greene, New York," *Cityscape* 4, no. 2 (1998), pp. 179, 188, 192; Julie Lasky, "Fort Greene, Brooklyn: Riding the Wave of Gentrification," *New York Times*, Nov. 6, 2019; and analysis of household demographics above and below Myrtle Avenue from the Census Bureau's 2014–2018 American Community Survey data.

48 **the historic Queen Anne and Second Empire townhouses:** Winifred Curran, "Creative Destruction: City Policy and Urban Renewal in Fort Greene, Brooklyn" (master's thesis, Hunter College, The City University of New York, 1998).

48 **south of Myrtle, live the majority of Fort Greene's whites:** Census Bureau's 2014–2018 American Community Survey data.

49 **a term derived from *gentry*:** The word "gentrification" was coined by German-British sociologist and urban planner Ruth Glass in 1964. Jane Solomon, "When and Where Did the Word Gentrification Originate?," KQED.org, May 18, 2014. On etymology of gentry: Michael Weiss, Cornell University Department of Linguistics.

49 **selling for $2.1 million in 2017:** "81 Adelphi St, Brooklyn, NY 11205," Zillow.com, accessed Feb. 20, 2021.

49 **it was the nineteenth-century home:** Prithi Kanakamedala, "P.S. 67 Charles A. Dorsey School," placematters.net, Place Matters, City Lore, accessed Feb. 26, 2021.

49 **the same year that slavery in New York ended:** Even after 1827, dozens of Black people remained enslaved in New York, living with southerners who ignored abolition. Wilder, *Covenant with Color*, p. 19. On gradual abolition: Eric Foner, *Slavery and Freedom in Nineteenth-Century America* (New York: W. W. Norton, 2015), p. 44.

49 **the Board of Education, in 1845, admitted the free school:** Suzanne Spellen, "Building of the Day: 270 Union Avenue," *Brownstoner*, Feb. 21, 2012.

49 **moving it to Willoughby Street:** "Board of Education," *Brooklyn Daily Eagle*, April 15, 1847.

50 **Racial tensions had long been simmering:** Karen M. Staller, *New York's Newsboys: Charles Loring Brace and the Founding of the Children's Aid Society* (New York: Oxford University Press, 2020), pp. 248–50; Leslie M. Harris, *In the Shadow of Slavery: African American in New York City, 1626–1863* (Chicago: University of Chicago Press, 2003), p. 280.

50 **Brooklyn, by comparison, was a haven:** Scheiner, *Negro Mecca*, p. 20.

50 **thousands of Black families left Manhattan for Brooklyn:** Ibid., p. 34.

50 **This prominent tide included:** Carla L. Peterson, *Black Gotham: A Family History of African Americans in Nineteenth-Century New York City* (New Haven: Yale University

Press, 2011), p. 286; Harold Xavier Connolly, "Blacks in Brooklyn from 1900 to 1960" (Ph.D. dissertation, New York University, 1972), pp. 67, 348.

50 **the so-called Black Belt:** Robert Swan, "The Black Belt of Brooklyn," in Charlene Claye Van Derzee, ed., *An Introduction to the Black Contribution to the Development of Brooklyn* (New York: New Muse Community Museum of Brooklyn, 1977), p. 99.

50 **"most of the wealthy negroes":** "Wealthy Negro Citizens," *New York Times*, July 14, 1895.

50 **As many as seventy-one:** "The Census for 1890 reported 71 homes owned by Brooklyn Negroes as opposed to 21 for Manhattan Negroes." Scheiner, *Negro Mecca*, p. 34.

50 **forming the base of:** Connolly, "Blacks in Brooklyn," pp. 52–58.

50 **spiritual leadership:** New York City Landmarks Preservation Commission, *Fort Greene Historic District Designation Report* (New York: New York City Landmarks Preservation Commission, 1978), p. 17.

50 **and civil rights vanguard:** Connolly, "Blacks in Brooklyn," p. 348.

50 **These currents combined to spectacular effect on November 23, 1883:** "The Brooklyn School Opening," *New York Globe*, Dec. 1, 1883; "Events in Brooklyn: Summary of the Week's Local News," *Brooklyn Daily Eagle*, Nov. 25, 1888.

50 **Booker T. Washington would later visit the school:** Kanakamedala, "P.S. 67 Charles A. Dorsey School."

50 **appointing the first African American, Philip A. White, to the Board of Education:** Suzanne Spellen, "Building of the Day: 1634 Dean Street," *Brownstoner*, April 4, 2011.

50 **A few weeks later, White proposed a resolution:** Peterson, *Black Gotham*, p. 370.

51 **By then, the building had moldy ceilings:** Janet Upadhye, "Principal Brings School Back from the Brink of Closure," DNAinfo.com, March 17, 2014.

51 **Forty-one percent of the Roots students were white:** 2011–2016 Demographic Snapshot data accessed via New York City's "Open Data" website: opendata.cityofnewyork.us, Oct. 9, 2018.

51 **the Department of Education had targeted P.S. 67 for potential closure:** Ultimately, P.S. 67 remained open. That it was targeted: Philissa Cramer, "Dozens of Elementary and Middle Schools Told They Might Close," *Chalkbeat New York*, Oct. 3, 2012.

51 **in 1870 became the first female African American doctor:** "Susan Smith McKinney Steward, M.D., '1870 (1847–1918)," New York Medical College, accessed Feb. 26, 2021; David Gordon, "Black Woman Doctor Honored," *New York Times*, May 19, 1974.

51 **would be listed for sale in 2016 for nearly $2.7 million:** "205 DeKalb Avenue," Trulia.com, accessed Feb. 4, 2021.

51 **named for Simon Boerum:** Leonard Benardo and Jennifer Weiss, *Brooklyn by Name: How the Neighborhoods, Streets, Parks, Bridges, and More Got Their Names* (New York: New York University Press, 2006), p. 57.

51 **a man with three slaves:** New-York Historical Society, *Abstracts of Wills on File in the Surrogate's Office* (New York: New-York Historical Society, 1900), pp. 336–37.

51 **Peter Wyckoff, enslaver of seven:** Benardo and Weiss, *Brooklyn by Name*, p. 72; Peter Wyckoff of Brooklyn, Kings County, had seven slaves according to the 1800 census, per "New York Slavery Records Index," CUNY Academic Commons, 2017.

51 **Ditmas Park (four slaves):** Benardo and Weiss, *Brooklyn by Name*, p. 103; Jan Van Ditmarsen of Flatbush, Kings County, had four slaves according to the 1698 census, per "New York Slavery Records Index," CUNY Academic Commons, 2017.

51 **Luquer Street (thirteen):** Benardo and Weiss, *Brooklyn by Name*, p. 67; "Heads of Families at the First Census of the United States Taken in the Year 1790" (Washington, D.C.: Government Printing Office, 1907), p. 97.

51 **Van Brunt Street (seven):** Benardo and Weiss, *Brooklyn by Name*, p. 71; "Heads of Families at the First Census," p. 98.

51 **Cortelyou Road (two):** Benardo and Weiss, *Brooklyn by Name*, p. 106; *The Cortelyou Genealogy: A Record of Jacques Corteljou and of Many of his Descendants* (Lincoln, Neb.: Press of Brown Print. Service, 1942).

52 **Van Dam and Bayard streets are named for the owners of slave ships:** "New York Slavery Records Index," CUNY Academic Commons, 2017, pp. 484, 490–93, 496, 497, 499, 502, 505; that Peter Stuyvesant was director-general of the Dutch West India Company's New Netherland colony: "Part 1—Early Settlement and the Rise of Slavery in Colonial Dutch New Jersey," Montclair State University, montclair.edu, accessed Feb. 20, 2021; that these were the men for whom the neighborhood and streets were named: Benardo and Weiss, *Brooklyn by Name*, pp. 13, 29–30, 77.

52 **Even the McKinney school began with a slave-owning name:** Joshua Sands; see "Heads of Families at the First Census," p. 96; "Brooklyn Gets School," *New York Times*, March 10, 1960.

52 **"A chair is still a chair":** Luther Vandross, "A House Is Not a Home," *Luther Vandross* (Epic, 1982).

54 **She suffers from asthma, as do nearly seventy thousand public school children:** "Public School Children (5–14 Yrs Old) with Asthma," New York City Environment and Health Data Portal, the city's Department of Health and Mental Hygiene.

55 **Her class is reading:** Walter Dean Myers, *The Glory Field* (New York: Scholastic, 1994).

Chapter 6

58 **Everyone worked to pay the bills:** Interviews with Holmes and her cousin Benjamin Bailey.

58 **"Sometimes I feel like a motherless child":** Traditional African American spiritual.

59 **who took "mayoral control" of the city's sprawling public school system:** Ashley Hupfl, "Five Things to Know About Mayoral Control," City and State New York, June 13, 2016; Abby Goodnough, "Mayor Links Teacher Pay to Control of Schools," *New York Times*, March 9, 2002.

59 **More than three hundred miles of fresh bike lanes:** New York City Department of Transportation, *Cycling in the City: An Update on NYC Cycling Counts* (New York: New York City Department of Transportation, 2013), p. 2.

59 **Real estate has boomed:** Rachel S. Friedman, "The Construction Boom and Bust in New York City," *Monthly Labor Review* 134, no. 10 (2011), pp. 16–21.

59 **His administration will ultimately close 157 public schools while investing mightily in charters:** DOE.

59 **teachers are being eliminated with each passing year:** Interview with Holmes.

60 **a pale yellow eighteenth-century estate:** "Brief History of Gracie Mansion and Its Conservancy: 1799–Present," Gracie Mansion Conservancy, accessed Feb. 26, 2021.

61 **In a city with a 2 percent vacancy rate:** New York City's vacancy rate was 2.1 percent in the third quarter of 2012 and 2.4 percent in the third quarter of 2013. Ilaina Jonas, "U.S. Economy May Be Nipping at Apartment Sector," Reuters, Oct. 3, 2012; Dawn Wotapka, "New York City Rents Pass $3,000 Mark," *Wall Street Journal*, Oct. 1, 2013.

61 **on eleven pristine acres:** "Brief History," Gracie Mansion Conservancy.

61 **When Mayor Bloomberg tried to ban the sale of large sugary drinks:** Michael M. Grynbaum, "New York Plans to Ban Sale of Big Sizes of Sugary Drinks," *New York Times*, May 30, 2012.

62 **who pushed to rewrite the law so he could serve a third term:** Michael Barbaro and David W. Chen, "Bloomberg's Latest on Terms: 3 for Him, but Only 2 for Everyone Else," *New York Times*, Oct. 25, 2010.

62 **declaring Gracie "the people's house":** Jennifer Steinhauer, "With Mayor Out, the People Move In; New York Finds Many Uses for Gracie Mansion," *New York Times*, June 11, 2004.

62 and directing $7 million in private donations: Ibid.

62 a chandelier from the 1820s and a mahogany four-poster bed: Michael Barbaro, "Preparing Gracie Mansion for a New (Live-In?) Mayor," *New York Times*, Aug. 27, 2013.

62 Gracie's renovation brought a glitzy spread: Steven M. L. Aronson, "Amazing Gracie Mansion," *Architectural Digest* 60, no. 11 (November 2003).

62 In a city that has invested millions of dollars in "green spaces": In May 2003, Bloomberg allocated $25 million to "create new green spaces and improve parks throughout Lower Manhattan." Press release, "Downtown Parks Receive $25 Million," New York City Department of Parks and Recreation website, June 10, 2003.

62 Since Bloomberg took office, the number of homeless families has risen by 80 percent: DHS.

62 They are now staying in shelters for the longest period on record: In 2013, the average length of stay for homeless families was 13.5 months. DHS data.

62 "a much more pleasurable experience than they ever had before": Kate Taylor, "Mayor Offers Ideas for Why Homeless Numbers Are Up," City Room, *New York Times*, Aug. 23, 2012.

62 "running around and going into the walls": Family's DHS records.

62 have cited the Auburn shelter for more than four hundred violations: Analysis of city and state inspection reports from 2004 to 2013. The agencies that issued these violations include DHS, OTDA, HPD, and the city's Department of Health and Mental Hygiene.

63 a twelve-year-old boy at Auburn complained in writing: Auburn records, obtained through a FOIL request. In response to this child's "client complaint" and others filed, a spokesperson for the Mayor's Office told me, in 2013, that DHS was "unable to furnish any confidential information without signed consent from the parties involved."

63 The police were never notified: Official at NYPD.

Chapter 7

64 a gap that can leave the poorest child exposed to fewer words: While there is debate about the scope of the vocabulary gap—and even the concept itself—one study found that children "whose mothers graduated from college were exposed to 3,000 or so more words per day, translating into a four-million-word gap by 4 years of age between the highest and lowest [socioeconomic status] groups in our sample." Jill Gilkerson et al., "Mapping the Early Language Environment Using All-Day Recordings and Automated Analysis," *American Journal of Speech-Language Pathology* 26, no. 2 (2017), p. 261.

64 pledging to leave "no New Yorker behind": David W. Chen, "De Blasio, Announcing Mayoral Bid, Pledges to Help People City Hall Forgot," *New York Times*, Jan. 27, 2013.

65 de Blasio was seven years old when his parents' marriage ended: Michael Scherer and John Wagner, "New York Mayor Bill de Blasio Adds His Name to the Democratic Presidential Field," *Washington Post*, May 16, 2019.

65 His father, a Harvard-trained economist: Javier C. Hernández, "From His Father's Decline, de Blasio 'Learned What Not to Do,'" *New York Times*, Oct. 13, 2013.

65 aligning himself with the Sandinistas in Nicaragua: Javier C. Hernández, "A Mayoral Hopeful Now, de Blasio Was Once a Young Leftist," *New York Times*, Sept. 22, 2013.

65 the first African American elected to the office: Jaclyn Diaz, "David Dinkins, New York City's 1st Black Mayor, Dies at 93," NPR.com, Nov. 24, 2020.

65 "Let's be honest about where we are today": Chen, "De Blasio, Announcing Mayoral Bid."

65 More than fifty-five thousand people are now sleeping in city shelters: In February 2013, there were 56,911 people staying in the five shelter systems administered by New York City agencies; the vast majority of these people (50,353) were in DHS shelters.

65 "you can arrive in your private jet at Kennedy Airport": Sam Roberts, "City's Shelter-

ing of Out-of-Town Homeless, and Mayor's Remark, Stir Debate," *New York Times*, March 17, 2013.

66 **one of the most bitter battles of his leadership:** Joe Coscarelli, "School-Bus Drivers to End Strike, Give Up on Bloomberg," *Intelligencer*, Feb. 15, 2013.

68 **"What happens to a dream deferred?":** Langston Hughes, "Harlem," *Montage of a Dream Deferred* (New York: Henry Holt, 1951), pp. 71–72.

Chapter 8

71 **"independent living plan":** DHS.

71 **The Tax Refund Offset Program will give Supreme's tax money either to these mothers:** OTDA officials.

73 **Dasani will be out of school for two weeks:** This suspension was never entered into DOE's records system, but I witnessed it.

Chapter 9

77 **Dasani was awake to the world:** All descriptions of Dasani as a small child, unless otherwise noted, are from interviews with her mother, her biological father, her stepfather, her two great-aunts (Margo and Linda), her two cousins once removed (Snow and Kalinda), her uncle Lamont, and Chanel's godmother, Sherry Humbert.

77 **Nearly half a century earlier, on November 14, 1953:** Joanie's birth certificate.

77 **Another thirty years would pass before the hospital closed:** United Press International, "Last Patient Gone from Cumberland," *New York Times*, Aug. 25, 1983; Barbara Basler, "City to Shift Homeless Families to a Brooklyn Site," *New York Times*, Nov. 8, 1985.

77 **returning by foot to the nearby projects:** Interview with Margo.

77 **The borough's Black population had recently doubled to 208,000:** John Louis Flateau, "Black Brooklyn: The Politics of Ethnicity, Class, and Gender" (Ph.D. dissertation, The City University of New York, 2005), p. 30; Wilder, *Covenant with Color*, pp. 23, 61, 178.

78 **June and Margaret Sykes:** All biographical details about June and Margaret Sykes, unless otherwise noted, are taken from June's military, Civilian Conservation Corps, and SSA records, his death certificate, Margaret's birth certificate, and interviews with June's former employers, as well as with three of the Sykes children and two of their grandchildren.

78 **Robert Moses, had another vision:** Curran, "Creative Destruction," p. 31.

78 **closing hundreds of worksites between 1945 and 1955:** Ibid.

78 **a collection of thirty-five brick buildings that opened in 1942:** Thomas J. Campanella, *Brooklyn: The Once and Future City* (New York: Princeton University Press, 2019), pp. 368, 370.

78 **the same year Moses, joined the city's planning commission:** "Mayor Names Moses to Planning Body," *New York Times*, Nov. 23, 1941.

78 **whom he considered "inherently 'dirty'":** Robert A. Caro, *The Power Broker: Robert Moses and the Fall of New York* (New York: Vintage Books, 1975), p. 318.

78 **Of the 255 playgrounds Moses built in New York City in the 1930s:** Ibid., p. 510.

78 **only a quarter of her neighbors were white:** Campanella, *Brooklyn: The Once and Future City*, p. 375.

78 **"rotting $20,000,000 slum":** Joseph Martin, Dominick Peluso, and Sydney Mirkin, "The Housing That Your Jack Built Is Now Tobacco Road," *Daily News*, Feb. 19, 1957.

78 **dividing the projects in half:** Campanella, *Brooklyn: The Once and Future City*, p. 379.

78 **in a fifth-floor corner unit at 29 Fleet Walk:** Joanie's birth certificate.

78 **a tight-knit flock:** Descriptions of Joanie's childhood are from interviews with five Sykes family members, including her sisters Margo and Linda as well as her childhood friend Linda.

78 **"down by the courts"**: Interviews with Margo and the childhood friend, Linda.

79 **just a few miles from the Virginia shore where America's first slaves landed:** The enslaved landed at Old Point Comfort in 1619; the World War II troops departed from Hampton Roads, Virginia, in 1944. Beth Austin, *1619: Virginia's First Africans* (Hampton, Va.: Hampton History Museum, 2018), p. 7; Ivan J. Houston, *Black Warriors: The Buffalo Soldiers of World War II: Memories of the Only Negro Infantry Division to Fight in Europe During World War II* (Bloomington: iUniverse, 2009), pp. 21–23.

79 **staggered up the gangplank of a ship bound for Africa:** Interview with Ivan J. Houston; Houston, *Black Warriors*, p. 23.

79 **Wesley Junior Sykes was twenty-three years old:** June's birth and death certificates.

79 **the 92nd Infantry, an all-Black division:** Abby Callard, "Memoirs of a World War II Buffalo Soldier," *Smithsonian Magazine*, Nov. 6, 2009.

79 **joining thirty-five hundred other African American troops:** Interviews with Houston and Michael E. Lynch, a senior historian at the U.S. Army Heritage and Education Center.

79 **was the first to be called to duty:** Houston, *Black Warriors*, p. 34.

79 **as part of the only Black division to fight in Europe:** Ibid.

79 **The men were quiet, their faces drawn:** Interview with Houston; Houston, *Black Warriors*, p. 23.

79 **Most were from the rural South:** Gail Buckley, *American Patriots: The Story of Blacks in the Military from the Revolution to Desert Storm* (New York: Random House, 2001), pp. 258–59.

79 **A Black serviceman could be lynched:** Equal Justice Initiative, *Lynching in America: Targeting Black Veterans* (Montgomery, Ala.: Equal Justice Initiative, 2017), p. 4; Chad L. Williams, "Vanguards of the New Negro: African American Veterans and Post–World War I Racial Militancy," *The Journal of African American History* 92, no. 3 (2007), pp. 347–70.

79 **his father—the senior Wesley Sykes—had registered:** Wesley Sykes's World War I registration card.

80 **an angry mob had attacked a Black veteran:** "Six Witnesses Fail To Implicate Any of Lynching Party," *The News and Observer*, Dec. 29, 1919.

80 **"souvenir hunters":** Irving Cheek, "Outsider Linked Up with Lynching," *The News and Observer*, Dec. 31, 1919.

80 **"breaks the monotony":** "What the Playmakers Are Doing," *Goldsboro Daily Argus*, Jan. 14, 1922.

80 **The Sykes surname traces back to a white slave owner:** The search for African American ancestors is fraught with reminders that 150 years ago "Black people weren't considered people," in the words of the journalist Nicole Ellis. The 1870 census was the first to include African descendants by name. Before that, they existed as the registered "property" of their enslavers, in estate records, slave schedules, wills, and other documents. To trace the Sykes family's ancestry, I hired the genealogist Diane L. Richard to help me find and analyze hundreds of historical records dating back to the 1700s, including deeds of gifts, court minutes, bills of sale, probate records, and nineteenth-century census counts. Nicole Ellis, "Descendants: A *Washington Post* Original Series," *Washington Post*, Feb. 25, 2020.

80 **In the North Carolina of the 1830s:** Heather Andrea Williams, "How Slavery Affected African American Families," Freedom's Story, TeacherServe, National Humanities Center, accessed Feb. 26, 2021.

81 **Albert had been murdered by gunshot:** "Murder in Wayne: Tragedy in Colored Family in Granthaus Township," *Wilmington Morning Star*, May 1, 1910.

81 **"colored man of notorious character":** Ibid.

81 **The young June was soon working the fields:** June worked as a drugstore delivery boy

for two years and as a seasonal farm worker for eight. Civilian Conservation Corps records.

81 **His chance came at age twenty:** Ibid.

81 **June began sending $15:** Ibid.

81 **A light rain fell as the ship unmoored:** Interview with Houston.

81 **Army bases, buses, even blood banks remained segregated:** It was not until March 1943 that the War Department banned the segregation of recreational facilities; in July 1944, the department also ordered the federal government's vehicles desegregated. Buckley, *American Patriots*, p. 260; Ira Katznelson, *When Affirmative Action Was White: An Untold History of Racial Inequality in Twentieth-Century America* (W. W. Norton, 2005), p. 90.

81 **more than 1.2 million African Americans served:** "African Americans in World War II: Fighting for a Double Victory," The National WWII Museum, accessed Feb. 26, 2021; Chelsea Brasted, "America's Oldest Living WWII Veteran Faced Hostility Abroad—and at Home," *National Geographic*, May 11, 2020.

81 **"victory over our enemies at home and victory over our enemies on the battlefields abroad":** "The Courier's Double 'V' for a Double Victory Campaign Gets Country-Wide Support," *Pittsburgh Courier*, Feb. 14, 1942.

81 **Black recruits found themselves under the command of white southerners:** Robert W. Kesting, "Conspiracy to Discredit the Black Buffaloes: The 92nd Infantry in World War II," *The Journal of Negro History* 72, no. ½ (1987), p. 4.

81 **officers must show an "ability to handle negroes":** Michael E. Lynch, *Edward M. Almond and the U.S. Army: From the 92nd Infantry Division to the X Corps* (Lexington: University Press of Kentucky, 2019), p. 63.

81 **Most Black troops were relegated to service positions:** "African Americans in World War II," The National WWII Museum.

81 **who joined the 370th as an auto mechanic:** My description of June's military service is based on records from the U.S. Department of Veterans Affairs (including his military discharge form), the Civilian Conservation Corps, and the National Archives of St. Louis, as well as on interviews with Houston and Lynch, both of whom helped me analyze these records.

81 **had been fighting for America since the Revolutionary War:** Ploski and Williams, *Negro Almanac*, p. 541.

81 **segregated into their own regiments after the Civil War:** After the Civil War, Congress passed a law on July 28, 1866, creating two African American cavalry regiments and four infantry regiments. "The Proud Legacy of the Buffalo Soldiers," National Museum of African American History and Culture, nmaahc.si.edu/blog-post/proud-legacy-buffalo-soldiers, accessed Feb. 26, 2021.

81 **sent west in 1867 to exert control over Native Americans:** "Buffalo Soldiers," History.com, A&E Television Networks, Dec. 7, 2017.

82 **who referred to the Black troops as Buffalo Soldiers:** Ibid.

82 **recent invasion of Normandy had claimed 2,501 Americans:** The Normandy invasion of June 6, 1944, killed 4,414 Allied troops, including 2,501 Americans. Thousands of others were wounded or went missing in action. The National D-Day Memorial Foundation; Office of the Press Secretary, "Fact Sheet: Normandy Landings," The White House, June 6, 2014.

82 **After eight days at sea:** Unless otherwise noted, details about Houston and the 370th Regiment's passage through Italy are based on interviews with Houston and on his book *Black Warriors*, pp. 26–29, 38–39, 55.

82 **using the forced labor of fifteen thousand captives:** Smithsonian Institution, *World War II Map by Map* (New York: Dorling Kindersley, 2019), p. 240.

83 **survived three major battles:** June's military discharge form.

83 **June carried a rifle:** Interviews with Houston and Lynch.

83 **He would later tell his grandchildren:** Interviews with Margo, Linda, and Lamont.

83 **More than five hundred of his comrades were killed:** Hondon B. Hargrove, *Buffalo Soldiers in Italy: Black Americans in World War II* (Jefferson, N.C.: McFarland, 1985), p. 192.

83 **June's regiment had liberated two cities:** They liberated Lucca, Pontremoli, and several smaller towns and villages. Houston, *Black Warriors*, pp. 58–75, 185.

83 **the Buffalo Soldiers' heroics would be taught in Italian grade schools:** Interview with Ivan A. Houston, the son of Ivan J. Houston, who co-produced the documentary *With One Tied Hand* (United States: Pacific Film Foundation, 2016) about Houston's service as a Buffalo Soldier.

83 **"When I take off my uniform":** Langston Hughes, Arnold Rampersad, and David Ernest Roessel, *The Collected Poems of Langston Hughes* (New York: Vintage Books, 1995), pp. 303–304.

84 **"There was a Buffalo Soldier":** Bob Marley and the Wailers, "Buffalo Soldier," *Confrontation* (Island Records, 1983).

84 **June left the military with three Bronze Service Stars:** June's military discharge records.

84 **allowing millions of veterans to go to college:** "G.I. Bill of Rights," *National Archives Foundation*, 2021.

84 **The GI Bill drove the creation of middle-class America:** Katznelson, *When Affirmative Action Was White*, p. 113.

84 **They were largely denied the GI Bill supports:** Edward Humes, "How the GI Bill Shunted Blacks into Vocational Training," *The Journal of Blacks in Higher Education*, no. 53 (2006), pp. 94–98; Lizabeth Cohen, *A Consumers' Republic: The Politics of Mass Consumption in Postwar America* (New York: Random House, 2004), pp. 166–69.

84 **Job training programs catered overwhelmingly to whites:** Ibid.

84 **answered to a Jim Crow South:** Katznelson, *When Affirmative Action Was White*, p. 114.

84 **joining the 6 million African Americans:** Isabel Wilkerson, *The Warmth of Other Suns: The Epic Story of America's Great Migration* (New York: Random House, 2010), p. 9.

84 **Brooklyn's largest Black enclave:** John R. Logan, Weiwei Zhang, and Miao Chunyu, "Emergent Ghettos: Black Neighborhoods in New York and Chicago, 1880–1940," *American Journal of Sociology* 120, no. 4 (2015), pp. 1067, 1082, Figure 5; Bureau of Community Statistical Services, *Brooklyn Communities: Population Characteristics and Neighborhood Social Resources*, vol. I (New York: Community Council of Greater New York, 1959), p. 100.

84 **Labor unions tended to exclude Black workers:** In 1930, at least twenty-two of the nation's labor unions excluded Black members. By 1950, when June Sykes was working in Brooklyn, nine unions continued to ban African Americans, while other unions excluded them by voting against their proposed memberships or by ignoring their applications altogether. Ray Marshall, "The Negro and Organized Labor," *The Journal of Negro Education* 32, no. 4 (1963), pp. 375–76.

85 **when 94 percent of the profession was white:** 1950 census data.

85 **June had worked for seventeen companies:** June's SSA records.

85 **bringing him a total income of $2,900:** Ibid.

85 **Black janitors earned 41 percent less than white mechanics:** In 1950, Black janitors earned $1,480 and white mechanics earned $2,518. The yearly gap between these two incomes was $1,038. Over twenty years, adjusting for inflation, this gap came to $25,391 (equivalent to $192,350 in 2019 dollars). Analysis by Wimer, based on 1950 census data accessed through IPUMS at the University of Minnesota.

85 "depress real estate values": "Afro-American Realty," *New York Times*, July 27, 1904.

85 which had 150,000 members: Wilder, *Covenant with Color*, p. 121.

85 visited a church in Bed-Stuy in 1929: Ibid., p. 129.

85 the city withheld sufficient policing and other services: Ibid., p. 196; Connolly, "Blacks in Brooklyn," pp. 165–75.

85 the federal Home Owners' Loan Corporation began color-coding American cities: "Introduction, Mapping Inequality: Redlining in New Deal America," University of Richmond Digital Scholarship Lab, University of Richmond, accessed Feb. 26, 2021.

85 Brooklyn fell into decline as whites left: Wilder, *Covenant with Color*, pp. 212–14.

85 restrictive covenants prevented Blacks from buying homes: Bruce Lambert, "At 50, Levittown Contends with Its Legacy of Bias," *New York Times*, Dec. 28, 1997.

85 less than 1 percent went to nonwhite veterans: In the 1950 census, among veterans identified by race, 70,875 were approved for mortgages in the New York and northeastern New Jersey suburbs; only 631 of those mortgages went to nonwhite veterans. 1950 census data; Lizabeth Cohen, *A Consumers' Republic*, p. 171.

86 White American families would eventually amass a median net worth: Tracy Jan, "White Families Have Nearly 10 Times the Net Worth of Black Families. And the Gap Is Growing," *Washington Post*, Sept. 28, 2017.

86 In 1952, he and Margaret landed a subsidized apartment: Interviews with Margo and other family members, corroborated by Joanie Sykes's birth certificate.

86 This was the largest of the nation's so-called "projects": Campanella, *Brooklyn: The Once and Future City*, p. 375.

86 "the forgotten man at the bottom of the economic pyramid": In a radio address on April 7, 1932, President Franklin Delano Roosevelt told listeners, "These unhappy times call for the building of plans that rest upon the forgotten, the unorganized but the indispensable units of economic power, for plans like those of 1917 that build from the bottom up and not from the top down, that put their faith once more in the forgotten man at the bottom of the economic pyramid." "Radio Address re a National Program of Restoration," April 7, 1932, Franklin D. Roosevelt, Master Speech File, 1898–1945, File 469, Franklin D. Roosevelt Presidential Library and Museum.

86 most of the apartments went to white defense workers: Edward Weinfeld, "Purpose of Houses Changed by War to a Workers' Project," *Brooklyn Daily Eagle*, Aug. 16, 1942.

86 But the Navy Yard had also been redlined, along with part of Fort Greene: Wilder, *Covenant with Color*, pp. 188–89.

86 Brooklyn was on its way to becoming the largest ghetto: Wilder, *Covenant with Color*, p. 177; Connolly, "Blacks in Brooklyn," pp. 148–49, 155–56.

86 "one of the best laborers": Interview with John Liuzzo.

86 leading his wife to apply for welfare: Interviews with Peter and John Liuzzo.

86 denied public aid to families with "a man in the house": This rule varied from state to state. In New York City, welfare workers were required "to make unannounced visits to determine if fathers were living in the home—if evidence of a male presence was found, cases were closed and welfare checks discontinued." Alma Carten, "The Racist Roots of Welfare Reform," *The New Republic*, Aug. 22, 2016.

87 The closest public pool was forty blocks away: "History of Parks' Swimming Pools," New York City Department of Parks and Recreation website, accessed Feb. 24, 2021; Google Maps.

87 the civil rights movement, which had found a northern base in Brooklyn: Lilly Tuttle, "Civil Rights in Brooklyn," Museum of the City of New York, Oct. 25, 2016; Tamar W. Carroll, *Mobilizing New York: AIDS, Antipoverty, and Feminist Activism* (Chapel Hill: University of North Carolina Press, 2015), p. 50; Flateau, "Black Brooklyn," pp. 50–51.

87 setting off the first major uprising of the civil rights era: Hansi Lo Wang, "New York's

'Night of Birmingham Horror' Sparked a Summer of Riots," *All Things Considered*, NPR, July 18, 2014; Walter Rucker and James Nathaniel Upton, eds., *Encyclopedia of American Race Riots*, vols. 1 & 2 (Westport, Conn.: Greenwood Press, 2007), pp. 73–74, 478–79.

87   **riots swept through Brooklyn and cities across America:** Lorraine Boissoneault, "Martin Luther King Jr.'s Assassination Sparked Uprisings in Cities Across America," *Smithsonian Magazine*, April 4, 2018.

87   **"A riot . . . is the language of the unheard":** Martin Luther King, Jr., interview with Mike Wallace, *60 Minutes*, Sept. 27, 1966.

Chapter 10

89   **She needed a name:** Interview with Margo.

89   **the Housing Authority evicted the Sykes family:** Interviews with Margo, Linda, and another Sykes family member.

89   **Brownsville, one of the poorest parts of a city in decline:** Craig Baerwald et al., *At Home in Brownsville Studio: A Plan for Transforming Public Housing* (New York: Hunter College Masters of Urban Planning, 2014), p. 18; Kim Phillips-Fein, "The Legacy of the 1970s Fiscal Crisis," *The Nation*, April 16, 2013.

89   **a seismic shift that would hit African Americans especially hard:** "Because of their disproportionate representation in manufacturing jobs, African American men suffered disproportionately from the decline of American manufacturing after 1980." Kenneth G. Dau-Schmidt and Ryland Sherman, "The Employment and Economic Advancement of African-Americans in the Twentieth Century," *Articles by Indiana University Bloomington's Maurer School of Law Faculty* 1292 (2013), pp. 102–103; William Julius Wilson, *The Truly Disadvantaged: The Inner City, the Underclass, and Public Policy* (Chicago: University of Chicago Press, 1990), pp. 42–43, 135; Gerald Taylor, "Black Factory Workers 'Profoundly and Disproportionally' Felt the Pain of Job Losses," Alliance for American Manufacturing, Oct. 6, 2016.

90   **finding low-skill work in the automobile, rubber, and steel industries:** Wilson, *Truly Disadvantaged*, pp. 12, 42, 135, 148.

90   **As unemployment soared in America's inner cities:** Ibid., p. 3.

90   **Black middle-class families were migrating to the suburbs:** Ibid., pp. 7, 17.

90   **which had opened jobs and neighborhoods to those with college degrees:** Ibid., pp. 7–8, 109–15; Robert Greenstein, "Prisoners of the Economy," *New York Times*, Oct. 25, 1987.

90   **"the underclass":** William Julius Wilson, *The Declining Significance of Race: Blacks and Changing American Institutions* (Chicago: University of Chicago Press, 1980), pp. 1–2, 154.

90   **what Wilson called "maladaptive behaviors":** William Julius Wilson, "Social Theory and the Concept 'Underclass,'" in David B. Grusky and Ravi Kanbur, eds., *Poverty and Inequality* (Stanford: Stanford University Press, 2006), p. 106.

90   **had reached striking new heights by the mid-1970s:** Wilson, *Truly Disadvantaged*, p. 3.

90   **"culture is a response to social structural constraints":** Ibid., p. 61.

90   **"Ford to City: Drop Dead":** Frank Van Riper, "Ford to City: Drop Dead," *Daily News*, Oct. 30, 1975.

90   **slashed municipal services and eventually closed public hospitals:** Robert D. McFadden, "Edward I. Koch, a Mayor as Brash, Shrewd and Colorful as the City He Led, Dies at 88," *New York Times*, Feb. 1, 2013; Ronald Sullivan, "A City Hospital in Fort Greene Will Be Closed," *New York Times*, Aug. 11, 1983.

90   **a smooth-talking construction worker:** Interviews with Sherry and Margo.

90   **still married to a woman from South Carolina:** Court records from a lawsuit filed by Sherry in the Supreme Court of the State of New York, County of Richmond.

91 **their own mother, Margaret, began charging them $50 each:** Interviews with Margo and Linda.

91 **took jobs assembling foosball figurines:** Margo's SSA records.

91 **She gave her baby girl to Sonny Boy:** Interviews with Sherry, Margo, Chanel, and other family members.

92 **Sonny Boy was earning about $400 a week:** Court records.

92 **a seven-story teardown project at Bellevue Hospital's Building F:** Municipal Archives, New York City.

92 **At around 10 A.M., the sound of falling debris:** Court records.

93 **Joanie was living three miles west:** Interview with Margo.

93 **and the landlord refused to fix it:** Interview with Joe Robinson.

93 **She survived on welfare checks and cash:** Interview with Margo; Joanie's HRA records.

93 **at a predominantly white school in neighboring Howard Beach:** In 1983, Chanel attended P.S. 146 in Howard Beach. DOE records. According to the 1980 census, 99 percent of Howard Beach residents were white. Virginia Byrne, "Howard Beach Blacks Have Mixed Emotions About Living There," AP News, Feb. 8, 1987.

94 **Crack had surfaced in America by the early 1980s:** For the early 1980s: "DEA History, 1980–1985," U.S. Drug Enforcement Administration, accessed Feb. 26, 2021; for Miami and Los Angeles: Albert Samaha, "Cheaper, More Addictive, and Highly Profitable: How Crack Took Over NYC in the '80s," *Village Voice*, Aug. 12, 2014.

94 **While coke remained a glamour drug, selling for $100 per gram:** Crack sold from $2.50 to $5, depending on the source. For $3: J. H. Lowinson, P. Ruiz, R. B. Millman, and J. G. Langrod, eds., *Substance Abuse: A Comprehensive Textbook*, 4th ed. (Philadelphia: Lippincott Williams and Wilkins, 2006), p. 112.

94 **Joanie showed more control:** Interviews with Chanel, Margo, and Robinson.

94 **Margo had less discipline:** Interviews with Chanel and Margo.

94 **brought a surge of dopamine:** Eric J. Nestler, "The Neurobiology of Cocaine Addiction," *Science & Practice Perspectives* 3, no. 1 (2005), p. 5.

94 **emphasized deterrence rather than treatment:** "Just Say No," History.com, A&E Television Networks, May 31, 2017.

95 **"Hang in there, whites. Just say no!":** Dave Chappelle, "Sticks & Stones," August 2019, Pilot Boy Productions, 2019.

95 **making punishment for crack possession (common among the poor) one hundred times more harsh:** Under the Anti–Drug Abuse Act of 1986, the mandatory minimum sentence for distributing 5 grams of crack was five years in prison—the same sentence given for distributing 500 grams of powder cocaine, hence the so-called "100-to-1 disparity." While most crack users were white, the vast majority of people incarcerated for crack have been African American. Crack cocaine "is more accessible for poor Americans, many of whom are African Americans. Conversely, powder cocaine is much more expensive and tends to be used by more affluent white Americans." Deborah J. Vagins and Jesselyn McCurdy, *Cracks in the System: Twenty Years of the Unjust Federal Crack Cocaine Law* (Washington, D.C.: American Civil Liberties Union, 2006), p. i. See also Jamie Fellner, "Race, Drugs, and Law Enforcement in the United States," *Stanford Law & Policy Review* 20, no. 2 (2009), pp. 264–65; "Crack Cocaine Myths and Facts," Criminal Justice Policy Foundation, accessed Feb. 23, 2021.

95 **Even first-time crack offenders landed mandatory minimum sentences of five to ten years:** In the case of bodily harm or death caused by the use of crack, the mandatory minimum sentence was twenty years (Anti–Drug Abuse Act of 1986).

95 **a disproportionately Black and Latino group:** In 1990, African Americans were 11 percent of the U.S. population, but 46 percent of the prison population (with 331,880 Black people incarcerated in a prison population totaling 715,649). Latinos accounted for 9 percent of the general U.S. population but 13 percent of the prison population

(with 95,498 incarcerated). It is also important to note that Native Americans were 0.7 percent of the U.S. population but 0.9 percent of the prison population (with 6,471 incarcerated). By comparison, white non-Hispanic Americans comprised 76 percent of the U.S. population and 38 percent of the incarcerated. Put another way: In 1990, for every one thousand Americans in each racial or ethnic group, there were eleven Black, four Latino, and four Native Americans incarcerated for every white person. Louis W. Jankowski, "Number of Inmates/Residents in State and Federal Correctional Facilities, by Race and Hispanic Origin, June 29, 1990," *Correctional Populations in the United States, 1990* (NCJ 134946, Washington, D.C., 1992), p. 50, table 4.7; 1990 census data.

95 **this population would surpass a million:** Associated Press, "U.S. Has Highest Rate of Imprisonment in World," *New York Times,* Jan. 7, 1991.

95 **The United States had claimed the highest incarceration rate:** Ibid.

95 **a male cousin lured her into a basement bathroom:** Interview with Chanel.

97 **On April 30, 1990, she took her daughter:** Joanie's DHS records.

97 **aid to the poor "shall be provided by the state":** New York State Constitution.

97 **known as SBLs among aides to Mayor Ed Koch:** Interview with Goldfein.

97 **A third of this population:** Joel Blau, *The Visible Poor: Homelessness in the United States* (New York: Oxford University Press, 1992), p. 86; Jonathan M. Soffer, *Ed Koch and the Rebuilding of New York City* (New York: Columbia University Press, 2010), p. 280.

97 **were closing to make way for luxury buildings:** Deirdre Carmody, "The City Sees No Solutions for Homeless," *New York Times,* Oct. 10, 1984.

97 **an Irish cook who had lost his job:** Blau, *Visible Poor,* p. 99.

97 **filed a class-action lawsuit that established New York's constitutional right to shelter:** "The Callahan Legacy: Callahan v. Carey and the Legal Right to Shelter," Coalition for the Homeless, accessed Feb. 26, 2021.

97 **Callahan died on the streets of the Lower East Side:** Ibid.

97 **This was the dawn of "modern homelessness":** Ibid.

97 **a word that entered popular discourse in the 1980s:** Mitchel Levitas, "Homeless in America," *New York Times Magazine,* June 10, 1990; Kim Hopper, "Homelessness Old and New: The Matter of Definition," *Housing Policy Debate* 2, no. 3 (1991), pp. 774, 798.

97 **One population was disproportionately hit: African Americans:** Marian Moser Jones, "Does Race Matter in Addressing Homelessness? A Review of the Literature," *World Medical & Health Policy* 8, no. 2 (2016), pp. 139–56.

97 **"We'll move out of the shelter":** Tracy Chapman, "Fast Car," *Tracy Chapman* (Elektra, 1988).

98 **"peeling like dead skin in summer":** Patti Smith, *Just Kids* (New York: HarperCollins, 2010), pp. 85–86.

98 **He was buried with military honors:** June's death certificate; interviews with Margo and Linda.

98 **Margaret, was now living in Canarsie:** Interview with Margo, corroborated by public housing records and Chanel's DOE records.

98 **which took its name from the Dutch enslavers:** Benardo and Weiss, *Brooklyn by Name,* p. 3.

98 **Joe had dropped out of community college and was dealing crack:** Interview with Robinson.

98 **Every few weeks, a new cache of drugs arrived:** Interviews with Chanel and Margo.

99 **Crack had reordered the local economy:** Samaha, "Cheaper, More Addictive, and Highly Profitable."

99 **more than twenty-two hundred people had been killed:** Donatella Lorch, "Record Year for Killings Jolts Officials in New York," *New York Times,* Dec. 31, 1990.

99 **It was the bloodiest year in modern New York history:** Fox Butterfield, "U.S. Crime Rate Rose 2% in 2001 After 10 Years of Decreases," *New York Times,* Oct. 29, 2002;

Mayor's Office press release, "Mayor Bloomberg and Police Commissioner Kelly An-nounce 2013 Saw the Fewest Murders and Fewest Shootings in Recorded City History at NYPD Graduation Ceremony," City of New York, Dec. 27, 2013.

100 **By age fifteen, Chanel had attended seven different schools:** Chanel's DOE records.

100 **The dental office charged Medicaid $235:** Chanel's Medicaid records.

100 **Joe, had gone to prison for killing a man:** Interview with Robinson; prison records.

100 **where a medical exam revealed HIV in his blood:** Interviews with Chanel and Margo.

100 **She spent her final weeks at Presbyterian Hospital:** Interviews with Chanel and Margo.

101 **He had died in a car accident:** Interviews with Margo and Chanel.

101 **five months after AIDS became the leading cause:** Gretchen Gavett, "Timeline: 30 Years of AIDS in Black America," *Frontline*, Public Broadcasting Service, July 10, 2012.

101 **thanks to an antiretroviral drug:** Interviews with Margo and other family members.

Chapter 11

103 **The alternative was a child welfare system that segregated:** Nina Bernstein, *The Lost Children of Wilder: The Epic Struggle to Change Foster Care* (New York: Vintage Books, 2002).

104 **The term "child abuse" had surfaced in the 1960s:** Larry Wolff, "The Battered-Child Syndrome: 50 Years Later," *Huffington Post*, Jan. 4, 2013; C. Henry Kempe et al., "The Battered-Child Syndrome," *Journal of the American Medical Association*, 181, no. 1 (1962), pp. 17–24.

104 **sparked a national outcry, leading to mandatory child abuse reporting laws:** Joyce, "Crime of Parenting While Poor."

104 **the plaintiff, in 1973, of a landmark class-action lawsuit:** Richard Severo, "Church Groups See Danger in Child-Care Bias Lawsuit," *New York Times*, March 16, 1975.

104 **Children were flooding the city's foster care system:** Michael Oreskes, Suzanne Daley, and Sara Rimer, "A System Overloaded: The Foster-Care Crisis," *New York Times*, March 15, 1987.

104 **News outlets sounded the alarm of America's "crack babies":** Janine Jackson, "Reex-amining 'Crack Baby' Myth—Without Taking Responsibility," Fairness & Accuracy In Reporting, July 1, 2013.

104 **These reports stemmed from a single medical study:** Vann R. Newkirk II, "What the 'Crack Baby' Panic Reveals About the Opioid Epidemic," *The Atlantic*, July 16, 2017.

104 **prenatal exposure to crack causes subtle—if any—differences:** Maia Szalavitz, "'Crack Babies' Don't Necessarily Turn into Troubled Teens," *Time*, May 28, 2013; "Crack Cocaine Myths and Facts."

104 **pregnant drug users became the target of law enforcement:** Lynn M. Paltrow, David S. Cohen, and Corinne A. Carey, *Year 2000 Overview: Governmental Responses to Preg-nant Women Who Use Alcohol or Other Drugs* (Women's Law Project, National Advo-cates for Pregnant Women, October 2000), p. 16.

104 **the number of foster children in New York City reached a record high:** David Tobis, *From Pariahs to Partners: How Parents and Their Allies Changed New York City's Child Welfare System* (New York: Oxford University Press, 2013), p. 21.

104 **a child with roots at the Auburn shelter:** Lizette Alvarez, "The Life and Love of a Single Father," *New York Times*, Nov. 29, 1995.

105 **Elisa was tortured by her mother:** Lizette Alvarez, "A Mother's Tale: Drugs, Despair and Violence," *New York Times*, Nov. 27, 1995.

105 **the authorities called it the worst case of child abuse:** Joyce Purnick, "Elisa's Death: A Year Later, Hints of Hope," *New York Times*, Nov. 21, 1996.

105 **"A Shameful Death":** *Time*, Dec. 11, 1995.

105   **Vowing to reform the system:** David Firestone, "Giuliani Is Forming a New City Agency on Child Welfare," *New York Times*, Jan. 12, 1996.

105   **with 13,207 admissions in 1997 alone:** Timothy Ross and Anne Lifflander, *The Experiences of New York City Foster Children in HIV/AIDS Clinical Trials* (New York: Vera Institute of Justice, 2009), p. 66.

105   **Their $657 rent was covered by the city's Housing Authority:** Joanie's HRA and NYCHA records.

105   **sending hundreds of thousands of single mothers back to work across America:** In the three years following welfare reform, at least 2 million Americans left the rolls, although it is unclear how many of these people (the majority of them single mothers) went back to work. One way to gauge this is with employment data. During that same period, from 1996 to 1999, the number of unemployed single mothers fell by 773,000 (from 3,486,000 to 2,713,000), while the number of employed single mothers grew by 883,000 (from 6,150,000 to 7,033,000). Research indicates that more than half of the "welfare leavers" found work, but often struggled to keep their jobs in an unstable, low-paying labor market (a pattern that also existed before welfare reform). Welfare reform was not solely responsible for this three-year rise in employment, which began before the law was signed. Analysis provided by Arloc Sherman, vice president of Data Analysis and Research for the Center on Budget and Policy Priorities (CBPP), of data from the Bureau of Labor Statistics; CBPP analysis of figures compiled from the U.S. Department of Health and Human Services and the U.S. House of Representatives Committee on Ways and Means provided by Sherman.

105   **"Welfare is time limited":** Joanie's HRA records.

105   **was hired, in the fall of 2000, as a janitor:** Joanie's Metropolitan Transportation Authority (MTA) records.

105   **a starting salary of $22,816:** Joanie's HRA records.

106   **"It was some crazy shit":** Interview with Clarence Greenwood.

106   **Whites were still a rarity:** Between 2000 and 2018, the percentage of white people living in Bedford-Stuyvesant skyrocketed from 2.4 percent in 2000 to 30.1 percent in 2018—a 1,150 percent increase. "State of the City 2019: Bedford Stuyvesant BK03 Neighborhood Profile," New York University Furman Center for Real Estate and Urban Policy, accessed Feb. 26, 2021.

107   **Chanel's path into the Bloods had started a year earlier:** Interviews with Chanel and another former member of the Bloods.

107   **She had been working there as a cashier:** Chanel's SSA records.

107   **as memorialized in the 1991 film *Boyz N the Hood*:** *Boyz N the Hood*, directed by John Singleton (United States: Columbia Pictures, 1991).

107   **a New Yorker named Omar Portee had spent time with the gang in LA:** Chris Hedges, "Old Colors, New Battle Cry," *New York Times*, Jan. 31, 2000.

107   **they were the most violent gang in New York City:** Daniel Browne, Mark Woltman, and Tomas Hunt, *Old Problem, New Eyes: Youth Insights on Gangs in New York City: A Report by Public Advocate Betsy Gotbaum* (New York: Office of the New York City Public Advocate, 2007), p. 4.

108   **Male recruits had to "cut" their way in:** Interview with Chanel; also see "The Gang Manual," published by NYPD circa 2000–2001, when Bernard B. Kerik was the city's police commissioner, accessed via publicintelligence.net on Feb. 27, 2021.

109   **He would soon sign a deal with DreamWorks:** David Segal, "Citizen Cope's Record Year," *Washington Post*, Jan. 28, 2002.

109   **The man who would become Dasani's father:** Ramel is identified only by his street name. All biographical information about Ramel is from interviews with him and Chanel, and from Ramel's criminal records.

110 which cost Chanel $300 per day: Chanel's drug treatment records.

110 wiping off graffiti and removing gum from the seats: Joanie's MTA records.

110 "Baby girl delivered alive": Dasani's hospital records.

Chapter 12

112 where his older brother, Shamell, was now serving time for dealing crack: Shamell's criminal records.

112 Dasani was three months old when she and her parents became officially homeless: Chanel's DHS records.

113 "I know you have a little life in you yet": Maxwell, "This Woman's Work," *Now* (Columbia, 2001).

113 Chanel remained with her at Odyssey House: Chanel's Odyssey House records.

113 She was now earning more than $34,000: Joanie's MTA records.

114 constantly "disrespecting" her: NYPD Domestic Incident Report.

114 Chanel still had to pass "eligibility review": Daniel Browne, Mark Woltman, and Daliz Pérez-Cabezas, *Turned Away: The Impact of the Late-Arrival Placement Policy on Families with Children* (New York: Office of the New York City Public Advocate, 2008), pp. 5, 7; interview with Goldfein.

114 in 1990, when the city sheltered more than 6,700 homeless children: For data through September 2011, "figures for homeless families, children, and adult family members reflect end-of-month census data" taken from DHS, HRA, and NYCStat shelter census reports. "New York City Homeless Municipal Shelter Population, 1983–Present," Coalition for the Homeless, p. 3, accessed Feb. 26, 2021.

114 Dasani and her sister were joining the ranks of more than 16,700 children: Coalition for the Homeless Advocacy Department, "New York City Homeless Municipal Shelter Population, 1983–Present," p. 8.

115 one of the richest men in the world: In 2001, *Forbes* ranked Bloomberg the 82nd-richest person in the world: "#29, Bloomberg, Michael Rubens," *Forbes*, accessed Feb. 23, 2021.

115 After coming to New York in 1966: All biographical details about Bloomberg, unless otherwise noted, are based on the following: Eleanor Randolph, *The Many Lives of Michael Bloomberg* (New York: Simon and Schuster, 2019); Dean E. Murphy, "Bloomberg a Man of Contradictions, but with a Single Focus," *New York Times*, Nov. 26, 2001; Adam Nagourney, "Bloomberg Edges Green in Race for Mayor," *New York Times*, Nov. 7, 2001; Michael Barbaro, "The Bullpen Bloomberg Built: Candidates Debate Its Future," *New York Times*, March 22, 2013; Michael Barbaro and Kitty Bennett, "Cost of Being Mayor? $650 Million, If He's Rich," *New York Times*, Dec. 29, 2013.

115 he drew quick applause for the creation of 311: Winnie Hu, "New Yorkers Love to Complain, and Hot Line Takes Advantage," *New York Times*, Dec. 1, 2003.

115 the mayor considered placing families on retired cruise ships: Leslie Kaufman, "Officials Tour Cruise Ships in a Search for Shelter Space," *New York Times*, Nov. 21, 2002.

115 "We would have to remove bars and discos which are inappropriate for shelter": Ibid.

115 Bloomberg sent homeless families to . . . Bronx House of Detention for Men: Jennifer Steinhauer, "Mayor's Style Is Tested in Sending Homeless to Old Jail," *New York Times*, Aug. 16, 2002.

116 "Our own policies needlessly encourage entry and prolong dependence on shelters": Leslie Kaufman, "Mayor Urges Major Overhaul for Homeless," *New York Times*, June 24, 2004.

116 For decades, the city had helped homeless families jump the waitlist: DHS and Coalition for the Homeless.

116 **Only a small fraction of those families returned to shelters:** A study by the Vera Institute of Justice looked at homeless families in 1998 who left shelters with long-term subsidized housing and tracked them over the next five years. Only 11.5 percent of the families returned to a shelter. Nancy Smith et al., *Understanding Family Homelessness in New York City: An In-Depth Study of Families' Experiences Before and After Shelter* (Washington, D.C.: Vera Institute of Justice, 2005), p. 12, table 5.

116 **Bloomberg adopted a new set of policies:** Christin Durham and Martha Johnson, *Innovations in NYC Health & Human Services Policy: Homelessness Prevention, Intake, and Shelter for Single Adults and Families* (New York: Urban Institute, 2014).

116 **Promising to make "chronic homelessness effectively extinct":** Dina Temple-Raston, "Bloomberg Vows to Make Chronic Homelessness 'Extinct,'" *New York Sun*, June 24, 2004.

116 **Bloomberg revamped the shelter system:** During Bloomberg's tenure, his administration spent nearly $5 billion on shelter services, creating 7,500 added units or beds. Mayor's Office, 2013.

116 **a city-run "innovation lab" that would spend $662 million:** Mayor's Office, 2013.

116 **"fraud investigators":** Samantha M. Shapiro, "The Children in the Shadows: New York City's Homeless Students," *New York Times*, Sept. 9, 2020.

116 **The investigators paid house visits:** Interview with Goldfein.

116 **an applicant was told to sleep in a relative's bathtub:** Ibid.

Chapter 13

121 **He was the lone parent of two small children:** All biographical details about Supreme are from interviews with him, as well as from records spanning his life, including child protection, court, prison, police, Medicaid, and HRA records.

121 **two-year-old Khaliq and a baby girl he called Nana:** Early biographical details about the oldest four children are from interviews with their parents and other relatives, as well as from their school, hospital, family court, ACS, HRA, and DHS records.

121 **She suffered from a hereditary eye disease:** Nana was diagnosed with familial exudative vitreoretinopathy. Nana's medical records.

122 **In an autopsy:** Kylia Gordon's autopsy report.

124 **founded by Clarence Smith, a veteran of the Korean War:** Bradley R. Gooding, "Poor Righteous Teaching: The Story of the FBI and the Five Percenters," *Ex Post Facto* (2001), pp. 57, 70; Autodidact 17, "Allah, the Father's Assassination: 48 Years Later," *New York Amsterdam News*, July 13, 2017.

124 **whose ranks were said to include Busta Rhymes, Mobb Deep, members of the Wu-Tang Clan:** Robert Tanner, "'Five Percent' Adherents Spread Faith—or Fantasy," *Los Angeles Times*, Jan. 3, 1999; The RZA, *The Wu-Tang Manual* (New York: Penguin, 2005), p. 43; Tai Gooden, "Showtime's New Wu-Tang Docu-Series Highlights How 5 Percent Nation Influenced the Group," *Bustle*, May 10, 2019; Simon Vozick-Levinson, "Erykah Badu on Covering Drake, Duetting with André 3000, Her New Mixtape," *Rolling Stone*, Jan. 12, 2016.

124 **as later immortalized by Lin-Manuel Miranda in *Hamilton*:** Lin-Manuel Miranda, "My Shot," recorded 2015, Atlantic Recording Corporation, track 3 on *Hamilton* (Original Broadway Cast Recording).

126 **went to the city clerk's office to get married:** Chanel and Supreme's marriage certificate.

Chapter 14

129 **A fresh start came in the summer of 2006:** Family's DHS file.

129 **the hospital had found traces of marijuana:** ACS records and interviews with Chanel and Supreme.

129 **The practice of drug-screening newborns:** Gail L. Zellman et al., "A Search for Guidance: Examining Prenatal Substance Exposure Protocols," *Maternal and Child Health Journal* 6, no. 3 (2002), pp. 205–12; Oren Yaniv, "Weed Out: More Than a Dozen City Maternity Wards Regularly Test New Moms for Marijuana and Other Drugs," *Daily News*, Dec. 29, 2012.

130 **None of these skills were captured on her report card:** Dasani's DOE records.

Chapter 15

131 **A few minutes after 9 A.M., she set down her bucket:** Joanie's MTA records.

131 **Joanie kept up appearances:** Interviews with Chanel, Dasani, Linda, and Margo.

132 **she had been paying rent with the city's time-limited subsidy:** Chanel's HRA records.

132 **"gasping for breath & unable to speak in complete sentences":** Joanie's EMT Prehospital Care Report.

132 **At 1:15 A.M., Joanie was pronounced dead:** Joanie's death certificate.

133 **Joanie had died of cardiac arrest brought on by atherosclerosis:** Joanie's death certificate and accompanying medical report.

133 **Her years of crack use had made her vulnerable to this heart disease:** Keren Bachi et al., "Vascular Disease in Cocaine Addiction," *Atherosclerosis* 262 (2017), pp. 154–62.

133 **Memories of this come in fragments:** Interviews with Chanel, Margo, Supreme, Dasani, and her siblings.

134 **"How long have you known the deceased?":** Joanie's MTA records.

134 **she had earned a total of $280,752:** Ibid.

134 **Chanel's portion of the inheritance came to $49,000:** Interviews with Chanel and Lamont.

134 **realtors steered African Americans to the economically depressed North Shore:** Steven V. Roberts, "Bias Is Charged in Housing on S.I.," *New York Times*, Jan. 20, 1967.

134 **The island remains New York City's most segregated borough:** Elizabeth Bennett, "Creating Racial Equity in New York City's Most Segregated Borough," *Grantmakers in the Arts Reader* 31, no. 2 (2020); Mireya Navarro, "Segregation Issue Complicates de Blasio's Housing Push," *New York Times*, April 14, 2016; analysis of census data by author and U.S. Army Major (ret.) Danny Sjursen.

135 **voted by a 65 percent margin to secede:** Eleanor Randolph, "'Forgotten Borough' Steps Toward Divorce," *Washington Post*, Dec. 5, 1993.

135 **locals call it the Mason-Dixon Line:** Joseph Berger and Ian Urbina, "Along with Population and Diversity, Stress Rises on Staten I.," *New York Times*, Sept. 25, 2003.

135 **the white enclaves that, in 2016 and 2020, would vote resoundingly for Donald J. Trump:** Matthew Bloch et al., "An Extremely Detailed Map of the 2016 Election," *New York Times*, July 25, 2018; Alice Park et al., "An Extremely Detailed Map of 2020 Election," *New York Times*, Feb. 20, 2021.

135 **"You had breathing space":** Joshua Jelly-Schapiro, "Wu-Tang's RZA on the Mysterious Land of Shaolin: Staten Island," Literary Hub, Oct. 12, 2016.

135 **which they renamed Shaolin Land:** Ibid.; Wu-Tang Clan, "C.R.E.A.M.," RCA Records, *Enter the Wu-Tang*, 1993.

Chapter 16

136 **the family's $1,481 rent would be paid in full:** The family's lease and HRA records.

137 **where she had come by ambulance on May 9, 2009:** Chanel's Staten Island University Hospital records.

137 **the tide of white Americans who had fallen to the same fate:** "Opioid Overdose," Centers for Disease Control and Prevention, accessed Feb. 25, 2021; Helena Hansen and Julie Netherland, "Is the Prescription Opioid Epidemic a White Problem?," *American Journal of Public Health* 106, vol. 12 (2016), pp. 2127–29.

138   **Chanel as a park maintenance employee:** Chanel's SSA records.

138   **"She looked deeply in the sky":** Dasani's "Grade 3 Early Performance Assessment in Language Arts Student Response Book."

138   **in 2011, Bloomberg would end Advantage after the state withdrew its funding:** John Surico, "De Blasio's Homelessness Reset: Advantage Lessons Learned," *Gotham Gazette*, April 4, 2014.

138   **More than a quarter of the families who signed up for Advantage:** Mosi Secret, "Clock Ticks for a Key Homeless Program," *New York Times*, May 31, 2011; Mireya Navarro, "In New York, Having a Job, or 2, Doesn't Mean Having a Home," *New York Times*, Sept. 17, 2013.

138   **had cost $65.5 million to build:** Mosi Secret, "A New First Stop for Homeless Families," City Room, *New York Times*, May 3, 2011.

139   **Of the city's 152 family shelters:** 2013 data from DHS.

139   **the so-called "root shock" of the serially displaced:** Root shock is "the traumatic stress reaction to the destruction of all or part of one's emotional ecosystem." Mindy Thompson Fullilove, *Root Shock: How Tearing Up City Neighborhoods Hurts America, and What We Can Do About It* (New York: New Village Press, 2004), p. 9.

139   **"the longest-term stayers":** In 2010, Auburn was among four "Next Step" family shelters providing "intensive case management" to families who had stayed in the city's shelter system for extended periods. The program began in 2007, when DHS identified nearly fifty families who had been in city shelters for more than five years. Julie Bosman, "A Shelter for Families in Need of a Push," *New York Times*, March 21, 2010; DHS press release, "DHS Unveils Reform Package Centering on Work and Self-Sufficiency," April 25, 2007.

139   **Auburn's only housing specialist had died a year earlier:** State inspection reports.

139   **just as Brooklyn was becoming one of the most expensive rental markets in America:** Jorge Rivas, "Brooklyn Is the Second Most Expensive Place to Live in the U.S.," *Colorlines*, Sept. 7, 2012; Cate Corcoran, "Brooklyn Second Most Expensive Place to Live," *Brownstoner*, Sept. 6, 2012.

139   **even as drugs, guns, and lovers came in through the fire escape:** Interviews with Auburn residents.

140   **the same summer that this man touched Chanel's breast:** Chanel's Auburn case file; "client complaint" records.

140   **Yet he kept his job and soon got a raise:** City payroll data.

141   **She had spent her childhood in the same apartment:** Interviews with Staraisa and her mother, Bonita.

142   **a legal synthetic opioid:** Methadone was developed in Germany in the 1930s but pioneered to treat heroin addiction in 1964 by Vincent Dole, Mary Nyswander, Mary Jeanne Kreek, and two colleagues at the Rockefeller University. Herman Joseph and Joycelyn Sue Woods, "Changing the Treatment Direction for Opiate Addiction: Dr. Dole's Research," *Substance Use & Misuse* 53, no. 2 (2018), p. 181; "Fifty Years After Landmark Methadone Discovery, Stigmas and Misunderstandings Persist," The Rockefeller University, Dec. 9, 2016. For how methadone works, see Richard A. Rettig and Adam Yarmolinsky, eds., *Federal Regulation of Methadone Treatment* (Washington, D.C.: National Academies Press, 1995), pp. 18, 42–43, 93.

142   **on March 14, 2011, Supreme punched his wife in the face:** Family's Auburn records.

143   **When they walked into Room 449 on September 7, they found most of their possessions gone:** Family's Auburn records and interviews with family.

Chapter 17

144   **"All of my belongs went in garbbage":** Client complaint report filed by Chanel at Auburn; family's DHS case file.

144   **She was soon in handcuffs and charged—wrongfully, she says:** Interview with Chanel, as well as NYPD and criminal court records.

145   **For child maltreatment cases in New York's family court:** Interviews with Goldfein and Chris Gottlieb, co-director of New York University School of Law's Family Defense Clinic.

145   **He was "not convinced," he told the judge:** Family court transcript.

146   **earning her first income in years—$1,098 per month:** Chanel's DHS and SSA records.

146   **she stayed in the neonatal intensive care unit:** Interview with Chanel.

146   **"methadone taper down":** Lee-Lee's hospital records.

148   **Sheena had made good enough grades:** Interviews with Sheena and Sherry.

148   **Dasani flunked out of the fifth grade:** Dasani's DOE records.

148   **The city's Department of Education had given Dorsey a D rating:** 2011–2012 City-wide Progress Report accessed via New York City's "Open Data" website: opendata.cityofnewyork.us, June 11, 2019.

148   **Brooklyn's first school for Black children was in danger of being closed:** Cramer, "Dozens of Elementary and Middle Schools."

Chapter 18

152   **The local precinct will investigate six murders:** From January to August 2013, six people were murdered in the 88th Precinct, which includes the neighborhood of Fort Greene. Office of the Deputy Commissioner, Public Information.

155   **The top 5 percent of residents earn 76 times the income:** Analysis by Beveridge and Weber-Stoger.

155   **A growing tax base can improve public schools and parks:** Richard G. Sims, "School Funding, Taxes, and Economic Growth An Analysis of the 50 States" (National Education Association Research Working Paper, Washington, D.C., 2004), p. 1; Lance Freeman, *There Goes the 'Hood: Views of Gentrification from the Ground Up* (Philadelphia: Temple University Press, 2011), p. 99; "The Cost of Local Government in Philadelphia," PEW Charitable Trusts, March 20, 2019.

155   **"the geography of opportunity":** Quentin Brummet and Davin Reed, "The Effects of Gentrification on the Well-Being and Opportunity of Original Resident Adults and Children" (Federal Reserve Bank of Philadelphia Working Paper No. 19–30, Philadelphia, 2019), p. 1.

155   **"Would we prefer a city in which the wealthy and the poor":** Interview with Ingrid Gould Ellen.

155   **The early pioneers of Fort Greene's gentrification:** Themis Chronopoulos, "African Americans, Gentrification, and Neoliberal Urbanization: The Case of Fort Greene, Brooklyn," *Journal of African American Studies* 20 (2016), p. 303.

155   **among them Chris Rock, Erykah Badu:** Ibid., 310.

155   **Branford Marsalis:** Peter Watrous, "Here's Branford," *New York Times Magazine*, May 3, 1992.

155   **whose homegrown 1986 film:** *She's Gotta Have It*, directed by Spike Lee (United States: Island Pictures, 1986).

155   **"Black Mecca":** Chronopoulos, "African Americans, Gentrification," p. 310.

155   **Richard Wright had written passages of his landmark 1940 novel, *Native Son*:** Nelson George, "'I Feel Like a Native Son,'" *New York Times*, June 19, 2005; Stephen Brown, "Richard Wright: Inspired by the Neighborhood," Patch.com, Feb. 16, 2011.

155   **Much of it began in 2003, with Mayor Bloomberg's plan:** Diane Cardwell, "City Has a $100 Million Plan to Develop Downtown Brooklyn," *New York Times*, April 15, 2003.

155   **developers broke ground on nineteen luxury buildings:** *My Brooklyn*, directed by Kelly Anderson (United States: New Day Films, 2013).

155   **Within a decade, the neighborhood's real estate prices had doubled:** Analysis by Bev-

eridge and Weber-Stoger. Real estate change provided by Miller Samuel Inc. and Douglas Elliman.

156   **its portion of white residents had jumped by 80 percent:** Ibid.

156   **an estimated three-quarters of Fort Greene's Black-owned businesses closed:** Stacey A. Sutton, "The Spatial Politics of Black Business Closure in Central Brooklyn," in Mia Bay and Ann Fabian, eds., *Race and Retail: Consumption Across the Color Line* (New Brunswick, N.J.: Rutgers University Press, 2015), p. 210.

156   **Brooklyn was seeing the opposite of white flight:** Chronopoulos, "What's Happened," p. 549.

156   **The very boundaries of neighborhoods that were once marked in red:** Suzanne Spellen, "From Redlining to Predatory Lending: A Secret Economic History of Brooklyn," *Brownstoner*, March 30, 2016.

156   **now contain some of the hottest real estate:** Colvin Grannum, "Inclusion Through Homeownership," in Christopher Herbert, Jonathan Spader, Jennifer Molinsky, and Shannon Rieger, eds., *A Shared Future: Fostering Communities of Inclusion in an Era of Inequality* (Cambridge, Mass.: President and Fellows of Harvard College, 2018), pp. 355–56; Dennis Holt, "Report: 2011 Was a Boom Year for Brooklyn Real Estate," *Brooklyn Daily Eagle*, April 6, 2012.

156   **"Then comes motherfuckin' Christopher Columbus Syndrome":** Joe Coscarelli, "Spike Lee's Amazing Rant Against Gentrification: 'We Been Here!,'" *Intelligencer*, Feb. 25, 2014.

156   **same forces are reshaping Bed-Stuy:** Sam Roberts, "Striking Change in Bedford-Stuyvesant as the White Population Soars," *New York Times*, Aug. 4, 2011.

158   ***Diners, Drive-Ins and Dives*:** Show directed by Steven Bortko, featuring Guy Fieri, Page Productions, aired Nov. 4, 2006 on The Food Network.

159   **The police took him to the emergency room of Lutheran Medical Center:** ACS records.

Chapter 19

162   **"I'ma always want you":** 112 featuring The Notorious B.I.G. and Mase, "Only You (Bad Boy Remix)," *Only You (Remix)* (Bad Boy Entertainment, 1996).

162   **a year before he was murdered:** Dana Ford, "Notorious B.I.G. Autopsy Released, 15 Years After His Death," CNN, Dec. 7, 2012.

165   **The teacher's story begins with her mother:** All biographical details of Hester's life, unless otherwise noted, are from interviews with her.

165   **Miss Hester was eleven years old when Brooklyn's schools began to desegregate:** *Hart v. Community School Board of Brooklyn*, New York School District #21, 497 F.2d 1027 (2nd Cir., 1974).

166   **winning a scholarship to SUNY Cortland:** SUNY Cortland staff.

166   **two master's degrees from Touro College in 2004:** Touro College database.

167   **her cousin once removed, Cakes, was shot dead:** Interviews with Chanel and Margo.

167   **Shakesha was raped and smothered by her boyfriend:** Wayne Toppin's Queens County Criminal Court records; Courtney Dentch, "Two murdered in separate Hollis disputes," QNS.com, March 27, 2003.

167   **Sheena, who graduated from Bates:** Bates College staff.

Chapter 20

170   **There is a lakeside camp in Upstate New York:** Camp Homeward Bound, Coalition for the Homeless.

174   **"She's living in a world and it's on fire":** Alicia Keys, "Girl on Fire," *Girl on Fire* (RCA, 2012).

175   **she can reap $10 per child in carfare through Medicaid:** In 2013, the Advanced Psy-

chotherapy and Behavioral Health Services clinic in Brooklyn was issuing carfare to patients covered by Medicaid. According to the state's Health Department, cash reimbursements through Medicaid for transportation costs are illegal.

177 **"Do you want to kill yourself?":** Interview with Khaliq.

Chapter 21

179 **the children skip school (as required by homeless services):** The city's long-standing policy, until 2016, was that all family members must be present at the intake office whenever a family was logged out or had to reapply for shelter after being found ineligible. Legal Aid Society.

180 **it was children who gave rise to America's modern welfare program:** By the late 1800s, the work of "child-saving" charities and Jacob Riis's seminal book, *How The Other Half Lives,* had sparked a public outcry over the plight of New York City's child vagrants. This was instrumental in shaping the Progressive movement's agenda, which led, in 1909, to the first White House Conference on the Care of Dependent Children—a meeting that birthed the "mother's pension" movement, America's first version of federal cash aid, laying the foundations of the modern welfare state. I have pieced together this sequence based on a wide literature, including Irwin Garfinkel and Sara S. McLanahan, *Single Mothers and Their Children: A New American Dilemma* (Washington, D.C.: Urban Institute, 1986), p. 101; Dorothy Roberts, *Shattered Bonds: The Color of Child Welfare* (New York: Basic Books, 2009), p. 174; Libba Gage Moore, "Mothers' Pensions: The Origins of the Relationship Between Women and the Welfare State" (Ph.D. dissertation, University of Massachusetts, 1986), p. 1; and *Proceedings of the Conference on the Care of Dependent Children Held at Washington D.C., January 25, 26, 1909* (Washington, D.C.: U.S. Government Printing Office, 1909), p. 5.

181 **the "worthy" and the "unworthy":** John E. Hansan, "Poor Relief in the Early America," Social Welfare History Project, Virginia Commonwealth University, accessed Feb. 26, 2021.

181 **By the nineteenth century, a new system emerged:** David M. Schneider and Albert Deutsch, *The History of Public Welfare in New York State, 1867–1940* (Montclair, N.J.: Patterson Smith, 1969), p. 8.

181 **where a staggering 3.6 million immigrants:** Robert Ernst, *Immigrant Life in New York City, 1825–1863* (Syracuse, N.Y.: Syracuse University Press, 1994), p. 187, appendix II, table 7.

181 **a term that morphed into "tenements":** Staller, *New York's Newsboys,* pp. 78–79.

181 **"One young immigrant described how his family of eight":** Ibid., p. 81.

181 **forming a children's world:** "Unlike today, the teeming milieu of the New York streets in the mid-nineteenth century was in large part a children's world." Christine Stansell, "Women, Children and the Uses of the Streets: Classes and Gender Conflict in New York City: 1850–1860," *Feminist Studies* 8, no. 2 (1982), p. 312.

181 **as many as thirty thousand homeless children wandered the city:** Timothy J. Gilfoyle, "Street-Rats and Gutter-Snipes: Child Pickpockets and Street Culture in New York City, 1850–1900," *Journal of Social History* 37, no. 4 (2004), p. 855.

181 **a wayward tribe of "street Arabs," "waifs," and "gutter snipes":** Robert G. Waite, "'Street Arabs, Gutter Snipes, Waifs': The Problem of Wayward, Abandoned and Destitute Children in New York City, 1840–1920," *New York History Review,* July 11, 2012.

181 **a phrase coined by Mark Twain:** Mark Twain and Charles Dudley Warner, *The Gilded Age: A Tale of To-day* (Hartford: American Publishing Company, 1873); Tracy Wuster, "'There's Millions in It!': *The Gilded Age* and the Economy of Satire," *The Mark Twain Annual* 11, no. 1 (2013), p. 1.

182 **with half of the nation's wealth concentrated in the hands of the one percent:** Michael D'Antonio, *Hershey: Milton S. Hershey's Extraordinary Life of Wealth, Empire,*

and Utopian Dreams (New York: Simon and Schuster, 2006), p. 86; Edward T. O'Donnell, "Are We Living in the Gilded Age 2.0?," History.com, June 15, 2018.

182 **in the "seat of the empire":** "From George Washington to James Duane, 10 April 1785," Founders Online, National Archives, accessed Feb. 26, 2021.

182 **who came to be known as the father of American foster care:** Daphne Eviatar, "Suffer the Children," *The Nation*, May 10, 2001.

182 **launching a movement to "place out" New York's street children:** Staller, *New York's Newsboys*, p. 18.

182 **As many as two hundred thousand children boarded these trains:** Rebecca S. Trammell, "Orphan Train Myths and Legal Reality," *The Modern American* 5, no. 2 (2009), p. 4.

182 **were leaving white "ignorant Roman-Catholic" families:** In 1872, Charles Loring Brace wrote, "To all words of spiritual warning or help there came the chilling formalism of the ignorant Roman Catholic in reply, implying that certain outward acts made the soul right with its creator." *The Dangerous Classes of New York, and Twenty Years' Work Among Them* (New York: Wynkoop and Hallenbeck, 1872), p. 154.

182 **"a good home in the West":** Ibid., p. 234.

182 **worked in arrangements reeking of indentured servitude:** Trammell, "Orphan Train Myths and Legal Reality," p. 6; Joyce, "Crime of Parenting While Poor."

182 **"emigration as a cure for pauperism":** Brace, *Dangerous Classes of New York*, p. 245.

182 **Most of these children were not even orphans:** Bernstein, *Lost Children of Wilder*, p. 198; Stansell, "Women, Children and the Uses of the Streets," pp. 320, 327; Staller, *New York's Newsboys*, pp. 19–20.

182 **about 93,000 children were living in orphanages and as many as 75,000 more in foster homes or facilities for juvenile delinquents:** *Proceedings of the Conference*, p. 5.

182 **On January 25, 1909, some two hundred charity workers:** Trammell, "Orphan Train Myths and Legal Reality," p. 8; *Proceedings of the Conference*, p. 20.

182 **"There can be no more important subject from the standpoint of the nation":** *Proceedings of the Conference*, p. 35.

182 **Most of the nation's Black children still lived in the South:** William C. Hunt, U.S. Department of Commerce, *Thirteenth Census of the United States Taken in the Year 1910*, vol. 1: *Population 1910: General Report and Analysis* (Washington, D.C.: Government Printing Office, 1913), p. 135.

182 **one of only two African Americans included at the conference:** Andrew Billingsley and Jeanne M. Giovannoni, *Children of the Storm: Black Children and American Child Welfare* (New York: Harcourt, 1972), p. 72.

183 **"The negro, in some way, has inherited":** *Proceedings of the Conference*, p. 115.

183 **children had been treated like miniature adults:** Children's Bureau, Administration for Children and Families, U.S. Department of Health and Human Services, "Centennial Series: An Evolving View of Childhood," *Children's Bureau Express* 12, no. 4 (2011).

183 **The "work" of young children was to play:** Carolyn Ann Williams-Roberson, "Granville Stanley Hall on the Education of the Elementary School Child" (Ph.D. dissertation, Loyola University Chicago, 1994), p. 52.

183 **"Century of the Child":** Ellen Key, *The Century of the Child* (New York: G. P. Putnam's Sons, 1909).

183 **"should not be broken up for reasons of poverty":** *Proceedings of the Conference*, p. 193.

183 **Roosevelt's meeting spurred a national movement:** Garfinkel and McLanahan, *Single Mothers and Their Children*, pp. 97–99; *Proceedings of the Conference*, p. 9.

183 **America's first welfare mothers were overwhelmingly white:** Garfinkel and McLanahan, *Single Mothers and Their Children*, p. 99; Moore, "Mothers' Pensions," p. 157;

U.S. Department of Labor and the Children's Bureau, *Mother's Aid, 1931: Bureau Publication No. 220* (Washington, D.C.: Government Printing Office, 1933), p. 10.

183 **by 1971, when Dasani's grandmother Joanie walked into a welfare office:** Interview with Margo. (HRA could not locate Joanie's welfare records prior to 1987).

183 **created by President Franklin D. Roosevelt in 1935:** Garfinkel and McLanahan, *Single Mothers and Their Children*, p. 87.

183 **greatly expanded three decades later by the Great Society legislation:** Garfinkel and McLanahan, *Single Mothers and Their Children*, p. 111.

184 **Black women had to fight to join welfare's rolls:** Gene Demby, "The Mothers Who Fought to Radically Reimagine Welfare," NPR.com, June 9, 2019; Moore, "Mothers' Pensions," p. 114.

184 **became the base for a national welfare rights movement:** Jason DeParle, *American Dream: Three Women, Ten Kids, and a Nation's Drive to End Welfare* (New York: Penguin Books, 2004), p. 89.

184 **By 1975, 11 million Americans were receiving welfare cash:** Gilbert Crouse et al., *Welfare Indicators and Risk Factors: Thirteenth Report to Congress* (Washington, D.C.: Office of Human Services Policy, U.S. Department of Health and Human Services, 2014), pp. II-12, table IND 3a.

184 **Black families made up 44 percent of this group:** For 44 percent: Howard Oberheu, "Studies of the Characteristics of AFDC Recipients," *Social Security Bulletin* 40, no. 9 (1977), p. 18; for less than 10 percent: Gordon W. Green, Jr., Renee H. Miller, and John F. Coder, "Money Income and Poverty Status of Families and Persons in the United States: 1975 and 1974 Revisions," *Current Population Reports*, series P60-103(RV), advance report (Washington, D.C.: U.S. Government Printing Office, 1976), pp. 9–10.

184 **"In Chicago, they found a woman who holds the record":** "The Truth Behind the Lies of the Original 'Welfare Queen,'" *All Things Considered*, NPR, Dec. 20, 2013.

184 **she was identified as Linda Taylor:** Josh Levin, *The Queen: The Forgotten Life Behind an American Myth* (New York: Little, Brown, 2019).

184 **whose own welfare assistance would peak at $650 monthly:** Joanie's HRA records.

184 **By 1991, New York's welfare rolls were approaching one million:** Paul Lopatto, "New Yorkers Receiving Cash Assistance: A Nearly 60-Year Low?," New York City Independent Budget Office, Aug. 20, 2019.

184 **welfare was costing taxpayers an estimated $13 billion a year:** *Aid to Families with Dependent Children: The Baseline* (Washington, D.C.: U.S. Department of Health and Human Services, 1998), p. 64, Table 4.2.

184 **vow to "end welfare as we know it":** DeParle, *American Dream*, p. 4.

185 **President Clinton signed the Personal Responsibility and Work Opportunity Reconciliation Act:** "The Personal Responsibility and Work Opportunity Reconciliation Act of 1996," Office of the Assistant Secretary for Planning and Evaluation, U.S. Department of Health and Human Services, Sept. 1, 1996.

185 **facing time limits on cash and a mandate to look for work:** Center on Budget and Policy Priorities, *Policy Basics: Temporary Assistance for Needy Families* (Washington, D.C., Center on Budget and Policy Priorities, 2020), p. 4.

185 **from "Income Support Centers" to "Job Centers":** Rebecca L. Scharf et al., "The Wages of Welfare Reform: A Report on New York City's Job Centers," *Scholarly Works* 54, no. 4 (1999), p. 473.

185 **declaring the welfare system too "user friendly":** Mayor Rudolph Giuliani, "Reaching Out to All New Yorkers by Restoring Work to the Center of City Life" (speech, New York, N.Y., July 20, 1998), accessed via nyc.gov.

185 **new sanctions created a culture of deterrence:** Helen Strom and Afua Atta-Mensah, *Culture of Deterrence: Voices of NYC Public Assistance Recipients* (New York: Safety Net Project, Urban Justice Center, 2014).

185   more than 6 million Americans—mostly women and children—had left welfare's rolls: In 1996, around 12 million people received monthly cash welfare benefits. By 2001, that number had dropped by more than half, to around 5.6 million. Crouse et al, *Welfare Indicators*, p. A-7, table TANF 2.

185   In New York City, the rolls had dropped by more than half: Nina Bernstein, "Manhattan: New Welfare Report," *New York Times*, Aug. 24, 2001.

186   New York, one of the nation's archetypal "safety net" states: Lynne Fender et al., *Assessing the New Federalism State Update No. 12: Recent Changes in New York Welfare and Work, Child Care, and Child Welfare Systems* (Washington, D.C.: Urban Institute, 2002), pp. 4–5.

186   New Yorkers have greater access to public healthcare, food stamps: Adam McCann, "States with the Most and Least Medicaid Coverage," *WalletHub*, accessed Feb. 26, 2021; E. J. McMahon, "NY Ranks High in Welfare Benefits," Empire Center for Public Policy, Aug. 19, 2013.

186   New York City is the only American metropolis that guarantees the legal right to shelter: Legal Aid Society and Coalition for the Homeless.

186   Chanel offers to "punch that bitch in the face": Family's DHS file.

Chapter 22

192   It has a limited partnership with Nike: Nike Inc.

194   Giant went to prison in 1989 on two felony convictions: Interview with Giant and criminal records.

195   joined by Malcolm X's grandson, Malik: Kia Gregory and Damien Cave, "Troubled Life in Malcolm X's Shadow Comes to a Violent End," *New York Times*, May 10, 2013.

198   Much of his wrath is reserved for six-year-old Papa: Interviews with children.

Chapter 23

200   Supreme's first memories are of dark spaces: This chapter is based on interviews with Supreme as well as on his school, ACS, criminal court, drug treatment, and medical records, his parents' child protection records, his grandmother's death certificate, and his sister's autopsy report.

200   an assailant burst into her home and shot her seven times: Supreme's grandmother's death certificate.

201   That year alone, 514 people were murdered in Brooklyn: *Homicide Analysis 1983* (New York: Crime Analysis Unit, Office of Management Analysis and Planning, NYPD), p. 2.

204   a jury had acquitted the Florida man: Lizette Alvarez and Cara Buckley, "Zimmerman Is Acquitted in Trayvon Martin Killing," *New York Times*, July 13, 2013.

204   whose death would spark the Black Lives Matter movement: Karen Grigsby Bates, "A Look Back at Trayvon Martin's Death, and the Movement It Inspired," NPR.com, July 31, 2018.

204   In the previous twelve years, officers had stopped and frisked more than 5 million New Yorkers: Christopher Dunn, "Stop & Frisk During the Bloomberg Administration 2002–2013" (New York: New York City Liberties Union, 2014) ed. Jennifer Carnig, p. 1.

204   most of them people of color from the city's poorest neighborhoods: Dunn, "Stop & Frisk During the Bloomberg Administration," pp. 4–5.

205   the city's stop-and-frisk practice is racially targeted: Joseph Goldstein, "Judge Rejects New York's Stop-and-Frisk Policy," *New York Times*, Aug. 12, 2013.

205   As Bloomberg vows to appeal the ruling: Ibid.

205   "end a stop-and-frisk era that unfairly targets people of color": NYForDeBlasio, "New Yorkers for de Blasio TV Ad: 'Dante,'" YouTube, Aug. 8, 2013, video.

205 **A nurse notes that he is "neatly groomed":** Supreme's Cornerstone of Medical Arts Center records.

Chapter 24

207 **"My baby's not breathing!":** Interviews with Aisha Whitlock (the mother of the deceased baby), Dasani, her siblings, Chanel, and state officials; 911 records and a state inspection report.
207 **assigning the family to a room that reached 102 degrees:** OTDA.
207 **Auburn's fire safety system is virtually inoperable:** Ibid.
207 **No young child with chronic breathing problems:** Report of Inspection by OTDA, Nov. 15, 2013.
209 **leading Chanel and her children into the store's private jail:** Interview with Chanel and the children; police records. Macy's declined to comment.
209 **the police take Chanel into custody:** Chanel's criminal records.
210 **federal law gives homeless children the right to stay in one school:** *Education of Homeless Children & Youth: The Guide to Their Rights* (Washington, D.C.: National Law Center on Homelessness and Poverty, 2011), p. 4.
211 **Bill de Blasio will win by a landslide:** "Election 2013: New York City Mayor," *New York Times*, Nov. 6, 2013.
211 **restoring Democratic Party rule to New York City:** Matt Flegenheimer, "How Bill de Blasio Went from Progressive Hope to Punching Bag," *New York Times Magazine*, Aug. 6, 2019.
212 *The New York Times* **publishes the first installment:** Andrea Elliott, "Invisible Child: Girl in the Shadows: Dasani's Homeless Life," *New York Times*, Dec. 9, 2013.
212 **"get to work on this right away":** Chester Soria, "De Blasio Picks City Govt Vet to Be Deputy Mayor for Health and Human Services," *Gotham Gazette*, Dec. 12, 2013.
212 **while privately expressing fury that the** *Times* **has tarnished his legacy:** A senior aide to Bloomberg.
212 **"This kid was dealt a bad hand":** Colin Campbell and Ross Barkan, "Bloomberg Defends Homeless Policies While Calling Dasani Story 'Extremely Atypical,'" *Observer*, Dec. 17, 2013.
212 **a rebuttal to the series in** *The Wall Street Journal:* Howard Wolfson and Linda Gibbs, "Bloomberg's Real Antipoverty Record," *Wall Street Journal*, Dec. 17, 2013.
212 **it dropped and then rose again after 2008:** According to Wimer's analysis of census data, the New York City poverty rate was 20.1 in 2002, dropped in 2005 to 19, rose the next year to 19.2, and then declined before rising again in 2009, after the Great Recession. The city's poverty rate returned to 20.1 in 2010.
212 **a million people had joined the city's food stamp rolls:** HRA data.
212 **which has created a trust for the children:** The "Invisible Child Trust" is managed by the CLC Foundation in Mount Kisco, New York.
213 **The school has taken heat from education officials:** Interview with Holmes.
213 **putting "the face of poverty":** Ross Barkan, "Dasani Drama: New York Times Denies Public Advocate Played Role in Dasani Story," *Observer*, Jan. 2, 2014.
214 **"This is Dasani Coates":** NYC Mayor's Office, "2014 New York City Inauguration," YouTube, Jan. 1, 2014, video.
214 **"When I'm in the White House":** Interviews with Dasani and Chanel.
215 **the city will remove more than four hundred children from Auburn:** Andrea Elliott and Rebecca R. Ruiz, "New York Is Removing over 400 Children from 2 Homeless Shelters," *New York Times*, Feb. 21, 2014.
215 **With the city's homeless population approaching a record sixty thousand:** In January 2014, there were 59,690 people staying in the five shelter systems administered by New York City agencies; nearly 53,000 of these people were in DHS shelters.

Chapter 25

216 **has just been suspended from P.S. 200:** Letter from Papa's school, shown to me by Chanel.

216 **missed an "employment-related appointment":** Chanel's HRA records.

216 **although she was never notified of any such requirement:** A review of Chanel's HRA records shows that the city's welfare agency failed to notify her of any employment-related appointment.

217 **De Blasio has cleared the way for universal prekindergarten:** William Neuman, "De Blasio Finds Biggest Win in Pre-K, but Also Lasting Consequences," *New York Times*, Oct. 31, 2017.

217 **recruited to his ranks a former political rival, Steven Banks:** Matthew Chayes, "Long-time Critic Named to Head NYC's HRA," *Newsday*, Feb. 28, 2014.

217 **Banks will eventually assume responsibility of the city's shelter system:** "Meet the Commissioner," Department of Social Services, City of New York.

217 **"make our government work for New Yorkers who need a helping hand":** Mayor's Office press release, "With Three Appointments, Mayor de Blasio Builds Out Leadership Team Dedicated to Expanding Opportunity For More New Yorkers," City of New York, Feb. 28, 2014.

218 **an epic fight in which he broke the television and pulled out a knife:** Interview with Chanel.

219 **Goldfein is a staff attorney at Legal Aid:** All biographical details about Goldfein are from interviews with him and news articles.

219 **Derrick DeBruce, a Black inmate in Alabama:** Kelsey Stein, "Federal Appeals Court Orders New Sentencing for Alabama Death Row Inmate Convicted in 1991 Execution-Style Shooting in Talladega," AL.com, July 16, 2014.

219 **Six weeks from now, in July 2014, they will score a victory:** Ibid.

220 **"causing pain and swelling," according to the police:** The Office of the Deputy Commissioner, Public Information.

220 **to moonlight as a music critic for *The Village Voice*:** Music archives, *The Village Voice*, "Josh Goldfein," Nov. 10, 1998–May 16, 2006.

221 **Two-thirds of all children living in city shelters are chronically absent:** Liz Pappas, *Not Reaching the Door: Homeless Students Face Many Hurdles on the Way to School* (New York: New York City Independent Budget Office, 2016), pp. 4–5.

Chapter 26

226 **Starting at age four, they can attend for free:** Milton Hershey School staff.

226 **whose founder and CEO, Eva Moskowitz, is at war with the new mayor:** Daniel Bergner, "The Battle for New York Schools: Eva Moskowitz vs. Mayor Bill de Blasio," *New York Times Magazine*, Sept. 3, 2014.

226 **In March, Moskowitz closed her twenty-two charter schools:** Al Baker and Javier C. Hernández, "De Blasio and Operator of Charter School Empire Do Battle," *New York Times*, March 4, 2014; Eliza Shapiro, "City's Charter Movement Gets the Albany Day It Wanted," Politico, March 5, 2014.

226 **Cuomo announced a deal on the state budget:** Thomas Kaplan and Javier C. Hernández, "State Budget Deal Reached; $300 Million for New York City Pre-K," *New York Times*, March 29, 2014.

226 **her first large crop of seniors would graduate:** Success Academy spokesperson.

230 **the doctor concluded that he suffers from a mood disorder:** Supreme's medical records from Bellevue Hospital Center.

230 **had been fueled by Mayor Bloomberg's antismoking campaign:** Joseph Goldstein, "A Cigarette for 75 Cents, 2 for $1: The Brisk, Shady Sale of 'Loosies,'" *New York Times*,

April 4, 2011; Ryan Jaslow, "NYC Raises Smoking Age to 21, Sets Cigarette Pack Minimum Price at $10.50," CBS News, Nov. 19, 2013.

230   **the father of five children and two stepchildren:** Rich Schapiro and Dareh Gregorian, "Eric Garner's 1-Year-Old Daughter Will Never Be Accepted into His Family: Widow," *Daily News,* July 3, 2015; Al Baker, J. David Goodman, and Benjamin Mueller, "Beyond the Chokehold: The Path to Eric Garner's Death," *New York Times,* June 13, 2015.

233   **for $1.2 million (nearly double its value the previous year):** Property records for Hester's former address in Bedford-Stuyvesant.

233   **more than sixty-four thousand New Yorkers now in city shelters:** In September 2014, there were 64,759 people staying in the five shelter systems administered by New York City agencies; more than 57,000 of these people were in DHS shelters.

233   **The city's lack of affordable housing is the primary reason:** In 2014, eviction was the number one reason people entered the city's shelter system, according to DHS. "The primary forces driving New York City's homelessness problem are similar to those in other urban areas of the U.S.: poverty and a lack of affordable housing": Mayor's Office, "Turning the Tide on Homelessness in New York City" (Office of the Deputy Mayor for Health and Human Services and the Department of Social Services, 2017), p. 3.

234   **But most of the rent will be covered by the voucher:** Family's HPD records.

Chapter 27

236   **"It was the third of September":** The Temptations, "Papa Was a Rollin' Stone," *All Directions* (Gordy, 1972).

237   **Nearly half of the neighborhood's residents live below the poverty line:** 91 Laurel Avenue is located in Staten Island's Census Tract 29, where 45 percent of 4,674 families had incomes below the federal poverty level in 2014–2018. Analysis of the 2014–2018 data from the Census Bureau's American Community Survey.

238   **a grand jury declines to indict the white officer:** Monica Davey and Julie Bosman, "Protests Flare After Ferguson Police Officer Not Indicted," *New York Times,* Nov. 24, 2014.

238   **The officer charged in Eric Garner's death is spared indictment:** J. David Goodman and Al Baker, "Wave of Protests After Grand Jury Doesn't Indict Officer in Eric Garner Chokehold Case," *New York Times,* Dec. 3, 2014.

238   **marching to the Barclays Center:** Christopher Robbins, "Photos: Protesters Attempt 'Royal Shutdown' Outside Barclays Center," *Gothamist,* Dec. 9, 2014.

241   **There are thirty-seven such schools in New York City:** DOE spokesperson; Anna Sussman, "Suspension Trap," Type Investigations, April 28, 2011.

241   **Mount Loretto in Staten Island:** David Bird, "Grim Life of Newsboys in the 1800's Depicted in Trade Center Show," *New York Times,* Dec. 12, 1997.

Chapter 28

246   **with a population of 14,500:** World Population Review data, 2021.

247   **that draws more than 3 million visitors yearly:** Tsz Yin (Gigi) Au et al., *2016 Theme Index and Museum Index: Global Attractions Attendance Report,* ed. Judith Rubin (California: Themed Entertainment Association and AECOM, 2017), p. 31.

247   **Milton Hershey had a troubled childhood:** My depiction of Hershey's life is based on interviews with Susan Alger, the Milton Hershey School historian, and on two books: D'Antonio, *Hershey* and James D. McMahon, Jr., *Milton Hershey School* (Charleston, S.C.: Arcadia Publishing, 2007). See also *The Man Behind the Chocolate Bar: An Introduction to Milton S. Hershey 1857–1945* (Hershey: The Hershey Story, The Museum on Chocolate Avenue).

247   **Fanny took to "stripping" the neighbors' cows:** D'Antonio, *Hershey,* p. 14.

247   **Milton went hungry at times, or lacked proper shoes:** Ibid., pp. 21–26.

248 **opened a candy shop near Hell's Kitchen:** Interview with Alger; D'Antonio, *Hershey*, p. 50.

248 **where ragged children:** Jacob A. Riis, *How The Other Half Lives* (New York: Charles Scribner's Sons, 1890).

248 **There were no federal laws:** Child Welfare Information Gateway, "About CAPTA: A Legislative History" (Washington, D.C.: U.S. Department of Health and Human Services, Children's Bureau, 2019), p. 1.

248 **the Manhattan case of nine-year-old Mary Ellen:** There are varying accounts of Mary Ellen's age. The facts of her case are taken from Eric A. Shelman and Stephen Lazoritz, *The Mary Ellen Wilson Child Abuse Case and the Beginning of Children's Rights in 19th Century America* (Jefferson, N.C.: McFarland, 2005); Lela B. Costin, "Unraveling the Mary Ellen Legend: Origins of the 'Cruelty' Movement," *Social Service Review* 65, no. 2 (1991), pp. 203–23; Sallie A. Watkins, "The Mary Ellen Myth: Correcting Child Welfare History," *Social Work* 35, no. 6 (1990), pp. 500–503.

248 **no government office tasked with preventing child abuse:** Lela B. Costin, Howard Jacob Karger, and David Stoesz, *The Politics of Child Abuse in America* (New York: Oxford University Press, 1997), pp. 207, 219.

248 **leading to the creation of the first nongovernmental organization:** The New York Society for the Prevention of Cruelty to Children.

249 **"especially for children":** Charles W. Lobdell, "Hershey," *Liberty Magazine*, Sept. 13, 1924, p. 48.

249 **"If you want to make money":** "Milton Snavely Hershey in Philadelphia, 1876–1882," Hershey Community Archives, Sept. 6, 2018.

249 **No one knew how to make this delicacy affordable:** D'Antonio, *Hershey*, pp. 48, 95–96.

249 **milk chocolate required binding two incompatible ingredients:** D'Antonio, *Hershey*, p. 95.

249 **In 1897, Milton bought the property for $10,311:** Interview with Alger.

249 **His breakthrough came in 1900:** Hershey sold his first "Hershey bar" in 1900, according to Alger. A second breakthrough came in 1903, when he perfected his milk chocolate recipe with the help of John Schmalbach. D'Antonio, *Hershey*, p. 107.

249 **Milton sold his caramel company for $1 million:** D'Antonio, *Hershey*, p. 90.

249 **selling for five cents apiece:** Ibid., p. 114.

250 **"the Henry Ford of chocolate":** John Luciew, "The Hershey Co. Prepares to Break Ties with Iconic Past to Ensure Survival," PennLive.com, June 2, 2010.

250 **marrying Catherine "Kitty" Sweeney:** D'Antonio, *Hershey*, pp. 80–81, 145.

250 **modeled after the village built by the Cadbury chocolate family:** Jonathan Birchall, "Hershey's legacy is a sweet story," *Financial Times*, Dec. 4, 2009.

250 **while abstaining from any "offensive purpose or occupation":** D'Antonio, *Hershey*, p. 116.

250 **Milton's ultimate experiment and proudest legacy:** "But the school was his proudest achievement." Daniel Golden, "What Were Milton Hershey's Wishes? Question Hinders His Wealthy School," *Wall Street Journal*, Aug. 12, 1999.

250 **"poor, healthy, white, male orphans":** Hershey Industrial School Deed of Trust, 1909, provided by Scullin.

250 **"Those boys must grow up with the feeling that they have a real home":** Alexander Gottlieb, "An Old-Fashioned Millionaire," *Brooklyn Daily Eagle*, Feb. 17, 1929. (All other references to "Gottlieb" in the notes are to Chris Gottlieb of NYU.)

250 **the first crop of orphans, ages four to eight:** Interview with Alger; D'Antonio, *Hershey*.

251 **in 1923, Milton gave $60 million:** "M. S. Hershey Gives $60,000,000 Trust for an Orphanage," *New York Times*, Nov. 9, 1923.

251 **"It's a sin for a man to die rich":** D'Antonio, *Hershey*, p. 128.

251   **More than nine thousand children have graduated:** All facts about the Hershey school, unless otherwise noted, pertain to 2015 (the year that Dasani enrolled) and were provided by the school's administrators.

251   **which can be spent only on the school:** Hershey Industrial School Deed of Trust.

251   **was valued at $12.2 billion:** The trust had grown to $17,587,508,487 by 2020; IRS Forms 990 (federal nonprofit tax returns) for 2015 and 2020, Milton Hershey School and School Trust.

251   **the Milton Hershey School has little regulatory oversight:** Mark Rosenman, "The Chocolate Trust: Deception, Indenture and Secrets at the $12 Billion Milton Hershey School," *Philanthropy News Digest*, June 5, 2015; D'Antonio, *Hershey*, p. 250.

251   **the school's academic program weakened and enrollment declined:** D'Antonio, *Hershey*, p. 250.

252   **spent more than $250 million revamping the campus:** Ibid.

252   **when the trust bought a $12 million golf course:** Bob Fernandez, "Hershey School's Purchase of Golf Course Helped Investors," *Philadelphia Inquirer*, Oct. 3, 2010.

252   **A probe by the state attorney general:** Paul Smith, "Attorney General Announces Milton Hershey Trust and Milton Hershey School Reforms," FOX 43, May 8, 2013; Nick Malawskey, "Pennsylvania's Attorney General: No penalties, but Reforms for Hershey Trust," PennLive.com, May 9, 2013.

252   **More than two thousand children live in suburban-looking villages:** In addition to data provided by Lisa Scullin, a senior administrator of the Milton Hershey School, descriptions of the school are based on my direct observation and on interviews with Dasani, Hershey's houseparents, students, alumni, administrators, teachers, coaches, and other staff.

252   **earns $17,207, well below the federal poverty line:** In 2015, the federal poverty line for a family of four was $24,257, according to 2015 census data.

252   **Hundreds of students have avoided foster care by enrolling at Hershey:** Interview with Scullin.

253   **the richest private school for children in America:** Bob Fernandez, "No Candy-Coating Lack of Charity at Hershey School," *Philadelphia Inquirer*, Nov. 6, 2016.

253   **tuition at Phillips Exeter Academy is 45 percent less:** In the 2014–15 academic year, tuition at Phillips Exeter Academy was $46,030. "Phillips Exeter Academy Financial Report 2015," p. 6.

253   **Gurt grew up at the Hershey school:** Interview with Scullin.

256   **Tabitha is standing near her forty-two-year-old husband:** All biographical details about the McQuiddys are from interviews with Tabitha and Jason McQuiddy.

Chapter 29

258   **Dasani lies awake:** During Dasani's enrollment at Hershey, I made fourteen trips to see her. Most of the scenes I describe are from direct observation. This scene and a few others were reconstructed from interviews with Dasani and, when possible, corroborated by passages from her daily journal, texts, emails, photos, and video, in addition to ACS case notes and interviews with students and staff at the school.

260   **came to Hershey in 2006 after his father tried to kill his mother:** Hershey administrators.

261   **"I think it's getting to the point":** Barenaked Ladies, "Call and Answer," *Stunt* (Reprise Records, 1998).

262   **the local public schools had high ratings:** In 2007, the *Pittsburgh Business Times* ranked the Derry Township School District twenty-third out of the 498 public school districts in Pennsylvania: "Three of Top School Districts in State Hail from Allegheny County," *Pittsburgh Business Times*, May 23, 2007.

263   **fourteen-year-old Abbie Bartels:** Details about Abbie Bartels are based on court

records, my correspondence with a lawyer for the Bartels family, news articles, and interviews with a senior school administrator.

263 **threatened to hurt herself:** A senior Hershey administrator, citing court records from *Wartluft v. Milton Hershey Sch.*, Civil No. 1:16-CV-2145 (Middle District, Pennsylvania, 2020).

263 **"high level of need currently beyond our programming":** Ibid.

264 **"serious emotional and behavioral problems":** When Dasani enrolled at Hershey in 2015, the school did not accept students with "serious emotional and behavioral problems," according to its website. By 2020, the website stated that students must "be free of serious behavioral problems that are likely to disrupt life in the classroom or student home life at MHS."

264 **Only a third of the students are in psychotherapy, and 14 percent take psychotropic medications:** Interview with Scullin.

264 **the McQuiddys and their two sons drove to her house:** Interview with a senior Hershey administrator, corroborated by a lawyer for Bartels. (Due to ongoing litigation, the Hershey school did not allow the McQuiddys to comment on the case.)

264 **after missing several days of medication while in her family's care:** A senior Hershey administrator, citing court records from *Wartluft v. Milton Hershey Sch.*

264 **a lawsuit by her family, and a segment on CNN:** Bob Fernandez, "Judge Dismisses Case Against Hershey School in Girl's Death," *Philadelphia Inquirer*, March 19, 2020; "14 year old Abbie Bartels hung herself one year ago after being banned from graduation," YouTube, July 4, 2014; *Anderson Cooper 360*, CNN, July 1, 2014.

264 **Critics of the school find its rules draconian:** Hershey's most prominent critic is Ric Fouad, an alumnus whose nonprofit "Protect the Hersheys' Children" seeks to reform the school.

264 **one in ten children:** Interview with Scullin.

266 **In the 1982 film:** *Annie*, directed by John Huston (United States: Columbia Pictures, 1982).

266 **a new *Annie* premiered:** *Annie*, directed by Will Gluck (United States: Columbia Pictures, 2014).

267 **The only person to see Papa leave:** My account of Papa's departure is based on interviews with Papa, video of him retracing his steps the day after he ran away, as well as on interviews with Papa's parents, siblings, and school principal, in addition to Richmond University Medical Center records, ACS investigative notes, and my direct observation of Papa in the hospital.

268 **Bruschi (who is white) grew up in Stapleton:** Interview with Lou Bruschi.

268 **when much of the neighborhood was Italian American:** Alan S. Oser, "Stapleton," *New York Times*, June 6, 1982; Michael J. Fressola, "Beyond Meatballs and Big Ang: The Italian Tale of Staten Island to Be Examined at CFA," SILive.com, Sept. 23, 2014.

269 **the vast majority of Bruschi's students are from poor Black or Latino families:** In the 2014–15 academic year, the student population at P.S. 78 was 43 percent Black, 49 percent Hispanic, and more than 93 percent of all students were living in poverty. 2011–2016 Demographic Snapshot data accessed via New York City's "Open Data" website: opendata.cityofnewyork.us, Oct. 9, 2018.

269 **a nickel-sized wound in his scalp:** ACS records.

269 **about fifty students at any given time are being monitored by the agency:** Interview with Bruschi. While ACS did not disclose the number of active cases at this school, an agency official said that between 2016 and 2019, P.S. 78 made an average of 31 yearly reports of suspected child abuse or neglect. In any given year, that would comprise about one in 25 of the school's students, but this does not include students with former ACS cases or those with active ACS cases who have enrolled at the school.

269 **the second-highest number of children citywide:** In 2015, nearly fifty thousand chil-

dren were enrolled in ACS-contracted preventive services in New York City. The North Shore's "Staten Island Community District 1," where Dasani's family lived, had 2,062 children enrolled in preventive services. This was the second highest number in the city, after East New York's community district, "Brooklyn 5," which had 2,215 children enrolled.

269 **with 20 percent quitting ACS after their first year:** On average, another nine percent of ACS caseworkers leave in their second year and 3.5 percent leave in their third year. The median length for caseworkers is between four and five years. ACS data.

270 **The officers agree:** ACS and hospital records.

270 **"What happens if you do something bad?":** ACS records.

Chapter 30

276 **psychologist Abraham Maslow, who in 1943 created the "Hierarchy of Needs":** A. H. Maslow, "A Theory of Human Motivation," *Psychological Review* 50, no. 4 (1943), pp. 370–96.

277 **when chocolate sales had slipped and Hershey's employees needed work:** "Milton S. Hershey: The Man Behind the Chocolate," Milton Hershey School's website, accessed March 2, 2021; D'Antonio, *Hershey*, p. 197.

278 **Poor children tend to live with chronic stress:** Johannes Haushofer and Ernst Fehr, "On the psychology of poverty," *Science* 344, no. 6186 (2011), pp. 862–67; Martha E. Wadsworth et al., "An Indirect Effects Model of the Association Between Poverty and Child Functioning: The Role of Children's Poverty-Related Stress," *Journal of Loss and Trauma* 13, no. 2-3 (2008), pp. 156–85; Catherine DeCarlo Santiago, Martha E. Wadsworth, and Jessica Stump, "Socioeconomic Status, Neighborhood Disadvantage, and Poverty-Related Stress: Prospective Effects on Psychological Syndromes Among Diverse Low-Income Families," *Journal of Economic Psychology* 32, no. 2 (2011), pp. 218–30; Daniel Brisson et al., "A Systematic Review of the Association Between Poverty and Biomarkers of Toxic Stress," *Journal of Evidence-Based Social Work* 17, no. 6 (2020), pp. 696–713.

279 **the brain scans of seventy-seven infants:** Jamie L. Hanson et al., "Family Poverty Affects the Rate of Human Infant Brain Growth," *PLOS ONE* 8, no. 12 (2013); interview with Pollak.

279 **Chronic stress also produces higher amounts of cortisol:** Christopher F. Sharpley, James R. McFarland, and Andrzej Slominski, "Stress-Linked Cortisol Concentrations in Hair: What We Know and What We Need to Know," *Reviews in the Neurosciences* 23, no. 1 (2011), p. 112.

279 **known for pioneering the "growth mindset":** Carol S. Dweck, *Mindset: The New Psychology of Success* (New York: Random House, 2006).

279 **when children think that their intellectual abilities can improve:** Interview with Dweck.

280 **Kali grew up on the outskirts of Philadelphia:** Interview with Kali.

285 **Julie spent her childhood in Chambersburg:** Interview with Julie Williams.

286 **"a very engaging and outgoing young lady":** During Dasani's enrollment at Hershey, I did not attend any of her counseling sessions or talk to her about these sessions. My description of Dasani's relationship with Julie Williams is based on interviews with Dasani and Julie in 2020, three years after their therapeutic relationship ended. This quote is from Julie's "summary of psychotherapy" which was provided to me by Dasani—not by the Hershey school.

289 **the "parentified" child:** Linda Burton, "Childhood Adultification in Economically Disadvantaged Families: A Conceptual Model," *Family Relations* 56, no. 4 (2007), pp. 329–45; Gregory J. Jurkovic, *Lost Childhoods: The Plight of the Parentified Child* (New York: Routledge, 2014), pp. 51, 53.

289 **firstborn children tend to take on:** Interview with child psychiatrist Lea DeFrancisci Lis.

Chapter 31

291 **built in 1931 as a "children's court":** Department of Citywide Administrative Services, City of New York.

291 **a child protection system:** Among experts, "child welfare" and "child protection" are used interchangeably to describe the public system that investigates suspected abuse or neglect, monitors families, and provides services including foster care. In this book, I describe this system as "child protection" to avoid confusion with the general welfare system.

291 **"Madam," says the judge:** Family court transcript, March 27, 2015.

292 **has three major players:** Tobis, *From Pariahs to Partners*, p. 5.

292 **enter this system with one anonymous tip:** Interviews with child protection advocates, lawyers, and ACS officials.

292 **a "preponderance" of evidence:** This was the evidentiary standard used in New York's family court until 2020. For the change in standard, see Chris Gottlieb, "Major Reform of New York's Child Abuse and Maltreatment Register," *New York Law Journal*, May 26, 2020.

292 **54,302 investigations:** Data provided by ACS.

293 **will remove 3,232 children:** Ibid.

293 **more than 94 percent of whom are Black, Hispanic, Asian, or "other":** Ibid.

293 **Over half of all Black children in America are subjected to at least one child protection probe before turning eighteen:** According to research drawn from 2015 census data and a federal database of neglect and abuse cases. Hyunil Kim et al., "Lifetime Prevalence of Investigating Child Maltreatment Among US Children," *American Journal of Public Health* 107, no. 2 (2017), p. 277.

293 **They are 2.4 times more likely than whites:** Christopher Wildeman, Frank R. Edwards, and Sara Wakefield, "The Cumulative Prevalence of Termination of Parental Rights for U.S. Children, 2000–2016," *Child Maltreatment* 25, no. 1 (2020), p. 33.

293 **a foster care population of more than 427,000 children:** U.S. Department of Health and Human Services, *The AFCARS Report: Preliminary Estimates for FY 2016 as of Oct 20, 2017* (Washington, D.C.: Office of the Administration for Children and Families, Children's Bureau, U.S. Department of Health and Human Services, 2017), p. 1.

293 **nicknamed this practice Jane Crow:** Stephanie Clifford and Jessica Silver-Greenberg, "Foster Care as Punishment: The New Reality of 'Jane Crow,'" *New York Times*, July 21, 2017.

293 **the "targeted" child:** "Childhood Maltreatment Among Children with Disabilities," Centers for Disease Control and Prevention, U.S. Department of Health and Human Services, Sept. 18, 2019; Alice Kenny, "The Cinderella Phenomenon: When One Child Is the Target of Abuse," ACEsConnection, July 10, 2020.

294 **A sixty-six-year-old native of Manhattan:** All biographical details about Judge Arnold Lim were provided to me in emails from the judge, via his former clerk.

294 **a public interest law firm represents the majority of poor parents:** In New York City, parents can be represented, free of charge, by one of four public interest law firms: The Bronx Defenders, Brooklyn Defender Services, the Center for Family Representation, and the Neighborhood Defender Service of Harlem, or else by private attorneys who are members of the Assigned Counsel Plan (18-B Panel). Children are assigned an attorney free of charge, mainly from the Legal Aid Society, but also from Lawyers for Children, the Children's Law Center, or the 18-B panel (attorneys in private practice). Interview with attorney David Lansner; New York Bar Association Guide, 2012.

294 **They work in every borough except Staten Island:** On very rare occasions, Staten Is-

land Legal Services has represented poor parents in child abuse and neglect cases, but this was not an option for Chanel in 2015.

294 **paid by the city at $75 per hour:** Fees are set by the state and paid by the city, according to an administrator for the office of New York City's Assigned Counsel Plan.

295 **For twenty years, Yost served with the New York Police Department:** NYPD spokesperson.

295 **as a deep undercover operative in east Brooklyn:** All biographical details about Glenn Yost are taken from interviews with him, as well as from public records and news articles.

301 **Blood is seeping from the toddler's mouth:** The account of Lee-Lee's seizure is based on interviews with Dasani, Chanel, and other family members, and on direct observation by me at the hospital.

303 **Mayor de Blasio will soon announce that he wants this encampment and seventy-nine others cleared:** Jennifer Fermino, "Exclusive: Mayor de Blasio Takes Tour of Filthy, Needle-Ridden Bronx Drug Den—Vows to Clean Up Homeless Encampments," *Daily News*, Sept. 4, 2015.

306 **"He had never learned to run properly, but he was long-legged for a ten-year-old":** Katherine Paterson, *Bridge to Terabithia* (New York: Harper Collins, 2008), p. 4.

306 **gave a TED Talk originally titled "The Key to Success? Grit":** Interview with Angela Duckworth. At her request, TED changed the title of her talk to "Grit: The Power of Passion and Perseverance." It was filmed in April 2013. TED.com.

306 **more than 22 million views:** As of Feb. 23, 2021, Duckworth's talk had 22,730,579 views on the TED website and 7,564,020 on YouTube.

306 **Success, according to Duckworth, hinges not solely on talent or IQ:** Interview with Duckworth; Angela Duckworth, *Grit: The Power of Passion and Perseverance* (New York: Scribner, 2016).

307 **For a pilot study on "strategic self-control":** Interview with Duckworth.

307 **"Mr. Hershey, in my view":** Milton Hershey School, "'Grit' Presentation at Milton Hershey School," YouTube, Aug. 14, 2014.

307 **"If a man does not like the work he does, he is not a success":** Lobdell, "Hershey," p. 48.

307 **"When you tackle a job, stick to it until you have won the battle":** Milton Hershey, quoting his mother; Carter Nicholson, "Hershey—the Friend of Orphan Boys," *Success*, October 1927.

307 **Milton called this "character building":** Hershey Community Archives.

307 **now an offensive tackle for the Seattle Seahawks:** In 2017, Gilliam left the Seahawks for the San Francisco 49ers. "Offensive Lineman Garry Gilliam Signs With San Francisco 49ers," Seahawks.com, April 18, 2017.

308 **Those who had moved before age thirteen did better:** Raj Chetty, Nathaniel Hendren, and Lawrence Katz, "The Effects of Exposure to Better Neighborhoods on Children: New Evidence from the Moving to Opportunity Project," *American Economic Review*, 106, no. 4 (2016).

308 **"The start has a tremendous influence on a boy's later life":** This quote appeared in *McClure's Magazine* in April 1924.

308 **"Grit is living life like it's a marathon":** Angela Duckworth, "Grit: The Power of Passion and Perseverance," TED.com, April 2013.

Chapter 32

311 **Ward, who was seven when she left her home:** Interview with Fonati Ward.

313 **Among the first code-switchers studied by linguists:** Erica J. Benson, "The Neglected Early History of Codeswitching Research in the United States," *Language & Communication*, 21, no. 1 (2001), p. 28.

315 **where she admitted to recent "opiate use":** Chanel's Mount Sinai Beth Israel records.

315 **Filling this role, on contract with ACS, are 63 nonprofit organizations:** In 2015, the agency contracted 57 nonprofit organizations to provide 180 prevention service programs for families; some of those nonprofits also provided foster care services, including residential programs and therapeutic family foster care. In total, there were 63 unique nonprofit organizations providing ACS with either prevention, foster care, or both. ACS official.

316 **The vast majority of families complete services:** Between 70 and 80 percent of families successfully complete preventive services, which means that the family has met one or more of its goals. ACS data.

316 **New York City's foster care numbers have dropped significantly:** ACS data.

316 **preventive spending has nearly tripled:** Ibid.

316 **The agency's investment . . . has been touted as a national model:** Interviews with Gottlieb and Nora McCarthy, founder of the parent advocacy organization Rise. In 2011, ACS began implementing eleven evidence-based models of preventive care, the largest such program in the country and "pioneering in scope for the field of child welfare." Fernando Clara, Kamalii Yeh García, and Alison Metz, *Implementing Evidence-Based Child Welfare: The New York City Experience* (New York: Casey Family Programs, 2017), p. 7.

316 **"stabilize families at risk of a crisis":** "Description & History," ACS website, accessed March 2, 2021.

316 **ACS is currently spending, in 2015, about $532 million on foster care:** $532 million is the rounded total of spending on foster care services ($494,060,000) plus spending on foster care support ($37,546,000). *Report of the Finance Division on . . . the Fiscal 2017 Preliminary Mayor's Management Report for the Administration for Children's Services* (New York: New York City Council, 2017), p. 3.

316 **Around 44 percent of ACS's budget depends on federal funds:** *Report on the Fiscal Year 2015 Executive Budget for the Administration for Children's Services* (New York: New York City Council, 2014), p. 2.

316 **the federal government is giving ten times as much money to programs that separate families:** Interview with Richard Wexler, executive director of the National Coalition for Child Protection Reform, citing *Title IV-E Spending by Child Welfare Agencies*, Child Trends, December 2018, p. 2.

316 **orphans were called "foundlings" because they were found on the streets:** Oxford English Dictionary, 2021.

316 **"Guard this little one":** Glenn Collins, "Glimpses of Heartache, and Stories of Survival," *New York Times*, Sept. 3, 2007.

317 **a Catholic offshoot of the orphan train movement:** New-York Historical Society Museum and Library, "Guide to the Records of the New York Foundling Hospital 1869–2009," NYU Digital Library Technologies, New York University, Dec. 5, 2019.

317 **nuns brought babies of "indeterminate race" to the Museum of Natural History:** Bernstein, *Lost Children of Wilder*, p. 149; David Rosner and Gerald Markowitz, "Race, Foster Care, and the Politics of Abandonment in New York City," *American Journal of Public Health*, 87, no. 11 (1997), pp. 1844–49.

317 **A Black baby was far less likely to be adopted:** Rosner and Markowitz, "Race, Foster Care," p. 1848.

317 **"that all children, adults, and families can have the opportunity to reach their full potential":** "Our Why," New York Foundling website, accessed March 2, 2021.

317 **Foundling is the second-largest foster care provider:** ACS data.

317 **a $133 million annual budget:** IRS Form 990 (federal nonprofit tax return) for 2015, New York Foundling, "Total expenses," p. 1.

318 for children with cognitive delays, severe emotional problems, and other challenges: "District 75," DOE website, accessed March 2, 2021.

319 he is stopped by a teacher, "wrestled to the ground": Khaliq's Staten Island University Hospital records.

319 "You have been seen for a grief reaction (grieving)": Ibid.

323 Khaliq's body crashes to the ground: This account is based on ACS records and interviews with Khaliq, his parents, and siblings, as well as on ACS records. The subsequent scene of Khaliq at the hospital is based on direct observation by me and on ACS records.

323 Unlike weed, K2 tends not to show up on drug tests: "Synthetic Cannabinoids (K2/Spice) DrugFacts," National Institute on Drug Abuse, National Institutes of Health, U.S. Department of Health and Human Services website, June 2020.

326 he has been screened for drugs fifty-three times, always testing negative: Supreme's Medicaid and drug treatment records; interview with Supreme. The negative test results were over the course of 18.5 consecutive months, from October 2013 through March 2015.

326 Excluding one parent is almost always less traumatic than breaking up a family: Interviews with ACS officials and Gottlieb.

Chapter 33

330 Since last year, the city has spent over $1 million renovating Auburn: DHS data in response to a FOIL request.

331 which requires a $101 security deposit for a day pass: Lyft spokesperson.

331 She lost her own children to foster care: Interview with Barbara.

331 "crepitus suprapatellar effusions": Chanel's hospital records.

332 "the activation of public space through the insertion of participatory objects": Stereotank is a design studio founded by Marcelo Ertorteguy and Sara Valente, per Stereotank's website.

335 Hair tests can detect up to ninety days of drug use: Gennaro Selvaggi, Antonio G. Spagnalo, and Anna Elander, "A Review of Illicit Psychoactive Drug Use in Elective Surgery Patients: Detection, Effects, and Policy," International Journal of Surgery 48 (2017), pp. 161–62.

335 trace remnants of drugs . . . absorbed from the person's bloodstream: Pascal Kintz, Alberto Salomone, and Marco Vincenti, eds., Hair Analysis in Clinical and Forensic Toxicology (London: Academic Press, 2015), pp. 6–7, 47–48.

335 a "hair color bias": James A. Bourland, "Hair Pigmentation Literature Review" (presentation to the Drug Testing Advisory Board Meeting, Rockville, Md., Sept. 3, 2014), p. 6; Chad Randolph Borges, "Roles of Drug Basicity, Melanin Binding, and Cellular Transport in Drug Incorporation into Hair" (Ph.D. dissertation, University of Utah, Department of Pharmacology and Toxicology, 2001).

335 Black people tend to have more melanin in their hair: Leah Samuel, "Hair Testing for Drug Use Gains Traction," Scientific American, Nov. 1, 2016.

337 Marisol grew up in Queens: While ACS did not permit Marisol Quintero to discuss the case of Dasani's family, Marisol provided biographical details about her life and work.

338 like the M15 . . . making sixty-six stops: M15 East Harlem–South Ferry route, MTA.

339 "I am trying to clean my life up from opiates": Chanel's Mount Sinai Beth Israel records.

341 Everything is in her name: According to Chanel's apartment lease, her HRA records, and her Con Edison records.

342 when poor families enter the child protection system, the opposite tends to happen: Interviews with Gottlieb and other child protection experts, including McCarthy.

342 "hides the systemic reasons for poor families' hardships": Dorothy Roberts, "Why Child Welfare Is a Civil Rights Issue," The Family Defender 3, no. 2 (2009), p. 7.

343 **The $14.5 million facility offers a meditation room:** "Stephen's Legacy Lives On," LIHerald.com, Dec. 2, 2009; "Mother and Child Program," New York Foundling, accessed Feb. 23, 2021.

343 **He has no way of knowing that John has called in sick:** While John told me that he had called in sick, this was not noted in Foundling's records.

343 **at 7:52 A.M., Supreme enters the Island Food Market on Broad Street:** This account is based on interviews with Supreme, as well as on police and criminal court records.

Chapter 34

347 **the new Pixar animation *Inside Out*:** *Inside Out*, directed by Pete Docter (United States: Walt Disney Studios Motion Pictures, Pixar Animation Studios, 2015).

349 **ACS appears to be unaware of the arrest:** There is no indication in the family's ACS or Foundling records that caseworkers were aware of Supreme's arrest on June 20, 2015. ACS learned of the arrest more than three months later, according to a family court transcript from Oct. 7, 2015.

349 **"Single father with 8 children in need of food!":** Supreme's HRA records.

349 **The welfare agency should issue an emergency food grant—as required by law:** New York Codes, Rules and Regulations 351.8(c)(3) & 351.8(c)(4).

349 **his request is denied:** A spokesperson for HRA said that Supreme's request was rejected "for failing to comply with eligibility requirements"—namely that Supreme had missed a mandatory substance use assessment appointment "required under federal and state law." While it is correct that Supreme missed one substance use assessment, this is not grounds for rejecting his emergency request for food aid. According to HRA Policy Directive #12-29-ELI: "At application, social service agencies are required to assess a reported emergency situation. If an immediate need is identified it must be addressed and, whenever possible, resolved on the same day."

350 **She is living in a homeless shelter, in the same neighborhood where her life began:** Chanel was assigned to the HELP Women's Center, located at 116 Williams Avenue in Brooklyn—formerly the site of P.S. 63, which closed in 1980; David Bird, "Shelter for Men Opened by City at Brooklyn Site," *New York Times*, Oct. 22, 1981.

351 **The average ACS caseworker oversees nearly ten families:** *Child Welfare Indicators Annual Report 2015* (New York: The Council of the City of New York, 2015), pp.1–4.

351 **Marisol will work an estimated 252 hours in overtime:** Citywide payroll data (2015) accessed Nov. 13, 2020, via New York City's "Open Data" website: opendata.cityof newyork.us.

351 **an agency that will spend more than $29 million just in overtime pay:** Between fiscal years 2015 and 2019, ACS doubled its overtime spending, from $29.5 million in 2015 to $60 million in 2019. Analysis of 2021 reports from the city's Finance Division and *Fiscal 2020 Preliminary Mayor's Management Report for the Administration for Children's Services* (New York: The Council of the City of New York, 2020), p. 14.

351 **the president and CEO of Foundling will earn $572,902:** IRS Form 990 (federal nonprofit tax return), New York Foundling, 2015.

352 **for the movie:** *Akeelah and the Bee*, directed by Doug Atchison (United States: Lionsgate Films, 2006).

353 **a white supremacist had gunned down nine Black worshippers:** Debbie Elliott, "5 Years After Charleston Church Massacre, What Have We Learned?," NPR.com, June 17, 2020.

353 **textbooks have minimized the role of slavery:** Joe Heim, "What Do Students Learn About Slavery? It Depends Where They Live," *Washington Post*, Aug. 28, 2019.

353 **a geography book depicts slaves as "workers":** Michael Schaub, "Texas Textbook Calling Slaves 'Immigrants' to Be Changed, After Mom's Complaint," *Los Angeles Times*, Oct. 5, 2015.

354 **the cartoon show:** *Daniel Tiger's Neighborhood*, created by Angela Santomero, aired Sept. 3, 2012, in broadcast syndication, on PBS Kids, 9 Story Media Group.

355 **Her last known drug test . . . came back clean:** Chanel's drug treatment counselor at the Staten Island University Methadone Maintenance Treatment Program showed Chanel the results the previous week, during a visit I attended.

356 **Marisol has no records:** In order to access Chanel's records, ACS was required to submit a Health Insurance Portability and Accountability Act (HIPAA) form to Chanel's clinic, signed by Chanel. On June 24, Chanel signed a HIPAA giving her clinic permission to speak with her Foundling prevention worker. On July 6, Chanel met with Marisol, who made no mention (during a conversation that Chanel recorded) of Chanel's HIPAA. A week later, on the morning of Chanel's July 13 court appearance, Marisol told Chanel that she had not signed the necessary consent.

356 **the city will agree to pay Garner's family $5.9 million:** J. David Goodman, "Eric Garner Case Is Settled by New York City for $5.9 Million," *New York Times*, July 13, 2015.

356 **the officer who choked him is still working:** Daniel Pantaleo kept his job for nearly five years after Garner's death and was fired in 2019. Ashley Southall, "Daniel Pantaleo, Officer Who Held Eric Garner in Chokehold, Is Fired," *New York Times*, Aug. 19, 2019.

359 **Jonathan and Melissa Akers draw from a deeper well:** All biographical details about the Akerses are from interviews with Jonathan and Melissa Akers.

360 **gangs like the Roman Lords:** Interview with Jonathan Akers; Greg Donaldson, "Hoops in the 'Hood Brings Brownsville a New Concept," *New York Times*, Aug. 8, 1993.

Chapter 35

363 *Man's Search for Meaning:* Viktor Emil Frankl, *Man's Search for Meaning* (Boston: Beacon Press, 2006).

365 **This is the highest point in all five boroughs, rising 404 feet skyward:** United States Geological Survey, U.S. Department of the Interior.

366 **A woman has plunged to her death:** "Woman Killed After Plunging in Front of Moving Subway Train in Brooklyn," *Daily News*, Aug. 30, 2015.

367 **A white fourteen-year-old native of Royersford:** Interview with Ashley.

368 **Natalya Trejos (whose LinkedIn profile lists, among her tasks, "coordinating evictions with local Marshal's office"):** Natalya Trejos's LinkedIn profile, accessed via LinkedIn.com on Nov. 23, 2020.

369 **On Chanel's lease, the landlord is listed as "GRI 89 Laurel LLC":** HPD records.

369 **a Wall Street banker:** "Rising Stars 2020," *Private Debt Investor*, Oct. 1, 2020.

369 **bought 91 Laurel:** Property transfer tax documents for lot 3, block 562, in Staten Island, New York, June 4, 2013.

369 **a market value that would rise by 70 percent over five years:** In 2013, the property sold for $351,500 (Office of Richmond County Clerk). By 2018, the property's value had risen to $596,000 (New York City's Department of Finance, Market Value History).

369 **Her job was to conduct the initial investigation:** ACS data.

369 **ACS made an error:** Analysis by Lansner, Gottlieb, and Linda Lowe, the family's case supervisor at Foundling. In interviews, ACS officials said that even therapy-based preventive programs are responsible for helping families meet concrete needs, such as accessing government benefits and fixing housing problems.

370 **The sequence begins on August 29, 2015:** My description of these events is based on interviews with Supreme and the children, their text messages, and direct observation by me, as well as on the family's ACS, Foundling, DOE, HRA, and HPD records, and Chanel's Con Edison and DOC records.

371 **files seven complaints with the city's housing and preservation department:** Supreme's 311 records and Chanel's HPD records.

371 **Again, the welfare agency refuses to assist him:** On Sept. 14, 2015, an HRA caseworker denied Supreme's emergency request for "food stamps" (the Supplemental Nutrition Assistance Program, known as SNAP). In Supreme's HRA records, the caseworker wrote, "You will get regular SNAP benefits this month," noting that the children's food stamps were going to an eleven-digit HRA "case number." All welfare recipients are given a case number. But the number cited by the worker on Sept. 14 corresponded to Chanel's case, whereas Supreme had not received food stamps in three months. According to an HRA spokesperson, Supreme's request for public assistance was finally approved two weeks later, on Sept. 30, 2015.

372 **"Peace miss Debi Rose":** Email from Supreme to the office of Councilwoman Debi Rose on September 16, 2015, at 5:39 p.m. When questioned about this, Rose's spokesperson said that she receives hundreds of emails a day and did not recall seeing Supreme's message.

Chapter 36

374 **a "retroactive" food stamp benefit totaling $3,812:** HRA records.

374 **"hazardous":** Family court transcript, Oct. 6, 2015.

375 **Supreme has made perfect attendance at his drug treatment:** ACS records.

375 **By October 6, his fate is sealed:** My description of the events leading up to and on October 6 is based on interviews with Supreme, Chanel, and the children, written accounts by Avianna and Nana, direct observation by me on October 6, 2015, family court documents and transcripts, the family's ACS, Foundling, HRA, HPD, and DOE records, and Supreme's drug treatment and criminal records.

375 **"It is a safety issue at this point":** Family court transcript, Oct. 16, 2015.

381 **joining 364 children to pass through this month:** According to ACS data, received in response to a FOIL request.

381 **Scoppetta had been a foster child in the 1930s:** Sam Roberts, "Nicholas Scoppetta, Former Foster Child Who Led Child Welfare Agency, Dies at 83," *New York Times,* March 24, 2016.

381 **He spent that first night in a facility:** Nicholas Scoppetta, interview by Terry Gross, *Fresh Air,* NPR, July 22, 1997.

381 **"One of the traumatic events for me":** Julie Kracov, "Foster the Children: Nicholas Scoppetta Makes Sure the Kids are Alright," *Observer,* Observer Media, Oct. 24, 2013.

381 **Scoppetta became the first-ever commissioner of ACS:** Steven Lee Myers, "Advocate with a Heart," *New York Times,* Jan. 12, 1996.

381 **the center bearing Scoppetta's name is now a dreaded place:** Heather Holland, "Kids Went Missing 1,600 Times from One City-Run Children's Facility," DNAinfo, Sept. 15, 2014.

381 **Those who act out are sometimes sent across the street:** Michael Fitzgerald, "Is New York State Responsible for Some Long Stayers at the City's Temporary Foster Home? City Child Welfare Commissioner Thinks So," *The Imprint,* March 28, 2019; Susan Edelman and Rachel Petty, "'Disturbed' kids at city foster-care center 'drugged' at hospital," *New York Post,* July 31, 2016.

381 **sometimes in handcuffs:** Holland, "Kids Went Missing 1,600 Times."

381 **children ran away . . . nearly sixteen hundred times:** Ibid.

383 **"Come on," she says. "Your case is ready":** Interview with Supreme, whose subsequent arrest is corroborated by Judge Lim's comments in family court.

384 **joining nearly fifteen thousand other children to enter the system this year:** In 2015, the city's daily average of foster children was 11,098, with a total of 14,949 children who were in foster care for at least one day. ACS data.

385 **Today they find fourteen housing violations:** All inspections and cited violations of the

family's rental property were provided by HPD's Division of Code Enforcement and verified by a spokesperson for HPD.

Chapter 37

389 **the film:** *Unbroken*, directed by Angelina Jolie (United States: Universal Pictures, 2014).

389 **stranding him . . . for forty-seven days before the Japanese Navy captured Louis:** Laura Hillenbrand, *Unbroken: A World War II Story of Survival, Resilience, and Redemption* (New York: Random House, 2010).

390 **They begin with polite conversation:** This scene was reconstructed from interviews with Dasani and ACS records.

394 **"I'm going to kill them both, I promise":** ACS records and interview with Supreme.

395 **a British slave owner who came to Virginia in 1712:** Willie Lynch, *The Willie Lynch Letter and the Making of a Slave* (Ravenio Books, 2011); William Jelani Cobb, "Is Willie Lynch's Letter Real?," Ferris State University, May 2004.

395 **Louis Farrakhan's 1995 address::** "Minister Louis Farrakhan, 'Million Man March,' (16 October 1995)," Voices of Democracy, University of Maryland, accessed Feb. 10, 2021.

395 **Kendrick Lamar's 2015 album:** Kendrick Lamar, "Complexion (A Zulu Love)," *To Pimp a Butterfly* (Top Dawg Entertainment, Aftermath Entertainment, Interscope Records, 2015).

400 **which must be defended at any cost:** Interviews with Dasani and Chanel; Elijah Anderson, *Code of the Street: Decency, Violence, and the Moral Life of the Inner City* (New York: W. W. Norton, 1999).

400 **Palmyra is a small working-class town:** 2015 census data.

402 **A fifty-six-year-old native of the New Jersey suburbs:** All biographical details about Lowe are from interviews with her.

402 **At least a dozen caseworkers have passed through her life:** ACS records.

404 **When the caseworkers are out of earshot, Chanel turns to Nana:** I was able to attend this visit at the request of Chanel and Supreme, who introduced me as a "friend," though the family's Foundling supervisor, Lowe, noted that I was also a reporter. Within a few months, both ACS and Foundling had banned me from visits, despite my "very strong bond with the children," as Lowe noted in the case file, adding, "Ms. Elliott is in the process of writing a book and NY Foundling does not give any permission to be involved."

405 **Rarely are the funds enough, and no amount of money makes fostering an easy job:** A 2018 study recommends that New York increase its foster care rates by up to 54 percent. Haksoon Ahn et al., "Estimating minimum adequate foster care costs for children in the United States," *Children and Youth Services Review* 84 (2018), p. 62.

405 **These labels determine a foster parent's stipend:** All information about foster child labels, stipends paid to foster parents in New York City, and funds paid to foster agencies was provided by ACS.

405 **But only 470 families . . . are enrolled in the homemaking program:** ACS data.

406 **the burden is on ACS to inform parents of such a service:** "The individual or responsible adult member of a family eligible to receive homemaker service shall be informed by the caseworker of the nature of such service . . ." New York Codes, Rules and Regulations, Title 18, section 460.2.

407 **child welfare law under President Clinton in 1997:** Katharine Q. Seelye, "Clinton to Approve Sweeping Shift in Adoption," *New York Times*, Nov. 17, 1997.

407 **the crime bill would later haunt the presidential bids of Hillary Clinton and Joe Biden:** Todd S. Purdum, "The Crime-Bill Debate Shows How Short Americans' Memories Are," *The Atlantic*, Sept. 12, 2019.

407 **once a child has spent fifteen months in foster care:** Under federal law, states must move to terminate parental rights when a child "has been in foster care under the re-

sponsibility of the state for 15 of the most recent 22 months," or when a court makes certain determinations, with limited exceptions. Adoption and Safe Families Act of 1997, 42 U.S.C. § 1305 note (1997).

407 **more than half a million children were languishing in foster care:** *The AFCARS Report: Final Estimates for FY 1998 through FY 2002 (12)* (Washington, D.C.: Administration for Children and Families, Children's Bureau, U.S. Department of Health and Human Services, 2006), p. 1.

407 **a population that has since dropped by 24 percent:** Of the 71.4 million children in the U.S. in 1998, 559,000 were in foster care. By 2015, that number had dropped to 427,444 (out of 73.6 million children total). For data on the U.S. child population in 1998 and 2015: "POP1 Child Population: Number of Children (in Millions) Ages 0–17 in the United States by Age, 1950–2019 and Projected 2020–2050" (Federal Interagency Forum on Child and Family Statistics, accessed through childstats.gov). For foster care data from 1998 and 2015: *The AFCARS Report: Final Estimates for FY 1998 through FY 2002 (12)*, and *The AFCARS Report: Preliminary FY1 2016 Estimates as of Oct 20, 2017 (23)* (Washington, D.C.: Administration for Children and Families, Children's Bureau, U.S. Department of Health and Human Services, 2017), p. 1.

407 **more than sixty-two thousand children had been rendered orphans:** *The AFCARS Report: Preliminary FY1 2016 Estimates as of Oct 20, 2017*, p. 1.

Chapter 38

409 **Themis, the goddess of divine law and order:** In Egypt, she was Maat; the Romans called her Justitia. Randy Kennedy, "That Lady with the Scales Poses for Her Portraits," *New York Times*, Dec. 15, 2010.

412 **"Betcha can't whip like me":** iAmDLOW, "Do It Like Me Challenge prod by @NunMajorBeats," YouTube, Sept. 29, 2015, video.

414 **At around noon, a sixty-three-year-old white woman:** The description of this attack is based on interviews with Khaliq, as well as on his police, family court, and ACS records, and on news articles.

415 **The attackers, as reported in the press, tend to be Black teenagers:** Thomas Sowell, "Thugs Target Jews in Sick 'Knockout' Game," *New York Post*, Nov. 19, 2013; Associated Press, "Deadly 'Knockout' Game Gains National Prominence," Syracuse.com, Nov. 22, 2013.

415 **prompted the Reverend Al Sharpton to condemn the game:** Georgett Roberts and Michael Gartland, "Al Sharpton Condemns 'Knockout' Attacks," *New York Post*, Nov. 23, 2013.

415 **"Assault on Woman Prompts 'Knockout Game' Concerns":** Eddie D'Anna, "Watch: Assault on Woman Prompts 'Knockout Game' Concerns," *Staten Island Advance*, Nov. 25, 2015.

416 **"very helpful, not disrespectful":** ACS records.

417 **On December 7, 2015, a detective visits Khaliq's school in Staten Island:** The account of Khaliq's arrest is based on interviews with Khaliq and Lowe, as well as on police, ACS, and Foundling records.

418 **Chief Keef . . . who grew up in Chicago:** Dan Hyman, "Chief Keef vs. Chicago: Why the Rapper Has Become Public Enemy No. 1," *Billboard*, July 30, 2015.

418 **after forty-five people were fatally shot over Easter weekend:** Per Liljas, "Feds Step In After 45 People Shot in Chicago over Easter Weekend," *Time*, April 22, 2014.

418 **"is ridin' through New York":** Chief Keef, "Faneto," *Back from the Dead 2* (Glo Gang, 2014).

419 **where Auntie Joan has overseen a rocky transition:** Interview with Joan; Foundling records.

420   The *Advance* runs a story with a photograph of Avianna: "Dreyfus Intermediate Students Pay It Forward," SILive.com, Jan. 15, 2016.

425   **she and Supreme have been blunting their pain with drugs:** A month earlier, in December 2015, Supreme had tested positive for marijuana. In March 2016, he enrolled in a detox center—the same month that Chanel tested positive for opiates. The following August, according to family court transcripts, Chanel told a drug counselor that she had a two-year history of intranasal heroin use. She denies having said this.

Chapter 39

427   **A lethal blizzard:** "East Coast Digs Out from Epic Blizzard," CBS News, Jan. 24, 2016.

428   **arrested three weeks ago and charged with possession of cocaine:** Elvis Byrd, Jr.'s criminal court records.

428   **physically and emotionally abused her for "many years":** Sherrie Byrd's civil court records.

429   **a child drowned on the premises:** Marc Santora and Nate Schweber, "Drowned Boy, 3, Climbed Fence to Get Into a Pool," *New York Times*, July 25, 2014.

429   **found her baby son . . . floating facedown:** Ibid.

429   **investigators revoked Mrs. Byrd's daycare license:** Greg B. Smith, "Exclusive: New York City Day Care Violations Can Slip Through the Cracks, Leading Parents to Think Their Kids Are Safer than They Are," *Daily News*, Feb. 11, 2016.

429   **Elvis Byrd walks into the house:** This account is based on ACS, Foundling, and police records, as well as on interviews with Supreme, Avianna, Nana, and Sherrie Byrd. According to ACS, Elvis Byrd admitted that "he got into the face of Avianna and told her not to disrespect him," broke furniture, and may have pushed Nana, but he denied calling the girls names. His son, Elvis Jr., told ACS that he entered the house after the incident happened. The agency made a finding of inadequate guardianship. ACS investigative records.

434   **"I can't even hear you because these kids are being so loud":** Khaliq's court records.

434   **The woman's "disrespectful" tone gets "under my skin":** Letter from Khaliq.

434   **he punches a woman outside a deli before robbing her:** Khaliq's court records.

434   **"a bloody nose for no reason":** ACS records.

434   **Khaliq is like two different boys, she tells his caseworker:** ACS records.

434   **getting off a bus on Hylan Boulevard:** Khaliq's court records.

435   **He faces three charges of assault and six robbery-related charges:** Khaliq's court records.

435   **the Boys Town staff had found a razor in his room:** ACS records.

Chapter 40

446   *Ruptura* **is the Latin origin of "rupture":** The word "rupture" entered the English language in the fifteenth century from Middle or Anglo-Norman French, and ultimately goes back to the Latin word *ruptūra*. Analysis by Michael Weiss and Nicholas Zair, Cambridge University Faculty Classics.

446   **Nightmares hound the children:** Maya and Papa's Foundling records.

447   **a letter arrives at Foundling, signed by a doctor:** Nana's Foundling records.

447   **who has examined Nana at the foster mother's behest:** Interviews with Nana and Avianna.

447   **The doctor's diagnosis is later reversed:** Interview with Nana.

449   **this is clearly a depiction of Supreme's gold teeth:** Interview with Papa.

449   **"Can I lay by your side, next to you":** Sam Smith, "Lay Me Down," *In the Lonely Hour* (Capitol Records and Method Records, 2014).

Chapter 41

453 **a nod to the movie ATL:** *ATL,* directed by Chris Robinson (Warner Bros. Pictures, 2006).

457 **landlords had served Chanel with an eviction notice:** Housing court records.

457 **Supreme and Chanel have repeatedly broken the building's rules:** Interviews with Chanel, Supreme, and the landlords.

Chapter 42

463 **The counties surrounding Hershey will vote overwhelmingly for Trump:** Matthew Bloch, Larry Buchanan, Josh Katz, and Kevin Quealy, "An Extremely Detailed Map of the 2016 Election," *New York Times,* July 25, 2018.

463 **serving an eighteen-month sentence at a secure detention facility:** ACS records.

463 **With that, the foster mother draws new boundaries:** Interviews with Avianna, Chanel, and Dasani.

466 **Dasani faces an assault charge (which is later dropped):** ACS records.

Chapter 43

469 **Denise, an African American teacher who works in special education:** Interview with Denise.

469 **More than thirty-three hundred students attend the high school:** Facts about Wagner provided by DOE.

477 **Papa goes quiet, making "grunting noises," notes the medic:** My account of the events leading to Papa's hospitalizations in April and May is based on ACS records and Richmond University Medical Center records.

479 **landing a gig at the White House:** Paul Williams, "DJ Fussyman Music Mogul in the Making," *Living Staten Island,* Early Fall 2017.

479 **A forty-foot mural of the boy's face covers a brick wall in Stapleton:** NYC Arts Cypher, "Cypher Fest: Surprise! Portrait with DJ Fussyman," YouTube, Oct 13, 2016, video.

479 **"He was a fussy baby":** Interview with Lakema Freeland, Fussy's mother.

479 **the disassembled parts of a .38-millimeter revolver:** Interview with Chanel.

Chapter 44

482 **"Subway Slasher: Psycho Slices Mom at Grand Central":** May 29, 2017, *New York Post* Covers Archive; Tina Moore, Nick Fugallo, and Max Jaeger, "Homeless Woman Accused of Rage-Filled Subway Slashing," *New York Post,* May 28, 2017.

482 **the ACS commissioner had stepped down and three employees were fired:** "3 ACS Employees Fired, Independent Monitor Ordered After Probe of Zymere Perkins Case," CBS Local, Dec. 13, 2016.

482 **convicted . . . of smothering her eight-pound baby:** Press release, "DA Vance: Tiona Rodriguez Pleads Guilty to Killing Newborn Son Found in Her Bag at Herald Square Victoria's Secret," Manhattan District Attorney's Office, Jan. 17, 2018.

485 **an apparent heart attack:** Interview with Bailey.

486 **a white Brooklyn artist:** Pamela Wong, "Brooklyn Artist Katie Merz Chosen to Create 80 Flatbush Mural," *Bklyner,* Sept. 22, 2017.

Chapter 45

498 **the school's Haitian-born assistant principal:** All biographical details about Jean Etienne are from interviews with him.

499 **Lansner, a prominent seventy-one-year-old lawyer:** All biographical details about Lansner are based on interviews with him, Gottlieb, and other child protection experts and

from news articles including, by Leslie Kaufman, "City Often Took Children Without Consulting Court," *New York Times*, Oct. 28, 2004. See also *Nicholas v. Williams*, 203 F. Supp. 2d 153 (E.D.N.Y. 2002).

500   **"the classic parent at the mercy of the system because she doesn't bow down":** Interview with McCarthy.

500   **Lansner wanted to help the family "because it was Dasani":** Interview with Lansner.

501   **a routine that requires transporting the mayor:** J. David Goodman, "What's Keeping the Mayor from Going Green? His Gym Routine," *New York Times*, June 2, 2017.

501   **a Black homeless woman named Nathylin Flowers Adesegun:** Kathleen Culliton, "'I'm Doing My Workout,' Mayor Tells Homeless Woman Seeking Help," Patch.com, Oct. 5, 2018.

501   **de Blasio's public approval ratings have dropped to 42 percent—down 18 points:** Quinnipiac University Poll, April 3, 2019; Quinnipiac University Poll, May 17, 2017.

501   **the mayor has left a trail of disappointments:** Alex Shephard, "Bill de Blasio Has Failed," *The New Republic*, June 2, 2020; Luis Ferré-Sadurní, "New York City's Public Housing Is in Crisis. Will Washington Take Control?," *New York Times*, Dec. 25, 2018; Nikita Stewart, "New York's Toughest Homeless Problem," *New York Times*, May 30, 2019; Flegenheimer, "How Bill de Blasio Went."

502   **cut deals with developers at the expense of low-income New Yorkers:** Flegenheimer, "How Bill de Blasio Went"; Andrew Rice, "How Are You Enjoying the De Blasio Revolution?" *New York Magazine*, Dec. 28, 2015; Nikita Stewart, Jeffery C. Mays, and Matthew Haag, "Facing Homeless Crisis, New York Aims for 1,000 New Apartments a Year," *New York Times*, Dec. 12, 2019.

502   **currently more than seventy-two thousand homeless New Yorkers:** In March 2019, there were 72,520 people staying in the five shelter systems administered by New York City agencies; more than 63,000 of them were in DHS shelters.

502   **a Brooklyn prankster will post a sign:** Jeffery C. Mays and William Neuman, "De Blasio for President? 'Nah,'" *New York Times*, May 10, 2019.

511   **the killing of George Floyd:** Derrick Bryson Taylor, "George Floyd Protests: A Timeline," *New York Times*, March 28, 2021.

511   **and thousands of others protested at Barclays Center:** Edgar Sandoval, "Protests Flare in Brooklyn over Floyd Death as de Blasio Appeals for Calm," *New York Times*, May 30, 2020.

511   **as Mayor de Blasio stood back defending them:** Henry Austin, Suzanne Ciechalski, and Tom Winter, "New York Mayor Bill de Blasio Defends Police After Video Shows NYPD SUV Driving into Protesters," NBC News, May 31, 2020.

512   **a movement to abolish the child protection system:** Eileen Grench, "NYC Child Welfare Officials Helped Get Her Fired over Social Media Posts. Activism Got Her Back on the Job," *The City*, Feb. 11, 2021.

Afterword

517   **Alex Kotlowitz's 1991 classic:** Alex Kotlowitz, *There Are No Children Here: The Story of Two Boys Growing Up in the Other America* (New York: Anchor Books, 1991).

517   **One in five American children was living in poverty:** "Information on Poverty and Income Statistics: A Summary of 2014 Current Population Survey Data," U.S. Department of Health and Human Services, Office of the Assistant Secretary for Planning and Evaluation, Sept. 16, 2014.

517   **the highest child poverty rate, in 2012, of any wealthy country after Romania:** By 2018, the United States had the fourth-highest child poverty rate, after Israel, Chile, and Romania. For 2012, see: Peter Adamson, *Measuring Child Poverty: New League Tables of Child Poverty in the World's Rich Countries*, Innocenti Report Card 10 (Florence,

Italy: UNICEF Innocenti Research Centre, 2012), p. 3, Figure 1b. For 2018, see: "Poverty Rate," Organisation for Economic Co-operation and Development, accessed April 12, 2021, via data.oecd.org.

518   **America's poor children (numbering 16 million in 2012)**: The number of American children in poverty has declined in recent years, dropping to 10.5 million in 2019. Child poverty rose again in 2020 during the coronavirus pandemic. For 16 million children: Census data, 2012. For 10.5 million: Deja Thomas and Richard Fry, "Prior to COVID-19, Child Poverty Rates Had Reached Record Lows in U.S.," Pew Research Center, Nov. 30, 2020. During the pandemic: Priyanka Boghani, "How Covid Has Impacted Poverty in America," *Frontline*, Dec. 8, 2020.

519   **a "representative" child, one whose family reflected demographic trends**: Children's Defense Fund, *Child Poverty in America 2012: National Analysis* (Washington, D.C.: Children's Defense Fund, 2013), p. 2. Also see Arloc Sherman, Danilo Trisi, and Matt Broaddus, *Census Data Show Poverty and Inequality Remained High in 2012 and Median Income Was Stagnant, but Fewer Americans Were Uninsured* (Washington, D.C., Center on Budget and Policy Priorities, 2013), p. 8; Lindsay M. Monte, "Multiplied Disadvantage: Multiple Partner Fertility and Economic Wellbeing into the Great Recession" (paper presented at the Population Association of America Annual Conference, Boston, Mass., May 2014), p. 1.

520   **Old English—*understandan***: Brent Vine, University of California, Los Angeles Department of Classics and Program in Indo-European Studies.

521   **Under the section titled "Personal Relations with Sources"**: "Ethical Journalism: A Handbook of Values and Practices for the News and Editorial Departments," *New York Times*.

522   **the twenty-five-page "statement on method"**: Mitchell Duneier, *Sidewalk* (New York: Farrar, Straus and Giroux, 1999), pp. 333–57.

522   **"We must remind ourselves . . . ," Lee Ann had written**: Lee Ann Fujii, "Research Ethics 101: Dilemmas and Responsibilities," *PS: Political Science & Politics* 45, no. 4 (2012), pp. 722.

523   **During economic downturns, it is often the poorest Americans who are the most charitable**: Bill Chappell, "Some Americans Boosted Charitable Giving In Recession; The Rich Did Not," *The Two-Way*, NPR.com, Oct. 6, 2014.

524   **To be poor is to be surveilled**: Virginia Eubanks, *Automating Inequality: How High-Tech Tools Profile, Police, and Punish the Poor* (New York: St. Martin's Press, 2017).

524   **The same children were cycling through these systems**: "Research on the Intersection of Families, Housing, and the Child Welfare System," U.S. Department of Housing and Urban Development, Office of Policy Development and Research, Aug. 3, 2012.

index

INVISIBLE
CHILD

ANDREA ELLIOTT

Random
House
Book Club

Because
Stories Are
Better Shared

™

A BOOK CLUB GUIDE

Questions and Topics for Discussion

1. Why is this book called *Invisible Child*? What makes Dasani and her siblings—and their parents—unseen?

2. How does America's history of racism inform the story of Dasani's family? Which government policies and social inequities have impacted this family over time?

3. Is Fort Greene a single neighborhood or two separate places? Discuss the upsides and downsides to gentrification, contrasting the wealthy part of Fort Greene with the area where Dasani lives. Does proximity to wealth improve Dasani's life or make it more difficult?

4. Discuss the role of the author, Andrea Elliott, in reporting and writing this story. What are some of the ethical challenges of a project like this? Did you feel Elliott's presence while reading the book?

5. Elliott writes that Dasani's parents, depending on your perspective, are "either 'working the system' or 'making ends meet.'" Did you share one of these opinions before you started reading? Did your opinion change after reading the book?

6. Dasani's family is repeatedly displaced. What impact does this have on Dasani and her siblings?

7. Dasani has developed an arsenal of skills to help her survive—from her command of household chores to her analysis of case-workers' vocal intonations and facial expressions. "None of these skills were captured on her report card," Elliott writes. Should

schools evaluate students solely on their academic performance or on a range of life skills?

8. Does *Invisible Child* complicate the popular American refrain that you should "pull yourself up by your bootstraps"? Does it challenge the argument that government aid is the only solution to poverty?

9. Elliott writes, "Dasani is well versed in city politics, not because she follows the news. She is simply forced to notice what other children miss." How much did you know about local politics when you were Dasani's age? In what other ways is Dasani forced to grow up quickly?

10. Should Chanel and Supreme have lost custody of their children? In what ways might the child protection system help a family like Dasani's? How does the system fall short, or even harm families?

11. Discuss the importance of positive role models and their impact on Dasani's life—especially African American women like Faith Hester, the Brooklyn school teacher, and Julie Williams, the therapist at the Milton Hershey School. What are the limits of a role model's influence on a child's life?

12. What ultimately caused Dasani to leave Hershey? Could anything have been done to prevent that outcome?

13. Does achieving conventional success require Dasani to disconnect from her family, culture, or identity? Is that a price worth paying, or even a fair price to ask?

14. Dasani has a complicated relationship with her mother, Chanel—just as Chanel had with her own mother, Joanie. How might this mother-daughter dynamic help or hinder a family living on the edge?

15. It's common for survivors of trauma to escape their pain by drinking or taking drugs. What events might have triggered Chanel and Supreme's dependence on drugs? Did their struggles with addiction impact your view of them as parents?

16. How did you feel at the end of the book? What kind of trajectory do you see for Dasani and her siblings?

17. What surprised you most about Dasani's story?

PHOTO: NINA SUBIN

ANDREA ELLIOTT is an investigative reporter for *The New York Times* and a former staff writer at *The Miami Herald*. Her reporting has been awarded a Pulitzer Prize, a George Polk Award, a Scripps Howard Award, and prizes from the Overseas Press Club and the American Society of Newspaper Editors. She has served as an Emerson fellow at New America, a visiting journalist at the Russell Sage Foundation, a visitor scholar at the Columbia Population Research Center, and is the recipient of a Whiting Foundation grant. In 2015, she received Columbia University's Medal for Excellence, given to one alumnus or alumna under the age of forty-five. She lives in New York City. This is her first book.

andrea-elliott.com
Twitter: @andreafelliott

about the type

This book was set in Electra, a typeface designed for Linotype by W. A. Dwiggins, the renowned type designer (1880–1956). Electra is a fluid typeface, avoiding the contrasts of thick and thin strokes that are prevalent in most modern typefaces.